Calvin's Ecclesiology

Calvin's Ecclesiology

A Study in the History of Doctrine

Tadataka Maruyama

William B. Eerdmans Publishing Company
Grand Rapids, Michigan

Wm. B. Eerdmans Publishing Co.
4035 Park East Court SE, Grand Rapids, Michigan 49546
www.eerdmans.com

Published 2022
Printed in the United States of America

28 27 26 25 24 23 22   1 2 3 4 5 6 7

ISBN 978-0-8028-8185-4

Library of Congress Cataloging-in-Publication Data

A catalog record for this book is available from the Library of Congress.

To the precious memory of Han and Nelson van den Blink

Contents

FOREWORD

Tadataka Maruyama is already known as having made an important contribution to the historical study of Reformed ecclesiology in his monograph *The Ecclesiology of Theodore Beza* (1978). His study of Calvin's ecclesiology advances our understanding of the place and importance of the doctrine of the church in Calvin's thought and contributes substantially to Calvin studies in general. Given its contextual approach to Calvin's work and writings and its chronological organization, it reveals the connections between Calvin's doctrine of the church and engagement with practical matters of church governance and order in Geneva—and given this view of Calvin's immersion in the work of church reform it also provides an entrance into Calvin's life and work beyond just the topic of ecclesiology. The work can and should be studied for its contribution to a specific area of Calvin studies, but it can and ought to be read as an engaging point of entry into the study of Calvin's life and work.

Despite its central place in Calvin's work in and for the Reformation in Geneva, his ecclesiology has received comparatively less attention than other doctrinal topics. To be sure there are quite a few articles that discuss Calvin's doctrine of the church, often as ecumenical exercises, less frequently with close attention to the development of his doctrine in context. Whereas monographs analyzing Calvin's understanding of predestination abound, with the topics of Christology, Scripture, and justification not far behind in numbers of monographs, Calvin's views on the nature, organization, and administration of the church have not received major monographic attention since Benjamin Milner's work in 1970. The shorter essays devoted to Calvin's doctrine of the church also tend either to present it doctrinally as a finished product or to examine only one aspect of ecclesiology. Maruyama's study examines the many aspects of Calvin's ecclesiology and does so in the context of the developing Reformation in Geneva. It also draws on extant research into separate aspects of ecclesiology, such as preaching and sacraments, the functions of the Genevan consistory, and the impact of religion on society in Geneva during Calvin's time.

Although the focus of the work is Calvin's ecclesiology, Maruyama's wide grasp of the literature and his attention to context also render the book a major contribution to the biographical study of Calvin. This is a carefully argued work that evidences a mastery of the primary sources in their original language and a firm grasp of the scholarly state of the question. Maruyama provides an approach to the subject via significant stages in Calvin's life that is both sound and convincing. His work is perhaps best characterized as a study in intellectual history that effectively sets Calvin's developing views on the doctrine of the church into the context of sixteenth-century Geneva and of Reformed debate and formulation. Identification of the work as "intellectual history" indicates that it is not a piece of confessional historiography that ignores historical context. It is also not a work of social history, although unlike a purely doctrinal study, Maruyama is cognizant of the contributions of social and institutional historians.

The organization of Maruyama's work underlines the identification as intellectual history. There are four chronologically arranged chapters, the first examining Calvin's academic formation, his conversion, and his early "catholic" ecclesiology, with emphasis on Calvin's reading of the credal article on the "Holy Catholic Church," its marks, rites, and powers together with Calvin's understanding of Christian freedom. Here Maruyama insightfully reads Calvin's characterization of "adversaries" of the faith as a reflection on Guillaume Budé's criticism of early Protestantism in his *Transition to Christianity*, at the same time that he analyzes Budé's work as representative of a humanist approach in between the Reform and its most bitter antagonists.

The first chapter evidences a significant knowledge of the backgrounds and contexts of Calvin's education, notably emphasizing the initial experience of an opposition between the arts faculty under which Calvin studied and the theological faculty and the subsequent experience of Montaigu, which tended away from the humanist models toward preparation for church office. The chapter also contains a highly nuanced approach to Calvin's conversion that carefully surveys both Calvin's early writings and his context and applies its conclusions to the issue of church reform and a view of Calvin's early ecclesiological understanding, with the first edition of the *Institutes* serving as a basis for detailing Calvin's early but carefully formulated position. The author's attention to the limitations imposed by the documents is to be commended given the tendency of much "Calvin scholarship" to view the Reformer's thoughts as entirely of a piece, with little change of mind throughout his career. In other words, what Maruyama consistently avoids is reading Calvin's thought through the lens of the 1559 *Institutes*.

The second chapter lines out the contribution of Guillaume Farel and Genevan context, with attention to Farel's Lefèvrian roots in the reformist approach of the Meaux circle, Farel's own developing ecclesiology, and the documents of church reform written by Farel and Calvin. The chapter concludes with a section on the practice of Catholic ecclesiology in the Caroli affair and Calvin's *Two Epistles* (1537). Maruyama's analysis of the documents reveals the complexity of Calvin's early development—perhaps most notably in this chapter in the analysis of the *Two Epistles*, where Maruyama offers a deep and detailed contextual analysis that could stand by itself as a major essay on documents. Once again, there is a clear and up-to-date mastery of sources, both primary and secondary.

In his third chapter, Maruyama takes on the issue of Calvin's developments in Strasbourg, between his earliest work in Geneva and his later work, after his return, as the leading Reformer. Here again, Maruyama engages the most recent scholarship both on Calvin and his time in Strasbourg and on the Reformation in Strasbourg as directed largely by Martin Bucer. The chapter presents a careful study of the various ecclesiologies that Calvin would have encountered—Bucer's own, a more Lutheran approach, and an Anabaptist view. The detail and analysis here are excellent, including a refined analysis of Bucer's own position as it developed and a careful analysis of Bucer's relationship to Calvin, including an examination of the scholarship on Bucer's influence that marks out major differences between Bucer and Calvin, based in part on recently discovered materials.

The fourth and final chapter examines the later history of Calvin's work in Geneva around the nodal point of 1555, which marks Calvin's victory over opposition in Geneva and offers a detailed picture of the maturing ecclesiology that emerges in several stages from Calvin's later *Institutes* and exegetical works. Building on a point made originally by Doumergue, Maruyama emphasizes the importance of the third edition of the *Institutes* (1543) for Calvin's development: Here the doctrine of the church builds on Calvin's vision for the church on his return to Geneva and, although much expanded in 1559, achieves the substance of Calvin's fully developed ecclesiology. Among other points noted by Maruyama, it is here in the 1543 text that Calvin fully addressed the Roman charge of schism, pointing out that if Christ is truly the head of the church, drawing closer to Christ and away from Rome could hardly be identified as schismatic. Here again, the grasp of materials is outstanding, use of the events and publications of 1555 as a focal point is convincing, and the exposition is carefully well contextualized.

In sum, Maruyama's work is a masterful account of the early Reformation context and its impact on Calvin as well as Calvin's impact on the shaping of a Reformation ecclesiology in Geneva and beyond. His chronicle of Calvin's progress from a "Catholic" to a "Reformed" ecclesiology is compelling. And his in-depth analysis of documents in their context provides a significant and most welcome advance in scholarship on Calvin and the Genevan Reformation.

Richard A. Muller
Lowell, Michigan

Acknowledgments

This book is mine, yet at the same time, it is not mine.

It is mine in the sense that I am fully responsible for its contents. The methodology I employed to understand Calvin's ecclesiology; the interpretations I inferred in examining the original texts of Calvin and his contemporaries; the critical appraisals I applied to the wealth of academic works, past and present, in Calvin scholarship; and the narrative descriptions I used to portray the development of Calvin's ecclesiology in historical context—all are mine. I am also responsible for possibly unnoticed errors in it.

Concurrently, this book is not mine in the sense that several external factors have contributed to shape its current form. Such are the cases of the Calvin texts with which I have grappled to comprehend the author's intended meanings, of academic influences that I received in my primary theological formation in the 1960s and 1970s, as well as my secondary and postretirement reorientation into current Calvin scholarship, and of some professional assistance I had for finalizing the text as it now stands.

Calvin's ecclesiology was once a possible topic of my doctoral dissertation under a noted Calvin scholar's guidance. When I encountered the difficulty of understanding the somewhat enigmatic Reformer Calvin and his original texts relevant to ecclesiology, and because the field of Calvin studies was crowded with a host of prominent and mostly theological interpretations, I opted for the less-researched field of Beza studies. Thanks to a research opportunity in Geneva, I wrote a dissertation that was later published as *The Ecclesiology of Theodore Beza* (Geneva: Droz, 1978). After my retirement, when I returned to tackle afresh Calvin's ecclesiology, I found the twenty-first-century field of Calvin studies had morphed into that of multidisciplinary studies. Facing this challenging scene, my primary methodological option was to read the original Calvin texts as much as possible in their historical context in order to comprehend Reformer Calvin and his ecclesiology. This resulted in innumerable hours of dialoguing with Calvin through his texts and letting them dictate the main tenets of my narrative. Calvin as a Reformer of France and the development of his ecclesiology in three stages are just two discoveries in this process.

Influences during my primary theological formation inevitably formed my basic stance as a researcher. Among many, I count major inspiration from four professors under whom I studied and researched. I received an initiation into historical theology from Professor Paul Woolley of Westminster Theological Seminary. Known as the most fair-minded teacher at Westminster by the seminarians, Professor Woolley's lectures were historically sound and unbiased and marked by his love for Christ's church. Professor Jaroslav Pelikan, Yale University's Professor of Ecclesiastical History, was my main reason to study at Yale Divinity School. His Divinity lectures on "History of Christian Doctrine" were electrifying and distinguished by his scope of the whole of Christendom, his depth of insightful knowledge of the world surrounding the formation of Christian doctrine, and the width of his interdisciplinary research in theology, history, literature, philosophy, and social sciences. I tried to apply his methodology, later elaborated in his major work, *The Christian Tradition: A History of the Development of Doctrine* (5 vols., Chicago: University of Chicago Press, 1971–89), to my work on Beza mentioned above and to my current work on Calvin. Professor Edward Dowey, a renowned scholar of the Protestant Reformation and especially Calvin, and the author of *The Knowledge of God in Calvin's Theology* (New York: Columbia University Press, 1952) was the mentor of my doctoral studies at Princeton Theological Seminary. His lectures and seminars on Calvin were always marked by the depth of his scholarship, which reflected a thorough investigation into Calvin's commentaries and the *Institutes*. In particular, with great intensity, he taught me how to read Calvin's *Institutes*. Professor Pierre Fraenkel of the Theology faculty of the University of Geneva was my research advisor during my two-year residence at its Institute for the History of the Reformation (IHR). As seen in his *Testimonia Patrum: The Tradition of the Patristic Argument in the Theology of Philip Melanchthon* (Geneva: Droz, 1961), his in-depth familiarity with the theological traditions of Western Christendom, as well as his sincere efforts to bridge the Roman Catholic and Protestant heritages, were exemplary. To these scholars I humbly acknowledge my indebtedness.

I am grateful for the assistance given to me by three professionals who have read the entire manuscript. The Rev. Dr. Kendall Clark Baker of the United Church of Christ examined its overall structure, contents, and literary composition and gave me many suggestions for its improvement. Dr. David S. Sytsma of Tokyo Christian University, a specialist in historical theology, provided a good critical review that included many insightful suggestions for improvement and useful information on the most recent research. I am especially grateful for Ms. Stevi Hamill of Seattle, Washington. Well versed in the fields of linguistics, philosophy, and theology, she diligently worked over the manuscript, written by the present author with English as a second language, and wonderfully turned it into a modern readable work.

This book has a history of its own. An earlier version of my work on Calvin was published in Japanese as *Calvin's Reformation Ecclesiology* (Tokyo: Kyobunkwan, 2015). Although this book is a revised and enlarged version and is written for the wider English readership in mind, it shares the basic structure and contents with the Japanese version. In this regard, I am grateful to Kyobunkwan for kindly acknowledging its publication by Eerdmans. When I first approached Eerdmans through the courteous mediation of Dr. R. David Nelson of Baker Academic, Eerdmans's editor-in-chief, Dr. James Ernest, took up my cause. I owe a particular debt to Dr. Ernest, who is a scholar in historical theology in his own right, for his keen interest in my work and constant encouragement in the entire process from my submission of the manuscript to the prospect of its publication. It was also his recommendation that paved the way for Dr. Richard A. Muller, Professor Emeritus, Calvin Theological Seminary, to kindly write a foreword for this book. As a noted Calvin scholar, Professor Muller has shown his keen interest and profound knowledge in many aspects of Calvin studies, some of which my book has also touched on. I am especially grateful for his foreword, which will certainly be helpful for English readership in understanding my presentation of Calvin's ecclesiology.

A special thanks is due to Eerdmans's editors and staff members, Amy Kent, Laurel Draper, and Alexis Cutler, and to copyeditor Alexander Freeman-Diehm, for their professional courtesy and expertise. I was privileged to have frequently used the University of Washington libraries, especially the Suzzallo and Allen Libraries, which were a gold mine for my research. When the book's narrative quotes scriptural passages, they are taken from *The Holy Bible: New Revised Standard Version* (New York and Oxford: Oxford University Press, 1989). Lastly, I am above all grateful to my wife, Meredith, who has read my manuscript at various stages and several times for corrections and improvement. My daughter Kimi Maruyama, a computer expert, became my tutor to help me put this work in modern printable form.

This book is dedicated to the memory of Rev. Dr. Arie Johannes (Han) and Mrs. Katherine Nelson Mooers van den Blink. In 1967, at the very first event of

Princeton Theological Seminary's doctoral program, the Faculty's invitational dinner for the entering doctoral candidates and their spouses, while gathering outside the dining hall, Han and Nelson sought me out and introduced themselves. Soon afterward, they invited an international student from Indonesia and myself to their family dinner and introduced us to their well-mannered and lovely children, Jan, Sarah, and Katherine. There I learned that Han's parents, missionaries from the Netherlands to Indonesia, Han, and his brother were forced to spend several years (1942–45) in a concentration camp of the occupying Japanese Army. Han and Nelson kept inviting me to their home and soon I became like an adopted member of the family. When Meredith and I became engaged, furthermore, Han, as a Presbyterian minister and majoring in pastoral theology, counselled us and then traveled to New Hampshire with his entire family to officiate at our wedding. After our graduation, the Van den Blinks in the United States kept in touch with the Maruyamas in Japan. At every Christmas season Nelson remembered us with the gift of an always interesting and unique Christmas tree ornament. Years later on the occasion of Katherine's wedding, Han, then an Episcopalian minister, and I had the chance for private and intensive discussions for hours, which were then continued with the exchange of many emails over a period of a year or two. The topics included our Christian life, the mysteries of God, Christ, the Spirit, and the church, the Reformation, Calvin, our experiences of the war in which Han revealed his sufferings amidst the horrors of the concentration camp, eternal life, the resurrection of the body, and so forth. While Nelson and Han have now passed into history, their memory will remain forever precious to me.

Tadataka Maruyama
Christmas 2021

Abbreviations

I. Reformation Studies: Primary Sources and References

ASD *Desiderii Erasmi Roterodami Opera Omnia*. Amsterdam: North-Holland Publishing Co., 1969–.

BDS Stupperich, R., et al., eds. Series I: *Martin Bucers Deutsche Schriften*. Gütersloh: Gerd Mohn/Paris: Presses Universitaires de France, 1960–.

BOL Wendel, F., et al., eds. Series II: *Martini Buceri Opera Latina*. Leiden: Brill/Paris: Presses Universitaires de France/Gütersloh: C. Bertelsmann Verlag, 1954–.

CR: Melanchthon

Bretschneider, K. G., and H. E. Bindseil, eds. *Philippi Melanthonis opera quae supersunt omnia, Corpus reformatorum*. Vols. 1–28. Halle: C. A. Schwetschke und Sohn, 1834–1860.

CR: Zwingli

Egli, E., et al., eds. *Huldreich Zwinglis sämtliche Werke, Corpus reformatorum*. Vols. 88–. Berlin, Leipzig, Zurich: C. A. Schwetschke und Sohn, 1905–.

Creeds and Confessions

Pelikan, J., and V. Hotchkiss, eds. *Creeds and Confessions of Faith in the Christian Tradition*. 3 vols. New Haven and London: Yale University Press, 2003.

OER Hillerbrand, H. J., et al., eds. *The Oxford Encyclopedia of the Reformation*. 4 vols. New York and Oxford: Oxford University Press, 1996.

WA Knaake, J. K. F., et al., eds. *D. Martin Luthers Werke: Kritische Gesamtausgabe*. Weimar: Hermann Bohlau, 1883–.

II. Calvin: Primary Sources and References

Battles, trans., *Institution*

Calvin, John. *Institution of the Christian Religion.* (English translation of *BC* 36/1.) Translated by F. L. Battles. Atlanta: John Knox Press, 1975.

BC Peter, R., and J.-F. Gilmont, eds. *Bibliotheca Calviniana. Les oeuvres de Jean Calvin publiées au XVIe siècle.* 3 vols. Geneva: Droz, 1991–2000.

Benoît, ed., *Institution*

Calvin, Jean. *Institution de la religion Chrestienne,* (*BC* 60/8). 5 vols. Edited by J.-D. Benoît. Paris: J. Vrin, 1957–63.

CO Baum, G., E. Cunitz, and E. Reuss, eds. *Ioannis Calvini opera quae supersunt omnia.* 59 vols. (*Corpus reformatorum.* Vols. 29–87). Brunsvigae: Schwetschke, 1863–1900.

COR *Ioannis Calvini opera omnia. Denuo recognita et adnotatione critica instructanotisque illustrata, Conventus internationalis studiis Calvinianis*, Geneva: Droz, 1992–.

Series I: *Institutio Christianae religionis*

Series II: *Opera exegetica*

Series III: *Scripta ecclesiastica*

Series IV: *Scripta didactica et polemica*

Series VI: *Epistolae*

(For example, Series II: *Opera exegetica.* Vol. 13 [*Commentarius in Epistolam Pauli ad Romanos*] is cited as *COR* II-13.)

Institutes, ed. McNeill

McNeill, J. T, ed. *John Calvin. Institutes of the Christian Religion.* (English translation of *BC* 59/4.) 2 vols. Translated by F. L. Battles. Philadelphia: Westminster Press, 1960.

Institutio

Calvinus, Joannes. *Institutio Christianae religionis* (*BC* 59/4), *OS*, 3–5. Edited by P. Barth and W. Niesel. Munich: Chr. Kaiser, 1957–62.

OS Barth, P., and G. Niesel, eds. *Calvini opera selecta.* 5 vols. Munich: Chr. Kaiser, 1926–36.

III. Calvin: Secondary Sources

Balke, *Calvin and the Anabaptist*

Balke, Willem. *Calvin and the Anabaptist Radicals.* Translated by W. J. Heynen. Grand Rapids: Eerdmans, 1981.

Bouwsma, *Calvin*
Bouwsma, William J. *John Calvin: A Sixteenth Century Portrait.* Oxford: Oxford University Press, 1988.

Doumergue, *Jean Calvin*
Doumergue, Émile. *Jean Calvin: Les hommes et les choses de son temps.* 7 vols. Lausanne, 1899–1917; Neuilly: G. Bridel, 1926–27.

Farge, *Orthodoxy*
Farge, James K. *Orthodoxy and Reform in Early Reformation France: The Faculty of Theology of Paris, 1500–1543.* Leiden: Brill, 1985.

Ganoczy, *Calvin*
Ganoczy, Alexandre. *Calvin: théologien de l'église et du ministère.* Paris: Éditions du Cerf, 1964.

Ganoczy, *Young Calvin*
Ganoczy, Alexandre. *The Young Calvin.* Translated by D. Foxgrover and W. Provo. Edinburgh: T&T Clark, 1987.

Gordon, *Calvin*
Gordon, Bruce. *Calvin.* New Haven: Yale University Press, 2009.

Herminjard, *Correspondance*
Herminjard, A. L. *Correspondance des réformateurs dans les pays de langue française.* 7 vols. Geneva and Paris: H. Georg, 1866–86.

Higman, *Lire et découvrir*
Higman, Francis. *Lire et découvrir: La circulation des idées au temps de la Réforme.* Geneva: Droz, 1998.

Höpfl, *Christian Polity*
Höpfl, Harro. *The Christian Polity of John Calvin.* Cambridge: Cambridge University Press, 1982.

Kelley, *The Beginning*
Kelley, Donald R. *The Beginning of Ideology: Consciousness and Society in the French Reformation.* Cambridge: Cambridge University Press, 1981.

Maruyama, *The Ecclesiology*
Maruyama, Tadataka. *The Ecclesiology of Theodore Beza.* Geneva: Droz, 1978.

McGrath, *A Life*
McGrath, Alister E. *A Life of John Calvin.* Oxford: Blackwell, 1990.

McKee, *Elders*
McKee, Elsie A. *Elders and the Plural Ministry: The Role of Exegetical History in Illuminating John Calvin's Theology.* Geneva: Droz, 1988.

Milner, *Calvin's Doctrine*
Milner, Benjamin C. *Calvin's Doctrine of the Church.* Leiden: Brill, 1970.

Muller, *The Unaccommodated*
Muller, Richard A. *The Unaccommodated Calvin: Studies in the Foundation of a Theological Tradition*. Oxford: Oxford University Press, 2000.

Mullett, *John Calvin*
Mullett, Michael A. *John Calvin*. London and New York: Routledge, 2016.

Oberman, *The Dawn*
Oberman, Heiko A. *The Dawn of the Reformation: Essays in Late Medieval and Early Reformation Thought*. Edinburgh: T&T Clark, 1992.

Oberman, "Initia Calvini"
Oberman, Heiko A. "Initia Calvini: The Matrix of Calvin's Reformation." *Mededelingen van de Afdeling Letterkunde* 54 (1991): 109–47.

Oberman, *John Calvin*
Oberman, Heiko A. *John Calvin and the Reformation of the Refugees*. Geneva: Droz, 2009.

Parker, *John Calvin*
Parker, Thomas H. L. *John Calvin: A Biography*. Philadelphia: Westminster, 1975.

Steinmetz, *Calvin*
Steinmetz, David. *Calvin in Context*. Oxford: Oxford University Press, 1995.

Tuininga, *Calvin's Political Theology*
Tuininga, Matthew J. *Calvin's Political Theology and the Public Engagement of the Church: Christ's Two Kingdoms*. Cambridge: Cambridge University Press, 2017.

Wendel, *Calvin*
Wendel, François. *Calvin: The Origins and Development of His Religious Thought*. Translated by P. Mairet. New York: Harper & Row, 1963.

Zachman, *Image and Word*
Zachman, Randall C. *Image and Word in the Theology of John Calvin*. Notre Dame: University of Notre Dame Press, 2007.

Introduction

French Reformer Jean Calvin (1509–64) was best known for his work in Geneva, the city of his exile. By the time his career as the Reformer of Geneva began in 1536, however, the story of his early academic formation in humanities and law, studies in Bible and church fathers, "sudden conversion" to Evangelicalism, and exile first to Basel and later to Geneva, had taken place in the background of the early French Reformation. In addition, his reformatory career of three decades, from the mid-1530s to the mid-1560s, never lost sight of and vision for reforming the church in his homeland. Even his expanded vision for an Evangelical Europe never seemed to betray his French identity. Furthermore, this period coincided with the crisis of European Christendom: its church unity threatened, its schism intensified, and its final breakdown into Roman Catholicism and Protestantism. As a native of France, located in the center of Europe, and a second-generation reformer having inherited the initial reforms of Luther, Zwingli, and others, this was the challenging age that Calvin had to face and in which he formed his concept of the church. From this historical perspective, this study of Calvin's ecclesiology, "a study in the history of doctrine," faces two unavoidable challenges: one concerns his textual materials and those of others relevant to the topic; the other concerns the intrinsic development of his ecclesiology in this context.

Concerning the first challenge, this study will address as its main feature Calvin's primary materials, both Latin and French, that are relevant for understanding his ecclesiology, and that need to be carefully selected and critically examined in their historical context as well as on the basis of recent Calvin scholarship. This study cannot assume all of the materials as one corpus, and deduce from it his comprehensive and harmonized concept of the church. Even though the final *Institutes* of 1559 presented a so-called "Calvin's ecclesiology," it was historically conditioned material and hardly represented the whole picture of his ecclesiology. Each of the *Institutes* of 1536, 1539, and 1543 also contributed in its unique way to the formation of his ecclesiology. Likewise, the selective method of either emphasizing some materials or ignoring others serves the purpose of this study. The same method should be applied to the non-Calvin materials of his day, which were particularly important as determinant factors for the formation of his ecclesiology.

As to the second challenge, which concerns the substantive nature of Calvin's concept of the church, this study proposes a three-stage development of his ecclesiology. In each stage, he focused on a particular "mode" of the church and formulated an ecclesiology which he deemed met the need and challenge of the time. The first mode, which this study calls "Catholic ecclesiology," focused on the church's catholicity. This formed the basic stratum of his ecclesiology and its clear expression was found in the first *Institutes* (1536), where the suprahistorical church of "the whole number of the elect" and the historical church of "the congregation of believers" were depicted as the two images of the Catholic church. The second mode, which this study calls "Reformed ecclesiology," was an ecclesiology exclusively focused on the form of the church in history. If "Catholic ecclesiology" was an ideal of the French humanists and Calvin as a humanist theologian, "Reformed ecclesiology" was the work of the recognized Reformer Calvin. Its articulated expression was found in the third *Institutes* (1543), the most important edition concerning his ecclesiology. Upon the stratum of "Catholic ecclesiology," he formulated "the legitimate form of the church," which was thoroughly based on his interpretation of biblical principles and was distinguishable from the form of the Lutheran Church. It was directly in opposition to the forms of the Roman Catholic Church and Anabaptist congregations. The third mode is termed "Reformation ecclesiology," the expression by which this study assumes that Calvin, in the last phase of his reformatory career, faced the reality of Evangelical Christianity in Europe and found "the Reformation church" not only in disarray but also oppressed by the Roman Catholic Church and its princes. This mode found its expression in his lectures and commentaries on the Old Testament prophetic books, including the Psalms, and in the final *Institutes* (1559). He articulated the image of the Reformation church by focusing on the church's prophetic and eschatological dimension. Portraying Europe as a theater of God's providence, for example, Calvin viewed the Reformation church as an eschatological reality and depicted it as two concurrent images:

one, the church as the theater's noble "orchestra"; and the other, "the church under the cross" of the suffering Christ.

Chapter 1, "Academic Formation and Catholic Ecclesiology," traces Calvin's academic formation and initial ecclesiological development within the historical background of the early French Reformation. The period under examination (1523–35) spans from the time of his matriculation at the University of Paris to that of completing the writing of his first major theological work, the 1536 *Institutes*, in the city of his exile, Basel. During this period, he studied the basics of humanities and theology in Paris, law in Orléans and Bourges, advanced humanities studies at the Collège Royal in Paris, and biblical and theological studies on his own. This was the time when French society witnessed the emerging force of evangelical humanism represented by Lefèvre and his associates, as well as the influence of the reform concepts of Erasmus, Luther, Zwingli, Bucer, and others. The earliest manifestation of the humanist reform, tacitly approved by King Francis I and enthusiastically supported by his sister, Marguerite, was in the Meaux reform (1521–25) led by Lefèvre and the Lefèvrians. By the time Calvin associated himself with the evangelical humanists, as chapter 1 assumes, evangelical humanism was experiencing a polarization process between moderate and radical evangelical humanists. Chapter 1 also assumes that Calvin's so-called "sudden conversion" was not simply a turning to "Lefèvrian evangelicalism" but more precisely a radical transition from moderate to radical evangelical humanism, a position fully compatible with the Evangelicalism of Luther and Zwingli.

Against this background of the early French Reformation, chapter 1 examines Calvin's earlier works: the Seneca commentary (1532), his first and last work of humanist aspiration; the first draft of *Psychopannychia* (1534–35, delayed publication in 1542), his first attempt in biblical and theological studies; and the first *Institutes* (1536). Concerning the first *Institutes*—the work of a young humanist scholar who had mastered biblical and patristic studies and the Evangelical theology of Luther, Zwingli, Bucer, and others in a short period of time—chapter 1 takes a unique approach in examining his early ecclesiology. Firstly, it considers the first *Institutes*—incomplete in comparison to the final *Institutes* (1559)—as a work of major importance that presented Catholic ecclesiology as the basic stratum of Calvin's ecclesiology as a whole. Secondly, since Calvin intended the first *Institutes* to be his theological manifesto, in a Europe that he pictured in crisis or as "Europe afflicted," this study begins its ecclesiological inquiry with his teaching of the Lord's Supper (ch. 4), a symbol of the church's catholic unity, and examines his teaching in the historical context of the ancient church's Christological formation. Especially on the knotty issue of Christ's presence in the Supper, Calvin presented a biblical and catholic "framework" for evangelical teaching. Although his position presented the Christology of the Antiochene school over against that of the Alexandrian school, he attempted to mediate the conflicting teachings of Luther and Zwingli within the framework of Chalcedonian orthodox Christology. Thirdly, this study analyzes Calvin's Catholic ecclesiology as consisting of two distinctive concepts of the church: "the whole number of the elect" in the catechetical "instruction" section (chs. 1–4) and "the congregation of believers" in the polemical "apology" section (chs. 5–6). Especially in chapter 6 ("Christian Freedom, Ecclesiastical Power, and Political Administration"), which formed his apology for Catholic ecclesiology, he presented for the first time his notion of church reform in the context of Christ's kingdom and Christian freedom. Fourthly, concerning the difficult problem of placing the dedicatory epistle to Francis I, this study takes it as an extension of chapter 6 applied practically to the French context, thus, as an epilogue to the first *Institutes*. It also postulates "our enemies" in the dedicatory epistle to be reform-minded humanists, represented in famous humanist scholar Budé's *Transition to Christianity* (1535).

Chapter 2, "The Early Genevan Reformation and Practice of Catholic Ecclesiology," examines Calvin's ecclesiology in his first reformatory work (1536–38) in Geneva. This short period began with his unintended detention in Geneva by its chief pastor, Guillaume Farel, and ended with their expulsion from the city. Although the scene of their work was the city of Geneva, they were French exiles and were offspring of the early French Reformation. As far as Calvin's ecclesiology was concerned, this period provided a test case for his Catholic ecclesiology in the historical context of the early French Reformation, as well as his "first" Genevan reform. Chapter 2 does not take the historical "fancy" view, long cherished by some Calvin researchers, that he had led the early Genevan reform. Instead, it regards Farel as both a leading representative of radical evangelical humanism in France and the leader of the Genevan reform. Accordingly, it begins its inquiry with Farel's humanist mentor, Lefèvre, and his ecclesiological formation in France. It proceeds to examine Farel's formation in Lefèvrianism and the Evangelicalism of Luther, Oecolampadius, and Zwingli, as well as focusing on his ecclesiology in his main work, *The Summary* (1529). As a result, chapter 2 postulates Lefèvre's ecclesiology and reform concept, represented in the Meaux reform and by the Lefèvrians, as the first and primary type of church reform; Farel's radicalized Lefèvrianism and Evangelicalism as the second type; and Calvin's Catholic ecclesiology, sharing the same radicalism and Evangelicalism with Farel but with his own unique formation, as the third type of church reform in the early French Reformation.

Chapter 2 examines the three Genevan reformatory documents (1537), the *Instruction* (catechism), the *Confession*, and the *Articles* (ecclesiastical ordinance). In rejecting the traditional notion of Calvin's authorship of all the documents, it takes the view of recent Calvin scholarship: Calvin's sole authorship of the *Instruction* and Farel's main authorship of the *Confession* and the *Articles*, with some contributions by Calvin. It also tentatively concludes that the early Genevan Reformation was led mainly by Farel, a theologian in his own right, and that Farel's radical congregationalism and Calvin's Catholic ecclesiology were quite distinct.

During this period, the unique character of Calvin's Catholic ecclesiology as the third type in the early French Reformation manifested itself in the Caroli affair and *Two Epistles* (1537), which Calvin published in the midst of the Caroli affair. This affair was unique in the sense that Caroli was a Paris Doctor of Theology who had turned from moderate evangelical humanism to Evangelicalism in France and was also an exile serving as chief pastor of the Lausanne church. The affair started with Caroli's charge against Farel and Calvin of Arian heresy and became a major crisis of the Genevan reform. The affair was also unique in the sense that it was Calvin, not Farel, who had led the Genevan apology against Caroli's charge of Trinitarian unorthodoxy. Calvin's apology clearly demonstrated how his Catholic ecclesiology was founded upon thorough biblicism. In *Two Epistles*, a controversial and often-neglected work, Calvin attempted a forceful apology aimed at the moderate reformist group of the Lefèvrians. He exposed their identity, challenged them to make the either-or choice of Christ's kingdom or the Pope's kingdom, and demonstrated his uncompromising and practical activism. Although the first Genevan reform failed, for Calvin it was a testing time for his "consistent biblicism" and "practical activism," which were to become two pillars of his future work as a Reformer of the church.

Chapter 3, "The Strasbourg Period and a Transition to New Ecclesiologies," examines Calvin's ecclesiological formation in the short yet important transitional period (1538–41). It was a preparatory stage for the future "Reformer of Geneva" and, as a pastor of the French refugee church, he took his first step toward becoming a "Reformer of France." And in Strasbourg, a pivotal center of political and religious communication in Europe, he nurtured his own vision of being a "Reformer of Europe." From the perspective of his ecclesiology, this transitional period signified the progress from his basic stratum of "Catholic ecclesiology" to what we will discuss in the next chapter, his Reformed ecclesiology and Reformation ecclesiology.

In view of Calvin's ecclesiological formation, what makes his Strasbourg period so meaningful was the close presence of a unique Reformer, Martin Bucer, who took Calvin in, arranged for him to be a pastor of the French congregation, made him a lecturer of the Bible in the Academy, and paved the way for him to meet the Lutheran princes and theologians and even to participate in the religious unification colloquies in Germany for the sake of the French Reformation. Unlike in the case of Luther, his relationship with Bucer was personal. In this regard, chapter 3 begins its inquiry with Bucer's ecclesiological formation under the heading "Bucer's Strasbourg." The inquiry covers Bucer's formation before, during, and after Calvin's Strasbourg period and finds two distinctive directions for church reform, namely, "the Reformation of a local church" and "the Reformation of the European Christian world." The former direction is exemplified by his famous publication *Concerning True Pastoral Care* (1538) and in his controversial involvement in the "Christian Society movement" (1546–49), and the latter by his reformatory work for England, *Of the Kingdom of Christ* (1551).

Chapter 3 then proceeds to examine the knotty topic of "Bucer and Calvin." There is no doubt that the whole outlook of Calvin's ecclesiology found close affinity with no other major Reformer but Bucer. They shared similar ideas of Christ's kingdom, its relation with church and state, the importance of the word, the sacraments, and discipline for church reform, and their emphasis on practical Christianity. From this background, many researchers have associated Calvin's theological formation with Bucer and have developed the so-called "Bucer's influence" theory, especially acknowledging that Calvin learned about the church from Bucer. The theory has been convincingly presented in the mid-twentieth century by a Strasbourg historian, Wendel, a Catholic Calvin scholar; Ganoczy, a Bucer scholar; van't Spijker; and others, and its effects are widely dispersed today. Exclusively focusing on ecclesiology, chapter 3 challenges this theory and critically evaluates it in the context of such issues as the contemporary Roman Catholic Church under papal rule, the future of the French Reformation, Calvin's consistent biblicism, and his practical activism. Especially on the crucial issue of the Roman Catholic Church being the "church of Christ" (due partly to having been able to examine Bucer's unpublished manuscript document, *Theological Advice*, which was only recently made public and was unavailable to the main formulators of the "Bucer's influence" theory), chapter 3 notices a basic difference between Bucer and Calvin. If we are to acknowledge Bucer's contribution to Calvin's ecclesiology, however, chapter 3 indicates two distinctive directions of church reform. Namely, the ideas of the Reformation of the local church and that of the European Christian world are Bucer's most important contributions.

The second *Institutes* (1539) and the *Romans Commentary* (1540) were two academic achievements of Calvin's Strasbourg period. They marked the beginning of two distinctive series of dogmatic formulations of theological loci and exegetical expositions of Scripture. With regard to the second *Institutes*, chapter 3 focuses on Calvin's basic concept of the church and his apology against the Anabaptists, and concludes that the second *Institutes* and its French translation (1541) pave the way for the third *Institutes* (1543). The *Romans Commentary* was not just the first commentary to be published, but it was meant to be a "prototype" for all the remaining printed works of sermons, lectures, and commentaries on the biblical books. Calvin developed a unique notion of salvation history as the history of justification by faith, as well as his concept of the church, based upon this history. In the final analysis, this historical perspective of salvation history was to provide the framework for both his Reformed and Reformation ecclesiologies.

Chapter 4, "Reformed Ecclesiology and Reformation Ecclesiology," examines the final stage of Calvin's ecclesiological formation in the long and eventful period (1541–64) of his second Genevan reform. It takes a unique approach to this examination and pursues three major themes, each of them illustrating a certain aspect of his ecclesiological formation. Firstly, chapter 4 traces the theme of Calvin's images as "Reformer of Geneva," "Reformer of France," and "Reformer of Europe." Under this theme, a critical evaluation is made of such topics as the *Genevan Ecclesiastical Ordinance* (1541); the year 1555 as a turning point and 1559 as the apex of the Genevan reform; the organization of the French Reformed Church (1559); and the question of Calvin as "Luther's heir." Secondly, another theme concerns the division of this period into two halves, centered on the year 1555. The division, though it may sound artificial, was well founded in the histories of Geneva, France, and Europe. In addition, with regard to Calvin's own history of exegetical works, the pre-1555 period concentrated on the New Testament books and the post-1555 period on the Old Testament books, especially the prophetic books, including the Psalms. Thirdly, corresponding to the above two themes, the last theme concerns the formation of two distinctive ecclesiological modes: Reformed ecclesiology and Reformation ecclesiology. Chapter 4 considers them as representations of the two directions of the Evangelical Reformation, the Reformation of the local church and that of the European Christian world, which Calvin had inherited from Bucer.

In its substance, Calvin's Reformed ecclesiology is what has been distinctively known as "Calvin's ecclesiology," formulated first in the third *Institutes* and later to be found in book 4 of his final *Institutes* (1559). Although it is undoubtedly an ecclesiology of Reformed theology, its formation is seen in a particular historical context. Having experienced the Strasbourg period and participated in the church unification colloquies, Calvin came to realize an urgent need to formulate the external "form" of the Evangelical churches that would be able to counter the Roman Catholic hierarchy. His realization was partly based upon the conviction that the first-generation Reformers, having been successful in formulating basic scriptural teachings on the church's nature and identity, had not sufficiently presented "the legitimate form of the church" based upon Scripture and the ancient church tradition. This was the substance of Reformed ecclesiology that he presented in the third *Institutes* as well as in his *First Corinthians Commentary* as a test case for the practice of Reformed ecclesiology.

The final mode of Calvin's ecclesiology, Reformation ecclesiology, is not a theological but a historical concept. This means that he envisioned the entire Evangelical church of his age, from Luther's to his own, in the framework of God's salvation history and placed his own ideas of the Reformation church and its identity and reform in that historical frame. As to the substance of Reformation ecclesiology, chapter 4 focuses on Calvin's exegetical works of the prophetic books, especially the Psalms, and the substantive revisions of the *Institutes* consisting in rearranging the previous material and supplementing it with new material, which resulted in book 4 of the final *Institutes*. His vision of the Reformation church presupposed God's salvation history unfolding in the historical process, assumed the Reformation church as a unified reality despite some discords, especially over the Lord's Supper, in the Evangelical churches, and defined the church in history strictly as under the leadership of the Triune God. Above all, his vision placed the reality of "church and state" under the spiritual kingdom of Christ, and, accordingly, the triangular relationship (Christ's kingdom–church, Christ's kingdom–state, and church-state) assumed prophetic and eschatological features. On the one hand, the Reformation church was viewed as "the orchestra" in the European theater and "the living and visible image" of Christ's kingdom. On the other hand, it was viewed as "a remnant," or the church "under the cross" and "in resistance." Besides the *Psalms Commentary* (1557) and the final *Institutes*, chapter 4 uses his *Lectures on Daniel* (1561) for understanding the Reformation church's prophetic dimension.

Chapter 1

Academic Formation and Catholic Ecclesiology

Our first chapter examines Calvin's academic formation in arts, law, and theology and their relation to his concept of the church. The actual period of our examination spans from 1523, when he matriculated at the University of Paris, to 1535, when he completed his first theological work, the 1536 *Institutes of the Christian Religion* in the city of his exile, Basel. During this period, Calvin studied the basics of arts and theology in Paris and law at the law faculties of Orléans and Bourges, returned to Paris for advanced art studies at the Collège Royal, and experienced a sudden conversion as well as a consequent focusing on biblical and theological studies.

This chapter examines in particular the 1536 *Institutes* in which, we assume, the basic stratum of Calvin's ecclesiology, "Catholic ecclesiology," takes shape. It is generally assumed that any study into his formative period faces considerable difficulties due to the paucity of historical documents and Calvin's own silence about himself. Only two documents containing some autobiographical recollections are extant and both are works posterior to this period. The one penned closer to this period is his famous *Reply to Sadoleto* (1539). The other, written in his last years, is the preface to the *Psalms Commentary* (1557). In both cases, the autobiographical descriptions are said to be brief and rather obscure. Indeed, the *Reply to Sadoleto* contains a note saying that he would not speak much about himself. Concerning the preface's descriptions, the biographer Gordon remarks that the descriptions are "utterly devoid of sentimentality." He also characterizes Calvin in his formative years as an "enigmatic figure."[1] Keeping these difficulties in mind, in the following three sections we shall examine Calvin's academic formation, the period from his sudden conversion to his exile in Basel, and the authoring of his first *Institutes*.

Section 1. Academic Formation

The academic formation of the young Calvin from Noyon, the Picardy region of France, took place during his motherland's turbulent history—a period that historian Salmon generalizes as "society in crisis." The Concordat of Bologna, signed by King Francis I and Pope Leo X in 1516, signaled the opening of a new age in which the king accelerated his control of French ecclesiastical appointments as well as church hierarchy. By patronizing the humanist studies, Francis promoted a moderate church reform. The papacy, on the other hand, gained the rights of the ecclesiastical benefices, the French Church's economic foundation. As a result, the French Church was said to have fallen into the most corrupt state in its history.[2] It is hard to imagine that the sensitive young man's early formation could escape the reflections of this age. In this section, we shall briefly examine Calvin's formation in the following four historical stages: Calvin's college days in Paris, the period of his studies in law, attending lectures at the Collège Royal, and his first publication, a commentary on Seneca's *De clementia*.

1. The Early French Reformation

It can be safely assumed that the early French Reformation was one of the chief motifs of which Calvin in his academic formation was keenly conscious. During his university student days (1523–28) as a candidate for ecclesiastical office, France, under the rising influences of national pride and humanism, increasingly recognized the urgency of church reform and witnessed the initial influx of Luther's and Zwingli's Evangelical ideas. It is likely that during his law school days (1528–31) the discipline of French jurisprudence experienced an upsurge of reformatory sentiment. Even the humanist studies on which he had concentrated during this period, especially at the Collège Royal, were widely

1. *OS* 1:460: "de me non libenter loquor." Cf. Oberman, "Initia Calvini," 111–14; Gordon, *Calvin*, 1–2, 4.

2. J. H. M. Salmon, *Society in Crisis: France in the Sixteenth Century* (New York: St. Martin's Press, 1975), 80.

recognized as bearers of reform. Thus, his self-instruction from this background into the field of theology was not an unexpected course. Furthermore, the fruit of his theological studies, the first *Institutes*, is recognized as the first systematic presentation of Evangelicalism in the French Reformation. The concept of the church in the early French Reformation, however, bore some features uniquely distinct from the Lutheran Reformation that had advanced in the German territories under the Holy Roman Empire and from the reformation of the imperial cities represented by Zwingli's Zurich, Oecolampadius's Basel, and Bucer's Strasbourg. France was a major power located in the center of Europe that confronted the Holy Roman Empire, the papal curia, and the kingdoms of Spain and England. Correspondingly, there was a strong sentiment in the church, based on its catholicity as well as Gallicanism, which promoted the French Church's autonomy within the family of the Roman Catholic Church.

This sentiment was enhanced by the above-mentioned Concordat of Bologna. On the one hand, the king strengthened his control of the French Church against the papal curia and, on the other hand, the papal curia assured the French Church's Roman Catholic character as well as its control over the church's economic resources.[3] Even though the Concordat was not the occasion to advance church reform as a national policy, it certainly secured room for the king to promote church reform based on late medieval conciliarism. French kings had historically given support for claiming the national church's autonomy and for keeping papal dominance over France in check. In addition, Francis's own patronage of the humanist studies contributed to church reform. In the conciliar tradition, there was a conceptual distinction between the Catholic Church and the Roman Church, with the Roman Church considered as a member of the Catholic church. Similarly, the French Church claimed to be a member of the Catholic church, distinct from the Roman Church. Furthermore, humanist studies under the patronages of the king and his sister, Marguerite, tended to distinguish not only between the Catholic church and the Roman Church, but also between the ancient catholic church and the late medieval Roman Catholic Church, promoting the restoration of the ancient Catholic church's tradition as a core of church reform. This awareness of the Catholic church tradition was the ideal of French humanism as well as the early French Reformation, and it was assumedly shared by the young Calvin.

The resurging awareness of the church catholic manifested in French humanism is well illustrated by the early work of Lefèvre d'Étaples, *Commentaries*

3. J. Parsons, *The Church in the Republic: Gallicanism and Political Ideology in Renaissance France* (Washington, DC: Catholic University of America Press, 2004), 33–36.

on the Four Gospels (1522), which appealed for the restoration of the long extant ancient Catholic church.[4] Out of this humanist tradition led by Erasmus and Lefèvre, there appeared the reform movement that advocated for the restoration of the church catholic, pure gospel proclamation, and the recovery of evangelical worship. Its representative case was the Meaux reformist group led by Cardinal Guillaume Briçonnet and Lefèvre that was extensively involved in the practical reform of Briçonnet's Meaux bishopric. In fact, Calvin's university days coincided with this period of church reform at Meaux, a suburb of Paris, from its apex to setback and then disappearance.[5]

In the background of Calvin's academic formation, however, there were other forces at work around the French reform movement. The Theological Faculty of the University of Paris, popularly known as the Sorbonne, claimed itself to be a main defender of the Roman Catholic Church. On the opposite side, the influence of the Evangelicalism of Luther and Zwingli, which envisioned a reform far more radical than the humanist reform, was beginning to be felt. In the milieu of the threefold conflicting forces, the Paris Theological Faculty took initiatives to suppress the early French Reformation. Its operations were exemplified by the judgment of heresy against Luther (1521), the heresy inquiry in the case of Lefèvre and the Meaux reform (1525), and the judgment of heresy against Erasmus (1527). Its main argument against them asserted that pairing humanist studies and reform would inevitably result in the Lutheran heresy. It often cooperated with the royal judicial system, especially the Parlement of Paris, for that suppression.[6]

In this historical context, we find a polarization within the French reform movement: a moderate position seeking church reform within the framework of the current French Church, and a more radical position advocating a thorough reform of the Church, including the positive evaluation and application of the Evangelical reform of Luther and Zwingli. In our study we shall call these two groups the moderate evangelical humanists and the radical evangelical humanists. If we take the case of the Meaux reform (1521–25) and its associates, for example, Brinçonnet, Lefèvre, and a leading reformist Gérard Roussel, who

4. Lefèvre d'Étaples, *Commentarii initiatorii in quatuor evangelia* (1521). Cf. F. Simon, *The French Renaissance*, trans. H. G. Hall (New York: St. Martin's Press, 1969), 155–78, esp. 177–78.

5. Cf. Gordon, *Calvin*, 14–17.

6. Farge, *Orthodoxy*, 3–4, 165–69, 171–77, 183–96. Our study uses the official title, "the Faculty of Theology of Paris" or "the Paris Theological Faculty," instead of "the Sorbonne," which was historically a misnomer. Since some professors of theology belonged to and many lectures in theology were held at the Collège de Sorbonne, "the Sorbonne" was used as an alias or a derogatory name in Calvin's days.

later became the court preacher of Marguerite and was appointed as Bishop of Oloron, were regarded as the former. Louis de Berquin, who was known both for his translations of Erasmus and Luther and as a satirical author against the Paris Theological Faculty, a Paris Doctor Pierre Caroli, and Guillaume Farel, who was a disciple of Lefèvre and later became the reformer of Neuchâtel, Geneva, and Lausanne in French-speaking Switzerland, were regarded as the latter.[7]

2. *Paris University Days*

The historical certainty concerning Calvin's life in this period is limited to a few facts. A fourteen-year-old youth matriculated at the Collège de la Marche in 1523, moved to the prestigious Collège de Montaigu within a few months, and, after four years of study there, graduated with a degree (*licencié en arts*) in 1528. From this inadequate picture, researchers have advanced ratiocinations concerning his academic formation as well as his personal profile by using his own later recollections, secondary materials, and contextual evidence. In our study, however, from our interest in the formation of his ecclesiology, we shall selectively focus on the following three points.

(i) The first point is to acknowledge that Calvin's basic education in the arts can well be understood within the scheme of its opposition to the University's Theological Faculty. In the history of medieval university education, Renaissance humanism arose as a reforming force out of the basic study of the humanities, and its influences had later permeated the professional studies of theology, law, and medicine. Calvin's days at the university witnessed the increasing conflict between the reform ideas of humanists and the Theological Faculty, which was alarmed by their influence. In Paris, in August 1523, the month of Calvin's matriculation, for example, an Augustinian monk was burned to death for the charge of Lutheran heresy, and royal intervention forced the release of Berquin, a reformer who had been imprisoned by the collusion of the Faculty and the Parlement of Paris.[8] In rejoicing over Berquin's release, the university students staged a comedy, "La Farce des théologastres," which was considered to be patterned after Berquin's condemned satire against the Faculty. The play's plot satirized the Faculty by calling it the Sorbonne and

7. Oberman, "Initia Calvini," 143–44; Higman, *Lire et découvrir*, 622–23; Gordon, *Calvin*, 14–17.

8. Cf. Farge, *Orthodoxy*, 173–74. Louis de Berquin's satire (*Apologia adversus calumniatores Lutheri, alias speculum theologastrorum*) ridiculed the theological professors who determined Luther a heretic as "quack theologians" and was possibly the origin of the students' satirical play ("La Farce des théologastres").

set the reformist group of Luther and the French humanists over against the Faculty.[9] If these events symbolized Calvin's initiation into university life, the expulsion of Erasmus's humanistic work, *Colloquies*, from the entire university curriculum in 1528, orchestrated by Noël Beda, syndic of the Faculty, certainly marked an epilogue for Calvin's university days.[10]

Among humanist influences that had assumedly touched Calvin in this period, we may count two cases as historically more verifiable: the basic instructions in grammar and rhetoric received at La Marche from Mathurin Cordier, to whom Calvin later dedicated his *Commentary on the First Thessalonians* (1550), and his friendship with humanist reformist and his elder cousin, Pierre Robert Olivétan, whose French translation of the Bible afforded an occasion for Calvin to write two prefaces in 1535. Among other humanist influences, Calvin researchers have advanced ratiocinations of a few notable cases: the late medieval lay reform movement, Devotio Moderna, which appealed to returning to the Bible and Augustine and was said to be influential at Montaigu in Calvin's time; the characteristically anti-Pelagian Scotism; the Neo-Augustinianism of John Major (Mair), a philosopher from Scotland and a leading professor at Montaigu (1525–31). However, the overall picture is that Calvin was predominantly influenced by humanism, the trend of the times, and that the humanist trend can be understood in sharp opposition to the Paris Theological Faculty.[11]

(ii) The second point concerns Calvin's studies at the Collège de Montaigu where he had spent his life from 14 to 18 years of age. Montaigu was known for being a prestigious Collège during this period. Its reputation was largely due to the educational reforms of Jean Standonck, its rector at the end of the previous century, as well as to Noël Beda, rector at the turn of the century, who was known for rigorous studies and strict observance of the rules. Incidentally, there were several Montaigu residents who later became famous: Erasmus had a short stay a few years ahead of Calvin. François Rabelais and Ignatius Loyola, a founder of the Jesuit Order, also roughly coincided with Calvin's time.

On the other hand, the reputation of Montaigu definitely did not rest on its humanist studies but on its role as a preparatory school for candidates to the ecclesiastical offices. In fact, many candidates resided there and upon their graduation advanced to theological studies. Due to this close affiliation with the Theological Faculty, Montaigu was also known for its spirit of de-

9. Q. Breen, *John Calvin: A Study in French Humanism*, 2nd ed. (Hamden, CT: Archon Books, 1968), 28–29. In the play, along with the personifications of Faith and Reason, the Roman god Mercury (Berquin) appeared as an emissary of Germany and defended Luther, Erasmus, and Lefèvre.

10. Cf. Farge, *Orthodoxy*, 195–96.

11. Cf. McGrath, *A Life*, 27–28, 34–35; Bouwsma, *Calvin*, 12–13.

fending the church establishment and their conservatism was prevalent. For example, "La Farce des théologastres" satirized Montaigu as an accomplice of the Collège de Sorbonne where the theological courses were concentrated. John Major, Montaigu's philosopher and professor in the Theological Faculty, criticized the humanist studies for bringing in "a great army of pestilential heretics." He later joined the heresy inquest of Erasmus.[12] Furthermore, a controversial anti-Lutheran work, *Adversus Clandestinos Lutheranos* (1529) of Noël Beda, Montaigu's previous rector during Calvin's time and current syndic of the Theological Faculty, determined that the humanist studies of Erasmus, Lefèvre and others were the chief instigators of the Lutheran heresy. It is not certain how a sentiment such as Beda's was accepted at Montaigu. Despite Calvin's own silence about his Montaigu period, we can safely assume that his academic formation was conducted in the tension between reactionary theology and reform-minded humanist studies.[13]

Judging from the college's spirit and its close affiliation with the Theological Faculty, exactly what the subjects of Calvin's studies were as well as what he had learned at Montaigu is a matter of conjecture. In addition to the basic humanities (grammar, logic, rhetoric, mathematics, music, geometry, and astronomy), we can assume that he familiarized himself with the philosophical and theological studies of traditional Thomism and the current Nominalism, Neo-Augustinianism, and the Devotio Moderna. Among the current humanists, the influence of Erasmus and Lefèvre can be assumed. Concerning the influence of Erasmus upon the young Calvin, from the classical work of Doumergue to the modern study of Bouwsma, researchers have generally agreed.[14] Concerning Lefèvre's influence, it is hard to imagine that Calvin, as a candidate of the ecclesiastical offices, would not have been acquainted with Lefèvre's biblical works (the Psalms, the Pauline and Catholic Epistles). These works were all published before Calvin's matriculation at the University. Yet, due to his silence on Lefèvre's works, the influence has not been fully established.[15] Concerning

12. Cf. Breen, *John Calvin*, 28; Farge, *Orthodoxy*, 179, 194.

13. Noël Beda, *Apologia adversus clandestinos Lutheranos*. Cf. Gordon, *Calvin*, 7–8; Farge, *Orthodoxy*, 198; Bouwsma, *Calvin*, 12. Bouwsma considers the school spirit of Montaigu "hardly a humanist academy" and the humanist influence upon Calvin through his like-minded teachers and friends.

14. Doumergue, *Jean Calvin*, 1; Bouwsma, *Calvin*, 13–14.

15. Many researchers who have placed Calvin in his historical context, from Wendel (*Calvin*, 41: "the reformism of Lefèvre") to the most recent, Gordon (*Calvin*, 57–62: "a Lefèvrian evangelicalism"), have associated Calvin's academic formation with Lefèvre and his sympathizers. Although both Wendel (130) and Gordon (57–62) see no significant imprints of Lefèvre in the first *Institutes*, Oberman ("Initia Calvini," 114) points out Calvin's

Neo-Augustinianism, since Reuter's study, Major's considerable influence has received some attention. But as some objections persist, researchers seem to have not yet reached a conclusion.[16] Concerning the question of whether Calvin could have taken some advanced theological studies while he was at Montaigu, many researchers find this unlikely, largely due to the undergraduate's limitation of time and the demands of the theological faculty curriculum.[17] In addition, since the above-mentioned preface to his Psalm commentary described his formation at Montaigu as "the study of philosophy" (*philosophiae studium*), besides the studies of humanities and classical philosophy, it encompassed the basic courses in Scholastic philosophy as preparatory to advanced theological studies. Incidentally, the same preface attributed his father's wish for Calvin to abandon the expected major in theology and to proceed in the study of law.[18] However, since there is no other historical evidence besides Calvin's attestation uttered thirty years after the actual incident, we can rather assume that Calvin, after having studied the basics of theology and yet having been troubled in the conflict between humanist studies and conservative theology, gradually opted to abandon theology and to advance to a law major. Furthermore, he chose not to study canon law in Paris but civil law in Orléans, a center of humanist studies and a city away from the capital.

(iii) The third point deals with the most difficult question from the perspective of historical documentation, namely, Calvin's relationship with the greatest religious problem of the time, "the issue of Luther," hotly debated especially in the capital and at the University. In particular, at the University of Paris, the initial involvement with the issue was occasioned by the theological examination of

---

relationship with Lefèvre as an overlooked research field vis-à-vis that with Erasmus and Budé. We will examine Lefèvre in connection with Guillaume Farel in chapter 2.

16. See K. Reuter's thesis of Major's influence on Calvin's formation (*Das Grundverständnis der Theologie Calvins* [Neukirchen: Neukirchner Verlag, 1963], 20–28), as well as some negative reviews of the Reuter thesis by A. N. S. Lane (*John Calvin: Student of the Church Fathers*, Edinburgh: T&T Clark, 1999, 88–89), Ganoczy (*Young Calvin*, 61), and Oberman ("Initia Calvini," 120–23). A. E. McGrath's fresh defense of the Reuter thesis ("John Calvin and Late Mediaeval Thought: A Study in Late Mediaeval Influences upon Calvin's Theological Development," *Archiv für Reformationsgeschichte* 77 [1986]: 58–78) is also useful.

17. Ganoczy, *Young Calvin*, 59–60, 177; Oberman, "Initia Calvini," 116. Cf. Farge, *Orthodoxy*, 13–28. Generally speaking, the students in theology, after humanity studies in grammar, philosophy, and science, attended the colleges of Sorbonne or Navarre where the theological courses were concentrated. Ganoczy's view that for an undergraduate like Calvin it was practically impossible to pursue theology seems to be supported by Farge's analysis of the Paris Theological Faculty's curriculum. Accordingly, Ganoczy's view of Calvin as "a lay theologian" or the self-taught theologian seems to be justified.

18. *CO* 31:21.

the Leipzig Disputation between Johann Eck and Martin Luther (1519). The request to examine was made by the Catholic Church, upon the agreement of both participants, to the two universities of Paris and Erfurt. The disputation's major focus was on papal primacy and infallibility of the Catholic Church as well as the related topics of the ecclesiastical constitution and councils. Incidentally, Luther considered the true Catholic church as Christ's kingdom, the pope an antichrist, and papal hierarchy a historical product unwarranted by divine authority.

While Erfurt declined to take up the request, the University of Paris, as a proud consultant of Christendom, did so. Upon examining the disputation as well as Luther's works, the Theological Faculty finally issued its heresy judgment against Luther (*Determinatio*) in April 1521. Since the final judgment was delayed, the examination was able to take into consideration Luther's three great reform tracts of 1520, especially *On the Babylonian Captivity of the Church*, which attacked the papal church and its sacramental system. The examination's overall themes were the doctrines of the church and the sacraments. Since the *Determinatio* was repeatedly published and its German, Dutch, and French translations were made available, this was the document to which Calvin would surely have had access. Furthermore, the Theological Faculty moved to exclude Luther's books from the university curriculum. The Parlement of Paris issued a decree to prohibit the possession and reading of his books on the suspicion of his being a heretic in August 1523, when Calvin matriculated. Although it is hard to imagine Calvin as a candidate for ecclesiastical offices and uninterested in the Luther issue, researchers seem to be divided as to what extent his formation was influenced by it.[19] For sure, in the tradition of French humanism, Lefèvre's position did not consider Luther a heretic. On the other hand, as Calvin recollected later in the preface to his *Psalms Commentary*, the conditions before his conversion were "pertinaciously addicted to the superstitions of the Papacy." It can be assumed that his university days left no room for the suggestions of the Luther reception, not even for Lefèvre's reformist ideas.[20]

3. *Studies in Law*

(i) After graduating from the University of Paris, Calvin studied law at the Universities of Orléans and Bourges, received his "*licencié en lois*," and established

19. Cf. Farge, *Orthodoxy*, 125–30, 165–70.

20. *CO* 31:21. Cf. Wendel, *Calvin*, 20; Ganoczy, *Young Calvin*, 49, 55, 61–62; McGrath, *A Life*, 40–50; Gordon, *Calvin*, 12–13, 17. As to Calvin's academic formation, Ganoczy and McGrath positively relate it with the problem of Luther; but Gordon, considering Calvin's position unverifiable, does not relate it.

himself as a jurist. The law school at Orléans was a prestigious institution established in the thirteenth century and the oldest such institution north of Italy. In his immediate background, Calvin knew the former graduate of Orléans, Guillaume Budé, a most prestigious French legal scholar (*Annotationes in Pandectas*, 1508) and Hellenist (*Commentarii linguae graecae*, 1529). Budé introduced a new humanist methodology, incorporating philological and exegetical precision into the study of law. Of fifteenth-century origin in the capital of the old Berry, the law school at Bourges was known for its close ties with the royal household, was under the patronage of Marguerite of Navarre, and was a recognized center for humanist studies along with Orléans. At Orléans, Calvin studied under his compatriot scholar, Pierre de L'Estoile, and at Bourges under an Italian scholar who shared Budé's new methodology, Andrea Alciati. Mullett's recent Calvin biography characterizes L'Estoile as "the pious conservative Catholic senior cleric and academically traditionalist law professor" and Alciati as "a leading pioneer . . . of a humanistic analysis of the *Corpus juris* based on linguistic, philological and stylistic content and historical, social and cultural context."

As far as Calvin's formation is concerned, many researchers consider his law school days as a means to worldly success or "the lost years," and instead focus on the humanist studies to which he had rapidly inclined during this period. This aspect is noteworthy for the fact that Orléans and Bourges were known as enclaves of the humanists and reformists. After finishing his law studies, Calvin returned to Paris and attended some lectures at the newly established Collège Royal for higher humanist studies. It should also be noted that the law studies themselves had some bearing upon his later formation, especially in theology. In this connection, citing Calvin's later recollection of his law studies in the preface to his *Psalms Commentary*, Millet highlights the importance of Calvin's law studies for "a different direction" which God's providence showed him and "other studies," namely, higher humanist studies and the biblical and theological studies, which he was to later pursue. Gordon's biography notices that Calvin drew on such theological notions as the role of the Holy Spirit as "witness," the nature of justification, God as "legislator" and "judge," and Christ as the "perpetual advocate" from his law studies. Thanks to his legal studies Calvin had begun to cultivate the linguistic, historical methodology that he had learned from L'Estoile and Alciati and that he will later apply to his innovative biblical interpretations.[21]

21. Mullett, *John Calvin*, 11; O. Millet, *Calvin et la dynamique de la parole: Étude de rhétorique réformée* (Paris: Classiques Garnier, 2019), 37, 39–42, 54–55; Gordon, *Calvin*, 21–22.

(ii) Granted that Calvin used legal concepts for his later formation in theology, what exactly did his studies under L'Estoile and Alciati mean for his intellectual formation, especially for his attitude toward the religious issues of the time? The basic humanist assumptions employed in the theology of Erasmus and Luther called them to lay aside current Scholastic theology, instead returning to the traditions of Scripture and the ancient church. A similar return was observed in the studies of civil law at this time. McGrath calls what Calvin had studied "French legal humanism." It was a movement to return to the traditions of the old French and ancient Roman laws in order to establish a new legal system as a part of the centralization of government under Francis I. L'Estoile and Alciati were the leaders of this movement.[22] Although both scholars shared the same methodology of studying the civil law (*corpus iuris civilis*) in connection with the old French and the ancient Roman laws, in actual legal hermeneutics they represented two different traditions. Calvin had studied one tradition under L'Estoile and the other under Alciati. For instance, L'Estoile favored a more traditional method of studying civil law in compiling the old legal cases and interpretations. Alciati, representing Italian humanism, took a more thoroughly humanist approach, comparing civil law with ancient Roman law and tracing the development of legal concepts.[23] When a dispute arose between the interpretations of both scholars, Calvin was asked to write a preface to *Antapologia* (1531), an anti-Alciati work of his friend Nicolas Duchemin who defended the French scholar. It is interesting to note that Calvin, while responding to his friend's expectations by praising L'Estoile as the greatest scholar of the present age, never denied Alciati and instead tried to mediate both sides. According to Gordon, here were manifested Calvin's "intellectual independence" and "unwillingness to submit to the intellectual agenda of another" as well as nationalistic spirit for L'Estoile who favored the French Church over the Roman Church.[24] It should be noted, however, that L'Estoile was a religious traditionalist who, as a vicar of the Bishop of Orléans, later persecuted the Lutherans and denied the Evangelical reforms.

(iii) A more positive impact upon Calvin's intellectual formation in this period was his association with the humanists. This group included the German classicist Melchior Wolmar, under whom Calvin studied Greek in Orléans, his elder cousin and reformist Olivétan from his Paris days, and his school fellows Duchemin, François de Connan, and François Daniel. At the time of Calvin's

22. McGrath, *A Life*, 58–59.
23. Gordon, *Calvin*, 20.
24. Gordon, *Calvin*, 20–21.

encounter in Orléans, Wolmar was known as a Lutheran, and, since Wolmar had moved to Bourges by Marguerite's invitation in 1529, Calvin had received Wolmar's instructions in classical Greek during his entire law school days. When he later dedicated his *Second Corinthians Commentary* (1548) as a witness of this association, its dedicatory epistle recollected the studies of this period as "Greek literatures together with legal study," and thanked Wolmar for the basic humanist studies that proved useful in his later years.[25] Although acknowledging Wolmar's contributions, however, the epistle was totally silent on his influence on faith, which was assumedly a great concern for the later Reformer of Geneva. If, after having studied the classics in Paris, Wolmar became known as a Lutheran and escaped the pressures in the capital by moving to Orléans, and as Calvin seemed to be following him as his teacher to Orléans and Bourges, there remains the question of what the epistle did not mention, since Calvin would soon become his teacher's fellow Evangelical after his conversion. While many researchers have connected Calvin's development to Evangelicalism and subsequent conversion to Wolmar's influence, there are some interpretations that question this assumption and consider it historically unfounded.[26]

As far as Calvin's association with Olivétan is concerned, on the other hand, a more positive, though not clear-cut, influence could be seen since Olivétan had gone through a similar journey to Evangelicalism ahead of him. As indicated in his prefaces to Olivétan's French Bible, which we will analyze later, this association had lasted for the entire period of his Paris days and legal studies. However, there is here an issue concerning a testimony of historical importance in the Calvin biography by Beza—Calvin's later successor in Geneva, who was ten years younger than Calvin and had stayed during this period at Wolmar's residence for tutelage, where he met Calvin for the first time. In connection with Calvin's move to Orléans, Beza's biography mentions that Olivétan advised Calvin to turn to "true religion." The biography asserts that it was because of this advice that Calvin made a turn to the studies of the Bible.[27]

25. *CO* 12:365.

26. Among the advocates of a cautious approach on this issue—besides Wendel (*Calvin*, 23), Breen (*John Calvin*, 42), and Ganoczy (*Young Calvin*, 67–68)—Gordon (*Calvin*, 19) acknowledges Wolmar only as "first teacher of Greek." Interestingly, Theodore Beza described Wolmar's contribution to Calvin (*Vita Calvini*, *CO* 21:122) as limited to Greek literature, at the same level attributed in Calvin's dedicatory epistle.

27. *CO* 21:121: "de vera religione admonitus legendis sacris libris se tradere." Despite Beza's knowledge of Calvin in the Orléans period, the validity of his memory as a ten-year-old boy can be questioned. Since Doumergue (*Jean Calvin*, 1:117) portrayed Olivétan as "a mysterious figure," many scholars have discounted Olivétan's influence on Calvin in

The verification issue of this testimony aside, it seems possible to interpret that the advice was an occasion for Calvin to turn to biblical studies as the basis for evangelicalism, since the term "true religion" suggested the position of the radical rather than the moderate evangelical humanists within the early French Reformation. Lastly, although the above-mentioned school fellows of his law studies were interested in reform, they seemed to have remained moderates. In sharp contrast, during this period or immediately after, Calvin experienced his conversion, which indicated his decisive turn to a radical evangelical position.[28]

4. Studies at the Collège Royal and the Commentary on Seneca's De clementia

In 1530, Francis I, gathering a group of scholars in the trilingual fields (Greek, Hebrew, and Latin), finally established the Collège Royal for higher humanistic learning in the University of Paris. Due to the Collège's initial stage of limited faculty, lack of requirements for admission, and free auditing, Calvin's studies there were considered to be irregular and limited to Pierre Danes's Greek and François Vatable's Hebrew language courses during the years from 1531 to 1533.[29] During this period, since Calvin visited Orléans at least twice, it is assumed that he received a degree in law, or became a professional "*licencié*."[30] Also, at the occasion of his father's death in May 1531, he seemed to have chosen to proceed to higher humanist learning, and his Seneca commentary could be placed as a result of this process.[31] We should ask what this period meant for Calvin's academic formation as well as his ecclesiology.

Orléans, and Gordon (*Calvin*, 18–19) considers Beza's statement, if it were true, "an attractive possibility," but "conjecture." On the other hand, Ganoczy (*Young Calvin*, 64–65) and F. Higman ("Olivétan, Pierre Robert," *OER* 3:174–75), referring to the humanist or the Lefèvrian background, cautiously affirm the possibility of Beza's statement.

28. Cf. Gordon, *Calvin*, 29–30; Wendel, *Calvin*, 23; Ganoczy, *Young Calvin*, 68–69.

29. Cf. Breen, *John Calvin*, 63–65; Wendel, *Calvin*, 26; Ganoczy, *Young Calvin*, 69, 72. According to Ganoczy, among the readers in Greek and Hebrew (Pierre Danes, Jacque Toussain, François Vatable, Agatha Guidacerius), Danes and Vatable, who were Lefèvrians, urged the exegesis of the original text to the auditors.

30. Concerning Calvin's legal studies, many scholars, including Wendel (*Calvin*, 26), consider them to have been completed at Orléans.

31. Although Wendel (*Calvin*, 26) and others make a ratiocination that Calvin turned himself over to concentrated humanist studies on the occasion of his father's death, both Calvin's own preface to the Psalms commentary and Beza's *Vita Calvini* did not refer to this connection.

(1) Studies at the Collège Royal

(i) First, either in the advanced learning of basic humanities or in the professional studies of law and theology, there existed some interdisciplinary communication and cooperation by means of humanities studies. In this regard, therefore, Calvin's move from the study of law to that of advanced humanities could be understood. Guillaume Budé, advisor to the king, whose recommendation paved the way for the establishment of the Collège Royal, was an exemplar for the young Calvin. For him, Budé was a prominent senior of the Orléans law school, a progenitor of Roman law in French legal circles, an established Hellenist, and a well-known author of the *Commentarii linguae graecae* (1529). Although this kind of cooperation could well be witnessed among the humanists, the reverse side of the picture was that there existed in the professional studies an antagonistic spirit against the humanities, as exemplified by the Paris Theological Faculty's naming Erasmus "a mere rhetorician" unqualified in the field of theology.[32]

(ii) Second, although Calvin's auditing of Greek and Hebrew courses was in itself a study in classics, it could also be associated with biblical studies that were in conflict with official Catholic theology. In fact, in its heresy inquiry against Erasmus, the Paris Theological Faculty criticized his studies in Greek language and his critical editions of the Greek Bible and Latin translation. This inquiry resulted in the intervention of the king's palace to defend the study of the humanities. In opposition to the establishment of the Collège Royal in 1530, the Theological Faculty chastised the thesis that studies in Greek and Hebrew were indispensable for biblical studies and preaching as "erroneous and impious." Furthermore, in 1534, at the proposal of the faculty's syndic Beda, the Parlement of Paris summoned the professors of Greek and Hebrew of the Collège Royal and forbade their criticism of the Vulgate Bible.[33] Under these circumstances, as suggested by Ganoczy, Calvin's auditing was "a proof of courage" indicating his spiritual stirring for biblical studies, and the whole course of his study at the Collège Royal might point to the shared common concern of evangelical humanists such as Lefèvre for reform.[34]

(iii) Lastly, it has been said that there are few materials, other than the Seneca commentary, that can substantiate Calvin's intellectual trajectory in this

32. Breen, *John Calvin*, 61; H. A. Oberman, *The Two Reformations*, ed. D. Weinstein (New Haven: Yale University Press, 2003), 126; Farge, *Orthodoxy*, 187.

33. Farge, *Orthodoxy*, 186–96, 205–6.

34. Ganoczy, *Young Calvin*, 72.

period. In particular, the difficulty in tracing his development is compounded in the year-and-a-half period of "vacuum" from April 1532 to October 1534 when he returned to Paris. But there is a letter of intercession that could have been written during this period addressed to Martin Bucer in Strasbourg, for the sake of Calvin's French humanist friend who was a refugee charged with Anabaptism in the city. If we assume that the letter dated only as "September 4th, at Noyon" was written between 1532 and 1534, its composition would roughly correspond to the period in which Bucer's Strasbourg had struggled with and finally repelled Anabaptist challenges by establishing the *Strasbourg Ecclesiastical Ordinances* (1534), thus suggesting the seriousness of the charge (*suspicio anabaptismi*) against the friend. Though believing in the friend's innocence, in view of the charge's seriousness, Calvin appealed for a spirit of toleration, which he extensively discussed in his Seneca commentary. The letter furthermore reflected his evangelical humanism as well as the ideal of the church catholic.[35] It is particularly noteworthy that the letter seemed unintentionally to reveal the division between the moderate evangelical humanist group to which Calvin belonged and the radical evangelical humanists of his friend. Calling traditional Catholicism "servitude," Calvin described his friend, who was highly esteemed among French humanists, as no longer able to submit voluntarily to that servitude "which we are still enduring" and going into exile without a hope of returning to the homeland.[36] This sentence might be interpreted as a reflection of the polarization then taking place in the evangelical humanist movement.

(2) The Commentary on Seneca's De clementia

Although Calvin's first publication, the Seneca commentary, is no doubt important for assessing his intellectual development, its evaluation as to his religious formation varies widely. On the one hand, from the viewpoint of consistency

35. *COR* VI-1:131–33. Cf. Ganoczy, *Young Calvin*, 87–91; Balke, *Calvin and the Anabaptist*, 34–35. The editors of *COR* VI-1 take the letter originated in 1536 and sent from Nyon, a town north of Geneva, instead of Noyon in France. In view of the letter's general tone, and especially the sentence quoted that more suitably depicted Calvin before his conversion and exile, we take the letter as originating in the period of 1532–34.

36. *COR* VI-1:132: "Tamen, cum non posset submittere diutius cervices isti voluntariae servituti, quam adhuc ferimus, demigravit ad vos in nullam spem reditus." Although the editors acknowledge the expression, "bondage which even yet we bear," unnatural to Calvin's personal situation after his exile, their footnote interprets Calvin speaking in general terms "as a French man," and not personally.

between humanism and theology, there are positive evaluations of the work as "the culmination of Calvin's youthful humanism" and his "pagan apprenticeship" to the Christian life. On the other hand, those who emphasize the difference between Renaissance humanism and the Reformation say that the career of a professional man of letters "has begun and ended with this work" and that it was "a poisoned chalice."[37] Among the scholars who emphasize historical research on Calvin's intellectual formation, there are many approaches to analyze this work: Wendel considers it original as a humanistic work; Oberman urges us to read it as a book of the age, especially "in the context of the politically turbulent situation in France"; Höpfl analyzes it as the combined work of law and humanities studies and focuses on its political concepts.[38] In this study, however, we view it in the context of the early French Reformation, considering it particularly as a work of his moderate evangelical humanist period.

(i) First of all, under the current of the northern Renaissance in which humanities studies had increasingly been drawn toward religion and ethics, "the resurgence of Stoic philosophy" could be seen among humanists such as Erasmus and Budé. In this context, Calvin, aspiring to establish himself as a humanist scholar, took advantage of the times with his Seneca commentary. As a matter of fact, there was a testimony that "a certain Calvin" lectured on Seneca and was well received at the Collège de Fortet where he might have taken residence while auditing lectures at the Collège Royal.[39] The reasons why he felt a strong affinity with the currently popular Stoicism can be guessed: the earnest Stoic posture toward ethics; its conformation theory that stressed unity and equity in mankind and societies; its enthusiasm for the study of truth; its avoidance of magical ceremonies in religion; and the belief in and respect for a supreme deity. In particular, it is noteworthy that Stoic social conformation theory, which sought harmony for overcoming religious and ethnic boundaries, was opened to the ideal of the church catholic shared among French evangelical humanists. The Seneca commentary, however, mainly revealed Calvin to be a humanist

37. *L. annei Senecae, . . . , libri duo de clementia, . . .* , 1532: *BC* 32/1. Among researchers, some examples of a positive view are found in Breen, *John Calvin*, 67; F. L. Battles, *Interpreting John Calvin* (Grand Rapids: Baker Books, 1996), 84; T. F. Torrance, *The Hermeneutics of John Calvin* (Edinburgh: Scottish Academic Press, 1988), 133–40. Some negative views are found in Höpfl, *Christian Polity*, 7, 19, McGrath, *A Life*, 60–61, Gordon, *Calvin*, 30.

38. Cf. Wendel, *Calvin*, 27–37; Oberman, "Initia Calvini," 139–42; Höpfl, *Christian Polity*, 7–18.

39. Oberman, "Initia Calvini," 140n119. The witness was Claude d'Espence, the regent at the Collège de Beauvais, an Erasmian, who later became a Catholic apologist against the Calvinist influences in the French Church.

scholar. There was no substantial evidence whatsoever that indicated either the violent religious conflicts suggested by his later "sudden conversion" or the manifestation of his evangelical belief made clear after the conversion.[40]

(ii) Secondly, besides the Seneca commentary being a product of Calvin's legal and humanities studies, it was also a book of the times in the sense that it dealt with the "church and state" issue that was regarded as an important issue among French magistrates as well as humanists. In particular, the humanist studies on Roman law that Calvin received directly from L'Estoile and Alciati were welcomed in the courts of Francis I who sought to strengthen his absolutistic right in opposition to papal supremacy, and therefore their points of contact could be considered. For example, the personal history of Roman Stoic philosopher Seneca, who was an advisor to Emperor Nero in his "good rule" period and later victimized by Nero in his "bad rule" period, was well known among contemporary Christians and later church fathers. Likewise, religious tolerance was a serious issue for sixteenth-century humanists—especially for French evangelical humanists who had been under the king's protection and had continued to advance their reform programs, and whose Meaux reform was severely damaged by attacks of conservatives during the king's captivity in Spain (1525–26). Lefèvre, a leader of the moderates, was later rescued from the prosecuting Parlement of Paris by the king's intervention, but Berquin, a representative of the radical humanists, was executed in 1529 while the king turned his back. Furthermore, at the time Calvin's commentary on Seneca appeared, the king's oppressive measures against radical evangelical humanists were strengthened and the issue of religious tolerance became an existential issue for them.[41]

If Calvin tried to present a kind of "advice to princes" following the examples of Budé's *Institution du Prince* and Erasmus's *Institutio Principis Christiani*, his book showed no evidence of appeals to the monarch for tolerance or mercy beyond what Seneca's *De clementia* did. To this point, an interesting element appeared in Calvin's textual interpretation in which he drew the proposition "princes are unbound from laws" (*princeps legibus solutus est*) from the in-

40. Cf. Wendel, *Calvin*, 27–28; Ganoczy, *Young Calvin*, 74; Balke, *Calvin and the Anabaptist*, 24; Battles, *Interpreting John Calvin*, 65–85. There were only three biblical references, including the reference to Romans 13 (*CO* 5:18), in which Calvin stated that "our religion" likewise confessed the same. As to the patristic references, Augustine's *City of God* was referred to over a dozen times only in order to support Seneca's arguments. One noticeable comment might be on the theme of "misericordia" (*CO* 5:154, 156–57) in which Calvin opposed the Christian view over Seneca's view of identifying it as a human infirmity unfit to deities.

41. Cf. Farge, *Orthodoxy*, 152–56, 183–85, 198; R. J. Knecht, "Francis I of France," *OER* 2:132.

terpretation of Roman law according to the Justinian Codes, and he agreed with Budé, Alciati, and the court jurists in defending the monarchic absolutist claims.[42] In the background of the king's protection of humanists in opposition to the coordination of the Parlement of Paris and the Theological Faculty, as Monter indicates, this proposition was shared among the moderate evangelical humanists. Calvin, as one of them, expressed his hope for the king's role. Or, as Höpfl notices, the way in which Calvin affirmed the proposition "rather formally" could be an indication of his vacillation between the proposition's intimation of a king "unbound from laws" and that of a king as "the upholder and guardian of the law." His two references, the traditional distinction between a good king's rule according to law and a tyrant's claim of being above law, together with his citation of Romans 13 for the biblical principle of all princely authorities deriving from God, indicated this vacillation.[43]

(iii) Thirdly, it is noteworthy that Calvin's commentary on Seneca, though a book of the times, did not directly mention certain topics that were noticeable issues in France at this time. Since the commentary was not meant to be a defense of the Christian faith, for example, it neglected medieval theories on church and state. Instead, it addressed the Justinian Codes, which were in line with Roman law and from which the above-mentioned proposition was taken. This was in the tradition of canon law that portrayed states as existing in a condition of depravity resulting from the fall, and therefore to be placed under the authority of the church. This was naturally propagated by the papal church as well as its theological institutions. Also, the commentary on Seneca understandably did not mention Niccolò Machiavelli's *The Prince* (*Il principe*, 1513 in the original Italian, posthumous publication in 1532). While the traditions of the Justinian Codes and canon law both presupposed the church and state relationship as God-given, *The Prince* denied this presupposition from historical analyses of human societies, positioned religion (the church) as a part of the state institution, and freed the duties of the prince from the conscriptions of religious faith and ethics. Although both works of Calvin and Machiavelli were published in the same year, for Calvin *The Prince* represented the opposite of his understanding of religion and the Christian antiquities. As the evaluation of *The Prince* among humanists including Erasmus was rather low and its Latin translation appeared late in 1553, Calvin seemed to have felt no serious threats from it. Furthermore, it seems to be an enigma that the

42. *CO* 5:23, 67. Cf. Breen, *John Calvin*, 83–85; Wendel, *Calvin*, 30.

43. W. Monter, *Judging the French Reformation: Heresy Trials by Sixteenth-Century Parlements* (Cambridge, MA, and London: Harvard University Press, 1999), 58–84; Höpfl, *Christian Polity*, 14–17. Cf. *CO* 5:18, 67, 89–90, 98.

commentary lacked any reference to the Luther issue that, as we discussed above, was a serious problem for the moderate evangelical humanists. It also lacked any appeal for religious tolerance or for mercy from the king who had intensified his suppression of radical evangelical humanists. Rather, can we ask why Calvin's maiden publication would miss such a great opportunity?[44]

(iv) Lastly, even though the Seneca commentary is insignificant for insight into Calvin's theological formation, we should ask whether it suggested any indication of Calvin as future Reformer of the church. Höpfl, who recognizes in it a glimpse of the future "Reformer and ecclesiastical politician," takes notice of two concepts. Concerning the definition of a state or a city, firstly, Calvin referred to Seneca's citation of Aristotle's *Politics* and formulated his own definition as "an assembly [*concilium*] or society [*coetus*] of men associated by law." Rephrasing "an assembly or company" as "community [*societas*]," he further cautioned that all "societies" were not to be called states except the ones that were based upon right morals and just laws. Likewise, those who do not keep the laws were not worthy of a state and could be expelled from it.[45] This kind of communal concept of a state could be seen reflected in the first *Institutes* that defined the church as "God's community [*societas*] and people [*populus*]" and the state that could be constituted in the tripartite structure of magistrate, law, and people who were ruled by law.[46] Secondly, Calvin's concept concerning the lawbreakers in the community was formulated as the tripartite aim of the law, which was to say, the lawbreaker's punishment should result in his rectification; his punishment should be a warning to the community; and his expulsion as a last resort should serve for the security of the community.[47] This concept was also used for church discipline and excommunication in the first *Institutes*.[48]

Section 2. From a "Sudden Conversion" to Exile in Basel

In the history of the early French Reformation, the years 1533 and 1534 were generally considered a decisive turning point in which both hope and anxiety

44. Breen, *John Calvin*, 84–85, 134–37. As far as the *Institutes* is concerned, there seems to be no reference to Machiavelli in the first edition, but an implicit reference is found in the last edition (*Institutio* 4.20.1: *OS* 5:471: "The flatterers of princes, immoderately praising their power, do not hesitate to set them against the rule of God himself.")

45. *CO* 5:96. Cf. Höpfl, *Christian Polity*, 16.

46. *OS* 1:86, 260.

47. *CO* 5:132. Cf. Höpfl, *Christian Polity*, 18.

48. *OS* 1:89–90.

for reform converged. Reflecting this picture, the domestic religious policy of Francis I protected the moderate evangelical humanists and checked the overreactions of the Paris Theological Faculty on the one hand, but on the other hand turned to an overt suppression of the domestic reform movements of the radical evangelical humanists. His policy was especially hardened on the occasions of the inaugural address of Paris University's new rector, Nicolas Cop (October 1533) and the Placards affair (October 1534). As a foreign policy measure against the Holy Roman Emperor, likewise, Francis I met Pope Clement VII and confirmed the papal tie at Marseilles in 1533. In the next year he sought religious compromise with the German Protestant princes. In the reform movement itself, the polarization between the moderate and radical groups among evangelical humanists became decisive, exposing the conflicting choices of whether to seek reform within the current Catholic Church under the king's leadership or to suffer persecution, execution, and exile.

A personal history of Gérard Roussel, a moderate reformist, exemplifies the cases of evangelical humanists. When the Meaux reform came under suppression while the king was imprisoned in Spain in 1525, Roussel and his teacher Lefèvre took refuge in Strasbourg where they had witnessed the reality of the Evangelical Reformation. After the king's release from Spain, Roussel returned to France and became a court preacher of Marguerite of Angoulême. While his evangelical Lent sermon of 1533 excited the Parisians, the Theological Faculty charged it as a grave error of Lutheranism and despite the king's intervention he was imprisoned for three months. The outcome of this last-mentioned event also reflected the fluid and transitory character of the times. While the Faculty's syndic Beda who led the Roussel prosecution suffered the loss of his position and banishment from Paris, Roussel under the protection of Marguerite (now Queen of Navarre) became Bishop of Oloron later in 1536.[49]

Furthermore, it should be noted that this period coincided with radical changes in Calvin's life, in which he experienced a rapid inclination into the studies of the Bible, church fathers, and theology, a "sudden conversion," a flight from Paris in connection with the Cop address, his exile in Basel, and the writing of his first *Institutes*. During this period, unquestionably, his early theology, especially his concept of the church, was formed.

49. Cf. F. Higman, "Roussel, Gérard," *OER* 3:452–53; Ganoczy, *Young Calvin*, 76–78; Farge, *Orthodoxy*, 200–204. According to Ganoczy, being acquainted with Roussel during the auditor period of the Royal Readers, Calvin became an admirer of Roussel as a leader of the reformist group. For his later relationship with Roussel, see below chapter 2, section 3 on *Two Epistles*.

1. A "Sudden Conversion"

(i) Despite the fact that Calvin's conversion was a decisive factor for assessing his academic formation and career as a Reformer, researchers face the difficulty of its historical evasiveness.[50] For example, little is said even in Calvin's own work about the reality of his conversion. While the preface to his *Psalms Commentary* (1557), a work of some twenty years after the event, described it as a "sudden conversion," suggesting a change at a certain time; his apologetic work of several years later, the *Reply to Sadoleto* (1539) described it as a serial process. The traditional, theological interpretation portraying it as a dramatic change from the Catholic to the Protestant faith, or the change of allegiance from the Roman Catholic Church to the Evangelical church, has been challenged by historical criticism. There have been many attempts in recent years to resolve this difficulty, but there seems to be no established theory. In the following pages, we will illustrate this point by citing recent research by McGrath, Gordon, and Bouwsma.

Well aware of the problem posed by recent research, McGrath takes a position closer to the traditional view, and interprets Calvin's conversion basically as the process "from a humanist to a reformer," indicating not only "merely a private and interior religious experience" but also "an outward, observable and radical shift in institutional allegiance."[51] Assuming the traditional "sudden conversion" view as unsustainable in the light of historical criticism and proposing an interpretation sustainable within its limits, Gordon first supposes the *Reply to Sadoleto* as the original material describing a historical process from the Roman Catholic Church to Evangelicalism. Then he cites Calvin's "sudden conversion" in the preface to the *Psalms Commentary* as "not a private act but an act of the Church," patterned after the example of the apostle Paul's conversion. According to Gordon, historically the conversion was meant to be the beginning of this process, occurring throughout Calvin's auditing at the Collège Royal and ending with "a Lefèvrian evangelicalism."[52] Bouwsma's interpretation, as a personal and psychological analysis, rejects any parallel equivalent to the conversions of the apostle Paul and Augustine that were recorded as historical events, and proposes that such historical investigations into the young

50. Despite the fact that many attempts have been made since Doumergue (*Jean Calvin*, 1:345), who initially pointed out the historical difficulty of assessing Calvin's conversion, Calvin researchers in general tend to avoid this knotty issue even today.

51. McGrath, *A Life*, 68–70.

52. Gordon, *Calvin*, 33–35.

Calvin can be ignored. Furthermore, he interprets Calvin's "sudden conversion" as an unexpected event, and its reality only as "a shift and quickening of his interests" in the circle of the French evangelical humanists. Although Bouwsma admits that the conversion resulted in a shift toward biblical and theological studies, his thoroughly personal and ahistorical interpretation suggests the shift as relating neither to a confessional statement nor ecclesiastical allegiance, but only as an event in Calvin's personal academic history.[53]

Each of the above-mentioned three types represents a fresh approach to comprehending Calvin's conversion and seems to have its characteristic advantage as well as disadvantage. But whether any of them present a holistic image of the conversion remains a question. While McGrath's theological interpretation, for example, may be able to illustrate the common factors with Luther's and Zwingli's conversions, it seems to be too general to pinpoint the conversion of the French humanist Calvin. As to the more historically conscious interpretation of Gordon, is it appropriate to view the end point of the conversion as a Lefèvrian humanism, thus underestimating Calvin, who advanced to write the *Institutes* after the conversion? In the case of Bouwsma's interpretation, although successful in describing Calvin's conversion as "a sixteenth century portrait" (the subtitle of Bouwsma's book), an impression lingers that the conversion is portrayed as being too isolated from the historical context of the early French Reformation. In our quest for Calvin's early formation, can we sufficiently evaluate the conversion as a transition from the seeker of humanistic recognition in his Seneca commentary to the author of the *Institutes*, or the transition in which the humanities studies—what Wendel calls Calvin's "goal" before his conversion—became his "means" for theology afterward?[54]

As conversion primarily means the change of mind before the divine, is there room for an interpretation that can take into account some suprahistorical elements? Such is the case of Oberman who interprets Calvin's term "sudden" in the context of the medieval terminology as "God-given," or initiated by God, and the conversion itself as "this soul-rendering experience that gives way to the resuscitating power of God."[55] Furthermore, as Calvin's

53. Bouwsma, *Calvin*, 10–11.

54. Wendel, *Calvin*, 44. Cf. Mullett, *John Calvin*, 14–17, esp. 16. Mullett's biography presents a similar view: "The gradual evolution of a mind from a conventional earlier Catholicism, through a Christian humanist phase in the style of the Catholic reformist Lefèvre d'Étaples, into the eventual full acceptance of the doctrines of the Reformation."

55. Oberman, *The Dawn*, 264; Oberman, "Initia Calvini," 130–31. Cf. Torrance, *The Hermeneutics of John Calvin*, 79n85. Emphasizing Calvin's late medieval background like Oberman, Torrance notices a semantic similarity of the "subita conversio" between the De-

conversion could ultimately be associated with his calling, is an interpretation such as Ganoczy's possible, who takes it basically as a "spiritual awakening" but more substantially as "a response to a call to reform the Church"?[56] As an attempt to view it holistically, we propose to place it in the historical context of the early French Reformation, particularly of the evangelical humanism in which the moderate and the radical groups were polarized. We interpret it as the converting process from moderate to radical evangelical humanism in which Calvin, having wrestled with both issues of Rome and Luther, began to formulate his early theology, especially his ecclesiology.

(ii) In French evangelical humanism, the nature of both the "Rome issue" and "Luther issue" had been gradually changed during the period of Calvin's academic formation. Since Lefèvre's *Commentaries on the Four Gospels* made a historical distinction between "the ideal ancient Catholic church" and "the current Roman Catholic Church" as well as the former's restoration and the latter's reformation, a variety of religious reformist ideas and movements, including the Meaux reform, had been attempted. Partly due to the king's increasing control of the French Church as well as his policy of keeping its Roman character, however, church reform had not substantially advanced. Since Luther's famous *Ninety-Five Theses* (1517) and the Paris Theological Faculty's heresy judgment, the *Determinatio* (1521), two main points of controversy seemed to emerge: the Mass as a pivot for the church's salvific system and the ministerial ordination by which the papal rule of the church was secured. Concerning the Mass, among the evangelical humanists since the Meaux reform, a distinction was commonly held between the simple and biblical Lord's Supper and the Catholic Mass. Above all, in the Placards affair a radical contrast between "a sacrament of Jesus Christ" and "the deceitful Papal Mass" was made. Concerning ordination based on the concept of papal primacy, the *Determinatio*, in its preface, avoided any judgment on papal primacy for the reason of church politics, but the main text judged Luther for denying "the church's authority and the ministerial order." And, during Calvin's Collège Royal period, at the request of the archbishop of Rouen, the Theological Faculty judged against the bishopric's *curé* and humanist Étienne Le Court for his denial of papal primacy.[57]

As to the "Luther issue," from the time of the *Determinatio* in the early 1520s Evangelicalism represented by Luther had infiltrated German territories

votio Moderna movement represented by Thomas à Kempis, who used the term as radical awareness of one's being justified before God, and Calvin's.

56. Ganoczy, *Young Calvin*, 242, 263–65.

57. Farge, *Orthodoxy*, 166–67, 198.

within the Empire and the imperial cities and territories in Switzerland. As Evangelicalism had been widely recognized as the Protestant Reformation in the late 1520s, it became increasingly difficult for French evangelical humanists to ignore it as an option for church reform. But, the king whom they had hoped to be a crucial factor for church reform was still keeping his suppressive stand against this issue, and arrests and executions of so-called Lutherans were occurring in various parts of the country. In addition, the emergence of a position that viewed church reform sufficiently completed with the French Church's autonomy and exclusion of heretics was noticeable, as exemplified by the growing conservatism of humanists such as Budé, whom we will discuss later in connection with Calvin's *Institutes*. On the other hand, however, it was also a fact that some of them continued to choose exile in Strasbourg, Zurich, Basel and elsewhere, and that the surge of "Lutheranism" was recognized by magistrates in over fifty cities and towns in France after the Placards affair.[58] Certainly, the king, in search of the cooperation of German Protestant princes through Melanchthon's intermediary, made clear that those whom he had been suppressing were not the Lutherans, but the so-called Sacramentarians such as the Zwinglians. Nevertheless, among evangelical humanists both groups were considered practically the same.

(iii) At this juncture, as we propose to view Calvin's conversion process as a transition from moderate to radical evangelical humanism, how can we relate his conversion to the Rome and Luther issues? To begin with, both moderate and radical groups shared common concepts such as the church's catholicity and a distinction between the ancient Catholic church and the current Roman Church. It is also not historically accurate to mold French evangelical humanists into two groups, as if they were distinguishable entities. Furthermore, there were no clear-cut marks as such between the two groups. Neither the choice to remain in the country nor to become exiles could be regarded as marks. In addition, even within one group, for example among the moderate evangelical humanists, there was a variety of positions concerning the Rome and Luther issues. There was Budé who, being close to the moderate group, sharply distinguished authentic humanist reform of the Roman Catholic Church from Evangelical reform, which he regarded as nonauthentic and excessive. There was also Lefèvre who avoided radical criticism against papalism, yet silently kept his positive evaluation toward the Evangelical Ref-

58. Kelley, *The Beginning*, 16–18, 24–25; Monter, *Judging the French Reformation*, 55–68; J. A. Reid, "French Evangelical Networks before 1555: Proto-churches?," in *La réforme en France et en Italie*, ed. P. Benedict, S. Seidel Menchi, and A. Tallon (Rome: École française de Rome, 2007), 105–24.

ormation. Even among those who were later known as Nicodemites, there were some who, in agreement with the radical group, remained in the country and engaged in evangelical reform.[59]

Having considered the above points, however, we cannot ignore the fact that the Rome and Luther issues exposed a number of differences among French evangelical humanists. In particular, for example, concerning the Rome issue, different responses could be seen concerning whether to regard the current Roman Catholic Church as a form of the ancient Catholic church or as a deviation of a papal church in need of radical reform. Among those who sought reform within the current church, both optimism in hoping for the possible restoration of Catholic Christianity and pessimism in forsaking it as impossible could be seen. Concerning the Luther issue, there was an undeniable split within the early French Reformation, with some viewing Luther's Evangelical Reformation as a continuous form of the ancient Catholic church, while others viewed it as an unauthentic deviation from it. As a matter of fact, this question seemed to imply the division of evangelical humanism into two groups. As an illustration of this point, Higman considers evangelicalism that sought reform within the current church as the mainstream of the French Reformation, calling it that of "Catholic liberals," and characterizing it as decisively "non-Lutheran."[60] If we regard Higman's "Catholic liberals" as an equivalent of our "moderate evangelical humanism," his characterization of them as "non-Lutheran" may suggest our "radical evangelical humanism" as being fully compatible with Luther's Evangelicalism. To sum up, we will test our assumption that Calvin's conversion served as a turning point from moderate to radical evangelical humanism in his personal trajectory from the time of the Cop address to his own exile in Basel.

2. *The Cop Address and After*

On All Saints' Day in 1533, sixteen years after Luther's *Ninety-Five Theses*, a son of the king's court physician and a medical professor of Paris University, Nicolas

59. Cf. H. A. Oberman, *The Impact of the Reformation* (Grand Rapids: Eerdmans, 1994), 187–94; Gordon, *Calvin*, 35–36. Oberman considers the Nicodemites "courageous alternative" to Calvin's "refugees' reformation" and cites Calvin's fellow law student in Orléans and friend, Antoine Fumée, as an example. Concerning the perplexing evaluations in Lefèvre research, confer a dictionary article: G. Bedouelle, "Lefèvre d'Étaples, Jacques," *OER* 2:415–16.

60. Higman, *Lire et découvrir*, 622–23. Like Higman, Oberman ("Initia Calvini," 144–46) traces the origin of French radical evangelicalism to the Lefèvrian circle, especially among Lefèvre's disciples who regarded the papal church as "Anti-Christ" and called for radical reform of the French Church.

Cop, delivered his inaugural address as the new rector on the pericopal text (Matt 5:1–12). The main point of the address was a mixture of "the philosophy of Christ" that brought to mind Erasmus's theme, and "justification by faith" based upon the law and gospel contrast that echoed Luther's Evangelical doctrine. As it carried a theological overtone, the existence of a ghostwriter was conjectured from the beginning. Especially among Cop's friends in the Paris evangelical humanist circle, Calvin's participation was rumored. As its challenging character reflected the tense conditions of the time, the address caricatured the Scholastic theologians of the Paris Theological Faculty who persecuted evangelical humanists as heretical Lutherans, calling them sophists and heretics ignorant of the philosophy of Christ. Likewise, it was an apology bold enough to claim the church's theology of self-justification as against the gospel and to honor those who had suffered for the sake of the gospel as "the blessed faithful."[61]

The reaction to the address, which caused an uproar in Parisian society, was swift. Upon the request of the Theological Faculty, which had been warning about "this damnable Lutheran sect which is infesting" the capital since Roussel's Easter sermon, the Parlement of Paris started an official inquiry. As the king's ire was made known, Cop was forced to seek exile in Basel and Calvin to take flight.[62] Since Cop was regarded as an Erasmian or Lefèvrian humanist, he could have been the sole author of the address. If we assume Cop to be either the author or the polisher of the final draft, and, if we also assume the substantial participation of Calvin who had increasingly inclined toward theological studies, this address could be said to be based on their common position as moderate evangelical humanists. But it could also be representing a position that did not exclude Luther's Evangelicalism for the sake of church unity and was open to some reformist ideas of the radical evangelical humanists. In other words, it could be a historic witness that tread a step further from the moderate toward the radical position. With this view in mind, we will focus on the following three points.

61. *OS* 1:4–10: "Concio academica." The traditional theory of Calvin's participation was questioned in the first half of the twentieth century. Wendel (*Calvin*, 40–41) cautiously questioned it and Ganoczy (*Young Calvin*, 81–82) rejected it outright. Partly due to a more recent study of J. Rott ("Documents Strasbourgeois concernant Calvin," *Regards contemporains sur Jean Calvin* [Paris, 1965], 42), B. Roussel ("François Lambert, Pierre Caroli, Guillaume Farel, et Jean Calvin (1530–1536)," in *Calvinus Servus Christi*, ed. W. H. Neuser [Budapest, 1988], 32–35), Oberman ("Initia Calvini," 143n132), McGrath (*A Life*, 64–66), and others tend to acknowledge the possible participation.

62. Farge (*Orthodoxy*, 204) considers that Cop and Calvin "had misjudged the climate for reform in Paris," and McGrath (*A Life*, 64) calls the address "a catastrophic error of judgment."

(i) First, there is the Erasmian expression in the address's opening, "What is so great is . . . the philosophy of Christ." This was its keynote as well as a manifestation of Erasmian or Lefèvrian humanism over against the Paris Theological Faculty that called Erasmus "a mere rhetorician" who equated theology with the philosophy of Christ.[63]

(ii) Second, the biggest issue of the address was the portion of it that interpreted the gospel of Christ through the Pauline theme of the law and gospel as well as through justification by faith. This was said to suggest a rough sketch of Luther's teaching. Because it was common knowledge that Luther's Evangelicalism meant total rejection of the papal system, some moderate evangelicals were quick to proscribe this topic and to regard evangelical reform as dangerous and schismatic. Since this portion was indeed a bold assertion, interpretations on it by modern researchers seem to vary widely. On the one hand, some researchers assume the participation of Calvin and see in it his transitional process from moderate to radical evangelicalism. On the other hand, rejecting his participation, some interpret it as merely expressing an expectation for an optimistic and peaceful reform. The question of Calvin's participation aside, however, the text seems to allow a middle ground between these two interpretations. That is to say, like the position of Berquin, who had been known as the translator of both Erasmus and Luther and who consistently appealed for the harmonious reform ideas of both reformers, the text could be said to represent an attempt to apply the fundamentals of Christ's philosophy to evangelical reform.[64]

(iii) Third, it is noticeable that, on the biblical text "Blessed are the peacemakers" (Matt 5:9), the address touched on the relation of the church's peace and unity with its reform. It is not an error to sum up this core point of the address as "the possibility of a peaceful reformation of the Church which would find room for an Erasmus as well as a Luther." But whether it sufficiently expresses the tenor of the address is another matter.[65] Certainly its text affirmed the idea of the church catholic by appealing "to keep peace, and to restore unity among opposing parties." Immediately after this affirmation, however, the text introduced a distinction between "spiritual peace" (*pax spiritualis*) and "worldly peace" (*pax mundi*). The two were remarkably contrasted. "Worldly peace" was a reform that eagerly removed the church's obvious abuses, but

63. *OS* 1:4. Cf. Farge, *Orthodoxy*, 187.

64. Two opposing examples referred to here are Karl Barth (*The Theology of John Calvin*, trans. G. W. Bromiley [Grand Rapids: Eerdmans, 1995], 142–44) and Ganoczy (*Young Calvin*, 81–82). For an analogy to Berquin, see M. Mann, *Érasme et les debuts de la réforme Française (1517–1536)* (Paris: H. Champion, 1934), 165.

65. Cf. Wendel, *Calvin*, 41–42.

left "the root of discord" (*radix discordiae*) untouched. "Spiritual peace," on the other hand, was a reform that, in removing the church's discords, never appealed to the means of threat, but "subjected all to harmonize to the word of truth."[66] If we can assume that "worldly peace" is a reference to the moderate evangelical reform that was hesitant to take the step for fundamental reform, "spiritual peace" could suggest the reform ideas of the radical evangelicals who would bring all issues, including those of Rome and Luther, to the test of God's word. To sum up the above considerations, it could be said that the address, while holding basically to a moderate position, took a step further toward the radical position of a more thorough reform, and that, regardless of whether Calvin participated or not, both Cop and Calvin shared this position at this juncture.

3. Psychopannychia

Thanks to the favor of his moderate evangelical humanist friend and priest Louis du Tillet, Calvin spent several months hiding in the country at the Du Tillet family residence near Angoulême, far southwest of the capital. During this time, he studied mainly the Bible and the church fathers by using the family library that was said to house several thousand volumes. The results of his studies included his first attempt at a theological topic, *Psychopannychia*, and possibly some preliminary research for his later first edition of the *Institutes*.[67] In the period during and after Angoulême, one noticeable event was his visit to the aging Lefèvre at Marguerite's court at Nérac in early 1534. Concerning this Nérac meeting, however, Calvin left no records, just like for other events such as the Meaux reform or the Lefèvrian circle of Paris, with which he was said to be associated.[68] As to another noticeable event, Calvin started legal procedures at his native Noyon Church to terminate the church benefice that had been a source of sustenance for his studies. If we interpret this action as due to his own voluntary decision and not forced upon him by the church

66. *OS* 1:9.

67. In a letter to François Daniel (*CO* 10b:37), a friend from the Orléans period and a lawyer considered to belong to the moderate evangelical humanist group, Calvin described his engagement in the "common studies" (*studio mutuo*). As Ganoczy (*Young Calvin*, 83–85) suggests, the studies were likely in "the Bible and the Fathers." The official title and text of the *Psychopannychia* are *Vivere apud Christum non dormire animis sanctos, qui in fide Christi decedunt* (*BC* 42/5; *CO* 5:165–232).

68. Although Colladon and Beza, biographers of Calvin, could have supplemented Calvin's silence, their accounts (*CO* 21:57, 123) only mentioned the fact of Calvin's visit.

that had come into conflict with his father and had excommunicated him, we are able to assume that the process of his conversion had already started and some decisive changes had taken place in his attitude toward the Roman Catholic Church. Concerning the traditional interpretation, which connected his changes with the termination of church benefices and produced an explanation for his turn to Protestant Evangelicalism, however, the evaluations of it by researchers have varied. We suggest that the core of these changes was a sign of his transition from moderate evangelical to radical evangelical humanism.[69] After his last visit to Noyon, Calvin resided from early summer to the fall of 1534 in Orléans, where he completed his first draft of the *Psychopannychia*.

To place the *Psychopannychia* in the course of Calvin's theological formation, we must confront several difficult problems before examining the text itself. Firstly, the book had had a complicated history before its considerably delayed final publication in 1542. For example, Calvin encountered some counsels of caution from Strasbourg's Wolfgang Capito and Martin Bucer who read its first draft with the preface dated "at Orléans, 1534" and the second draft of 1535, of which Calvin himself wrote to his friend as "a new book." Heeding their counsel, its publication was postponed. The main reason for their caution was said to be that the so-called dormant theory (the believer's soul sleeps from death until resurrection) was not a unique teaching of the Anabaptists as Calvin seemed to imply. As the teaching was shared by both Luther and Andreas Karlstadt, concern for the concord of Protestant Evangelicalism was to be heeded.[70] As the book's underlying tone and composition were from the first draft and its substantive materials were completed in the second draft, it could be considered a work of the last phase (1534–35) in Calvin's academic formation.

Secondly, even though assuming that Calvin had considerable knowledge of the Anabaptists by 1534–35, the question remains as to why he chose the dormant theory as the topic of his refutations. Since it was neither a main nor common teaching among the Anabaptists, though Michael Sattler who drafted

69. Cf. Wendel, *Calvin*, 42; Ganoczy, *Young Calvin*, 85; McGrath, *A Life*, 73–74; Gordon, *Calvin*, 39–40. A variety of interpretations of the connection between Calvin's conversion and the Noyon event can be seen: for example, Wendel's position is close to the traditional view; both Ganoczy and McGrath see the connection as a conjecture; and Gordon sees it in the two steps of Calvin's conversion process, one to "a Lefèvrian form of evangelical Christianity within the bounds of the Catholic church," and the other to the process of "turning his back on the Catholic church" in which the Noyon event took place.

70. Cf. Balke, *Calvin and the Anabaptist*, 31–32. Reference to a "new book" is found in Calvin's letter to Christopher Fabri (*CO* 10b:52).

the *Schleitheim Confession* held it, among Calvin researchers some are puzzled by his intention and seem to evaluate the book as "marginal." Although it was a fact that the infiltration of the dormant theory in the early French Reformation was feared and Calvin was asked to refute it, there is the question of the identity of Calvin's opponents. Researchers have proposed various views, such as the Platonists in the Lefèvrian circle (Oberman), and Michael Servetus (Gordon), who was Calvin's acquaintance from his Paris days and who studied medicine at the University.[71]

Lastly, there remains the biggest problem of all, namely, the question as to whether the book did not sufficiently reflect the author who was considered to have had a conversion to radical evangelical humanism or Protestant Evangelicalism by the time of its first draft, as many researchers have assumed. Even though it was Calvin's first theological work, he presented himself as a humanist scholar who was then using the same method as in his previous Seneca commentary and handling mainly biblical and patristic materials. He did not even use the anti-Anabaptist theological works of Luther and Zwingli. As a theological work, it was unquestionably transitional. Also, from our emphasis on Calvin's turning to radical evangelical humanism, as the work presented criticism of neither the Roman Catholic Church nor the positive reformist ideas, researchers view it as lacking "the slightest allusion to the author's religious transformation" and its author as "still wearing the mask of a Catholic."[72] Nevertheless, if we place the book in the historical context of the early French Reformation, it presented remarkably Calvin's clear idea of the church catholic, the exclusion of the Anabaptists from that church, and the contrast between his evangelical humanism and the Anabaptists. Or, if we focus on his turbulent personal history, we can see it as his "spiritual pilgrimage" when he experienced the decisive turn to become a radical evangelical humanist, the Placards affair, and his exile in Basel.[73] With the above considerations in mind, we will proceed to the examination of the text in the following three points.

(i) The first point concerns the first draft's preface that was kept in the 1542 publication. In that preface, Calvin made clear that a refutation of the dormant theory had been requested of him and that the theory was an ancient heresy first noticed in the ancient church, later transferred to the Arabs (in Islamic

71. Cf. G. H. Williams, *Spiritual and Anabaptist Writers* (Philadelphia: Westminster, 1977), 136–44; Balke, *Calvin and the Anabaptist*, 31–33, 35–37; Oberman, "Initia Calvini," 134–39; Gordon, *Calvin*, 43.

72. Examples of the negative view can be seen in Ganoczy (*Young Calvin*, 245) and McGrath (*A Life*, 73).

73. Cf. Gordon, *Calvin*, 42–46.

philosophy and theology), and in recent years inherited by the Anabaptists.[74] A problematic sentence appears in the portion where Calvin expressed his intention to handle the issue with a fair and tolerant mind. Despite his intention, he said, the current situation surrounding the discussions on religion was far from tolerant, and the ones who had received even the slightest criticism jointly cried out "the unity of the church being asunder, charity being violated." Since the book's main purpose was to refute the Anabaptists, the subjects of the quoted sentence could be the Anabaptists. In this case, however, the interpretation is unnatural since they did not believe the church's catholicity or unity and could not truthfully utter such a cry. Therefore, the sentence needs to be interpreted as Calvin's device to expose their hypocrisy. Another possible interpretation takes the sentence as a description of current religious discussions in general and the cry as a reaction to church reform for which the church's conditions or teachings were criticized.[75] In addition, it should be noticed that Calvin's own reaction to the cry was expressed, in his words, "we acknowledge no unity except in Christ and no charity except being in his bond." This is unnatural as a reference to the Anabaptists. Rather, it can be taken as a thorough reform proposal directed to the intolerant Catholic conservatives or to some of the moderate evangelical humanists who considered radical evangelicalism either unorthodox or excessive.[76]

(ii) The second point concerns Calvin's hermeneutical stance in the book's major portion where he interpreted the biblical passages and revealed the essence of his evangelicalism. In the first half of this portion, where he interpreted the biblical passages so as to refute the Anabaptists' dormant theory, he made an interesting comment. He summed up a simple biblical teaching in arguing that, while the souls of God's elect after death reside in heaven, fully awake and waiting for the final judgment, the souls of all the rest exist under the fear of God's judgment. Calvin went on to warn that "to inquire beyond this [the biblical teaching] is to sink oneself in the abyss of God's mystery."[77]

74. *CO* 5:169–72. Cf. *BC*, 113–16. Calvin's initial writing was occasioned by the request of his humanist friends and the acquisition of the tracts of Antoine Pocquet, an Anabaptist leader, on the same subject.

75. *CO* 5:171–72: "flebiliter deplorant scindi unitatem ecclesiae, violari caritatem." For example, Ganoczy (*Calvin*, 271) takes the former interpretation, but we consider the latter more fitting to Calvin's situation in 1534.

76. *CO* 5:172.

77. *CO* 5:201. Cf. Oberman, "Initia Calvini," 124–27. Oberman follows Bouwsma (*Calvin*, 45–48, et al.) who analyzes sixteenth-century humanist Calvin in terms of "abyss" and "labyrinth."

In the second half, where he examined the biblical passages that he claimed supported the dormant theory, he criticized the Anabaptists' interpretation of Genesis (3:9) as underestimating the effects of original sin, which, according to them, caused the loss of immortality but did not subject mankind to the judgment of God. According to Calvin, "the ones who claimed to escape God's judgment are to entrap themselves in one thousand abysses and they cannot escape from there."[78]

His hermeneutical stance as reflected in these sayings corresponded to the method used by his fellow evangelical humanists. Following the examples of Erasmus and Lefèvre, he contrasted the simple and Christocentric gospel teaching with the "abyss" and "labyrinth" of the Catholic Church's scholastic theology and salvific system, and he applied the same method to refute the Anabaptists. Above all, it should not be overlooked that Calvin clearly expressed his evangelical faith in the assumedly postconversion process. For example, he emphasized how the supporters of the dormant theory underestimated the salvific effect of Christ's redemptive death in the following saying: "Now, O dreamers, ponder to your heart for a while how Christ, who had died and [after his death] had worked for your salvation, could have been sleeping?"[79] For Calvin, the evangelical faith taught a "progress" (*cursus*) that was not simply based upon the philosophical notion of the soul's immortality or the Anabaptists' view conditioned by human death, but upon the progressive process directly connected with God's power and Christ's salvation. This alone could nurture the believer's soul while in life, keep it in Christ's presence after death, and bring it to its completion through the final judgment.[80]

(iii) The third point concerns Calvin's concept of God's kingdom, or the kingdom of Christ. This becomes the theme of an interesting expression in his early ecclesiology, which he entertained here in the polemical context of the Anabaptist dormant theory, and which he will later elaborate on as a key concept fully integrated in his mature ecclesiology. Particularly in this context, according to the current humanists' view of history, he posed biblical salvation history from God's creation to the eschatological end as the history of God's kingdom or the church and coupled it with the personal "progress" within the believer's soul. Using the metaphor of Christ's body and the believers as the church in Ephesians (4:13), for example, he described the kingdom–church relation in this way: "In short, the kingdom is the edification of the church as

78. *CO* 5:204. Cf. Oberman, "Initia Calvini," 130–31.

79. *CO* 5:191.

80. *CO* 5:210–11. Cf. Oberman, "Initial Calvini," 133, 137.

well as the progress of the believers."[81] He also described the kingdom as "the elect" or "the people." In this sense he said that, as the kingdom existed among the faithful on earth, eternal life had already begun among them there. However, the Anabaptists' view that severed this "progress" by the believers' death contradicted the biblical concept of the kingdom.[82] Furthermore, he used a few impressive descriptions: in connection with the metaphor of "a rich man and Lazarus" (Luke 16), "the church which resides as the foreigners on the earth"; and in connection with Hebrews (11:13), believers are "those who are residents in a foreign land and the unknown folk." These were fitting expressions of Calvin who was, at the time of composing the first and second drafts, either a fugitive or an exile, and who dreamed of the ancient church's restoration in France where the manifestation of the Evangelical church, though early signs of its germination were visible, was not fully materialized. Lastly, considering the dormant theory, Calvin confirmed his Evangelical commitment: "we" who inherited the teachings of the ancient church fathers who had faithfully kept the "the mystery" of the gospel should now engage in the refutation of this heresy.[83]

Even from the above limited considerations, we may come to a better understanding of the *Psychopannychia* in which Calvin not only refuted the Anabaptists' dormant theory but also tried to exclude Anabaptism from the teachings of the ancient church and the universal concept of the church catholic. In defending his evangelical position, he clearly distinguished it from that of the Anabaptists yet fully identified with the orthodox and Catholic tradition. In his defense, though implicitly, he kept in check the intolerant conservative Catholics and some moderate evangelical humanists who considered his evangelical position unorthodox. Furthermore, we may say that the book contained materials that presented a rough sketch of his early ecclesiology. Fragmentary expressions of concepts found there such as God's kingdom, the kingdom of Christ, the church's history, the elect, foreigners, and exile in a foreign land will find their places in the systematic presentation of his first *Institutes*.

4. *Exile in Basel*

The Placards affair of October 1534 is often called a watershed for the future of the French Reformation. The affair was a coordinated and widespread plot to spread tracts denouncing "the papal Mass" in sharp contrast to "the holy

81. *CO* 5:212.
82. *CO* 5:194, 197.
83. *CO* 5:214.

supper of Jesus Christ." These were posted in many cities of reformist spirit and even in the king's palace. As a result, it hardened the king, who previously had somewhat favored humanistic reform. The tracts energized Catholic conservatism spearheaded by the Paris Theological Faculty, drove the moderate evangelical humanists into a tight corner, and stigmatized the radical evangelical humanists as fugitives or exiles, thus making the polarization of the two humanist reformist groups definite.

(i) From an ecclesiological viewpoint, the aftermath of the affair clearly manifested a trend to exclude radical evangelical humanism, as well as the Evangelicalism of Luther and Zwingli, from the permissive boundary previously afforded by the French Reformation. This trend could be illustrated by Budé's well-known work, *Transition to Christianity*, which we will discuss later in connection with Calvin's first *Institutes*. From his official position as Francis I's counselor, Budé sharply distinguished between two movements: the humanistic studies originating in Hellenism and the reform patterned after the ancient church that had inherited the tradition of Hellenistic studies on the one hand, and Lutheran Evangelicalism and the radical French reformist movements of the Placards affair on the other. He appealed to the king for the latter's punishment.[84] Budé's case posed a serious danger not only of driving a wedge between the moderate and radical reformist groups but also of polarizing two great movements, Humanism and the Reformation. Since the tract of the Placards affair reflected the Zwinglian view of the Eucharist, it had the negative effect of exposing a discord within Protestant Evangelicalism between the Lutherans and the Zwinglians. The discord was even exploited in the king's appeasement policy toward Germany's Lutheran princes.[85]

It was in the historical context of this turbulent period that Calvin's Catholic ecclesiology was formed. Its overall picture was made clear in Basel where Calvin, after visiting Bucer and Capito in Strasbourg, settled in the city of his exile in January 1535. Although an important step for this ecclesiological formation had already been taken in the initial writing of the *Psychopannychia*, there he restrained himself from both criticizing papalism and defending Protestantism.[86] But in Basel, he composed two Latin and French prefaces

84. Cf. J. Bohatec, *Budé und Calvin: Studien zur Gedankenwelt des französischen Frühhumanismus* (Granz: Verlag Hermann Böhlaus Nachf, 1950), 121–41.

85. Cf. Ganoczy, *Young Calvin*, 98–100; Gordon, *Calvin*, 40–42; Farge, *Orthodoxy*, 206–8; C. Elwood, *The Body Broken: The Calvinist Doctrine of the Eucharist and the Symbolization of Power in the Sixteenth-Century France* (New York and Oxford: Oxford University Press, 1999), 27–29.

86. Cf. *CO* 5:171–72.

to his cousin Olivétan's French Bible, published at Neuchâtel in the French-speaking region of Switzerland. In these he described for the first time the current church not as a Catholic church but as a papal church, and he clearly identified his position with Protestant Evangelicalism.[87]

(ii) Calvin's two prefaces to Olivétan's Bible were minuscule in comparison to the first *Institutes*, the great accomplishment of his Basel period. However, they were important materials due to the fact that they were composed both during the last phase of his writing of the *Institutes* and in the close historical context of the early French Reformation. Above all, they expressed the convictions of a radical evangelical humanist.[88] Even though they took different literary formats, the Latin preface as a personal epistle with Calvin as the subject and the French preface as promotional literature for the studies of the Bible, both revealed glimpses of his early ecclesiology. In the Latin preface, for example, our attention is called to its opening greetings that could be called his first declaration to European Christendom. The greetings placed "John Calvin" at the head and was addressed "to all emperors, kings, princes, and gentlemen who are under Christ's sovereign power, greetings."[89] Though a humble exile, Calvin presented himself here as a young Evangelical who declared his allegiance to Christendom behind the shield of Christ's sovereignty. Just like the greetings, the text of the preface was permeated with his Evangelical convictions without any trace of his previous hesitation. We will examine the Latin text in the following three points of ecclesiological interest.

The first point posed by Calvin was a clear contrast between the ancient church of "the purer ages" and "the Roman popes and priests" (*Romani Pon-*

87. Cf. E. Droz, *Chemins de l'hérésie: Texts et Documents* (Geneva: Slatkine, 1970), 102–16; Millet, *Calvin et la dynamique*, 455–64; F. Higman, "Olivétan, Pierre Robert," *OER* 3:174–75. Although both Droz and Millet consider Calvin a "collaborator" of the publication, the extent of his involvement, besides the two prefaces, is not certain. Olivétan's French Bible inherited the philological tradition of Lefèvre's French Bible (1530–34). Olivétan was regarded to have moved from the Lefèvrian circle to the more radical position, exiled to Strasbourg, and engaged in the earlier evangelization in the French Swiss regions, including Geneva.

88. Although the texts consulted here are from the *CO* edition (*CO* 9:787–90, 791–821) based upon the later Beza source, as to the Latin preface that takes an epistolary form, the *COR* edition (*COR* VI-1:107–13) based upon the original Olivétan French Bible is also consulted. The editors of the *COR* text consider the writing of two prefaces in May 1535. Ganoczy (*Young Calvin*, 94–98), Backus and Chimelli (I. Backus and C. Chimelli, eds., *La vraie piété: Divers traités de Jean Calvin et confession de foi de Guillaume Farel* [Geneva: Labor et Fides, 1986], 17–23), and Gordon (*Calvin*, 55–57) provide good analyses on the historical background of the prefaces.

89. *COR* VI-1:107; *CO* 9:787.

tifeces et sacrificuli) who he considered to be both the prime instigators as well as obstacles that necessitated the current church reform.[90] Based upon the historical distinction between the Ancient and the current Roman Catholic Church, his evangelical orientation intended to exclude the papal church from what he considered to be the church catholic that had inherited the tradition of the ancient church.

The second point was another sharp contrast between the church hierarchy governed by "the Roman popes and priests" and "the order of teaching and learning" that God had established in his church by sending prophets and teachers and that was to be restored by church reform.[91] From the context of the French Reformation, this point could well reflect Calvin's wish to restore the French Catholic Church as sharply distinguished from the papal church.

The third point was his frequent use of the terms "people" or "the faithful people" as the equivalent of the church. These terms were known in Erasmus's idea of the church, and Calvin's use of them likely reflects his general background of humanist studies. In particular, as he suggested at the end of the preface, Olivétan's French translation was requested by Farel and Pierre Viret, reformers who had turned from being Lefèvre's disciples to the radical reformist position. Thus, a question could be asked about the preface's relation to Lefèvrianism. As we will examine in chapter 2, Lefèvre's basic concept of the church was also that of "the faithful people."[92]

The above three points seem to indicate a sketch of Calvin's idea of church reform. For example, he referred to "a certain voice" (the position of the Paris Theological Faculty?) that feared the provision of vernacular Bible translations to the simple people as dangerous, as entrusting the mystery of God to them. He refuted it by saying that God, who had made a prophet out of a shepherd and apostles out of fishermen, had established "the order of teaching and learning" in the church as "the school of God" where the people could hear and learn from those who taught the word of God.[93] Here Calvin considered the "freedom" witnessed by the church fathers as the tradition of the ancient church that let the people hear and learn freely from the word of God. This was opposed to the tyranny under the popes and priests who took God's word from the people and gave them "spoiled food" instead. Accordingly, in

90. *COR* VI-1:110–11; *CO* 9:788–89. Cf. Ganoczy, *Young Calvin*, 96.

91. *COR* VI-1:108–9; *CO* 9:788. Cf. Ganoczy, *Young Calvin*, 96.

92. *COR* VI-1:113; *CO* 9:790. For Lefèvre's idea of the church, see chapter 2, section 1 below.

93. *COR* VI-1:109. Cf. *CO* 9:787–88; Farge, *Orthodoxy*, 177–80.

relation to his idea of the ministry, while the main duty of Catholic priests was to officiate at religious ceremonies as "substitute foods," evangelical ministers as "prophets, teachers, and interpreters" enabled the people to hear and learn from God's word as "real food." This idea of evangelical ministers showed a close affinity with Lefèvre's concept of the church and its reform. It was also a clear manifestation of Protestant teaching on the ministry since Luther's *On the Babylonian Captivity of the Church* (1520) and was the theme that Calvin would later develop in his first *Institutes* as well as in *Two Epistles*, which we will take up in chapter 2.[94]

(iii) Unlike the sonorous Latin preface, the French preface, which was placed at the head of the New Testament in Olivétan's Bible, began with a familiar sentence, but without its subject, Calvin: "To all who love Jesus Christ and his gospel, greetings." Ganoczy calls the preface "a masterpiece of literary clarity and at the same time a magnificent testimony of a positive and enthusiastic evangelical spirit." Gordon calls it "the product of an original mind." This could well be said to be the first confession of Evangelical faith by Calvin.[95] For example, there appeared one remarkable sentence that expressed the deep mind of a twenty-five-year-old humanist scholar and clearly followed a pattern of his own conversion. The sentence took the theme of the redemptive power of Christ's death that brought life to a believer and transformed the dead into the living, and went on like this by using thirty-one pairs of antonyms:

> As such by him [Christ] rudeness is polished, wrath calmed down, darkness enlightened, injustice justified, weakness invigorated, despair consoled, sin forgiven, contempt defied, dread assured, debt cancelled, toil lightened, sadness gladdened, misfortune made blessed, difficulty eased, disorder ordered, division united, humiliation vindicated, rebellion subjugated,

94. *COR* VI-1:110–11. Cf. *CO* 9:788–89. On the ideas of the church and its reform, as we will see in chapter 2, a close parallelism can be assumed between Calvin's Latin preface and Lefèvre's ecclesiological expressions as well as his disciple Farel's *Summary* (1529).

95. *CO* 9:791. Cf. Ganoczy, *Young Calvin*, 96–98; Millet, *Calvin et la dynamique*, 459–64; Gordon, *Calvin*, 56–57; Muller, *The Unaccommodated*, 23–24. Instead of the critical edition (I. Backus and C. Chimelli, eds., *Vraie Piété*, 17–38), the *CO* text is used here. Ganoczy points out the importance of the hitherto neglected French preface in view of Calvin's theological development and considers it as his own confession. As to Calvin's theme of reform in the French preface, Millet succinctly expresses it thus: "Due to the power proper to [the scriptural] message, the reform of the church is accomplished as if it were by itself." Muller also considers it as the first manifestation of Calvin's principal exegetical theme, "grace and election" in salvation history, which is analogous to Bullinger's *De testamento seu foedere Dei* (1534).

> menace threatened, entrapment untrapped, assaults assailed, effort redoubled, combat combatted, war fought against, vengeance avenged, torment tormented, damnation damned, abyss sunk further, hell closed, death destroyed, and mortal made immortal.[96]

As far as Calvin's notion of the church was concerned, however, the French preface presented no elaboration like the Latin preface. Rather, we would call attention to the following points.

As to the first point, we notice that Calvin placed the church as God's people within the scope of salvation history from God's creation of the world to the end of times. At the creation, as Calvin described, man created in God's image was made "to humble himself," "to praise God with gladness," and "to glorify not himself but God alone." In the fall of man as well as the church, man was described as "being in ruin, without dignity and excellence" and the church as "being without the law of God's word, government, and discipline." God chose "a certain people" to declare his word, made a covenant with them as the elect people, upon the people's rebellion renewed "the new covenant" in Christ, and raised "a new elect people" from all corners of the world.[97] Above all, Calvin described salvation history as the history of a perpetual conflict to the end of times between believers belonging to "the Kingdom of God" and those "evildoers, rebels, and reprobate" in their disbelief.[98]

As to the second point to notice, Calvin posed a touchstone of "Bible, gospel, and Christ" for discerning true believers and the church. This touchstone was described by him as follows: "without the gospel we are not Christians; without the gospel all richness poverty; wisdom folly before God; strength feebleness; all human justice damnation of God." In the particular context of the French Church, he applied this touchstone not only to conservatives in the Church but also to moderate reformists. He criticized them for boasting of their "sure hope [for reform], perfect charity in the name of God, earnest love for their neighbors" and for condemning radical reformists. Calvin cried out against them: "O Christian gentlemen and ladies, . . . If you hold in contempt and despise to hear, discern, read, and retain this holy gospel, where is your hope?"[99]

96. *CO* 9:813: "Tellment que par luy rudesse est adoulcie, courroux appaisé, tenebres esclaircies, iniustice iustifée, . . . abysme abysmé, enfer enferré, mort morte, mortalité immortelle."

97. *CO* 9:791, 793, 795, 799.

98. *CO* 9:811.

99. *CO* 9:803, 807, 809. Ganoczy (*Young Calvin*, 98) notices in this portion of the preface some implicit critical comments against Briçonnet, Roussel, Daniel, Duchemin, Budé, Lefèvre, and other humanists.

As to the third point to notice, the preface attempted to offer an apology for those who had suffered persecutions, martyrdom, and exiles. At the same time, however, it tried to convince the readers that such sufferings were inevitable for the true church and appealed to them to learn that "from the example of Christ, only this way can lead them to the victory." For Calvin, as Oberman notes, God of salvation history revealed himself as a "fugitive" who traveled along with the Old Testament people in their exile in Sinai and sent Christ as the head of God's church to lead the New Testament church under the cross. Having heard the news of the martyrdom of his friend Étienne de la Forge (February 1535) in Paris, Calvin heartened his readers in saying, "Let us never be discouraged" by the deaths of "the true servants of God." He cited Tertullian's famous saying "the blood of the martyrs is the seed of the church." Here we can see a glimpse of Calvin's concept of the church as a sojourner and pilgrim on the pathway to heaven. This theme, which he developed throughout his life as a Reformer, seems to point to what Oberman calls "the Reformation of the refugees."[100]

Section 3. The Writing of the First *Institutes of the Christian Religion* and the Formation of Catholic Ecclesiology

The writing of the first *Institutes* was completed in the summer of 1535, but due to printing considerations, its publication was delayed until the following spring. It was the big accomplishment of Calvin's wandering period, from fugitive to exile, as well as the apex of his theological formation.[101] As far as his ecclesiological formation was concerned, the *Institutes* witnessed to the tentative completion of his Catholic ecclesiology, which was for him both an ideal of his evangelical humanism and a substructure of his own concept of the

100. *CO* 9:795: "Il les a accompaigné nuict et iour en leur fuite, estant comme fuitifz au milieu d'eulx"; *CO* 9:809, 811. Noticing the Christological significance of this quotation, Oberman ("Via Calvini: Unlocking the Enigma of John Calvin's Impact," *John Calvin*, 47) says that Calvin described "Christ himself as an exile or a fugitive, showing solidarity with his people as he accompanies them on the seemingly hopeless journey through the desert." In other articles ("Initia Calvini," 147; "*Europa Afflicta*: The Reformation of the Refugees," *Archiv für Reformationsgeschichte* 83 [1992]: 91–110), Oberman seems to have found in this theme of God in Christ as a refugee Calvin's overarching reform concept, namely, "the Reformation of the refugees."

101. For the text of the first *Institutes*, the *OS* edition (*OS* 1:11–280) is used. Battles's translation and endnotes are cited as Battles, trans., *Institution*.

church. His Catholic ecclesiology comprehended the church as the people of God or Christ in the entire scope of salvation history, from God's creation, the fall and redemption, the gospel, and to the end of times. Catholic ecclesiology was assumedly completed in the ancient church of the apostles and church fathers and its restoration was earnestly desired in Calvin's own time. As to his personal life, the publication of the *Institutes* corresponded to the year of Erasmus's and Lefèvre's deaths. It also signaled a generation change and perhaps the emergence of a new leader on the European stage.

(i) The publication year 1536 corresponded to the period in which the final breakup of European Christian society was taking place and when the French Reformation was also facing a crucial division between the old Catholic Church and the new Evangelicalism. Confronting this reality, Erasmus, who left the city of his residence, Basel, after its decisive introduction of Evangelical reform, lamented the reality, writing, "No one will undo this universal tragedy except God." Calvin, who chose Basel as the city of his exile for the sake of Evangelicalism and with the publication of his *Institutes*, challenged with indignation the slow progress of reform fifteen years after Luther's initial Reformation.[102] On the one hand, in mainstream Protestantism, this period witnessed strong indications of reform such as the German Lutheran territories consolidating themselves under the *Augsburg Confession* (1530) vis-à-vis the Catholic territories. At the same time, the City-Reformations of the Reformed wing were being established in Zurich, Basel, Strasbourg, and elsewhere. And the Church in England under Henry VIII was being separated from the Roman Catholic Church and cautiously siding with the Protestant Reformation through the *Ten Articles* (1536).

But the Radical Reformation, which offered serious challenges to mainstream Protestantism in the early Reformation period, was now facing a turning point due to the revolutionary upheaval at Münster (1534–35). On the Roman Catholic side, the reformist Pope Paul III promoted Gasparo Contarini to cardinal in 1535, who then chaired a commission to produce a reform proposal, the memorial *Concilium de Emendanda Ecclesia* (1537). Nonetheless the opposing Catholic conservatism also consolidated their counterreform moves. At this historical juncture, how did Calvin comprehend the bankruptcy of Western Christendom in Basel and what remedy did he try to offer by his *Institutes*?

(ii) Generally speaking, the first edition of Calvin's *Institutes* is often regarded as the preliminary step of his principal theological work for which

102. P. S. Allen, ed., *Opus epistolarum*, 9, no. 2343, cited in Kelley, *The Beginning*, 6. Cf. Ganoczy, *Young Calvin*, 232–33.

he compiled several editions over a period of a quarter century. Because the first edition is often cited in connection with the final and complete edition of the *Institutes* (1559), its originality has been underestimated. As a study in the history of doctrine, however, our ecclesiological inquiry attaches great importance to it and starts with its external and internal characteristics.

As to the external characteristics, firstly, the word "institution" (*institutio*) in its title indicates a "catechism." Derived from the Greek, this word was used by classical authors such as Quintilian and Lactantius, a church father often referred to as "a Christian Cicero" and as "the instruction in Christian faith" among Calvin's contemporaries Erasmus and Luther.[103] As a matter of fact, the first four chapters of the *Institutes* (law, faith, prayer, sacraments) consist of a catechism patterned after Luther's *Catechisms* (1528–29). Though not using the question-and-answer form, their content is clearly meant for instruction. This portion is intended to present sound arguments and to avoid being polemical, for example, by often using "we" as the subject of sentences; indicating conflicting views introduced by "certain ones"; referring to the Catholic polemists and the Anabaptists as "our opponents" or "the impious"; and avoiding personal names except for some heretics in the ancient church. In a sense, this portion corresponds to "a simple and elementary form of teaching," the expression used in the dedicatory epistle to the king that Calvin prefixed to the *Institutes*. However, as the same epistle also indicates that the author has to make his instruction "an apology" due to the fact that Evangelicalism was under attack, the last two chapters (the remaining five sacraments, Christian freedom, ecclesiastical power, political administration) present an apology full of fierce polemics.[104]

Accordingly, as one remarkable external characteristic, Calvin calls his work "institute" by combining the instructional and apologetic portions into one. Furthermore, this fundamental division also reflects the subjects treated, the methods, and the contents of the arguments presented. As we will examine later, a good example can be found in Calvin's concept of the church. Finally, since it was composed at the last phase of the writing, perhaps in August 1535, the dedicatory epistle is to be examined as an extension of the apologetic portion, chapters 5 and 6.

(iii) Unlike the external characteristics of the *Institutes*, the comprehension of its internal characteristics or the originality of its substance is not easy, as

103. Cf. Bouwsma, *Calvin*, 17; Gordon, *Calvin*, 57–58.

104. *OS* 1:21, 36. (Battles, trans., *Institution*, 1, 18.) Cf. Wendel, *Calvin*, 112, 144–45; Ganoczy, *Young Calvin*, 99; Battles, trans., *Institution*, "Introduction," xxix–xxx, xxxvi; Gordon, *Calvin*, 57–58.

many attempts have been exhausted on the nature of Calvin's early theology. For example, Wendel's *Calvin* (1950), regarded as an important work of modern historical research, considers the *Institutes* as the first result of "a Lefèvrian" Calvin who has experienced his conversion, attempted to write a theological book by using his humanist originality, and presented the instruction as a catechism and its application as an apology for the French Reformation.[105] Over against the trend of historical research represented by Wendel, Ganoczy's *Calvin théologien de l'église et du ministère* (1964) and *Le jeune Calvin* (1966) challenge the trend. The author emphasizes the originality of the *Institutes* by focusing on the fact that Calvin, as a humanist and law scholar, has mastered theology in a short period of time and as a self-taught, lay theologian. While, besides the predominant impressions of Luther, the theologies of Melanchthon, Zwingli, Bucer, and others are reflected in the *Institutes*, Ganoczy notices Calvin's theological creativity in integrating these impressions into one system. Today, there seems to be no common understanding on the nature of the first *Institutes*. However, a remark made in Gordon's recent biography is noteworthy: "The trained lawyer and the self-taught theologian were coming together. At the very moment he was making the case for true religion, he was setting out the legal framework of the Church."[106] While we consider Gordon's insight on "framework" applicable to Calvin's theology in general, as well as to his ecclesiology, we propose to examine Calvin's ecclesiology in the *Institutes* in the following four frameworks.

The first framework is the historical and religious reality of Calvin's age, expressed as "the divided body of Christ," in which his ecclesiology was formed. The conflicts of Roman Catholicism, mainstream Protestantism of the Lutheran and the Reformed churches, and the Radical Reformation revealed a vivid image of the divided Christendom, which Erasmus called the "universal tragedy" and Calvin "Europe afflicted." There was no other doctrinal controversy than the one over the sacraments, especially the Lord's Supper, that so vividly exposed this reality of the divided Christendom. Since the Lord's Supper in particular symbolized the internal unity of the church, accordingly, we begin our inquiry of Calvin's ecclesiology with his eucharistic doctrine. The reason for this method is our assumption that the young Calvin's theology in general and his eucharistic doctrine in particular was founded upon his unique understanding of the Christological definition of the Chalcedonian Council (451) and that there existed accordingly a parallelism between his

105. Wendel, *Calvin*, 111.

106. Ganoczy, *Calvin*, 36; Ganoczy, *Young Calvin*, 231–38; Gordon, *Calvin*, 60.

doctrines of the Eucharist and the church. As we will see later, the Chalcedonian orthodoxy on the relation between Christ's divinity and humanity was formulated by harmonizing the two opposing positions of the Alexandrian school ("union but not fusion") and the Antiochene school ("distinction but not separation"). According to Niesel, Calvin's Christology exerts dominant influence upon his understanding of the sacraments as well as the church.[107] The second framework is the biblical and catholic doctrine that Calvin identified with the theological and ecclesiological traditions of the Bible and of the ancient church, which he proposed to restore. To illustrate this point, we refer to chapter 2 of the *Institutes* where he formulated his own doctrinal understanding of God, Christ, the Holy Spirit, and the church by utilizing biblical witnesses, the Creeds of Nicea and Chalcedon, the church fathers, and his contemporary Evangelical theologians. The third is the polemical application of the framework by which he excluded the papal church from the tradition of the biblical and catholic doctrine as one extreme diversion, together with Anabaptism, what he calls its "subterfuge," as another extreme. This polemical two-sided exclusion was a characteristic noticeable not only in the *Institutes* but also in his theological works in general.[108] The fourth framework is perhaps his deepest personal concern, namely, the historical context of the French Reformation. Without recognizing this context in relation to Calvin, who drastically turned from moderate evangelical humanism represented by Lefèvre to radicalism and was at that time an exile, we may not clearly understand the first *Institutes*, especially its apologetic portion and the dedicatory epistle. To sum up, what we are to present from these four frameworks is no other than Calvin's Catholic ecclesiology.

With the above remarks in mind, we will try to sketch an overview of Calvin's early ecclesiology in the first *Institutes* under the following four headings. To start with, we will take an unorthodox approach for our ecclesiological

107. W. Niesel, *The Theology of Calvin*, trans. H. Knight (Philadelphia: Westminster, 1956), 246–50. Cf. Niesel, *The Theology of Calvin*, 115–18. Niesel considers "the Chalcedonian dogmatic definition" as key to understanding the "structural organization" of Calvin's theology. For example, he relates Calvin's Christological foundation to his notions of Scripture, the sacraments, justification and sanctification, the Holy Spirit, and so forth.

108. Cf. P. Fraenkel, *Testimonia Patrum: The Function of the Patristic Argument in the Theology of Philip Melanchthon* (Geneva: Droz, 1961), 313–15, esp. n. 32. According to Fraenkel, Melanchthon considered both the papal church and the Radical Reformation as "heresies" in view of the normative ancient church. Since this combination of two parties as heresies was a prevalent theme in Calvin's apologetics, it can be argued that either he followed Melanchthon's lead or he shared this combination with him as a common humanist argument.

inquiry and start with Calvin's doctrine of the sacraments (ch. 4), which reflects the religious reality of "the divided body of Christ" and provides a key to understanding his ecclesiology. Then we will focus on his ecclesiology under two headings, one in the "instruction" portion (ch. 2) that provides his sketch of Evangelical Christianity and the other in the "apology" portion (chs. 5–6) that proposes his notion of church reform for the first time. And finally, we will make an ecclesiological analysis of the dedicatory epistle to the king as his personal proposal for the reform of the French Church.

1. The Sacraments: "The Divided Body of Christ"

Since Luther attacked the core of the medieval salvific system of the Catholic Church, especially the doctrine of the Mass, the controversy over the Lord's Supper had become the great issue of the age. This was manifested not only between the Old and New Religions, but also among the Evangelicals as the dispute at the Marburg Colloquy (1529) between Luther and Zwingli prominently disclosed the Protestant discord. At the time of Calvin's writing the *Institutes*, although there had been some attempts by Melanchthon, Oecolampadius, Bucer and others to resolve the discord, no significant breakthrough was achieved. Due to the Placards affair, which categorically negated the Catholic Mass and could be an immediate background factor for Calvin's writing the *Institutes*, there was a pressing need for him to formulate the biblical and catholic teachings of the Lord's Supper.

In France, as Monter remarks, the political reality condemned the Zwinglian view suspected in the Placards affair as "sacramentarian," punishable in the French legal system as a heresy. Therefore, Calvin's formulation aimed, on the one hand, to exonerate Evangelicalism from the charge of "sacramentarianism." On the other hand, he sought to solidify his own view based upon his biblical studies and the readings of Augustine and other church fathers, Scholastic theologians, contemporary Catholic apologists, and French evangelical humanists.[109] On the Protestant side, he was said to have consulted

109. Cf. Monter, *Judging the French Reformation*, 69. According to Battles's endnotes (Battles, trans., *Institution*, 313–16), the Catholic apologists and works consulted by Calvin included, among others, the anti-Lutheran works of Johann Eck, *Enchiridion Locorum Communium adversus Lutherum*, 1525, 1532; Johannes Cochlaeus, *De Authoritate Ecclesiae*, 1524; Josse van Clichitoveus, *Antilutherus*, 1524; those of the French humanist apologists, Robert Ceneau (Bishop of Avranches), *Appendix ad Coena Dominicam*, 1534; Guillaume Budé, *De Transitu Hellenismi ad Christianismum*, 1535; and Jacopo Sadoleto (Bishop of Carpentras), *In Pauli Epistolam ad Romanos Commentariorum*, 1535.

as main sources, among others, Luther's *On the Babylonian Captivity of the Church* (1520), Melanchthon's *Loci Communes* (1521), Zwingli's *Commentary on True and False Religion* (1525), Bucer's *Four Gospels Commentary* (2nd ed., 1530), and the Anabaptist document *The Schleitheim Confession* (1527). His use of Bucer's commentary, in particular, was noteworthy because Bucer shifted here from the Zwinglian view to a more conciliatory position accommodating the sacraments as "the means of grace" and appreciating the Lutheran view of Christ's "real presence" in the Supper.[110] Nevertheless, unlike Bucer's attempt to conciliate the given and opposite views of Luther and Zwingli, Calvin's formulation was a fresh attempt to set the "framework" of the sacraments, thoroughly based upon the biblical and catholic understandings. As we will discuss later, the framework might present a parallelism to his ecclesiology.

(1) The Sacraments in General

(i) Calvin offered three points on the definition, purpose, and use of the sacraments. As to the first point of definition, he presented two descriptions: "an outward sign" (*signum externum*) by which the sacraments testified God's goodness toward the faithful and supported their weak faith; and "a testimony of God's grace" (*testimonium gratiae Dei*) declared by the sign. Since Calvin alternatively expressed "sign" and "testimony" as God's "promise" (*promissum*) or "covenant" (*foedus*), his two descriptions reflected the position of Augustine, who interpreted the sacraments as the outward sign and testimony of God's inward grace which preceded them, as well as the Augustinian tradition of Luther and Protestant Evangelicalism.[111] Interestingly, while he regarded the "substance" of the sacraments as God's "grace or promise," he called them "outward signs," an "appendix" that was only intended "to confirm and seal the promise itself" or the means by which God accommodated himself to the weakness of the faithful. Furthermore, it is noteworthy that Calvin had no hesitation in calling the sacraments "earthly elements." On the one hand, his perspective emphasized the necessity for the sacraments to testify to God's grace or promise as their substance. On the other hand, he rejected both the Catholic doctrine of the sacraments, which confused their "substance" with

110. Cf. Ganoczy, *Young Calvin*, 133–68; A. Lang, *Der Evangelienkommentar Martin Butzers und die Grundzüge seiner Theologie* (Leipzig: Dieterich'sche Verlagsbuchhandlung, 1900), 224–69. Bucer's mediating efforts resulted in the *Wittenberg Concord* (1536), the doctrinal accord on the sacraments reached between Lutheran and South German Reformed theologians.

111. *OS* 1:118–19. (Battles, trans., *Institution*, 118–19.)

"sign and testimony," and the Anabaptist teaching, which emphasized the presence of faith determining their signification.[112]

(ii) In the main portion on the sacraments in general, Calvin focused on their "purpose" and confirmed their traditional concept as the "means of grace" that both the Roman Catholic Church and mainstream Protestantism had inherited. In referring to Augustine's concept of sacrament as "a visible word" of God, he underlined the necessity of the sacraments as "exercises which make us more certain of the trustworthiness of God's word." Over this understanding of their "purpose" Calvin assumed opposition from two sides. On the one hand, as Catholic teaching affirmed that the sacraments might be offered to those who did not believe either in God or his word, he reiterated the purpose of the sacraments "to nourish, exercise, and increase faith."[113] On the other hand, he acknowledged some opposition from the Protestant side, saying that his understanding of the sacraments as a "means of grace" overly emphasized the sacramental rites and minimized both the role of the faith of believers and the work of the Holy Spirit that made the faith possible. His reactions to this opposition were mostly instructive and mediating. He proposed the comprehensive approach of integrating the declaration of God's word, the positive use of the sacraments, the role of the Holy Spirit and of faith in their administration. Yet, he clearly opposed the ritualism of the Catholic teaching that emphasized the sacraments in themselves, gave them their own "power" (*virtus*), and attributed to them their indispensable nature for the faithful. At the same time, he pointed out a danger of sacramentarianism on the Protestant side and appealed instead for total confidence in the sacraments as they set forth God's promise to us.[114] In this context, it is particularly interesting that Calvin, clearly referring to the sacramentarian tendency of Zwingli, rejected that position as "an error." From an etymological analysis of the term (*sacramentum*), Zwingli reduced the meaning of the sacrament to "an oath" that a

112. *OS* 1:118. (Battles, trans., *Institution*, 118.) Cf. Oberman, "The 'Extra' Dimension in the Theology of Calvin," *The Dawn*, 242–43. The bald expression, "earthly elements," is characteristically Calvin's.

113. *OS* 1:119–20. (Battles, trans., *Institution*, 119–20.) Both the *OS* editors' note (*OS* 5:263n3) and Battles, trans., *Institution* (361–62) suggest that Calvin's argument here reflected Bucer's Four Gospel Commentary of 1530 (*Enarrationes (perpetuae), in Sacra Quatuor Evangelia*, I, 18).

114. *OS* 1:120–21. (Battles, trans., *Institution*, 120–21.) According to the *OS* editors, Calvin was conscious of two positions under "a danger of Sacramentarianism": Zwingli's position in his *Commentary on True and False Religion* (*CR: Zwingli*, 3:761) that overemphasized the role of faith, and Schwenckfeld's position that overemphasized the Holy Spirit's operation in the sacraments.

soldier swore to his officer in ancient times and was applied to the Christian sacraments as the oath of the believers' allegiance to Christ.[115]

(iii) Concerning the "use" of the sacraments, Calvin posed a similar scheme of two extremes, Catholic sacramental teaching and a rigid sacramentarian view of Protestants such as the Anabaptists, with his own Augustinian Evangelicalism positioned in the middle. He considered the former dangerous as a diabolical teaching that attached to the sacraments "some sort of secret power." He regarded the latter as a view that weakened their "use" by only allowing them to attest to God's goodness shown in them and attributing no benefits "unless the Holy Spirit accompanies them."[116] Although we cannot avoid the impression that Calvin's general discussion on the sacraments was introductory and less developed, some of his characteristic remarks were noteworthy. In the last section of this portion, for example, he wrote that the sacraments were signs or ceremonies, common to both the Old and New Testaments, by which "the Lord wills to exercise and confirm the faith of his people." Their common purpose was "to direct and almost lead men by the hand to Christ, or rather, as images, to represent him and set him forth to be known." In the New Testament, "baptism attests to us that we have been cleansed and washed, and the Eucharistic Supper attests that we have been redeemed."[117]

(2) The Lord's Supper

Any researcher who reads Calvin's first exposition on the Lord's Supper inevitably encounters this simple question: where does the young humanist scholar stand on the tradition of the eucharistic teaching of the Christian church? As we will see, Calvin considers a basic issue of the biblical teaching to be the "ex-

115. *OS* 1:121–22. (Battles, trans., *Institution*, 121–22.) Cf. G. W. Locher, *Zwingli's Thought: New Perspectives* (Leiden: Brill, 1981), 220–22, 224–28; Ganoczy, *Young Calvin*, 125–58; P. Opitz, "Calvin in the Context of the Swiss Reformation: Detecting the Traces," in *Calvinus Pastor Ecclesiae*, ed. H. S. Selderhuis and A. Huijgen (Göttingen: Vandenhoeck & Ruprecht, 2016), 23–25. Locher's concise analysis highlights Zwingli's unique views vis-à-vis Luther and Calvin. Although Calvin is critical of Zwingli's overemphasis on "faith" and sacramental symbolism in the doctrine of the Lord's Supper, Ganoczy argues that there is a wide range of agreements between Zwingli and Calvin's 1536 *Institutes*. Opitz alludes that what the *Institutes* criticizes was Zwingli's earlier view of the Lord's Supper expressed in his *Commentaries*, which later Zwingli himself considered insufficient and revised. More than Ganoczy, Opitz emphasizes the common ground between the two Reformers and concludes that "the older Calvin grew, the more explicitly he avowed his allegiance to Zwingli."

116. *OS* 1:123–24. (Battles, trans., *Institution*, 123–24.)

117. *OS* 1:124–27. (Battles, trans., *Institution*, 124–27.)

change" (*commutatio*) between what is Christ's and what is and is to be the communicant's in the Supper. Where is Calvin's notion of the "exchange" to be placed in that tradition? It is said that, in rejecting the Catholic eucharistic doctrine, he presents the biblical and catholic "framework" for the Evangelical teaching of Christ's "presence" in the Supper and from this framework mediates the conflicting teachings of Luther and Zwingli. How is his attempt possible and is it to be understood in that tradition? In order to assess Calvin's eucharistic teaching and its implication for his ecclesiology, we will first sketch his teaching in general and Christ's presence in particular, and then proceed to examine his notion of Christ's eucharistic presence in the historical context of the sixteenth century.

An Evangelical Teaching and Its Christological Background

(i) Calvin began by presenting a brief definition, "the bread sanctified in Christ's body, and the wine sanctified in his blood," and called the sacrament "the Lord's Supper" (*coena Domini*) or "Eucharist" (*eucharistia*).[118] Concerning its "purpose" and "use," he then affirmed two points: the Lord's Supper was instituted to confirm that Christ's body and blood offered and shed on the cross was "handed to us, as now to be ours and also forever to be so"; and it was meant to be "exercises of faith" to protect, arouse, and increase faith. The first point could be called the principle of exchange. As Calvin himself described it, it was "the exchange, which out of his measureless goodness he has made with us." Christ's wealth and immortality were to be ours. In exchange our weakness and death were to be his, which brought us the "use" of making us "the children of God" with Christ. Furthermore, he described the reality of this exchange in the sacrament as being "just as if Christ himself was present and was set before our gaze and touched by our hands," or, by our eating and drinking, Christ becoming "one substance with us."[119] Concerning the second

118. *OS* 1:136. (Battles, trans., *Institution*, 137.) According to Ganoczy (*Young Calvin*, 153), Calvin's designations, the Lord's Supper and Eucharist, reflected Zwingli's position expressed in his *Commentary* (*CR: Zwingli*, 3:775) rather than that of Luther who retained the term "Mass" in *On the Babylonian Captivity of the Church* and the *Small Catechism*. However, as we will examine in chapter 2, it should be remembered that Calvin's terms were used in Lefèvre and his circle that was Calvin's humanist background.

119. *OS* 1:137. (Battles, trans., *Institution*, 139–40.) As Battles's endnote (*Institution*, 368) suggests, Calvin's notion of "exercise of faith" might reflect the Lutheran emphasis expressed by Luther's *On the Babylonian Captivity of the Church* and Melanchthon's *Loci Communes* (*CR: Melanchthon*, 21:40–44). Calvin's own emphasis on "commutatio" and "una nobiscum substantia" was clearly distinct from Zwingli's "commemoratio" as well as Lefèvre's "memoria et imitatio," as we will see in chapter 2.

point of "the exercise of faith," he carefully described the process by which Christ's body and blood became the food of believers for their spiritual life through their faithful participation in the sacrament.[120] In this connection, Calvin referred to the interpretation of John's Gospel, chapter 6, which was then one of the focal points in the dispute between the Lutherans and the Zwinglians. To the biblical text in which Christ called himself "the bread of life" and declared that "the one who eats this bread will live forever" (35, 58), Calvin applied a historical interpretation to his text. He said that Christ's declaration was not referring to the sacrament but was to be taken as a "promise" that was fulfilled after Christ's institution of the sacrament at the Last Supper and his cross. Then he implicitly criticized Zwingli and Bucer who read the sacramental significations into the text.[121]

(ii) What we discussed above concerns Calvin's primary understanding of the Lord's Supper based upon his notion of the "exchange" between Christ and the believers. From there he proceeded to the issue of Christ's "presence" (*praesens/praesentia*) in the sacrament. Though a secondary issue, this had caused trouble since the time of the ancient church. Calvin tried to formulate his own view after examining various theories, and he aimed to set the biblical and catholic "framework" on it. Though he considered the various theories on the "presence" only as the appendices to "the simplicity of the Bible," he nonetheless listed some main theories as follows (as quoted from the editors' note of *Calvini Opera Selecta*): the body of Christ was present "really or substantially" (*realiter ac substantialiter*: the Catholics and Luther); with "the same dimensions in which he hung on the cross" (the Scholastics); with "a transubstantiation" (*transubstantiatio*: Lombard and the fourth Lateran Council); as "the bread itself" (*panem ipsum*: Luther); "only as sign and figure" (*signum tantum et figuram*: Zwingli).[122] However, his main aim was not to try to make scholastic analyses of them, but to formulate the biblical and catholic "framework" for the presence.

Concerning Christ's presence in the Supper, Calvin applied what he had developed on Christology in the preceding expositions of the Apostles' Creed in chapter 2 to the doctrine of the Lord's Supper here in chapter 4. Before we

120. *OS* 1:137–38. (Battles, trans., *Institution*, 140.) Battles's endnote (*Institution*, 369) considers that Calvin consulted Luther in this portion.

121. *OS* 1:138–39. (Battles, trans., *Institution*, 141.) Cf. *OS* 5:346n1. Although Calvin was here apprehensive about the connection of Christ's sayings with the Lord's Supper advocated by Zwingli and Bucer, his final rejection of this connection appeared in his *John's Gospel Commentary* of 1553 (*BC* 53/5: *COR* II-11/1:217–18 on 6:54).

122. *OS* 1:139. (Battles, trans., *Institution*, 141–42.)

analyze Calvin's discussions, however, it is helpful to include a brief and preliminary summary of the history of orthodox Christological formation from the Nicene Creed (325/381), which confirmed Christ's divinity with the formula "one substance [*homoousios*] with the Father," to the Definition of Chalcedon (451), which tentatively concluded the Christological controversies.

(iii) It is said that the Christology of Chalcedonian orthodoxy was the result of the conflicts and compromises between the two major ancient schools of theology: the school of Antioch that interpreted Christ's incarnation as the logos "became a man," and the school of Alexandria that interpreted it as the logos "took the flesh." These two schools represented two streams of Christian teachings. If the opposing two schools could be visualized as an ellipse with two foci, the Chalcedonian orthodoxy narrowed the elliptical circle in order to exclude as unorthodox the extreme views of the two schools by confirming both Christ's complete divinity and complete humanity as in the theory of the "one person in two natures." On the one hand, the Antiochene school affirmed Christ's complete historical and corporal humanity along with his divinity as confirmed by the Nicene Creed, thus representing the position emphasizing the distinction of Christ's two natures. By overemphasizing this distinction, however, the school's extreme left-wing of Nestorianism was considered to be teaching the "two persons in two natures" theory and was condemned as heresy in view of the two negatives, "indivisibly" and "inseparably" in the Chalcedonian definition. On the other hand, the Alexandrian school represented the position that viewed the "one person in two natures" theory from the perspective of Christ's divinity. Since the school emphasized the hypostatic union of the two natures, there were tendencies to view their distinction less clearly and to view Christ's humanity somewhat deified after his incarnation. Accordingly, the other two negatives of the Chalcedonian definition, "unconfusedly" and "unchangeably," rejected the school's extreme right-wing Eutyches as the heresy of Monophysitism.

Of course, beyond the framework of Chalcedonian orthodox Christology, there existed far more extreme heretical positions. For example, at the far-left side of the Antiochene position was Arianism, which acknowledged Christ's complete humanity but denied his complete divinity. At the far-right side of the Alexandrian position was the "kenosis" theory of Marcion and Gnosticism, which denied Christ's incarnation and complete humanity. As a matter of fact, in his expositions of the Apostles' Creed in chapter 2, Calvin acknowledged the general framework of Chalcedonian orthodoxy and called it "mysteries." There he called the orthodox Alexandrian position on Christ's two natures as "natures united, not comingled" (principle of "union but not fusion"), and the orthodox Antiochene position as "not to separate, but to distinguish" Christ's two natures (principle of "distinction but not separation"). At the same time, he illustrated Alexandria's far right, extreme heretical position of Manichaeism that taught a dualistic Christ with an incomplete human nature, and Antioch's far left, extreme position, by Nestorius's "two Christs" theory.[123]

(iv) At this juncture, we should note that, in the background of the Reformation debates on the relation between Christology and the doctrine of the Lord's Supper, and especially on the question of the "presence," there was a long history in Western Christendom of developing Chalcedonian orthodoxy into the Roman Catholic dogma of the Mass. In other words, as noted by Pelikan, it was the hermeneutical history concerning the relation between the body of Christ born of Mary, crucified on the cross and sitting at the right hand of God after his resurrection, and the body and blood offered as a sacrifice in the Mass. Since the ancient church, there had been a tension at eucharistic celebrations, whether its elements, bread and wine, pointed to things that were not there or things that were to change into something else. In the West, this tension developed into the ninth-century controversy between the symbolic theory of Ratramnus and the transformational theory of Radbertus. Although the controversy itself was on the interpretation of Augustine's eucharistic doctrine, it also reflected the Christological controversy between the schools of Antioch and Alexandria. Ratramnus took Christ's humanity after the resurrection, sitting at God's right hand in heaven, and interpreted the element of bread as symbolizing that body. On the other hand, Radbertus, in emphasizing the hypostatic union of the two natures, interpreted the element as undergoing some substantial changes in the Mass. While Radbertus's theory became predominant in the Catholic Church, the position of identifying Christ's body in history and in the Mass developed into the Catholic dogma of transubstantiation at the fourth Lateran Council (1215) and was codified in Thomas Aquinas's *Summa*. Denying this identification was regarded as heterodoxy, but was transmitted into late medieval theology and the Reformation.[124] In particular, the Reformation debate on the Lord's Supper between Luther and Zwingli, though they both rejected the Catholic dogma of transubstantiation, was intended to present the Evangelical understanding of Christ's "presence." However, Luther suspected Nestorian (extreme Antiochene) tendencies in Zwingli while Zwingli pointed to "kenosis" (extreme Alexandrian)

123. *OS* 1:80–82. (Battles, trans., *Institution*, 71–74.) Cf. J. Pelikan, *The Christian Tradition: A History of the Development of Doctrine*, 5 vols. (Chicago and London: University of Chicago Press, 1971–89), 1:226–76.

124. Cf. Pelikan, *The Christian Tradition*, 3:184–204; 4:52–59.

tendencies as well as papist remnants in Luther's consubstantiation theory. Although Luther and Zwingli both stood on Chalcedonian orthodoxy, it could be said that, as to the issue of Christ's "presence," their positions reflected the characteristics of the Alexandrian and the Antiochene schools. As we will discuss below, Calvin seemed to have understood the historical context of this issue.

Calvin on Christ's Presence in the Supper

(i) After these preliminary remarks, as we come back to Calvin's discussions on the first point of Christ's presence in general, we notice the Antiochene characteristics, "distinction but not separation" of Christ's divinity and humanity in the sacrament. He applied the idea of "exchange," which he used in his discussions on the sacraments in general to the particular issue of the "presence," and considered that Christ's complete humanity, shown in his incarnation, sufferings and cross, and ascension, was necessarily presented "truly and effectively" in the Lord's Supper. In other words, he said, in order for the believer to complete one's salvation through one's bodily resurrection, it was absolutely essential for Christ's resurrected body "to be contained in a place, to possess its own dimension, and to have its own shape." In short, this body could not be in the Supper.[125]

From this starting point, as if he were apprehensive of the opposite Alexandrian school's unclear distinction between the divine and the human natures, he questioned the two theories of Christ's body after his ascension. One theory considered the body's dimension as "extended as far and wide as heaven and earth," and the other considered it a "glorious and immortal" unbound by place, shape, or dimension. When Calvin questioned them as if they presented a danger of raising "Marcion from hell," though without naming anyone, he seemed to point to Luther and his followers. Especially, the latter theory of Christ's "glorious and immortal" body in the sacrament could be a reference to Kaspar von Schwenckfeld, who turned from Luther's eucharistic view to the Spiritualist position. While cautioning Schwenckfeld's adverse effects upon Evangelicalism and calling him a "madman," Calvin presented a lengthy and severe refutation. Nevertheless, his discussions on this point were generally conscious of the orthodox consensus and seemed to follow the guideline of

125. *OS* 1:139–40. (Battles, trans., *Institution*, 141–43.) Calvin's notion to connect Christ's perfect humanity with the believers' future salvific needs was already expressed in chapter 2 (*OS* 1:78: Battles, trans., *Institution*, 69). For this notion, see Oberman, "The 'Extra' Dimension," *The Dawn*, 240–41.

the "communication of properties" (*communicatio idiomatum*) in which what was true to Christ's divinity or humanity was to be communicated to what was true to his humanity or divinity.[126]

Taking the Antiochene Christology as his starting point, Calvin proceeded to set the framework of his biblical and catholic teachings on the Lord's Supper. In particular, he tried to place the opposing positions of both Luther's and Zwingli's basic assumptions within it. However, his framework was neither simply taking a middle course between the opposing positions nor presenting some points agreeable to both. Rather, it was what he himself thought the biblical and catholic teachings should be. For example, on the one hand, he described Christ's body after the resurrection under "the condition of flesh that it must subsist in one definite place, with its own size and form," thus affirming Zwingli's basic assumption, that Christ's body after the ascension resided in heaven. On the other hand, as if he were solicitous to please Luther, he interpreted Christ "at the right hand of God" as "he reigns in the Father's power and majesty and glory." In this sense, Calvin called Christ's rule the "kingdom" (*regnum*) and described both Christ with his heavenly body as "thus uncircumscribed, Christ can exert his power wherever he pleases, in heaven and on earth" and his earthly rule as "he is always able to be among his own people to live in them, sustain them, strengthen, quicken, keep them, as if he were present in the body."

Here appeared Calvin's unique and characteristic Christology in connection with both the kingdom of Christ and the Lord's Supper. As to the kingdom of Christ, Calvin already interpreted Christ's ascension in chapter 2 as the historical beginning of Christ's kingdom and, as we will see later, his notion of the kingdom was to bear a fundamental impact upon his ecclesiology. As to the Lord's Supper, he described his notion of the heavenly Christ, with his risen body, exerting his rule over heaven and earth as "something further beyond the body" (*etiam extra carnem*). This description was to be known as the so-called "*extra Calvinisticum*" issue in the later eucharistic controversy between the Lutherans and the Calvinists in which Calvin was accused of Nestorianism.[127] If this notion of Calvin showed consideration to Luther's fundamental assumption, he tried to further press his own position by using

126. *OS* 1:140–42. (Battles, trans., *Institution*, 143–45.)

127. *OS* 1:142. (Battles, trans., *Institution*, 145.) Cf. *OS* 1:84 (Battles, trans., *Institution*, 76); E. D. Willis, *Calvin's Catholic Christology: The Function of the So-Called Extra Calvinisticum in Calvin's Theology* (Leiden: Brill, 1966), 8–23, 61–100; Oberman, "The 'Extra' Dimension," *The Dawn*, 245–55.

one negative and one positive sentence. Christ's "presence" in the Lord's Supper was negatively described as "the very substance (*substantia*) of his body or the true and natural (*verum et naturale*) body of Christ is not given there" and positively described as "all those benefits which Christ has supplied us within his body." As to the effect of the "presence," furthermore, it was to lead believers to "an undoubted assurance of eternal life and . . . of the immortality of our flesh."[128]

(ii) To the second point of Christ's presence, Calvin took up the interpretation of the biblical text, "this is my body" and "this is my blood" (Matt 26:26, 28). With an anonymous reference to Luther, he pointed to the problem of "some intransigent person" (*quis morosulus*) who refused to compromise on the text's literal expressions. The historical precedence at the Marburg Colloquy (1529) sought Evangelical accord between Luther and Zwingli but disagreed only on the one issue of Christ's presence in the Supper. Luther insisted on his interpretation of his key text's "is" (*est*) and accused Zwingli, Oecolampadius, and others who took it as "signifies" (*significat*) Christ's body in heaven, of being sacramentarians. Calvin's brief treatment of Luther's problem was not polemical but exceptionally took a dialogue form by using the first and second person singular. For example, as if perplexed by Luther's view, he said that "you . . . deprive him [Christ] of his true flesh," but finally appealed for the catholic consensus by going beyond the different interpretations and basing it upon Paul's commendation of the "analogy of faith" (*analogia fidei*: Rom 12:3).[129]

Unlike this amicable treatment, however, he took a sharply polemical stand against the Catholic teaching on the Mass which, in interpreting the same biblical text, argued that "both [Christ's] soul and divinity are together with the body and cannot be separated from it: consequently, we must adore Christ there," and deduced from this argument the "adoration" of the host at the Mass. The focal point of his criticism was that the Catholic teaching on the Mass was not "catholic" but a deviation from the apostolic church's catholic teaching, consequently turning the adoration of Christ "spiritually in heavenly glory" into the idolatry of adoring the host at the Mass.[130] Calvin's intention behind his criticism seemed to be directed against the Catholic teaching going far

128. *OS* 1:142–43. (Battles, trans., *Institution*, 145–46.) Cf. Ganoczy, *Young Calvin*, 144–49. Calvin's use of "power" and "show/exhibit" seemed to indicate his unique view conceived from the Antiochene perspective. His view was further elaborated in the 1539 edition (*CO* 1:1000–1003) and was completed in the 1559 edition (*Institutio* 4.17.8–10: *OS* 5:349–52) with a new emphasis on "the secret power of the Holy Spirit."

129. *OS* 1:143. (Battles, trans., *Institution*, 146.)

130. *OS* 1:143–45. (Battles, trans., *Institution*, 146–48.)

beyond the Alexandrian school's orthodox position of Christ's two natures, "union but not fusion," into a danger of the "fusion" of the two natures.

(iii) To the third point of the presence issue, Calvin took up another phrase in Christ's institution of the Supper, "(Do this) in remembrance of me" (Luke 22:19), and implicitly tried to make up for Zwingli's symbolic interpretation by placing the notion of "memorial," which the symbolic interpretation emphasized, in the correct signification. At the same time, his discussion on this notion could be a point of contact with his own background, especially Lefèvrianism. As we will examine in the next chapter, although Lefèvre's eucharistic teaching basically used symbolic interpretation, he emphasized its spiritual and practical implications. In this respect, Calvin could have inherited some Lefèvrian emphases. For example, acknowledging that the Lord's Supper carried the purpose of "memorial" elements such as gratitude to God or the proclamation of Christ's death (1 Cor 11:26), Calvin emphasized the additional elements that could inspire believers to "love, peace, and concord," and that could be said to be the sacrament's practical signification and applications. Surprisingly, he spent several paragraphs on this theme of "love, peace, and concord," which could be taken as the sincere appeal of the young humanist or Lefèvrian Calvin who was confronting the religious reality of Europe as the "broken body of Christ." Since he recognized that this theme was also found in the tradition of the ancient church, he quoted the church fathers, especially Augustine, and emphasized the sacrament's dual implication. Namely, for those who sought "love, peace, and concord" it became "spiritual food, sweet and delicate," but for those who did not, "a deadly poison." He closed his discussions with a charge to the communicants to examine themselves, to serve each other, and to commune together.[131]

(iv) After presenting his understandings of the biblical and catholic doctrine of the Lord's Supper, Calvin proceeded to its "framework" as a practical application, namely, to exclude the papal church and the Anabaptists from the "framework" as two extremes. As to the first, he examined the issue of the qualifications of communicants, and charged that the papal church first questioned their "worthiness" and, in order to determine whether they were in a "state of grace" or not, the church forced them to go through the erroneous

131. *OS* 1:145–47. (Battles, trans., *Institution*, 148–51.) Calvin had maintained the theme of "love, peace, and concord" up to the final edition (*Institutio* 4.17.38: *OS* 5:402). References cited here included *Didache* and Augustine's *Homilies on the Gospel of John*. Battles (*Institution*, 372–73) considers that Calvin consulted Latin translations of Luther's sermons on the Lord's Supper and *Betbüchlein* (1522: *Enchiridion precationum*, 1525, 1529).

sacramental process of "contrition, confession, and satisfaction." On the other hand, the assumedly Anabaptist position demanded of the communicants "a perfection of faith" or a perfection that "would make the sacrament void and superfluous."[132] In addition, he listed erroneous practices of the papal church: the obligation to receive communion at least once a year, which he called "a veritable invention of the devil"; the communion of one symbol (element) based on a sophistry that "a body contains blood"; the private Mass which destroyed the fellowship of Christ with his church of believers; and so forth. Especially, he directed his sharpest criticism to the Mass, claiming that the Catholic Church was fraudulently substituting the Lord's Supper for the Mass as "a sacrifice and offering to obtain forgiveness of sins" officiated by the priests. He held that the countless repetitions of sacrifice and offering at the Mass essentially wiped out the significance of Christ's once and for all sufferings and death on the cross.[133]

As we have seen a glimpse of Calvin's early doctrine of the Lord's Supper, we have noticed several characteristics. Firstly, the self-taught theologian presented a biblical and catholic teaching of the Lord's Supper, based upon humanist methods and using the materials from the biblical, patristic, and medieval sources as well as contemporary sources of Luther, Zwingli, perhaps Lefèvre and others. There he proved himself to be, although as yet unrefined, a considerable theologian. Secondly, in his discussions on the sacrament's "definition," "purpose," and "use," he characteristically tried to keep a balance between doctrine and practice, considering the idea of "exchange" between Christ and the believers as the primary "purpose," and boldly defining the hottest controversy of Christ's "presence" as a secondary issue. Over the controversy within Protestant Evangelicalism, his unique notion of Christ's body in heaven, which was to be known later as "something further beyond the body," became a marked characteristic of his theology.

Nevertheless, a reason why we examine his eucharistic teaching prior to his ecclesiology is an assumption that Calvin regarded the biblical and catholic framework of the Lord's Supper as a framework that could also be applied to his Catholic ecclesiology. In this sense, we consider that the significant characteristic of chapter 4 of the first *Institutes* was his application of the ancient church's Christological consensus via the Nicene and Chalcedonian Creeds to his current problem of Christ's "presence" in the sacrament. Certainly, it was true that, due to the discussions in the "instruction" portion, he consistently avoided

132. *OS* 1:147–49. (Battles, trans., *Institution*, 151–52.)
133. *OS* 1:149–56. (Battles, trans., *Institution*, 152–61.)

name calling. He was apprehensive of Luther's consubstantiation theory as not properly appreciative of Christ's humanity, and he was apprehensive of Zwingli's symbolic theory as unsatisfactory in the salvific significations given to Christ's presence. But it was also true that Calvin regarded both positions of Luther and Zwingli within the catholic framework and his intention was certainly not to associate them with Marcion's Docetism and Nestorius's "two persons in two natures" theory. What he tried to achieve above all in chapter 4 was to establish a balanced biblical and catholic eucharistic doctrine that should be confirmed in Protestant Evangelicalism and French evangelical humanism as inheritors of the tradition of the ancient church. In a sense, this doctrine was as an important element of his Catholic ecclesiology as well as a personal remedy to the European religious problem of "the divided body of Christ."

2. *The Fundamentals of Catholic Ecclesiology: Chapter 2, Expositions on the Fourth Article of the Apostles' Creed*

Like his doctrine of the Lord's Supper, Calvin's ecclesiology in the first *Institutes* was formulated in his deep awareness of "the divided body of Christ." The Reformation conflict over the concept of the church revealed a deep chasm between the Roman Catholic and Protestant religions, as well as between the mainstream and Radical Reformation in Protestantism. Likewise, due to his background of the French Reformation, as we will examine later in the dedicatory epistle to the king, there was a reality that his "opponents" were accusing Protestant Evangelicalism of introducing "new" and "uncertain" doctrines into the church, bringing in schism, confusion, and license, and falling into its own self-contradiction of claiming that the true church had always been existent, all while denying the authority of the only existent Roman Catholic Church. In Calvin's mind, there was an awareness that Anabaptists, whom he called the Roman Catholic Church's "troops in ambush," were attacking Evangelicalism from behind by causing "discord and doctrinal quarrels."

As we proceed to examine Calvin's Catholic ecclesiology, it is necessary to recall the structural characteristic of the *Institutes*. While the main body of the *Institutes* was divided into two portions of "instruction" and "apology," his chief discussion on the fundamentals of the church was concentrated in chapter 2 of the first portion. Their practical applications are found in the second portion, especially chapter 6 on Christian liberty, ecclesiastical power, and political administration. There, Calvin not only distinguished the natures of his discussions accordingly, but also used two different concepts of the church, namely, the suprahistorical reality of the church based upon God's election in the first portion, and the church gathered in the historical process on earth in the second portion. He further integrated the two concepts into one catholic reality and presented it as what this study calls Catholic ecclesiology. Generally speaking, there seems to be a kind of consensus among Calvin researchers that acknowledges primarily the former concept in the first *Institutes* and calls it the "invisible" church. But this study will consider the coexistence of the two concepts, which many researchers seem to overlook, as a key to the understanding of his early ecclesiology.[134] Accordingly, we will analyze the first concept in this section as "the fundamentals of Catholic ecclesiology," and the second concept in the next section as "an apology of Catholic ecclesiology."

(1) The "Holy Catholic Church"

As mentioned above, Calvin borrowed the structure of the "instruction" portion from Luther's *Catechisms*. Concerning structural differences, Luther's *Catechisms* placed ecclesiology in the third article, the Holy Spirit, of the Apostles' Creed. The *Institutes* separated ecclesiology from the doctrine of the Holy Spirit and placed it at the head of the fourth article. While Luther evangelically interpreted the creed's phrase, "holy, Catholic church" as "holy Christian church," Calvin retained the term, "Catholic," and emphasized the church's catholicity.[135] At the beginning of his expositions on the church, he tried to present the church's fundamental definition as "the whole number of the elect" (*universus electorum numerus*). This bold expression was assumed to have followed Augustine's lead. The concept itself was also held by Luther

134. As early as 1917, Doumergue (*Jean Calvin*, 5:5, 11) noticed two distinctive notions of the church used in the first *Institutes*, one in chapter 2 ("*universum electorum*") and the other in chapters 5 and 6 ("*coetus fidelium*"). Concerning the history of the formation of the *Institutes*, however, a predominant theory held by researchers from early Wendel (*Calvin*, 294–95) and Ganoczy (*Calvin*, 184–91, 200, 202–3) to recent Gordon (*Calvin*, 57–59, 98) has focused on the "invisible church" of the elect as the basic notion of the church in the first *Institutes*. According to this theory, furthermore, through contacts and influences of Bucer, Calvin shifted the ecclesiological emphasis from the invisible to the visible church, notably in the second and third editions of the *Institutes*. Following Doumergue's initial insight, our study considers the catechetical and apologetic divisions as well as the coexistence of two distinctive notions of the church in the first *Institutes* as a key to his early ecclesiology.

135. *OS* 1:86. (Battles, trans., *Institution*, 78.) For Luther's interpretation of the Apostles' Creed in both the Small and Large Catechism, see *The Book of Concord*, trans. and ed. T. G. Tappert (Philadelphia: Fortress Press, 1959), 345, 415. Reflecting Luther's view, the *Augsburg Confession* composed by Melanchthon (Article 7, German text) reads "one holy Christian church" (*The Book of Concord*, 32).

and Bucer, but was categorically distinct from "the congregation of believers," the basic Protestant understanding of the church since Luther. Here it is noteworthy that, throughout his expositions on the fourth article, Calvin consistently used the biblical texts as his primary source. He did not use, for example, the invisible-visible notion of the church customarily used in Scholastic theology, but connected the definition with its manifestations in the church in history.[136]

As a supplementation to the fundamental definition, he referred to the church's catholicity and uniqueness or oneness. As to catholicity, for example, God's elect were described in terms of universality as "whether angels or men; of men, whether dead or still living; of the living, in whatever lands they live, or wherever among the nations they have been scattered."[137] He further identified the Catholic church with "society" or "one people of God" of which Christ was said to be the "Leader," "Ruler," and "Head." Here appeared Calvin's unique view that the suprahistorical election of God and the historical people of God were combined in terms of Christ and both were representing the unique reality of the Catholic church. Furthermore, as he described the reason for God to choose the elect "in order that all might be gathered into God's Kingdom," for him "the whole number of the elect" was not only expressing the reality of the Catholic church but also that of the kingdom of Christ, the theme that he was to develop further during his life, especially in connection with his ecclesiology.[138] It should be noted, as we will examine below, that

136. *OS* 1:86. (Battles, trans., *Institution*, 78.) Cf. S. H. Hendrix, *Ecclesia in Via: Ecclesiological Developments in the Medieval Psalms Exegesis and the Dictata super Psalterium (1513–1515) of Martin Luther* (Leiden: Brill, 1974), 155–60; Wendel, *Calvin*, 139–40; Ganoczy, *Young Calvin*, 159–60. According to Hendrix, Luther in his *First Psalms Lectures* (1513–15) focused on "the congregation of the faithful" as the chief biblical notion of the church. Along with it, however, Luther also used other notions such as the church of the elect as well as the invisible/visible church, which reflected his Augustinian and Scholastic background. Both Wendel and Ganoczy connect Calvin's basic notion of the church with the historically closer background of Bucer. Confer n. 139 below.

137. *OS* 1:86. (Battles, trans., *Institution*, 78.) Although the reference to angels was a traditional notion, it was not found in the *Four Gospel Commentaries* of Bucer who emphasized the connection of God's election with faith. Calvin dropped the reference in the second edition (*CO* 1:537–39).

138. *OS* 1:86. (Battles, trans., *Institution*, 78.) In examining Calvin's first *Institutes*, D. N. Wiley ("The Church as the Elect in the Theology of Calvin," in *John Calvin and the Church: A Prism of Reform*, ed. T. George [Louisville: Westminster John Knox, 1990], 99–103) recognizes the coexistence of the "invisible and visible" church concepts and notes Calvin's emphasis on the "visible" church.

Calvin later connected this reality of the church with another concept of the church, "the congregation of believers," as the manifestation of this reality. In short, for Calvin, Catholic ecclesiology represented the churchly reality that was expressed by the combination of God's elect, Christ's kingdom, and the congregation of believers.[139]

Calvin's expositions on the Apostles' Creed, in comparison to the four words (one, holy, catholic, and apostolic) used by the posterior Nicene Creed, placed the predominant emphasis on the church's catholicity, nominally treated its oneness and holiness, and ignored almost totally its apostolicity. For example, the church's oneness was expressed as the elect gathered in one body of Christ or as those "who live together in one faith, hope, and love, and in the same Spirit of God, called to the inheritance of eternal life." As to the church's holiness, Calvin's description was moderate and only referred to the sanctification of the elect.[140] It was also true that another expression of the Apostles' Creed, "the communion of saints," was also described in terms of God's election and the church's catholicity, and its entity was briefly described as "in the Catholic church all the elect (who with true faith worship God together) have reciprocal communication and participation in all goods."[141]

(2) Manifestations and Marks of the Catholic Church

Having defined the concept of the Catholic church, Calvin tackled the difficult question of its manifestations in history and the marks that ought to be used to discern it. Generally speaking, his discussions on this problem reflected the Evangelical position of Luther, Zwingli, and Bucer. However, as the first

139. As the emphasis is on the integration of the church of the elect and the church in history, its precedent can be found, for example, in Bucer's *Four Gospels Commentary* of 1530 (*Enarrationes [perpetuae]*, II, 73r). E. A. McKee (*The Pastoral Ministry and Worship in Calvin's Geneva* [Geneva: Droz, 2016], 17–23) rightly sees a similar combination of the church of the elect and "membership in the church" in the text under consideration.

140. *OS* 1:86. (Battles, trans., *Institution*, 78.) Our study considers "catholicity" fundamental to Calvin's notion of the church and disagrees with Ganoczy (*Calvin*, 186–87; *Young Calvin*, 160–61) who takes the church's "oneness/unity" as fundamental.

141. *OS* 1:91–92. (Battles, trans., *Institution*, 85–86.) Calvin dropped this viewpoint in the Apostles' Creed of "communion of saints" as that of the elect in the revision of the second edition (*CO* 1:540–42: *Institutio* 4.1.3: *OS* 5:4–7) in favor of the emphasis on the communion of the faithful. As seen in the final edition, however, a new emphasis was added on "God's election" (*electio Dei*) as the ultimate end of, and on "Christ's firmness" (*firmitudo Christi*) as the secondary foundation of the "communion of saints."

presentations of a self-taught theologian, the discussions display the impression of theoretical insufficiency since some of the points expressed there were to be corrected, supplemented, and deleted in the succeeding editions of the *Institutes*. His intention behind them is not always clearly understood, but we will analyze them in the following four points.

(i) Firstly, he affirmed that the Catholic church was to be manifested in the historical process of the elect's "calling, justification, and sanctification," and due to the certainty of God's election this process was said to advance to its final stage, the so-called "perseverance of the saints." If this reasoning was *a priori*, he affirmed, the *a posteriori* reasoning was not necessarily true. He warned that "it is not for us to determine for certain whether others are of the church, nor to distinguish the elect from the reprobate."[142]

(ii) Secondly, in addition to the elect's individual process, Calvin also emphasized their collective process as God's people or the relationship between their catholic faith and God's election. Since Calvin affirmed that God's sovereign election chose believers for his church, his people, and the body of Christ, he concluded, "we are among God's elect and of the church, if we partake in Christ." Nevertheless, he criticized the Catholic apologists who used a reverse reasoning for their claim that the "power of the keys" (Matt 16:19) given to the ministers of the word could determine who were of the church or not.[143]

(iii) Thirdly, Calvin proceeded to the difficult question of discerning the Catholic church by the church's external marks. As background, he seemed to regard the two-marks theory (declaration of God's word and administration of the sacraments) expressed in the Augsburg Confession of the Lutheran Church as an Evangelical consensus. Since he based his concept of the Catholic church on God's election, however, he was going to face different issues due to the Augsburg Confession, which considered the congregation of believers as a starting point. In other words, he took a dialectic approach. On the one hand, he considered the final identity of the Catholic church based upon God's election impossible to discern by humans because "the elect cannot be recognized by us with the assurance of faith." On the other hand, "yet Scripture describes certain sure marks to us" by which it was requested for us to discern "the elect of God, the children of God, the people of God, and the church of

142. *OS* 1:86–88. (Battles, trans., *Institution*, 79–81.) As far as Calvin's argument in this portion was concerned, its conceptual analogy with Bucer's *Four Gospels Commentary* suggested by Ganoczy (*Young Calvin*, 160–62) and Battles (trans., *Institution*, 349–50) seems to be evident.

143. *OS* 1:88–89. (Battles, trans., *Institution*, 81–83.)

God." In more practical terms, he affirmed that, on the one hand, "all who profess with us the same God and Christ by confession of faith, example of life and participation in the sacraments, ought by some sort of judgment of love (*caritatis iudicium*) to be deemed elect and members of the church." On the other hand, some of them were deemed not to be of the church according to the marks of their deeds or the use of excommunications.[144]

In this description, the first problem was what Calvin meant by "judgment of love." It could be understood that by this phrase he meant it not as a definitive judgment but that of the church based upon its common and brotherly estimate. The second problem was, by the phrase "confession of faith, example of life and participation in the sacraments," whether he proposed a three-marks theory (the word of God, the administration of the sacraments, and church discipline) or not. In other words, since the Augsburg Confession listed only two as the church's objective and essential marks, the question is whether Calvin proposed the three marks as indications of what the Catholic church based upon God's election should be. Furthermore, if he intentionally listed the three with a recognition of the two objective marks of Luther, Melanchthon, and Zwingli, it could be an indication of his originality or the influence of Bucer who initiated his ecclesiology from God's election and presented three marks in his *Four Gospels Commentary* (1530), which was believed to be used by Calvin.[145] However, it should be noted that, in the discussions before and after the above quotation, Calvin referred to two objective marks. In addition, we need to recognize the persistent tension between the objective two and the subjective three marks in his basic understanding of the church. For example, in his dedicatory epistle to the king, which we will examine later, Calvin referred to two marks with a clear recognition of the Augsburg Confession. But his *Reply to Sadoleto* referred to three marks. Nevertheless, his conception of the Catholic church based upon God's election as well as the notion of three marks will retreat. The systematic presentation of his ecclesiology based upon the objective two marks will commence from the second edition of the

144. *OS* 1:89–90. (Battles, trans., *Institution*, 83–84.)

145. Bucer, *Enarrationes (perpetuae)*, II, 73r. Cf. Ganoczy, *Young Calvin*, 161; Battles, trans., *Institution*, 350. Since Doumergue (*Jean Calvin*, 5:23–31) proposed the three-marks theory, although distinguishing the two marks of God's word and the sacraments as "essential" and the third mark of discipline as "indispensable," the theory has gained a stream of supporters. As far as the first *Institutes* is concerned, noting Bucer's influence on this, both Ganoczy and Battles consider the three marks by which Calvin depicted the matured church in Christ and led by the Holy Spirit. Instead of theorizing the two or the three marks of the church, McKee (*The Pastoral Ministry*, 19–20) sees here "the distinction between the marks of the church and the marks of Christians" and considers it Calvin's "creative insight."

Institutes (1539). Therefore, his formal position could be appropriately stated as the two-marks theory.[146]

(iv) Fourthly, Calvin's discussions on church discipline, especially excommunication, were conscious of the Catholic disciplinary system and Anabaptist rigorism, but were general and brief. There, the tripartite aim of the law that he expressed first in the commentary on Seneca was brought up in connection with excommunication. The disciplined believers should not profane God again, should not influence others adversely, and might be led to repentance. Since God's election was ultimately beyond human comprehension, the excommunicated should not be regarded as forsaken by God or without hope of salvation, but should be fairly treated according to the law of God.[147]

As we have briefly sketched the fundamentals of Calvin's catholic concept of the church, we have noticed there the underlying tone of Augustine, Luther's ecclesiology, points of contact with Bucer, and also its incomplete and transitory character as an Evangelical ecclesiology. Yet at the same time, Calvin's fundamentals reveal his Christological foundation, namely the Chalcedonian definition from the Antiochene approach ("distinction but not separation"). We have also noticed unique notions such as the Catholic church defined in terms of God's election and its manifestations in history, the dialectic concept of the oneness of "the whole number of God's elect," the kingdom of Christ, and the church as the body of Christ. From these fundamentals, on the one hand, Calvin could call the church of God's election "the Catholic church, the mystical body of Christ" (*ecclesia catholica, corpus Christi mysticum*). On the other hand, he repudiated the papal church as guilty of making an induction from its historical existence to God's election and of identifying itself as the Catholic church and deifying its hierarchy.[148]

146. *OS* 1:89–90, 91. (Battles, trans., *Institution*, 83–84, 85.) Cf. the dedicatory epistle: *OS* 1:31. (Battles, trans., *Institution*, 12.) In the second edition of 1539 (*CO* 1:543–44), Calvin retained the text that implied "three marks." Immediately after the retained text, however, referring clearly to the "marks of the church" (*symbola/notae ecclesiae*), he presented "two marks" of the church. It should be also noted that the discussion on two marks was in the context of the "mixed church" (*ecclesia multitudinis*) of the elect and the nonelect, and not that of the "Catholic church" of the elect, and that church discipline was treated as the "fruit" (*fructus*) or "sinew" (*vinculum*) of two marks for organizing the church in history. Among Calvin researchers who mention the "three marks" of Calvin, such as Oberman (*John Calvin*, 26–27) and R. White ("Oil and Vinegar: Calvin on Church Discipline," *Scottish Journal of Theology* 38 [1985]: 25–26), there seems to be a general tendency to distinguish the first two fundamental marks from the third mark as their "fruit" or the "form" needed for organizing the church.

147. *OS* 1:89–91. (Battles, trans., *Institution*, 83–85.)

148. *OS* 1:91–92. (Battles, trans., *Institution*, 85–86.)

3. Apology for Catholic Ecclesiology: Chapters 5 and 6

Calvin's concept of the church in the "apology" portion of the first *Institutes* exclusively dealt with the reality of the church in history and the Christian world in Europe. As Doumergue notices this "change" of tone from "the whole number of the elect" to "the congregation of believers," Calvin theoretically distinguished the church as "a physical thing" (*res carnalis*) from the church as "the mystical body" (*corpus mysticum*) of Christ. Nonetheless both concepts, distinguished but not separated, pointed to the one Catholic church. The signification of these concepts could be distinguished as the Catholic church's theoretical "fundamentals" and the "apology" for its manifestations in history. As far as the structure of the "apology" portion was concerned, chapter 5 (the remaining five sacraments) substantially corresponded to Luther's *On the Babylonian Captivity of the Church* (1520). The three points of chapter 6 (Christian freedom, ecclesiastical power, and political administration) were the themes dealt with in Luther's *On the Freedom of a Christian* (1520) and *On Secular Authority* (1523). It could be said accordingly that Calvin inherited Protestant Evangelicalism represented by Luther as well as by other Reformers such as Zwingli and Bucer. He applied this to formulate afresh his own Evangelical church concept and social teachings in the historical context, as well as perspectives quite different from those of his predecessors. Concerning the nature of the "apology," Ganoczy summarizes chapter 5 as "critique and ideal of the ecclesiastical structures" and chapter 6 as "the outline of Calvin's plan for reformation." Thus, the "apology" portion was the first concrete presentation of his church reform ideas.[149] Before we examine his "apology" in the following pages, it is useful to call the reader's attention to three characteristics in the "apology."

(i) The first characteristic concerns the fact that the "apology" portion never mentioned God's election or the elect, but described the church in history from the perspective of "believers." In this portion, for example, the predominant descriptions of the church are "the church of believers" (*fidelium ecclesia*), "the gathering of believers" (*coetus fidelium*), "the gathering of believing people" (*coetus fidelium populi*), and others.[150] One focal point of the problem is how

149. Cf. Doumergue, *Jean Calvin*, 5:11–13, 23–25; Ganoczy, *Young Calvin*, 215–38. Doumergue suggests the coexistence of two notions in Calvin (the "objective element" of "the congregation of believers" and "the subjective element" of "the whole number of the elect") as evidence of Luther's and Bucer's influence. Our study places the two notions in the background of Calvin's Antiochene Christology.

150. *OS* 1:156, 159, 237, 243; 1:156, 160; 1:187. (Battles, trans., *Institution*, 160, 164, 258, 266; 160, 166; 198.)

Calvin distinguished and related these two church concepts: the church of the elect and the congregation of believers. The widely accepted view among researchers assumes only the first concept, ignoring the coexistence of two as in the first *Institutes*, and refers to the appearance of the second concept only from the second edition of the *Institutes*. This view is unacceptable from material evidence. Furthermore, the view that acknowledges the coexistence but does not explain the theological necessity of why and how Calvin distinguished and related them also is insufficient.[151] In order to assess this necessity, besides the ecclesiological analyses of the text itself, research into Calvin's wider philosophical and theological background is needed. At this juncture, however, what we can suggest is the parallelism existing between his eucharistic doctrine and ecclesiology. One example is his Antiochene Christology which started to distinguish Christ's divine and human natures and then related them; this parallels his discussions on the sacraments in general that distinguished the "substance" of the sacraments (God's grace/promise) from their rites (signs/testimonies) and called the latter "earthly elements." Concerning Christ's "presence" in the Lord's Supper, his distinction between Christ's body in heaven and the sacrament's bread and wine as "earthly elements" parallels his notion of Christ's body exerting its manifestations in heaven and earth. From these examples, we can see that an ecclesiological parallelism exists between the church of the elect and the congregation of believers.

(ii) The second characteristic is the theme that provides coherence to his "apology" portion, namely, the kingdom of Christ. The theme is not clearly seen in chapter 2 in the expositions of the Apostles' Creed. However, it is predominantly present in the "apology" portion, especially chapter 6, in connection with the topics of ecclesiastical power and political administration, that is, the so-called "church and state" or "two kingdoms" perspective. The concept of Christ's kingdom itself was a biblical notion found chiefly in the Pauline epistles, was inherited by the church fathers, and was transmitted into the tradition of the medieval Catholic Church as the basis of the "church and state" or "two kingdoms" perspective primarily through Augustine's *City*

151. For the predominant theory, see note 134 above. An early example of the latter case is found in Doumergue (*Jean Calvin*, 5:11–12) who considers Calvin's two ideas "absolutely distinct," but does not go further to relate them. Among Calvin's theological precedents, Bucer seemed to be a notable case of interrelating the church of the elect and the congregation of the faithful as early as in his 1527 *Gospels Commentary* (*Enarrationum in Evangelia Matthaei, Marci, & Lucae*, II, 179–80, 181v–82v). Since Bucer tended to relate two ideas as one unitary reality, without making a clear and conceptual distinction, it may be problematic to view Bucer as Calvin's precedent on this point.

of God. In the young Calvin's background of Evangelicalism, Luther's "two kingdoms-regiments" theory attempted a fresh and soteriological reinterpretation of "church and state," attributing to the church the administration of the gospel, and to the state that of the law. Over against Luther, who sharply distinguished the two administrations and tended to associate Christ's kingdom predominantly with the church, Zwingli and Bucer emphasized the role of Christ's kingdom in both "church and state." For example, as to the church and state relationship, Zwingli followed the traditions of the Swiss Confederation's ideal and advocated a closer identity of church and state. Furthermore, under a proposition, "Christ's Kingdom is external" (*regnum Christi etiam externam*), he closely associated Christ's kingdom with the magistracy as a major player in church reform. Like Zwingli, Bucer also affirmed Christ's kingdom exerting its influence equally in both church and state as its manifestations. As a matter of fact, in the process of the Strasbourg Reformation in the early 1530s, Bucer defended the magisterial role in church reform against his colleague, Antonius Engelbrecht, who followed the Lutheran notion of Christ's kingdom. Unlike Zwingli, however, he emphasized the church's spiritual government as independent from the magistracy. This emphasis resulted in his long struggle with the city magistracy on the issue of church discipline. Since Ganoczy's comparative analysis of Bucer's notion of Christ's kingdom as a source of Calvin's notion in the first *Institutes*, the affinity of their notions has been widely acknowledged.[152]

(iii) The third characteristic concerns a crucial question: How did the young Calvin relate Christ's kingdom with the historical reality of the earthly two kingdoms, that is, church and state as spiritual kingdom and civil kingdom? In other words, this question is about the relationship between his notion of Christ's kingdom and his two kingdoms theory. In order to ascertain this relationship accurately, it is essential to examine it in the following two historically given contexts in which he formulated his first cohesive social teachings. One is his Antiochene Christology, which we have previously examined in connection with his eucharistic doctrine and suggested its parallel implication on his ecclesiology. Like the instance of Christ's resurrected body in heaven and its manifested presence in the Lord's Supper, Calvin followed the

152. Cf. H. R. Lavater, "Regnum Christi Etiam Externam—Huldrych Zwinglis Brief vom 4. Mai 1528 an Ambrosius Blarer in Konstanz," *Zwingliana* 15 (1981): 338–43; Locher, *Zwingli's Thought: New Perspectives*, 228–29; Ganoczy, *Young Calvin*, 159–60; Tuininga, *Calvin's Political Theology*, 41–47, 56–60. Tuininga considers Zwingli's two kingdoms theory as a representative Reformed view, yet distinctive from the Bucer-Calvin view. He also considers Calvin's view in terms of "Bucer's influence."

Antiochene principle of "distinction but not separation." He first ontologically distinguished Christ's transcendent kingdom from its earthly manifestations, church and state. Then he closely related Christ's kingdom to them individually. If we can diagram this relationship, Christ's kingdom and its two earthly manifestations form an equilateral triangle, Christ's kingdom occupying the top point and the other two the bottom points. In this triangular scheme, three sets of lines between two points (Christ's kingdom—the church, Christ's kingdom—state, and church—state) are kept in the tension of "distinction but not separation." In this regard, on the one hand, Calvin's teaching is too comprehensive to be simply represented by the earthly two kingdoms theory. On the other hand, due exactly to his Antiochene background, his teaching distinguishes itself from those of Luther, Zwingli, and even Bucer.

The second context concerns the historical reality of the mid-1530s, in which Calvin's original teaching was decisively formulated in sharp opposition to both Roman Catholic ecclesiasticism and the Münster Anabaptist revolution. As we will examine Calvin's texts, over against the Catholics, he accused them of identifying Christ's kingdom with their church institution, thus usurping Christ's unique prerogative. Over against the Münster Anabaptists, he also accused them of claiming their revolution as an earthly realization of Christ's kingdom, thus committing "a Jewish vanity to seek and enclose Christ's kingdom within the element of this world." It is this apologetic stance against the two extreme positions of the Catholics and the Münster Anabaptists that also distinguishes his unique teaching from those of Luther, Zwingli, and Bucer. For example, unlike Luther and Bucer, who tend to closely identify Christ's kingdom with the church, Calvin avoids any uncritical identification. Instead, he carefully delineates their close relationship. Unlike Zwingli, who closely associates Christ's kingdom with the magistracy, he checks overdrawn associations by emphasizing the spiritual nature of Christ's kingdom. In short, in the first *Institutes* the young Calvin encompasses both Christ's kingdom and the two earthly kingdoms into a cohesive teaching so as to view the whole reality of the Christian world of his day.[153]

153. On the last point of our discussion, two recent and serious works that examine Calvin's two kingdoms theory can be seen as illustrations: D. VanDrunen, *Natural Law and the Two Kingdoms: A Study in the Development of Reformed Social Thought* (Grand Rapids: Eerdmans, 2010), 70–82; Tuininga, *Calvin's Political Theology*, 61–69. Since both works focus on Calvin's social teachings and his Christ's kingdom doctrine is not their primary concern, naturally they concentrate on his notion of two kingdoms as an independent theory. In addition, they notice little of or give no significance to either Calvin's distinctive teaching in the first *Institutes* or the historical context in which it was formulated. First, VanDrunen's

(1) Five Remaining Rites

Calvin spent the largest number of pages of the first *Institutes* on chapter 5, his refutation of what the Roman Catholic Church called the sacraments of confirmation, penance, extreme unction, ecclesiastical orders, and marriage—five out of seven rites of the Church's sacramental system. His main thrust was to expose that the Catholic institution had dominated the church through these false rites that were diversions from the tradition of the Bible and the ancient church. In general, his discussions followed the anti-Catholic polemics of Luther, Melanchthon, Zwingli, and Bucer, but some interesting insights of his early ecclesiology might be seen in his more extensive discussions on penance and ecclesiastical orders.

Penance

Since Luther's *Ninety-Five Theses* and *On the Babylonian Captivity of the Church*, the rite of penance as the core of the Catholic salvific system was the focal point of Evangelical attacks. With this recognition, Calvin presented an

work assumes Calvin's teaching remaining unchanged from the first to the last *Institutes* (70n5, the assertion that we consider basically correct). Although the work carefully distinguishes Christ's kingdom from "its present institutional expression in the church," on the one hand, its main thrust is on the close association between them. On the other hand, by emphasizing the redemptive and spiritual nature of Christ's kingdom, it pictures the civil magistracy as distinctive from Christ's kingdom and cites Calvin's own texts for support, but without mentioning that the texts originally appear in Calvin's anti–Münster Anabaptist attack. As far as the first *Institutes* is concerned, we worry whether VanDrunen's work is either able to properly cope with Calvin's vehement attack on the Catholic identification of their institution with Christ's kingdom or is reading too much of Luther's initial emphases into Calvin's position. On the contrary, Tuininga's work correctly represents Calvin' s two kingdoms theory as "Christ's two kingdoms" (its subtitle) and it even examines the first *Institutes*, but with a sweeping statement that the *Institutes* "contained the Frenchman's classic statement of the kingdoms concept, but it said very little about the institutional form a reformed church should take, and it did not say much about the role civil magistrates should play in the process of reformation." Following the "Bucer's influence" theory (which we will examine in chapter 3 below), furthermore, the work emphasizes "Calvin's legacy: the autonomy and integrity of the spiritual kingdom of Christ, which is to say, the church" (62), just as Bucer's would affirm. Judging from Calvin's theological background as Antiochene Christology, which is quite distinctive from Bucer's Thomistic background, and his severe criticism against the Catholic institution's claim of Christ's kingdom, we wonder whether or not the work reads too much Bucer into Calvin's early formation and uncritically identifies the church with Christ's kingdom. On this point, confer n. 169 and n. 175 below.

Evangelical view, without naming Luther or the Augsburg Confession formulated by Melanchthon. He argued that "certain men well versed in penance" affirmed the biblical "penance" consisting of two elements, namely, "mortification" with the awareness of God's judgment and the believers' own sins and "vivification" by faith.[154] Following this lead, Calvin criticized the Catholic penance that turned what was originally meant to be the believers' voluntary deeds into the penitential system of "contrition of heart, confession of mouth, and satisfaction of works," as defined by Scholastic theologians. This resulted in robbing believers of their freedom and giving ceaseless pain to their souls.

In particular, Calvin's severe criticism was directed against the Catholic view of "the power of the keys" and the abuse of power in claiming that it belonged exclusively to the order of priests.[155] In discussions on this point, his first writings on the crucial issue of the power of the keys appeared. Generally speaking, three biblical texts were considered to be important for the understanding of this power, namely, Matthew 16:19 and 18:17–18 and John 20:22–23. Calvin took the first and third texts as belonging to one series and distinguished it from the second text as belonging to another series. In this twofold theory, Calvin interpreted the first series as referring to the power to be exercised in the proclamation of God's word and the power that Christ "promised" to Peter in the first text (Matt 16). After his resurrection, he "gave" it to all the apostles by giving them the Holy Spirit as the third text (John 20) testified. He further distinguished it from the power to be exercised in church discipline as prescribed in the second text (Matt 18). With this distinction, which could also be found in Bucer's writings, Calvin accused the papal church of ignoring the distinction and abusing the texts concerning the declaration of the word by applying it to the Church's disciplinary system of penance. The basic distinction also had some bearing on his own ideas of the ministers of the word and their relationship with the congregation in matters of discipline.[156] Furthermore, his interpretation of the second text of Matthew 18, especially the "church" in the phrase "tell it to the church" (17), was noteworthy. As Bucer considered Evangelical church discipline by the "assembly" or "people" gathered in Christ's name and led by the Holy Spirit as an ideal form, Calvin likewise took the "church" in the text as not referring to some priests but to

154. *OS* 1:170, 171. (Battles, trans., *Institution*, 177, 179.)

155. *OS* 1:184, 185, 187. (Battles, trans., *Institution*, 194, 195, 197–98.)

156. *OS* 1:185–87. (Battles, trans., *Institution*, 195–98.) Cf. Ganoczy, *Young Calvin*, 165–67; White, "Oil and Vinegar," 26–27. A precedent of the two serial interpretations could be found in Bucer's 1527 Gospels Commentary (*Enarrationum in Evangelia Matthaei, Marci, & Lucae*, II, 179v–81v, 215v).

the "assembly of the believing people." Thus, he not only proposed a congregational principle in church discipline but also emphasized the Holy Spirit's role in church discipline by saying, "I deny that the power of the keys belongs to any persons who have not received the Holy Spirit."[157] This last point, since he would later revise some aspects of it, should be considered transitory.

Ecclesiastical Orders

Calvin's first exposition on ecclesiastical orders could be approached from two angles, namely, his refutation of Catholic doctrine and the formation of his own doctrine. Regarding the first aspect, his writings followed the general guideline of his Evangelical predecessors and, in comparison with his later systematic presentation, they were merely an outline. The basic tone of his refutation was that the Catholic doctrine was a departure from the biblical notion. Particularly he criticized two points that it introduced, the distinction of "clerics" and "laymen" and the substitution of the biblical notion of minister with its own inventions. On the first point, he cited two biblical texts, 1 Peter 3:9 and 5:3, that were used by Luther in his teaching of the priesthood of all believers. Calvin affirmed that, since the biblical notion of "clergy" or "cleric" originally referred to the ministry (*ministerium*) of the whole people of God, the Catholic doctrine abused it for the exclusive rule of the clerics.[158] On the second point of substitution, his criticism was directed against the "seven orders," especially the highest order of "deacon" and "priest." The Catholic doctrine substituted the biblical office of deacon for a supplementary office of "priest." Furthermore, the biblical ministry of "priest," which chiefly consisted in the proclamation of the word and the administration of the sacraments, was

157. *OS* 1:187–88. (Battles, trans., *Institution*, 198–99.) Cf. Bucer, *Enarrationum in Evangelia Matthaei, Marci, & Lucae*, II, 214r-v; W. van't Spijker, *The Ecclesiastical Offices in the Thought of Martin Bucer*, trans. J. Vriend and L. D. Biema (Leiden: Brill, 1996), 73–74. Bucer maintained the congregational principle in church discipline and proposed its ideal form, though yet presently impossible, of the cooperation between the people who "completely surrender themselves to Christ" (*qui sese penitus Christo dediderint*) and the like-minded magistracy. As far as Calvin's text was concerned, the former sentence, stressing the congregational discipline of "the believing folk," was omitted in the extensively revised edition of 1543 (*CO* 1:712), but the latter sentence, referring to the Holy Spirit, survived in the final edition (*Institutio* 3.4.20: *OS* 4:109).

158. *OS* 1:206–7. (Battles, trans., *Institution*, 220–21.) Cf. Ganoczy, *Young Calvin*, 217–18. The identification of "clerics" (1 Peter 5:3) with "the whole people of God" (*universa Dei plebes*) was dropped in the final edition (*Institutio* 4.4.9: *OS* 5:65–66), even though an equivalent term, "the whole church" (*tota ecclesia*) was retained.

replaced with an office like the Judaic priesthood "to perform the sacrifice of Christ's body and blood on the altar, to say prayers, and to bless God's gifts." For him it was simply the usurpation of Christ's office of high priest who alone could make intercessions to God for sinners and offer sacrifices to God, as well as the negligence of the office to preach the gospel to believers.[159] As to the related issue of distinguishing "bishop" (*episcopus*) and "presbyter/priest" (*presbyter/sacerdos*) that Catholic doctrine had made into two different orders, Calvin repudiated the Catholic notion that the bishops were the successors of the twelve apostles and that the presbyters/priests were the successors of the "seventy" sent by Christ. He affirmed the two orders as basically the same office of preaching the gospel and administering the sacraments.[160]

As far as the formation of Calvin's own doctrine of ministry was concerned, his anti-Catholic polemics in chapter 5 provided only a transitory shape. Its full and developed form was to be seen in the third edition of the *Institutes* (1543), written after his reformatory experiences in both Geneva and Strasbourg. Nonetheless a glimpse of his basic assumptions on doctrine appeared here. Over and against Catholic doctrine, for example, he assumed that the Bible taught "bishop" and "priest" as the same office and in one grade, that such various expressions found in the Bible as "bishop," "presbyter," "priest," and "pastor" basically referred to the same office of God's word and the sacraments, and that they all were equally the "ministers of the church."[161] From these assumptions, as well as his studies of the Bible and Catholic sources of the *Decretals*, he made a judgment of historical perspective that the basic aim of the Catholic ministerial system was "to shape one religion out of Christianity, Judaism and paganism by sewing patches together."[162] As to the "historical episcopacy," namely, the process of church history in which the office of bishop was considered a different order from that of priest, his position was flexible and nuanced due to his apparent consideration for the religious reality of the time. In clearly rejecting the notion of bishops as the successors of the apos-

159. *OS* 1:209–10. (Battles, trans., *Institution*, 223–24.)

160. *OS* 1:211–12. (Battles, trans., *Institution*, 226–27.)

161. *OS* 1:210, 212–13. (Battles, trans., *Institution*, 225–28.)

162. *OS* 1:213–18, esp. 217. (Battles, trans., *Institution*, 228–34.) To shape one religion "out of Christianity and Judaism and Paganism" is Calvin's fundamental judgment against the papal church. Bouwsma (*Calvin*, 43–44) suggests the mixing of religions as Calvin's psychological abhorrence of the Catholic Church's religious practices. Calvin clearly defined the New Testament ministry primarily as the inheritor of the Old Testament's prophetic office rather than that of the sacerdotal office as practiced by the papal church's priests in the Mass. For an apologetic aspect of this issue, see chapter 2, section 3 on *Two Epistles* below.

tles, for instance, he considered the office of the apostles as commissioned by Christ to the entire world, which distinguished it from the offices of bishop and priest who were sent to a certain region or an individual church.[163] As to the ordination of priests, he rejected the Catholic claim of bishops having the exclusive right to ordain. Rather, he suggested the possibility of ordination by a bishop, the vote of a few responsible persons, the decision of a magistrate, the common vote of the people, an assembly of elders, or the advice of some faithful bishops.[164]

(2) Christian Freedom, Ecclesiastical Power, and Political Administration

Chapter 6 of the first *Institutes* is perhaps the most important source for understanding Calvin's early ecclesiology. We have summarized above the main theme of the "apology" portion in two points, namely, the usurpation of Christ's kingdom by both the Catholic sacramental system as the papal kingdom and its "troops in ambush," the Anabaptists, and the violation of the freedom of believers. Since Calvin refuted the Catholic claim that their sacramental system was a necessary matter for the believer's salvation in chapter 5, his discussions in chapter 6 dealt with the second point, the violation of freedom as a matter of moral and social concern for believers.

Incidentally, the title of chapter 6 seems rather strange, because the relationship of the three topics is not self-explanatory and, as we will see later, the descriptions he chose are not easily understood. Granted that the three topics were found in Luther's *On the Freedom of a Christian* and *On the Babylonian Captivity of the Church*, questions still remain. Why did he arrange the topics in this order? And what thought pattern of his was suggested by the title? As an explanation, we propose that he presented his unique and comprehensive view of the Christian world, starting with the perspectives of Christ's kingdom and Christian freedom, and then proceeded to the topics of ecclesiastical power and political administration as two foci of the "church and state" notion that provided the fundamental structure to the current Christian world. For example, on the topic of ecclesiastical power, he said of papal dominance that "thus the Kingdom of Christ is invaded; thus freedom given by him to the consciences of believers is utterly oppressed and cast down." On political administration, he said of the Münster Anabaptists that "it is a Jewish vanity to seek and enclose Christ's Kingdom within the elements of this world." In the

163. *OS* 1:211–12. (Battles, trans., *Institution*, 226–27.) Cf. Ganoczy, *Young Calvin*, 217–18.
164. *OS* 1:213–14. (Battles, trans., *Institution*, 228–29.)

context of his refutation of the papal church and the Anabaptists, therefore, he proposed to regard Christian freedom as "a spiritual fruit which we gather from Christ's grace" and "to keep within its own limits all that freedom."[165] As the last quotation suggests, what he proposed was not just adhering to Luther's idea of Christian freedom, but rather it served as a fresh presentation of this practical reform's direction in the existent religious confusion 15 years after Luther's original proposal. In other words, he proposed to place his notions of Christ's kingdom and Christian freedom, especially his characteristic notion of "adiaphora," in the historical context of a new era in which Christian freedom was abused within Evangelicalism on the one hand, and the abuse was criticized for causing license and social disorder by Catholic opponents on the other hand.[166]

Christian Freedom

Calvin's discussions on this topic have two focal points. One was to clearly present a framework of Christian freedom and its signification and to keep Christian freedom "within its own limits." The other was to apply the framework to the practical lives of believers in the context of ecclesiastical power and political administration.

(i) The first point is a historical question: How did Calvin view his notion of Christian freedom vis-à-vis Luther, who closely tied it with justification by faith, and how did Calvin present his new interpretation with his own emphases? For Luther the relationship between justification by faith and Christian freedom was close and dynamic in the sense that a believer justified by faith was like "a lord" freed from the laws and obliged to none, yet at the same time like "a servant" bound still under the laws and obliged to serve all. Calvin accepted Luther's emphasis of this close relationship as "a matter of prime

165. *OS* 1:233, 259. (Battles, trans., *Institution*, 253, 285.) Höpfl's treatment of chapter 6 (*Christian Polity*, 34–55) represents the typical position of old Calvin scholarship: for example, the Calvin of the first *Institutes* is viewed as an inexperienced and immature theologian, and his theological notions are mostly measured by first-generation Reformers such as Luther and Zwingli. One unique feature of chapter 6 is the young Calvin's fresh critique of his contemporary Christian world from the biblical perspective of Christ's kingdom. As a historian of political thought, Höpfl almost totally ignores Calvin's comprehensive and pervasive notion of Christ's kingdom. In this unique perspective of Christ's kingdom, we assume that Calvin's treatment of church and state is considerably distinctive from Luther's and Zwingli's views.

166. Cf. *WA* 6:543; Ganoczy, *Young Calvin*, 216.

necessity," for without understanding it "neither Christ nor gospel truth is rightly known." But he also focused on the issues of the abuse of freedom and its rightful and practical use according to the scriptural rules and the consciences of believers.

In particular, Calvin presented a tripartite notion of Christian freedom: the first two theses were Luther's "freedom from the law" and "freedom to serve neighbors," and the third concerned the matters that were "adiaphora." This was an area that Luther dared not step into and that was basically indifferent to the concern for salvation, leaving it to the free decision of believers. In his work, Calvin added his own emphases on the first two theses and concentrated his discussions on the third issue of "adiaphora." As an emphasis on the first thesis, for example, he used Ephesians (1:4–5), which was not used by Luther in connection to this issue, and defined the aim of "freedom from the law" as "in sanctification." He interpreted the second thesis with a new emphasis on voluntarily obeying and serving "the will of God." Over against his reinterpretation, naturally, some researchers may rightly criticize it as suppression of or aversion to Luther's teaching.[167] As a reminder, however, there was a historical precedence in which Luther's original teaching on Christian freedom was questioned and subjected to practical revisions, especially, in the face of the Peasants' War and the rise of Anabaptism. In Saxony, for example, there occurred an incident in which a congregation chose ministers out of its fold against the traditional custom of ministerial appointments. On this occasion Luther wrote *The Right and Power of a Christian Congregation or Community* (1523) and defended the congregational right to appoint its ministers from his principles of justification by faith, priesthood of all believers, and Christian freedom. In later history, however, his radical congregational position was revised in view of a more coherent ministry-congregation relationship.[168] In Calvin's background of the French Reformation, as our examination of the dedicatory epistle to the king will show, not only Catholic apologists but also evangelical humanists like Budé characterized the Evangelicalism of Luther

167. *OS* 1:223–33, esp. 224–25. (Battles, trans., *Institution*, 241–53.) Calvin was said to have taken the tripartite notion of Christian freedom from Melanchthon's *Loci communes*. On Calvin's notion of Christian freedom in general and that of "adiaphora" in particular, Höpfl (*Christian Polity*, 35–38) considers that Calvin deviated from Luther's original principle of Christian freedom and also weakened Luther's notion of the priesthood of all believers. Bouwsma (*Calvin*, 50) seems to have followed Höpfl's lead.

168. *WA* 11:409. P. Blickle (*From the Communal Reformation to the Revolution of the Common Man*, trans. Beat Kümin [Leiden: Brill, 1998], 13) notices the revolutionary nature of Luther's small work and characterizes its idea as "Communal Reformation."

as "a new movement" that caused disturbances in the church and his teaching of justification by faith as "freedom of no restraint." Even the king agreed with the accusation. In this historical context, Calvin attempted a new approach to the concept of Christian freedom. Although his attempt was but an underdeveloped sketch, it should receive due recognition.

(ii) The second point was on the knotty problem of "adiaphora," the issue "indifferent" to the believer's salvation and the last element of tripartite Christian freedom. The thrust of Calvin's new approach could be summarized as giving Christological signification to Christian freedom and providing a framework not only for the private lives of believers but also for the entirety of the Christian world. In other words, it was a bold attempt to place "adiaphora" as an underlying model for the following two topics of "church and state." Ecclesiastical institutions, orders, and rites discussed under the second topic of ecclesiastical power and the forms of secular government discussed under the third topic of political administration were regarded fundamentally as matters of "adiaphora." It was true that he discussed problems generally treated under "adiaphora," such as superstitions, regarding weak brothers, scandals, and modesty, but the question was his underlying framework. In order to understand this framework, we propose to examine it from two perspectives: one from its Christological foundation, namely, the notion of Christ's kingdom; and the other from the relationship of Christ's kingdom with ecclesiastical institutions and civil government.

As to the first perspective of Christ's kingdom, as we examined Calvin's notion of Christ's presence in the Lord's Supper, his concept supposed a twofold reality of Christ's kingdom analogous to his Antiochene understanding ("distinction, but not separation") of Christ's resurrected body in heaven and his presence in the Supper. As Calvin understood it, the kingdom of the Eternal Logos, Christ, was primarily a transcendent reality that could not be univocally identified with any earthly institution or government. At the same time, however, the kingdom of the Logos incarnate was an immanent reality, manifesting itself as the image of the transcendent kingdom and able to represent it in earthly institutions or government.

At the end of his discussions on Christian freedom, Calvin mentioned "a two-fold government in man," corresponding to both man's "soul" and "present life." He then related the church and state to Christ's kingdom and concluded that they could be "the spiritual kingdom" and "the political kingdom." In the eucharistic doctrine, Calvin distinguished and related three realities: Christ's resurrected body in heaven, his presence in the Supper, and the rite of the Supper itself as the "earthly element." If we can correctly use

Calvin's eucharistic doctrine as an analogy, we assume that he also postulated three realities: Christ's transcendent kingdom, its manifestations or images in church and state as Christ's "spiritual kingdom" and "political kingdom," and ecclesiastical institutions and civil government as matters of "adiaphora." In this framework, as mentioned above, the relationship between Christ's transcendent kingdom, its manifestation in the church (Christ's spiritual kingdom) and its other manifestation in the state (Christ's political kingdom) could be understood as a triangular relationship. The first two relationships, between Christ's transcendent kingdom and the church and between that and the state, could be seen as parallel. In both relationships, Christ's kingdom was to function as a decisive factor, defining how the church and the state should be. The third relationship between the church and the state could be properly understood as that of Christ's two kingdoms, spiritual and political.[169]

169. *OS* 1:226, 227–28, 233. (Battles, trans., *Institution*, 245, 246, 252.) One of the latest contributions to *Calviniana*, Tuininga's *Calvin's Political Theology* is an important work. Tuininga carefully pursues his goal of delineating in full Calvin's "political theology" and its implications, and applies them to the current issue of the church's "public engagement." The work's merit should be primarily assessed in the pursuit of this goal. What makes his work unusual and unique, however, is his methodological use of Calvin's notion of Christ's kingdom. Only in this limited scope do his work and our study share a point of contact on such Calvin notions as Christ's kingdom, the church, and "church and state." Although Tuininga does not examine the Christological foundation of Calvin's notion of Christ's kingdom, he is thoroughly aware of the issues surrounding the notion, including the historical background of Christ's two kingdoms theory, and attempts his own interpretation of it. In chapter 3 ("The Kingdom of Christ," 92–139), for example, he defines Christ's kingdom (92) as "the consummation of God's purpose for creation and for human beings" and enumerates "Calvin's bedrock doctrines" such as "creation, humanity, sin, preservation, natural law, the restoration of the world, the Spirit, the kingdom of Christ, and hope," which he considers important for understanding Calvin's notion. On the "spiritual" kingdom of Christ, furthermore, he interprets the meaning of "spiritual" in this way (119–20): "1) the power of the kingdom is that of the Holy Spirit, 2) the kingdom completes creation's eschatological purpose, and 3) the kingdom will be consummated only at Christ's return." As this brief sketch indicates, throughout the discussions Tuininga seems to emphasize three points: the immanent presence of Christ's kingdom in history (creation, restoration, and consummation), the power of the Holy Spirit that realizes that presence, and the kingdom's eschatological nature. Although these are legitimate emphases in themselves, we wonder whether these can sufficiently present the whole scope of Calvin's notion, or whether Tuininga misses other crucially important emphases. Our concern can be expressed in three points: (1) Christ's kingdom is primarily a transcendent reality and the immanent kingdom Tuininga focuses on can be viewed as its manifestation or "image" in history. (2) The kingdom's power is primarily in God's or Christ's word and, in the case of the church, the ministry of the word. In Calvin's theology, the Holy Spirit is basically understood as Christ's Spirit and the Spir-

As to the perspective of the general relation of Christ's kingdom to the second and third topics of chapter 6, we will take note of three theses that appeared in the discussion on Christian freedom. The first appeared at the beginning of the discussion, "we are bound before God by no religious obligation to outward things of themselves indifferent." The second, "Christian freedom, in all its parts, is a spiritual thing." And the third appeared at the end, "whatever we have said concerning Christian freedom pertains to this spiritual kingdom." If we understand them correctly, the first thesis affirmed his principle that outward things in themselves were indifferent to salvation. The second affirmed that nonetheless, in relation to the moral and social lives of believers, their decisions on "adiaphora" were neither neutral nor secular, but spiritual. As a conclusion, the third affirmed that the whole scope of Christian freedom was deeply related to the spiritual rule of Christ's kingdom. It should be noted here that Calvin almost exclusively took polemical aim at the Roman Catholic Church in the second topic and at the Münster Anabaptists in the third topic.

In his discussion on the second topic, Calvin defined Christ's kingdom as the rule governed by "one King . . . and one law of freedom, namely, the holy word of the gospel." From this viewpoint he accused the papists of usurping Christ's spiritual kingdom and violating the freedom of believers by elevating the basically "adiaphora" matters of ecclesiastical institutions, orders, rites, and laws of their own making to be "spiritual," therefore matters indispensable for the salvation of believers. At the beginning of his discussion on the third topic, Calvin made a startling statement, "Christ's spiritual kingdom and the civil jurisdiction are things completely different." In implicitly refuting the Münster Anabaptist revolution, he accused the Anabaptists of appealing to Christian freedom and of claiming to establish their church to be "a spiritual kingdom" in Münster as nothing more than "a Jewish vanity to seek and enclose Christ's kingdom within the elements of this world." In both cases of the papists and the Anabaptists, the very nature of Christ's spiritual kingdom was replaced by what he considered to be "adiaphora." Perhaps this was the reason he presented a framework of placing the topic of Christian freedom first and

---

it's operation is closely tied to the word. Tuininga's emphasis on the Holy Spirit, however, serves well for his understanding the kingdom's immanent nature and his goal of studying Calvin's political theology. As Oberman notes the "extra" dimension in Calvin's theology (*The Dawn*, 239), Christ's kingdom reveals its "secret" and "incomprehensible" nature as "the rule of Christ obtains *etiam extra ecclesiam*." (3) Corresponding to Calvin's close correlation between the word and the Spirit, the nature of Christ's kingdom is both "prophetic" and "eschatological." This point will be seen below in our discussion on ecclesiastical power.

then, from the perspective of Christ's kingdom and Christian freedom, especially "adiaphora," proceeded to the topics of ecclesiastical power and political administration.[170]

Ecclesiastical Power

Calvin began the second topic with this sentence: "Whatever we have said concerning Christian freedom pertains to this spiritual kingdom." Then, he set his apologetic sight on the papal claim of "the power which those who wish to seem pastors of the church usurp for themselves." Thus, the context of his polemics was Christian freedom, the issue was Christ's spiritual kingdom, and the focal point was ecclesiastical power. First of all, Calvin considered papal ecclesiastical power to have "usurped" what was proper to Christ's kingdom. Furthermore, he considered that the "usurped" power was claimed to be instituted in the church's own constitutions, laws, human tradition, ecclesiastical councils, customs, rites, jurisdiction, and so forth, which were elevated to the status of having salvific power and described as "traps to catch and ensnare souls," "tyranny," "innumerable," and "limitless."[171] Over against papal ecclesiastical power, he then presented the real power of Christ's spiritual kingdom as "one law of freedom, namely, the holy word of the gospel." In the context of the word as the kingdom's power, he further discussed the church's ministry of the word, the ministers, and the congregation of believers. Although he added his critical comments on the papal government and institutions, his intention seemed to be to present the real image of the church as Christ's spiritual kingdom within the whole scope of the church's existence in history. In this image, around the axis of the power of the word, Christ's lordship, the Holy Spirit's operation, the ministry of the word, the ministers, the congregation of believers, and the church's government and institutions were to occupy their proper places. In fact, we believe, Calvin presented here for the first time a rudimental sketch of the image of Christ's spiritual kingdom. From the themes of Christ's word and the Holy Spirit, the image acquired two basic natures of Christ's kingdom, namely, the prophetic and the eschatological. As a result, his unique view was a thorough refutation of medieval Catholicism that viewed

170. *OS* 1:233, 258–59. (Battles, trans., *Institution*, 252, 285–86.) The scheme of three topics in chapter 6 was maintained in the second edition of 1539 where each topic acquired a chapter. In the third edition of 1543, however, the topic of Christian freedom was separated from the other two topics and the scheme became less clear.

171. *OS* 1:233–34, 239, 244, 250; 234, 242, 248, 250. (Battles, trans., *Institution*, 253–54, 260–61, 266–67, 274; 254, 264, 272, 274.)

"church and state" from the worldview of the Dionysian hierarchy and identified Christ's kingdom primarily with the superior hierarchy of the church. It was also distinctive from Luther's two kingdoms-regiments theory that theologically interpreted the church and state relation in terms of the "Gospel and Law" dichotomy and viewed Christ's kingdom more closely identified with the church and less with the state, which he considered a necessary evil. Furthermore, it was different from Zwingli's "divine and human justice" theory that viewed the church as narrowly associated with divine justice, while attributing both divine and human justice to the state and identifying Christ's kingdom primarily with the state in saying that "the Kingdom of Christ is external." Throughout his reformatory works, Calvin amplified this image of Christ's kingdom as an important notion of his theology.[172] From this viewpoint, we note the following three points.

(i) The first point touched on the basic characteristic of Calvin's early ecclesiology, namely, Christ's kingdom and the word as its power in relation to the church in history. The church's ministry, ministers, government, and institutions were to be arranged in accordance with this characteristic. First of all, it is noticeable that Calvin's extraordinary emphasis was on the "given" and "*extra*" nature of the word. What would make the church Christ's church and his spiritual kingdom was the word, which was not the church's own, but that which was given from above. As Calvin said, "this power has been given for upbuilding" of the church; the church was to use it as "the ministry of the word"; and "whatever authority and dignity Scripture accords to either prophets or priests, or apostles, or successors of apostles, is wholly given not to the men themselves, but to the ministry . . . or to the word."[173]

Calvin stressed the word's powerful and prophetic nature. In this context, surprisingly, the first scriptural text he used from the Prophets was Jeremiah 1:10: "[God] set his prophets over nations and kingdoms, to pluck up and to root out, to destroy and to overthrow, to build and to plant." It was a well-known text that Pope Boniface VIII, in the conflict with Philip IV of France, used as a prooftext for papal supremacy in the famous bull *Unam sanctam* (1302). In it, the Pope claimed that the Holy Catholic Church held both the "spiritual" and the "temporal" swords and that no salvation was possible unless

172. *OS* 1:233–27, 243–46. (Battles, trans., *Institution*, 252–59, 265–69.) In chapter 6 of the first *Institutes*, Calvin places the predominant emphasis on the word as the power of Christ's kingdom, what we call the prophetic theme. He also relates the operation of the Holy Spirit to the congregation of believers and the process of their sanctification and consummation, what we may call the eschatological theme.

173. *OS* 1:234. (Battles, trans., *Institution*, 254.)

one subjected oneself to the Church's supreme head, the Pope. Fully aware of the historical implications of this text, Calvin dared to cite the text, not in the context of his overt attack against papal supremacy, but in a defense of the legitimacy of ecclesiastical power. Furthermore, he grounded the legitimacy in the fact that "[the Lord] had put his words into their [prophets'] mouths," citing many texts from the prophets who challenged the corrupt priests of the Old Testament. In recognition of the ministry of such prophets as Jeremiah, Isaiah, and Ezekiel over against the corrupted class of priests, he especially criticized the papal church as guilty of substituting the prophetic ministry of the word for the priestly ministry of what the church called the sacraments. In sharp contrast to the priests of the papal church, Calvin positioned the Evangelical pastors as "successors of apostles." He described the charge committed to them that they "may boldly dare do all things by God's word; . . . may compel all worldly power, glory, loftiness to yield to and obey his majesty; . . . may build up Christ's household and cast down Satan's kingdom; may feed the sheep and kill the wolves; . . . may bind and loose; and finally may launch lightnings and thunderbolts; but do all things in God's word." What we see here is none other than the prophetic image of Christ's spiritual kingdom.[174]

Concerning the relationship between Christ's spiritual kingdom and the church's institutions and order, Calvin's basic stance viewed the identification of these two distinctive realities as a papal error. He cited Prophet Jeremiah's warning, "Do not trust in these deceptive words: 'This is the temple of the Lord, the temple of the Lord, the temple of the Lord'" (7:4), as an example of Jewish people's false confidence. Calvin made the point that, while God's word was neither heard nor trusted in the temple, the priests and people conflated the institutions of "temple, ceremonies, and priestly functions" with divine worship itself. In this context, his affirmation appeared: "since the church is Christ's Kingdom, and he reigns by his word alone" (*cum ecclesia regnum sit*

174. *OS* 1:234–35, 237. (Battles, trans., *Institution*, 254–25, 258.) Cf. G. Digard et al., eds., *Les Registres de Boniface VIII*, vol. 3 [Athens and Rome, 1921], 889–90; H. Berger, "Das Papsttum als Antichrist," in *Calvins Geschichits Auffassung* (Zurich: Zwingli Verlag, 1955), 73–91; Tuininga, *Calvin's Political Theology*, 92–139; Zachman, *Image and Word*, 1–22. Berger provides a comprehensive analysis of Calvin's view on the papacy as the antichrist and Satan's kingdom. Concerning Calvin's predominant emphasis on the word as the spiritual kingdom's power and its "prophetic" and "given" character in the first *Institutes*, we wonder whether Tuininga misses Calvin's emphasis at the expense of the kingdom's innate immanence in history. As to Calvin's notion of relating the kingdom with its manifestation or image as Christ's word of the gospel in the church, Zachman provides an introductory reference to Calvin's background.

Christi, regnet autem non nisi per verbum suum). This bold, yet perhaps exceptional, affirmation identifies the church with Christ's kingdom, asserting the kingdom's close connection with the word, not with the church institution, which alone was to make the church Christ's spiritual kingdom. It should also be noted that this issue appeared in a rhetorical question in which Calvin referred to this false identification as "deceptive words" (Jer 7:8–15), and that this discussion was in the larger context of emphasizing the ministry of the word, which was considered the "scepter" of Christ's kingdom.[175]

(ii) The second point concerned the role of the Holy Spirit in Christ's kingdom and the Spirit's relation to ecclesiastical power. Calvin discussed the Spirit's role in the church in the context of the papal claim that the Catholic Church's tradition, holiness, disciplinary system, councils, observances, and so forth were not only governed by the Holy Spirit but were also of its own making. Over against this claim, Calvin stressed the inseparable conjunction as well as immanent presence of Christ's "promise" (word) and the Holy Spirit. Whoever questioned this authority of the church, Calvin argued, was "impious and contentious not only to the church but also to the 'Spirit of Christ,' by whose direction the church is without doubt ruled." If Calvin viewed Christ's word as

175. *OS* 1:243–44. (Battles, trans., *Institution*, 262–63.) One of the modern interpreters of Calvin's theory on Christ's kingdoms, P. Wilcox ("The Progress of the Kingdom of Christ in Calvin's Exposition of the Prophets," in *Calvinus Sincerioris Religionis Vindex*, ed. W. H. Neuser and B. G. Armstrong [Kirksville: Sixteenth Century Journal Publishers, 1997], 320) uses such texts as Psalms (87: argumentum; *CO* 31:800) and Amos (9:13, *CO* 43:172) and argues that Calvin can assert without qualification that "the church is Christ's Kingdom." "The church" in this context is said to be "the institutional (or visible) church." For detail, see chapter 4, n. 197 below. The latest interpreter, Tuininga (*Calvin's Political Theology*, ch. 5, "Christ's Spiritual Kingdom," esp. 182–97) states: "one of Calvin's most emphatic claims throughout his works is that the church is Christ's kingdom" (182). Although Tuininga seems to be well aware of the issue of identification and carefully says that "Calvin does not entirely equate the two concepts" or that "Calvin often uses the terms kingdom and church interchangeably" (182n2) and so forth, the main thrust of his presentation is a univocal identification. Historically speaking, since Calvin's notion of Christ's spiritual kingdom was formulated in the context of what he considered the papal error of identifying their church institutions with Christ's kingdom, it should be remembered that he was always suspect of such univocal identification. As we will see later in chapter 4, section 2, "Reformed Ecclesiology," furthermore, Calvin tackled the identification issue in different ways and distinguished the visible church's "title" (that which concerned the church's fundamental and indispensable constitution) and its "form" (that which concerned its external appearance in institutions and order, being subject to change in history). Retrospectively speaking, what Calvin discussed here under the second topic of ecclesiastical power concerned only the external "form" that could be a manifestation of Christ's kingdom but could hardly be univocally identified with it.

given from above, he distinctively attributed the role of guiding and governing the church to "the Spirit of Christ." In this way, it can be said that Christ's word and the Holy Spirit inseparably founded ecclesiastical power.[176]

In particular, against the papal claim of the church being holy because it was governed by the Holy Spirit, its general councils infallible, and participation in its ceremonies indispensable for salvation, Calvin made a two-sided apology. On the one hand, he characterized the papal argument as asserting that "inasmuch as the church is governed by the Spirit of the Lord, it can proceed safely without the word." On the other hand, Calvin closely related the Spirit to Christ's word, church government, and what he termed "the church of believers" or "the whole people of believers." For example, he said that "the church has the amplest promises that she is never to be forsaken by Christ, her spouse, but guided by his Spirit into all truth" and that "the Lord is ever present with his people and governs them by his Spirit."[177] In this context, Calvin introduced an analogy between the Old Testament priests "who have shaken off and cast away obedience to God's word," and whom prophets stood against, and contemporary Catholic priests. Interestingly, Calvin characterized disobedient priests as if they had said, "the Spirit of God dwells continuously in them, that the church subsists in them, and dies with them." He then pointed out the same claim put forward by Catholic priests. If Calvin understood that the permanent and immanent presence of Christ's word and his Spirit constituted ecclesiastical power, the Spirit's governing presence in the church highlighted the eschatological perspective of Christ's kingdom.[178]

(iii) The third point concerned two aspects of church government to which Calvin paid special attention in his anti-Catholic discussion, namely, the power of jurisdiction exercised by bishops and the power of church councils to establish doctrines. As to the first aspect, we have mentioned that he showed a rather flexible attitude toward the so-called historical episcopacy in chapter 5, but here he criticized the papal church for elevating bishops as superior ministers after the pattern of the Old Testament high priests, allowing them to exercise spiritual power in the ruling of the church. His verdict was expressed in a terse sentence, "the spiritual power on which the pope with his whole entourage (*papa cum toto suo regno*) preens himself is an impious tyranny opposed to God's word and unjust toward his people."[179]

As to church councils, despite some positive evaluations that he attributed

176. *OS* 1:239. (Battles, trans., *Institution*, 260–61.)

177. *OS* 1:242–43. (Battles, trans., *Institution*, 264–66.)

178. *OS* 1:246. (Battles, trans., *Institution*, 269.)

179. *OS* 1:250. (Battles, trans., *Institution*, 274.) Cf. Ganoczy, *Young Calvin*, 220–21, 223–24.

to the catholic councils of the ancient church, he maintained a noticeably cool and negative attitude toward church councils in general. Some of his reasoning for this attitude included the following: councils did not always follow God's word alone; they claimed to be guided by the Holy Spirit, nonetheless they established nonbiblical doctrines and rules; their decisions were oftentimes contradictory and subject to later revisions; and even "those ancient and purer councils" were influenced by the spirit of their times and subject to errors.[180] One particularly noticeable point was his cool attitude toward late medieval conciliarism. At the time, conciliarism as a church reform movement was still strong and the French Church was one of the chief advocates for it. But in his discussion on this issue, none of the conciliar theses such as "a Council is above a Pope" could be found. Since even Reformers such as Luther, Melanchthon, and Bucer sought the possibility of conciliar solutions, Calvin's general distrust in church councils was remarkable. In a nutshell, his critique of papal church government could be expressed as the replacement of Christ's governance by his word and his Spirit by the church institution of general councils.[181]

Political Administration

The last topic of the first *Institutes*, "political administration," was in itself unique. It was unique in the sense that, while the last-mentioned discussion on ecclesiastical power was to be subjected to extensive revisions and replacements in succeeding editions, "political administration" was to be retained without major revisions until the last edition in 1559. In a sense this retention is a puzzle. Calvin likely wrote on this topic in 1535 when Anabaptism, especially its branch of the Münster revolution, was a real threat to both Catholicism and the main Protestant churches. In this historical context, he expressed his first theological understanding of political government within a particular and unique conceptual framework and apologetic aim—that is, the framework of Christ's kingdom and Christian freedom, especially the notion of "adiaphora,"

180. *OS* 1:239, 246–47. (Battles, trans., *Institution*, 265, 269–70.) Cf. Ganoczy, *Young Calvin*, 216. As an example of interconciliar contradictions, Calvin referred to the Synod of Constantinople (754, Calvin incorrectly called it "Council") summoned by Byzantine Emperor Constantine V, son of Leo III, which advanced the iconoclastic policy, and the Second Council of Nicea (787) called by Empress Irene, which formalized the legitimacy of image worship in both the Eastern and the Western churches. Calvin's reference to the Second Council of Nicea will become a relevant point when we discuss Lefèvre, who affirmed the Second Nicene position and Calvin's *Two Epistles* that challenged the Lefèvrian position of the moderate reformists on worship (chapter 2, sections 1.1 and 3.2 below).

181. *OS*, 1, 233, 246–47. (Battles, trans., *Institution*, 253, 269–71.) Cf. Bouwsma, *Calvin*, 43, 204.

and apologetics almost exclusively aimed at Anabaptism. In 1559, due to his repeated rearrangements of the contents of the first *Institutes*, the final edition lost the original conceptual framework of chapter 6 and the Anabaptist movement as a whole, further dispersed and marginalized, was no longer considered a serious threat. Nonetheless he retained the original text, with only a few additions. One possible additional reason for this retention was his fear of the growing political control over religion in general and church government in particular, such as Lutheranism in Germany, Zwinglianism in Switzerland, and Anglicanism in England, thus resulting in violation of his ideas about Christ's kingdom and Christian freedom.

The interpretation of the topic, "political administration," has posed many difficulties. Accordingly, its evaluations have varied among Calvin researchers. Generally speaking, among theological researchers who value the first edition's importance, there seems to be a tendency to either ignore or underestimate Calvin's treatment of this topic. Even researchers in the field of political science who do pay attention to it have often found in it a mindset that could not escape the medieval framework, as well as theoretical underdevelopment. Furthermore, more recent interdisciplinary studies seem to lack an established evaluation of it.[182] What will be presented in the following pages is but an attempt to evaluate positively its uniqueness from the perspective of Calvin's notions of Christ's kingdom and Christian freedom, especially "adiaphora." We will focus on three points, namely, the section's topic, the introductory portion, and the main body of the text in three parts (the magistrate, civil laws, and the people as subjects).

(i) As to the first point, Calvin's choice of topic was unique in the sense

182. Cf. Wendel, *Calvin*, 111–49, 308–10; Ganoczy, *Young Calvin*, 215–30; Höpfl, *Christian Polity*, 52–54; F. Oakley, "Christian Obedience and Authority, 1520–1700," in *The Cambridge History of Political Thought, 1450–1700*, ed. J. H. Barns (Cambridge: Cambridge University Press, 1991), 185–87. To mention only a few examples, Wendel and Ganoczy are two of the writers who ignored this topic's importance in the first *Institutes*. Wendel's conclusion (310: "nearer to Luther's personal ideas, and to the conception worked out by Bucer") is far from satisfactory. Höpfl and Oakley are two cases of negative evaluation. Viewing Calvin's notion on the church-state relation from the perspective of Luther's two kingdoms theory, Höpfl concludes that Calvin failed "as an architect of ecclesiastical polity." Oakley places Calvin's view in the medieval context and sees his insistence on church discipline and anti-Anabaptist stand parallel to medieval clericalism and *Corpus Christianum*. Exceptionally, the latest interdisciplinary study, Tuininga's *Calvin's Political Theology* (ch. 6: "Christ's Political Government," 228–43), analyses the last chapter of the final *Institutes*, carefully and in full, as one of Calvin's "early formations" on the topic. His analysis of the original 1536 text takes note of Calvin's contextual treatment of Christ's kingdom and apologetic aim against the Anabaptists.

of its imbalance. While he chose the term "power" (*potestas*) for the previous topic, "ecclesiastical power," he used "administration" (*administratio*) for this topic, "political administration," instead of "political power." As we have seen in his discussion on Christian freedom, in which he characterized the "church and state" framework as "the spiritual kingdom" and "the political kingdom," he could have chosen "political power." In fact, Peter Lombard's *Sententiarum*, familiar to Calvin as a basic theological text in his Paris University days, Melanchthon's *Loci communes*, likely used for the writing of the first *Institutes*, and Machiavelli's *Il principe*, although seemingly ignored at this time, all commonly used the term "the magisterial power." A nuanced look at the term *administration* indicates a "government" that administered political power under a superior or sovereign.[183] Although it seems difficult to explain this imbalance, we will try to find an explanation from his notion of the "church and state" or "two kingdoms" framework in which he placed Christ's kingdom above "church and state" and set the relationships of "kingdom and church" and "kingdom and state" as parallel. In this parallelism, as we have mentioned above, the church or its institutional structure, together with the magistrate or his administration, were both considered "ministers" of Christ's kingdom and, at the same time for the life of believers, were both regarded "adiaphora" for their salvation. The imbalance in this parallelism can be explained as follows: Only in the kingdom and church relationship is the kingdom's power, the ministry of God's word, entrusted to the church, while none of such spiritual and divine power is entrusted to the magistrate or his administration. It should be noted that, just like Calvin characterized the Roman Catholic Church as guilty of deifying church structures and called it "the Papal kingdom," he warned here against the same deification of any political powers and tried to place "political administration" in a right relationship with Christ's kingdom.[184]

183. *OS* 1:232–33. (Battles, trans., *Institution*, 252–53.) Cf. Bouwsma, *Calvin*, 210. Without noticing this unbalance, Bouwsma considers the term "administration" as a common usage of the time, namely, a "rightly ordered state."

184. Calvin's concept of "political administration" is unique on at least two accounts: first, to place it in the context of the spiritual kingdom of Christ, and second, to view it as an extension of Christian freedom, especially of adiaphora. In addition to Luther and Zwingli as mentioned, it should be noted that many researchers have regarded Bucer's comprehensive and dynamic theory of Christ's kingdom as Calvin's precedent. In a closer analysis, however, we cannot consider both theories identical. For example, Bucer seemed to have a tendency to closely identify Christ's kingdom with the historical realities of both church and state, as can be seen in his defense for the "Christian societies" movement in Strasbourg and in his *De Regno Christi* (1550) for England. Already early in the first *Institutes*, on the other hand,

(ii) As to the second point, the introductory portion (only two pages in *Calvini Opera Selecta*) articulated Calvin's concept of political government from a particular historical perspective. In clear contrast to the previous topic in which he accused the papal church of abuse of ecclesiastical power, here he treated the challenge from another extreme, the Anabaptists. At the beginning, for example, a decisive sentence affirmed that "Christ's spiritual Kingdom and the civil jurisdiction are things completely distinct." This could well be a general statement against the mixture of the sacred and profane, but the context suggested otherwise. In an apparent reference to the revolutionary upheaval at Münster, for example, he described the upheaval as "a Jewish vanity to seek and enclose Christ's Kingdom within the elements of this world." In his discussion on the previous topic, he called the papal church's efforts to dignify the church structure as "the stupid confidence of the Jews" and to deify the church's "traditions" and "mysteries" as "either partly Jewish or Gentile observances." Here he applied the same logic to the Anabaptists. Also, in a possible reference to the *Schleitheim Confession*, he rejected the Anabaptist position that regarded the civil government, law, and court useless for those believers who died to the world. Furthermore, he rejected their position that denied the magisterial role in the church on the basis of the church's "perfection," that is, "there ought to be such great perfection in the church of God that its government should suffice for law."[185] Thus, the whole discussion in the introductory portion pointed to the historical context of the time in which Calvin wrote the *Institutes* and the Münster upheaval became a great challenge not only to Protestant Evangelical teaching on "church and state" but also to the French Reformation.

The introductory portion revealed another aspect of Calvin's concept of political administration, formed around the themes of Christ's kingdom and Christian freedom. In this context, he narrowly defined the "use" of political administration as "the duty of rightly establishing religion," then first distinguished it from and next related it to the theme of Christ's kingdom. With regard to their distinction, he said negatively, as far as Christian freedom warranted by Christ's kingdom was concerned, "it makes no difference

Calvin seemed to avoid this kind of close identification and had viewed Christ's kingdom in a tension vis-à-vis both church and state.

185. *OS* 1:258–60. (Battles, trans., *Institution*, 284–86.) "Perfection in the church" in the last quotation may be a reference to Article 6 of the *Schleitheim Confession* (*Creeds and Confessions*, 2:699) where "the perfection of Christ" is antithetically contrasted to the secular state. In the later refutation of Article 6 (*Brieve Instruction*, 1544: *BC* 44/7, *CO* 7:80–81), Calvin associated the confession's "perfection of Christ" with the Anabaptist claim of the New Testament church's perfection over against the Old Testament church.

what your condition among men may be or under what nation's laws you live, since the Kingdom of Christ does not at all consist in these things."[186] As to their relatedness, he affirmed the role of political administration in the lives of believers but on the condition that it was useful as a minimum essential "so long as we live among men" and "as pilgrims upon the earth while we aspire to the true fatherland."[187] From the above points, it can be said that Calvin's perspective on political administration was quite distinct from the ordinary theories on civil government. It was narrowly meant for those who had already become members of Christ's kingdom and for how they ought to live in the historical context of the church and civil government so as to guard their Christian freedom.

(iii) The third point concerned three subjects discussed in the main text on political administration. Calvin briefly described them as "the magistrate, who is the protector and guardian of the laws; the laws, according to which he governs; the people, who are governed by the laws and obey the magistrate." This brief statement clearly indicated that their core was to be the laws. Furthermore, the entire text put forth the notion that "Christian politics" (*Christiana politia*) should be governed by the laws. Incidentally, Calvin used exactly the same concept of the magistrate as "the protector and guardian of the laws" in his Seneca commentary. In that previous work, however, it was balanced by another concept, "princes are unbound from laws," which was taken out of the *Justinian Codes* in defense of the monarchy's absolute power. Calvin was said to be hesitant in choosing between the two concepts. In his first *Institutes*, however, he showed no trace of such hesitation but consistently affirmed that Christian politics should be governed by the laws and that it should not be mixed with nor aimed at ruling religion.[188]

As to the first subject concerning the magistrate, Calvin discussed his "function," "calling," "duty," and "power." He meticulously took aim to refute the Anabaptist position that rejected the "church and state" framework. Concerning the magistrate's "duty," for example, he cited the text used by Luther and Zwingli (John 10:35, "If those to whom the word of God came were called

186. *OS* 1:259. (Battles, trans., *Institution*, 285.) "The duty of rightly establishing religion" (*recte constituendae religionis cura*) appears in *OS* 1:260: Battles, trans., *Institution*, 287.

187. *OS* 1:259. (Battles, trans., *Institution*, 286.)

188. *OS* 1:260. (Battles, trans., *Institution*, 287.) Cf. Höpfl, *Christian Polity*, 14–17; Bouwsma, *Calvin*, 63, 207; n. 42 above. Höpfl suggests Calvin's hesitation and Bouwsma considers Calvin's view common to that of contemporary humanists and makes a fair assessment: Calvin "accepted the political absolutism dominant in his time, but he was no apologist for it."

'gods'") and affirmed the divine origin of the magistrates. He said that "they have a mandate from God, having been invested with divine authority, and are wholly God's representatives, in a manner, acting as his viceregents." To this point, he also referred to Romans 13:4 where the apostle Paul called them "ministers of God," as well as to 12:8 where Paul was said to attribute God's gift to "one who rules" (*qui praeest*) as "Christ's servants for the upbuilding of the church."[189]

As to the magistrate's "calling," Calvin affirmed the authenticity of the magistrate's office as "a calling, not only holy and lawful before God, but also the most sacred and by far the most honorable of all callings" and the magistrates themselves as "ministers of divine justice," "vicars of God," and "deputies of God." All of Calvin's discussions here were apparently directed against the Anabaptists' particular claim, which he phrased as "all Christians are forbidden to engage in kingdoms and governments" (cf. *Schleitheim Confession*, 6). As he had assumed that Christian freedom could stand firm regardless of the political situations or laws under which believers were to live, he also denied any difference in the "calling" of magistrates, whether they were in monarchies, aristocracies, or democracies.[190]

Concerning the second subject of the laws, as Calvin himself said "as in passing," his discussions were not only exceptionally brief but also directed toward a particular viewpoint. That is, the framework of Christ's kingdom and Christian freedom. At the beginning of the section, he stated "the laws, stoutest sinews of the commonwealth or, as Cicero calls them, the souls, without which the magistracy cannot stand." In clear contrast to his discussions on ecclesiastical power that began with the statement that the church ought to be governed by Christ and "one law of freedom, namely, the holy word of the gospel," here he posed a question concerning "with what laws a Christian state ought to be governed." In another contrast, as he had charged the papal church with violating Christ's kingdom and said that "the laws they frame they call 'spiritual,' . . . and declare them necessary for eternal life," here he was to discuss the signification of the laws that could not violate Christian freedom guaranteed by Christ's kingdom.[191]

189. *OS* 1:261. (Battles, trans., *Institution*, 287–88.)

190. *OS* 1:261–63. (Battles, trans., *Institution*, 288–90.) Cf. *Creeds and Confessions*, 2:699–701.

191. *OS* 1:267. (Battles, trans., *Institution*, 296.) Cf. *OS* 1:233. (Battles, trans., *Institution*, 253.) As for the term "sinews," in the third edition of 1543 and later editions (*Institutio* 4.12.1: *OS* 1:212) Calvin had used it for ecclesiastical discipline that was to bind the members together.

Here, Calvin introduced a thesis: "A commonwealth is duly framed which, neglecting the political system of Moses, is ruled by the common laws of nations." This could be an application of what he had said at the beginning of the section, namely, Christ's kingdom stood firm everywhere regardless of political and legal systems.[192] He then referred to the triple division theory of the laws that was notably used by Thomas Aquinas in the Scholastic tradition and Melanchthon on the Protestant Evangelical side to divide the Old Testament laws into moral, ceremonial, and judicial laws. The moral law of Moses was said to be "the true and eternal rule of righteousness, prescribed for men of all nations and times" and to have two aims: "one of which simply commands us to worship God with pure faith and piety; the other, to embrace men with sincere affection."[193] In sharp contrast to the moral law, he considered the ceremonial laws as "the tutelage of the Jews" for promoting their piety until the coming of Christ and the judicial laws as "definite formulas of equity and justice" for preserving love among them. Both laws were said to be in force only for a limited period of time, with no need for other nations to employ them. Interestingly, Calvin wrote that God "through the hand of Moses did not give that law to be proclaimed among all nations." In other words, Calvin affirmed that nations were not only free from Jewish ceremonial and judicial laws but also to be recognized as legitimate so long as they upheld the principles of worship and love. In addition, as he had rejected the papal church's ceremonies and jurisdictions as Jewish or Pagan "mixtures," he affirmed all believers who upheld the same principles of the moral law to be able to exercise their Christian freedom irrespective of the ceremonial and judicial laws.[194]

Concerning the third subject of the people, Calvin's discussions reflected a particular situation in which he found himself as an exile and apologist for the sake of Protestant Evangelicalism and in which he was obliged to refute the Anabaptists. Conscious of the Anabaptist challenge of the separation of Christians from the world, he described the "people" as "the common society of Christians." He then stated the gist of his argument by addressing issues of

192. *OS* 1:268. (Battles, trans., *Institution*, 296.) Cf. I. J. Hesselink, *Calvin's First Catechism: A Commentary* (Louisville: Westminster John Knox, 1997), 243–45. Tuininga (*Calvin's Political Theology*, 238–39) interprets Calvin's reference to "the political system of Moses" in this way: "His primary concern in discussing political laws is not to call the magistrate to enforce the laws of scripture or promote Christian virtue but to nullify dogmatic attempt to impose biblical laws on Christian governments."

193. *OS* 1:268. (Battles, trans., *Institution*, 296–97.)

194. *OS* 1:268, 270. (Battles, trans., *Institution*, 297, 299.) Hesselink (*Calvin's Concept*, 247) considers Calvin's refusal "to take Old Testament legislation as a norm for civil government" as "a radical and significant break."

"usefulness," which the magistrates and the laws could accord to the people, and of "deference" and "obedience," which private Christians owed to their magistrates. Although these issues were urgent and important topics for Protestant Evangelicalism as well as French evangelical humanism, his discussions did not emphasize them and rather gave an impression of self-restraint and idealism. One of the reasons for this could be his image of Christians as those that, though belonging to Christ's kingdom, were obliged to live on earth as "pilgrims" and to practice their faith according to Christ's gospel as well as before political administration. With this eschatological perspective, Calvin seemed to view Christians' involvement with civil government as conditioned by two factors: On the one hand, Christ's kingdom and civil government were "things completely different" yet not opposing each other; on the other hand, for Christians as pilgrims aspiring to heaven, involvement in government was feasible as long as it was "useful" for them.[195]

The most serious contemporary issues were people's "deference" and "obedience," which touched on the problem of resistance to the magistrates. As Calvin's opening statement on the magistrates as "ministers and representatives of God" suggested, his discussions seemed to give an impression of reserved conservatism. At the time of his writing the *Institutes*, there was certainly the need for both Protestant Evangelicalism and the French Reformation to distinguish themselves from the tumults caused by the Münster Anabaptists. His conservatism can be an object of criticism in that he was too preoccupied with the Anabaptist challenges and failed to develop what he had cultivated in his humanist and legal studies, as well as the ideas expressed in his Seneca commentary.[196] In addition, the perspective of Christ's kingdom as his persistent theme was not sufficiently presented in the discussions here. As far as his argument's aim was concerned, however, he clearly presented two well-balanced propositions to both Christian society and the magistrates. Concerning the first proposition, which was to oblige people to give "deference" and "obedience" to magistrates, he rejected the Anabaptist view of the magistracy that he characterized as "a kind of necessary evil." Then he idealized a magistrate as "shepherd of his people, guardian of peace, protector of righteousness, and avenger of innocence," urging complete Christian obedience not only in word and deed but also in heartfelt moderation.[197]

195. *OS* 1:270. (Battles, trans., *Institution*, 299.) Cf. *OS* 1:259. (Battles, trans., *Institution*, 286.)

196. *OS* 1:273. (Battles, trans., *Institution*, 302–3.) Cf. Höpfl, *Christian Polity*, 52–53.

197. *OS* 1:273–74. (Battles, trans., *Institution*, 303–4.) According to Battles (*Institution*, 432), the expression "a kind of necessary evil" was not taken from the *Schleitheim Confession* (Article 4), but from Zwingli's refutation of the confession (*In Catabaptistarum Strophas Elenchus*, 1527).

Concerning the second proposition on the self-moderation of magistrates, as well as concerns for the limit of Christian obedience, he brought up the idea of "mutual obligation" between the people and the magistrates. On the one hand, he rejected the view that no obedience was due to unjust magistrates. He urged the people to obey the unjust and persecuting magistrates, not to seek their own solutions, and to appeal for the help of God "in whose hand are hearts of kings and the changing of kingdoms."[198] On the other hand, with a warning before God, "Let princes hear and be afraid," Calvin urged them to be aware of God's ultimate judgment on them. In this context, he brought up the issue of the limit of Christian obedience or resistance, introducing the traditional distinction between private and public persons. Although the right of resistance was not accorded to private persons, he acknowledged the right accorded to constitutional magistrates, what he described as "the magistrates of the people," to protect people's freedom. That is, he recognized the lawful institutions of restraint against the abuse of princely powers. Notably, he referred not only to three ancient cases of Sparta, Rome, and Athens but also to the case of his contemporary French "three estates."[199]

Calvin's reference to the "three estates" with a phrase, "perhaps, as things now are," was said to have some impact upon the subsequent development of the French Reformation. The reference was noteworthy in the sense that, at the time of his writing, the "three estates" had not been held for thirty years during which the foundation of the absolutistic rule of Francis I was laid down. Here could be seen Calvin's mixed thoughts on both expectation and criticism: expectation for the "three estates" to check the abuse of the king's power, and criticism if the expectation was betrayed. As a matter of fact, he called the "three estates" the "protector" of the people's freedom ordained by God. On the one hand, he writes, "I am so far from forbidding them to withstand, in accordance with their duty, the fierce licentiousness of kings." On the other hand, if not, "their dissimulation involves nefarious perfidy, for by it they dishonestly betray the freedom of the people."[200] As the last argument in the first *Institutes*, he then affirmed the "rule of exception" that the people's "obedience is never to lead us away from obedience to him [God]." He further admonished kings that their "commands" would never lead the people to disobey God's commands. He then admonished the people that their civic obedience ought

198. *OS* 1:277–78. (Battles, trans., *Institution*, 307–9.) Referring to J. Bohatec (*Calvins Lehre von Staat und Kirche*, 1937, 644–45; *Budé und Calvin*, 450–52), Battles (*Institution*, 433–34) considers Calvin's notion of "mutual obligation" common to his contemporary French evangelical humanists.

199. *OS* 1:278–79. (Battles, trans., *Institution*, 309–10.)

200. *OS* 1:279. (Battles, trans., *Institution*, 310–11.) Cf. *Institutes*, ed. McNeill, 1518n54.

to be always "in the Lord" and according to the heavenly edict, "We must obey God rather than men" (Acts 5:29).[201]

4. The Dedicatory Epistle to the King as an Epilogue

In the above-mentioned history of Calvin's *Institutes*, we have noticed that the first edition's dedicatory epistle and the third topic of political administration in chapter 6 had gone through the succeeding editions without major revisions. Their theoretical continuity was also noticeable as the writing process of the first *Institutes* suggested the step of finishing chapter 6 and then writing the epistle, perhaps in the summer of 1535. Despite this theoretical continuity, however, there was a difference in their applications. While chapter 6 was meant to be a general discussion for the European Christian world, the epistle to Francis I, by nature, was a particular discussion reflecting the volatile French religious situation after the Placards affair. In addition, the scope of the epistle itself was not reflecting the *Institutes* as a whole but was narrowly limited to three topics of chapter 6: Christian freedom, ecclesiastical power, and civil administration. While there has been a general assumption in Calvin research to view the epistle as a prologue to the entire *Institutes*, from the above-mentioned considerations, this study proposes that it be viewed as the first edition's epilogue.[202] From this perspective, in the following pages, we will discuss three aspects of the epistle, namely, its peculiar characteristics, an analysis of Budé's *Transition to Christianity* that can be considered an exemplar work of what Calvin called "our adversaries," and an ecclesiological analysis of the epistle.

201. *OS* 1:279–80. (Battles, trans., *Institution*, 310–11.) The last topic of chapter 6, "Political Administration," had practically survived without major revisions until the final edition. In this section, however, the final edition (*Institutio* 4.20.32: *OS* 5:502) inserted an important paragraph concerning the resistance theory. Citing Daniel (6:22–23) and others, Calvin took a decisive step forward and asserted that the faithful not only could resist the impious edict of a king but also should remind themselves that their observance of such an edict meant disobedience to the higher authority of God. In the historical context of France that was to lapse into the Wars of Religion in a few years, the paragraph was said to have become a guiding principle for the Huguenots.

202. Battles (*Institution*, "Introduction," li) rightly observes a close relationship between the dedicatory epistle and chapter 6 and considers the latter as the epistle's "conclusion." On the contrary, our study regards the epistle as "an epilogue" either of the entire book for Christendom as a whole, or of chapter 6 for a particular discussion of the French context. For the date of the epistle (August 23, 1535), see *COR* VI-1:33.

(1) Peculiar Characteristics of the Dedicatory Epistle

(i) There were several ordinarily unexpected characteristics in Calvin's epistle. As a dedicatory epistle was generally regarded as a testimony of the author's personal friendship or the patron's protection and reward, firstly, this epistle was meant to be the author's apology or appeal to Francis I. Secondly, the cover of the first *Institutes* read "Preface to the most Christian King of France." Thus, it is worth noting that Calvin called the epistle only a "preface" and inscribed only "of Noyon, author" under his name, the designation that he had already used in his first published work on Seneca. Thirdly, the fact that he did not use even his official title (*licencié en lois*) might indicate his position as a fugitive fleeing from the hand of the king, therefore appealing to him within the private author's book. Fourthly, the cover also indicated that the book was offered to the king "as a confession of faith." Although the *Institutes* contained a chapter on the expositions of the Apostles' Creed, the designation of the entire book as "a confession of faith" was unusual. As a possible explanation for this, it could be assumed that he was originally writing an educational book for his compatriots who were interested in the gospel and, thus, had no intention of an appeal to the king as such. The sudden change of the religious situation that he described in the epistle as "the fury of certain wicked persons has prevailed so far in your realm that there is no place in it for sound doctrine" might have urged him to write and present the book as an apology.

However, the most impressive characteristic of all was his scheme to make a litigating struggle out of the epistle by which he charged what he called "our adversaries" and defended the Evangelicals as the defendants. With what Millet calls "judicial rhetoric," Calvin, a legal expert, portrayed the royal palace as the king's "law court" (*tribunal*), the king as its "judge," the epistle as "a petition" for the king's hearing, perhaps he himself as "a lawyer" representing the Evangelicals who were persecuted for the charges of heresy and sedition, and the confession of faith as the defendants' "plea."[203] In fact, there were many expressions that suggested a court of law. Concerning Evangelical doctrine, for instance, he contended that a guilty verdict was meted out against the Evangelicals "without a hearing" and by ignoring their "confession" and "testimony." He asked "of what crime?" and "with what right?" they were convicted. For Calvin as a private citizen, of course, it was unrealistic to make a direct appeal to the king for a private hearing, and it

203. *OS* 1:19, 36. (Battles, trans., *Institution*, 1, 18.) Cf. Millet, *Calvin et la dynamique*, 474–77.

was even more unrealistic to regard the king and his palace as a just judge and law court. What then was his intention in employing such a metaphor?[204]

(ii) As to the first question we ask, who were "our adversaries" whom Calvin pretended to bring before the king's law court? Though they were not identified by him, to determine their portraits might help us to understand his intention as well as to know the readers to whom he intended to write his first *Institutes* and thus to persuade of the Evangelical cause. A key to unlocking this question might be found in his appeal at the end of the epistle: "O most noble king, . . . you may not incline an ear credulous beyond measure to their slanders."[205] In other words, he employed an expedient means to portray the king as a just and neutral judge, thus not responsible for the policy of persecuting the Evangelicals. He then supposed his "adversaries" as those who were close to the king and were able to advise him and to influence his religious policies, in short, as the "slanderers" responsible for the persecution.

From this assumption, many researchers, including Bohatec, have listed Robert Ceneau, Bishop of Avranches, the famous humanist scholar Budé, and Jacopo Sadoleto, Bishop of Carpentras (later, Cardinal) among the "adversaries," all of whom were widely known as humanist scholars and reform-minded leaders. They were close to the royal court, and some of them were regarded as comrades by the Protestant Evangelicals. However, they were said to have hardened their stance toward Protestant Evangelicalism after the Placards affair. Granted the right to visit the royal palace by the King's mother, Ceneau was known as the author of an apologetic work for the Catholic Mass. In this he appended the works of the Catholic apologist, Johannes Cochlaeus, contending the Münster upheaval as a natural result of Luther's teachings. Sadoleto, an Italian who had served as a close confidant to both Popes Leo X and Clement VII and was Bishop of Carpentras near Avignon at the time of Calvin's writing the *Institutes*, published and dedicated his *Romans Commentary* to Francis I in 1535. Sadoleto urged the king to uphold Catholic orthodoxy and to suppress Protestant Evangelicalism in its dedicatory epistle.[206]

204. *OS* 1:22–23. (Battles, trans., *Institution*, 2–3.)

205. *OS* 1:23, 35. (Battles, trans., *Institution*, 4, 17.)

206. Cf. Bohatec, *Budé und Calvin*, 127–41; Ganoczy, *Young Calvin*, 99; Balke, *Calvin and the Anabaptist*, 39–40; Battles, trans., *Institution*, 313–16. Since Ceneau's polemical work (*Axioma Catholicum / Appendix ad Coenam Dominicam*, 1534) was refuted by Bucer (*Opera Latina 5: Defensio adversus Axioma Catholicum*, 1534), it was possible that it was known to Calvin who was writing the *Institutes* in Basel. Whether Sadoleto's work (*In Pauli Epistolam ad Romanos Commentarium*) was known to Calvin by this time may be problematic. Although the original commentary, dated 1535, was acknowledged by Melanchthon's letter (September 25, 1535), the work's Pelagian tendency alarmed Erasmus, the Paris Theological

(iii) The figure more influential by far than the first two was Budé, the most well-known French Hellenist, holding the titles of advisor and "maître des requêtes" in Francis I's court. For Calvin, Budé was a former graduate of Orléans law school and a distinguished scholar of Roman law, an advocate for the royal lectureship, which later became the Collège de France, and an undisputed leader of humanist studies. Calvin praised him as the greatest humanist scholar and placed him ahead of Erasmus in his Seneca commentary, yet differed on his interpretation of the Seneca text. Even though Budé was known as a reform-minded humanist, his theological stance followed Cochlaeus's conservatism. His *Transition to Christianity* was published in March 1535 in Paris with the king's privilege. Its publication was said to have turned the trend of the times further against Protestant Evangelicalism in France and caused Germany's Melanchthon to express his disappointment and fear of its adverse effects. Although Calvin's work customarily used no proper names of his contemporaries, it was almost certain that Calvin read Budé's work during his writing of the *Institutes* in Basel. In addition, when he wrote at the beginning of the epistle that "I know with what horrible reports they [adversaries] have filled your [king's] ears and mind," Budé was likely prominent in his mind. With these considerations, one can assume that Calvin was conscious of Budé's slanderous accusations while writing the epistle and perhaps chapter 6.[207]

(2) Budé's Transition to Christianity

(i) *Transition to Christianity* was a work of dignified formality. Its character was well reflected in its cover page: at the top, "G. Budé of Paris" (G. Budaei Parisiensis) in large characters, then his official title; dedicated to "the invincible and most powerful Prince Francis, the most Christian King of France"; its title (*De Transitu Hellenismi ad Christianismum, Libri Tres*); and after the publication place and year, the king's privilege (*cum privilegio Regis*) in large

---

Faculty, and the papal curia. It went through several revisions and was officially published in 1536. Among Calvin's possible adversaries, Bohatec's choice of either Budé or Cochlaeus, whose views Budé shared, seems reasonable.

207. Guillaume Budé, *De Transitu Hellenismi ad Christianismum, Libri Tres*, 1535. Our study uses the text of *Opera Omnia Guilielmei Budaei* (4 vols., 1557; repr., Farnborough, 1966, 1:130–240) and also consults a bilingual text of the original Latin edition and its French translation by M. Lebel (Sherbrooke, Quebec: Éditions Paulines, 1973), hereafter Lebel edition. For the effects of Budé's publication, for example, see Wendel (*Calvin*, 130), Bouwsma (*Calvin*, 12–14, 117–18), and McGrath (*A Life*, 58–59). For Calvin's comment on Budé in his Seneca commentary, see Margaret Mann, *Érasme et les débuts de la réforme française* (Paris: H. Champion, 1934), 163–64; for Melanchthon's reaction, see Battles's endnote (*Institution*, 316).

characters. His dedicatory epistle, with the title "preface" (*praefatio*), assumed the book to be an occasion for the privileged advisor to give lectures to the king on the important topics of the times. In particular, Budé praised the king as the defender of orthodox faith as exemplified by his punitive measures taken after the Placards affair as well as his leading role in the sacred host procession and the Mass at Notre Dame (January 1535).[208] If Calvin read this work at the last stage of writing his *Institutes*, his awareness of it was even manifested in his own work's cover, which seemingly intended to stand in contrast to Budé's: at the top he placed the title (*Christianae Religionis Institutio*) in large characters; in the middle he used the same word, "preface," for the epistle to the king to whom he offered the book as "the confession of faith"; then, without his title he simply wrote "John Calvin of Noyon, author" (*Joanne Calvino, Noviodunensi, autore*).[209]

The main aim of Budé's *Transition to Christianity* was to propose the ultimate harmony of the Hellenist or the wider Humanist studies and classical Christianity by means of the historical concept of transition. As a book of the times, it signified both a crisis in which humanists were accused of collaborating with Protestant Evangelicalism after the Placards affair and an urgent appeal to the importance of humanist studies in France. As an apologetic work, its goal was to demonstrate the historical continuity from classical Christianity to contemporary Roman Catholicism. On the one hand, it denounced Luther's Evangelicalism as "a new movement," unorthodox and unreliable. On the other hand, it countered the accusation of the Paris Theological Faculty that Hellenist studies provided a nursery for paganism and the Lutheran heresy in the church. At the same time, it intended to maintain the humanist *via media* by rejecting both Catholic conservatism and Protestant Evangelicalism as two extremes.

(ii) As to its content, although each of the three books lacked a subject title, book 1 dealt with the basic relationship between Hellenism and Christianity as well as the former's transition to the latter. Budé considered the essence of Hellenism as what Aristotle called a "philosophy" of the search for the truth and its goal as man's "preparation for his death," and that of Christianity as

208. *De Transitu*, titulus, 1:130–33. All citations are hereafter taken from *Opera Omnia*, vol. 1. Cf. C. Elwood, *The Body Broken: The Calvinist Doctrine of the Eucharist and the Symbolization of Power in Sixteenth-Century France* (Oxford and New York: Oxford University Press, 1999), 27–28. Since the original title page is not included in the *Opera Omnia* text, the Lebel edition is consulted.

209. For the original title page of the first *Institutes*, the *Bibliotheca Calviniana* (*BC* 1, 37) is used.

a "philosophy of revelations" (*oraculorum philosophia*). In connection with these two philosophies, Budé dealt with such themes as life and death, immortality of soul, faith, truth, love, revelations, and others. In book 2, he discussed topics that Christian philosophy ought to address, such as revelations, Christ, Christ's death and resurrection, the freedom of will, salvation, and judgment. After touching on the current controversies on these topics, he appealed for obedience to the traditional Church and its faith. In sharp contrast to the two previous volumes, book 3 presented the personal Christian convictions of the author as a Hellenist. It held the basic assumption that, while classical philosophy aimed at the meditations on death, Christian philosophy was oriented toward the meditations on God which "we ought to recognize as the unique and absolute subject." Budé urged the faithful to use these two philosophies so as to be led to firm convictions of faith, hope, and love.[210]

It is not easy to determine how Budé placed his criticism of Protestant Evangelicalism in the scope of *Transition to Christianity*, and this is further obscured by the lack of not only the titles of the volumes but also the divisions of chapters and sections. In particular, his criticism seemed to be concentrated in two locations in book 1 (*Opera Budaei*, 1:149–54) and book 2 (1:172–81), but both locations were placed as marginal to the main thrust of his arguments. While there was no direct evidence of Calvin's reaction to Budé's criticism, it was true that, as we will examine later, a summary statement of his "adversaries" in the dedicatory epistle contained almost all the points of Budé's criticism. First, in book 1, Budé consistently characterized Luther's view in connection with the freedom of will issue as "freedom of no constraints" (*libertus dissoluta*), "new opinions" (*novae opiniones*), and his reformation as "new movements" (*res novae*). He also accused the Protestant Reformation of causing disrespect for church tradition concerning the Bible, church fathers, and church councils, as well as attacks on priestly order and the Mass.[211] In view of the fact that many humanists had joined the Reformation, furthermore, his utmost concern was said to be whether God intended through the "new movements . . . the reconstruction of Christianity and the reorganization of Classical studies," or not.[212] In book 2, his criticism was introduced in connection with what he viewed as the most disturbing matter, namely, that French humanists

210. Cf. *De Transitu*, 1:134–61, 162–211, 212–40. The Lebel edition ("Introduction," xxi–xliv) presents an outline of Budé's arguments.

211. *De Transitu*, 1:149–50, 152–53. Cf. Bohatec, *Budé und Calvin*, 95–100, 130–31; Battles, trans., *Institution*, 318.

212. *De Transitu*, 1:152, 154.

were considered "the pope's group or party" (*pontifica familia/gregales*). For Budé, who considered humanists to be the true interpreters of Christianity, an apology ought to distinguish their understanding of Christianity from the claimers of orthodoxy of both papalism and the "new movements," as well as their "theosophists" (*theosophos*) from the "theologians" (*theologos*) of both. Notably, his apology concluded that the "new movements" had nothing to contribute to their "Christianity."[213]

From this basic stance, Budé focused on the doctrines of the "new movements." First, he reworded "freedom of no constraints" from book 1 as "justification by faith" (*fidei iustificatio*) and acknowledged that this doctrine was welcomed in some corners of the church as a substitute for the papal salvific system. However, his intention was to denounce this doctrine as the primary cause of introducing heterogeneous rules into Christian spirituality, of destroying the ancient customs of church discipline and ceremonies, and of bringing laxity of faith and morals into the church. To this end, he mentioned church discipline within the "new movements" as effective in removing some superstitions from the church. However, he was particularly dismayed by the fact that their discipline forfeited the church's jurisdictional authority and instead introduced the rule of the believers' votes.[214] Second, he attacked the Protestant Reformation as "an insane and capital philosophy," with its core assertion being that it had restored the doctrines of the ancient church. For him, the "new movements" did not inherit the ancient church's schools and controversies. Instead of restoring the ancient church, they only offered rash and impious arguments while building their own "new spiritual structure" founded upon their "unbound license." For traditionalist Budé, their capital crime was their act of apostasy in abandoning the authoritative church, "the Lord's first bride, the unique parent of Christianity" (*sponsa domini prima, parens unicus Christianismi*) and taking "a mother" (*mater*) of their own taste.[215]

(iii) Our brief survey of Budé's *Transition to Christianity* has revealed some of his characteristic assumptions: a Gallicanist concept of the church distinguishing the French Catholic Church from the Roman-Papal Church; the superiority of humanism over both papalism that thought lightly of humanism, and Protestant Evangelicalism that he considered heterogeneous to humanism; and his confidence in the restoration of the ancient church. As to the "new movements," in particular, he regarded them as foreign imports and academically shallow disciplines contemptible of classical studies. Remarkably,

213. *De Transitu*, 1:171, 172–73.
214. *De Transitu*, 1:173, 174, 175, 178.
215. *De Transitu*, 1, 180.

his optimism for humanist reform was so extraordinary that he regarded the humanism of his times not only able to go back through the religious confusions of the last three centuries to reach classical Christianity and to restore it in the contemporary church, but also able to go forward for the next three centuries through the current religious controversies and disruptions and to maintain a superior position. A concluding remark of his criticism was especially characteristic: since what he considered "orthodoxy" (*orthodoxia*) could never be reached by "controversial spirit" (*loxodoxia*), he proposed the *via media* solution, rejecting both the papal and Protestant claims.[216] In French society after the Placards affair, especially in the academic world of French humanism that the king had been nurturing, the polarization of radical reformists and moderate or conservative reformists was accelerating. At this juncture, the challenge of *Transition to Christianity*, which represented a position quite different from what we have termed moderate evangelical humanism or Lefèvrianism, was widely felt. The following posits that Calvin's reaction to it can be seen directly in his dedicatory epistle and generally in the entire scope of his first *Institutes*.[217]

(3) An Ecclesiological Analysis of the Dedicatory Epistle

Before going into the analysis, we should ascertain two points concerning the nature of the adversaries' charges. The first point concerns the following paragraph in which Calvin seemed to summarize the charges:

> They call it [our doctrine] "new" and "of recent birth." They reproach it as "doubtful and uncertain." They ask what miracles have confirmed it. They inquire whether it is right for it to prevail against the agreement of so many holy fathers and against most ancient custom. They urge us to acknowledge that it is schismatic because it wages war against the church, or that the church was lifeless during the many centuries in which no such thing was heard. Finally, they say that there is no need of many arguments, for one can judge by its fruits what it is, seeing that it has engendered such a heap of sects, so many seditious tumults, such great licentiousness.

As the description used here did not correspond to the usual theological terms of Catholic apologists, but clearly indicated those of the humanists, it could suggest the profiles of the "adversaries." In this context, all the charges, except

216. *De Transitu*, 1, 175, 176, 182, 183.
217. Cf. Kelley, *The Beginning*, 15–16.

perhaps one of the confirmations by miracles, roughly corresponded to the criticism in Budé's *Transition to Christianity*.[218]

The second point concerns the nature of Calvin's response to the charge in his dedicatory epistle, which was thoroughly in accordance with the methodology of humanists. In other words, over against the charge of the adversaries that the Protestant Evangelicals assumed the Bible for their false doctrines, Calvin, citing the hermeneutical principle of "the rule of faith" (*regula fidei*), said that "if our interpretation be measured by this rule of faith, victory is in our hand." On the similar charge of misusing the church fathers, he also said that "if the contest were to be determined by patristic authority, the tide of victory would turn to our side." Over against the charge of Budé and other adversaries who advocated the "continuity" of the ancient church and the current Roman Catholic Church by appealing to patristic authority, Calvin raised the question of "discontinuity" instead of "continuity" or "transition" and boldly proposed that his Evangelicalism inherited and restored the tradition of the ancient church in accordance with the humanist method of biblical and patristic interpretation.[219] As seen in these two points, Calvin's first *Institutes* is characterized by a theology formed by humanist methodology and presented as a confession of faith to those intellectuals and humanists who were interested in church reform. Our assumption is that, at the last writing stage of the *Institutes*, Calvin faced the challenges of anti-Evangelical conservative humanists represented by Budé, as well as by some of the moderate evangelical humanists represented by Lefèvre. If so, in this particular context of the French Reformation, the dedicatory epistle indicated a new characterization of the *Institutes* as its "prologue." Yet at the same time, as an apology, it signaled a concluding remark of the *Institutes* as its "epilogue."

(i) Calvin seemed to respond to the charges of adversaries via the four issues of antiquity, historicity, catholicity, and society, which corresponded to the various aspects of Budé's charges that Protestant Evangelicalism was new

218. *OS* 1:25. (Battles, trans., *Institution*, 6.) Cf. Bohatec, *Budé und Calvin*, 131–33. As far as the above-mentioned two sections of Budé's attacks on the Evangelicals were concerned, there seemed to be no reference to "certification by miracles." However, as Bohatec suggests, Calvin could have interpreted Budé's defense of the Catholic Sacraments, including the Mass, which the Evangelicals attacked as false miracles, as Budé's demand for the Evangelicals to produce such "certification by miracles."

219. *OS* 1:24, 27. (Battles, trans., *Institution*, 4, 8.) Cf. Bohatec, *Budé und Calvin*, 133–34; J. van Oort, "John Calvin and the Church Fathers," in *The Reception of the Church Fathers in the West: From the Carolingians to the Maurists*, ed. I. Backus (Leiden: Brill, 1997), 2:663–66.

and uncertain, and lacked authentication by miracles: it was against the church fathers and tradition; it was schismatic; and it caused moral decay and social unrest. Although Calvin treated them as theological issues to a certain extent in the main text, especially in chapter 6 of the *Institutes*, here in the dedicatory epistle he did not go into theological arguments. Rather, he applied to them the terms and arguments of a court of law. Concerning the issue of antiquity, for example, he defended Evangelicalism as the restorer of the old and certain gospel, what the Roman law called "rehabilitation of right" (*jus postliminium*), the restoration of the lost item or right. Concerning the authentication by miracles which Catholic apologists had brought out, he argued that the miracles recorded in ancient historical sources were attributed to both the orthodox church fathers and heretics alike and that the argument itself was, apart from the church court, not useful in civil court.[220] Concerning the issue of historicity, he argued that Evangelicalism did respect authority of the church fathers and that "the greater part of what we are saying today meets their approval." On the argument that the adversaries appealed to the need of the church's decisions since the opinions of the fathers often differed, he called the argument "the subtleties of sophists" and reminded them that the fathers unanimously appealed to return to Scripture and to ask for its judgment.[221]

(ii) The most interesting issue from an ecclesiological perspective was that of catholicity. Calvin's basic stance on this issue was the idea of history, especially of church history, shared by both humanism and Protestant Evangelicalism. According to this idea, the history of the Christian church was divided into three periods of the church's purity, depravity, and restoration. The question was raised concerning church reform in the latter two periods, when reform took the form of restoring the ancient church of the first period, which would not be schismatic, but catholic. In the Reformation period, which coincided with Calvin's academic formation period, a noteworthy conflict on this issue was seen between the two church reform concepts of Luther and Erasmus. Luther emphasized the discontinuity of the second and third periods. He sought the two marks of God's word and the two sacraments of baptism and the Lord's Supper as the core of the church's catholicity as well as the restoration of the ancient church. He also proposed a reform of the Roman Catholic Church that he considered to be basically the church in the second period. In his later work, the *Explanatio symboli* (1533), Erasmus used the concept of "tranquility of the church hierarchy" as defense of the church's institutional continuity throughout

220. *OS* 1:25–27. (Battles, trans., *Institution*, 6–8.) Cf. Ganoczy, *Young Calvin*, 271–72.
221. *OS* 1:27–29. (Battles, trans., *Institution*, 8–11.)

the three periods and defended the catholicity of the contemporary Roman Catholic Church. On the issue of the church's catholicity, Calvin focused on Christ who had been continuously residing in the "people of all believers" and placed this position in opposition to that of the adversaries who acknowledged the church's catholicity only in the visible "form of the church" or "in the Papal seat of the Roman Church and the Episcopal order." As this position was shared among Catholic apologists as well as Budé and Erasmus, on the one hand, Calvin opposed it and acknowledged that the church catholic could "exist without the visible forms." Yet on the other hand, he shared with Luther the two marks of God's word and the sacraments for its manifestation.[222]

Even though Calvin's position on catholicity was basically the same as in the text of the *Institutes*, he added two new illustrations only found in the dedicatory epistle to counter the arguments of adversaries who emphasized the institutional continuity of the papacy and the infallibility of church councils. The first illustration was of the Sanhedrin, the Jewish highest council and legal court, which was involved in Jesus's death. He considered the council as the ecclesiastical council of the Old Testament period, and deduced from the case of Jesus's death the notion of the general fallibility of ecclesiastical councils that would later become a key to his theory on church councils. The second illustration concerned a reformed Council of Basel (1431–49) during which a conflict took place between Italian Pope Eugenius IV, who was deposed by the Council as a heretic, and Amadius VIII of Savoy, who was elected by the Council as antipope Felix V. The Council inherited the reform principle of the superiority of a council over a pope that was established in the Council of Constance (1414–18). The Council deposed Eugenius, who moved to dissolve it, and elected Amadius instead. But it ended in confusion and Amadius resigned. On the one hand, while acknowledging the Council's right to elect Amadius as an authentic pope, Calvin expressed his dismay about Amadius's resignation, writing "Amadius was appeased by a cardinal's hat, as a barking dog by a morsel." On the other hand, Calvin described Eugenius and papists at the Council as "these rebellious and obstinate heretics," and made a judgment of historical perspective that from them "have come forth all future popes, cardinals, bishops, abbots, and priests." Furthermore, he was conscious of contemporary papists who were anticonciliarists and generally denied the authenticity of the Council of Basel. He demanded that they show "another definition of the church's form," and to the king he asked for a judgment over

222. *OS* 1:31. (Battles, trans., *Institution*, 12–13.) Cf. Ganoczy, *Young Calvin*, 272; Erasmus, *Explanatio Symboli*, ASD V–1, 274. For Erasmus, see also chapter 2, n. 152.

their teaching that was nothing but "a deadly butchery of souls, a firebrand, a ruin, and a destruction of the church."[223] His clear apologetic intent was to appeal to conciliarism, which still resonated with the king's Gallicanism and the French Church, and to present to those humanists and intellectuals whom he considered the readers of his work a strongly worded antipapal position that indeed employed stronger wording than chapter 6 of the main text.

(iii) Concerning the last issue of society, Calvin described in general terms the adversaries' charge regarding "how many disturbances, tumults, and contentions the preaching of our doctrine has drawn along with it, and what fruits it now produces." But what he had in mind was the severest charge of all, namely, the charge of tumult in society and treason against the king. To the charge of social disturbance, Calvin's characteristic response was that he neither denied nor apologized for the disturbance taking place, but boldly attempted to explain its deepest and ultimate cause in religious matters by using the antagonistic scheme of the kingdom of Christ and that of Satan. In other words, since "a certain characteristic of the divine word, is that it never comes forth while Satan is at rest and sleeping," the advancement of God's word caused a two-sided reaction. On one side, just like light shined in darkness, God's word caused Satan to wake up from his sleep and let him respond violently to the word. On the other side, as a "stronger man [Christ] had troubled and assailed his [Satan's] Kingdom" (cf. Luke 11:22), "Satan began to shake off his accustomed drowsiness and to take up arms" and "stirred up men to action that thereby he might violently oppress the dawning truth."[224] In addition, Calvin pointed out another aspect of the cause in case Satan was not successful, saying that Satan changed his stratagems and attempted an ambush to arouse "disagreements and dogmatic contentions through his Catabaptists." This could be Calvin's determined attempt to dissociate Protestant Evangelicalism from the current Münster Anabaptist revolution, as well as his apology for countering the adversaries' attempt to associate the two in France. As the biblical case of Elijah who was accused of "troubling Israel" and of Christ who was condemned as if "to the Jews, Christ was seditious," Calvin contended it unfair to attribute the cause of current social disturbances to Evangelicalism.[225]

For Calvin a far more serious charge than social disturbance was the ultimate charge of treason. He described this as follows: "By this new gospel (for so they call it) men strive and seek only after the opportunity for seditions

223. *OS* 1:32–33. (Battles, trans., *Institution*, 13–15.)
224. *OS* 1:33. (Battles, trans., *Institution*, 15.) Cf. Bohatec, *Budé und Calvin*, 136–38.
225. *OS* 1:33–35. (Battles, trans., *Institution*, 15–17.)

and impunity for all crimes" or "the overthrow of [French] kingdom." His response was a total rejection of the charge as ungrounded. He declared: "we, from whom not one seditious word was ever heard." As mentioned above, he recognized the core of the issue as the slanderous charge to associate the current Münster revolution with Protestant Evangelicalism, and he not only denied the charge but assured that, if seditious acts like Münster were ever to take place in Francis's rule, "there are laws and legal penalties by which they may be severely restrained."[226] Although he did not offer further apologies on this, it was certain that he took the charge of treason as the most serious issue for Evangelicalism in France.

In fact, it was this very association that Francis's official diplomatic document, drafted by his ambassador to Germany, Guillaume du Bellay, in February 1535, used to justify his policy of eradicating the Evangelicals from his kingdom. Calvin himself suspected the existence of Cochlaeus's theological arguments and the justifications of Budé and other humanists of the king's policy to be behind the document.[227] It could also be said that Calvin's refutation of this association was his strongest personal motive to write the dedicatory epistle and the last topic of chapter 6. In his testimony twenty-five years later, in the preface to his commentary on Psalms, he revealed his motive for writing the first *Institutes.* He described a certain antagonistic document that attacked the French Evangelicals as "the Anabaptists or the seditious fellows" and his wish to liberate his fellow Evangelicals from the unjust accusations. Furthermore, the preface testified that, as some of them suffered their martyrdom, for Calvin to remain silent was nothing but the act of a coward and apostate.[228] In the last portion of the dedicatory epistle, as if it were his final pleading before a court of law, he made his last argument to counter the charge of treason. In both cases, whether the king listened to the pleading and showed his favor to the Evangelicals or, to the contrary, he listened to the advice of the adversaries and continued to follow his policy of persecuting the Evangelicals, Calvin pledged his obedience to the king. In the very last sentence, interestingly, he did not appeal for the king's "clemency" but pleaded for Christ to establish the king's rule "in righteousness" and "in equity."[229]

226. *OS* 1:35. (Battles, trans., *Institution*, 17–18.)

227. Concerning Calvin's particular apology in this section, Balke (*Calvin and the Anabaptist*, 41–46) considers it as Calvin's reaction to the adversaries' association of the Evangelicals with the Anabaptists, and Höpfl (*Christian Polity*, 21) sees it as Calvin's exposing of "this kind of lie" seen in diplomatic documents.

228. *CO* 31:23. Cf. Ganoczy, *Young Calvin*, 99; Gordon, *Calvin*, 57.

229. *OS* 1:36. (Battles, trans., *Institution*, 18–19.)

Concluding Remarks

(1) In summing up chapter 1, let us emphasize three key concepts: Calvin's academic formation, Catholic ecclesiology, and the first *Institutes*. These points help us to comprehend the whole scope of the chapter. His academic formation can be described in short as self-taught theology that utilized his background in humanities and law. As in the preceding cases of Erasmus, Zwingli, and Melanchthon, he wrote theology from a humanist perspective and methodology. Catholic ecclesiology was an ideal for sixteenth-century humanists. Calvin shared it with his fellow humanists and tried to express his own Catholic ecclesiology in his first theological work. As our subtitle, "A Study in the History of Doctrine," indicates, among all editions of the *Institutes* we consider the first to be the most important work for understanding the formation of his ecclesiology, and we regard his Catholic ecclesiology to be the basic stratum of his ecclesiology as a whole.

(2) Calvin's ecclesiological formation took place in two historical contexts, large and small: the French Reformation and his personal religious experiences. The period of his academic formation coincided with the early stage of the French Reformation and, in particular, with the emerging force of evangelical humanism represented by Lefèvre. It is notable that this was Calvin's intellectual background. While evangelical humanism went through a polarization process between the moderate and radical positions over the issue of church reform within the French Church, personally Calvin experienced "a sudden conversion" between the Cop address of 1533 and his exile in Basel of 1535. During this period, he decisively turned from moderate to radical evangelical humanism. Upholding the idea of Catholic ecclesiology, concerning the "Rome issue" he rejected the current Roman Catholic Church as the non-Catholic, papal church. Concerning the "Luther issue," he adhered himself to the Evangelicalism of Luther as the restorer of biblical and catholic faith.

(3) Calvin's first *Institutes*, which he completed for publication in 1535 in Basel, formally followed the example of Luther's *Catechisms*. Substantially, however, it was a combination of the catechetical "instruction" portion and the polemical "apology" portion. As to its contents, it was the work of a young humanist scholar who had mastered in a short period of time biblical studies and the Evangelical theology of Luther, Zwingli, Bucer, and others. Its noteworthy characteristic was not only in its formal and substantial uniqueness but also in its spirit or ethos, in which Calvin expressed his diagnosis of the current situation as "Europe afflicted." Our study began an examination of his ecclesiology in the *Institutes* with his treatment of the sacraments as an illus-

tration of this ethos. There we noticed the unique formation of his sacramental theology in the context of the conflicting Catholic and Protestant Evangelical positions. In particular, we noticed that, from his understanding of the ancient orthodox Christology with his Antiochene approach, he attempted to mediate between the Lutheran and the Zwinglian positions within the framework of biblical and catholic faith.

(4) Calvin's Catholic ecclesiology of the first *Institutes* was presented as a combination of two distinctive concepts of the church: "the whole number of the elect" in its "instruction" portion, and "the congregation of believers" in its "apology" portion. From his apologetic perspective, Christendom was placed in the center of the spectrum of "church and state," to the exclusion of the extreme positions of the papal church and the Anabaptists. As seen in the dedicatory epistle, which our study considered "an epilogue" to the *Institutes*, Calvin postulated the idea of Christ's kingdom which spiritually ruled over this spectrum of European Christendom. On the basis of this idea, he formulated his first and unique proposal of the reform of "church and state." The proposal was unique in the sense that it was firstly formulated from the perspectives of Christ's kingdom and Christian freedom, especially the notion of "adiaphora," and that it was secondly composed of two distinctive and unbalanced topics of "ecclesiastical power" and "political administration." As the succeeding editions of the *Institutes* proved, the first edition was not a finished product. However, historically it was a first and unique theological manifest of the French humanist, "Calvin in context."

Chapter 2

The Early Genevan Reformation and Practice of Catholic Ecclesiology

From his background in French humanism and legal studies, Calvin entered the stage of the European Reformation as a lay theologian and the author of the first *Institutes*. Unknown as a Reformer, this young humanist scholar was soon to be thrown into the actual scene of the Reformation. However, this did not occur in the cities of his choice for exile, Basel or Strasbourg, but Geneva, which had only recently joined in the Swiss Reformation dominated by Zwinglianism.[1]

Calvin did not voluntarily associate himself with the Genevan Reformation. It is generally assumed that his encounter with chief minister of Geneva, Guillaume Farel, in June 1536, was a decisive moment for him personally, as well as for the city of Geneva and the French Reformation. What did it mean for him, however, to participate in the reform of a particular city? In sharp contrast with the "sudden conversion" narrative portrayed as a personal transition from moderate to radical evangelical humanism that was surveyed in the previous chapter, to join with radical reformist Farel was nothing but a public manifestation of his religious affiliation. His recollection of this occasion twenty years later was recorded in the preface to his *Psalms Commentary*. Though he was unyielding in his choice of scholarly pursuit, he finally gave in to the intimidating Farel as well as to divine will, which he could not avoid admitting was behind the intimidations. Thus, he chose to join not with enthusiasm but hesitantly. Whether his choice was meant to be educational engagement, and

1. B. Gordon, *The Swiss Reformation* (Manchester and New York: Manchester University Press, 2002), 1–5, 152–53.

whether it can be assumed he intentionally chose the position of a lecturer of the Bible rather than pastor, the fact of active involvement in church reform was substantially the same. In this sense, he took the radical step from a biblical humanist to a Reformer.[2]

At the same time, the city of Geneva in its early reform was taking an unusual shape. In addition to the military alliance with neighboring Bern, which enabled the city to free itself from Savoy's rule and introduce Evangelicalism into its church, the church was to be led by the exiled French ministers, notably Farel and his associate Calvin who took the place of the Savoyard Catholic clergy. In the German-speaking Swiss cities, such as Zurich, Basel, and Bern, where the early city-oriented Swiss Reformation had advanced, churches were commonly led by the Reformers of their own breed. In French-speaking Geneva, where the Reformation's second stage was introduced, however, two notable leaders of the church had their common background in the early French Reformation, even though they did not share common ideas of church reform. In this chapter, accordingly, we will focus on three aspects of the early Genevan Reformation. Section 1 will examine Lefèvrianism, which was Farel's immediate ideological origin as well as Calvin's general academic background, and Farel's transition from Lefèvrianism to Evangelicalism. Section 2 will attempt an ecclesiological analysis of three church documents that Farel, Calvin, and others presented to the Genevan magistrates in 1537. And section 3 will examine the Caroli affair in which Calvin played a predominant role and his publication of *Two Epistles* (*Epistolae Duae*) as cases for the practice of his Catholic ecclesiology.

Section 1. Lefèvrianism and Evangelicalism in Farel

(i) In order to elucidate the nature of the early Genevan Reformation, it is necessary to ascertain Farel's academic and ecclesiological formation vis-à-vis Calvin's formation as examined in chapter 1. The traditional claim that Calvin led the early Genevan Reformation and was the sole or primary author of the three documents considered to be primary sources of the early Genevan Reformation (a catechism titled *Instruction*, the *Confession of Faith*,

2. *CO* 31:26. Cf. Wendel, *Calvin*, 48–50; H. Heyer, *Guillaume Farel: Essai sur le développement de ses idées théologiques* (Geneva: Ramboz et Schuchardt, 1872), 40; Ganoczy, *Young Calvin*, 108. Ganoczy considers that the position of "lecturer" is Calvin's own choice, due to his feeling of unpreparedness to be a pastor.

and the ecclesiastical ordinances often designated as the *Articles*), is regarded as untenable from historical investigations. Instead, the currently held view affirms both the *Confession* and *Articles* originating with Farel, even though a possibility of Calvin's coauthorship is acknowledged.[3] What then was Farel's significance in the early Genevan Reformation?

In a sense, Farel was a forerunner of Calvin. Despite the fact that Farel himself had taken a path to Evangelicalism similar to Calvin's, although ten years prior to Calvin, he had quite different ideas about church reform when he encountered Calvin in 1536. Farel studied at the University of Paris, at the Collège du Cardinal Lemoine where a famous humanist scholar, Lefèvre, had nurtured many students until his retirement in 1508. Later, in the footsteps of Lefèvre, he taught humanities at the same Collège and, like his mentor, even engaged in biblical and theological studies as well as participating in the French Reformation. As in Calvin's case of transition from moderate to radical evangelical humanism, Farel, facing his own personal crises, joined the Meaux reform led by Lefèvre and experienced a similar transition in the 1520s.[4]

(ii) In our previous analyses of the first *Institutes*, we have noticed that Calvin, in addition to the Bible and church fathers, had selectively studied Reformers such as Luther, Melanchthon, Zwingli, Bucer, and others and formulated his own theology. Farel's case took a similar path through the readings of Luther as well as personal associations with Oecolampadius, Zwingli, and Bucer. At the last stage of his theological formation, as our examination of Genevan church documents will indicate, Farel had undoubtedly reached his own unique church reform concepts that were in some aspects different from Calvin's. This can be explained by Farel's formation in Evangelicalism during the formative stage of the Reformation in the 1520s, while Calvin's formation took place in the 1530s when the Reformation was more established. Farel had actually experienced Evangelical church reform for more than ten years prior to his engagement in Geneva. Furthermore, perhaps as the most distinctive factor of Farel's formation, he was a close disciple of Lefèvre and had inherited and radicalized his teacher's ideas. Likewise, Calvin was known to be associated with the Lefèvrian humanist circle in Paris. He was personally associated with its member, Gérard Roussel, and at the time of writing the *In-*

3. *Instruction et confession de foy*; *OS* 1:378–417; *COR* III-2:1–113; *BC* 37/2. *Confession de la foy*; *OS* 1:418–26; *Articles concernant l'organisation de l'église*; *OS* 1:369–77. Although having recognized the issue of authorship, both *CO* and *OS* included all three documents in the Calvin collections, but *COR* and *BC* include only the *Instruction*.

4. Cf. Heyer, *Guillaume Farel*, 9–12.

stitutes certainly had access to the achievement of Lefèvre's important biblical studies. Unfortunately, however, the extent and depth of Lefèvrian influence on Calvin has not been established.[5] In this section, accordingly, we will focus first on Lefèvre's ideas about the church and its reform, including addressing its impact on the Meaux reform, and then we will examine Farel's concept of the church. Before going into our main discussion, we will comment briefly on Farel's place in the early French Reformation.

(iii) Even though critical reevaluation of Farel has been sought for a long time, Farel research has been delayed, as witnessed by the critical edition of his works begun only recently. Thus, evaluations of Farel by researchers are not yet firmly established. For example, the editors of volume 1 of the critical edition make a severe judgment on Farel's reform as "an incendiary" (*boutefeu*), his theology in comparison with Calvin as "an insignificant theologian" (*piètre théologien*), and his work as a whole as nonoriginal. A leader of historical research in Reformation studies, Oberman, calls Farel a Reformer of instigation and a prophetic type or a troublemaker. And the recent biographer of Calvin, Gordon, characterizes Farel's reformatory work akin to the pattern of the radical message of the Placards affair.[6] Over and against these evaluations, Higman considers Farel "a pioneering French reformer" or, "the true father of the French Reformation." Higman seems to base his positive evaluation upon a distinction between the French Reformation's prereformation stage (Lefèvre and the Meaux reform) and its premier stage headed by Farel, who withdrew from the Meaux reform and turned to Evangelicalism.[7] This tendency to separate Farel from his background of Lefèvre and the Meaux reform can also be seen in the recent work of Zuidema and Van Raalte (*Early French Reform: The Theology and Spirituality of Guillaume Farel*) that characterizes Farel as a unique theologian in his own right prior to Calvin, as well as a pioneer of the French Reformation.[8] Our study considers Farel as an heir of the tradition

5. References to Lefèvre's exegetical works are in his commentaries on Psalms (1509), the Pauline Epistles (1512), the Four Gospels (1522), and the Catholic Epistles (1524). Lefèvre's influence on Calvin's theological and exegetical studies seems to remain an unexplored field.

6. Guillaume Farel, *Traités Messins* (*Oeuvres imprimées*, Tome 1), ed. Reinhard Bodenmann and Françoise Briegel (Geneva: Droz, 2009), "Introduction générale," ix, xi; H. A. Oberman, "Calvin and Farel: The Dynamics of Legitimation in Early Calvinism," *Journal of Early Modern History* 2 (1998): 52; Gordon, *Calvin*, 65.

7. F. Higman, "Farel, Guillaume," *OER* 2:99–100; Higman, *Lire et découvrir*, 62–63.

8. J. Zuidema and T. Van Raalte, *Early French Reform: The Theology and Spirituality of Guillaume Farel* (Farnham, Surrey: Ashgate, 2011), 3–30. Unfortunately, this work fails to relate Farel with his ideological root of Lefèvrianism.

of Lefèvre and the Meaux reform, with the characteristic mark of his reform concept being the radicalization of that tradition toward the Evangelicalism of Luther and Zwingli. In a final analysis, our study will present the tradition of Lefèvre and the Meaux reform, Farel, and Calvin's first *Institutes* as three distinctive types of reform in the early French Reformation.

1. Lefèvrianism

A French humanist and a contemporary of Erasmus, Jacques Lefèvre d'Étaples (Jacob Faber Stapulensis) distinguished himself in four consecutive academic fields of philosophy, medieval mystical theology, patristic studies, and biblical studies. However, his point of contact with the early French Reformation was said to be in the last stage of his biblical studies. A turning point in his life came in 1508 when he retired from his professorship at the Collège du Cardinal Lemoine and moved to Saint-Germain-des-Prés, the famous abbey in Paris, and became fully engaged in biblical studies and writing. This move was occasioned by his old disciple, Bishop Guillaume Briçonnet, who acquired the abbotship of the monastery in 1508 and then invited Lefèvre and his disciples to join him. At the abbey, Farel, a youth of aristocratic stock from Gap in southeastern France who was to matriculate at the University of Paris the next year, began to receive Lefèvre's guidance in both academic discipline and spirituality.[9]

Lefèvre's Early Biblical Works

(i) In 1509 the first fruit of Lefèvre's biblical studies came as the publication of the *Quincuplex Psalterium*, a synopsis of five Latin texts of the Psalter that

9. For Lefèvre's academic background and achievement, confer a basic study by Augustin Renaudet (*Humanisme et Renaissance* [Geneva: Droz, 1958], 201–16), Rice's precise introductory article (introduction to *The Prefatory Epistles of Jacques Lefèvre d'Étaples and Related Texts*, ed. E. F. Rice Jr. [New York: Columbia University Press, 1972], xi–xxv), and another article on Lefèvre's mystical works ("Jacques Lefèvre d'Étaples and the Medieval Christian Mystics," in *Florilegium Historiale*, ed. J. G. Rowe and W. H. Stockdale [Toronto: University of Toronto Press, 1971], 89–124). Also see a comprehensive work of Hughes (P. E. Hughes, *Lefèvre: Pioneer of Ecclesiastical Renewal in France* [Grand Rapids: Eerdmans, 1984], 1–68), and Bedouelle's recent introductory article (G. Bedouelle, "Jacques Lefèvre d'Étaples," in *The Reformation Theologians: An Introduction to Theology in the Early Modern Period*, ed. C. Lindberg [Oxford: Blackwell, 2002], 19–33). Incidentally, a joint study on Farel (*Guillaume Farel, 1489–1565: Biographie nouvelle*, Neuchâtel and Paris [Geneva: Slatkine Reprints], 1930, 99–101) considers Farel's matriculation to the University of Paris in 1509, a year after Lefèvre's retirement.

was said to accord him recognition as a biblical scholar, to open to him the new field of hermeneutics, and above all to enable him to take a step toward evangelicalism. This work was known to Luther who used in the *First Psalms Lectures* (1513–15) in Wittenberg, and also to Zurich's Zwingli. The book was significant in the sense that it took in advance some of the Reformation's hermeneutical principles, such as God as the author of the Bible (Psalms), Christ as the hermeneutical key to the texts, and the Holy Spirit as that which inspired the writers, providing a contrast between "carnal interpretation" based upon human reason and "spiritual interpretation" illuminated by the Holy Spirit. Lefèvre's Christocentric theses—that Christ is the spirit of the whole Scripture (*totius scripturae spiritus*), that Scripture without Christ is only literature and letter that kills, and that truly Christ is the life-giving spirit—were indeed noteworthy hermeneutic principles in his age.[10]

From the perspective of ecclesiology, especially noteworthy was Lefèvre's basic definition of the Psalms as "praise of the synagogue and church community" (*laus communis synagogue et ecclesiae*) and the "Psalm of David" as the "Psalm concerning Christ" (*psalmus de Christo*). Besides this Christocentric theme of the church's praise, Lefèvre consistently expressed the church as "the congregation of the faithful" (*congregatio fidelium*), "the faithful people" (*populus fidelis*), and "the elect people" (*populus electi*). He emphasized the substantive identity of the "congregation or people" of the Old and New Testaments. And he paired the history of the Old Testament people described in the Psalms with that of the New Testament Christian church. Accordingly, the "love of God" described in the Psalms was equivalent to the "love of Christ" as the "bridegroom" of his "bride" the church, right worship of God was the equivalent of "the evangelical doctrine," and the reform of the congregation or people was equivalent to "the reformation."[11] It could be said from a historical

10. We use a photocopy of the 1513 edition (Jacques Lefèvre d'Étaples, *Quincuplex Psalterium* [Geneva: Droz, 1979]). This work covers the entire 150 Psalms and each page of the text contrasts three main Psalms texts (French, Roman, and Hebrew) on the top and the commentary below includes "Titulus"; "Expositio"; "Concordia," which examines the New Testament citations of the Psalms; and "Adverte," which includes exegetical comments. Lefèvre's Christological exegesis on Psalm 31:9 caused a controversy involving Erasmus. The quotation here is taken from the prefatory letter to the 1524 Psalms edition (Rice, ed., *Prefatory Epistles*, 476). For Lefèvre's hermeneutics of the Psalms commentary, see H. A. Oberman, *Forerunners of the Reformation: The Shape of Late Medieval Thought* (New York: Rinehart and Winston, 1966), 281–301; Hughes, *Lefèvre*, 56–68; and S. M. Porrer, ed., *Jacques Lefèvre d'Étaples and the Three Maries Debates* (Geneva: Droz, 2009), 24–25.

11. *Quincuplex Psalterium*, 6r (Ps 4/5), 9v (Ps 8/9), 32v (Ps 21/22), 34v (Ps 22/23), 69r (Ps 44/45), 108r (Ps 73/74), 147r (Ps 101/102).

perspective that Lefèvre's church concept was inherited by Luther's "congregation of believers," which was the principal definition of the church in the Reformation, as well as by Farel's congregationalist concept and perhaps by Calvin's church concept expressed in the apology portion of the first *Institutes*.

(ii) Lefèvre took a step further into the field of theology by publishing *St. Paul's XIV Epistles* (*St. Pauli Epistolae XIV*, 1512). The work was based upon the official Vulgate text and accompanied by his own Latin translation in consultation with Greek texts. To each of the Pauline epistles, including Hebrews, he added a "commentary" (*commentarius*) on the text as well as an "examination" (*examinatio*) that amounted to textual criticism. Appearing four years prior to Erasmus's famous Greek New Testament (*Novum instrumentum*, 1516), it questioned Jerome's authorship of the Vulgate translation, criticized the fourfold meanings of the text favored by Scholasticism, and emphasized the combination of the text's literal and spiritual exegesis based upon the Christocentric hermeneutic principle. What he had intended was to separate humanist hermeneutics from the fourfold meanings of Scholasticism. This is what Erasmus would do later in his Greek New Testament in ridiculing Scholastic theologians as those who were satisfied with "Jerome's interpretation." As a "forerunner" of the Reformation, Lefèvre made his contribution by emphasizing and restoring the study of the original texts of Scripture which, in turn, refreshed Catholic theology at the beginning of the French Reformation.[12]

Concerning the theory of justification, for example, though the work contained some bold references to what was to be later known as Luther's teaching of justification by faith, there were other references that acknowledged the salvific efficacy of good works. Thus, the work as a whole seemed to favor the double justification theory.[13] Concerning the Lord's Supper, the work contained neither extensive arguments on the subject nor clear criticism of the Mass or transubstantiation, but it did show some remarkable notions that could be viewed as challenging the official teachings of the Catholic Church. Commenting on Hebrews chapter 7 (26–28), for example, Lefèvre emphasized the once-and-for-all nature of Christ's sacrifice on the cross, encouraged the celebration of the Lord's Supper to be the "memory or recollection" (*memoria*

12. Oberman, *Forerunners*, 297–307; Rice, *Prefatory Epistles*, xx–xxi; Hughes, *Lefèvre*, 69–81; Porrer, *Jacques Lefèvre d'Étaples*, 25–28. Cf. Erasmus, *Methodus*, LB V, 78B: "Mihi satis est interpretatio Hieronymi."

13. Concerning comparison with Luther on justification, Hughes (*Lefèvre*, 96–98) emphasizes affinity, while a more acceptable view of the double justification theory is presented by Rice (Rice, *Prefatory Epistles*, xxii–xxiii; "Jacques Lefèvre d'Étaples and the Medieval Christian Mystics," 98–99); Bedouelle ("Jacques Lefèvre d'Étaples," 26), and others.

ac recordatio) of Christ's sacrifice instead of the current priestly repetitions of the sacrifice in the Mass, and emphatically announced that there should be no "other mystery" (*aliud mysterium*) in the celebration except the memory of Christ's death. On Hebrews chapter 10 (11–12), likewise, he reiterated that, in the New Testament sacrament of the Lord's Supper, the priest's duty should not be like that of Old Testament priests who repeated sacrifice, but should be the exercise of frequent "memory and imitation" (*memoria et imitatio*) or "imitation of innumerable benefits" (*imitatio inumera beneficia*) of Christ's sacrifice until his second coming. It was indeed a witness of Lefèvre's radicalism that, at the dawn of the Reformation in 1512, he challenged the Catholic Mass and appealed to the faithful communicants to remember Christ's sacrificial love as well as the practice of one's own love toward one's neighbors.[14] Nonetheless, despite some radical notions found here and there, his first theological work, which could also be the first source to ascertain his ecclesiology, showed no radicalism as such. Rather, he seemed to have avoided theologically explicit comments on the Catholic Church or its church structure, and even his comments on the Pauline texts relevant to the notion of the church focused on the linguistic analyses and spiritual meanings of the texts.[15]

(iii) The second stage of Lefèvre's trajectory to evangelicalism was his leadership in the Meaux reform. The reform movement had roughly spanned from the time his patron, Briçonnet, started serious reform of his Meaux bishopric around 1521, through its apex and crisis in 1523, to its practical dissolution in 1525. The movement was recognized by King Francis I and enthusiastically supported by his sister Marguerite of Angoulême. Since its chief aim was educational reform of the parish based upon the French Bible, accordingly its characteristic feature took the form of a preaching movement. Lefèvre's activity during this period could be viewed from two aspects, namely, his leadership of the Meaux reform and his biblical studies. Concerning the first aspect, he moved his residence to the bishopric in 1521, gathered a reformist group of associates around him, and led the reform. Among the so-called "Meaux group," what we called the French evangelical humanists in the previous chapter, were

14. Jacob Faber Stapulensis, *S. Pauli Epistolae XIV ex Vulgata, Adiecta Intelligentia ex Graeco, cum Commentariis* (Stuttgart: Frommann Helzboog, 1978), 243r, 250v. Cf. Hughes, *Lefèvre*, 87–92; Bedouelle, "Jacques Lefèvre d'Étaples," 27–28. In these texts, while Hughes sees affinity with Zwingli's eucharistic view, Bedouelle rejects it and rather sees harmony with the contemporary Catholic position.

15. Our impression is drawn from an examination of the key Pauline texts on the church (Rom 12:4–8; 1 Cor 12:27–31; Eph 1:20–23, 4:10–11, 5:26–29; Col 1:15–20) and their corresponding comments (97r–97v, 125v–126v, 163v–164v, 168r, 170v–171r, 182v–183r).

Louis de Berquin, a well-known translator of Erasmus and Luther, Lefèvre's disciples Gérard Roussel, Guillaume Farel, as well as the unusual cases of Paris theological doctors, Pierre Caroli and Martial Mazurier (Masurier). In general, the group's aim was practical parish reform within the framework of the existing Catholic Church.[16] Concerning the second aspect, the result of his biblical studies had established his reputation both as a biblical scholar and a controversialist. Having already caused the "three Marias controversy" by publishing *On Mary Magdalene* (*De Maria Magdalena*) in 1518, during this period he published two important works, *Commentaries on the Four Gospels* (*Commentarii initiatorii in quatuor Evangelia*, 1522) and the French translation of the New Testament (*Nouveau Testament*, 1523), which left a considerable imprint upon the early French Reformation.

(iv) The "three Marias controversy," which began right after Luther's *Ninety-Five Theses*, was about the current practice of venerating Mary Magdalene. Lefèvre understood this practice as combining the biblical figure of Mary Magdalene with the other two Marys (Mary of Bethany and a woman who anointed Jesus's feet with oil) into one Saint Mary whom he judged as unbiblical. Although his intention was to academically question the biblical authenticity of the church practice, the issue became a big controversy involving Beda of the Paris Faculty of Theology and Bishop John Fisher of England.[17] An interesting aspect of the controversy was that Lefèvre posted at the end of *On Mary Magdalene* a dialogue with his "special and close friend" in which he expressed his own view on the veneration of the saints. Incidentally, there has been a theory that this "friend" was indeed Farel who, in his later recollection, recorded his advice to Lefèvre which accused him of "papal idolatry" and, as a result, caused Lefèvre to turn to serious biblical studies.[18] Besides this identity issue of the

16. Cf. Hughes, *Lefèvre*, 94–96, 133–34; J. E. Olson, "Briçonnet, Guillaume," *OER* 1:216–17; Henry Heller, "Meaux," *OER* 3:36–37; J. K. Farge, *Biographical Register of Paris Doctors of Theology, 1500–1536* (Toronto: Pontifical Institute of Mediaeval Studies, 1980), 65–71, 318–21. The Meaux Diocese's condition at the time of Briçonnet's appointment was as such that more than half of the 130 clerics were considered either absent clerics or unfit for preaching. Those who were called by Lefèvre were thought to be the "evangelical humanists." Among them, the ordained priests such as Roussel and Caroli were appointed to parishes, but the unordained like Farel received the permit for preaching. It was said that, throughout the Diocese, the biblical preaching in French had been regularly heard between 1518 and 1523.

17. For this controversy, see Porrer's comments as well as the interlinear Latin text in this English translation (Porrer, ed., *Jacques Lefèvre d'Étaples*, 33–50, 155–253).

18. Guillaume Farel, *Du vray usage de la croix de Iesus-Christ* (Geneva: Kessinger Publishing, 1865/1980), 129–30, 170–73. Farel's testimony was not intended to be a historical record. On the validity of the testimony, Porrer (*Jacques Lefèvre d'Étaples*, 50n151) cautiously

"friend," crucially important was Lefèvre's intention to record the dialogue. Although officially he was said to have avoided making his view on venerating the statues and images of Christ or the saints known, in the dialogue he recorded his friend's witness on this subject. As the witness, his friend acknowledged that he did bend his knees before the statues of the saints, just like the faithful did in his day. In his "spirit" (*mens*), however, he held that he worshipped Christ present behind the statues. From this point, then, Lefèvre introduced his own distinction between "to worship" (*adorare*) and "to venerate" (*venerare*). In emphasizing this distinction, he cited the friend's comment on the Virgin Mary, "while by spirit venerating her as Mother of God, it is to worship God's and the Virgin's son [Christ] positively and with all might."[19]

The distinction, which was thought to be Lefèvre's own, perhaps originated in the transitional period from his philosophical to biblical studies during which he translated into Latin part 3 of *The Fount of Wisdom*, a main work of Greek theologian John of Damascus (Johannes Damascenus), titled *The Orthodox Faith* (*De Orthodoxa Fide*) in 1507. John of Damascus was a chief contributor in establishing the orthodox dogma on the veneration of icons during the Second Council of Nicea (the seventh ecumenical council, 787) that practically put an end to the iconoclastic controversy in Eastern Christendom. His main argument was based upon a Christological emphasis of the incarnation. From this point he discussed the unique nature of Christian worship in distinction from Old Testament worship under the commandment against image-worship (Exod 20:4–5). Since God himself nullified the second commandment of the Law in Christ's incarnation, John of Damascus argued, in Christian worship the faithful could "worship" Christ (and his mother and the saints) in the veneration of his icon. We assume that Lefèvre used this Christological argument in his search for the identity of his evangelicalism. In the polarization of the moderate and radical humanists described in the previous chapter, the issue of this distinction between worship and veneration had become crucially important along with the issues of "Rome" and "Luther," and Lefèvre could have supplied the theoretical basis for the moderate humanists. In other words, the issue was either to accept this distinction, which was

---

questions it, but Van Raalte (Zuidema and Van Raalte, *Early French Reform*, 72–74) takes it affirmatively.

19. Porrer, ed., *Jacques Lefèvre d'Étaples*, 243–51, esp. 248: "quam mens veneretur vt dei matrem; dei autem virginisque filium, tota prona, pro virili adoret." Despite the fact that Lefèvre raised the issue of the Mary Magdalene cult, the book concluded with his own affirmation of the Virgin Mary cult by the phrase, "veneramus sum." Since Farel later rejected this distinction, Roussel might be more suitable for this "friend."

the official doctrine of the Roman Catholic Church for justifying the current Catholic practices, or to reject it and to judge Catholic practices as idolatry. In the prospect of the French Reformation, it was a crucial point against which Calvin would take a critical stand in the first piece of *Two Epistles* on worship and in his later anti-Nicodemite works.[20]

Lefèvre on Church Reform

(i) In his trajectory to evangelicalism around 1519, it is said that Lefèvre experienced a turning point concerning his view on the so-called human traditions of the church in the midst of the three Marys controversy. Clear evidences of this change could be seen in his works of the Meaux reform period, *Commentaries on the Four Gospels*, and the French translation of the New Testament. In the preface "To Christian Readers," the *Commentaries* declared the basic tone of evangelicalism:

> The word of Christ is the word of God, the gospel of peace, liberty, and joy, the gospel of salvation, redemption, and life. That is, [the gospel of] peace out of perpetual war, liberty out of cruelest bondage, joy out of endless sorrow, and furthermore, [the gospel of] salvation out of total perdition, redemption out of the most wretched captivity, and then, life out of endless death.

Referring to "human commands and teachings" (Col 2:22), the preface then implicitly criticized the Catholic teaching on human traditions and affirmed that "the word of God is sufficient." Since "the Early Church made no regulations except the gospel," there was no need of creaturely, human makings and teachings in Christian worship.[21] Although the basic evangelical tone

20. Cf. Pelikan, *The Christian Tradition*, 2:106–7, 118–20, 132; J. W. Brush, "Lefèvre d'Étaples: Three Phases of His Life and Work," in *Reformation Studies*, ed. F. H. Littell (Richmond: John Knox, 1962), 122; Hughes, *Lefèvre*, 28–29.

21. Rice, ed., *The Prefatory Epistles*, 434–37, esp. 434: "Verbum autem Christi verbum Dei est, evangelium pacis, libertatis et laetitiae evangelium salutis, redemptionis et vitae. Pacis, inquam, ex bello perpetuo, libertatis ex durissima servitude, Laetitiae ex luctu indeficiente, salutis ex summa perditione, redemptionis ex miserrima captivitate, et denique vitae ex intermina morte." (Translation is our own.) Cf. Farge, *Orthodoxy*, 172; Hughes, *Lefèvre*, 154–56. According to Rice (441n8), the last quotation ("Primaria Ecclesia . . . nullam regulam praeter Evangelium novit.") was listed as the first of eleven errors drawn up by the Theological Faculty of Paris against Lefèvre.

declared in the preface can be seen at every turn, as to comments that indicate Lefèvre's evangelical concept of the church, we will selectively focus on three commentaries from Matthew's Gospel.

Commenting on "strive first for the kingdom of God and his righteousness" (6:33), Lefèvre declared that "God's kingdom is the kingdom of Christ, his justice is justice of the new law" and expressed his own view of double justification. Since justice in the gospel was double, consisting in both "justification by works" and "justification by faith," the former justice was acquired by the faithful in imitating Christ's examples and keeping his commandments, and the latter was nothing but grace, justified by God and faith and resulting in good works.[22] Commenting on the parable of the mustard seed (13:31–32) to which he claimed to add "spiritual understanding," some interesting aspects of his evangelical concept of the church appeared. For example, "a mustard seed" was interpreted as "God's word, faith in Christ, the new law, holy and innocent religion," "sower" as "Christ the Lord," "field" as "understanding of the faithful," and a "seed" sown in a good field as Christianity, which was grown from its smallest beginning and was contrasted with other religions of superstitions and errors. Furthermore, the grown up "tree" was interpreted as "people gathered together by faith, the universal church of believers from the whole world," and its "branches" as "particular churches" in various countries.[23] It is interesting to notice here that Lefèvre conceived both the universal (Catholic) church and the particular churches from the basic perspective of faithful believers.

(ii) Even though Lefèvre's *Commentaries* had no explicitly critical comments on the Roman Catholic Church's teachings and hierarchical structure, a challenging exception could be seen in his comment on the Petrine text (16:16–19). From his comment we are not certain whether he was conscious of Erasmus's *New Testament* (1st edition of 1516 or 2nd edition of 1519) or not, but if he were indeed, the comment presented a clearer evangelical interpretation than Erasmus did. Lefèvre began his comment with Peter's confession, "You are the Messiah, the Son of the living God," which he interpreted as a "confession of being not from man but infused from God," thus emphasizing its God-given nature. Then he went on to connect Peter with the "rock," and affirmed that due to the confession's God-given nature Jesus gave Simon the

22. *Commentarii Initiatorii in Quatuor Evangelia*, 32v: "Regnum dei, regnum Christi. Iustitia eius, iustitia novae legis. Et haec duplex: quaedam operum, quam imitando Christum, et mandata eius implendo, assequimur. Altera fidei, qua a deo et iustificamur. Et haec iustitia, gratiae est, et fidem consummatam sequitur, ut opera bona virtus." Our text is not the first edition (1522), but the second Basel edition (1523).

23. *Commentarii Initiatorii in Quatuor Evangelia*, 61v.

name, Peter, denoting the "rock." The comment's conclusion on this point, however, was quite radical. It affirmed that, as seen in Peter as an example, "the Lord founds his own church on the rock, that is, true and solid faith" of all believers. The comment implicitly rejected the view that made Peter's faith an "unwavering exemplar," citing the text (16:23) in which Jesus rebuked Peter right after his confession. Lefèvre expanded the implication of the text's "rock" to the faith of all believers by citing the last part of the Sermon on the Mount, "everyone then who hears these words of mine . . . builds his house on rock" (7:24). Though Lefèvre's interpretation of "rock" emphatically pointed to the faith of all believers, it should be remembered that his comment also left room for Augustine's interpretation of "rock" as Christ based upon the Pauline text of 1 Corinthians (10:4). This could be an indication that he was consciously challenging Erasmus's interpretation that cited Augustine's interpretation but ultimately rejected it.[24]

Secondly, Lefèvre's comment on the issue of "the keys of the kingdom of heaven" (16:19) or "the power of the keys" was noteworthy as to his evangelical concept of the church. Here, the comment defined "the keys" as "the keys of faith" (*clavis fidei*), then interpreted "binding and loosing" which was theologically interpreted as the exercise of the power of the keys to determine and to forgive sin "not belonging to Peter, but to Christ," emphasizing the exercise of the keys based not on Peter's will but on the best and infallible will of Christ. Lastly, the comment concluded with a statement, "not Peter alone received it [the power of the keys], but all others who would build the church by faith and according to the Lord's will have received it." Lefèvre's comment on the Petrine text as a whole clearly went beyond the logical and rhetorical analyses and presented a far more radical evangelical position than Erasmus's polished and balanced hermeneutics.[25]

24. *Commentarii Initiatorii in Quatuor Evangelia*, 74r–74v. As Renaudet (*Humanisme et Renaissance*, 211–12) and Bedouelle ("Jacques Lefèvre d'Étaples," 25) indicate, Lefèvre's biblical hermeneutics differed considerably from that of Erasmus. Since his comment on the Hebrews in the *St. Paul's 14 Epistles* caused a controversy with Erasmus, it was said that he had taken notice of Erasmus's hermeneutics. If he was conscious of Erasmus's interpretations on this text, he countered them by adding the concluding passage of the Sermon on the Mount, Jesus's scolding of Peter, and Paul's testimony, which were not used by Erasmus. His focus could be on Erasmus's interpretation of Peter's confession: Erasmus took it as Peter's "profession of solid faith" (*hoc est solidam istam fidei professionem*) as his own view in the first edition of the *New Testament*, but in the second edition altered it by adding a phrase, "steadfast Peter represented the solid faith of the church" (*Petrus saxeus solidam ecclesiae fidem repraesent*), an interpretation more aligned with the Roman Catholic view.

25. *Commentarii Initiatorii in Quatuor Evangelia*, 74v. The fact that Lefèvre left room

In particular, what was noticeable was Lefèvre's consistent accent on the theme of believers and their congregation, the theme that was echoed in the Meaux reform emphasizing the raising of the parish faithful who heard the Bible, learned its teachings, and practiced them, as well as in Farel's congregationalism that we will describe later. As a matter of course, the *Commentaries* was subjected to the heresy hearing of the Paris Theological Faculty. In 1526, the Faculty's leading member Beda also attacked Lefèvre's *St. Paul's 14 Epistles* along with Erasmus's *New Testament Paraphrases* as heretical works. While Erasmus responded to Beda with a series of exchanges, Lefèvre avoided dispute and maintained his silence under the protection of the royal household.[26]

(iii) The French translation of the New Testament appeared at the peak of the Meaux reform in 1523. The preface to its first part (the Gospels) was regarded as a masterpiece in which an aging humanist scholar freely expressed his conviction of evangelical faith. At the head of the preface, Lefèvre quoted "an acceptable time . . . a day of salvation" (2 Cor 6:2) and declared that "Jesus-Christ" (*Jesuchrist*) wished "the gospel to be purely announced in the entire world." By vernacular translation of the Bible, he said, "simplest members of the body of Jesus-Christ [the church] . . . could be assured of the evangelical truth." Touching on the necessity of reform and its guideline, furthermore, he affirmed that "in order to rectify the faults of Christianity, . . . one has to turn himself to him [Christ] in abandoning all confidence in creatures as well as in all human traditions which are not able to bring salvation, and in solely following the word of God which is spirit and life." Here we may find a terminal point of Lefèvre's trajectory to evangelicalism, and may conclude that as an amateur theologian he had reached a position close to Luther's Evangelicalism. In this respect, we also witness here a kind of radicalism that later enabled Farel to make his transition to Evangelicalism, as we will describe below.[27]

---

for Augustine's interpretation of "this rock" as "Christ himself" can be seen as his objection to Erasmus's view that "strictly speaking our interpretation of the words differs from Augustine's." Furthermore, one can see in Lefèvre's interpretation of "rock" and "the keys," which extended the text's implication to faithful believers in general, his objection to Cyprian's interpretation of Peter as "rock," "the one for all [believers]" (*unus pro omnibus*). While Erasmus added this reference to Cyprian as "Divine Cyprian" (*divus Cyprianus*) in the second edition of the *New Testament*, Lefèvre seemed to ignore Cyprian completely.

26. Farge, *Orthodoxy*, 171, 191–95; Renaudet, *Humanisme et Renaissance*, 213–14; Bedouelle, "Jacques Lefèvre d'Étaples," 30–31. Oberman's evaluation on Lefèvre (*Forerunners*, 291), "an admirer of Zwingli, familiar with Farel and the young Calvin, Faber [Lefèvre] never identified himself openly with the cause of the Reformation," needs to be balanced with regard to his contribution to the early French Reformation.

27. Rice, ed., *The Prefatory Epistles*, 449–50. Cf. Renaudet, *Humanisme et Renaissance*,

2. *Farel's Trajectory from the Meaux Reform to Evangelicalism*

(i) At the time Farel joined the Meaux reform in 1521 at Lefèvre's request, he was undoubtedly a Lefèvrian. In addition, the Collège du Cardinal Lemoine, where he had taught for several years following in his teacher's footsteps, was known as a prominent school of Lutheran influence. However, both the exact nature of Farel's involvement with the Meaux reform and the reason for his exit from the reform movement in 1522, a year before its apex and crisis of 1523, remain complex problems that need to be answered. In the previous chapter, we posed the two issues of "Rome" and "Luther" as touchstones for distinguishing the positions of the moderate and radical evangelical humanists in the early French Reformation. Concerning the "Rome" issue, the Meaux reform could hardly take an official stand since both Briçonnet and Lefèvre were close to the royal household and knew the king's religious policy that acknowledged the Roman papacy.

As reform had advanced into practical parish life, however, problems touching on the "Rome" issue, such as human traditions, caused tension within the movement. In addition, as we have seen, Lefèvre's rejection of human traditions was well known by this time, and the external influence from Evangelicalism of Luther and Zwingli was also felt by the movement. An important primary source of the Meaux reform, *The Epistles and the Gospels* (*Epistres et evangiles*, 1525) revealed some interesting pictures of the reform movement. This work, which was said to be coauthored by Lefèvre and his disciples, divided the church calendar into fifty-two Sundays, starting from Advent. For each Sunday it provided the New Testament passages from the epistles and the gospels, adding some comments on the passages and a summary of a preached message called "Exhortation." Its content as a whole depicted the movement's thoroughly evangelical and spiritual characteristic. It limited references to the Holy Mother and saints regularly seen in the Church Calendar, and expressed, though not overtly, such evangelical notions as justification by faith, Christian

213; Hughes, *Lefèvre*, 156–57. Lefèvre's historic French translation of the New Testament was published in two separate volumes in 1523. As early as August, it became an occasion for the Paris Theological Faculty's induction of the ban on the French translations of the Vulgate Bible. Its contribution to the Meaux reform and the French Reformation was widely affirmed. Rice (*The Prefatory Epistles*, xxiii–xxiv) considers Lefèvre's radicalism "under the influence of the Germans and Swiss." Citing Beda's derogatory remark about Lefèvre as "humanista theologizans," Rice provides a fair and overall assessment of Lefèvre's theology: "the complex play in his thought of tradition and innovation; and it cunningly places the professional teacher of philosophy and the liberal arts who reserved the best of his passion for amateur theology."

freedom, and the need for spiritual reform. For example, the twenty-third Sunday after Pentecost on the Philippians text (3:21) assured the faithful that "[Jesus Christ] will *reform* our humble body in conformity with the body of his glory according to the operation of his power."[28] Nonetheless, due to the hostile circumstances of the times for any humanist reform, it carefully avoided any references to the current Church structure or teachings, so as to be accepted by the French Church.

Despite the official heresy judgment of the Paris Theological Faculty, the "Luther" issue was not easily stilled. Infiltration of Luther's teaching was seen among the French humanists, and even at Meaux the need to counter it was felt inevitable. From the beginning, Briçonnet wanted a moderate type of reform and his swift reaction to the movement's radicalization and acceptance of Luther's teaching took the form of an Episcopal Decree (October) to the bishopric and a Prohibition (December) to the ministers in 1523. According to them, Luther's teaching was labeled a heresy disturbing "the Catholic Church's purity." As "a new teaching," it was criticized as disregarding church discipline by means of advocating for the self-determination of believers and attacking the veneration of the Holy Mother and saints. To the ministers, warning of the risk of excommunication, the Prohibition banned the preaching of "the Lutheran pest." From this occasion on, the Meaux reform stumbled as a preaching movement and Briçonnet gradually distanced himself from the reform. But interestingly he kept close ties with Lefèvre.[29] The case of Lefèvre, considered more progressive in church reform than Briçonnet, was unique in the sense that he had kept his silence without making any pronouncements, either approval or disapproval, on both Luther's teaching and the papacy or Mass. Yet he kept hoping for sincere reform of the French Church. The case of Farel, who inherited the radical aspects of Lefèvrianism, was quite different. He had obviously seen the movement's nonradical nature as well as its limits and decided to leave the movement a year before Briçonnet's countermeasures in 1522. In 1523, Farel chose exile in Basel.[30]

28. *Epistres & Evangiles*, 350. Cf. M. Mann, *Érasme et les débuts de la réforme française*, 108–10. We use here the later revised text of the Vingle edition (Jacques Lefèvre d'Étaples and his disciples, *Epistres & Evangiles pour les cinquante et deux dimenches de l'an*, ed. G. Bedouelle and F. Giacone [Leiden: Brill, 1976]) and not the original Du Bois edition of 1525. According to the editors, a prominent candidate for the anonymous "reviser" is Gérard Roussel.

29. *Epistres et Evangiles*, xix; Hughes, *Lefèvre*, 134–38; Bedouelle, "Jacques Lefèvre d'Étaples," 21. Cf. Screech, ed., *Épistres & Évangiles* (Facsimile, Du Bois edition), Geneva, 1964, 9–10, esp. n. 7.

30. Cf. P. Benedict, *Christ's Churches Purely Reformed: A Social History of Calvinism*

(ii) As to prospects for the future reform of the French Church, although Lefèvre was assumedly optimistic and Farel was definitely pessimistic, the real issue that separated these two cases seems to be more complex. On this issue, it seems appropriate to note that Higman distinguishes Lefèvre's "radical, but non-schismatic, evangelicalism" from Farel's "radical and schismatic reform."[31] Thus, the Meaux reform movement as a whole met the historic year 1525 in which it saw not only its dissolution as a movement, but also its supporter Francis I's captivity in Spain; the Paris Theological Faculty's heresy investigations of Berquin, Lefèvre, Roussel, Caroli, and others; and the heresy judgment on Lefèvre's French *New Testament* and *The Epistles and Gospels*.[32]

Farel's activities for over ten years from his exit from the Meaux reform to the start of his reform in Geneva can be summarized as the "formation of his church reform concept and its practice." To survey his trajectory during this period, there were a series of notable events: his exile in Basel, his friendship with Basel's Oecolampadius, his fellowship with Zurich's Zwingli and Strasbourg's Bucer and Capito, the Disputation in Basel that occasioned a conflict with Erasmus in 1524, and his first publication, *The Lord's Prayer and the Apostles' Creed in French* (*Le Pater noster & le Credo en francoys*, 1524). Furthermore, Farel's trajectory included being expelled from Basel, his reform in the French city of Montbéliard, and his ordination there as an evangelical minister called by Oecolampadius and Duke Ulrich of Würtemberg, count of Montbéliard. His activities of evangelization afterward were mostly concentrated

(New Haven and London: Yale University Press, 2002), 78; Eire, *War against the Idols*, 182–89. The dating of Farel's exit from the Meaux reform is not certain. According to the joint research project on Farel biography (*Guillaume Farel*, 101–6), he departed in 1522 and returned to his native Gap for evangelical activities. P. G. Bietenholz (*Basel and France in the Sixteenth Century* [Geneva and Toronto: Droz, 1971], 91) estimates Farel's exile in Basel as early as June 1523. Interestingly, Benedict considers Farel the first disciple who translated Lefèvre's criticism of Catholic worship into its logical conclusion, the rejection of the Church itself. Eire theorizes that the Lefèvrian reform was inherited by two groups: one, the moderates of Roussel and others who had avoided schism and advocated for restrained reform; the other, the radicals headed by Farel who had followed the radicalism of Lefèvre's last years.

31. Higman, *Lire et découvrir*, 62. Cf. Screech, ed., *Épistres et Évangiles*, 17; Bedouelle, "Jacques Lefèvre d'Étaples," 31. Concerning Lefèvre's radicalism, like Higman, Screech admits it and concludes that Farel chose the path of "the fundamental reform" instead of his teacher's moderation. On the other hand, rejecting the presence of radicalism in Lefèvre, seemingly shortsighted Bedouelle concludes that for Lefèvre "a renewal and unified reading of the Bible ought to be enough for the needed reformation of the church."

32. Higman, *Lire et découvrir*, 15–17, 63; Hughes, *Lefèvre*, 163–79; Screech, ed., *Épistres et Évangiles*, 13–18.

in the French-speaking territories of Switzerland bordering France, especially, under the protection of Bern, which became a powerful Evangelical state in southern Switzerland. His activities were extended to the Pays de Vaud and Geneva. As the result of his evangelization, Neuchâtel in 1530 and Geneva and Lausanne in 1536 had turned to the Protestant faith. In 1529, as a tentative completion of his theological formation in this period, Farel published his main work, *Summary and Brief Exposition* (*Summaire et briefve declaration*).[33]

(iii) Since we will analyze Farel's *Summary* in the next section, here we will briefly focus on three points that seem to illustrate his notion of the church during this period. The first point concerned the first published work of the French Reformation as well as of Farel, *The Lord's Prayer and the Apostles' Creed in French*. Using the French translation text of Luther's *Prayer Book* (*Betbüchlein*, 1523), *The Lord's Prayer* was intended for use in his evangelical work in Montbéliard and was published in Basel.[34] In his exposition on the Apostles' Creed, which closely followed Luther's original text, Farel placed the creed's article on the church in the third division of the Holy Spirit and interpreted the creed's "the holy catholic church" as "only one shared holy Christian church," just as Luther did as "eyne heylige gemeyne Christliche kirche," by changing "catholic" into "Christian." Just as Luther interpreted the creed's "communion of the saints" as "die gemeyne odder Samlung der trummen glaubigen menschen auff erden," Farel similarly spoke of "the company of holy believing persons on earth."[35] Since we assume that Farel had inherited Lefèvre's basic concept of the church, "the congregation of believers," his interpretation could be meant as agreeing with Luther's notion and presenting it positively as an Evangelical notion.

33. On the theme of Farel's theological formation, there seems to be no substantive research. Although Heyer's above-mentioned classical study is still useful, the recent work of Zuidema and Van Raalte (*Early French Reform*, 3–15) provides a general sketch, but without going into his background of Lefèvrianism. Among others, two studies attempt a theological analysis of Farel's *Summaire*: H. H. Esser, "Die Stellung des '*Summaire*' von Guillaume Farel innerhalb der frühen reformierten Bekenntnisschriften," in *Reformiertes Erbe*, ed. H. Oberman et al. [*Zwingliana* 19.1] (Zurich, 1992), 1:93–114; and R. White, "An Early Doctrinal Handbook: Farel's *Summaire et Briefve Declaration*," *Westminster Theological Journal* 69 (2007): 21–38. Concerning the first edition of the *Summary*, Doumergue (*Jean Calvin*, 2:153–54) entertains the possibility of an earlier edition (1526) that is said to be lost, we take the generally accepted view of 1529. As to Farel's ordination, we follow Higman's article ("Farel, Guillaume," *OER* 2:99–100) and we do not take Kelly's position (*The Beginning*, 113) which, without providing references, assumes that Farel was ordained by the "popular ordination" of the Montbéliard Church.

34. Cf. F. Higman, ed., *Le Pater Noster et le Credo en françoys* (Geneva: Droz, 1982); its English translation in Zuidema and Van Raalte, *Early French Reform*, 105–16.

35. *WA* 10/2:393; Zuidema and Van Raalte, *Early French Reform*, 115.

The second point concerned Farel's association with the Reformers, especially Oecolampadius, Zwingli, Bucer, and Capito, and their possible contribution to Farel's ecclesiology. For example, it has often been assumed among researchers that Farel took Zwingli's view of the Lord's Supper, and that on the question of ecclesiology he was indebted to Oecolampadius. At the time of Farel's exile, Basel was a highly esteemed city of a famous university, Renaissance culture, and a center of publishing houses. Among its residents there were many humanists represented by the famous Erasmus, the Anabaptists, and free-thinkers of various sorts. As to its Reformation, its well-known Pastor Oecolampadius began to lecture on Isaiah at the university. Professionally trained in both law and theology, Oecolampadius was known as an excellent humanist, an associate of Erasmus in the publication of the monumental *New Testament* (1516), and the author of his own *Greek Grammar* (1518). As an ordained priest, while he was serving as a confessor at Weinsberg, which was under Duke Ulrich of Würtemberg, he had developed his ideas concerning church discipline. As to his Evangelicalism, he clearly sided with Luther in the conflict with the Catholic theologians. Yet he was also known as "a mediating theologian" in the case of the Luther-Zwingli conflict on the Lord's Supper, and as a Reformer of close association with the Anabaptists, such as Karlstadt, Balthasar Hubmaier, and Hans Denck.[36] As to Oecolampadius's actual relationship with Farel, he set the stage for Farel to hold a disputation on thirteen theses, including the issues of biblical authority, monastic order, and church liturgy. In 1524, he arranged meetings for Farel with Zwingli, Bucer, and Capito. He took care of Farel's conflict with Erasmus and opened the way for Farel to serve in Montbéliard after his expulsion from Basel. As to the complicated problem of his influence on Farel's ecclesiology, however, we will wait for our later analysis of the *Summary* as the primary material for our assessment.[37]

The third point concerned Farel's encounter with Erasmus in June 1524 and their heated exchange of opinions over his previous disputation in Basel. The conflict was occasioned by Farel's criticism in the disputation in which he not only criticized the Roman Catholic Church but also Erasmus, who enjoyed high esteem and wide support among humanists in the city. As a result, the conflict revealed a gap between the moderate reformist position of Erasmus and that of Farel and Oecolampadius, which was more open to Luther's Evan-

36. Cf. E. Staehelin, *Das theologische Lebenswerk Johannnes Oekolampads* (Leipzig, 1939; New York and London: Johnson, 1971), 68, 97, 120–21; R. C. Walton, "Oecolampadius, Johannes," *OER* 3:169–71; T. A. Fudge, "Icarus of Basel? Oecolampadius and the Early Swiss Reformation," *Journal of Religious History* 21 (1997): 272–75.

37. Cf. Heyer, *Guillaume Farel*, 18–27; Zuidema and Van Raalte, *Early French Reform*, 9–11.

gelicalism. In particular, according to Augustijn's examination of this conflict, a noticeable difference appeared concerning Farel's seventh thesis on the Disputation on human traditions. While Farel insisted on the need to remove such practices unwarranted by Scripture from the church, Erasmus challenged him over the need of an objective standard to discern human traditions and upheld the possibility of the church's right to judge and to retain some church practices as permissible. Concerning an objective standard of Scripture, Farel was said to appeal to the principle of the Holy Spirit by decrying against Erasmus "the Holy Spirit, the Holy Spirit," insisting that those who were led and illuminated by the Holy Spirit could have spiritual understanding of Scripture. While Farel's position could be roughly interpreted as Augustine's principle of "Scripture interprets Scripture," Erasmus was said to insist that room be accorded for judgments of scriptural interpreters on the text, as well as for the church's decisions led by the Holy Spirit on the matters of indifference.[38] The fact that the encounter was not a public event but a private discussion and, above all, that its record came solely from Erasmus, could be problematic to researchers. However, it is interesting to note that the conflict revealed different views on human traditions between Erasmus and the Lefèvrianism that Farel had inherited.

3. *An Ecclesiological Analysis of Farel's Summary*

The *Summary* (1529) remained not only the representative work of Farel's early reformatory activities but also the sole work, though in various editions, which presented his theology as a whole in a rather systematic form. Nonetheless, it was not intended to be a systematic theology in a professional sense, but a compilation of major apologetic points, practical guidelines, declarations, and witnesses gathered from his reformatory activities since 1524. The period before and after the publication of Farel's work was what Higman considers "the key" for assessment of the early French Reformation, the period in which

38. P. G. Bietenholz, *Basel and France*, 42–43; C. Augustijn, "Erasmus und Farel in Konflikt," in *Erasmus: Der Humanist als Theologe und Kirchenreformer* (Leiden, New York and Cologne: Brill, 1996), 233–41. Cf. Herminjard, *Correspondance*, 1, no. 91, 194: "Opprimit ille Evangelium, qui illud incerium facit, ac illum pudet Christi"; Doumergue, *Jean Calvin*, 2:152–53. While Bietenholz views this conflict as that between Erasmianism and the Evangelicalism of Oecolampadius and Farel, Augustijn views it basically as the ideological conflict between Erasmus and the Lefèvrian Farel. Furthermore, Augustijn's historical analysis places this conflict as a preliminary skirmish for Erasmus's launching of the anti-Lutheran polemic on free will in the following year.

Lefèvrianism underwent a polarizing process between the "non-schismatic" and "schismatic" groups. Farel's work was considered the representative of the latter group. In addition, along with Calvin's first *Institutes*, this was a primary source for understanding the early Genevan Reformation, especially its three church documents that we will analyze in our next section. In view of this context, the following pages will examine the second edition of Farel's *Summary* (1534) that was closer to the Genevan Reformation.[39]

The general characteristic of the *Summary* could be said to be a combination of Lefèvrianism as its basic stratum and Evangelicalism selectively taken from Luther, Zwingli, Oecolampadius, and others. Lefèvre's characteristic notions were reflected in the work's overall structure and main doctrines of Scripture, Christ, faith, and especially in the antithetical presentation of materials observed in the first fifteen of the work's entire forty-two chapters. The presentation was meant to contrast sharply between the true and false religions and had been widely used by Lefèvre in his biblical commentaries, as well as in *The Epistles and Gospels*. In the *Summary*, the contrast was seen in "God and man" (1–2), "Christ in his divinity and humanity" (3), "Law and gospel" (4–5), "sin and justice" (6–7), "flesh and spirit" (8–9), "unbelief and faith" (10–11), "good works and grace" (12–13), and "human traditions and scripture" (14–15).[40] The *Summary*'s point of contact with Luther's teachings could be especially seen in its clear Evangelical notions of Scripture and salvation. Although the notions could also be seen in Lefèvre, it showed no evidence of ambiguity about the doctrine of justification by faith or hesitation to step into the "Rome" issue as seen in Lefèvre's work. In general, Farel's understanding of the sacraments was seemingly based upon Lefèvrianism, but was also aligned with Zwingli's and Oecolampadius's view that he was said to take up at the time of his exile in Basel. As to the Lord's Supper, Farel described it as "the holy table of our Lord" and contrasted it with the Catholic Mass as "Satan's invention." Over against

39. Although the photocopy of the original edition (A. Piaget, ed., *Summaire et briefve declaration* [Paris: Droz, 1935]) and the modern French edition (A.-L. Hofer, ed., *Sommaire et brève declaration* [Neuchâtel: Droz, 1980]) are available, we use the second edition edited by Baum (J.-G. Baum, ed., *Le Sommaire de Guillaume Farel* [Geneva: Jules-Guillaume Fick, 1867]). Our references to the text will be headed with the original title (*Summaire*), then chapters and pages in the Baum edition. For the historical context of its publication, confer Higman's article (*Lire et découvrir*, "Dates-clé de la Réforme française: *Le Sommaire* de Guillaume Farel et *La somme de l'escripture saincte*," 53–63) and Zuidema and Van Raalte, *Early French Reform*, 3–15.

40. Although both White ("An Early Doctrinal Handbook," 23) and Zuidema and Van Raalte (*Early French Reform*, 19–20) notice this antithetical presentation, they do not trace its origin back to Lefèvre and the *Epistles and Gospels*.

the Mass as the repeated "sacrifice" of Christ, he emphasized Lefèvre's emphasis of the Supper's memorial aspect, remembering Christ's sacrificial death on the cross, as well as exercising Christ's love among Christians. As to the technical issue of Christ's presence in the Supper, there was no elaboration on the issue. But Farel does employ an expression that could be taken as Zwingli's emphasis on Christ's bodily presence after his ascension: ". . . heaven, where he [Lord Jesus] *is presently sitting* [*est de present assis*] at the right hand of his Father." The overall impression of Farel's view on the sacraments, especially on the Lord's Supper, however, is Lefèvrian: since he characterized the participation of the believers in the Supper as "recollecting and remembering" (*racomptantz & rememorantz*) Christ's death, the expression could reflect "memory or recollection" and "memory and imitation" of Lefèvre's *St. Paul's XIV Epistles*.[41]

Out of forty-two chapters in total, what we may call the second part of the *Summary*, chapters 16–36, presented Farel's basic ideas concerning the church, even though it could hardly be called a systematic presentation or an ecclesiology. This part could be divided into three sections. It began with a section on the church and its power and sacraments (16–18), followed by an apologetic section on the Catholic teachings on the sacraments, good works, and veneration of the saints (19–31), and concluded with a section on excommunication and pastors in the Evangelical church (32–36). Except for the last two chapters, each chapter presented a clear contrast between the Catholic teaching and the Evangelical teaching. We assume that this part as a whole reflected Farel's comprehensive concept of the church in a sketch that represented a unique type in the early French Reformation, distinctive from both Lefèvrianism and Calvin's ecclesiology. In the following pages, we will examine the three sections in order to ascertain his overall concept of the church.

Basic Ideas of the Church, Chapters 16–18

(i) The first section concerned Farel's basic ideas of the church, its power, and sacraments (16–18). Concerning this section's structure, first of all, since the *Summary* neither cited nor used the Apostles' Creed, chapter 16 on the church had no reference to the creed's "the holy Catholic church" or the concept of

41. *Summaire*, chs. 18–19. (Zudema and Van Raalte, *Early French Reform*, 34–37.) Cf. Heyer, *Guillaume Farel*, 58; C. Elwood, *The Body Broken: The Calvinist Doctrine of the Eucharist and the Symbolization of Power in Sixteenth-Century France* (New York and Oxford: Oxford University Press, 1999), 31–32; E. Jacobs, "Die Abendmahlslehre Wilhelm Farels," in *Actes du Colloque Guillaume Farel*, ed. P. Barthel et al. (Geneva: Droz, 1983), 1:161–71.

catholicity of the church. Secondly, if we look at this section from the notion of the church's marks, as chapter 17, "The Keys of the Heavenly Kingdom," dealt with God's word and chapter 18 with the sacraments, these two chapters seemingly presented the two-marks theory of the church that Farel likely inherited from his Reformation background of Luther, Zwingli, and Oecolampadius. From a careful analysis of the text, however, an overall picture of Farel's ideas of the church seemed to emerge. Basically, he had inherited the concepts of Lefèvre and the Meaux reform, radicalized them, and selectively incorporated the Evangelical concepts of Luther and others into them. Concerning chapter 16, for example, by using a characteristic Lefèvrian term "Jesus-Christ" (*Jesuchrist*) Farel defined the church:

> The Church of Jesus-Christ is the holy congregation of the faithful who by true faith are united and incorporated into Jesus-Christ, of whom they are members. And even though Jesus is the true Son of God, all his members are, by him, sons of God. Jesus is the head, and true Christians are his body. He is the bridegroom; the faithful are his bride whom he has purified by his blood. His blood gave life to his body and saved his people from their sins.[42]

This definition, "the congregation of believers," was inherited from Lefèvre, shared with Luther and Zwingli, and was to be present later in the Genevan *Confession of Faith.*

Concerning this definition, an interesting point regarding the church's holiness appeared. Referring to Ephesians, especially the passage (5:27) where the wedding analogy of Christ and his spouse the church was referenced, Farel said, "Jesus is the head, and true Christians are his body. He is the bridegroom [*lespoux*], believers are his bride [*espouse*] whom he has purified by his blood." In other words, he interpreted the Ephesians passage "the church . . . in splendor, without a spot or wrinkle" as "Christian believers" in their historical existence.[43] In this connection, another interesting point appeared.

42. Zuidema and Van Raalte, *Early French Reform*, 132. The French text can be found in *Summaire*, chs. 16, 31: "Leglise de Iesuchrist est la saincte congregation des fideles, qui par vraye foy sont vniz & incorporez a Iesuchrist, duquel ilz sont membres. Et pourtant que Iesus est vray filz de Dieu, tous ses membres par luy sont filz de Dieu. Iesus est le chief, les vrays chrestiens sont son corps. Il est lespouz, les fides son espouse, laquelle il a purgee par son sang, donnant salut a son corps, sauuant son peuple de leurs pechez." Cf. *Confession de la foy*, *OS* 1:424.

43. *Summaire*, 31. Although Lefèvre's comments on Ephesians (5:26–27; *S. Pauli Epistolae XIV*, 171v–172r) interpreted "Christ's bride" to be "the church" and not "believers," the

In Farel's background of Lefèvre, Luther, Zwingli, and Oecolampadius, the historical concept of the church as the "congregation of believers" was often contrasted with its opposite, suprahistorical concept of the "assembly of the elect." However, this chapter had no reference to the elect at all, and the only reference to the elect appeared in the *Summary*'s very last chapter on the day of judgment.[44] This could mean that Farel emphasized only one side of the Augustinian synthesis of the elect and believers, accordingly showed no interest in the church's suprahistorical reality or catholicity, and instead focused on the historical and objective reality of the church. Although he titled the chapter "The Church," he chose "the faithful members of Jesus" instead of "the church" as the subject of many sentences in the chapter. For example, the idea that faithful members should live not for themselves but "for others" and the church's ministry of exhortation, correction, and so forth was described from the congregational viewpoint as the ministry of faithful members, as well as "for edification of others." In short, the chapter's two characteristic notions of congregational principle and the service of believers to others were what he had inherited as the ideals of the church from Lefèvre and the Meaux reform, which he then adopted for the Evangelical church.[45]

(ii) As Farel titled the next chapter (17) "The Keys of the Kingdom of Heaven" and described "the keys" as "the knowledge of God, the word of God, the holy gospel and the pasture of souls," it is reasonable to assume that he presented the chapter as the first mark of the church. In terms of "believers," here again he focused on believers as those to whom God sent the Holy Spirit, enabled them to understand Scripture, and gave them the keys through their hearing of the gospel. Accordingly, he emphasized the decisive role of believers to whom the door of heaven was opened, while the door was closed to those who did not believe.[46] There seem to be two noticeable points in this

Epistles and the Gospels (e.g., *Epistres et Evangiles*, 3A, 14; Cf. 59B, 338–39) often expressed the believers' regeneration and sanctification in terms of their nuptial union with Christ.

44. Farel's *Summary* shared with the *Epistles and Gospels* two interesting notions concerning the elect: a predominant emphasis on believers and their congregation, but not on the elect; however, the elect were mentioned in the eschatological context, as the *Epistles and Gospel* (*Epistres et Evangiles*, 3A, 13. Cf. 56B, 324; 59B, 338) affirmed that "Les secrets de la justification serent revéles au dernier jour. Ne jugeons donc pas."

45. *Summaire*, chs. 16, 32. (Zuidema and Van Raalte, *Early French Reform*, 132–33.) Cf. *Epistres et Evangiles*, 12A, 62–63: "l'union et concorde soit si grande entre lesditz membres du corps que tout ce que l'ung faict est ordonné au proffit et a l'utilité de l'autre"; 56A, 321: "Portez les charges et fardeaux l'ung de l'autre et ainsi vous acomplirez la loy de Christ"; 69B, 385–86.

46. *Summaire*, chs. 17, 33. (Zuidema and Van Raalte, *Early French Reform*, 133–34.)

chapter. The first point concerned an instance of omission. In the traditional field of theology, when the question of the keys was discussed, the primary scriptural text was Matthew 16 (or 18, which contained the same wordings), but this chapter did not refer to the above text. Likewise, the keys were usually associated with the office of ecclesiastical ministers, but the chapter had no reference to ministers. This point indicated a significant contrast with those who had traditional training in theology, such as Erasmus, Luther, Zwingli, and Bucer, who usually associated the keys with the office of ministers in their interpreting and preaching God's word. It is likely that Farel's position reflected the congregational principle of the Lefèvrian tradition in which believers were viewed as those who were able to directly interpret Scripture, to decide upon the meanings of Scripture, and accordingly to judge to accept or reject the traditional teachings of the church. We will see this again in connection with his notions of excommunication and ministerial office.[47] The second point concerned Farel's unique understanding of the keys not only as God's word and the gospel but also as "the pasture of souls." The image of a pasture could be a reflection of Lefèvre's above-mentioned *Commentaries on the Four Gospels* that viewed the church as a pasture where Christ was pastor and believers were his sheep who could feed on God's word and nourish themselves. At the end of the chapter, Farel mentioned the preaching of God's word as the corrective aspect of the keys and described it as "the pasture for poor souls." He affirmed that preaching (keys) enabled believers (poor souls) "to correct error, purify the heart, and . . . discern and know the voice of the pastor from that of a murderer."[48]

(iii) From the same congregational perspective, Farel presented the chapter on the sacraments (18), which he likely considered the second mark of the church. Concerning the definition of the sacraments, his unique expression, "signs and public attestations of things which were to be of believers" (*signes & protestations des choses qui doiuent ester es fideles*), was noticeable. A reason

47. *Epistres et Evangiles*, 39B, 224: "par lequel [Christ's] auctorité irrevocable est donnée a ung-chascun chrestien de juger et penser, quant on ordonne ou qu'on propose aucune chose, si c'est conformement a l'evangile ou non, et se il est consonant, le debvons recepvoir, sinon constamment le rejecter"; 47B, 269–70.

48. *Summaire*, chs. 17, 33–34. (Zuidema and Van Raalte, *Early French Reform*, 133–34.) Farel's understanding of the church and the keys can be generally placed in the historical setting of Lefèvre and the *Epistles and Gospels*. As to the keys' operation in believers, however, his emphasis on believers' response to God's word seems to echo Zwingli's view of the keys as the preaching of God's word. For this confer Zwingli, *Auslegen und Gründe der Schlussreden* (1523): *CR: Zwingli*, 2:373–75.

for its uniqueness was that, instead of the traditional "sign of grace," he used the indirect expression, "of things which were to be of believers," focusing on believers who were receiving God's grace. In the following sentence, which expressed the "purpose" of the sacraments, he focused on the recipients of the sacraments by saying, "[the sacraments which are] serving to and enabling [believers] to maintain, increase, and support the love of each other." Just like the previous chapter on the keys, here the emphasis was on the benefits for believers and for their service of love to others. By the same token, the meaning of baptism was expressed by the believers "confessing the desire to follow and live" as Christ's disciples. And the Lord's Supper was expressed, as we have seen above, by the believers "recollecting and remembering" Christ's death. From these emphases on the fideistic, memorial, and confessing participation of the believers in the sacraments, it is reasonable for some researchers to identify Farel's view with the position of Zwingli and Oecolampadius.[49] In a deeper analysis, however, Farel's view was closely following the memorial understanding of the sacraments shown in Lefèvrianism. As we have seen, for example, in a clear reference against the repetition of sacrifices in the Mass, Lefèvre's *St. Paul's XIV Epistles* affirmed that there should be no other mystery in the Lord's Supper than "memory or recollection" as well as "endless memory" or "imitation" of Christ's death on the cross.[50] In the same manner, Farel's *Summary* affirmed that believers were to receive baptism "in the sign of the fact" that they followed Christ and devoted all to him. He affirmed that believers were to participate in the Lord's Supper in order to be one body with Christ in "recollecting and remembering" his sacrifice and in serving to others by "imitating" his example. In this basically memorial understanding of the sacraments, emphasis was not on the sacraments as "means of grace" but on the believers' participation in them.[51]

Apology against the Catholic Teachings, Chapters 19–32

(i) The second section, a fairly lengthy apologetic portion from chapter 19 ("The Mass") to chapter 32 ("Excommuning"), focused mainly on the Catholic sacramental system as well as what Farel called "human traditions" in contrasting

49. *Summaire*, chs. 18, 34–35. (Zuidema and Van Raalte, *Early French Reform*, 134–35.) From this text, White ("An Early Doctrinal Handbook," 32) considers that Zwingli's influence on Farel was considerable.

50. *S. Pauli Epistolae XIV*, 243r (Heb 7:26–28); 250v (Heb 10:11–12). Cf. n. 14 above; Hughes, *Lefèvre*, 87–88.

51. *Summaire*, chs. 18, 34–35. (Zuidema and Van Raalte, *Early French Reform*, 134–35.)

Catholic and Evangelical teachings. In general, however, his apology reflected both Lefèvrianism and the Evangelicalism of Luther and others. As we have mentioned in connection with Lefèvre, the topic of human traditions was a crucial issue for both Lefèvre and the Meaux reform. Farel's *Summary* also treated the topic in chapter 14, "The Doctrine and Tradition of Men," in contrast to chapter 15 ("Scripture"). As he characterized it, the Catholic "human doctrine (and tradition) wants to mix itself with the things of God concerning the salvation of soul." His apologetics was to contrast this mixed religion of the Catholic Church with the religion of Scripture. Furthermore, he urged the faithful believers to examine Catholic "doctrine and tradition" in detail from Scripture, as he said, "in testing all their ordinances . . . constitutions and customs."[52]

(ii) The last chapter (32) of the apologetic portion was perhaps the most unique, yet the most difficult to understand, in the entire *Summary*. The chapter was titled "Excommuning" (*excommuniement*) instead of the traditional "excommunication." In the first sentence of the chapter, however, Farel used this term as a synonym of "excommunication"—"excommuning or excommunication is barring from our Lord's table." By choosing the "excommuning" for the chapter's title and in its text, he might have tried to express his narrower understanding of excommunication as the exclusion of the unworthy from the communion table of the believers, as well as the congregational aspect of church discipline. Throughout discussions, he made no allusions to magisterial involvement in the disciplinary process. At the same time, apologetically, he intended to make a contrast between what he called "the evangelical excommuning" and the authoritarian Catholic excommunication. In both cases, his intention was an emphasis on the communal and congregational aspect rather than the churchly and institutional aspect of church discipline.[53] Furthermore, he was narrowly defining "the evangelical excommuning" as what the Catholic Church had traditionally called "minor excommunication," and he seemingly avoided referring to the wider implication of excommunication that involved both churchly exclusion from the Supper and social sanctions.

52. *Summaire*, chs. 14, 27–28. (Zuidema and Van Raalte, *Early French Reform*, 130–31.)

53. *Summaire*, chs. 32, 78–81. (Zuidema and Van Raalte, *Early French Reform*, 156–57.) Cf. P. Opitz, "Calvin in the Context of the Swiss Reformation: Detecting the Traces," in *Calvinus Pastor Ecclesiae*, ed. H. S. Selderhuis and A. Huijgen (Göttingen: Vandenhoeck & Ruprecht, 2016), 18–19. Although we assume Farel's congregationalism was rooted in the French background of Lefèvre, as suggested by Opitz, there is a possibility that Farel knew Zwingli's earlier notion of congregational excommunication. Opitz cites Zwingli's 1523 expression: "excommunicationis potestas non est magistratus; nam totius ecclesiae est." *CR*: Zwingli, 3:879.

(iii) As to the next question of identifying the unworthy, clearly referring to the guideline of Matthew 18 (15–18), Farel considered the unworthy those who were unrepentant even after the triple steps of a single person's advice, the warning of two or three, and the admonition of "the entire congregation." As expected from his congregational principle, he interpreted the text's "church" (18:17) as "the entire congregation."[54] To this end, he urged the congregation to exercise "correction friendly and full of love" in hopes that the unworthy be restored to the communion of believers. Just as he signified the Lord's Supper as "memory and imitation" or remembering, imitating, and exercising the sacrificial love of Jesus, in "excommuning," which was the opposite image of the Lord's Supper, the exercise of the same love ought to be applied. Farel called it "friendly correction." In this "correction," he further claimed that "evangelical excommuning" was clearly discernible from "the method of excommunication of the pope and bishops."[55] Although Farel's view of "excommuning" could be identified with Lefèvrianism, as some researchers have assumed, Farel might have used Oecolampadius's view here. The assumption was partly due to the fact that Oecolampadius tried to introduce a church discipline in the Basel church that was quite different from the Zwinglian type in Zurich, which was to be exercised by "the whole church" or "the whole congregation" and according to the principle of medicinal and brotherly excommunication. However, it

54. *Summaire*, chs. 32, 78. (Zuidema and Van Raalte, *Early French Reform*, 156.) As to the French term "excommuniement," how and why Farel used it in distinction from "excommunication" cannot be ascertained from the text. Here we use the translation "excommuning," used by Zuidema and Van Raalte (*Early French Reform*, 156).

55. *Summaire*, chs. 32, 78–80. (Zuidema and Van Raalte, *Early French Reform*, 156–57.) Cf. White, "An Early Doctrinal Handbook," 33; Zuidema and Van Raalte, *Early French Reform*, 25. Church discipline, which Farel here defined "excommuniement," could be reflecting the common understanding of the Lefèvrians. Lefèvre's Gospel commentary on Matthew 18 (*Commentarii initiatorii*, 81v–82r) presents a radical interpretation of the fraternal and congregational discipline based upon the principle of "love" (*charitas*): the entire disciplinary process (18:15–17) was summarized as "the duty of brotherly love"; a lengthy portion on the use of the keys (18:18) was also unfolded in terms of brotherly love; and lastly fraternal discipline was connected to the subsequent saying of Jesus (18:19–20): "Where two or three are gathered in my name." Idealistically Lefèvre described a well-disciplined congregation as "refuge for the salvation of brothers." The *Epistles and Gospels* (*Epistres et Evangiles*, 56A, 524–25), which usually avoided any overtly critical remarks on Catholic disciplinary practice, defined a Christian congregation as "gathering with Jesus-Christ" (*compagnie avec Jesuchrist*) and suggested a kind of caring and correcting community: "Il [Christ] nous enseigne aussi par vraye amour et charité, en toute patien supporter les faultes et inffirmitéz de noz prochains." Incidentally, neither White nor Zuidema and Van Raalte notice Farel's peculiar view of discipline or trace its historical background.

seems difficult to historically assess this assumption and it should be remembered that Oecolampadius's understanding assumed church discipline as an ecclesial system as well as "the unity of the church" that promoted cooperation of ministers, representatives of congregations, and magistrates. All these points were not necessarily congenial to Farel's rather radical congregationalism and the church situation that the *Summary* portrayed.[56]

An Image of the Evangelical Church, Chapters 33–42

The third section, the last portion of the *Summary*, was not intended to be an anti-Catholic apology as such but rather some guidelines for the Evangelical church. As Farel chose the many topics of pastors, sword (magistracy), marriage, instruction of children, preparation for death, resurrection, and the Day of Judgment, we will analyze selectively the two topics of pastors and magistracy that reflect Farel's ecclesiological insights and an image of the Evangelical church.

(i) The topic of pastors occupied four chapters (33–36; false pastors, good pastors, pastors' power, and obligation to pastors). This alone suggested its importance for Farel. In detailed analyses, the weight of his discussions was not so much on the status of pastors or their office but on their place in or relationship with the congregation. There were no discussions on the biblical foundation of their office and the process from their calling by God to their installation by the church, but the focus was their role and function in the congregation. For instance, Farel portrayed false pastors and good pastors in an analogy of shepherd and sheep: false pastors were wolves coming to the congregation in sheep's skin, not speaking God's word, but feeding for themselves; good pastors were shepherds who, after the example of the great shepherd Christ, sacrificed themselves for their sheep, nourished them, and served them for the sake of God's love.[57]

Above all, unique and important was chapter 35, "Concerning the Power of Pastors." Its uniqueness derived from how the topic, the power of pastors, was contrasted with the power of the congregation that was hearing their preaching. When Farel defined that "the entire power of pastors is to edify, instruct

56. Cf. Oecolampadius, *Briefe und Akten zum Leben Oecolampads*, ed. E. Staehelin, Leipzig, 1927–31, II, 495, 518; A. Demura, "Church Discipline according to Johannes Oecolampadius in the Setting of His Life and Thought" (ThD dissertation, Princeton Theological Seminary, 1964), 161–80; D. Poythress, *Reformer of Basel: The Life, Thought, and Influence of Johannes Oecolampadius* (Grand Rapids: Reformation Heritage Books, 2011), 51–52, 100–101.

57. *Summaire*, chs. 33, 81–86. (Zuidema and Van Raalte, *Early French Reform*, 157–58.)

well, and teach the people by the pure and simple word of God," for example, the marginal reference of the definition was 1 Corinthians 10 (perhaps 10:33: "not seeking my own advantage, but that of many, so that they may be saved"). Since the "power" of pastors in this definition could well be replaced by their "duty," Farel's intention was to relate the power of pastors not to their status or administrative power but to their "function" in relation to the congregation. He went on to draw the conclusion, "when true pastors purely evangelize, God speaks in them with such great power that believers have life eternal and nonbelievers are silenced."[58]

Relatedly, there was another interesting reference to the capability of believers in clear contrast to the power of pastors. As Farel affirmed, "the true Christian who is founded on the true rock can read and hear anything." Since there was no marginal reference provided here, it is not certain what he was referring to by "the true rock." If he had Matthew 16 in mind, "the true rock" could mean Christ or the believers' confession of Christ. Or if Matthew 7:24 ("everyone then who hears these words of mine . . . built his house on rock"), which was the passage Lefèvre's *Commentaries on the Four Gospels* related to the Petrine text of Matthew 16, it could mean the believers' true understanding of God's word. In both cases, his emphasis was on the believing congregation's ability to read and hear God's word in their own language. This affirmation was a reflection of Lefèvrian reform and the Protestant reformatory principle of Luther, or perhaps his own anticlerical sentiment.[59] In fact, after the affirmation, using the first-person singular, he mentioned his search for the evangelical conviction in his humanist days when he was not ordained as a Catholic priest, followed by a lengthy criticism of the Catholic ministerial order.[60]

(ii) Chapter 36, "To What Extent One Is Obliged to True Pastors and What Obedience and Honor Is Owed to Them," further highlighted Farel's unique view. While he affirmed the "true Christian" as having the ability to "read and hear anything" in the previous chapter, the head of this chapter declared: "those who hear good pastors should test and judge all that has been said,

58. *Summaire*, chs. 35, 86. (Zuidema and Van Raalte, *Early French Reform*, 160.)

59. *Summaire*, chs. 35, 87: "Le vray Chrestien qui est fonde sur la vraye pierre, peult tout lire & ouyr." (Zuidema and Van Raalte, *Early French Reform*, 160.) Cf. Lefèvre, *Commentarii Initiatorii*, 74v (on the keys in Matt 18:18): "Neque eas salus a domine accepit Petrus, sed etiam caeteri omnes, qui in fide aedificauerunt supra CHRISTUM iuxta CHRISTI domini uoluntatem, ecclesiam"; *Epistres et Evangiles*, 39B, 224 (see n. 47 above). Among possible references to "rock" such as Romans 9:33, 1 Peter 2:6, etc., we consider here a reference to Matthew 16 that Farel did not use in connection with pastoral power.

60. *Summaire*, chs. 87–91. (Zuidema and Van Raalte, *Early French Reform*, 160–62.)

and consider diligently whether the saying is of the word of God; then they should firmly keep and believe it; not because of who has brought it, but as much as it is the word of God." This bold affirmation, which we may call the congregational right to audit pastors, could be interpreted as a rather radical application of the Evangelical principle to allow believers free exercise of interpreting Scripture. At the same time, it could be said to be his follow-up of the Meaux reform tradition that urged the faithful to guard against the teaching of Catholic priests and to test it from Scripture, which he was currently applying to the Evangelical congregation.[61] Furthermore, he postulated two cases of pastor's teaching, one not in accordance with Scripture and the other in agreement with Scripture. In the former case, he urged believers not to believe, even if the teaching was brought by "one of the greatest apostles of God or an angel from heaven." From there he drew a general conclusion that "one does not need to receive anything which is not clearly proved by scripture." In the latter case, he recommended the congregation to follow pastors just as they did God, and to support pastors, even though they should avoid the special treatments formerly given to the Catholic priests.[62] From what we have surveyed above, it could be said that Farel's view of Evangelical pastors vis-à-vis the congregation represented a far more radical congregationalism than the positions of Luther, Zwingli, Bucer, and Oecolampadius. From his background of critical attitude toward the ministerial dominance of the Catholic Church, perhaps, he warned against the introduction of a similar dominance in the Evangelical church by limiting the ministerial role to its "function" in relation to the congregation. In conclusion, we assume, Farel's radicalism in part was rooted in Lefèvrianism and the Meaux reform.

(iii) Chapter 37 on magistracy began with: "we are composed with two very opposite things, namely, soul and body."[63] This approach to the issue of magistracy was quite distinct from what he could have seen as the Evangelical interpretations of church and state, such as Luther's two kingdoms theory and Zwingli's divine and human justice theory. It was also distinct from Calvin's later work of the first *Institutes* that we examined earlier. First, as the title of

61. *Summaire*, chs. 36, 91–92. (Zuidema and Van Raalte, *Early French Reform*, 162.) Confer nn. 47, 58 above. On this point, White ("An Early Doctrinal Handbook," 34) exceptionally makes three references to the *Epistles and Gospels* (*Épistres et Évangiles*, 3A, 13; 39B, 224; 47B, 269–70) and emphasizes Farel's association with the Meaux reform.

62. *Summaire*, chs. 36, 92. (Zuidema and Van Raalte, *Early French Reform*, 163.) As mentioned above, this point was one of Farel's theses for the Basel Disputation.

63. *Summaire*, chs. 37, 93. Quotation in English is taken from Zuidema and Van Raalte (*Early French Reform*, 163).

the chapter, "Of the Sword, the Power of Justice and Corporeal Supremacy," especially the use of the term "sword" instead of "magistracy," suggested, his view of magistracy was based upon soul-body dualism. In fact, his discussion began with a sharp distinction between the world of "the soul and the spirit" and that of "the body." Briefly, he described the former as the world that had brought to man the knowledge of God by faith and a transition from death to life, from sin to justice, from God's wrath to adoption as his children. This was also the world where the faithful, by their spirit, were free from the constrictions of the superior/inferior relationship, such as husband and wife, man and woman, and lord and servant.[64]

The chapter's main argument, of course, rested on the other world of "the body" where man was subjected to the fall and all the human constrictions, and where, according to "the ordinance of God," corporeal superiors were to rule by the sword for justice and protection of human bodies and goods. Since the faithful believers were to live in these two worlds, accordingly, due to the rule of the soul they could not claim to be completely free from human constrictions, but at the same time "the faithful can have temporal lordship, own slaves, and bear the sword for the due administration of justice."[65] Certainly, at the end of this chapter Farel affirmed magisterial power as being from God and therefore to be respected and, citing Romans 13, that the magistrates were "ministers of God." This biblical reference, however, was seemingly used in a limited sense, placing magistrates as executioners of God's wrath against evildoers or as administrators of the material world created by "God's ordinance." But the main thrust of his argument was separation of the worlds of soul and body, as he warned of the "mixing and confusing," of "the freedom of the spirit with the flesh, the nourishment and rule of the pasture of the soul with that of the body." Nevertheless, it was not certain exactly how he did relate the two worlds nor his basic understanding of church and state. On the one hand, there were several indications of consciously aligning his position with the Evangelical understandings of Luther, Zwingli, and others. In this respect, such a statement concerning the subject's duty to his temporal lord as "by the confession and public attestation which he made at baptism, promising to keep

64. *Summaire*, 93–94. (Zuidema and Van Raalte, *Early French Reform*, 165.)

65. *Summaire*, 94–97. The last quotation (Zuidema and Van Raalte, *Early French Reform*, 165) indicates Farel's awareness of the Anabaptist position. His constant use of "sword" instead of "magistrate" suggests the Anabaptists' use of the term. However, his position is distinct from mainstream Reformers such as Luther, Zwingli, Melanchthon, Oecolampadius, Bucer, and later Calvin, and may point to his background of Lefèvrianism. On this, confer n. 67 below.

the law of our savior, he is bound to serve his lord as before," could be interpreted as his stance against the Anabaptists.[66] On the other hand, however, there were such statements as "if the whole world had true knowledge of God and love for each other was firmly planted in the heart, . . . there should be no need of sword." It is also difficult to assess what he meant in saying, "Jesus has his kingdom in the midst of his enemies."

Thus, we may suggest a possible root of Farel's understanding in Lefèvre's worldview that sharply separated the worlds of spirit and flesh and comprehended the church as a superior sphere of spirit over the inferior sphere of the world where the sword ruled. In fact, Lefèvre's commentary on Romans 13 mentioned two "supreme powers" (*summae potestates*), namely, the "power of church ministers" (*ecclesiastica*) and that of "secular rulers" (*secularis*), and from this antithetical scheme he discussed the magistracy. It is noteworthy that there he used the theory of hierarchies used by the Pseudo-Dionysian writings (*Celestial Hierarchy*, *Ecclesiastical Hierarchy*, and *Divine Names*) that he himself had earlier edited and published, and in which he presented the traditional view of the Roman Catholic Church as a copy of the celestial hierarchy that was to be served by the inferior hierarchy of the magistrates.[67] If Farel was in part influenced by Lefèvre's view, although his view was generally in the Evangelical orientation, we assume that he was either unsuccessful in presenting a clear Evangelical position on the church and state framework or incapable of freeing himself from his former teacher's influence.

Section 2. Three Documents of the Genevan Church

On January 16, 1537, a group of church leaders headed by Farel officially presented ecclesiastical ordinances (*Articles concernant l'organisation de l'église*)

66. *Summaire*, chs. 37, 97–99. (Zuidema and Van Raalte, *Early French Reform*, 163–66.) As to the last quotation, Farel could be aware of the *Schleitheim Confession* (art. 6) that admitted "the sword" as God's ordinance but regarded it "outside the perfection of Christ." (*Creeds and Confessions*, 2:699.)

67. *S. Pauli Epistolae XIV*, 98r-v, on Romans 13. In the exposition of the text, Lefèvre never used the terms "magisterium" or "magister." Even his quotation from the Vulgate text (Rom 13:4) substituted "the servant (minister) of God" (*Dei minister*) with "the maidservant of God" (*Dei ministra*). For Lefèvre's Dionysian world view, see Rice's introduction to *The Prefatory Epistles* (xxi), in which he says that "Lefèvre believed passionately and erroneously in the authenticity of the Dionysian corpus . . . that the Dionysius of the Areopagite mentioned in the Book of Acts."

to the city's syndics, along with a confession of faith (*Confession de la foy*) and a catechism (*Instruction et confession de foy*). As historical materials, the three documents belonged to the tradition of the Reformed Reformation that had advanced prior to Geneva in Zurich, Basel, Bern in Switzerland, and Strasbourg in South Germany. In fact, they marked a fresh impression on the Reformed tradition. As an assortment of the ordinances, the confession, and a catechism, they presented a rather comprehensive church reform plan. In particular, their presentation included ideas such as autonomous church discipline unsuccessfully attempted in Basel and Strasbourg. The catechism was considered to be a summary of Calvin's first *Institutes*, and it was a clear and wholesome example of Reformed theology in French. As indicated earlier, traditionally these documents were assumed to be of Calvin's authorship, and as such they were analyzed as a part of his reformatory concepts. Since Labarthe's preliminary study in the 1960s, the substantial start of Farel research, and the recent works of van Stam and others, however, an established theory assumes today that the two documents, the *Articles* and the *Confession*, though Calvin's cooperation was not excluded, were basically authored by Farel.[68]

Before going into our analysis of the three documents, we make two assumptions. The first assumption concerns the chronological order of the three documents, which is as complicated as the issue of their authorship and is uncertain. Although the *Articles* was officially presented to the city for discussion in January 1537, either its preliminary form or the final form itself had already been presented to the city's Small Council for prior examination on November 10, 1536. It is uncertain whether the *Confession* and the *Instruction*

68. Cf. R. M. Kingdon, "Confessionalism in Calvin's Geneva," *Archiv für Reformationsgeschichte* 98 (2006): 109. Concerning the authorship of the three documents, which had been traditionally attributed to Calvin, between the initial examination of Labarthe in the 1960s (O. Labarthe, "La relation entre le premier catéchisme de Calvin et la première Confession de foi de Genève," unpublished thesis, Geneva, 1967) and the recent thorough study of van Stam in 2000 (F. P. van Stam, "Die Genfer Artikel von Januar 1537: aus Calvins order Farels Feder?," *Zwingliana* 27 [2000]: 87–101), a kind of consensus has emerged: Calvin's authorship of both the *Confession* and the *Articles* has receded and instead Farel's authorship has become a predominant view. More recent studies (e.g., Muller, *The Unaccommodated*, 26–27n59; C. Augustijn et al., "Calvin in the Light of the Earlier Letters," in *Calvinus Praeceptor Ecclesiae*, ed. H. J. Selderhuis [Geneva: Droz, 2004], 150–57), accept this view, with the possibility of Calvin's coauthorship. In this respect, even in some recent studies, the first Genevan reform is viewed from the perspective of Calvin's leading role rather than Farel's. As to the three documents, for example, Mullett (*John Calvin*, 54–56) ignores Geneva's chief pastor Farel's role on one side, and considers the *Articles* "almost certainly drawn up by Calvin," on the other side.

were made available by that date and presented along with the *Articles*. If we assume Calvin's sole authorship of the *Instruction* and Farel's primary authorship of the *Confession* (that had in its title the phrase "being extracted" from the *Instruction*) and the *Articles*, with the possibility of Farel and Calvin in collaboration, the possible chronological order can be either *Articles/Instruction/Confession* or *Instruction/Confession/Articles*. Despite this issue of chronological order, however, our study will choose to first examine Calvin's reform concept expressed in the *Instruction*, then that of Farel in the *Confession*, and finally the *Articles* as their concrete reform proposal.[69] Secondly, we assume that Farel and Calvin had by this time read each other's previous works. By the time he persuaded Calvin to stay in Geneva, Farel knew of Calvin's *Institutes*. And by the time of his appointment in Geneva in September 1536, Calvin had knowledge of Farel's *Summary*.

1. Catechism: Instruction et confession de foy

The 1537 Genevan catechism took as its official title the *Instruction and Confession of Faith*. Its author was Calvin who, as a humanist, customarily thought and wrote in Latin. It was assumed that he wrote a summary of his *Institutes* in a Latin original, and therefore it was his own French translation of the original.[70] The *Instruction* clearly presented Evangelical theology in a nutshell. Even its style betrayed the influence of Latin, its content of precise expressions and without unnecessary repetitions was typically Calvin's own, and *prima facie* it distinguished itself from the other two documents. Since it was written on the occasion of his official installation as Lecturer in Scripture and its intention was instructional in the form of a short summary of his *Institutes*, it witnessed the author's fresh efforts in adding new supplements and explanations, omitting cumbersome theological arguments, and avoiding sharp attacks against Catholic theology. From the perspective of Calvin's theological formation, perhaps it could take a middle position between his first *Institutes*, which was

69. Cf. *BC* 1, 45; van Stam, "Die Genfer Artikel," 91; *COR* III-2:xii–xv. Concerning the composition dates of the *Catechism* and the *Confession* as well as the order of the Latin and French texts of the *Catechism*, we follow here the views of the editors of both *BC* and *COR* III-2. However, to place Calvin's drafting of the *Instruction* in 1537 and not in 1536 "as a complement to the *Articles*" (S. M. Manetsch, *Calvin's Company of Pastors: Pastoral Care and the Emerging Reformed Church, 1536–1609* [Oxford and New York: Oxford University Press, 2013], 19) seems untenable.

70. For the text, we use the *Renewed Calvini Opera* (*COR* III-2:1–113) with the *Opera Selecta* (*OS* 1:378–417) as a reference.

a manifestation of his Evangelical theology, and the second edition (1539) that was intended as a textbook in theology.[71]

For the preparation of the *Instruction*, it has been suggested that, besides the actual situation of the Genevan Church and Farel's *Summary*, Calvin was possibly aware of the outcome of the Lausanne Disputation (early October 1536) in which he participated as Farel's attendant. Occasioned by Bern's military occupation of the Pays de Vaud, the Disputation was regarded as a part of Bern's religious policy to convert Vaud to Evangelicalism. Since it was attended by participants of both sides, including many leading members of the Catholic Church in Vaud, and its official record, though prepared by the Evangelical side, was kept in its almost complete form, it has been considered an important document for the history of the Reformed church in French-speaking Switzerland, as well as that of the French Reformation. The Disputation was based upon the ten articles in French that Farel prepared in consultation with the Bernese authority, and was led by Farel and his protégé, Pierre Viret, who was also considered a Lefèvrian. It was attended, on the Evangelical side, by Paris theological doctor Pierre Caroli, who was an exile in Switzerland after the Placards affair, and Antoine Marcourt, Pastor of the Neuchâtel Church, who was regarded as an author of the placard. Its focal points of discussion turned out to be the topics of the church, the sacraments, and the ecclesiastical order, with Calvin making some contributions on the issue of the Catholic Mass.[72]

In the following pages, we will examine Calvin's church reform concept in three main points: the *Instruction*'s structure, its basic ideas concerning the church, and its last four chapters (the church's pastor and his power, human

71. *CO* 22:13–16 ("Notice préliminaire"); I. J. Hesselink, *Calvin's First Catechism: A Commentary* (Louisville: Westminster John Knox, 1997), 39–42; Muller, *The Unaccommodated*, 26–27. For Calvin's official title in the Church, see Wendel, *Calvin*, 50n12. Incidentally, there is a kind of puzzle in the *Instruction*, that is, while Calvin had attacked Catholicism in the main text of the *Institutes*, why did he restrain the provocative elements and, in particular, why did he eliminate a portion corresponding to chapter 5 ("False Sacraments") of the *Institutes* in the *Instruction*? This point was said to cause Farel to complain against Calvin.

72. For the text of the Lausanne Disputation, we use the official record, A. Piaget, ed., *Les Actes de la Dispute de Lausanne 1536* (Neuchâtel: Secrétariat de l'Université, 1928), hereafter cited as Piaget, *Les Actes*. For the English translation of the 10 articles, see "The Lausanne Articles, 1536" in *Creeds and Confessions*, 2:292–95. The following references are useful: É. Junod, ed., *La Dispute de Lausanne (1536). La théologie réformée après Zwingli avant Calvin* (Lausanne: E. Junod, 1988); F. Higman, "La Dispute de Lausanne, Carrefour de la Réformation française," in *Lire et découvrir*, 605–17; F. P. van Stam, "The Group of Meaux as the First Target of Farel and Calvin's Anti-Nicodemism," *Bibliothèque d'Humanisme et Renaissance* 68 (2006): 253–75.

traditions, excommunication, and magistrates). Since there are some conceptual differences between the *Instruction*'s last four chapters and the corresponding five chapters of the *Confession*, which we basically attribute to Farel, a comparison of the two documents will be included in our examination of the *Confession*.

(i) Concerning the first point of structure, generally speaking, the *Instruction* followed the logical flow of the first *Institutes*. Since the *Instruction* as a catechism could not expect its readers to have the basic theological knowledge that was presupposed for the *Institutes*, we assume that both supplement and elimination were felt necessary for Calvin. As to supplement, three focal points or *loci* were newly added, namely, "the difference between false and true religion" in connection with the knowledge of God, "free will" in connection with the knowledge of man, and "the law is a step toward Christ" as a bridge between the doctrine of justification and that of faith.[73] A case of interesting supplement was the point "Concerning Election and Predestination," placed between the two points of justification by faith and true faith, in which Calvin delineated the distinction between the elect and the reprobate as "the sublime secret of the divine plan." In his *Institutes*, he certainly mentioned the issue of the reprobate in the expression that "God works in the reprobate" and called the issue "a difficult and involved question," but he avoided stepping into a clear distinction between the elect and the reprobate. In the *Instruction*, however, he obviously felt the need to present this point more clearly and strengthen this doctrine by adding another new point, "faith is God's gift." Or, it could be Calvin's response to Farel's *Summary* that never related justification by faith with God's election.[74]

As to noticeable points of the *Institutes* that Calvin eliminated in the *Instruction*, there were two major issues; one was the entire chapter 5 on false sacraments and the other was the first point of chapter 6 on Christian freedom. Concerning the first issue, it could be assumed that Calvin considered the cumbersome theological arguments of chapter 5 difficult and unfit for the catechism, but unquestionably his consideration weakened the anti-Catholic nature of the *Instruction*'s apologetics. Concerning the second issue of not making Christian freedom an independent point in the *Instruction*, since Christian freedom had been a Reformation principle since Luther, omitting the issue could be serious enough to give the impression of the retreat of the

73. *COR* III-2:3, 7–9, 29–31; *OS* 1:379, 381, 389–90. For an English translation of the text, as a reference we use Hesselink's *Calvin's First Catechism*, which incorporates F. L. Battles's translation of the 1538 Latin Catechism.

74. *COR* III-2:31–37; *OS* 1:390–93. Cf. *OS* 1:73. (Battles, trans., *Institution*, 63.)

Reformation idea or the danger of a legalistic understanding of the gospel. It was true that, out of three elements (freedom from judgment of the law, freedom to observe the law, and freedom regarding the so-called "adiaphora") that constituted Christian freedom, the *Instruction* did refer to the first and second elements in connection with the point of "true faith." While not calling it Christian freedom, the *Instruction* referred to the first element as the work of the Holy Spirit, who gave to a believer "true faith" as "God's gift" that freed the believer from the judgment of the law. In the process of the Christian's sanctification, it also referred to freedom by which the believer could "obey the law by faith."[75] It was also true that, since the second edition of the *Institutes* (1539) made the point of Christian freedom into an independent chapter with the same content as in the first edition, there were no grounds for Calvin to have changed his position. As a result, the lack of an independent point on Christian freedom in the *Instruction* remained curious. We can offer only a few suggestions. One speculation is that, as we examined in the previous chapter, the apologetic scheme of Christian freedom, especially of "adiaphora," by which Calvin presented both topics of ecclesiastical power and political administration, was considered by him to be too difficult to leave in the *Instruction*. Another speculation is that, as he had found in Farel's *Summary* an individualistic notion of Christian freedom and emphasis on congregational freedom in church polity, he was afraid of their adverse effects on the Genevan Church, and therefore refrained from emphasizing Christian freedom.

(ii) The second point concerned the church concept, namely, whether the conceptual balance carefully maintained in the first *Institutes* between the church of the elect and the church in history had also been kept in the *Instruction* or not. In the previous chapter, we saw in the first *Institutes* the two church concepts balanced in the notion of the church's catholicity. In other words, Calvin had balanced them as the "fundamentals" and "apologetics" of his "Catholic ecclesiology." He defined the church of the elect as "the whole number of the elect" in his exposition on the "holy Catholic church" of the Apostles' Creed (ch. 2), and the church in history as "the congregation of believers" in the apologetic section (chs. 5–6). In the *Instruction*, he commented on the creed's "holy Catholic church" in this way: "by the bond of faith the entire elect are conjoined in one Church, society, and God's people, of which Christ our savior is the chief conductor, prince, and, as if, head of the body," and "this society is catholic, that is, universal." Regarding another creedal expression of "the communion of the saints," the *Instruction* described it not only

75. *COR* III-2:35–41; *OS* 1:391–94.

as "the communion of believers" but also as "the entire elect are gathered and formed into one body." As to the last quotation, since its equivalent expression was not found in the *Institutes*, Calvin seemed to stress a two-sided emphasis in this section: on one side, the suprahistorical election of God was the sole foundation of both the "holy Catholic church" and the "communion of the saints"; on the other side, the church of the elect was to be visibly manifested in the church, communion, society, and people in history.[76]

Why this double-sided emphasis? As one reason, we suppose that he was concerned about the visible and congregational emphasis laid on the church by his colleagues, especially Farel and Viret. Farel's *Summary* mentioned neither the relation of God's election with the church in history nor the idea of the church's catholicity. At the Lausanne Disputation, both the ten articles prepared by Farel and Viret's exposition on the third article (the church) showed a similar tendency of radical congregationalism.[77] Nonetheless, as we will examine later, the last four points of the *Instruction* strictly emphasized the church in history without referring to the elect, but instead using the terms "believers" and the "company of believers." Thus, the *Instruction* as a whole generally kept the balance of the two concepts, the church of the elect and the church in history. Calvin's dominant and new emphasis, however, was on God's election as the foundation of the church and its manifestation in history that united the two concepts.[78]

(iii) The third point concerned the last four points of the *Instruction*: the first three (the pastors of the church and their power, human traditions, excommunication) corresponded to the second topic (ecclesiastical power) of chapter 6 of the *Institutes*; and the fourth (magistracy) to the third topic (political administration).[79] As to their contents, though simplification by abbreviating and omitting some polemical and apologetic arguments of the *Institutes* was seen, there was no ideological development in the *Instruction*. Nonetheless, several changes, such as newly added emphases or shifts of emphases, were noticeable. The changes seemed to indicate Calvin's adaptation to the reality

76. *COR* III-2:61; *OS* 1:401.

77. Piaget, *Les Actes*, 147–52. Cf. Higman, "La dispute de Lausanne," *Lire et découvrir*, 609. Noteworthy are the third article, "La saincte escripture appelle l'eglise de Dieu tous ceux qui croient qu'ilz sont racheptez du seul sang de Jesuchrist . . . Le quell, estant retire de nous par sa presence corporelle," and Viret's explanation on "the Catholic church" in the Apostles' Creed: "nous declare que l'eglise universelle n'est autre chose que la communaulte de tous les fideles qui sont sur la terre."

78. *COR* III-2:107; *OS* 1:415.

79. *COR* III-2:103–4; *OS* 1:413–17.

of the ongoing Genevan Reformation. For example, as to the first three focal points, by simplifying the complex arguments of the *Institutes*, a new emphasis came forward, namely, that the duty of pastors was comprehensive and covered the examination of the church traditions as well as church discipline. In other words, the power of the keys that the pastors were to exercise combined two major areas of church government: doctrine and practice (discipline). Another example was seen as a shift of emphasis concerning the ministry of pastors. As we have seen in the previous chapter, the first *Institutes* dealt with the issue of ministry in the context of Catholic ecclesiasticism. Accordingly, Calvin's apologetics began with the power of God's word over against Catholic ministerial authority. He emphasized Christ as the executioner of the church's power, the word of God as power itself, regarded the power exercised by ministers as "ministry of God's word," and attributed to ministers only "authority or dignity."[80] However, the *Instruction* emphasized the fundamental importance of ministers and argued that, just as God's word and the sacraments were indispensable for the church, Christ wished the "human ministry" (*le ministere des hommes*) and "pastors" (*pasteurs*) to be properly instituted in the church. Thus, the power that ministers exercised was to be "totally comprehended in and limited to the ministry of the word."[81]

Here, it should be noticed that, in the title of the point concerning pastors, Calvin used the phrase "their [pastors'] power" (*leur puissance*) and that in the Latin edition of the *Instruction* published later in 1538 he also used the term "power" (*potestas*). If the use of the French words for "power" (*puissance*) and "authority" (*autorite*) were reflecting the traditional and customary distinction of two Latin words (*potestas/auctoritas*), Calvin's fresh use of "power" suggested a shift of emphasis on the importance of ministry. It should also be remembered that Farel's *Summary* did attribute "power" to the pastors, but the power of pastors was coupled with the power of the congregation.[82] In addition, Calvin stressed the comprehensive nature of the ministry of pastors by saying that the pastors were "to instruct the people publicly and privately in pure doctrine, to administer the sacraments and to teach them by the best example concerning holiness and purity of life," and interestingly he rephrased this by saying "this discipline and this order" (*ceste discipline et cest ordre*). We have seen that Calvin regarded the word and the sacraments as the two marks

80. *OS* 1:234–36.

81. *COR* III-2:103–5; *OS* 1:413–14.

82. *CO* 5:351. Cf. *Summaire*, chs. 35, 86–87. (Zuidema and Van Raalte, *Early French Reform*, 160–61.)

of the church, but here in the *Instruction* he called the two marks "this order" in distinction from "this discipline." This phrase was, we assume, the first indication of what we may call his two-series theory concerning the marks of the church, that is, while limiting the official two marks of the church to the word and the sacraments, he added discipline to the marks of the ministerial duty.[83] Furthermore, he warned that any slander against "this discipline and this order" was to be considered an act against God and a schismatic behavior against the church, and he highlighted the ministry's authority by referring to the power of the keys text (Matt 16:19).[84]

What did Calvin's shift of emphasis signify in the historical context of the early Genevan Reformation? Two assumptions can be made concerning his intention. On the one hand, it could be his reaction to Zwingli's caesaropapistic tendency of church polity in which the ministry was narrowly limited to the area of preaching and the sacraments, and that of discipline was primarily attributed to the magistrates. On the other hand, it could be his effort to rectify the congregational tendency that viewed the ministry subservient to the more fundamental power of the congregation. As we described in our examination of chapter 6 of the first *Institutes*, these two tendencies were considered extreme positions in his Catholic ecclesiology and Christ's kingdom theory that portrayed both church and state as "God's minister" within each autonomous jurisdiction. The first tendency of Zwinglianism was officially accepted by Bern, and in French-speaking Switzerland its influence was seen

83. The previous chapter noticed the rudimentary coexistence of the two- and three-marks notions of the church in the first *Institutes*. In the development of his theological thought, we assume, Calvin had developed a two-series notion of the church's marks. The two-marks notion, which concerned the essential identification of the church, was clearly formulated in chapter 4 of the 1539 *Institutes* (*CO* 1:542–45; *Institutio* 4.1.7–11), where the two marks were designated as "the order approved by the Lord." The three-marks notion, which concerned the external "form" of the church, became prominent in the context of the church's ministerial duties and its full expression was first seen in chapter 8 of the 1543 *Institutes* (*CO* 1:565, 623; *Institutio* 4.3.6, 4.7.23). The 1537 *Instruction* or the 1538 Latin *Catechism* could be viewed as the early stage of this development. Incidentally, our study on Beza (Maruyama, *The Ecclesiology*, 24n17) already noticed Calvin's two-series notion as his "theological insight."

84. A reference to the "heretical acts" (*injurieux . . . comme heretiques*) and the full citation of the power of the keys passage are not found in the corresponding section of the first *Institutes*. Traditionally, the passage (Matt 16:19) had been associated with the ministerial order and the medieval Catholic Church used it as "the Petrine text" for the defense of the papal lordship over the universal church. Calvin took issue with this claim in his first *Institutes* (*OS* 1:185, 188). The use of the passage in connection with the ministerial order in the *Instruction* here was noteworthy because this connection was absent in Farel's *Summary*.

in the Neuchâtel Church and its pastor Marcourt, as well as in Lausanne and Geneva.[85] The second tendency could be seen in Farel's *Summary*, where his Lefèvrian congregationalism focused on the "function" of pastors to preach the word and administer the sacraments and considered their "power" derived from that of the congregation. In addition, with regard to the Lausanne Disputation, it could be Calvin's reaction to Viret's exposition on the fifth article, "the said [Evangelical] church also recognizes no minister except the one who preaches the word of God and administers the sacraments," on which Viret delivered his anti-Catholic apologetics from a strict congregational stand.[86] As a whole, the *Instruction*'s point "the pastors of the church and their power" marked a new direction of Calvin's ecclesiology or a decisive first step toward his Reformed ecclesiology.

2. *Confession of Faith:* Confession de la foy

Among the three Genevan documents, besides the *Articles* that proposed the actual plan for reform of the existing Roman Catholic Church in Geneva, the *Confession*'s importance rested in the fact that it not only declared the doctrinal mark of a forthcoming Evangelical church but also was to be forced upon the citizens for their consent.[87] As we have assumed earlier, it was reasonable to

85. Cf. Gordon, *The Swiss Reformation*, 150, 152–54; G. Berthoud, *Antoine Marcourt: Réformateur et Pamphlétaire du "Livre des Marchans" aux Placards de 1534* (Geneva: Droz, 1973), 24–33. According to Berthoud, Marcourt, successor of Farel at the Neuchâtel Church and author of the famous 1534 Pamphlet, was known as a Zwinglian and was in conflict with Farel over the issue of the magisterial role in church government. Incidentally, Marcourt was the Genevan magistracy's choice for the church's chief pastor after the expulsion of Farel and Calvin in 1538.

86. Piaget, *Les Actes*, 276–80. In the exposition of the fifth article on the ministry, Viret defined the "body of Jesus-Christ" as composed of the faithful believers. Furthermore, he viewed the ministry necessary for nourishing the faithful and from this aspect he attacked the Catholic priests who did not nourish them. His utilitarian notion of the ministry at the close of the exposition (*tout ce que n'est de leur office apartient proprement aux fideles*) was noteworthy.

87. The *Confession*'s full title reads: CONFESSION DE LA FOY LAQUELLE TOUS BOURGEOIS ET HABITANS DE GENEVE ET SUBIECTS DU PAYS DOIBVENT IURER DE GARDER ET TENIR EXTRAICTE DE LINSTRUCTION DONT ON USE EN LEGLISE DE LA DICTE VILLE. (*OS* 1:418.) For the text of the *Confession*, we use the *Opera Selecta* (*OS* 1:418–26) and consult with *Calvini Opera* (*CO* 37:693–700) and Backus and Chimelli, eds., *La vraie piété*, 45–53. Backus and Chimelli use the *CO* text and consider the *Confession* as authored by Farel. For its English translation, we use *Creeds and Confessions*, 2:311–19, which bases the translation on the *CO* text.

attribute the origin of the *Articles* and *Confession* to Farel, the actual leader of the early Genevan Reformation and the Church's chief pastor, and that of the *Instruction* to Calvin as a young instructor of the Bible. Even if we accept this assumption, however, it was possible for Farel to have consulted with Calvin's *Institutes* and *Instruction* when he composed the *Confession*. In fact, the *Articles* and *Confession* both manifested some cooperative characteristics, if not coauthorship, of both Farel and Calvin. In the following pages, focusing only on the ecclesiological elements of the *Confession*, we will examine two points: first, the meaning of a peculiar expression in the *Confession*'s full title, namely, "extracted from the *Instruction*" (*extraicte de l'instruction*); second, an analysis of the *Confession*'s last five articles that roughly correspond to the *Instruction*'s last four points. Concerning the second point, we will consult the Latin text of the *Confession* that Calvin translated and edited from the French original and published in 1538 as an appendix to his own original Latin *Catechism*.[88]

(i) Concerning the first point of "extraction" from the *Instruction*, the *Confession* was indeed a mixed work. It contained some elements that were either borrowed from or assimilated with the *Instruction*. Yet at the same time it definitely retained Farel's characteristic reform concepts. As to the *Confession*'s structure, it did not follow Farel's *Summary* which employed the antithetical presentation (God and man, Christ's divinity and humanity, the law and the gospel, sin and justification, etc.), but took the soteriological scheme of the *Instruction* (God, the law, man, faith in Jesus Christ, salvation). Nevertheless, while the *Instruction* placed at its head such educational concerns as the knowledge of God and true and false religion, the *Confession* by its nature presented first the confession of faith in Scripture as "rule of our faith and religion." Such Evangelical emphases could be seen everywhere. Secondly, there were several doctrinal assertions for which Farel did not insist on expressing his own views in the *Summary*, but rather seemed to have assimilated them with the *Instruction*. A clear example of this could be seen in the articles on the sacraments. As we have pointed out in our analysis of the *Summary*, Farel understood the sacraments by the Lefèvrian emphases of the faith-oriented and memorial aspects and took Zwingli's symbolic view concerning Christ's presence in the Lord's Supper. In the *Confession*, however, the sacraments were clearly presented in the churchly framework that was characteristic in the *Instruction* but was not seen in the *Summary*. In addition, the *Confession* defined the sacraments by using two terms from the *Instruct*ion that were

88. Ioannes Calvinus, *Catechismus, sive Christianae religionis institutio* (*BC* 38/1). The editor of *Bibliotheca Calviniana* tentatively considers Farel as the French *Confession*'s author.

characteristically Calvin's but were not found in the *Summary*: the sacraments were instituted for the "exercises of faith" (*exercices de foy*), and what they presented was God's "promises" (*promesses*). As a particularly interesting point concerning their purpose, the *Confession* did not use the Lefèvrian theme of "keeping mutual love and increasing it" that Farel's *Summary* had so strongly emphasized, but instead used the terms found in the *Instruction*. For example, the purpose of baptism was to signify "the cleansing" of the sins of believers and the "mortification" of their bodies. As to the purpose of the Lord's Supper, furthermore, using Calvin's term "communication," the *Confession* defined it as "the truly spiritual communion" between Christ and believers, instead of the Lefèvrian notion of the "memory and imitation" by believers of Christ's sacrificial death that the *Summary* employed. Nonetheless, it should be noted that the *Confession* added some characteristic emphases of Farel's congregationalism. For example, he emphasized that the Lord's Supper should be celebrated "in the company of the faithful" so that "all those who wish to have Jesus for their life" could celebrate.[89]

(ii) The second point concerned the *Confession*'s last five articles (17–21: human traditions, the church, excommunication, ministers of the word, magistrates). Although sharing with the *Instruction* a common Evangelical conviction, the *Confession* showed some discrepancies in its order of argument as well as content. Concerning the order of argument, even though the *Confession* followed the order of the *Instruction* up to the articles on the sacraments, here it preferred the order of the *Summary* (chs. 14, 16, 32, 33–36, 37). As a result, the *Instruction* treated pastors first. Then, in connection with the power of pastors, it treated the topics of both human traditions and excommunication. On the other hand, as the *Confession* treated human traditions and excommunication first and then ministers of the word, it gave an impression that ministry was dissociated from the doctrinal judgment of human traditions and the practical exercise of excommunication.[90] As to its content, it seemed

89. *OS* 1:422–23; *Creeds and Confessions*, 2:316. Cf. *Summaire*, chs. 18, 34–36; *COR* III-2:95–101; *OS* 1:411–13. "Spiritual communication" was the notion that Calvin used in the first *Institutes* to supplement Zwingli's view, which sharply contrasted Christ's presence in heaven with his absence in the Lord's Supper. It was significant for Farel, who had taken Zwingli's view in the *Summary*, to incorporate Calvin's notion in the *Confession*.

90. *OS* 1:423–26; *Creeds and Confessions*, 2:317–19. Cf. *COR* III-2:103–11; *OS* 1:413–17. Augustijn, Burger, and van Stam ("Calvin in the Light of the Early Letters," 153) incorrectly assume that Farel "altered" the order as well as the content of Calvin's *Instruction* and considered excommunication an ordinary means for the church and its ministry. The fact was that, while Calvin's *Instruction* closely followed the order of his first *Institutes*, Farel's

to have assimilated the *Instruction*'s two articles of "human traditions," and "magistrates." Yet, in the three articles of "the church," "excommunication," and "ministers of the word," the document either emphasized Farel's own views or checked Calvin's views, thus suggesting different church reform ideas between Farel and Calvin.

Among the two clear cases of assimilation with the *Instruction*, the first article was on "human traditions" (17), an issue that was very close to the hearts of both Farel and Calvin. On this issue there was no substantive difference between Farel's *Summary* (ch. 14: "doctrine and tradition of men") and Calvin's *Instruction* (human traditions), but the difference appeared in their approaches to the issue. Farel treated the issue in the antithetical and general framework of "doctrine and tradition of men" versus "holy scripture" (ch. 15), and from his Biblicist position defined human doctrine and tradition as a mixture of human teachings with "the things of God." On the other hand, Calvin's *Instruction* saw the issue from the soteriological viewpoint of Christian freedom, especially of adiaphora. Accordingly, from 1 Corinthians 14 (40: "all things should be done decently and in order") he excluded from the discussion of this issue "civil observances" instituted for the order and peace of Christian assemblies, which were basically indifferent to salvation. Then, he focused upon how these indifferent things turned into "spiritual laws" to bind Christian conscience, as was done in the Catholic Church. Regarding this issue, the *Confession* followed Calvin's approach. It used the *Instruction*'s terms for the article heading ("human traditions"). It excluded from the discussion the ordinances that were necessary for the external governing of the church. And it took issue only with all "laws and regulations" that were never commanded by God, yet were destroying "Christian freedom."[91] The most obvious case of assimilation with the *Instruction*, if not Calvin's authorship, could be the *Confession*'s last article on magistracy (21). Corresponding to the term "magistracy" (*magistrat*) of the *Instruction*, the *Confession* used "magistrates" (*magistratz*) instead of the *Summary*'s "sword." Also, it positively defined their position as "a Christian vocation" and designated them as God's "vicars and lieutenants," perhaps corresponding to the *Instruction*'s "ministers and lieutenants."[92]

(iii) Among the *Confession*'s last five articles, besides the points of assimilation with the *Instruction*, the three articles "the church" (18), "excommunica-

Confession likewise followed that of his *Summary* and emphasized the congregational role in excommunication at the expense of the ministerial role.

91. *OS* 1:423–24. Cf. *Summaire*, chs. 14, 27–28; *COR* III-2:107; *OS* 1:415.

92. *OS* 1:425–26. Cf. *Summaire*, chs. 37, 93–94; *COR* III-2:109–11; *OS* 1:416–17.

tion" (19), and "ministers of the word" (20), in particular, suggested a different understanding of church reform. Assuming Farel's overall authorship of the *Confession*, the article on "the church" had a rather unique background. While Calvin's first *Institutes* used the Apostles' Creed as basically scriptural teaching, Farel's *Summary*, though citing and expounding on the Ten Commandments and the Lord's prayer, did not cite the Creed, perhaps, from the Biblicist point of view. Due to a concern for harmony with the *Instruction*, however, the *Confession* cited the Creed in Article 6 (salvation in Jesus), using the phrase "holy universal church" (*la saincte Eglise universelle*), thus avoiding the term "Catholic" that the *Instruction* used. Unlike Calvin's *Instruction* that treated the basic concept of the church under the creedal expressions of "the holy Catholic church, the communion of saints" and did not have an entry on the church in its last portion, Farel obviously felt the need to make a confessional statement on the church and placed a brief article on the church in the *Confession*'s last portion. This placement was characteristically Farel's. The article was placed after the articles on the sacraments. Just like in the *Summary*, it also showed no indication of the church's catholicity. The church it described here was the church in history, which was congruent with Farel's congregational view of the church.[93]

As to the content of the article on the church, there were three noticeable points of interest. The first point was its opening statement, "While there is only one church of Jesus-Christ." Since this church was further defined as "companies of the faithful" or "assemblies," Farel emphasized the church's congregational principle as well as the individuality of its members. This could well be his effort to counterbalance the *Instruction* in which Calvin interpreted the creed's "holy Catholic church and the communion of saints" in terms of God's election, but at the same time the church of the elect was to be "gathered and formed into one body" in history, thus emphasizing the church's catholicity as well as its unity.[94] The second point concerned the church's two marks of the word and the sacraments that the article presented as a clear indication of the church of Jesus-Christ. This was perhaps Farel's intention to supplement the *Instruction*, where Calvin did not present the two-marks theory clearly, even though he did earlier in his *Institutes*. As to the third point,

93. *OS* 1:424. Cf. *COR* III-2:61; *OS* 1:400–401; *OS* 1:420. Farel's congregational concept of the church is correctly described by White ("An Early Doctrinal Handbook," 31–32) as "individualistic pneumatology" and "a high degree of visibility" of the congregation of believers.

94. *OS* 1:424; *Creeds and Confessions*, 2:317. Cf. *COR* III-2:61; *OS* 1:400–401; also n. 77 above.

the article presented its sharpest attack against the Roman Catholic Church: "the churches governed by the ordinances of the pope are rather synagogues of the devil than Christian churches." Incidentally, this statement, the most radical anti-Catholic expression even among the three Genevan documents, reflected one of the main points of Farel's and Viret's apologetics at the Lausanne Disputation. Interestingly, however, in his translation of the *Confession* into Latin, Calvin eliminated this statement as part of his editorial effort.[95]

The article of "excommunication" (19) could also be said to be a clear case of assimilation, yet at the same time it was written in such a way as to show Farel's overall style and mentality. For example, the article employed the *Instruction*'s term for its title as well as in its text, using "the discipline of excommunication" instead of the narrower concept of "excommuning" or exclusion from the Lord's table preferred in the *Summary.* It also used Calvin's characteristic notion of triple purpose for excommunication. At the same time, Farel's unique emphasis could be seen with regard to "the discipline of excommunication." The ministerial role was never mentioned in this discipline. Instead, the discipline was described as "a thing holy and salutary among the faithful" from the congregational point of view. Another example of Farel's originality could be seen in the *Confession*'s use of Calvin's triple purpose itself. Calvin's *Instruction*, just like his first *Institutes*, described the triple purpose of excommunication in the following order: Christ's honor not to be despised by the wicked, other members not to be contaminated by the conversation with the wicked, and after being ashamed and having repented, the wicked to be restored. In particular, he stressed the first purpose because "the church is the body of Christ." On the contrary, the *Confession* exchanged the first and second purposes, thus making the second purpose, which was a preventive measure in the *Instruction*, as the primary purpose ahead of Christ's honor that was only cursorily mentioned. Furthermore, it enlarged the significance of the purpose of preventing adverse

95. *OS* 1:424; *Creeds and Confessions*, 2:317. Cf. *CO* 5:360. Concerning this statement, since Calvin considered the basic nature of Catholicism as a mixture of Christianity, Judaism, and heathenism in the first *Institutes*, he could agree with the meaning of the statement. As to his intention regarding its omission in the Latin *Confession*, it might reflect his concern for the statement's suitability in an official confession of faith. Van Stam ("The Group of Meaux," 256–57nn18, 20) considers this statement the first expression of Farel's criticism against the Nicodemist group of Meaux in the French Reformation and assumes that Calvin "afterward" followed Farel's position. Van Stam's interpretation may face difficulties due to the fact that, as we have seen in our previous chapter, Calvin's first *Institutes*, especially in chapter 4 and the apology section of chapters 5 and 6, had reached the same radical position that Farel's statement implied.

effects of the wicked into a positive measure of expelling them from the community. Perhaps interpreting Jesus's saying in Matthew 18 (15–17) as "what is expedient according to the ordinance of God," it considered this expulsion measure divinely sanctioned. Accordingly, it went on to list twelve items against which excommunication could be applied. Then, if those who were excommunicated showed no signs of repentance, it concluded that they were to be "separated from the communion of the faithful." However, the most characteristic feature of this article was the list itself. While Calvin's *Instruction* had a similar list with moral faults such as "open fornicators, adulterers, thieves," the *Confession* placed at the list's head "all manifest idolaters, blasphemers." Since these terms likely meant "Catholic believers" according to Farel's terminology, the *Confession* made clear a posture of expelling them from the Genevan Church.[96] This point will be taken up again in our analysis of the *Articles*.

The article on "ministers of the word" (20) was likewise clearly conscious of the *Instruction*, yet added Farel's own emphases and counterbalance. Its opening sentence was formulated with a forceful negative, "we do not reject any other pastors of the church who are the faithful ministers of God's word," which indicated its challenging nature and perception from the congregation's side. Here, Farel was following the line of arguments presented in the *Summary* where he focused on the "function" of pastors in the congregation and in the fifth Article of the Lausanne Disputation that declared no other ministers to be recognized legitimate than those who preach the word and administer the sacraments. Accordingly, the article affirmed the double function of ministers in a challengingly practical fashion: they were to nourish "the flock of Jesus-Christ on the one hand with instruction, admonition, consolation, exhortation, and accusation" as well as to resist "all false doctrines and deceptions of the devil." Furthermore, it showed a clear awareness of what Calvin had emphasized on the same topic in the *Instruction*, namely, the God-given nature of ministers and their indispensability, as well as their all-round function (preaching, the sacraments, and discipline) in the church. On the indispensability of ministers, for example, the article said that "the true ministers of the word" were "messengers and ambassadors of God" and it was "necessary to listen to them." "But on the other hand," it warned that those false prophets who spoke of themselves and despised the purity of the gospel were "ravaging wolves" unworthy of the title of pastors and were to be expelled from God's

96. *OS* 1:424–25, esp. 424: "Cest affin que les meschans par leur conversation damnable ne corrumpent les bons et ne deshonorent nostre Seigneur, et aussy que ayans honte ilz se retournent a penitence"; *Creeds and Confessions*, 2:317–18. Cf. *COR* III-2:107–9; *OS* 1:415–16.

people.[97] This challenging stance of Farel's could be interpreted as an attempt to check the young Calvin's naivete, or as his warning against the introduction of ministerial dominance in the Evangelical churches, or even as a sign of the anticlericalism mentality witnessed in Lefèvre and the Meaux reform. In any case, this article unquestionably revealed a conceptual difference between the *Instruction* and the *Confession*.

3. Ecclesiastical Ordinance: Articles concernant l'organisation de l'église

Among the three documents of 1537, the ecclesiastical ordinance "Articles concerning the Organization of the Church" is the most important for the Genevan Reformation, yet its authorship and evaluation have remained mostly unsettled and confused.[98] In serious research of recent years, for example, articles by van Stam (2000) and by Augustijn et al. (2004) proposed a theory of Farel's basic authorship with the possibility of Calvin's coauthorship. Gordon's recent Calvin biography (2009) inclined to take "the more experienced Farel" as its primary author. The most comprehensive research on this issue so far, the van Stam article, presented a convincing argument for the *Articles* through its text's hermeneutic and theological analyses as well as its background examinations of Calvin's *Institutes* and *Instruction* and Farel's *Summary* and *Confession*.[99]

If we accept this recent scholarship, there seem to be two possible conclusions: the one, Farel as a radical Lefèvrian Evangelical was a theologian in his own right; the other, the early Genevan Reformation was led by Farel rather than by Calvin. In the following pages, focusing on the formation of Calvin's ideas about church reform, we will examine the most problematic aspects of the *Articles* under three points: the relation between the sacraments and church discipline, especially between the Lord's Supper and excommunication, the process of executing excommunication, and the church reform guideline seen in the system of church discipline.

97. *OS* 1:425; *Creeds and Confessions*, 2:318. A part of the translation here is ours. Cf. *Summaire*, chs. 34–35, 83–91; *COR* III-2:103–5; *OS* 1:413–15.

98. For the text of the *Articles*, two editions (*COR* VI-1:157–70; *OS* 1:369–77) are used. They represent two different sources, the former the Genevan City Council record and the latter the record of the Genevan Church copyists. For the sources, confer *COR* VI-1:153–54 and for the authorship of the *Articles*, confer van Stam, "Die Genfer Artikel," *Zwingliana* 27 (2000): 90n17.

99. *COR* VI-1:153–54. Cf. van Stam, "Die Genfer Artikel," 87–100, esp. 98–99; Augustijn et al., "Calvin in the Light," 151–54; Gordon, *Calvin*, 72.

The Lord's Supper and Excommunication

(i) The core of the first point is the question about how the *Articles* related two statements placed in its preamble: one, "it is certain that a church cannot be said well-ordered and ruled unless the holy Supper of our Lord is often and frequently celebrated there"; the other, "in order to maintain the church well in its integrity, discipline of excommunication is necessary." Since excommunication was placed as the first of the four proposals of the *Articles* (excommunication, psalm singing, education of children, and marriage court) and the first proposal occupied two-thirds of the entire text, the relation between the Lord's Supper and excommunication was obviously considered a core issue. In the background of the first proposal, as suggested by Opitz, we find the Reformed context of South Germany and Switzerland. Since the 1520s, Strasbourg's Bucer and Capito, Zurich's Zwingli, Basel's Oecolampadius, and others had been negotiating for a consensus on the form of excommunication. In the Basel meeting of 1530, instead of a consensus, "a typically Swiss solution" was reached that recommended each city to adopt its own form as appropriate to its own circumstance. Farel and Calvin might have taken advantage of this solution.[100] Generally speaking, in areas and cities where Evangelical reform was introduced, the abolition of the Catholic Mass and the introduction of the evangelical Lord's Supper were considered as the official start of the Reformation, and the placement of the Lord's Supper as the first topic of the ordinance was not exceptional. However, to celebrate the Lord's Supper frequently and to relate it directly with the severest form of discipline (excommunication) indicated the radical nature of church reform.

Concerning frequent celebration, as we have seen in our examination of the *Summary* (ch. 18; the sacraments), it could be understood as Farel's adaptation of the Lefèvrian notion of communion as "unlimited memory" or "countless grace" to the Evangelical church situation. It was also seen in his concluding remarks at the Lausanne Disputation. Likewise, it was presented in Calvin's first *Institutes* where the celebration of the Supper was to "frequently return

100. *OS* 1:369. Cf. P. Opitz, "Calvin in the Context of the Swiss Reformation," 18–20; Ganoczy, *Young Calvin*, 113; van Stam, "Die Genfer Artikel," 87; Augustijn et al., "Calvin in the Light," 151; A. Demura, "Calvin's and Oecolampadius' Concept of Church Discipline," in *Calvinus Ecclesiae Genevensis Custos*, ed. W. H. Neuser (Frankfurt: Verlag Peter Lang, 1984), 187–89. On the question of the number of proposals, we follow Ganoczy's analysis: one "premise" (frequent communion) and four propositions. On the assumption of Calvin's authorship of the *Articles*, Demura examines the *Articles* from Oecolampadius's concept of church discipline.

in memory to Christ's passion" or "at least once a week." In this regard he was either in agreement with Farel or had also inherited the Lefèvrian notion. In addition, it should be noted that there was the precedence of the *Basel Ecclesiastical Ordinance* (1529) in which the weekly celebration, in rotating parishes, was proposed.[101] Concerning the direct connection of the Lord's Supper with excommunication, as we have pointed out in our examination of the *Summary* (ch. 32), what Farel had in mind could be Lefèvrian tradition that interpreted the Lord's Supper as "memory and imitation" of Christ's redemptive love and church discipline. Exclusion from the Lord's Supper, as well as reception of the disciplined repentant, was understood as a practice of the same love. It could also be suggested that, in the churches Farel had evangelized after his exit from the Meaux reform, the customary process of church reform went on like this: his attack on the Mass, introduction of the evangelical sacraments, and practice of church discipline. On the other hand, Calvin's first *Institutes* referred to an example of the evangelical order of worship at the end of chapter 4 ("The Sacraments"). In this order, the sacramental celebration and church discipline were closely tied. Before distributing bread and wine, the celebrant was to cite the words of Christ's institution and to declare the "promise" offered in the sacrament. "At the same time," Calvin said, the celebrant "should excommunicate all who are debarred from it by the Lord's prohibition." In this respect, Calvin was in basic agreement with Farel.[102]

(ii) If the frequent celebration of the Lord's Supper and its direct connection with excommunication were indeed what Farel and Calvin understood as the direction of the early Genevan Reformation, what was the meaning of this? There are at least two questions to be raised. Where was the position of Farel and Calvin to be placed in the history of the Reformation? And, what was the significance of this position for the formation of the Evangelical church to which the Genevan *Articles* aimed? As to the first question, our study has suggested the historical context of the early French Reformation, in particular, Lefèvrianism and its radicalization seen in Farel. However, our study has also admitted that the exact extent of Lefèvrian influence on Farel or Calvin needs to be historically substantiated. Another point of contact that some researchers have suggested was the Basel Reformer Oecolampadius. As we have mentioned earlier, Farel had close personal contact with him after his withdrawal from

101. *Summaire*, chs. 18, 34–36 (Zuidema and Van Raalte, *Early French Reform*, 134–35); Piaget, *Les Actes*, 408 cited in *COR* VI-1:157n2; *OS* 1:149–50, 161.

102. *Summaire*, chs. 18, 34–35 (Zuidema and Van Raalte, *Early French Reform*, 134); chs. 32, 78–81 (Zuidema and Van Raalte, *Early French Reform*, 156–57); *OS* 1:161.

the Meaux reform. In the case of Calvin, Wendel suggests the possibility of his knowing Oecolampadius's concepts of the Lord's Supper and church discipline. After his exile in post-Oecolampadius Basel, Calvin might either have had contacts with the latter's disciples or have read his posthumous Latin publication (1536). Here again, the nature of his influence on either Farel or Calvin has not yet been fully substantiated, and further research seems needed.[103] Therefore, we will mainly focus on the second question and examine the text of the *Articles* for the Genevan Church.

First of all, the direct connection of the Lord's Supper and excommunication as a church reform concept seems to presuppose a kind of community characterized by the sacrament and church discipline. As to the Lord's Supper, the *Articles* affirmed that the first proposal's aim was to establish "the congregation of Christians" (*la congregation des crestiens*) by means of the weekly communion of believers. "The congregation" was also described as "participants of Jesus' body and blood, of his death and life, of his Spirit and all goods." It was to be realized by communion as a "frequent exercise of our faith and charity," and not by the Catholic Church's practice of communion two or three times a year. Furthermore, its goal was idealistically set as "living like the Christians, being a gathering in peace and brotherly unity just like members of the same body."[104] As the primary characteristic of these statements, the church was described from the

103. Cf. Wendel, *Calvin*, 143. The posthumous Latin publication (*DD Ioannis Oecolampadii et Huldreichi Zwingli Epistolarum, Libri Quatuor*, Basel, 1536) was intended to highlight two Reformers' views on such questions as the Lord's Supper and church discipline. It included the Latin edition of Oecolampadius's comprehensive proposal on the introduction of church discipline in Basel: *Oratio de Reducenda Excommunicatione*. Cf. E. Staehelin, *Das theologische Lebenswerk Johannes Oekolampads* (Leipzig: M. Heinsius Nachfolger, 1939), 506–11. An Oecolampadius scholar, Kuhr (O. Kuhr, "Calvin and Basel: The Significance of Oecolampadius and the Basel Discipline Ordinance for the Institution of Ecclesiastical Discipline in Geneva," *Scottish Bulletin of Evangelical Theology* 16 [1998]: 22–26), assumes Calvin is the chief author of the *Articles* and asserts its clear parallel to the *Basel Reformation Ordinance* of 1529. However, two points in particular do not seem to be supported by the text of the *Articles*: (1) "the *Articles* demand some men ["deputez"] of moral integrity should be appointed from the congregation"; (2) "deputez" and ministers as "representatives from both congregation and ministry" form "a mixed ecclesiastical court for the exercise of church discipline." As we will examine later, on the first point Kuhr misses the fact that "deputez" were selected and appointed by the magistracy and not by the congregation. On the second point, the text was not clear about the form of the disciplinary agency. As we acknowledge Farel's main authorship of the *Articles* as well as his imprecise descriptions of the disciplinary process, we wonder if Kuhr might read too much parallelism with the *Basel Ecclesiastical Ordinance* and Calvin's later *Genevan Ordinance* of 1541 in the text of the *Articles*.

104. *COR* VI-1:160; *OS* 1:370.

viewpoint of its members and that of their participation in the Lord's Supper. In the first *Institutes*, Calvin conceived of the church from the perspective of God's election and the Lord's Supper from the principle of "the exchange which out of his [Christ's] measureless goodness he has made with us," and accordingly emphasized the sacrament as a "means of grace." In clear contrast, Farel's *Summary* presented a congregational concept of the church and emphasized the Lord's Supper as believers' memorializing and imitating Christ's sacrifice and love. In this comparison, the description of the church in the *Articles* as a sacramental community clearly pointed to Farel rather than to Calvin.[105]

Concerning excommunication, the *Articles* proposed "discipline of excommunication" as the primary means to establish "the congregation of Christians" in Geneva. It also affirmed that "the Lord's Supper which was ordained and justly established for conjoining the members of our Lord Jesus-Christ with their head as well as with themselves in one body and one spirit should not be tainted and contaminated," as well as that, "this communion should be of approved members of Jesus-Christ." Its main emphasis, therefore, was on the direct connection of the congregation, the sacraments, and excommunication. Accordingly, excommunication was defined as a teleological device for the true congregation. Also noticeable in its proposal of excommunication were the key terms it repeatedly used, namely, believers' "communion" and their "coming to the communing."[106] To view the Lord's Supper from the congregational perspective and excommunication as a teleological device seems to point to Farel. The relation that we suggested earlier between this thought pattern and Lefèvrianism or Oecolampadius has not been fully substantiated. As far as Oecolampadius was concerned, however, judging only from his *Oration* (*Oratio de Reducenda Excommunicatione*, 1530) regarding the introduction of excommunication in the Basel Church, he did not present such a teleological argument but consistently emphasized its use "for improving morality" of the community. In the case of Calvin, likewise, perhaps due to his twofold understanding of the keys or hermeneutical distinction between doctrine (Matt 16, the sacraments included) and practice (Matt 18, excommunication), he did not conceptually connect excommunication as a teleological device with the Lord's Supper either in the section of the first *Institutes* that deals with the purpose of excommunication or in the *Instruction*.[107]

105. Cf. *OS* 1:137 (confer ch. 1, n. 119); *Summaire*, chs. 18–19, 34–41 (n. 41 above).

106. *COR* VI-1:161–62; *OS* 1:371–72. Cf. van Stam, "Die Genfer Artikel," 97n47.

107. Cf. Oecolampadius's *Oratio* referred in n. 103 above; *COR* III-2:99–101, 107; *OS* 1:412–13, 415.

(iii) The *Articles* seems to have its own textual problem in the first proposal on the Lord's Supper and excommunication. According to the *Renewed Opera Calvini*, the text of this section (*COR* VI-1:157–68, lines 1–219) is composed of ten paragraphs. From the text's critical analysis, these paragraphs can be divided into three portions: the first (par. 1–5), preamble and the connection between the Lord's Supper and excommunication; the second (6–7), the biblical foundation and a history of excommunication; and the third (8–10), the process of introducing excommunication into the Genevan Church. While the first and the third portions, as we have partially seen above, suggest Farel's overall composition, the second short portion seems to distinguish itself from the other two and to suggest Calvin's own composition or Farel's use of Calvin material.

There are at least three indications that enable us to suggest this possibility. Firstly, the second portion's style in French is both concise and precise, its content partly recapitulates a point made in the first portion with a different expression, and it includes the phrase, "the kingdom of pope" (*royaulme du pape*), which Calvin customarily used in contrast to Christ's kingdom.[108] Secondly, as we have earlier compared Calvin's *Instruction* and the *Confession* concerning the list of wrongdoings to which excommunication can be applied, the second portion does not follow the *Confession*'s list that places "manifested idolaters, blasphemers" (which we have interpreted as believers of the Catholic faith) at the head. Instead, it aligns with the *Instruction* that lists moral wrongdoings in general and, as part of excommunication's biblical basis, it quotes a list from 1 Corinthians (5:11). Thirdly, as both the *Instruction* and the *Confession* refer to the so-called triple aims of excommunication, the *Articles* also refers to it, but in a very interesting way. We have noticed that Calvin's *Instruction*, just like his *Institutes*, arranges the three aims as such: that Christ's honor not be violated, that the adverse effects of wrongdoers upon other members be prevented, and having been ashamed and repented, that the wrongdoers be restored. The *Confession* exchanges the first and second aims, and makes the second aim, which is a preventive measure in Calvin, into a major principle of excluding the wrongdoers (especially, the Catholic believers) from the community. In this background, the second portion arranges a new order: it restores Christ's honor to the primary aim; it even places the restoration of wrongdoers in second place and quotes, according to the *COR* editors' footnote, an excerpt from Calvin's first *Institutes*; and it places

108. *COR* VI-1:163 (l. 113)–164 (l. 143); *OS* 1:372 (l. 1 4)–373 (l. 6). Concerning paragraphs, we follow the *COR* text. The reference to Christ's kingdom in this section is not conclusive evidence, since a similar reference is also found in the succeeding portion.

the *Confession*'s primary aim of exclusion as the last in order.[109] If our above-mentioned suggestions were correct, there is a possibility that Calvin might have had reservations on two counts, namely, to consider excommunication as a teleological device for establishing the Evangelical church and its Lord's Supper, and to regard the Catholic believers per se as the object of excommunication. We may even assume that, as a young instructor in Scripture, he had high expectations for the educational reform of the church and the conversion of the Catholics through instruction in the Evangelical faith.

Process of Excommunication

(i) The second point concerned the process of executing excommunication in the actual setting of the Genevan Church. Concerning the text that occupied the last portion of the first proposal, due to the fact that it was likely composed by Farel and reflected the early and fluid situation of the Reformation, it showed some signs of conceptual ambiguity and lack of concreteness. For convenience's sake, it will be presented here as a three-step process. As the first step, the magistracy was to select a certain number of "persons of good life and good esteem among all the faithful" from the city's four parishes, whom the text later identified as "deputies" (*desputés*), and have them oversee the conduct of the parishioners. As the second step, based on the guideline of Matthew 18 (15–17), when deputies found wrongdoings to be disciplined, they joined with ministers and jointly censured. If censure was not effective, they "would notify the church" (*signiffera a leglise*), and with their assent ministers reported to the "congregation" (*lassemblee*) for the discipline of the wrongdoers. As the third step, when the disciplined did not obey the church, it would become "time to bar the communion" (*temps de lexcommunier*). Though they were allowed to hear the sermons, they were excluded from "the communion of the Supper" as well as from "the company of Christians."[110]

(ii) In this process, there were some problematic points. As to the first step, for example, the official title and number of what the text designated as "deputies" were not clearly stated, nor whether they represented the magistracy or the church. As to the second step, the use of both "church" and "congregation" in the text added confusion. If the first, "church," was meant to be the

109. *COR* VI-1:163–64, esp. 164n53; *OS* 1:372–73. Cf. *OS* 1:424–25. Concerning difference in the lists of evildoers, Augustijn et al. ("Calvin in the Light," 153–54) notice the difference and relate it to "Farel's sharply anti-Catholic tendency."

110. *COR* VI-1:165–66; *OS* 1:373.

magistracy as representing the Genevan Church, what was the relation between "deputies" and "ministers," and were they to form a church court as the representatives of the state and the church? Since both Farel and Calvin were expected to be, to a certain degree, familiar with the cases of introducing the disciplinary system in Oecolampadius's Basel or Bucer's Strasbourg, the case of the *Articles* was extraordinary. Incidentally, the above-mentioned *Oration* of Oecolampadius interpreted "the church" ("tell it to the church," Matt 18:17) as a church court based upon the cooperative idea of ministers and elders, and it proposed the court's composition as four ministers, four magisterial representatives, and four congregational representatives. Bucer's original draft of the *Strasbourg Ecclesiastical Ordinances* (1533) proposed to set up a church court (*Ersamen Raht*) composed of three church officials, three ministers, and two representatives of the city councils.[111] Furthermore, even though "deputies" were selected and appointed by the magistracy and the three-step process presupposed the cooperation of "deputies," ministers, and congregations, excommunication as a whole was conceived from the narrow perspective of the congregation. Of course, the text did not present the radical congregational oversight of excommunication that Farel had proposed in the *Summary*, and indeed there were no Evangelical congregations in Geneva at this time. Yet at the same time, the text did not present either ministerial leadership or magisterial intervention as being in control of the process of excommunication.

(iii) The core question was, therefore, whether the process of excommunication was narrowly conceived as congregational and churchly excommunication focused upon the barring of the wrongdoers from communion, or was it holistically conceived as communal excommunication involving both the church and the magistrates. In this regard, an important sentence appeared at the end of the three-step process as a summary statement: "Truly, this seems to be a good means for us to regain excommunication in our church and to keep it in its entirety. And without this correction, the church cannot go forward."[112] In connection with this quotation, noticeably, the *Articles* urged magisterial actions in response to the disciplinary process so that "such contempt and mockery of God and his gospel" by those who have rejected discipline should not go unpunished. Then, it went on to describe magisterial actions and their implications in the Christian community. In this description, the term "ex-

111. For Oecolampadius's proposal in the *Oratio*, confer Staehelin, *Das theologische Lebenswerk*, 509. For Bucer's original proposal, confer *BDS* 5:25–26, 402; F. Wendel, *L'Église de Strasbourg* (Paris: Presses universitaires de France, 1942), 167–68.

112. *COR* VI-1:165 (l. 151)–166 (l. 185); *OS* 1:373 (l. 16)–374 (l. 11).

communication" was not applied to magisterial actions that were contrasted with "excommunication of our congregation" (*excommunication de nostre assemblee*).[113] Thus, magisterial actions were not conceived as a part of the process of excommunication and were also conceptually distinguished from congregational and churchly discipline.

Guideline for Church Reform

(i) The third point concerned the key proposal of the *Articles* of the guideline for reforming the Genevan Church. It was a two-sided proposal in which the magistracy, upon receiving the result of the disciplinary process of excommunication, was to discern those who were unfit for the church and to let the citizen make his confessional stand clear. On the one hand, the proposal urged the magistracy to support and enforce what the church had judged on the cases of excommunication. Since those who ignored the church's disciplinary process or stubbornly adhered to "all superstitions" (Catholic believers) still coexisted in the Church, the magistracy was to discern "who was of the church of Jesus-Christ or not" according to "excommunication of our congregation." On the other hand, as the *Articles* declared that "there is no greater element of division than faith," the proposal referred to the magistracy's own responsibility to maintain the community of faith in one accord. The responsibility was to force the inhabitants to make their confession stand clear so that those who loved the gospel and "those who love the kingdom of pope more than the kingdom of Jesus-Christ" could be separated.[114]

So far we have left two difficult questions unanswered. One concerns the place of the church reform concepts expressed in the *Articles* within the history of the Reformed Reformation. The other concerns the relation of the *Articles* to a particularly distinctive concept of the Reformed Reformation, namely, that of autonomous church discipline.

(ii) As to the first question, the issue of excommunication had a complex background in the Reformed Reformation. The issue was unavoidable when the practice of God's word and the ethical implications of the Evangelical teachings were emphasized as characteristic marks of the Reformation. In addition, it had come to the forefront as Oecolampadius and Bucer had tried to restore the Evangelical and churchly practice of excommunication as a reaction, in part, to Zwingli's disciplinary notion that had left the whole issue in the care of the

113. *COR* VI-1:166 (ll. 188–90); [*OS* 1:374 (ll. 15–17)].

114. *COR* VI-1:166–68; *OS* 1:374–75.

magistrates. Even for the Genevan magistrates who had won their political independence and Evangelical Reformation with the help of Zwinglian Bern, the primary concern was to avoid the two extremes of both the Catholic episcopal monopoly of church discipline and the rigidly congregational practice of the Anabaptists so as to keep excommunication under their control. As the first proposal of *Articles* can be historically placed against this background, such knotty problems as the proposal's originality, Oecolampadius's or Bucer's influence upon Farel or Calvin, and others must be addressed.[115]

Concerning Oecolampadius's influence, however, our analysis has suggested that these elements in the *Articles* were not necessarily congruent with his reformatory ideas: the tendency to regard excommunication as a means to establish the Evangelical church and its Lord's Supper, to consider the narrowly conceived excommunication of barring from communion as the congregation's possessory right, and to judge the Catholic faith per se as an object of excommunication. Of course, it was generally practiced in the churches where the magistracy introduced the Evangelical Reformation to discern the allegiance of church members to the old or the new faith, to enforce the confession of faith, and, if necessary, to force their involuntary or voluntary expulsions. For sure, Farel was well versed in these practices in the various churches where he had served for over ten years before his appointment in Geneva. In addition, the reality of Geneva that Farel and Calvin faced was "division of faith" as the *Articles* described. Its immediate priority was to discern "those who love the kingdom of pope more than the Kingdom of Jesus-Christ." Nonetheless, the proposal of the *Articles* as a whole, with its unique disciplinary concepts and emphases, represented a radical development in the history of the Reformed Reformation. And the reason for this, as we have suggested, seemed to point mainly to Farel's congregationalism and his Lefèvrian background.[116]

115. In recent scholarship that acknowledges Oecolampadius's influence upon Farel's and Calvin's concept of church discipline, for example, we can list the following works: A. Demura, "Calvin's and Farel's Concept," 187–89; J. W. Baker, "Christian Discipline and the Early Reformed Tradition: Bullinger and Calvin," in *Calviniana: Ideas and Influence of Jean Calvin*, ed. R. V. Schnucker (Kirksville: Sixteenth Century Journal Publishers, 1988), 110–11; O. Kuhr, "Calvin and Basel," 22–26; D. Poythress, *Reformer of Basel: The Life, Thought, and Influence of Johannes Oecolampadius* (Grand Rapids: Reformation Heritage Books, 2011), 46–48. From our study's point of view, the most affirmative view of Baker who seems to assume Farel and Calvin's coauthorship of the *Articles* and sees in it Oecolampadius's influence to the extent that "the only missing elements were the Consistory and the use of the term 'elders'" seems too simplistic. On the other hand, works such as those of van Stam ("Die Genfer Artikel," 99) and Augustijn et al. ("Calvin in the Light," 151–52), which assume the chief authorship of Farel as well as Oecolampadius's influence upon him, need to be taken seriously.

116. Cf. *COR* VI-1:167; *OS* 1:374; Ganoczy, *Young Calvin*, 113–14.

(iii) The second question of autonomous ecclesiastical discipline has historically been a complex issue that has been framed by Calvin researchers in the following way. In his second Genevan Reformation, after his three-year interim period (1538–41) in Strasbourg, Calvin had set up a system of autonomous discipline in Geneva that neither Oecolampadius nor Bucer had achieved. Then the question is asked regarding how to relate that achievement with the 1537 *Articles*. Especially among researchers who assume Calvin's authorship of the *Articles*, they have taken the methodology of reading into what Calvin had later achieved in the 1540s back to the first Genevan Reformation and finding in the *Articles* some early manifestations of autonomous discipline or the influence of Oecolampadius or Bucer.

As a study in the history of doctrine, on the contrary, our study has traced the early development of Calvin's concept of the church and related it to the *Articles*. In assuming Farel's overall authorship, it has also found the document to be a co-opted work, a mixture of what Calvin could agree with Farel on and of what he was hesitant about or what he was presenting as his own view to check Farel. As we have seen, Calvin could agree with the two main theses of the *Articles*; the close relationship of the Lord's Supper with excommunication, and the narrowly conceived excommunication as exclusion from communion that should belong to the church as indicated by the phrase, "excommunication of our congregation." As a matter of fact, in the first *Institutes* he interpreted the Matthew 18:17 text as "the discipline of excommunication which is entrusted to the church" and the term "the church" as "the assembly of believers."[117] Regarding these two theses, it can be said that he shared the notion of the *Articles* of a kind of autonomous and congregational excommunication. Of course, the concept of autonomous ecclesiastical discipline itself was not unique to the Reformed tradition. The Roman Catholic Church had historically practiced it with the emphasis on the church's predominance over the political powers. And the Anabaptists, who rejected the traditional church-state notion, practiced it in their separatist congregations as an extreme form of autonomous and congregational discipline. The real issue, however, was whether this excommunication was the same as the historical Reformed notion of autonomous ecclesiastical discipline or, if not the same, its early expression of it.

If we are able to attribute any uniqueness to what Oecolampadius and Bucer had proposed, it ought to be what the Reformed Reformation, facing the new reality of the emergence of both Evangelical churches and secular powers and accordingly creating the integral social teachings, had formulated. It was a new type of holistic church discipline based upon the cooperative notion of

117. *OS* 1:187. (Battles, trans., *Institution*, 197–98.)

both church and state. In more concrete terms, on the one hand the new type rejected both the Catholic and the Anabaptist church discipline as two extreme forms, on the other hand it balanced Zwingli's magistracy-oriented notion with the New Testament notion of the church's elders as representatives of both church and state, and thus interpreted this integration as autonomous church discipline.[118] Within this background, the *Articles* did not formulate any notion of "integration" but instead emphasized the notion of "distinction" as the congregational right over excommunication. If this was due largely to Farel's congregationalism, as we have suggested, it was not necessarily congruent with the Reformed notion of autonomous discipline or that of Oecolampadius and Bucer. Though the *Articles* presupposed a kind of cooperation of church and state in a wider concept of church discipline, it presented a premature form of cooperation for Calvin who had presented in his first *Institutes* an integral notion of the church and state as "God's ministers" under the scheme of Christ's kingdom. Even in his *Instruction* addressed to the Genevan situation, in reacting to Zwingli's notion of discipline and checking Farel's congregational polity, he emphasized ministerial autonomy in connection with church discipline. In this respect, his *Institutes* and *Instruction* both connotatively showed a basis for what was known as the Reformed notion of autonomous church discipline that was to be presented, in his case, in his later *Genevan Ecclesiastical Ordinances* (1541).

Strictly speaking, the subsequent history of the three documents presented to the magistracy in January 1537 is not the object of this analysis. According to Wendel's concise description, the events took place as follows: in March the magistracy finally accepted the *Articles* and soon afterward also accepted and made public the *Confession*. But difficulties arose in the process of collecting the assents of citizens through both the official visitations to each household and the collective persuasions at the cathedral. In July the magistracy, in fear of a volatile situation, abandoned the core element of the *Articles*, namely, the introduction of excommunication in the church. According to Wendel, the failure of Farel and Calvin was largely due to the fact that the *Articles* sharply distinguished the Reformed Evangelicals and the Catholic believers still hold-

118. For example, Gäbler's dictionary article (U. Gäbler, "Oekolampad, Johannes," in *Theologische Realenzyklopädie* [Berlin and New York: de Gruyter, 1995], 25, 29–36) considers Oecolampadius's disciplinary concept comprehensive and balanced. According to him, Oecolampadius balanced the magisterial disciplinary right and the church's relatively autonomous right in terms of the biblical notion of "elders" gathered in the ecclesiastical court, and in this respect he had contributed to the characteristic development of the Reformed Reformation in the southern parts of Germany and Switzerland.

ing a strong influence in the city. Farel and Calvin did not give the magistrates enough room to cope with the middle majority. Assuming Calvin's authorship of the three documents, Wendel attributes partial responsibility for failure to Calvin's "political inexperience." Among more recent researchers, the rather simplistic views of Farel's "radicalism," Calvin's "inexperience," and their misjudgment of the current situation of Geneva and its surroundings as reason for their expulsion have been entertained.[119]

As we have seen above, however, the core of the issue rested mainly on the radical nature of the proposal itself of the *Articles*, especially on two points that we have considered to be Farel's position. Firstly, as the expression "excommunication of our congregation" suggested, the proposal's insistence on the narrowly conceived excommunication as the congregation's own right caused the magistracy to rethink the issue. Even though the exclusion from communion itself was a churchly exercise, it was not so for Bern's Zwinglian polity, and fear of reintroducing ministerial control over excommunication was widely felt in Geneva. Therefore, the magistracy, led by a pro-Bern faction, was forced to abandon the proposal and to accept the Zwinglian polity. Secondly, the magistracy also reacted to the radical proposal of the *Articles* concerning the objects of excommunication. In particular, as seen in the *Confession* and the *Articles*, Farel's push to regard the Catholic faith per se as a possible object of excommunication had brought resistance and confusion in the city. Although we have suggested the possibility that Calvin did not share the same conviction with Farel on these two points, as a coauthor of the proposal he could not be excused from his responsibility. However, the whole reformatory process that would eventually lead to their expulsion from the city in the following year was certainly a lesson for Calvin who was later to establish a system of autonomous church discipline in the same city of Geneva.

Section 3. Practice of Catholic Ecclesiology

Since the early Genevan Reformation had been led by Farel, for Calvin it was a transitory period. As to its substantive documents, only the *Instruction* was authored by Calvin while the rest were primarily authored by Farel, although

119. Wendel, *Calvin*, 52–53. Cf. R. M. Kingdon, "Confessionalism in Calvin's Geneva," *Archiv für Reformationsgeschichte* 98 (2006): 110–12; C. Burger, "Calvin's Correspondence during His Stay in Strasbourg," in *John Calvin: The Strasbourg Years (1538–1541)*, ed. M. Arnold (Eugene, OR: Wipf & Stock, 2016), 26–27.

there was the possibility of Calvin's coauthorship. Thus, they could hardly represent the case for Calvin's "practice of Catholic ecclesiology." Among the events taking place and the publications appearing during this period, however, there were two exceptions that clearly indicated Calvin's case and were primarily led by Calvin's initiative with Farel on the sidelines. They were the Caroli affair and the publication of Calvin's *Two Epistles*.

The Caroli affair was occasioned by Caroli's accusation against Farel and Calvin of engaging in the Trinitarian heresy of Arianism, as well as his official appeal to the authorities of Bern regarding their Arianism. Caroli, a Paris theological Doctor, was an exile from France because of his Evangelical convictions. As the chief pastor of the Lausanne Church recently installed by Bern, he made his accusation in the beginning of 1537. Calvin, with his official title of "Lecturer of holy Scripture in the Church of Geneva," was to take a predominant role in the ensuing controversy for the defense of the Genevan Church. *Two Epistles*, published in March 1537, was based upon two original letters that he wrote before his arrival in Geneva and that he made into two open letters without addressees or personal references in the text. It was clearly addressed to the moderate evangelical humanist group in France. One common denominator of the Caroli affair and *Two Epistles* was the Lefèvrian background of Farel and Calvin, as well as perhaps that of Caroli. In spite of the fact that Calvin researchers, with various reasoning, have either ignored or slighted the significance of these two events, our study acknowledges their importance for the early Genevan Reformation and considers them indicative of the future formation of Calvin's ecclesiology. In other words, the Caroli affair pointed in the direction of Calvin's consistent biblicism, and *Two Epistles* pointed to that of his uncompromising practical activism. Above all, they proved to be not only examples of Calvin's practice of Catholic ecclesiology but also of his Evangelicalism that clearly distinguished itself from moderate Lefèvrianism. As a result, our following examination will consider Calvin's Catholic ecclesiology as the third type of ecclesiology present in the early French Reformation, along with the types of moderate Lefèvrianism and its radicalization in Farel's Evangelicalism.

1. Caroli Affair

After the Bernese authority accepted Caroli's appeal, the Caroli affair had evolved into a significant religious controversy over the orthodoxy of the Genevan Church, directly involving the magistracies and churches of Bern, Lausanne, and Geneva. The affair was also closely watched by Zurich, Basel, and Strasbourg where the Reformed Reformation had advanced. The affair's development can be sketched as follows: (a) in order to solve the controversy, an ecclesiastical synod was called in Lausanne in May 1537; (b) for that occasion Calvin wrote an apology in Latin, the "Genevan preachers' confession of faith concerning the Trinity," for the Genevan Church and presented it to Bern; (c) at the synod, Caroli refused to accept the apology for its lack of technical terms such as "Trinity" and "persons" in its main text; (d) another synod was called to settle the controversy in Bern in September; (e) for this occasion Calvin presented again the same apology with two freshly written "appendices" on the Trinity and persons; (f) as the synod accepted them, the charge against Geneva was cleared and the outcome was made known to the churches concerned. Although the Caroli affair was officially closed due to this outcome and Caroli's subsequent banishment from the Lausanne Church, its aftereffects lasted until 1545 when Caroli wrote a comprehensive apology, which was then refuted by Calvin. During this period, Caroli returned to the Roman Catholic Church, withdrew again from it, and then returned to the Evangelical fold. In the Reformed circles of Basel and Strasbourg, some Reformers mediated for the reconciliation of Caroli and Calvin.[120]

In the whole process of the affair, noticeably it was not Farel, chief pastor, but Calvin, the instructor in Scripture, who had played a predominant role both in defending the Genevan Church and negotiating not only with the Bernese ministers and magistrates, but also with Zurich, Basel, and Strasbourg for Geneva's favor.[121] It was also noteworthy that Calvin wrote most of the materials coming from the Genevan Church. Acknowledging the problematic aspects in Farel's writings to which Caroli mainly made his accusation, Calvin presented his own writings for the common defense of Farel and himself. In his letter to the Bernese ministers reporting the Lausanne meeting in which Caroli made the initial accusation, for example, he was said to respond to the accusation by presenting an excerpt from his *Instruction* (or perhaps the original Latin text) on the topic of the Trinity as "our confession of faith," not

120. *COR* III-2:145–52; *CO* 9:703–10. For the text of the *Confession on the Trinity* (*Confessio Genevensium Praedicatorum de Trinitate*), we use the *COR* edition; an introduction by the editor M. Vial and a comment on the Caroli affair by the editors (C. Augustijn and F. P. van Stam) of *COR* VI-1 (171–72) are useful. The 1545 publications are Caroli's *Refutatio Blasphemiae Farellistarus* and Calvin's defense of Farel in the name of the Genevan Minister, Nicholas des Gallars, *Pro G. Farello adversus Petri Caroli, Defensio* (*BC* 45/10).

121. Cf. *COR* VI-1:174n12. According to the editors, Caroli's complaints about Farel's unorthodoxy had been known to Bern's Haller, Basel's Grynaeus, and others before his official appeal to Bern.

from Farel's *Confession*. Caroli, however, rejected the excerpt as an insufficient statement on the Trinity and instead requested the official subscription of the Genevan ministers to the Catholic Creeds, especially the Creed of Nicea and the Athanasian Creed.[122] As a countermeasure to the Caroli affair and its aftereffects, Calvin published the original Latin text of the *Instruction* as the *Catechism* (*Catechismus, sive Christianae Religionis Institutio*) with designation of "John Calvin, Author" in 1538 and appended his own Latin translation of Farel's *Confession*. In this translation, interestingly, Calvin changed all of Farel's stereotyped French designations such as "Jesus-Christ" (*Jesuchrist*) and "Jesus" (*Iesus*) into "Christ" (*Christus*), thus emphasizing Christ's divinity. In the preface of this publication, he seemed to distance Farel's *Confession* from the controversy and instead used his own *Instruction* or the 1538 *Catechism*.[123] What did his apologetic maneuver mean for the early Genevan Reformation or for the prospect of the French Reformation? In order to respond to this question, we will focus on three aspects of the Caroli affair, namely, the significance of the affair itself, the accusation of Arian heresy, and Calvin's apology of the Catholic doctrine of the Trinity.[124]

(1) Significance of the Caroli Affair

The simple question "What is the Caroli affair in essence?" has been made obscure in Calvin research due to several factors. First, for Calvin, the affair is viewed as a minor event in passing, as well as a false charge from which he is eventually cleared. Second, the portrait of Caroli has contributed to difficulty in understanding him historically. As a matter of fact, Caroli, a Paris Doctor in theology and a member of the Theological Faculty's Consortium, was an atypical figure. He joined the humanist reform movement of Meaux, was forced into exile after the Placards affair, and became the chief pastor of Lau-

122. *COR* VI-1:175. This Latin letter (epistle # 32), addressed to the Bernese ministers, included the sentence that Calvin was said to quote from his *Instruction* in the initial meeting with Caroli. The fact that this quotation in Latin was found verbatim in his Latin edition of the 1538 *Catechism* (*COR* III-2:44; *CO* 5:337) suggests that, as the editors of *COR* VI-1 and our study assume, the Latin text of the *Instruction* was already extant in February 1537 when the letter was sent to Bern and that Calvin wrote the Latin catechism first and then prepared its French text for the Genevan magistrates.

123. Cf. the Latin *Catechism*'s text: *Catechismus, sive Christianae Religionis Institutio*, 1538, *BC* 38/1; *COR* III-2:3–113 and its prefatory epistle: *COR* III-2:115–21; *COR* VI-1:279–90; *OS* 1:426–32.

124. Texts consulted here include Farel's *Summary*, Calvin's first *Institutes*, and the French and Latin texts of the Genevan Church's three documents.

sanne. Lastly, Calvin's refusal to subscribe to the Catholic Creeds, especially the Athanasian Creed, the most anti-Arian creed among them, has been viewed as "inexplicable" by some Calvin researchers.[125]

(i) In general, the Caroli affair can be viewed as a controversy between a theologian professionally trained in Scholastic theology and the humanists who had turned to biblical and theological studies. The real picture, however, was not so simplistic. To start with, the nature of Caroli's biblical evangelicalism needs to be correctly understood. The first known starting point of his evangelical activities was his involvement with the Meaux reform (1522–25) and subsequently his sermons preached in Meaux which became subjected to the Paris Theological Faculty's heresy inquiries. Unlike many humanists who had joined or were related to the reform, he had never been taught by Lefèvre. One possible reason for his involvement was that, being originally from the Meaux Bishopric, he agreed with the reform ideas of Briçonnet and Lefèvre. The Theological Faculty had examined the content of Caroli's sermons twice, in 1523 and 1524, and found in them problematic elements such as criticism of the Mass, petitions to the Virgin Mary and saints, emphasis on justification by faith, and the practical use of the Bible for the life of the faithful. Judging from these elements, which were characteristics of the Meaux reform, he could possibly have been a Lefèvrian at this time.[126]

After the Meaux reform's dissolution in 1525, Caroli continued his preaching activities under the protection of Marguerite. In 1529 he completed his French Bible, and in its preface to the readers he included the preface of Luther's *Psalm Commentary* published in the previous year. He was known for his evangelical activities and was generally considered one of the leaders in the early French Reformation.[127] However, there was no historical evidence that suggested that he had had a similar experience of transition from the moderate to the radical evangelical humanism seen in Farel or had a clear confessional stand on the issues of "Rome" and "Luther." Likewise, there has been no estab-

125. For Caroli's biographical notes, see J. K. Farge, *Biographical Register of Paris Doctors of Theology, 1500–1536* (Toronto: Pontifical Institutes of Mediaeval Studies, 1980), 65–71. Doumergue's treatment on the Caroli affair (*Jean Calvin*, 2:252–68) presents a typical viewpoint of the earlier works, focusing on Caroli's atypical character and behavior. For Calvin's view on the Catholic Creeds, see W. Nijenhuis, "Calvin's Attitude towards the Symbols of the Early Church during the Conflict with Caroli," in *Ecclesia Reformata: Studies on the Reformation* (Leiden: Brill, 1972), 73–114.

126. Farge, *Biographical Register*, 66–68; Doumergue, *Jean Calvin*, 2:252–53; Ganoczy, *Young Calvin*, 115; Farge, *Orthodoxy*, 172–73; F. Higman, "Caroli, Pierre," *OER* 1:265–66.

127. Cf. Farge, *Biographical Register*, 68.

lished evaluation of his postexile activities in the Protestant Reformation. On the one hand, there is a negative evaluation by Ganoczy who considers that Caroli, unlike Luther and Zwingli, could have never taken a clear stance of "anti-Rome" and "anti-Catholic Church." On the other hand, Farge's brief yet so far most comprehensive analysis of Caroli's reformist concept takes notice of Caroli's view expressed in the above-mentioned Lausanne Disputation (1536). This is especially apparent in his three affirmations of salvation by faith and not by works, the authority of Scripture and its use, and the Eucharist as memorial and not sacrifice. Farge concludes that Caroli had clearly expressed his Evangelical and anti-Catholic view.[128] Incidentally, after the Lausanne Disputation ended in an Evangelical victory as planned, the Bernese authority appointed Caroli to be chief pastor of the Lausanne Church. However, this appointment had caused friction in both the Lausanne and Genevan Churches and had possibly become a distant cause of the Caroli affair. The appointment passed over Pierre Viret whom both Farel and the Genevan Church had recommended to be the chief pastor. Viret was a native originally from the Pays de Vaud, studied at the University of Paris, and was likely a Lefèvrian. Later, he helped Farel's evangelization in the French-speaking regions of Switzerland. He was engaged in the early evangelizing activities in Lausanne and led the Lausanne Disputation along with Farel. After Caroli's appointment, in addition, Viret and other ministers criticized Caroli's pastorate as "papist and authoritarian."[129]

(ii) Another factor in the background of the Caroli affair was the politically and religiously precarious situation of Geneva. As Geneva's independence from Savoy's religious overlord was achieved in 1535 by its military alliance with Bern, Geneva was politically surrounded not only by Bern but also by France, which allied with Bern in repelling the Savoyards, and by Savoy, which was still closely watching the Genevan development and retaining the nominal Bishop of Geneva. In the alliance with Bern, religiously, Geneva had to cope with Bernese demands of conformity in church organization and worship between the two churches. In this situation, Bern played a leading role in the Caroli affair. Chief pastor of Bern, Caspar Megander, presided at the synod in Lausanne,

128. Cf. Ganoczy, *Young Calvin*, 115; Farge, *Biographical Register*, 68–69.

129. Cf. R. D. Linder, "Viret, Pierre," *OER* 4:236–37; M. W. Bruening, "Pierre Viret and Geneva," *Archiv für Reformationsgeschichte* 99 (2008): 176–80. Although it is generally assumed that Viret studied in the Collège de Montaigu in the same year Calvin graduated and afterward turned to evangelicalism in Paris, his precise relationship with Lefèvrianism, Farel, and Calvin was uncertain. His accusations against Caroli in Lausanne included Caroli's practice of prayers for the dead, psychopannichiaism, "curious and useless dogma" (*COR* VI-1:173), and others.

and the dispute was officially settled in Bern.[130] Calvin recognized the affair to be a major threat, both politically and religiously, to the future of the Genevan Reformation. He especially feared its adverse effects upon the Reformed Reformation that had spread into South Germany and the German-speaking regions of Switzerland, as well as upon the orthodoxy of Evangelicalism that was permeating France and French-speaking Switzerland. His apology for the Genevan Church and efforts to persuade Bern, Zurich, Basel, and Strasbourg could be seen as a practical aspect of his Catholic ecclesiology.

(iii) What exactly was the nature of Caroli's accusation and that of Calvin's response? The concern of Caroli's accusation was not so much with his academic background of Scholasticism but with the Catholic faith of the ancient church that the humanists generally considered the golden age of Christianity. Acknowledging that the Evangelicalism of Farel and Calvin was founded on biblicism, Caroli questioned their Evangelicalism as to whether it correctly represented the Catholic and orthodox faith of the ancient church. Since he had known Farel from the days of the Meaux reform, had worked together with him on early evangelical works in Geneva, and was surely familiar with Farel's *Summary* and the three Genevan Church documents, what he questioned was the relation between their biblicism and their understanding of the Catholic faith of the ancient church. In other words, their teachings on God and Christ expressed in their writings were not only falling short of the Catholic faith but also expressed the error of Arianism that the ancient church had rejected.

By this time, Caroli must have known that the biblicism of Erasmus, Luther, and Lefèvre had accepted the authority of the ancient Catholic Creeds, and that even the Lutheran confession of faith, the Augsburg Confession, accepted the *Confession of Nicea* as the basic doctrinal standard for the Lutheran Church. From this traditionalist stand, he urged the Genevan ministers to officially subscribe to the Catholic Creeds.[131] Fully aware of the issue of the relation between biblical authority and the tradition of the ancient church, Calvin dared to reject Caroli's request of official subscription and formulated his own apology of the Trinitarian dogma. As a result, his apology presented his unique biblicism that was distinctive from that of Luther and even different from

130. W. G. Naphy, *Calvin and the Consolidation of the Genevan Reformation* (Manchester and New York: Manchester University Press, 1994), 20–21, 25–27; Gordon, *The Swiss Reformation*, 152–54; E. W. Monter, "Savoy," *OER* 3:488–89; E. Campi and C. Moser, "'Loved and Feared': Calvin and the Swiss Confederation," in *John Calvin's Impact on Church and Society, 1509–2009*, ed. M. E. Hirzel and M. Sullmann (Grand Rapids: Eerdmans, 2009), 15–17.

131. Cf. Farge, *Orthodoxy*, 170–77, 187–96.

that of Erasmus, Lefèvre, and Caroli. In the initial meeting, in which Caroli requested Farel and Calvin to subscribe to the Athanasian Creed as proof of their rejection of Arianism, Calvin responded that he would confess his belief in God on the basis of Scripture and not that of Athanasius's faith. In the *Genevan preachers' confession*, he formulated the doctrine of the Trinity without naming or using the creeds of Nicea and Athanasius, but expressed what the two creeds confessed to by exclusively using biblical testimonies.[132]

(2) Accusation of Arian Heresy

Historically, the core of the Caroli affair, the Arian heresy, or Arianism, had been a complex issue. Since Arius, who denied the true divinity of Jesus Christ, was condemned as a heretic at the Council of Nicea (325) and Arianism was likewise condemned at the Council of Constantinople (381), the history of the Arian heresy had evolved in Christendom. As Arius had become known as a heresiarch, the Arian heresy had evolved into an inclusive designation not only for Arianism but also for such unorthodox teachings as Adoptionism in Christology and Modalism in the Trinitarian doctrine. In the background of the Caroli affair, for example, when the Paris Theological Faculty began a heresy inquiry into Erasmus and Lefèvre, Erasmus was called an advocate of Arianism.[133] This case of the Theological Faculty could be likewise reflected in Caroli's charge against the humanists, Farel and Calvin. In fact, Calvin understood that Caroli's "Arianism" was a liberally used designation including the Modalist form of Sabellianism.[134] It was true that for Caroli, an orthodox theologian, the charge of Arianism could be dismissed by an official subscription to such anti-Arian creeds as the Nicean and the Athanasian. For Calvin's biblicism, however, unless the final authority of the Ancient Creeds in the matters of doctrine was confirmed, he could not accept Caroli's demand without reservation. Before examining Calvin's apology itself, however, there are two issues that made it complicated: first, the issue of Michael Servetus whose anti-Trinitarian view had become known in the background of the Caroli

132. *COR* VI-1:175; *COR* III-2:145–52. Cf. Ganoczy, *Young Calvin*, 114–15.

133. Farge, *Orthodoxy*, 187–89, 191; Rice, *Prefatory Epistles*, xviii–xxiv. The Paris Theological Faculty's heresy proceedings against Erasmus and Lefèvre took place when the faculty was led by its Syndic, Beda, and the charge of Arianism against Erasmus was based upon his criticism of the Catholic sacramental system that was interpreted as an attack on the divinity of Christ. As Rice remarks, "humanista theologizans" was also labeled at Lefèvre by Beda.

134. *COR* VI-1:208: "Itaque cum arrianae primum haereseos, Paulo post etiam sabellianae."

affair; second, the case of Geneva's chief pastor Farel whose writings Caroli seemingly attacked. In addition, we will briefly examine Calvin's position on the Trinity as expressed in his *Institutes* and *Instruction* as direct background materials of his apology.

(i) Servetus, a Spaniard, studied the humanities in Toulouse, traveled in Italy and Germany, and discussed the relation of God's logos to Christ with the church leaders of Basel and Strasbourg. In 1531, he anonymously composed a clandestine publication, the first work (*De Trinitatis Erroribus*) of his anti-Trinitarian view. Under the alias Michel de Villeneuve, he later studied medicine and anatomy at the University of Paris in the 1530s and was engaged in writing and medicine in Lyon and Vienne in southern France. Calvin was said to have known Servetus in Paris and to have referred to a few of Servetus's unorthodox opinions, likely taken from the clandestine publication, in his first *Institutes.* In the background of the Caroli affair, Servetus's publication began to be noticed in Reformed circles in southern Germany and Switzerland, and its influence was also felt and warned against in French-speaking Swiss Evangelical churches.[135] There was no evidence that Caroli had read Servetus's work at the beginning of the affair. However, it was possible that he might have suspected a parallel between Servetus's radical biblicism, which underlay his anti-Trinitarian teaching, and the biblicism of Farel and Calvin. By sharply separating the testimonies of Scripture and of the church fathers, for example, Servetus rejected the latter's orthodox teaching on the Trinity by appealing to the former's exclusive authority. Caroli might have suspected this kind of biblicism in Farel's and Calvin's refusal to subscribe to the Catholic Creeds. Furthermore, there was an actual case of Claude d'Aliod, once Farel's cominister in Neuchâtel and currently in Geneva, who was suspected of Servetus's influence. In February 1537, the Bernese authority urged Geneva to arrest and punish Aliod. In the Lausanne synod occasioned by Caroli's accusation, Aliod officially recanted the error upon Farel's persuasion.[136]

(ii) A far more serious problem for Calvin's apology was Farel's writings, in particular, his *Summary* and the *Confession*. After his exile in Switzerland, Caroli had worked closely with Farel and was well acquainted with his teachings. In May 1535, for instance, he joined Farel's early evangelical work in Geneva, and in June he participated with Farel in the theological disputation at Rive that was said to be a turning point for Geneva' s evangelization. Later in

135. Cf. Pelikan, *The Christian Tradition*, 4:323–24; J. Friedman, "Servetus, Michael," *OER* 4:48–49; Wendel, *Calvin*, 93–94.

136. Cf. *COR* III-2, "Introduction," 127; *COR* VI-1:208n2.

the same year, having read the *Summary*, Caroli reported that Farel and his association with Aliod became suspect of Arianism. The report had been known to the leaders of Bern, Zurich, and Basel, and in December Simon Grynaeus of Basel informed Farel directly.[137] For the professional theologian Caroli, the *Summary* was too careless in dealing with such a definitive doctrine as the Trinity and was an easy target. In fact, it had a considerable number of problems. Firstly, it did not use the ancient Catholic Creeds at all. Instead it described faith in God, Jesus-Christ, and the Holy Spirit by compiling scriptural testimonies. Secondly, it did not employ such technical terms used in the Nicene Creed as "Trinity" and "persons." In this respect, the *Summary* used a quite different approach from that of Calvin's *Institutes* which, following Luther's example, regarded the Apostles' Creed as closely expressing biblical teachings, and discussed the doctrine of the Trinity.[138] As to the content of the *Summary*, its chapters 1 ("God") and 3 ("Jesus-Christ") could be called into question concerning the relationship of God, Jesus-Christ as the Son of God, and the Holy Spirit. Its characteristic approach to this relationship could be summed up as the emphasis of individuality rather than unity of the three. From a starting point of God the Father, for example, Jesus-Christ and the Holy Spirit were understood as God's "functions." Its frequent use of the terms "Jesus-Christ" and "Jesus" instead of "Christ" could be viewed as falling far short of the orthodox Christology of Nicea. As to the Holy Spirit, there was no individual chapter attributed to it. Rather, the Holy Spirit was only referred to in chapter 9, "The Spirit and New Man." In this chapter, focusing on God's function, the Spirit was described in a peculiar expression as "'movement and affection' by which God renovates man, gives him grace, and justifies him through Jesus."[139]

From the above-mentioned characteristics, Caroli suspected Arianism or Sabellianism in the *Summary*. Furthermore, there were also basic problems in the *Confession* to which Caroli's criticism was concentrated in discussions during the affair.[140] Even though the *Confession* cited the Apostles' Creed as

137. Cf. Farge, *Biographical Register*, 69; *COR* VI-1:174n2; Herminjard, *Correspondance*, 3:174, 374, cited in Nijenhuis, "Calvin's Attitude," 79.

138. Doumergue, *Jean Calvin*, 2:261–62; Zuidema and Van Raalte, *Early French Reform*, 22–24. In noticing the absence of the Nicene terms on the Trinity in Farel's first edition of the *Summary*, both Doumergue and Zuidema insist that Farel corrected this shortcoming in his later post–Caroli affair editions.

139. *Summaire* (1534), chs. 1, 9–10; chs. 3, 10–12; chs. 9, 19–21. (Zuidema and Van Raalte, *Early French Reform*, 120–22, 126–27.) Cf. H. Heyer, *Guillaume Farel*, 45. The quotation is taken from Zuidema and Van Raalte, *Early French Reform*, 126.

140. *COR* VI-1:175n16. According to the editors' analysis of Caroli's 1545 Refutation

assimilation with the *Instruction* yet failed to use the Nicene terms "three persons" or "Trinity," it expressed faith in God, Christ, and the Holy Spirit in a far clearer way than the *Summary*. Nonetheless, Caroli's criticism could be directed to the following points: there was no basic description of God's relation to Christ the Son in Article 2, "One only God"; there was no individual article attributed to "Christ" or "Jesus-Christ"; and in Articles 6 to 8, which focused on Jesus-Christ's "function," the process of man's salvation was described as "Salvation in Jesus," "Justice in Jesus," and "Regeneration in Jesus."[141]

(iii) Since Calvin understood from the beginning of the Caroli affair that Caroli's criticism was not only directed at Farel but also at himself, an inquiry into Calvin's *Institutes* and *Instruction*, which he presented in the initial stage of the affair, is useful for the affair's background material. In this inquiry, the crucial question of whether or not the Trinitarian dispute between Caroli and Calvin represented two major positions of biblicism in the early French Reformation will be addressed.[142]

Calvin addressed the question of the Trinity in his first *Institutes*, chapter 2 on the exposition of the Apostles' Creed. As mentioned above, his use of the Creed followed Luther's example and was based upon his conviction of biblicism, which can be seen in that its content and terms closely corresponded to scriptural testimonies. As he acknowledged that this earliest Catholic Creed was formulated for the defense of the orthodox faith against dualistic Gnosticism and Docetism in the early Christian Church and, as a confessional statement, it was premature in expressing the Trinitarian dogma known later in the fourth century, he added an explanatory section prior to his exposition of the Creed itself. In this section, he expressed his conviction that the Trinitarian dogma was a doctrine witnessed and found in Scripture, and he related this scriptural stratum to the later development of the dogma, especially to the Catholic and orthodox faith expressed in the Nicene Creed. In using both Greek and Latin formulas, he explained the Catholic Trinitarian dogma as

(*Refutatio*, H 1r, H 2r), Caroli's initial attack focused on the *Confession*, of which our study assumes Farel's main authorship.

141. *OS* 1:420–21.

142. Wendel's assumption (Wendel, *Calvin*, 54) that Caroli started the accusation after having read both Farel's *Summary* and Calvin's *Institutes* may not be correct. According to Augustijn and van Stam (*COR* VI-1:255n28), Calvin's later recollection in his Defense (1545) mentioned Caroli's request for Calvin to present a copy of the *Institutes* for examination during the controversy. It might have been possible for Caroli to have added a new accusation of Sabellianism after the examination. Incidentally, Ganoczy (*Young Calvin*, 116) detects "a slight modalist tendency" in Calvin's Trinitarian theology.

"one *ousia*, three *hypostaseis*, that is, one substance, three subsistences in one substance" or "one substance, three persons."[143] In addition, perhaps referring to Servetus and others, he cautioned that "the heretics" who could not see these terms such as "ousia" and "hypostaseis" in Scripture and determined them of human invention had rejected the Nicene orthodoxy. Furthermore, he was well aware of the possibility that the rejection of heretics could be wrongly associated with the insistence by humanists on biblical authority or priority of scriptural witnesses over the doctrinal formulations of the church. He, therefore, made his position clear that the orthodox faith formulated by the Catholic church in the fourth century was to be accepted because it was based upon Scripture. To this point, he made an interesting remark: he called these terms not found in Scripture "the novelty of words" (*verborum novitas*) and defended the Nicene Council's use of them. He then affirmed:

> If, therefore, these terms were not rashly invented, they are rashly repudiated. Would that they had been buried, provided only among all men this faith were agreed on: that Father, Son, and Holy Spirit are one God, yet that the Son is not the Father, nor the Holy Spirit the Son; but they have been differentiated by a peculiar quality.

Just as much as Luther expressed his biblical scholar's sentiment by saying that he "hated homoousios" in the Nicene Creed, Calvin expressed his humanist spirit of biblicism by the phrase "would that they had been buried." As Pelikan, historian of Christian doctrine, suggests, here could be seen Calvin's biblicism, even more thorough than Luther's, as his fundamental conviction of scriptural priority by which even the Catholic faith of the past could be examined and reaffirmed in the context of the contemporary church. For our study we call this unique position Calvin's "consistent biblicism." In conclusion, he accepted the authority of the Nicene Creed on this ground: on the one hand, by employing "homoousios" the Creed effectively rejected Arius's "heteroousios" theory of God the Father and Christ the Son; on the other hand, it also rejected Sabellius's Modalist theory that God the Father took different modes of existence and manifested himself as the Son and the Holy Spirit.[144]

143. *OS* 1:72. (Battles, trans., *Institution*, 61.) Mullett's comment (*John Calvin*, 58), "Caroli, on the basis of allegedly scary references on the Trinity in the 1536 'Institute', accused the Genevans of subscribing to the heresies of Arius," is not correct. First of all, the main focus of Caroli's target was Farel, whom Calvin tried to defend. Secondly, Calvin did substantively treat the Trinity in his first *Institutes*.

144. *OS* 1:72, 74–75. (Battles, trans., *Institution*, 61, 65.) Cf. Pelikan, *The Christian Tradi-*

In this connection, lastly, two points in Caroli's accusation need to be examined in view of Calvin's Trinitarian position in the *Institutes*. As to the first point that the three Genevan Church documents lacked the term "Trinity," the *Institutes* did use the term effectively. In chapter 2, for example, it used the term four times: twice in the context of the first three articles of the Apostles' Creed referring to "three persons of the sacred Trinity" (*tribus personis sacrae trinitatis*), and twice in the context of refuting Arius and Sabellius.[145] As to the second point of Caroli's urging the Genevan ministers to subscribe to the Nicene and Athanasian Creeds, Calvin's view on the authority of the ancient councils expressed in the first *Institutes*, chapter 6, was noticeable. Calvin listed two reasons to support his position that even "those ancient and purer councils" could not be the final authority on matters of the church's doctrine: the Council of Nicea was illustrious for condemning the Arian heresy, yet still could not avoid conflicts and confusions; and to acknowledge their final authority would inevitably give room to the Roman Catholic Church's claim of the council's infallibility.[146] This was likely a reason for him to reject Caroli's demand for subscription.

Calvin's *Instruction* inherited the tenor of his Trinitarian teaching in the first *Institutes*. Being a catechism, however, it did not take in the abovementioned explanatory section, in which such terms as "ousios," "personae," and "homoousios" were used, placed prior to the exposition of the Apostles' Creed in the *Institutes*. A reason for this omission could be his concern that these terms could not serve the educational purpose of a catechism and that he, officially an "Instructor in scripture," tried to present Christian faith out of scriptural testimonies unfettered by the church's traditional formulations in doctrine and practice. In fact, in the article "Symbol of faith," the *Instruction* affirmed that the Apostles' Creed "contains nothing merely human but has been assembled from very sure testimonies of scripture." Then it defined the basic Trinitarian teaching, without referring to the Nicene formula, in

tion, 4:322–23: "Calvin had given the Nicene dogma of the Trinity a more thoroughgoing biblical documentation than it had received since the patristic era." Pelikan correctly interprets Calvin's notion of "buried" in comparison with Luther's synonymous phrase, "to hate homoousios" (*WA* 7:117) and succinctly describes Calvin's biblicism, which he suggests as thorough as or more thorough than Luther's. This portion including the phrase "utinam sepulta essent" (would that they had been buried) will survive in the final edition of the *Institutes* (*Institutio* 1.13.5: *OS* 3:113). However, Battles translates this phrase as "I could wish they were buried" in the 1559 *Institutes*.

145. *OS* 1:70, 75, 85. (Battles, trans., *Institution*, 59, 65, 77.)

146. *OS* 1:247. (Battles, trans., *Institution*, 270–71.)

this way: "when we name Father, Son, and Spirit, we are not fashioning three Gods, but in the simplest unity of God and Scripture and the very experience of godliness we are showing ourselves God the Father, his Son, and Spirit. . . . Let us contemplate the Father with his Son and Spirit."[147] Incidentally, this last quotation was likely what Calvin presented to Caroli for the defense of the Trinitarian view of the Genevan ministers at the initial meeting in Lausanne. Unsatisfied with the presentation, however, Caroli called the *Instruction* and *Confession* "new confessions of faith" and demanded the ministers subscribe to the Nicene and Athanasian Creeds. According to Caroli, at that meeting Calvin criticized some expressions such as "God of God, Light of Light" in the Nicene Creed as meaningless and "ridiculous battle-logic," and thus the subscription issue had become a major point of conflict.[148]

(3) Apology for Catholic Faith

The subscription issue had revealed the nature of Calvin's apology for Catholic faith. To be precise, the conflict between Caroli and Calvin was not simply between Catholic traditionalist and progressive humanist, but it was a manifestation of a deeper chasm between two streams of biblicism existing in the early French Reformation. As far as the ancient Catholic Creeds were concerned, Caroli as a Catholic theologian was beyond doubt a traditionalist. If he were at the same time a Lefèvrian humanist, however, he was well versed in the humanist tradition of Erasmus and Lefèvre, which held in high esteem the ancient church's theology and was critical of the current Scholastic theology.[149] For instance, Erasmus's new theological methodology (*Ratio seu compendium verae theologiae*), which was prefixed to the second edition of his *New Testament* (*Novum Testamentum*, 1519) and which advocated for biblical theology in place of Scholastic dogmaticism, was well known among the humanists. The new theology was based upon philological studies of the biblical text and focused on the studies of "oration" (*oratio*, *sermo*) rhetorically drawn from the text.[150] In the case of Lefèvre, a sharp contrast was made between (a) Scholasticism and the studies of the church fathers and mystical theology, (b) a dialectic theology based on "sic et non" and biblical theology based on hermeneutics

147. *COR* III-2:45 (ll. 25–33). Cf. *OS* 1:396; n. 124 above. Quotation in English is taken from Battles's translation in Hesselink, *Calvin's First Catechism*, 21.

148. *COR* VI-1:175–76; Caroli, *Refutatio*, B3v cited in *COR* VI-1:215n3.

149. Cf. Farge, *Biographical Register*, 66–70.

150. Cf. M. Hoffmann, *Rhetoric and Theology: The Hermeneutic of Erasmus* (Toronto: University of Toronto Press, 1994), 6–8.

and rhetoric, (c) knowledge (*scientia*) and wisdom (*sapientia*), (d) a systematic presentation of revealed truth and sacred doctrines drawn from Scripture itself, and (e) "summa theologia" and biblical commentaries.[151]

In addition, Caroli was surely paying close attention to the attacks against humanists from the traditional theology, especially the case of Erasmus's apology before the heresy inquiry of the Paris Theological Faculty. Labeled "the Arian heresy" by the faculty's syndic Beda, in his *Apology* (*Apologia*, 1525) Erasmus presented an interesting theory on the relation between biblical revelation and the development of church doctrine. Already in the previous year, he had written a book on Catholic faith (*Inquisitio de Fide*, 1524) in which, though indirectly, he defended Luther who professed the Apostles' Creed as "orthodox." In his *Apology*, however, Erasmus presented a full theory that God's revelation was not meant to be completed in Scripture. The same Spirit who had inspired biblical writers would continuously inspire the church fathers, councils, and theologians and would lead them to new understandings of the Christian faith. In this developmental theory of revelation, he related the authority of Scripture with the continuous development of Christian doctrine such as the Trinity, defending his own Trinitarian teaching in this continuity.[152] Erasmus's theory also revealed a biblicism that reflected the humanist spirit of attributing to history a normative value. In the Caroli affair, Calvin's apology likely faced the Erasmian type of biblicism.

(i) In the initial stage of the Caroli affair, when Caroli demanded that Farel and Calvin subscribe to the Catholic Creeds, it was not certain whether Caroli

151. Cf. Rice, *Prefatory Epistles*, xx–xxi.

152. C. R. Thompson, ed., *Inquisitio de Fide* (New Haven: Yale University Press, 1950), "Introduction," 39; Farge, *Orthodoxy*, 89; M. O. Boyle, *Erasmus on Language and Method in Theology* (Toronto and Buffalo: University of Toronto Press, 1977), 132–33. According to Boyle, Erasmus considered Scripture the "fountain" of God's revelation, the church fathers as those who had taken water from its "golden stream," and the Scholastics as those who had taken water from its "muddy stream." The final position Erasmus reached on the development of doctrine was found in his *Explanatio Symboli* (1533). This work could be known to both Caroli and Calvin. It was addressed to England under Henry VIII for the reconciliation of the Catholic and the Evangelical camps, and it affirmed the Holy Spirit not only as the revealer of the true doctrine but also, as a new emphasis, the guardian of church unity. On the other hand, Erasmus checked the Evangelicalism of the Lutheran and the Reformed Reformation by saying that "anyone who acknowledges the holy church curses and abjures every schismatic conspiracy against the peace of its hierarchy and also all covens of heretics." ASD V–1, 274. Quotation in English is taken from *Collected Works of Erasmus*, 70, 328. Cf. H. M. Pabel, *Erasmus' Vision of the Church* (Kirksville: Sixteenth Century Journal Publishers, 1995), 84.

had known Erasmus's *Apology* or developmental theory. However, there was circumstantial evidence that suggested the possibility of that knowledge; this was Caroli's exposition on the controversial issue of Christ's presence in the Lord's Supper at the Lausanne Disputation where he was considered an expert on theological issues by both the Catholic and Evangelical sides. In particular, the Catholic side, acknowledging that Farel and Viret had just interpreted "is" (*est*) in the Matthew text (26:26) as "signifies" (*significat*), especially requested Caroli's comment on this point. In sharp contrast to Farel's and Viret's interpretation of the text itself, Caroli presented a lecture-like historical analysis of the issue with two focal points. Concerning the first point, he affirmed that in the Roman Catholic Church's tradition there had been two major interpretations of "is," namely, to interpret it as "signification" or to interpret it "literally," and he objectively illustrated the conflict of the two interpretations by the eleventh-century controversy between Berengar of Tours and Hildebrand (later, Pope Gregory VII). Caroli considered that Berengar's interpretation, "this signifies my body," was supported by Jesus's Hebrew expression in the Bible and by the church fathers, but Hildebrand's interpretation, "this is converted to (*convertitur in*) my body," was not.[153] Concerning the second point, he used another illustration of William of Occam, Nominalist philosopher of the fourteenth century, who presented three possible interpretations of the "is" issue: the first was to interpret it as "signifies," the second, as "converted to," and the third as what he called "presence without transubstantiation." Caroli called the second interpretation transubstantiation theory or "determination of the Church" and criticized it. But he characterized the third interpretation, which was assumedly his own view, in this way: in the Lord's Supper, "by the gift of visible bread, Jesus gives himself invisibly to the soul and spirit of believers by faith"; likewise, the body of Jesus was presented "spiritually and invisibly" "to our spirit in order to be eaten by faith."[154]

There were a few characteristic aspects in Caroli's presentation. Firstly, what he called "determination of the Church" was not simply a theory, but the official Church dogma of transubstantiation established in the Fourth Lateran Council (1215). Without emphasizing this aspect, he objectively presented it as if it were one of three possible historical theories. Even though he rejected it as unwarranted by the testimonies of Scripture and the church fathers, his attitude toward the Catholic dogma was unique. Secondly, what he characterized as "presence without transubstantiation" was clearly distinguishable

153. Piaget, *Les Actes*, 328–29.
154. Piaget, *Les Actes*, 329–30.

from the view of Farel and Viret which was close to the Zwinglian view ("signifies"). As he described his own view as holding that the "bread . . . signifies and represents his [Jesus'] body," and emphasized the participant's faith, soul, and spirit, it could have affinity with Lefèvre's view.[155] Above all, the most characteristic aspect was the fact that he viewed the whole issue from the perspective of history rather than that of scriptural authority which Farel and Viret employed, offering various views in the history of Scripture, the church fathers, and the medieval church. In this respect, Caroli's view could come close to Erasmus's developmental theory.

In the Disputation, incidentally, Calvin took the floor immediately after Caroli's presentation. Not directly opposing Caroli but, as if, mildly criticizing him, Calvin took issue with Caroli's objective evaluation of Hildebrand and called him "the primary director toward this horrible transubstantiation." Further, he called those who had followed him and held the same view "poisoners, perjurers, slaughterers" who had brought miracles into the Mass, dissentions into the church, and the false teaching of mixing Christ's divinity and humanity. Farel followed Calvin and criticized Hildebrand "the Magician," quoted a biblical passage on Christ's bodily presence in heaven after his resurrection, which Caroli did not use in his presentation, and presented his own symbolic view of Christ's presence in the Lord Supper.[156]

(ii) Having covered some background material of Calvin's apology, we now come to the apology itself. The basic guideline of his apology was his biblicism that presupposed ultimate authority and norm of Scripture, assumed all fundamental Christian teachings such as the Trinity to be revealed in Scripture, and affirmed them to be proven from scriptural testimonies. His biblicism was clearly distinguishable from that of Erasmus, who regarded Scripture as a "fountain" of Christian doctrines and attributed normative value to the historical "development" of the doctrines. For Calvin it was imperative to "inherit" or "restore" rigorously the scriptural teachings. Already in his first *Institutes*, he had made his position clear: in God's word, which is the "object and target of faith," "God's mysteries pertaining to our salvation" are known. On the Trinity, for example, "scripture teaches us one God, not many. . . . The Father is God, the Son is God, and the Spirit is God, and there can be only one God."

155. Piaget, *Les Actes*, 330. Cf. Hughes, *Lefèvre*, 87–92; G. Bedouelle, "Jacques Lefèvre d'Étaples," 27–28.

156. Piaget, *Les Actes*, 330–32. "Murderer" in Calvin's list refers to Catholic priests celebrating the Mass and sacrificing Christ's body once again. As we will examine in the next section, *Two Epistles* depicts Catholic priests as "the butchers of Christ" (*carnifices Christi*).

His position also defended the orthodox Trinitarian doctrine, and rejected the heretical teachings. It affirmed that the Apostles' Creed later correctly inherited the scriptural norm as "the three persons of the sacred Trinity" and also "the ancient orthodox Fathers" [the Nicene Creed], even though using terms such as "ousia" and "hypostaseis" which were not found in Scripture, did the same.[157]

The same theme regarding the scriptural norm of the Trinity was found in Calvin's apologetic document, the *Genevan preachers' confession*. In its preface, the confession presented a general guideline that Christian doctrine such as the Trinity "should be diligently polished up to meet the right norm of scripture." Its main text dealt with three focal points; God's unity, God in three persons, and Christ's divinity and humanity. In each point Calvin tried to deduce a doctrinal affirmation exclusively from scriptural testimonies. On the first point, for example, what he had reached by this deduction was expressed in this way: "as being one with the church documents, we think that in the simplest unity of God there exist three *hypostaseis* in being subsistences" (*una cum ecclesiasticis scriptoribus in simplicissima Dei unitate sentimus has esse tres hypostases in subsistentias*). Interestingly, he generalized the Nicene Creed and others as "the church documents." In the Lausanne synod, it was this kind of biblicism against which Caroli sharply reacted and called the confession of the Genevan ministers insufficient as an expression of the Catholic faith.[158] Another noteworthy source was "A letter to readers" that Calvin prefixed to the *Instruction*'s original Latin text (*Catechismus*) published in 1538. This letter referred to the confessional statement on the Trinity adopted by the Genevan Church as "Catholic testification" (*catholica testificatio*) and affirmed it as "carefully and faithfully deduced from the pure word of God." The letter also defined the Trinity in a brief form, "in God's one essence, Triune persons" (*in una Dei essential personarum Trinitatem*), and it claimed the definition had "nothing to dissent from the orthodox consensus of the church."[159]

157. *OS* 1:69–70, 72. (Battles, trans., *Institution*, 58–60, 62.) Cf. Bouwsma, *Calvin*, 143–44. Bouwsma characterizes Calvin's full doctrine of original sin as "Copernican revolution," the characterization that clearly distinguished him among humanists. By this doctrine, Bouwsma asserts, Calvin could reject the superiority of Classical literatures, the church fathers, and church traditions as things of the past. The same characterization could be observed in Calvin's strict biblicism vis-à-vis Erasmus's and Caroli's developmental theory of doctrine.

158. *COR* III-2:145–46, 146–50; *CO* 9:703–4, 704–7. Doumergue (*Jean Calvin*, 2:259–60) characterizes Calvin's formulation of the Trinitarian dogma as "biblical conciseness" (*sobriété biblique*).

159. *COR* III-2:116–17.

(iii) The brief analysis above shows an outline of Calvin's apology for the Genevan Church. It also reveals a division of two distinctive streams of biblicism in the early French Reformation, the division of which Calvin was keenly aware in his conflict with Caroli. Historically, however, the Caroli affair did not end with the exoneration of the Genevan Church or Calvin and Farel. Rather, there remained two issues for the Genevan Church to deal with. The issues were crucial for the Church, which had just turned from the Roman Catholic to the Evangelical fold, and its orthodoxy was so severely challenged in the Caroli affair that Calvin was personally obliged to tackle them in the wider context of his apology. One was the necessity to define precisely the relation between the Genevan Church's scriptural foundation and the Catholic faith of the ancient church formulated in the Catholic Creeds. The other was the Catholic nature of Geneva's confessional stance. Granting that the Genevan Church had full rights to formulate its own doctrinal statement on the Trinity, how could the Church maintain its catholicity in doctrine with other churches, such as the Lutheran Church and the Reformed Churches of Bern, Zurich, Basel, and Strasbourg?

Concerning the first issue, Calvin took a stand of exclusiveness and sufficiency of scriptural foundation. In other words, for the Genevan Church, the doctrinal statement on the Trinity exclusively drawn up from scriptural witnesses was sufficient proof of its orthodoxy. As we have seen above, this was exactly what Calvin did in the main text of the *Genevan preachers' confession*. He called the faith expressed in it "orthodox and Catholic faith." Caroli considered this confession insufficient and reiterated his demand for the Genevan ministers to subscribe to the Nicene and Athanasian Creeds. However, it must have been known to both Caroli and Calvin that the Lutheran Church's Augsburg Confession took the Nicene Creed as the Church's primary doctrinal standard and that Luther himself, though critical of some expressions in the Nicene Creed, favored the Athanasian Creed.[160] In this historical context, without giving in to Caroli, Calvin nonetheless accommodated his demand. He kept the Genevan confession's main text intact, but he added two appendices on "Trinity" and "persons" in which he described the Nicene faith by using the creed's terminology. Notably, however, he called the two crucially important terms, "Trinity" and "persons" as "expression" (*vox*), which did not bear any

160. *Die drei Symbola oder Bekenntnis des Glaubens Christi, WA* 50:262–83. Among the ancient church's creeds, Luther valued most the Apostles' Creed, the Athanasian Creed, and the Te Deum, a Trinitarian hymn that was said to have come down from the tradition of Ambrose and Augustine.

dogmatic connotation, and titled the appendices "Concerning the expression of Trinity and the expression of persons." With this accommodation and without subscribing to the Creeds, he re-presented the *Genevan preachers' confession* to Bern and cleared the charge against the Genevan Church.[161] In clear contrast to his care for the Nicene Creed, he seemed to have totally ignored the Athanasian Creed in his apology. This was perhaps due to the fact that the Creed was never formulated in the church council and the Eastern Church never recognized it. Calvin followed the general consensus of humanists that it was not authored by Athanasius.[162]

In this connection, there was an interesting document that shed light on Calvin's insight on this issue. This was his letter of August 1537, in the name of the Genevan ministers, to the ministers of Zurich. The letter called Caroli a "Sorbonnist" and characterized his demand of subscription as denying the Genevan Church's freedom to formulate the same Trinitarian doctrine from scriptural testimonies. It was particularly noticeable that the letter tried to prove the Genevan Church's orthodoxy by referring to the *First Swiss Confession* (*Confessio Helvetica prior*, 1536) that Calvin and Farel had already officially accepted. This confession was considered to be a catholic creed among the Reformed churches in Switzerland. In its chapter 3 ("The Church Fathers"), the authority of the fathers was said to be accepted when they were teaching scriptural truth that was supported by scriptural testimonies. Chapter 6 ("God") expressed the faith in three "persons" in one "essence" of God without referring to the ancient Catholic Creeds at all. Curiously, furthermore, its description of the Trinity was close to what Calvin described as "in God's one essence, Triune persons." His reference to the *First Swiss Confession* was clearly meant to be his apology for the Catholic faith of the Reformed Evangelicals against Caroli.[163]

The second issue concerned Calvin's apology for the relationship between the ancient Catholic faith and the doctrinal standard of sixteenth-century Evangelical churches, both the Lutheran and the Reformed. As we have seen in

161. *COR* III-2:151; *CO* 9:707–8.

162. Cf. *COR* VI-1:175; J. N. D. Kelly, *The Athanasian Creed* (New York: Harper & Row, 1964), 109–14. Kelly traces the origin of this enigmatic creed to the Western Church of the sixth century and considers its main purpose the refutation of Arianism and its main characteristic the disuse of the Definition of Chalcedon.

163. *COR* VI-1:252–53, esp. n. 12. Cf. *Creeds and Confessions*, 2:283–84; T. George, "Helvetic Confessions," *OER* 2:219–22. The *First Helvetic Confession* was formulated in a conference held in Basel in which Zurich's Bullinger took a leading role. Besides the delegates from the Swiss Evangelical churches, Strasbourg's Bucer and Capito attended, and Calvin, then an exile in Basel, joined and became acquainted with Bullinger.

the previous chapter, Calvin demonstrated an early example of his apologetic posture in the presentation in his first *Institutes* of the Lord's Supper. On the conflict between Luther and Zwingli over Christ's presence in the Supper, in particular, Calvin tried to place both positions within the framework of the orthodox and Catholic faith, though pointing to their excessive aspects. Our study assumed that he comprehended the conflict of both positions in the context of the Alexandria-Antioch schools in the ancient church's Christological formation and that, even though from his own Antiochene school's perspective, he tried to fill the gap with Luther's Alexandrian position. In the Caroli affair, we also assume, Calvin understood the Trinitarian issue in the context of the ancient church's doctrinal formation, from the Nicene Creed to the Definition of Chalcedon, and applied this understanding when writing his apology for the Evangelical churches.

(iv) The ancient church's Trinitarian formation embodied a conflict between the two schools of Alexandria and Antioch concerning God's unity and trinity. Historically, this meant that there were two distinctive theological methodologies or hermeneutic principles implicitly existing in the Nicene Creed itself. On the one hand, the Alexandrian school's philosophical and speculative theology posed the question of God and his existence and successfully rejected Arianism by the use of terms such as "homoousios" and "hypostaseis." On the other hand, the Antioch school emphasized the Triune God's individuality and works, just like the Apostles' Creed, which was incorporated into the Nicene Creed, from the textual and historical studies of Scripture. The conflict was historically led by two theologians, Cyril of Alexandria who advocated for the ontological formation of the Trinity and Theodore of Mopsuestia who guarded the Triune God's individuality and works. In the final Definition of Chalcedon, Cyril's emphasis on the unity of divinity and humanity in Christ was considered orthodox. The extreme position of Eutyches, who held the deification of Christ's humanity due to its union with his divinity, was excluded from the definition. Likewise, Theodore's disciple Nestorius's extreme emphasis both on Christ's divinity and humanity, seen as holding the position of two natures and two personalities, was rejected.[164]

If we examine Calvin's Trinitarian teaching in the *Institutes* from the history of Trinitarian and Christological formation in the ancient church, his teaching can be characterized as taking the Antiochene school's approach that favored a biblical and historical understanding of the issue. For example, he first surveyed scriptural testimonies on the Trinity, then stated "the Father,

164. Cf. Pelikan, *The Christian Tradition*, 1:211–12, 228–32, 256–57.

Son, and Holy Spirit to be one God. For Father is God, the Son is God, and the Spirit is God." This logic characteristically indicated the Antiochene approach. Immediately after the above quotation, interestingly, he brought up the question of "the novelty of the words" such as "ousia" and "hypostaseis," which were characteristically Alexandrian terms. Finally, however, he admitted the merit of the Nicene Creed in rejecting Arianism even via these new words.[165] Calvin's awareness of this historical formation of the Catholic faith was also manifest in his main apologetic work in the Caroli affair, the *Genevan preachers' confession*. Especially noticeable was the confession's third part on Christ's divinity and humanity, a clear reference to the Definition of Chalcedon. In his discussion, he emphasized the Genevan Church's position on the Trinity and Christology as based not only upon scriptural testimonies but also upon "the consensus of the ancient church" (*veteri Ecclesiae consensus*) and that it was to be accepted as such. By the term "consensus," it was clear that he meant the formation of the orthodox and Catholic teachings from the Nicene Creed to the Definition of Chalcedon. He argued, furthermore, that while the Nicene Creed rejected Arianism, which represented a far extreme position of the Antiochene school, "the consensus of the ancient church" also rejected the dualistic and Docetic teachings of Marcion and Mani, which represented the more extreme positions of the Alexandrian school. He then concluded the third part with a note that emphasized that the Definition of Chalcedon excluded both Apollinarius and Nestorius as two extreme positions of the Alexandrian and Antiochene schools.[166]

In the final analysis, it can be said that the Caroli affair was the occasion on which Calvin set forth his apology for the orthodox and catholic Trinitarian theology of the Evangelical churches. Since Caroli was a theologian who turned from Lefèvrianism to the Protestant fold, furthermore, Calvin might have considered his apology a test case for the future of the French Reformation. For Calvin's own theological formation, however, the Caroli affair provided an opportunity to show his unique biblicism, which our study calls "consistent biblicism," coupled with his keen awareness of the Catholic faith. In particular, as we have noticed, his extraordinary biblicism was highlighted by his reference to the ancient Catholic Creeds, without naming them, as "church documents," by generalizing the Catholic Creeds as "the consent of the catholic church," and by providing two appendices on the Trinity and persons to the unchanged main text of the *Genevan preachers' confession*. All in all, this

165. *OS* 1:72. (Battles, trans., *Institution*, 61–62.) Cf. n. 144 above.
166. *COR* III-2:150; *CO* 9:707.

biblicism was an important aspect of his practice of Catholic ecclesiology, as well as the foundation of his theological works as a Reformer.

2. Two Epistles *(Epistolae duae)*

While the Caroli affair concerned Calvin's apology for the Catholic faith, *Two Epistles* concerned his apology for the reform of worship and ecclesiastical order. As mentioned above, the context of his apology in *Two Epistles* was the moderate reformist movement of Lefèvrianism. A crucial issue on the reform of worship was the Lefèvrian acceptance of the Catholic dogma promulgated at the Second Nicea Council (787) and its collateral distinction between worship and veneration. At the same time, *Two Epistles* itself became a historical root for his later involvement in the Nicodemite controversy of the 1540s.[167] *Two Epistles* was published in March 1537 in the midst of the Caroli affair and took the form of a compilation of two open letters with different titles. Obviously, they were taken from two original letters addressed to different persons in different contexts, but only after the two names of the addressees were suppressed and Calvin's editing added. Since Beza's *Life of Calvin* later revealed the two addressees as Nicolas Duchemin, a law schoolmate of Calvin's Orléans period, and Gérard Roussel, a leader of the Lefèvrian moderate reform, the addressee issue has been generally regarded as settled. With its opening call of "the most loving brother," the first letter, "On Fleeing the Illicit Rites of the Wicked and Observance of the Purity of Christian Religion," was meant to be his reply to Duchemin's request for an answer on this issue. With the opening call of "Dear friend," the second letter, "On the Duty of Christian Men in the Priesthood of the Papal Church, Its Administration or Abandonment," was written on the occasion of Roussel's ordination as Bishop of Oloron in February 1536. The two open letters were both aimed at a certain group that Calvin called "the moderators" (*moderatores*) or the moderate reformists. In the context of the early French Reformation, he placed the group between his Evangelicalism and the papists. Notably, in the "Preface to the readers," Calvin seemingly characterized the moderates by loosely referencing Ezekiel (33:31–33): "they hear your [the Lord's] words, but they will not obey them," and again, "they shall know

167. *De fugiendis impiorum illicitis sacris et puritate Christianae religionis observanda*; *De Christiani hominis officio in sacerdotiis papalis ecclesiae vel administrandis vel abiiciendis*. Cf. *BC* 37/1. The texts used here are from *COR* IV-4, *De fudiendis*, 1–64; *De . . . officio*, 65–136. The texts are also found in *Calvini Opera* (*CO* 5:233–312) and *Opera Selecta* (*OS* 1:287–362), but only the latter will be cited in parentheses.

that a prophet has been among them." Since this passage has been interpreted by some researchers to be his self-awareness as a prophet, if that were the case, *Two Epistles* was his challenge to the moderate reformists from this prophetic perspective concerning the future of the French Reformation. As a matter of fact, this passage was seemingly taken by the moderate reformists as an arrogant claim of Calvin's prophetic self-awareness and it became a point of criticism against him in the later Nicodemite controversy.[168]

(1) Problems concerning Two Epistles

Among Calvin's early works, there is no other work that is as problematic as *Two Epistles.* To start with, the work was considered problematic before and after its publication. In addition, it has been difficult to place it in the development of his theological thought, and, as a result, there is no common evaluation of it in the field of Calvin research. Although the work was basically Calvin's apology aimed at the moderate reformists in the early French Reformation, the methodological device of his apology was quite unique. By means of sharp contrast between papalism and his Evangelicalism, he showed the impossibility for the moderates to exercise any evangelical reforms within the papal church, and he urged them to make an either-or choice. His apology was a denial of moderate reform, such as the Meaux reform that had received a certain positive evaluation in the French Reformation, and there was even a question of whether or not the French Catholic Church under the papacy could be a Christian church. As a result, *Two Epistles* has been regarded a work of Calvin's extreme radicalism, and accordingly its negative evaluation seems to have survived until recently. On the contrary, this study considers it to be an important work that questioned the vision of the French Reformation and provided some insights into Calvin's own Catholic ecclesiology. Before we examine the text itself, we will try to clarify the nature of "problems" under the following three points, namely, his estimate of the moderates, his estimate of the papal church, and an example of the work's conflicting evaluations in Calvin research.

168. *CO* 21:127; *COR* IV-4:1, 49, 65; *COR* IV-4, "Introduction," xx–xxv. Cf. E. Droz, *Chemins de l'hérésie* (Geneva: Slatkine Reprints, 1970), 136–37. Droz interprets that Calvin identified himself with the role of the prophet Ezekiel. Although the editors, E. A. de Boer and F. P. van Stam of *COR* IV-4 (lxxxviiin7) interpret Calvin's reference of "a prophet" to Farel, we consider Droz's view more fitting to the text than the seemingly awkward reference to Farel. For the relationship between Calvin's prophetic self-awareness and the Nicodemite controversy, see chapter 4, section 1.2, esp. n. 69.

(i) The first point concerned Calvin's estimate of the moderates, which was questioned before and after publication. As the preface to *Two Epistles* (January 1537) made clear, the work took a two-step process for publication: the edited version of the original two letters was selectively circulated to solicit feedback, and then the final draft reflecting the feedback was prepared for publication. If we assume that the first edited version's circulation had begun before his appointment as "Lecturer of scripture" (September 1536), there might have been both positive and negative responses.[169] Among the negative responses, those from Strasbourg's Bucer and Capito, who had maintained their keen interest in the future of the French Reformation, were of particular importance. Capito's letter (end of 1536) to Calvin conveyed Bucer's concerns as well as a request for an early meeting to discuss the work. Capito's case was particularly noteworthy because he offered his house for Lefèvre's and Roussel's stay when they were exiled in Strasbourg after the collapse of the Meaux reform. Since both Lefèvre and Roussel were currently under the protection of Marguerite of Navarre, Capito was deeply worried about the publication's possible adverse effects in France for its implicit criticism of Lefèvrianism and Roussel.[170] Another case was an episode concerning the loss of Louis du Tillet's friendship after the publication. Du Tillet was Calvin's old friend and financial supporter who had assumedly experienced a similar transition from moderate to radical evangelical humanism and joined Calvin's work in Geneva. The publication was likely an important factor in losing Du Tillet's friendship. In the summer of 1537, he exited from the Genevan Reformation and returned, via Bucer's Strasbourg, to France, and there returned to the Catholic Church. His French correspondence with Calvin, referring to some passages from *Two Epistles*, criticized Calvin for being "in a rage" when he denied that the French Catholic Church was a Christian church. In conclusion, he said that he had no other choice but to call Calvin "a schismatic."[171] Even though the effect of *Two Epistles* on the French Reformation has not been properly examined, we consider the above two cases indicative of its problematic nature.

(ii) The second point concerned the fact that Calvin's *Two Epistles* created a stir regarding a huge controversial issue with which the Protestant Reformation had wrestled since Luther's initial reform, namely, whether the Ro-

169. *COR* IV-4:lxxxvii. (*OS* 1:288.) Cf. *COR* IV-4, "Introduction," xiii–xiv, xxxix, liii.

170. *COR* VI-1:149–50.

171. Cf. Gordon, *Calvin*, 92–94; *COR* IV-4, "Introduction," l–lii. For the exchanged French letters between Du Tillet and Calvin (*COR* VI-1, epistola # 57, 64, 75, 85), see the editors' introductory note (*COR* VI-1:310–11) to letter #57. Phrases quoted here are from Du Tillet's letter to Calvin in March 1538 (*COR* VI-1, ep. #64, 346; *CO* 10b, ep. #99, 166–67).

man Catholic Church should be regarded as a Christian church. Although Luther initially advocated reform of the Roman Catholic Church ruled by the pope, whom he considered the antichrist, as the Protestant Reformation advanced, he left this issue as a continuing question for Protestantism. By the time of the publication of *Two Epistles*, however, the positive answer of both Luther and Melanchthon on this issue was known. For example, Luther's *On the Private Mass and the Consecration of Priests* (1533) affirmed that even the sacrilegious church under papal rule could be considered "the sacred church" (*die heilige Kirche*) as long as it maintained baptism, the Bible, preaching, the forgiveness of sins, the Lord's Supper (even in the abnormal form of the Mass), ministers, and prayers. He portrayed an optimistic prospect that the veneration of saints, the Mass, and so forth were to be gradually corrected as the teachings of the Bible penetrated the church.[172] Over against the Lutheran position, the Reformed Churches of Zurich, Basel, and Strasbourg generally took a negative position on this question. This was partly due to the fact that their Reformation was basically the City-Reformation that enabled them to make more comprehensive transitions from Catholicism to Evangelicalism. One characteristic feature of their reform was to be practice-oriented, and clear distinctions from the old practices were implemented. In *The Old Faith* (1539), for example, comparing the papal church with Babylon, Bullinger acknowledged the existence of "the remnants" who had kept God's covenant even in the Roman Catholic Church, urged them to wait for those who could minister to them with God's word and to expect Christ's coming which would destroy the rule of the antichrist.[173]

Among the Reformed leaders, however, Bucer, who was known as a mediating Reformer, was an exceptional case. In fact, the French king was said to have had a plan to invite Bucer and Melanchthon to a theological consultation with theologians from the Paris Theological Faculty for the religious unity in the kingdom. Since we will closely examine Bucer's case in connection with Calvin's Strasbourg period (1538–41) in the next chapter, here we will mention in passing only two occasions in which Bucer was deeply involved and that

172. Cf. *Von der Winckelmesse und Pfarren Weghe*, *WA* 38:221; P. Fraenkel, *Testimonia Patrum: The Function of the Patristic Argument in the Theology of Philip Melanchthon* (Geneva: Droz, 1961), 291–92.

173. Bullinger, *Der alt gloub*, 1539, H7-H 8 cited in A. A. Garcia Archilla, *The Theology of History and Apologetic Historiography in Heinrich Bullinger: Faith in History* (San Francisco: Mellen, 1992), 35; H. A. Oberman, *Masters of the Reformation: The Emergence of a New Intellectual Climate in Europe*, trans. D. Martin (Cambridge: Cambridge University Press, 1981), 188–89.

clearly indicate his positive view on this question. One was his energetic participation in a series of religious colloquies (1540–41) held in Hagenau, Worms, and Regensburg under the auspices of the Holy Roman Emperor for church reunification in the Empire. Melanchthon, Bucer, and others represented the Protestant side and negotiated with the moderate reform Catholics led by Johann Gropper and Gasparo Contarini. Although the colloquies did not succeed, Bucer, as a determined advocate of reunification, and Gropper jointly produced the *Book of Regensburg*, an important document of compromise on the controversial doctrinal issues. The other was Bucer's unpublished and privately kept manuscript copies, *Theological Advice* (*Consilium Theologicum*), the existence of which had not been known to researchers until only recently. It was a memorandum on the reform of the church's liturgy and Christian life, and it significantly included in part a thorough refutation of Calvin's first piece of *Two Epistles*, "On Fleeing the Illicit Rites," without naming the title and its author. Reflecting Bucer's mediating position, on the one hand, it exposed the unbiblical nature of the current Catholic Church's hierarchy and liturgy. On the other hand, however, from Bucer's own understanding of the church and its liturgy, just like Luther, it concluded that "under the Papacy the churches of Christ exist" (*apud papistas esse Christi ecclesias*).[174]

(iii) As the third point, we will focus on the reception of *Two Epistles* in modern Calvin research, and we will indicate how difficult it is to place it in Calvin's theological and ecclesiological development. Among such prominent Calvin researchers as Wendel, Higman, and Gordon, for example, there is a tendency to view the radicalism of *Two Epistles* with puzzlement and, as a result, to ignore it or to belittle its significance for Calvin research. It seems that a part of this puzzlement is caused by their understanding of Calvin's early formation itself (his conversion, first *Institutes*, and position in the first Genevan reform), which they consider pointing to moderate "Lefèvrian reformism" or "Lefèvrian evangelicalism." As a result, the radicalism of *Two Epistles* is viewed as "marginal" and as "raw polemical invective."[175] Among published research

174. *Consilium Theologicum Privatim Conscriptum*: *BOL* 4, ed. P. Fraenkel (Leiden: Brill, 1988), "Introduction," xix–xxiv; F. Higman, "Bucer et les Nicodemites," in *Martin Bucer and Sixteenth Century Europe*, ed. C. Krieger and M. Lienhard (Leiden and New York: Brill, 1993), 645–47 (= Higman, *Lire et découvrir*, 637–39); *COR* IV-4, "Introduction," lvii–lviii. Bucer's work, which includes a refutation of Calvin's first epistle, will be examined in chapter 3, section 2 below.

175. Wendel, *Calvin*, 41, 47, 49–56, 111–12; Higman, "Bucer et les Nicodemites," 649–50 (= Higman, *Lire et découvrir*, 640); Gordon, *Calvin*, 57–62, 77–78. Higman's article examines *Two Epistles* in its comparison with Bucer's *Theological Advice* and characterizes Calvin's

that has seriously examined *Two Epistles* and has tried to solve this "problem" issue, two examples reaching two opposing conclusions are noteworthy. One is *The Young Calvin* by the Catholic Calvin scholar Ganoczy. The other is the article by van Stam, one of the editors of the Latin text of *Two Epistles* in the *Renewed Calvini Opera.*[176]

In his earlier and extensive work on Calvin's ecclesiology, *Calvin: théologien de l'église et du ministère*, Ganoczy highly evaluated Calvin's notion of the church's catholicity. In *The Young Calvin* he also considers *Two Epistles* basically a book that posed the question of "the church's unity and schism." According to him, what Calvin rejected in this work was not the Catholic church but the papal church, and the work as a whole was not advocating schism. This evaluation may have been influenced by Ganoczy's positive esteem of the first *Institutes* and its dedicatory epistle as a reform-proposal of the papal church that was for Calvin just "malformations" of the Catholic church.[177] Concerning the first epistle that dealt with the papal liturgy, Ganoczy admits that Calvin indeed advised the readers to avoid "idolatry, superstitions, and the sacrilegious Mass," but he insists that Calvin was not advocating secession from the Roman Catholic Church. He bases his argument on the assumption that Calvin considered such papal practices as the Mass as "malformations" in the church's external form. Concerning the second epistle that was occasioned by Roussel's episcopal ordination, Ganoczy's starting point is that Calvin was not rejecting the ordination itself in the Roman Catholic Church, but was criticizing evil practices surrounding papal ordinations. From this assumption, he considers the first half of the epistle as dealing with the ideal of biblical ministry. In spite of Calvin's vehement attacks concentrated in the second half, he concludes that

arguments as "evasive" and "too complicated" and Bucer's stand as "consistent." Sharing also the same sentiment of puzzlement, Droz (*Chemins de l'hérésie*, 145–55) calls Calvin of *Two Epistles* "an intransigent theorist," and Millet (*Calvin et la dynamique*, 491) views him as "a moralist and extremist."

176. Ganoczy, *Young Calvin*, 111–12, 274–76; F. P. van Stam, "The Group of Meaux as First Target of Farel and Calvin's Anti-Nicodemism," *Bibliothèque d'Humanisme et Renaissance* 63 (2006): 253–75. Cf. Augustijn et al., "Calvin in the Light," 139–57; *COR* IV-4, "Introduction," xi–lxi. Among other interpretations of *Two Epistles* or Nicodemism, Ginsburg's work (C. Ginzburg, *Il Nicodemismo* [Turin: Guilio Einaudi, 1970], 121–24) regards Nicodemism as a comprehensive system of thought, Millet's work (*Calvin et la dynamique de la parole*, 492–504) touches on *Two Epistles* from the perspective of Calvin's rhetorical tradition, and Eire's work (C. M. N. Eire, "Antisacerdotalism and the Young Calvin," in *Anticlericalism in Late Medieval and Early Modern Europe*, ed. P. A. Dykema and H. A. Oberman [Leiden: Brill, 1993], 583–603) examines the Roussel-Calvin relationship in the second epistle.

177. Ganoczy, *Young Calvin*, 252–66, 271–74.

the epistle's leading theme was "the ideal of pastoral ministry."[178] Accordingly, *Two Epistles* was congruent with Calvin's notion of the church's catholicity.

Van Stam's article, "The Group of Meaux," is historical research that considers Calvin's *Two Epistles* as the first of his works to express the anti-Catholic radicalism of Farel. Unlike Ganoczy, he narrowly defines the object of the attack of *Two Epistles* as the moderate Catholics, more specifically "the group of Meaux." Furthermore, he regards the work as Calvin's first expression of anti-Nicodemism, which as a historical movement is generally considered a phenomenon of the 1540s among researchers. There seems to be three assumptions used in van Stam's evaluation of *Two Epistles*. Firstly, he assumes that the radical anti-Catholic rhetoric or attacks on moderate Catholics seen in it was absent in Calvin's work of a few months earlier, the *Instruction*, as well as in his first *Institutes*. Secondly, he assumes that since the radical rhetoric of anti-Nicodemism suddenly appeared in Farel's *Confession*, in which he revised the moderate view of Calvin's *Instruction*, there was "a possible trigger" that caused Calvin to turn to radicalism within "a three-month period" between his *Instruction* and *Two Epistles*.[179] Thirdly, he considers the "trigger" to be the Lausanne Disputation that Farel and Viret led and supplies the following reasons for his assumption. The Disputation coincided with the period of the final redaction of *Two Epistles*. The "same context" and "similarity" were seen in both the Disputation and *Two Epistles*. In the final stage of the Disputation, without directly naming him, Farel made personal attacks on Roussel just like Calvin's second epistle did later. According to the conclusion he drew from these assumptions, Calvin had taken in Farel's radicalism, reflected it in his *Two Epistles*, and advocated both "complete secession" from the Roman Catholic Church and "early anti-Nicodemism."[180]

(2) Some Hermeneutical Confirmations

The above discussions have shown some problems surrounding *Two Epistles* and highlighted the difficulty of placing it in Calvin's early theological formation. Since this study has so far presented its views on Calvin's early theological formation, the first *Institutes*, and the first Genevan reform—views that are considerably different from those of the researchers mentioned above, espe-

178. Ganoczy, *Young Calvin*, 274–76.

179. Van Stam, "The Group of Meaux," 253–54. Already Wendel (*Calvin*, 47) and Droz (*Chemins*, 131–51, esp. 142) considered *Two Epistles* Calvin's first work of anti-Nicodemism.

180. Van Stam, "The Group of Meaux," 254–68.

cially from van Stam's comprehensive analysis—it will make the following three hermeneutical confirmations before it proceeds to examine the text itself.

(i) It can be generally assumed that the first draft of *Two Epistles*, which was composed at the latest by September 1536, could be placed in the context of the first *Institutes* and the dedicatory epistle; its final draft was composed after the Lausanne Disputation (early October 1536) for publication in March 1537; and, unlike the *Institutes* and the dedicatory epistle, its apologetic aim was rather narrowly directed to the moderate reformists in the French Church. After these factors are admitted, however, our first confirmation is that there existed fundamental coherence among the *Institutes*, the dedicatory epistle, and *Two Epistles* and that radicalism in *Two Epistles* could be placed in the context of Calvin's ideological development from the first *Institutes* and was not a strangely new element.

As seen in the previous chapter, our proposition assumes that what the first *Institutes* represented could not be characterized as Lefèvrianism or the position of the moderate evangelical humanists but rather more like radical Evangelicalism. This Evangelicalism was basically the same as Farel's position. Its radical character was consistent with the three Genevan documents, the main tenor of the Lausanne Disputation, and *Two Epistles*. In this respect, our proposition is to pose some questions about the hermeneutical methodology van Stam and others use. In the critical edition of *Two Epistles* of which van Stam is an editor, for example, despite the editors' thorough cross references to and from the first *Institutes*, there seems to be no clear presentation as to the theological identity of the *Institutes* or whether it represents Lefèvrianism or Calvin's own radical Evangelicalism. Concerning the three Genevan documents, van Stam's two assumptions can be questioned, that is, his move to start with the *Instruction* that is said to lack anti-Catholic polemics for the interpretation of *Two Epistles*, and his move to compare it with the *Confession* that is said to "rework" the *Instruction*'s shortcomings. For example, our analysis of the *Instruction* indicates that, for the sake of the educational goal of a catechism, Calvin possibly suppressed the anti-Catholic polemics already prevalent in chapters 5 and 6 of the *Institutes*. Furthermore, the *Confession* was said to be "extracted from" the *Instruction*, and not "reworked" as van Stam and others claim, and there was evidence of Farel's "assimilations" with it in the *Confession*. Our analysis certainly assumes that Farel was not complacent with the *Instruction*'s lack of anti-Catholic polemics, and he actually supplemented it in some cases. However, this technical concern should not be interpreted as Farel's questioning of Calvin's confessional stance.[181]

181. Van Stam, "The Group of Meaux," 257; van Stam, "Die Genfer Artikel," 96, 101. As one

Concerning the final draft of *Two Epistles*, furthermore, van Stam assumes the final draft's importance over the original letter. And he considers that, by taking the outcome of the Lausanne Disputation into consideration, changes brought into the final draft were "substantial." In this final draft, the editors of *Two Epistles* in the *Renewed Calvini Opera* conclude that Calvin completely aligned himself with the radicalism of Farel and Viret and joined the leaders of radical Evangelicalism.[182] As we will examine below, however, there is a fundamental difference between the nature of the Lausanne Disputation, which aimed to introduce Evangelicalism in the Pays de Vaud and unfolded a general anti-Catholic polemic, and *Two Epistles*, which was directed to a narrowly defined group of moderate reformists in France. In addition, van Stam's reference to Farel's anonymous personal attack against Roussel at the end of the Lausanne Disputation cannot be taken as evidence of Calvin's being influenced by the outcome of the Disputation. In fact, Calvin's original personal letter, the second epistle of *Two Epistles*, was written more than half a year before the Disputation that van Stam considers the "trigger." In that letter, we can see that he expressed the same radicalism against Roussel. The editors of *Two Epistles* have contributed considerably to historical research in Reformation studies, and van Stam in Calvin studies, and their view is not to be treated lightly. Since their views have been seemingly reflected in some more recent research, we dare to question it for the sake of further clarification of this issue.[183]

(ii) The second confirmation concerns the nature, purpose, and addressees of *Two Epistles*, the first work in which Calvin identified himself with his official title "Instructor of sacred Scripture in the Church of Geneva" (*Sacrarum literarum in Ecclesia Genevensi professor*). In recent years, *Two Epistles* has been variously viewed as Calvin's first polemical book, an apologetic work against Catholic conservatives and moderates, a declaration of his theological independence, an anti-Nicodemism work aimed at the Meaux group, and a compilation of his personal opinions expressed to Duchemin and Roussel.[184]

---

proof of his theory that Farel's *Confession* "reworked" Calvin's *Instruction* that was said to lack radical anti-Catholic polemics, van Stam refers to the presence of the phrase, "the Kingdom of pope," in the *Confession*. It is to be remembered, however, that Calvin's first *Institutes* (*OS* 1:237, 250) has already denoted the papal church as "Satanae regnum" and "papa cum toto suo regno."

182. *COR* IV-4, "Introduction," xix, xx, xxx, xl, xliii; van Stam, "The Group of Meaux," 254–61.

183. Augustijn et al., "Calvin in the Light," 154–55; Gordon, *Calvin*, 77–78. Although Gordon provides no reference for his remark ("Calvin had adopted the confrontational voice of Farel, who had encouraged his younger colleague to write polemically against the Catholic church"), he seems to reflect the theory of Augustijn and van Stam.

184. Cf. Augustijn et al., "Calvin in the Light," 154; van Stam, "The Group of Meaux," 272–75; Erie, "Antisacerdotalism and the Young Calvin," 600–603; Gordon, *Calvin*, 77–78.

However, it seems that some of the basic questions about it have not been sufficiently addressed. Unlike the first *Institutes*, which combined two elements of "instruction" and "apology," and the *Instruction*, which suppressed "apology" and focused on "instruction," *Two Epistles* concentrated on "apology" in the form of a practical and polemical treatise. Since its first epistle, "On Fleeing the Illicit Rites," dealt with Catholic liturgy that was closely related to the church's sacramental system and the second epistle, "On the Duty of Christian Men," dealt with priests whose primary duty was to officiate the liturgy, we are to recall Calvin's basic understanding of Catholic religion shown in the "apology" portion of the *Institutes*. Touching on these two subjects of the sacramental system, and ministerial order, he defined Roman Catholicism as a mixed religion devised from shaping "one religion out of Christianity and Judaism and paganism by sewing patches together."[185] This definition indicated his basic apologetic stance that permeated *Two Epistles*.

Concerning the main objective of *Two Epistles*, it has often been assumed that its objective was to attack the unbiblical character of papalism and its conservative theology, but this assumption is far from sufficient. Rather, by means of attacking papalism, we assume, the main objective was to expose the real identity of what Calvin called the "moderators" placed between papalism and Evangelicalism and to urge them to make an "either-or" choice. He depicted their real identity as those who knew well of the Evangelical faith and practice but who were either staying in the papal system due to unavoidable circumstances or intentionally staying by ratiocinating to justify their stay. In the first epistle, for example, it was the case of those who knew well of the heathen elements in the sacraments but continued to practice them as well as of those who used the Lefèvrian distinction of "worship" and "veneration" to justify their practice. Of course, this was a core issue that Calvin dramatized later in his anti-Nicodemite works of the 1540s.[186]

In the second epistle, Calvin likewise questioned whether the "moderate" clergy could officiate the idolatrous sacraments and ceremonies. In particular, he criticized the clerical role in the Mass as importing the Jewish priesthood into Christian ministry, and he called the celebrants of Christ's sacrifice in the

185. *OS* 1:157, 217. (Battles, trans., *Institution*, 161, 233.)

186. *COR* IV-4:32, 37–38. (*OS* 1:307, 309.) Cf. notes 19, 20 above. The "worship/adoration" and "veneration" distinction officially adopted in the Second Council of Nicea (787) was Lefèvre's justification to participate in the Catholic liturgy. In the current controversy, Calvin makes this distinction a key issue against the moderate reformists or Lefèvrianism and keeps it as a basic assumption in his Nicodemite controversy.

Mass "the butchers of Christ" (*Christi carnifices*).[187] In the context of the early French Reformation, the merit of *Two Epistles* was to expose the real image of the "moderates" who had become critical of the papal religion and yet had been unable to turn themselves to the Evangelical position that Calvin characterized as "our excessive severity" (*nostra acerbitas*), as well as to demonstrate the impossibility of their reformist position. In a final analysis, if the Caroli affair was an occasion for Calvin to demonstrate his "consistent biblicism" to the European Christian world, *Two Epistles* demonstrated his "practical activism" paired with his biblicism as the practice of his Catholic ecclesiology.[188]

It is not easy to identify to whom Calvin's two open epistles were addressed. If we were able to assume the three groups he had in mind, the first group could be the original addressees, Duchemin and Roussel. The second group could be Calvin's main target, namely, the group centered around "the moder-

187. *COR* IV-4:81. (*OS* 1:338.) Concerning Calvin's use of the term, "butcher" (*cernifex*), the editors' note (n. 83) refers to Farel's word (*la boucherye*) in the Lausanne Disputation (Piaget, *Les Actes*, 334; the word appears not in Farel's speech, but in Viret's), and implicitly suggests that Calvin in *Two Epistles* followed Farel's radicalism. If there were to be any references here, they should be to Calvin's use of "the butchers of Christ" (*Christi carnifices*) in his first *Institutes*, chapters 4 and 6 (*OS* 1:158, 233), both references in the context of the Mass celebration by Catholic priests. This seemingly indicates the problematic aspect of coeditor van Stam's use of the Lausanne Disputation as a hermeneutic prop for interpreting Calvin's *Two Epistles*.

188. *COR* IV-4:26–27. (*OS* 1:304.) Cf. D. F. Wright, "Why Was Calvin So Severe a Critic of Nicodemism?," in *Calvinus Evangelii Propugnator*, ed. D. F. Wright, A. N. S. Lane, and J. Balserak (Grand Rapids: Calvin Studies Society, 2006), 66–90. Wright's excellent article focuses on this very issue of Calvin's extremely rigorist stance in the Nicodemite controversy of the 1540s. It also traces the origin of Calvin's rigorist stance back to his earlier writings and experiences, including *On Fleeing the Illicit Rites* (1537), the 1536 *Institutes* (very cursorily at p. 88), and his visit to the Duchess of Ferrara (1535). Although we agree with its affirmation that Calvin's rigorist stance against such moderate reformists as Duchemin and Roussel is "multi-factorial," we wonder whether it goes back sufficiently to deeper roots, such as the Roman Catholic liturgical tradition itself and Lefèvre's stance on worship or Lefèvrianism that we consider major components of Nicodemism. As our previous analyses of Calvin's vehement attack on Catholic worship in the first *Institutes* (chs. 4–5) and Lefèvrianism indicate, we assume that the roots of Calvin's anti-Nicodemite rigorist stance go deeper into the very nature of the Christian church and its worship and the prospect of the French Reformation. "Our excessive severity" could be Calvin's self-scorning expression, which reflected his opponents' characterization of his position. The editors (*COR* IV-4, "Introduction," xlii–xliii) interpret this phrase as Calvin's defense of (or "speaking for") Farel's radical position to which Calvin had aligned since the Lausanne Disputation. And, moreover, they use it (especially the expression, "our") for their reconstruction of Calvin's process to become a radical like Farel by the time of the final editing and publication of *Two Epistles*.

ates." And the third group could be readers in general who could read the Latin text and were acquainted with the religious conditions of the time. Concerning the second group, since the first epistle's original addressee was Duchemin, who was nonclerical but a church-related professional who could exert his evangelical influence upon the faithful, the group could be broadly identified with the Lefèvrians or the moderate evangelical humanists.[189] As a matter of fact, the first epistle mentioned the Lefèvrian distinction of "worship" and "veneration." Since the second epistle had a paragraph that began with the call, "O Moderators" (*O moderatores*)—and that seemed to be Calvin's critical comment on the Meaux reform, the group could be more narrowly identified with those who had been associated with the "Meaux group."[190] The issue of the addressee's identity, however, was complex because in the text itself Calvin seemed to distinguish several groups and addressed them accordingly. This aspect could be seen particularly in the second epistle, for it was roughly divided into three parts: the opening part that retained characteristics of a private correspondence, the middle part as a treatise, and the closing part that was Calvin's personal challenge. Using second person singular, the opening part unfolded with relatively mild argument, and could be mainly from the original letter to Roussel. Using the third person singular and plural, the middle part concerned parish priests who were lower clergy than Bishop Roussel, the original addressee. It focused upon the reform of parish life, and it was likely added at the time of the final draft. More polemical and challenging than the previous parts was the third part. In using the second person singular as well as plural, it urged the main addressees of the epistle, supposedly Roussel and other moderates, to make a final choice, and it is possible that the text is from both the original letter and the final draft.[191]

(iii) The third confirmation concerns the concept of the church expressed in *Two Epistles*, especially in the second epistle. The dedicatory epistle of the

189. Cf. *COR* IV-4, "Introduction," xxi–xxv; F. Higman, "Roussel, Gérard," *OER* 3:452–53. It is not certain whether or not Duchemin was a Lefèvrian and was associated with the Meaux reform. However, it is certain that he was a law student and Calvin's senior at the humanist center Orléans and that, at the time of *Two Epistles*, he was a lawyer at the court of the reform-minded humanist Bishop of Le Mans, René du Bellay. It was possible, therefore, for Calvin to combine Duchemin and Roussel in one category of moderate reformism or Lefèvrianism.

190. Calvin's seemingly general criticism of the Meaux reform appears in *COR* IV-4:88 (ll. 788–98); *OS* 1:349.

191. *COR* IV-4:65 (l. 1)–87 (l. 530); 87 (l. 531)–104 (l. 959); 104 (l. 960)–118 (l. 1297). (*OS* 1:229–342; 342–53; 353–62.)

first *Institutes* succinctly expressed Calvin's basic church concept: "the church of Christ has lived and will live as long as Christ reigns at the right hand of his Father" and "against this church we now have no quarrel." In other words, Calvin affirmed that he was disputing the papal church and not the church of Christ. The church of Jesus Christ always had been existent in various times, places, and forms wherever the two marks of God's word and the sacraments were maintained.[192] The second epistle inherited this basic concept, and this fact could be illustrated by the following points. Firstly, the second epistle never used the term "catholic" (*catholica*) to designate the Roman Catholic Church but, by consistently calling it "the Papal church," Calvin refused to attribute "catholicity" to it. Over against the papal church, the second epistle posed "the church of Christ" (*eccleisia Christi*), or "the Christian church" (*ecclesia Christiana*), which could be more closely associated with "the kingdom of Christ" (*regnum Christi*).[193] Secondly, since the second epistle described the papal church in various ways such as "Roman seat" (*sedes Romana*), "Pope's kingdom" (*papae regnum*), "Satan's church" (*Sathana ecclesia*), and "camp of Anti-Christ" (*antichristi castrum*), the opposition of Christ's kingdom and the papal kingdom was Calvin's overarching conceptual structure, and under this structure he unfolded his apology.[194] Thirdly, Calvin related this structure to the reality of the French Church by way of a difficult question. He seemed to use a logic that we might call "dialectical duality." As long as the French Church obeyed Christ's kingdom, it remained "the church of Christ." While opposing Christ's kingdom and obeying the papal kingdom, it should be regarded as belonging to the "camp of anti-Christ." An illustration of this logic can be found in Calvin's question to a supposed disputant (Roussel) in the second epistle. In the *Institutes*, Calvin considered the Mass a weapon by which Satan could invade Christ's kingdom. In the second epistle he asked whether the disputant's officiating of the Mass was nothing but "handing the total kingdom of Christ over to Satan?"[195]

Calvin's conceptual structure, the opposition of Christ's kingdom and the papal kingdom, poses a serious difficulty to modern researchers. As a matter

192. *OS* 1:31. (Battles, trans., *Institution*, 12.)

193. *COR* IV-4:71, 90. (*OS* 1:332, 343.)

194. *COR* IV-4:91, 104, 117. (*OS* 1:344, 353, 361.)

195. *COR* IV-4:103–4. (*OS* 1:252–53.) Cf. *OS* 1:156. (Battles, trans., *Institution*, 160–61.) Here again, the editors' note (*COR* IV-4:103n204) only refers to Viret's and Farel's speeches at the Lausanne Disputation (Piaget, *Les Actes*, 124, 182–84, 199–200), but not to more appropriate references in Calvin's own *Institutes* (e.g., *OS* 1:156: Battles, trans., *Institution*, 160–61). Viret's and Farel's speeches concern the general contrast between the scriptural Lord's Supper and the sacrifice of the Mass, but not in the context of Christ's kingdom.

of fact, none of the above-mentioned interpretations of *Two Epistles* have examined this conceptual structure or his logic of "dialectical duality." For example, while Ganoczy's theological study poses the opposition of the Catholic Church and the papal church, it assumes that Calvin did not deny the former, but only denied the latter as the malformation of the former. In the context of the French Church's reality, however, the identity of what Ganoczy calls "Catholic Church" becomes an obscure existence without external identity.[196] Van Stam's historical study considers the Catholic church and the papal church as the same reality and interprets that Calvin, by adopting Farel's radicalism, denied this reality, and furthermore associated the moderates with it. Since his interpretation does not take the notion of Christ's kingdom, which Calvin repeatedly used, as well as the dialectical relation between the Catholic church and the French Church into consideration, Calvin's denial of the papal church is to be interpreted as the denial of the French Church.[197]

Some questions are to be raised here: Can we properly understand Calvin's radicalism from that of Farel who does not use the Christ's kingdom concept? Can we correctly interpret Calvin's delicate nuance in his apology exclusively aimed at the moderate group in the French Church? In fact, Calvin postulated that Christ's kingdom still existed in the French Church under the papacy and that, in the hope for that church's reform, he counted Duchemin and Roussel as evangelical reformists. He appealed to them for their loyalty to Christ's kingdom and urged them to make an either-or choice. For example, he carefully titled the second epistle "On the duty of Christian men in the priesthood of the Papal church, its administration or abandonment," and not "On abandoning the papal priesthood" as Ganoczy interprets. He was postulating Roussel and his group as "Christian men" and appealing to them to make their decision, even though at the end of the epistle he mentioned the possibility of his radical rejection of Roussel as a Christian. Furthermore, in the first epistle he assumed the readers to be "those who would belong to his [Christ's] kingdom" and urged them to "manifest piety by outward profession." This kind of delicate intention from Calvin needs to be noticed and not just ignored in the interpretation of *Two Epistles*.[198]

(3) An Ecclesiological Analysis of Two Epistles

Two Epistles is a compilation of Calvin's epistles on the themes of worship and ministry. In a strict sense, it is not a theological or polemical book but an

196. Ganoczy, *Young Calvin*, 274. Cf. n. 185 above.
197. Van Stam, "The Group of Meaux," 253; *COR* IV-4, "Personal Preface," ix–x.
198. *COR* IV-4:9. (*OS* 1:294.) Cf. Ganoczy, *Young Calvin*, 274.

apology characteristically based upon his consistent biblicism and practical activism. Concerning his biblicism, the first epistle neither uses philosophical concepts nor refers to the Second Council of Nicea, which canonized the adoration of icons, the transubstantiation theory dogmatized in the fourth Lateran Council, and Scholastic theology. But it does appeal to scriptural witnesses. The second epistle focuses on ministerial "duty" in connection with the practical reform of the church rather than ministerial "power" and "status." Concerning his activism, the first epistle focuses on what he calls "external profession," believers taking a clear stand concerning the Catholic liturgy. The second epistle deals with, among others, the clerical benefice and privileges, what Calvin calls "the most shameful thievery."[199] From this perspective of his biblicism and activism, we will attempt an ecclesiological analysis.

The First Epistle

The first epistle's broader historical context included the debate over the use of imagery in the Catholic liturgy, a practice that dogmatically could be traced back to the seventh ecumenical Council of Nicea (the Second Council of Nicea, 787). The council ended the long and complicated history of the iconoclastic controversy by rejecting the position that had regarded religious images as "idols" and by sanctioning the Christian use of icons and other objects deemed to be images of the divine and the sacred. Calvin had already touched on this issue, without referring to the Second Council of Nicea by name, in the first *Institutes*. The epistle's narrower historical context was the critical reactions to the use of imagery among the Evangelical Reformers. Although Luther, critical of the abuse of imagery in the Roman Catholic Church, took a moderate position on religious images, Reformers in South Germany and Switzerland, including Calvin, generally took the anti-imagery position and rejected the authority of the Second Council of Nicea.[200] The immediate background of the epistle, however, was the Lefèvrian acceptance of the Second Council of Nicea's core assumption as well as their accommodation to the Catholic liturgy. The first epistle was composed of an introduction and four sections in the main discussion, and the introduction referred to the (Duchemin's) request for Calvin's response to this issue, which could be summed up in the sentence mentioned

199. Cf. *COR* IV-4:9, 86. (*OS* 1:294, 341.)

200. For the iconoclastic controversy in the Eastern Church and the Second Council of Nicea, see Pelikan, *The Christian Tradition*, 2:91–145. For Calvin's treatment on the Second Council of Nicea, see J. R. Payton Jr., "Calvin and the Legitimation of Icons: His Treatment of the Seventh Ecumenical Council," *Archiv für Reformationsgeschichte* 84 (1993): 221–34. Although Payton traces Calvin's treatment historically, he does not refer to *Two Epistles*.

above, "those who would belong to his kingdom . . . must manifest piety by outward profession." The main discussion's first section concerned the mixing of heathen idolatry and superstitions within the papal church; the second section concerned Calvin's analysis of the current condition of the Catholic liturgy and his proposal for remedies; the third section concerned the letter's main focus, his refutation of the moderates' defense for participating in the liturgy; and the fourth section provided his advice on this issue. By limiting our focus to his ecclesiology, we will analyze the first and second sections under the first point, and the third section under the second point.[201]

(i) The first point concerned Calvin's apology aimed at the Catholic claim that their liturgical system centered around the seven sacraments was legitimate and certainly not idolatry. At the beginning of the first section, in opposition, he mentioned heathen idolatry and the church's superstitions. Calvin pointed out that Catholic liturgy was basically a mixture of these two elements. This argument continued his exposition on the second commandment of the Law in the first *Institutes*, chapter 1, where he defined Catholic liturgy as a syncretism of Christianity, Judaism, and heathenism. In a similar manner of argument, the first epistle concluded that what were called objects of "veneration" in Catholic liturgy actually corresponded to "wood or stone" and "similitude of gods" in heathen worship.[202] In contrast, he depicted the purity of worship in "the Christian church" and asked his "friend" (Duchemin) and readers, "our members are the members of Christ, shall we defile them by the worship of idols or by impure superstitions?"[203]

The second section concerned Calvin's advice to his "friend" and readers whom he considered evangelical believers in influential positions in the church. His argument seemed to reflect the notion of Christian liberty, especially that of adiaphora, which he had already treated in the first *Institutes*,

201. Introduction: (*COR* IV-4:1–12; *OS* 1:289–95), the main text #1: (*COR* IV-4:12–20; *OS* 1:295–300), #2: (*COR* IV-4:20–26; *OS* 1:300–304), #3: (*COR* IV-4:26–45; *OS* 1:304–14), #4: (*COR* IV-4:45–64; *OS* 1:314–28).

202. *COR* IV-4:12–14. (*OS* 1:295–96.) Cf. *OS* 1:42–45, 217. The editors' footnotes in this portion of the text provide no references to Calvin's *Institutes*. Judging from terms such as "wood or stone" and "images," in particular, the text to which the editors add notes 74 and 75 (*COR* IV-4:13) seems to reflect Calvin's own argument already expressed in the *Institutes*, chapter 2 (*OS* 1:43; Battles, trans., *Institution*, 26–27). To this text the editors only referred to the arguments of Viret and Farel in the Lausanne Disputation (Piaget, *Les Actes*, 290–97, 76). While their arguments are against Catholic worship in general, Calvin's arguments in the text are aimed at the moderate reformists and in the particular context of their Lefèvrian distinction of "worship/adoration" and "veneration."

203. *COR* IV-4:17. (*OS* 1:298.)

chapter 6. In the *Institutes*, the focus of his criticism was that the papal church made church laws and liturgy that were basically things of indifference to matters necessary for the salvation of believers and the binding of their consciences. To be precise, however, he said that "these things, superstition aside, are of themselves indifferent." Thus, he articulated that the superstitious elements in church laws, liturgy, and so on were excluded from the case of adiaphora.[204] Here in the second section addressed to evangelical readers, however, his discussion was guided by his concern that the general notion of adiaphora should not be abused by them. In particular, he called them "leaders" among the faithful, questioned the validity of their participation in the liturgy, and requested their response in three areas, namely, their responsibility, the forms of their "outward profession," and their choices in their participation. Concerning the responsibility of leaders, he argued, even if their participation was by the free exercise of their consciences, they were accountable when some believers followed their examples.[205] Concerning "outward profession," Calvin emphasized the integration of internal conviction and its external manifestation. He urged leaders that their internal conviction of liturgy not being evangelical was not sufficient, but must take the form of "outward profession" against it. Concerning the choices of leaders in adopting or avoiding images in the liturgy, "eating of meat," the sacraments of marriage or extreme unction, and "holy water," he urged them to make clear their "outward profession."[206]

At this point, he repeated what he had already expressed in the first *Institutes*, chapter 1, where he referred to the distinction between "to venerate" (*venerare*) the images and "to worship" (*adorare*) them. The distinction suggested his awareness of the Second Council of Nicea and the Lefèvrian position. In *Two Epistles*, however, the context of his argument was the practical issue of the leaders' act of "simulation." In this context, an interesting aspect of his liturgical reform appeared. Calvin pointed out the abuse and expansive interpretation of the Second Nicene canon by the Western Church. As a result, the abominable superstitions in the papal church had come to far exceed those of the heathen. He concluded that "the only method by which it [reform] will be accomplished will be by plucking it up by the roots."[207]

204. Cf. *OS* 1:226, 233, 242, 248, 250. (Battles, trans., *Institution*, 245, 253, 264–65, 272, 274.)

205. *COR* IV-4:20–21. (*OS* 1:300–301.) Cf. *OS* 1:250. (Battles, trans., *Institution*, 274.)

206. *COR* IV-4:22 (*OS* 1:302), 24–26. (*OS* 1:303–4.)

207. *COR* IV-4:23–24. (*OS* 1:302–3.) Cf. Pelikan, *The Christian Tradition*, 2:117–33, esp. 118, 122. Here Calvin seems to reflect the theory of the icon veneration advanced by John of Damascus and officially adopted in the Second Council of Nicea. On this, confer n. 20 above.

Although it was not certain whether he meant "plucking up by the roots" to be the evangelical reform or the eschatological intervention of God, it was certainly a reflection of his pessimism about the reform prospect of Catholic liturgy and ceremonies.

(ii) The second point concerned the epistle's third portion, in which Calvin refuted the argument of moderates to justify their participation in the Catholic liturgy, especially in the Mass. In this refutation, he assumed that the moderates were well aware of the difference between the Lord's Supper in Scripture and the current Catholic Mass, and they armed themselves with the reasoning of the "worship" and "veneration" distinction as well as the notion of adiaphora. He was well aware that they were acquainted with his adiaphora notion expounded in the *Institutes* and that they used it against him. Of three arguments Calvin raised against them, the first two concerned the Mass. He held that it could not be a matter of indifference because it was destroying the significance of Christ's cross and of the Lord's Supper that Christ instituted as a sacrament. Pointing out that he had already discussed these arguments in his *Institutes*, his refutation here was brief.[208] Since his third argument touched on the crucial issue of transubstantiation, unlike his theological arguments in the *Institutes*, he held that the practical issue of the Mass was the idolatry of its element, bread, consecrated and elevated by priests as the divine object of worship and venerated by the participants. His refutation basically reflected the argument in the *Institutes*, chapter 4 where the Mass was defined as a device to transfer God's glory to the created elements and to make idolatry out of the sacrament. However, an interesting remark that suggested his complex relationship with the moderates appeared: "let no one here object that it is not the bread that is adored, but Christ."[209] The last quotation suggested two things: first, that he had previously had a debate with the moderates over the issue of the "worship" and "veneration" distinction and the dogma of transubstantiation; second, as we have noted in Lefèvre above, that the Lefèvrian moderates typically equated the veneration of the sacred host with the worship of Christ. Here, he also argued the practical aspects of the issue, namely, that the element of bread should be offered to the participants for eating and not for venerating, that the body of Christ which the element signified should not be offered as the repeated sacrifice by priests, and that what was offered to participants was none other than the salvific "promise" to be received by faith.[210]

208. *COR* IV-4:31–32. (*OS* 1:307.)
209. *COR* IV-4:32. (*OS* 1:307.) Cf. *OS* 1:143–45. (Battles, trans., *Institution*, 144–48.)
210. *COR* IV-4:33–38. (*OS* 1:307–10.)

After having refuted the main argument of moderates that the participation in the Mass was a matter of indifference, Calvin took up their three new arguments, what he called their "new subterfuges." Their first argument was that, since the Mass was simply a "symbol" of Christ's death, the moderates could participate in it "as if" (*ac si*) they were partaking of the elements of the Lord's Supper.[211] Their second argument was that, since they understood the significance of the Mass as "memory" or "recollection" of Christ's death, they could receive from their participation in the Mass the same "benefit" (*usus*) as much as from the Lord's Supper. Calvin's refutation of the Lefèvrian notion was directed to their self-contradictions. He argued that, if they claimed to receive the same "benefit," they should avoid the Mass and choose the Lord's Supper as "outward manifestation."[212] Their third argument considered the Mass and other liturgies as "neutral rites" (*medii riti*) and insisted that the participants of the Mass could freely interpret it as either the Lord's Supper or the Mass. Here Calvin accused them of abusing his notion of indifference to justify their participation in the Mass. Besides the above-mentioned case of superstition excluded as the object of indifference, he rejected their argument as unskillful. He refuted their citations of three Old Testament images (the brazen serpent, Aaron's calf, Jeroboam's calves) by appealing to the examples of the prophets. Thus, Calvin's final verdict on the moderates depicted them as imitators of the biblical religion, betrayers of their own consciences, and idolaters by saying that their participation was no less sacrilegious than heathen worship.[213]

The above brief description of Calvin's apology indicated that the first epistle was quite distinctive from his previous works in the sense that it was aimed exclusively at a particular group of the moderates. Our last question left unanswered so far was the identity of the moderates. Although the "worship" and "veneration" distinction of the Second Council of Nicea was the official teaching of the Catholic Church, of the evangelical reformists in the French Reformation this position was distinctively held by Lefèvre and the Lefèvrians. In the first epistle's third section, for example, Calvin criticized the "moderates" and their practice of simulation and intentionally compared their position with his "our excessive severity" against idolatry. In the fourth section, his personal advice to his "friend" (Duchemin), furthermore, there was a refer-

211. *COR* IV-4:41, esp. ll. 900–901. (*OS* 1:312.)

212. *COR* IV-4:42. (*OS* 1:312–13.) Two terms, memory and recollection, may suggest Lefèvrian terminology. Farel's *Summary* uses the similar expressions, "racomptantz & rememorantz" (cf. n. 50 above).

213. *COR* IV-4:42–45. (*OS* 1:312–14.)

ence suggesting the same group. In the apocryphal book of Baruch (Jeremiah's Letter), chapter 6, there was a depiction of the Babylonian multitude worshipping their idol when captive Jews happened to be there. Jeremiah advised the Jews to say in their heart, "It is you, O Lord, whom we must worship." Calvin accused his opponents of interpreting the Prophet's advice as the recommendation of an "inward adoration of heart" (*cordis adoratio*), and by appealing to this case they defended their participation in the Mass. As we have seen above, he was aware of the fact that, in their participating in the Mass and the external "veneration" of the sacred objects, Lefèvre and the Lefèvrians insisted that they were "worshipping" Christ in their heart.[214] If our understanding of the identity of the moderates is correct, in the context of the early French Reformation, the first epistle can be interpreted as a manifestation of Calvin's final separation from moderate evangelical humanism or Lefèvrianism and, at the same time, the beginning of his anti-Nicodemite controversy.

The Second Epistle

Just like the first epistle, the second epistle was an apology addressed to those who had a basic understanding of evangelicalism. In particular, Calvin was writing to the original addressee (Roussel), and a reform-minded group including the moderates whom Calvin addressed as main interlocutors, and readers in general, especially those who were in the ministry of the church. Even though it was not meant to be an anti-Catholic polemical work, it unfolded a more thorough refutation of the Catholic hierarchy than his first *Institutes*. This was a more urgent and challenging appeal to the interlocutors to make their either-or decision. By way of illustration, for example, the epistle had a reference to an anti-Catholic acronym, ROMA (*Radix Omnium Malorum Avaricia*), that hinted at the New Testament passage, "the love of money is a root of all kinds of evil" (1 Tim 6:10). It also contained a paragraph

214. *COR* IV-4:26–27, 55–56. (*OS* 1:304, 322.) For Jeremiah's advice, "*Te oportet adorari, Domine*" (*COR* IV-4:55), the text of New Revised Standard Version (Baruch/the Letter of Jeremiah 6:6) is used. The editors' note suggests "the moderates" as "theologians of Meaux . . . Bucer and Capito." Payton's article ("Calvin and the Legitimation," 228–34), a study in conciliar history, traces Calvin's treatment on the Second Council of Nicea from the 1536 to the final 1559 editions of the *Institutes*. It especially focuses on Calvin's exposition in the 1539 edition (*Institutio*, 2, 8, 17–21) and his final view on the Second Council of Nicea (*Institutio*, 4, 9, 9) that mostly originated in the 1543 and 1550 editions of the *Institutes*. Our study considers that Calvin's view on the Second Council of Nicea can be appropriately viewed in the context of his reaction to moderate Lefèvrianism and the Nicodemite controversy.

that likely was the first appearance of Calvin's direct criticism of the Meaux reform.[215] As mentioned above in connection with "problems" concerning *Two Epistles*, the second epistle's interpretation is not an easy task. In the first *Institutes*, although Calvin had substantially dealt with the epistle's first main subject, the spiritual rule of clergy by means of the sacramental system, he did not elaborate on the second main subject, the clergy's benefices and privileges, except only to refer to it as "another kind of rule." Since the Concordat of Bologna (1515), which guaranteed King Francis I the right of clerical appointments and Pope Leo X that of the church's economic basis in France, however, the French Church was said to have fallen into the most corrupt condition in both its ministry and finance.[216] Against this historical background, Calvin's second epistle made a strenuous challenge with its three prominent themes, namely, the kingdom of Christ, church reform, and the clergy's personal decisions. We will follow these themes in the context of the epistle's three sections, the private communication with the original addressee (Roussel), the address to clergy in general at the parish level, and the section challenging the original addressee as well as the main interlocutors for their final decisions.

(i) In the opening section of private correspondence to his "friend" (Bishop Roussel), Calvin listed a bishop's duty under three headings: nurturing the church by the word of God, preventing Satan's incursion into the church, and demonstrating the path of sanctification to the faithful. These signified the bishop's duty as desiring Christ's kingdom and endeavoring toward its realization. In the closing section also addressed to his "friend," Calvin's challenge to him was harsh: "if you, while working in the camp of the Anti-Christ, are confident that you have your stand in the people of God, you are as if simultaneously hoping to participate in the heavenly kingdom with God's Son and in the sacrilegious excrements of larceny and robbery."[217] Yet, it should be noticed that Calvin acknowledged the legitimacy of the evangelical clergy's office itself. In his address to his "friend," he mentioned the ordination of his "friend" as "making an oath to God as well as to people in the sacrament." If

215. *COR* IV-4:108, 98. (*OS* 1:358, 349.) Cf. Augustijn et al., "Calvin in the Light," 155; van Stam, "The Group of Meaux," 264. Augustijn and van Stam regard the first appearance of the acronym (ROMA) in Calvin's works a key to understanding his turning to anti-Catholic radicalism and they theorize the influence of Farel who used this phrase in the Lausanne Disputation (Piaget, *Les Actes*, 366) upon Calvin.

216. *OS* 1:250. (Battles, trans., *Institution*, 275.) Cf. J. H. M. Salmon, *Society in Crisis: France in the Sixteenth Century* (New York: St. Martin's Press, 1975), 80; C. M. N. Eire, "Antisacerdotalism and the Young Calvin," 583–603.

217. *COR* IV-4:75, 117. (*OS* 1:335, 361.)

by "the sacrament" he meant "the sacrament of order" or that of episcopal installation, he acknowledged the legitimacy of the evangelical clergy.[218] His position was consistent with the first *Institutes*, chapter 5, where, in discussing the sacrament of order, he did not refer to the legitimacy issue, but only criticized the sacramental signification of the clergy, their hierarchical structure, and the unscriptural nature of their ordination ceremony. It was also consistent with the notion of catholicity in mainstream Protestantism in acknowledging the legitimacy of baptism as well as the ordinations of Luther, Zwingli, Bucer, and others received in the Roman Catholic Church.[219]

From this notion of catholicity, Calvin proceeded to describe the ideal of Christian ministry. In particular, he called his "friend" "an administrator" (*procurator*) of Christ's kingdom, "debtor to all" (*aliis debitor*), and "a watchman" (*custos*), "a guard" (*speculator*), "a dispenser of the mystery of heavenly wisdom" (*ad dispensanda coelesti sapientiae mysteria*) as a pastor over the church of God.[220] Nonetheless, he was severely critical about the reality surrounding the office of a bishop. Citing from the Old Testament prophet who urged the priests to be responsible for the "blood" of God's people and from the apostle Paul who declared that he was "not responsible for the blood of any," he emphasized the accountability of a bishop.[221] His criticism was especially directed to the celebration of the Mass that was daily exercised in bishoprics. He called the celebration itself nothing but "impiety and sacrilege" and a celebrant bishop "the butcher of Christ" who could be charged with "homicide" for he had crucified Christ again by repeatedly sacrificing him in the Mass. The benefices and privileges of bishops could not escape Calvin's criticism. In abusing them, a bishop was guilty of "the most impudent greed," and in the concluding portion of the first section, all bishops, including his "friend," were accused of committing the same crime.[222]

218. *COR* IV-4:80. (*OS* 1:338.) Since Calvin makes no differentiation, we interpret that he acknowledges the authenticity of the ordinations of Catholic priests in general rather than those of the limited cases of Roussel and other evangelical priests. On this point, there are conflicting interpretations: while Ganoczy (*Young Calvin*, 274) sees Calvin's "implicit" admission of the Catholic priests' authenticity, van Stam ("The Group of Meaux," 265–66; *COR* IV-4, "Introduction," xxvi, l) rejects it from Calvin's anti-Nicodemist position.

219. Cf. *OS* 1:205–20. (Battles, trans., *Institution*, 210–36.)

220. *COR* IV-4:71–72, 75. (*OS* 1:332–33, 335.) Cf. Ganoczy, *Calvin*, 388–89.

221. Two scriptural references cited by Calvin (Ezek 33:6; Acts 20:26) appear in the transitional section from his critical discussion of ministerial duties (*COR* IV-4:76–77: *OS* 1:336) to his personal challenge against Roussel (*COR* IV-4:78–87: *OS* 1:333–42).

222. Cf. *COR* IV-4:80–81, 85–86, 87. (*OS* 1:338, 341, 342.) For the notion of "the butchers of Christ," confer n. 187 above. Concerning Calvin's accusation of "murderer," if the edi-

(ii) The second theme of church reform became prominent, especially in the second section in which the ideal and reality of parish priests were focused on. First of all, Calvin signified their office as that of "stabilizing the kingdom of Christ," and then he contrasted their office's ideal and reality in the antithetical form of "should be . . . , but is . . ." (*sic . . . , ut . . .)*. For example, they should be presenting Christ the mediator to the faithful, but they were preoccupied with the saints. They should teach them to worship God alone, but they insisted on idolatrous practices, and so forth. As a result, he charged them with "joining in the church of Satan" by which they claimed themselves the rulers, boasted about themselves with attacks against God's truth, and chased God's people to the pillagers. If he meant the papal church by the expression "the church of Satan," his overall picture of evangelical priests serving in the papal church was extremely pessimistic.[223] Nonetheless, he dared to propose church reform against this background. His proposal could be summarized in three points, namely, "the sincerer preaching of God's word," "the true form of prayer," and "the true worship of God."[224] On the first point, for example, he envisioned the prospect of church reform in this way: "no matter how we consider the condition of the church today, unless the depths of wolves are removed, [the church] cannot be restored to Christ; unless [men] are freed from the snares, they cannot be brought back to God's pasture, unless men are torn up and liberated from the labyrinth of errors, they cannot be led to the right path."[225] Furthermore, on the third point, he emphasized the negative response of the faithful, namely, that they tried to stay away from idolatrous ceremonies, especially the Mass, and encouraged parish priests to prevent the faithful from participating in the Mass by showing their priestly examples and guidance.[226]

Up to this point in the second section, Calvin had been discussing church reform in general. However, here he focused on his main interlocutors, the evangelical clergy, who had not been able to commit themselves to reform, and rather took the position of deliberate circumspection. Their reasoning was said to be manifold: knowing the current condition of the church, the time of

tors' note (*COR* IV-1:85n105) is correct, here he uses the reference to Hebrews (6:6, "they are crucifying again the Son of God"), which is not found in the first *Institutes*. Since the reference is applied to the "deserters" (*apostates*) of faith, Calvin's use of it against Roussel seems extraordinary.

223. *COR* IV-4:90–91. (*OS* 1:343–44.)

224. *COR* IV-4:90–91. (*OS* 1:344–45.)

225. *COR* IV-4:92–93. (*OS* 1:345.)

226. *COR* IV-4:94. (*OS* 1:347.)

reform was not yet ripe; reform should be tried in maintaining church unity and considering opportune timing; the reform of superstition and idolatry should be preceded by biblical preaching that would take time; and so forth. Calvin's general response to such a position was to accuse them of ignoring the current condition and accommodating themselves to the status quo.[227]

In this context, interestingly, a paragraph appeared introduced by a vocative, "O Moderators" (*O moderatores*), which seemed to refer to the Meaux reform led by Lefèvre, Roussel, and others. The paragraph characterized the attempted reform as "contaminating, obscuring, confusing, disjoining, and exterminating God's word and the human spirit without reason and discretion." If the assumption of the "Moderators" being Lefèvre and evangelical humanists gathered around the Meaux reform was correct, Calvin's noticeably negative evaluation of the reform was astonishing.[228] As if he were talking to Roussel personally, he mentioned that those ministers who had led the reform advised the faithful to participate in idolatrous ceremonies. He continued by saying that their overconfident admonitions were received as a mere prologue (of reform); the reform had stumbled and disappeared; and, despite their selfish apologies, the abominable idolatries were still unchecked.[229] If we can assume this radical judgment to be Calvin's final and comprehensive evaluation of moderate evangelical humanism led by the Lefèvrians and the Meaux reform, his pessimism about the prospect of the French Reformation was indeed extraordinary. In the end of section two, a paragraph appeared consisting of six propositional sentences led by a phrase, "If by the Mass": for example, "if by the Mass the eternal priesthood of Christ was robbed"; "if [by the Mass] the Lord's Supper which was to present to us the memory of Christ's death was spoiled"; "finally, if sacrilegious elements were not removed from the Mass and the glory of God and Christ was hidden." To these propositions Calvin's answer was given in a question form: "Is it not that the total Kingdom of Christ be handed over to Satan?"[230]

(iii) The third theme of Calvin's personal challenge to Roussel and the moderate reformists appeared predominantly in the epistle's third section that mainly concerned clerical benefices and privileges. This topic corresponded in the beginning of the epistle to his calling the pope "Pluto of Rome," referring to the god of the underworld in ancient mythology, and also to the notion that

227. Cf. *COR* IV-4:95–97. (*OS* 1:347–49.) The editors' notes (95n167, 96n168) refer to Roussel's letter addressed from Meaux to Farel, who left the Meaux reform due to its non-radical nature and exiled in Basel.

228. *COR* IV-4:98 (ll. 788–98), esp. ll. 788–90. (*OS* 1:349.)

229. *COR* IV-4:98. (*OS* 1:349.)

230. *COR* IV-4:103 (ll. 921–32). (*OS* 1:352.)

the pope had been controlling the church and its clergy by means of benefices and privileges.[231] For example, he divided benefices into four categories of tithes, yearly allowances, special offerings, and spiritual rights, pointing to abuses in each case. As to tithes, he regarded its one tenth norm as the Catholic practice of "pseudo Levites." In connection with the donation of properties that constituted a greater part of the church's yearly allowances, he criticized a private Mass for the dead that claimed to rescue souls from purgatory. Concerning spiritual rights that he called a device to exploit the faithful, he regarded the pope who controlled these rights "the arch-pirate of Rome."[232]

A particularly noticeable reference was a Latin acronym "ROMA" that appeared in his criticism of special offerings. As mentioned above, this was a reference to the Pauline passage (1 Tim 6:10) from which the acronym was taken.[233] Concerning this reference, van Stam and other researchers consider it an important key to interpreting *Two Epistles*, but they regard its origin as uncertain. In the *Renewed Opera Calvini* volume's introduction to *Two Epistles*, for example, the editors, including van Stam, assume that Farel's "jest" possibly devised the acronym by connecting his anti-Catholic polemic and the Timothy passage in the Lausanne Disputation. According to the Disputation record, however, Farel himself who cited the passage in Latin said that "if a philosopher wishes, by one glance he will read ROMA there." And a reference to Luther's *Table Talks* provided in the editors' footnote also referred to the acronym, "as the ancient scholars (*veteres*) said," therefore, the acronym could hardly be devised as original by Farel.[234] Since it was difficult to reduce the acronym from the Vulgate text that used "desire" (*cupiditas*) at the end (*Radix enim omnium malorum est cupiditas*), it could be possible that among the humanists who translated the Greek word into "avarice" (*avaritia*) the acronym was noticed as a part of criticism against papal avarice. In this connection, Lefèvre's scriptural interpretation, which could be shared by both Farel and Calvin, was noteworthy. In his *St. Paul's XIV Epistles*, Lefèvre used two words in his commentary on the Timothy passage: in the formal comment part (*commentarius*) he used the official Vulgate's "desire" (*cupiditas*), but in the exegetical part (*examinatio*) in which he unfolded his own views, he introduced a new translation by saying that desire is what "in our ordinary usage we call avarice

231. *COR* IV-4:68. (*OS* 1:331.)

232. *COR* IV-4:104–10, esp. 110.

233. *COR* IV-4:108. (*OS* 1:356.)

234. *COR* IV-4:108n228. Cf. Piaget, *Les Actes*, 366: "que l'apostre escript: Radix Omnium Marolum Avaricia (I Timoth. 6), ou, si voulez philosopher par les premieres lectres, trouverez: ROMA"; *WA Tischreden* III, 3624: "Ideo veteres dixerunt: Roma Radix."

(*avaritia*)."[235] From this, we may be able to assume that in the Lefèvrian circle there was a basis from which the acronym could be circulated.

In the second half of the third section, Calvin made a final challenge to his "friend," mostly in dialogue form. To his "friend" who recently joined the highest rank (bishop) of the Catholic clergy and had pledged his allegiance to the pope, Calvin said plainly that it was not a "right way of living" (*recta vivendi via*) and urged him to choose the correct exercise of the episcopal office or to abandon it.[236] Furthermore, he inquired of his friend whether or not he was ready for exile, then challenged him with the final choice of either Christ's kingdom or remaining in the camp of the pope.[237]

It still remains difficult to determine what Calvin intended to achieve by publishing *Two Epistles*, even after having examined the above factors surrounding its publication and contents. It continuously reminds the reader of what an exceptional as well as extraordinary work it is. Yet the one thing that is certain about it is that his sense of crisis, especially surrounding the suppression of the germinal stage of the French Reformation after the Placards affair, can be easily observed in *Two Epistles*. It is also possible to see that, by means of putting forward what he called "our excessive severity," he encouraged the early evangelical movement not to disintegrate under pressure and not to end up in the compromise of the moderates. As many recent researchers have viewed *Two Epistles* as the first expression of Calvin's anti-Nicodemism, it could be said that he infused a powerful prophetic force into the prospect of the French Reformation.[238] From the viewpoint of his own formation of the church reform concept, *Two Epistles* was not a marginal work but a steppingstone for the future formation. If the Caroli affair demonstrated his rigorous biblicism, which even held the ancient formulas of the orthodox Trinitarian dogma as secondary and insisted on proving the same doctrine from scriptural witnesses, *Two Epistles* showed his practical Christianity on the issues of the church's worship and ministry, as well as his practical activism that aimed for an

235. *S. Pauli Epistolae XIV*, 211v, 213v: "Cupiditas, . . . nostri uno ferme vocabulo avaritiam nominavit." The editors (*COR* IV-4:108n228) refer to, besides Luther, Erasmus's annotation that lists both renderings of "cupiditas" and "avaritia," and to the Latin Bible of Robert Stephanus (Estienne) that renders "avaritia" instead of the Vulgate's "cupiditas."

236. *COR* IV-4:113, 115. (*OS* 1:358, 360.)

237. *COR* IV-4:116–17. (*OS* 1:360–61.) Cf. Ganoczy, *Young Calvin*, 276; Eire, "Antisacerdotalism," 601–3.

238. Cf. C. M. N. Eire, "Prelude to Sedition? Calvin's Attack on Nicodemism and Religious Compromise," *Archiv für Reformationsgeschichte* 76 (1985): 140–41; Wright, "Why Was Calvin So Severe," 77–81; n. 188 above.

uncompromising Evangelicalism. We assume, furthermore, that his biblicism and activism contributed to form the basis from which what we term his "Reformed ecclesiology" and "Reformation ecclesiology" will emerge, as we will discuss in chapter 4. Lastly, if we dare to mention a point of contact of *Two Epistles* with the Protestant Reformation in general or the Reformed Reformation in particular, historian Eire describes "Calvin's agenda" against Nicodemism, writing that "Calvin asserted the necessity of schism and laid a solid theological foundation" that influenced "Calvinist-inspired strife in England, Scotland, and the Netherlands during the second half of the sixteenth century."[239]

Concluding Remarks

(1) Chapter 2 is a test case for Calvin's "Catholic ecclesiology" in the historical context of the early French Reformation, as well as in his "first" Genevan Reformation. Since he joined the reform led by Farel in Geneva just after the publication of his first *Institutes*, chapter 2 examined Lefèvrianism as Farel's direct background, and has considered the French evangelical humanism represented by Lefèvre and the Meaux reform as the first and primary type of reform in the early French Reformation. From the fact that Farel, Lefèvre's disciple, had left the Meaux reform for its lack of radicalism and made a transition from moderate evangelical humanism to the radical evangelical position, we have considered Farel's reform as the second type. Concerning ecclesiology, for example, Farel inherited Lefèvre's basic concept of the church as the congregation of believers. However, as seen in his *Summary*, he radicalized the concept to the extent of congregational polity. On the other issues of "Rome" and "Luther" as well as the prospect of church reform within the French Catholic Church, the divergence between the two types was quite obvious.

(2) Concerning the three Genevan documents, over against the traditional view attributing them to Calvin's authorship, while we hold Calvin's sole authorship of the *Instruction*, we attribute both the *Confession* and the *Articles* to Farel's primary authorship, but with some possible assimilations with the *Instruction* and partial contributions by Calvin. Our examination of the three documents has made clear the basic working relationship between the two leading figures in the early Genevan Reformation. They shared a common ground of Evangelical theology and perhaps the common background of Lefèvrianism to a certain extent. As far as ecclesiology was concerned, how-

239. Eire, "Prelude to Sedition?," 141. Cf. Eire, *War against the Idols*, 171–75.

ever, Farel's congregational orientation in church polity and Calvin's Catholic ecclesiology were quite distinct. Our examination also suggests two tentative conclusions: the early Genevan Reformation was mainly led by Farel rather than Calvin; Calvin's Catholic ecclesiology can be considered as the third type of reform in the early French Reformation.

(3) The unique character of the third type, distinct from the other two, manifested itself in the Caroli affair and *Two Epistles* that section 3 has examined under the heading of Calvin's "Practice of Catholic Ecclesiology." We have focused on the significance of these two events in the early Genevan Reformation holding two assumptions. First, it was Calvin, not Farel, who had led the Genevan apology against Caroli's charge of Trinitarian unorthodoxy, and it was his apology that demonstrated that his Catholic ecclesiology was founded upon "consistent biblicism." Second, in *Two Epistles*, Calvin attempted a forceful apology aimed at the moderate reformist group of the Lefèvrians. He exposed their identity, challenged them to make the either-or choice of Christ's kingdom or the pope's kingdom and demonstrated his uncompromising and "practical activism." As a result, he opened up a path that led to his Nicodemite controversy of the 1540s. We assume that his biblicism and activism shown in these events were to become two pillars of his future work as a Reformer of the church.

(4) If we can borrow Oberman's view and attempt an overall evaluation of Calvin's ecclesiology in the first Genevan Reformation, it will be expressed in this fashion: having found "the true catholicity of the church" through his conversion, "Calvin shows how through the word and work of the Reformers of the first generation he learned increasingly to test the church of his time by the standard of the Church of the Gospel."[240] In this sense, his first Genevan period was a testing time for his biblicism and activism as well as a formative period upon which the future formation of his Reformed ecclesiology and Reformation ecclesiology was made possible.

240. H. A. Oberman, *The Two Reformations* (New Haven: Yale University Press, 2003), 129.

Chapter 3

The Strasbourg Period and a Transition to New Ecclesiologies

For both Calvin as a Reformer and in terms of his ecclesiology, the Strasbourg period between his forced exit from Geneva in 1538 and his resettling there in 1541 was one of transition. In 1538, he was a regional Reformer known by his first *Institutes* and recognized for his unsuccessful work with Farel in Geneva and his exiled engagements in his homeland's Reformation. After having settled in Strasbourg as the first pastor of the French congregation in that city, by 1541 Calvin was a Reformer both in name and reality: he had objectively observed the reality of the Strasbourg Reformation as well as the rapidly evolving situation of the early French Reformation beyond the border; he had acquired a firsthand knowledge of the Holy Roman Empire and the movements of the Lutheran and the Catholic camps within it; and he had become acquainted with Melanchthon and other Lutheran leaders in Germany as well as Bullinger and other Swiss Reformed leaders through the intermediaries of Bucer and Capito. In connection with this development, as many researchers have pointed out, his Strasbourg period had witnessed a transitional process in his ecclesiology, which could be characterized as a transition from somewhat book-learned and idealistic Catholic ecclesiology to an ecclesiology unsparingly reflecting both the micro- and macrorealities of the European Christian world. In this sense, Gordon's characterization of this period as "Discovering the church" is not far off target.[1] In current Calvin research, Gordon's characterization reflects the predominant understanding of Calvin's Strasbourg period, which is based upon the so-called "Bucer's in-

1. Gordon, *Calvin*, 82–102.

fluence" theory and assumes that, while Calvin had emphasized the invisible aspects of the church in his first *Institutes*, he learned from Bucer and "discovered" the visible realities of the church in Strasbourg. As we have pointed out in our previous chapters, however, this general characterization does not seem to do full justice to Calvin's Catholic ecclesiology that took into consideration the dialectic balance of the church of the elect and the church of believers in history in the first *Institutes.* This is demonstrated by Calvin's consistent biblicism and practical activism, seen in the Caroli affair and *Two Epistles*, as "practice of Catholic ecclesiology." The task we are facing here, therefore, is to take a fresh look at his Strasbourg period, especially the "Bucer's influence" theory, and to ascertain how his Catholic ecclesiology had evolved through his writings and activities in this period.

During Calvin's Strasbourg period, it could be said that the European Christian world itself had been facing a transition. For example, the religious colloquies held at Hagenau, Worms, and Regensburg (1540–41) symbolized this transition. Representing Emperor Charles V's goal to reunify the Catholic and the Lutheran Churches in Germany, the colloquies were practically the last attempts to avoid schism. Their success or failure could have had pan-European, international implications. In fact, the last colloquy held at the imperial Diet of Regensburg, which Calvin attended as an official member of the Strasbourg delegation, had agreed on the first five doctrinal articles of the *Book of Regensburg* prepared by Johannes Gropper and Bucer under the direction of the emperor. But the breakthrough agreement of the crucial fifth article on justification was later rejected by both Pope Paul III and Luther, and the colloquy stumbled in tackling the difficult issues of the sacraments and church authority. Afterward, the Catholic and Protestant camps were destined for military conflicts and the papal curia was to proceed to a general council led by the Pope.[2] Another example could be drawn from France and the French Reformation. As a historian of culture, Rothstein points out that French society had experienced significant changes around 1540 in the fields of industry, politics, language, history, and philosophy. She describes the spirit of these changes as "the idea of the new in the sense of moving forward, of going beyond the achievements of the past." Although she does not refer to the field of religion or theology, in responding to her theme Higman discusses new forms of religious engagement circa 1540. He focuses on changes in religious awareness and engagement among ordinary believers as a result of the Bible, religious

2. A. N. S. Lane, "Calvin and Article 5 of the Regensburg Colloquy," in *Calvinus Praeceptor Ecclesia*, ed. H. J. Selderhuis (Geneva: Droz, 2004), 233–63, esp., 236.

literature, catechisms, and hymnals that were now available to them in French. In this connection, Calvin's French edition of the *Institutes* (1541) prepared in Strasbourg was indeed a revolutionary step.[3] Although these are just two examples, they may help us to assume that Calvin sensed the changing air of history and began to pursue a responsive form of Christianity while in Strasbourg.

For Calvin, the three years in Strasbourg was perhaps the most peaceful and satisfactory time in his entire life. He was pastor of a congregation mostly composed of exiles and refugees from France. Other activities included his engagement with the Anabaptists in the city and its surrounding areas, lecturing on the New Testament at the Academy, and participating in the above-mentioned religious unification colloquies. During this time, he published the extensively revised second edition of the *Institutes* (1539) as well as the *Romans Commentary* (1540) that became the prototype of all succeeding commentaries on the Old and New Testaments. Important for the formation of French Reformer Calvin, above all, was that he lived in the free imperial city of Strasbourg itself. It was indeed a learning experience to have several scholars gathered together in this location: Matthias Zell, who introduced the initial reform into the city; Capito, a distinguished Hebrew scholar and known as a collaborator of Erasmus; Caspar Hedio, a doctor in theology specializing in church history and the church fathers; Johann Strum, a humanist pedagogue at the head of the Strasbourg Academy, who was a diplomat working between the French King and the Lutheran princes of Germany and an acquaintance of Calvin in his Paris years (1531–34); and especially Bucer as its chief pastor.[4]

3. M. Rothstein, introduction to *Charting Change in France around 1540*, ed. M. Rothstein (Selinsgrove: Susquehanna University Press, 2006), 9–39, esp. 16. Cf. F. Higman, "New Forms of Religious Engagement circa 1540," in *Charting Change in France around 1540*, ed. M. Rothstein, 119–40; C. Augustijn, "Calvin in Strasbourg," in *Calvinus Sacrae Scripturae Professor: Calvin as Confessor of Holy Scripture*, ed. W. H. Neuser (Grand Rapids: Eerdmans, 1994), 166–77. Characterizing Calvin's Strasbourg period "a radical transition," Augustijn presents a historical overview of Calvin's "development," including the "complex" problem of the Bucer-Calvin relationship.

4. J.-D. Benoît, "Calvin à Strasbourg," in *Calvin à Strasbourg*, Commission synodale de l'Église réformée d'Alsace et de Lorraine (Geneva: Éditions Labor, 1938), 16–17; M. Lienhard, "Strasbourg in Calvin's Time," in *John Calvin: The Strasbourg Years (1538–1541)*, ed. M. Arnold (Eugene, OR: Wipf & Stock, 2016), 11–22; F. H. Littell, "What Calvin Learned at Strassburg," in *The Heritage of John Calvin*, ed. J. H. Bratt (Grand Rapids: Eerdmans, 1973), 74–86; J. M. Kittleson, *Wolgang Capito: From Humanism to Rreformer* (Leiden: Brill, 1975); G. H. Williams, *The Radical Reformation*, 3rd ed. (Kirksville, MO: Truman State University Press, 2000), 915–18; B. S. Finsley, "Strum, Johann," *OER* 4:122–23; Millet, *Calvin et la dynamique*, 114–20. According to Millet, while Calvin was attending the Royal lectures, Strum

As Gordon's Calvin biography remarks, "the Strasbourg years witnessed a discernible broadening and deepening of Calvin's theology, and for this he owed much to Martin Bucer."[5]

With these preliminary remarks, in section 1: "Bucer's Strasbourg," this study will focus on the characteristics of the Strasbourg Reformation and Bucer's ecclesiology that we assume are indispensable for understanding Calvin's theological formation during this period. In section 2: "Bucer and Calvin," we will examine the so-called "Bucer's influence" theory and try to determine its rightful place. And, in connection with this theory, we will ascertain Calvin's consistent biblicism and practical activism in the historical context of his engagements in the French Reformation, the Genevan Reformation, and the religiously divided situation in Germany. In section 3: "The Second *Institutes* and the *Romans Commentary*," finally, we will examine the significance of the two publications from the viewpoint of his "transition to new ecclesiologies."

Section 1. Bucer's Strasbourg

The Strasbourg Reformation was a singularly historical event on two accounts. It occurred in a unique imperial free city, the uniqueness of which was even distinguished among the imperial cities of the times. And it was led by church leaders whose marked individualities were noticeable, especially by the unique figure of Martin Bucer whose theological formation, activities as a Reformer, and scope of theological notions were unparalleled even among major Reformers. First, the imperial city itself had exerted influence upon the nature of its Reformation. Known as "the most tolerant city" in Europe after the introduction of the Reformation, Strasbourg had tolerated several religiously diverse groups: the Catholic elements, the Lutherans who had been advocating for its close ties with Wittenberg and the Lutheran princes, the Reformed group that looked for its association with Zurich and other Swiss cities, the exiles and refugees like the above-mentioned Lefèvre and Roussel from France, and the Anabaptists and other radicals who had escaped persecution after the Peasants' War and had chosen this city for shelter.

Naturally, as the power politics of the city reflected the interests of these diverse groups, its chief magistrate, Jacob Strum, whom historian Brady calls

was teaching a course in dialectic and rhetoric at the University of Paris. In 1538 he joined Bucer and Capito in inviting Calvin to Strasbourg.

5. Gordon, *Calvin*, 88.

"a true Marsiglian" (follower of Marsilio of Padua), had advocated for the policy of Caesaropapism and checked a thorough religious reform proposed by Bucer and other Evangelical clergy, thus nurturing the anticlericalism and the spirit of moderation.[6] Furthermore, Brady remarks that the Strasbourg Reformation was taking shape in the city's conflicting power struggle between the "Zealots" and the "Politiques." The "Zealots" were those who had advocated for thorough Evangelical reform, for the Republican ideals of widely representing the citizenry, and for a closer diplomatic affiliation with the Swiss Protestant churches. On the other hand, the "Politiques" were advocates for moderate reform and the status quo, in order to maintain their political base of aristocrats and guilds, and wished to align with the Lutheran princes in order to protect the city's independence and privilege from the emperor. This was the reality of Bucer's Strasbourg in the 1520s when he began his reformatory work.[7]

Many Bucer researchers, as far as his ecclesiology is concerned, seem to distinguish two phases in his ecclesiological development, placing the dividing line at the *Strasbourg Ecclesiastical Ordinances* (1534) that officially declared that the city rejected the radical reform of Anabaptism and distinguished itself from the Lutheran reform. Following this customary assumption, we will survey his ecclesiology under the following two headings, "Ecclesiology of the Early Bucer" and the "*Strasbourg Ecclesiastical Ordinances* and the Later Bucer."

1. *Ecclesiology of the Early Bucer*

Among many designations attributed to Bucer, such as "Reformer of Strasbourg," "Reformer of Alsace," "Ecumenical theologian," "Practical theologian," "Erasmian Reformer," "Reformer between Luther and Zwingli," and "Father of Calvinism," two in particular are noteworthy from the perspective of his ecclesiology, "one Reformer with whom Anabaptists could expect to hold a genuine religious conversation," and "the first truly European churchman and

6. T. A. Brady Jr., *Protestant Politics: Jacob Strum (1489–1553) and the German Reformation* (Atlantic Highland, NJ: Humanities Press International, 1995), 15–52; Brady, *Ruling Class, Regime and Reformation at Strasbourg, 1520–1555* (Leiden: Brill, 1978), 199–208. In the *Defender of the Peace* (*Defensor pacis*), a political philosopher, Marsiglio (Marsilius) da Padoa (1275?–1342) challenged the prevailing high papal primacy on the grounds of Caesaropapism. He posed the power of Christian society (*Corpus Christianum*) as basically resting on its Christian members, with the temporal rulers as their representatives who could lead the people's religious life. The book was first published in 1522 and it exerted considerable influence on the early years of the Reformation.

7. Brady, *Ruling Class*, 208–9, 236–45; Brady, *Protestant Politics*, 104–16.

theologian."[8] The former is a theme predominantly seen in the early Bucer due to his theological "affinity" with the Anabaptists as well as his tolerant attitude toward them, quite distinct from the antagonism of Luther, Melanchthon, Zwingli, and Bullinger. The latter refers to the wide scope of Bucer's reformist vision predominantly seen in the later Bucer due to his sincere engagements in the Catholic-Protestant unification colloquies and the Reformation movements in Switzerland, France, England and elsewhere.

In addition, even in his early theological formation Bucer was an exceptional case among Reformers. As to his overall theological formation, for example, unlike Luther who was trained in the new theology of Nominalism as a friar of the Dominican order, Bucer was nurtured in the old theology of Thomism. It has been assumed that Thomism and its indivisible component, Aristotelian philosophy, had exerted wide influence upon Bucer's theology in general and that the influence had been seen in his theological and polemical treatises and commentaries. An illustration can be found in his exegesis of the power of the keys passages (Matt 16 and 18), of which an example can be taken from the later Bucer's anti-Catholic work against Bartholomaeus Latomus, *Two Writings against Latomus* (*Scripta duo adversaria . . . Latomi*, 1544). According to him, the church founded by Christ can be defined in two ways: its head, Christ, is a "Monarchy," and all of its powers belong to Christ; its body composed of members, however, is a "Republic" of which "power" (*potestas*) belongs to its "universal members of Christ" and its "authority" (*autoritas*) is exercised by its ministers. As the text's margin refers to Aristotle's *Politics*, this is an example of applying the Aristotelian distinction of "power" and "authority" to the concept of the church and its polity.[9] Incidentally, as we will see later, Calvin's biblicism

8. For the last two designations, see J. S. Oyer, "Bucer and the Anabaptists," in *Martin Bucer and Sixteenth Century Europe*, ed. C. Krieger and M. Lienhard (Leiden: Brill, 1993), 603–13, esp. 610, and M. Greschat, "Bucer, Martin," *OER* 1:223. For "Ecumenical theologian," see also D. F. Wright, trans. and ed., *Common Places of Martin Bucer* (Appleford, Abingdon: Courtenay Press, 1972), 17–71; for "Reformer between Luther and Zwingli," see M. Arnold and B. Hamm, eds., *Martin Bucer zwischen Luther und Zwingli* (Tübingen: J. C. B. Mohr, 2003); for "Father of Calvinism," see W. Pauck, "Calvin and Butzer," *Journal of Religion* 9 (1925): 256.

9. *Scripta Duo adversaria D. Bartholomaei Latomi*, 1544 (H. Pils, S. Ruderer, and P. Schaffrodt, eds., *Martin Bucer (1491–1551) Bibliographie*, hereafter cited as *Bucer Bibliographie* [Gütersloh: Gütersloher Verlag, 2005], no. 137), 157. Cf. *Refutatio Locorum Eckii*, *BOL* 1:255. For theological influence on Bucer in general, see C. Krieger, "Réflexions sur la place de la doctrine de la prédestination au sein de la théologie de Martin Bucer," in *Martin Bucer and Sixteenth Century Europe*, ed. C. Krieger and M. Lienhard (Leiden and New York: Brill, 1993), 83–99; for influence in biblical exegeses, see I. Backus's introduction to *Enarratio in*

was to take implicit issue with the Evangelical theologian Bucer's use of Thomistic and Aristotelian notions. Lastly, it should be noted as a distinctive factor that Bucer's theological formation came under the lasting influence of two dominant figures in the early Reformation, namely, Erasmus and Luther. Sent by the Dominican order to pursue doctoral studies in Heidelberg in 1517, Bucer became acquainted with Erasmus through their correspondence. Likewise, he met Luther in person at the Heidelberg Disputation (1518) and was said to have received a powerful and lasting impression of him.

(1) Erasmus, Luther, and Others

(i) It has been assumed that there were both "Erasmian" and "Lutheran" sides in Bucer's early Evangelical theology. As far as the one side was concerned, he was well acquainted with Erasmus's *New Testament* (*Novum Instrumentum*, 1516; *Novum Testamentum*, 1519) and the theological methodology (*Ratio Verae Theologiae*, 1519) attached to its second edition. For example, in his commentary on John's Gospel (*Enarratio in Evangelion Johannis*, 1528), he was known to have frequently used Erasmus's popular *Paraphrases* (*Paraphrasis*).[10] It was true that he openly sided with Luther after what was perhaps the most divisive controversy of the Reformation era between Erasmus and Luther on free will (1524–25). Against Erasmus's direct attack on the Strasbourg Reformation (*Epistola contra Pseudoevangelicos*, 1529), he wrote an apology (*Epistola Apologetica*, 1530) and let his separation from Erasmianism be known. However, it was also true that many Erasmian traits were manifested in Bucer's biblical hermeneutics, the basic understanding of Christianity as the practice of faith and love, the ideal of church unity, and so forth. Even in his later work (*De Vera Ecclesiarum . . . Reconciliatione & Compositione*, 1542), in which he passionately appealed for the possibility of reconciliation in church doctrine, liturgy, and discipline, he called Erasmus "Leader" of the Reformation along with Luther, crediting Erasmus's contribution in directing the faithful to read "the Bible and the Church Fathers" and not to follow ceremonies but rather "Christ and his faith."[11]

Evangelion Ioannis, *BOL* 2:xiii–xxxiii. For the *Scripta Duo* text here referred, see Maruyama, *The Ecclesiology*, 96n86.

10. For example, according to the editor I. Backus (*Enarratio in Evangelion Iohannis, 1528, 1530, 1536*: *BOL* 2:xiii, xvi) on John 4:38, Bucer used Erasmus's interpretation which stated that the ancient philosophers of Greece and Rome could be the foretellers of the Gospel.

11. *De Vera Ecclesiarum in Doctrina, Ceremoniis, et Disciplina Reconciliatione et Compositione*, 1543: *Bucer Bibliographie*, no. 125. Cf. "Martin Bucer, Von der Wiederereining

(ii) As to the other side of Bucer's formation, he had carefully followed the process of Luther (1519–21) from his *Ninety-Five Theses*, his excommunication, and to the Diet of Worms that pronounced the imperial ban against him. After he was involved in the reform of Weissenburg as "Luther's sympathizer," Bucer arrived in Strasbourg in 1523 and was soon involved in the city's Reformation. In his early days in Strasbourg, he was said to have regarded Luther as a Reformer equal to Erasmus and had kept the posture of "interpreter of Luther" by objectively observing Luther's moves. An interesting illustration of this point was his first Evangelical work, *That No One Should Live for Himself but for Others* (1525). As his letter to Luther indicated, he took the theme of the Law fulfilled in serving others from Luther's 1519 *Lectures on Galatians* (5:4). Yet, this work presented neither Luther's dialectic image of a Christian "being simultaneously justified and a sinner" nor his basic concept of the church as the "congregation of believers." Instead of Luther's sharp distinction between justification and sanctification, it emphasized Erasmus's theme of combining both in Christian practice.[12] Nevertheless, his initial electrifying impression of Luther at their meeting in Heidelberg, which he later related to a friend saying that Luther was "a real authentic theologian" and "what Erasmus only insinuates, he [Luther] teaches openly and freely," remained with him for his entire life.[13]

(iii) Besides Erasmus and Luther, there were other factors that had influenced the early Bucer's theological formation, including Zwingli's concepts of the Christian community and the Lord's Supper and Oecolampadius's

der Kirchen (1542)," *Archiv für Reformationsgeschichte* 31 (1934): 145–91, esp. 161. In the controversy over the nature of the Strasbourg reform, Erasmus's *Epistola contra Pseudoevangelicos*, 1529–30, and Bucer's response, *Epistola Apologetica*, 1530 (*Bucer Bibiliographie*, 42) were exchanged. F. Krüger ("Bucer und Erasmus," in *Martin Bucer*, ed. Krieger and Rienhard, 586–93) summarizes Erasmus's influence on Bucer in the following four points: to comprehend the Christian faith from the two foci of "faith and love"; to emphasize the unity of justification and sanctification; to hold a high view of church unity; and to signify the Lord's Supper as the symbol of church unity.

12. *Das ym selbs niemant, sonder anderen leben soll*, 1523 (*Bucer Bibliographie* 1): *BDS* 1:45–46, 48, 51, 61, 63, 66. Cf. Müller, "Einleitung," *BDS* 1:39. Cf. H.-A. Strohl, "Bucer, interprète de Luther," *Revue d'histoire et de philosophie religieuses* 19 (1939): 223–61; M. Brecht, "Bucer und Luther," in *Martin Bucer*, ed. Krieger and Lienhard, 351–58.

13. *Martini Buceri Opera Omnia*, Series III: *Correspondance de Martin Bucer* 1:54–56. The English translation used here is taken from D. F. Wright, trans. and ed., *Common Places of Martin Bucer* (Appleford, Abingdon: Courtenay Press, 1972), 19–20. Bucer's letter was addressed to Beatus Rhenanus, Erasmus's close friend who later edited Erasmus's complete works (1540) and authored his biography.

emphasis on the church's autonomous discipline. As to Zwingli's factors, the above-mentioned *That No One Should Live* was said to follow Zwingli's ideas of the Christian community. As a matter of fact, it postulated the Christian "community" (*Gemeynschaft*) as the place where God's elect believers and their services coexisted. It defined their services to others as well as to the whole community as "spiritual service," and it considered the ministers of God's word and the magistrates as "the most Christian status" (*christlichsten stand*) and their services to the entire community as the "common good" (*gemeynes nutzs*). In the early Bucer's most comprehensive work, *Ground and Reason* (*Grund und Ursach*, 1524), Bucer effectively used the key passage of Zwingli's eucharistic teaching, John 6:63 ("It is the spirit that gives life; the flesh is useless"), to signify the Lord's Supper not as a ceremony but as communion with Christ.[14] As to Oecolampadius's influence, during the course of the year 1530 Bucer gradually shifted his position of church discipline from his previous Zwinglian position that emphasized the predominant role of magistrates to Oecolampadius's position that stressed a more churchly and autonomous role in discipline. In 1531, he joined Oecolampadius and the Reformer of Constance, Thomas Blarer, in the Ulm Reformation, drafting the ordinance that proposed church discipline patterned after the early church and administered by a body of eight "ministers of Christian discipline" ("three from the city council, three from the community, and two pastors").[15]

(2) *The Anabaptists*

Bucer's relationship with the Anabaptists and other radicals in both positive communications and negative conflicts was quite unique even among his fellow mainstream Reformers. Without doubt it was a crucial factor in understanding his ecclesiological formation. Concerning the Anabaptists, long

14. *BDS* 1:44–45, 48, 51–53, 55–58; *Grund und Ursach* (*Bucer Bibliographie* 8), *BDS* 1:228–29, 257. Cf. F. Büsser, "Bucer und Zwingli," in *Martin Bucer and Sixteenth Century Europe*, ed. Krieger and Lienhard, 395–402.

15. Cf. F. Wendel, *L'Église de Strasbourg: sa constitution et son organisation, 1532–1535* (Paris: Presses universitaires de France, 1942), 155–56, 179–82; W. van't Spijker, *The Ecclesiastical Offices in the Thought of Martin Bucer*, trans. T. Vriend and L. D. Bierma (Leiden: Brill, 1996), 222–25; A. N. Burnett, *The Yoke of Christ: Martin Bucer and Christian Discipline* (Kirksville, MO: Northern Missouri University Press, 1994), 56–62. Concerning Bucer's shift of position, van't Spijker notes one factor in the Anabaptist challenge, namely, that the Evangelical churches lacked the church discipline taught in Scripture and practiced in the early church.

before Calvin made Strasbourg his residence in 1538, Bucer had been known as one of the most knowledgeable and experienced Reformers. As many Anabaptists and other radicals took refuge in Strasbourg, which Williams's *The Radical Reformation* calls "the most tolerant of the Reformation cities," Bucer's tolerant attitude toward them was well known. Especially among those whom Williams classifies as "the Evangelical Anabaptists," Bucer's friendship or sincere exchange of opinion with some of their leaders, such as Michael Sattler and Pilgram Marpeck, was extraordinary in view of the standard of the times. As to Sattler, who was regarded as the author of the *Schleitheim Confession*, Bucer called him "beloved friend" and considered his death after arrest and execution in Austria as that of "Christ's martyr." As to Marpeck, who was a leader of the Anabaptist congregation in Strasbourg, Bucer engaged in a series of closed discussions with him under the supervision of the city authority in 1532, which Mennonite scholar Oyer regards as one of the most substantial exchanges between the Anabaptist and the Reformed camps. Although they shared common reformatory notions, such as the emphasis on the Holy Spirit's reviving work among the faithful, the necessity of sanctification in the faithful and the church's moral renewal, and the indispensability of church discipline, the biggest conflicting topic was the scriptural authenticity of the city's reform process propagated by the magistracy and church leaders. Bucer took Marpeck's challenge as a total denial of the Strasbourg Reformation, and he proceeded to reject Anabaptism by establishing the *Strasbourg Ecclesiastical Ordinances* and other documents (1533–35).[16] In the following pages, we will focus on three characteristic points in Bucer's relationship of "communications and conflicts" with the Anabaptists.

(i) The first point concerned Bucer's selective attitude toward the Anabaptists. As we noted above, on the one hand, he kept an amicable attitude toward Sattler and Marpeck in spite of some marked differences. On the other hand, toward some Anabaptists who exerted a certain influence in Strasbourg, such as Melchoir Hofmann, Hans Denck, and Jacob Kautz, he had kept a confrontational attitude and rejected them in his writings. In addition to their common teachings of salvation for all, the unfettered freedom of the will, and apocalyptic eschatology, he considered their spiritualistic ideas of the church

16. Williams, *The Radical Reformation*, 377–83, 406–8, 422–30; *BDS* 2:253; A. N. Burnett, "Martin Bucer and the Anabaptist Context of Evangelical Confirmation," *Mennonite Quarterly Review* 68 (1994): 98–99; J. S. Oyer, "Bucer and the Anabaptists," in *Martin Bucer and Sixteenth Century Europe*, ed. C. Krieger and M. Lienhard (Leiden: Brill, 1993), 603–13; J. S. Oyer, "Bucer Opposes the Anabaptists," *Mennonite Quarterly Review* 68 (1994): 38–42.

most challenging, especially their refusal to attribute any salvific significance to the sacraments of baptism and the Lord's Supper, church discipline, and ministerial order. Some researchers, including Courvoisier, have assumed that "ties of intellectual relationship" or "theoretical affinity" undoubtedly existed between Bucer and the (Evangelical) Anabaptists.[17]

(ii) The second point was the fact that, despite this "theoretical affinity," confrontation over the idea of the church itself caused Bucer to make a decisive move for rejection. In the above-mentioned Bucer-Marpeck debates, he acknowledged the church as a mixed body of true believers and unbelievers, but affirmed that, as long as it maintained God's word and the sacraments of baptism and the Lord's Supper, it should be "the church of Christ." In opposition, Marpeck's confessional statement, *A Clear Response* (*Klarer Unterrich*, 1531), written as an apology against Bucer's position, challenged him on two accounts. Firstly, since Marpeck understood the relation between the Old and the New Testaments in terms of "promise and its fulfillment," as well as the relation between the Old and the New Testament churches in terms of "imperfection and perfection," he called what Bucer termed "a mixed church" nothing but "Evangelical Judaism" and the Strasbourg Church not a "Christian church."[18] Secondly, over against Bucer's use of the Zwinglian analogy between the Old Testament's circumcision and the current infant baptism, Marpeck introduced the difference between a "sign" and a "witness," calling circumcision and the New Testament "baptism by water" only a sign but not a witness. Even though circumcision and baptism were God-given signs, he assumed that, in order for a sign to be a witness, it required for God to add the Holy Spirit to it and for a believer to "accept, experience, and maintain" it in one's self. In this respect, infant baptism could not be worthy of New Testament baptism.[19]

(iii) The third point concerned the later Bucer's successful effort to bring the Anabaptists back into the state church system in Hessen, an exceptional achievement unparalleled among major Reformers. This case highlighted Bucer's accommodating efforts shown at the Marburg Anabaptist Disputation (1538) at which, after hesitation, he conceded to the Anabaptists' demand

17. J. Courvoisier, *La notion d'église chez Bucer dans son développement historique* (Paris: F. Alcan, 1933), 13. Bucer wrote such polemical works against Denck and Kautz, *Getrewe Warnung*, 1527 (*BDS* 2:225–58: *Bucer Bibliographie*, no. 26; cf. Williams, *The Radical Reformation*, 262–63) and against Hoffman, *Handlung gegen Melchior Hoffman*, 1533 (*BDS* 5:43–108: *Bucer Bibliographie*, no. 57).

18. P. Marpeck, *Rechenschaft seines Glaubens, Quellen zur Geschichte der Taufer* VII, Elsass 1 (Gütersloh: Gerd Mohn, 1959), 421, 423, 504.

19. *Marpeck, Rechenschaft*, 421, 439, 504.

to officially make discipline the third mark of the church by confirming that "there cannot be a church without discipline." In addition, he also assured the Anabaptists that the baptized infants would be catechized for confirmation as early as they were old enough.[20] In the later Bucer, even though there were references to the three marks of the church, in view of the Lutheran and Zwinglian positions of the two-marks theory, he customarily distinguished the first two "fundamental" marks from the third mark as their "fruit." But the later Bucer, who officially took the three-marks theory in Marburg, surely symbolized his mediatory position by encouraging Erasmus to come into the Protestant fold, the separatist Anabaptists to return to the church catholic, and the Lutherans and the Reformed in Germany to move forward to the reunification colloquies with the Catholics in the 1540s.

2. *Strasbourg Ecclesiastical Ordinances and the Later Bucer*

(1) Ecclesiastical Ordinances

The apex of the Strasbourg Reformation was centered in the 1534 *Ecclesiastical Ordinances* that signaled the establishment of the Reformed Church in distinction from the Lutheran Church and in the rejection of the Anabaptist and radical challenges. The *Ordinances* was preceded by the *XVI Articles* (1533) that provided doctrinal consensus for the reform synod's deliberations and was followed by the *Disciplinary Ordinances* (1535). In the historical context of the Protestant Reformation, this reformatory process (1533–35) produced a church polity clearly different from that of the Anabaptists and distinct from both Lutheran and Zwinglian positions. In the context of Strasbourg's city reformation, however, the process witnessed Bucer's ecclesiology, experiencing both its ideals and the reality of its concessions and retreats, and marked the major achievement of the early Bucer as well as the beginning of the later Bucer.

(i) The first document of the reformatory process, the *XVI Articles*, was the doctrinal standard for church reform drafted by the church synod and accepted by the magistracy without major revisions. For the interest of ecclesiology,

20. *Ordenung der Christlichen Kirchenzucht. Für die Kirchen im Fürstenthumb Hessen*, 1539, *BDS* 7:265. Cf. H. Eells, *Martin Bucer* (New Haven: Yale University Press, 1931), 155–56; van't Spijker, *The Ecclesiastical Offices*, 206–13; Williams, *The Radical Reformation*, 675–76; K. R. Davis, "No Discipline, No Church: Anabaptist Contribution to the Reformed Theology," *Sixteenth Century Journal* 12 (1982): 54–55. Eells considers that Bucer developed a system of confirmation between 1534 and 1539 and acknowledges the legitimacy of Bucer's designation as "father of evangelical confirmation."

noteworthy were articles on external/internal preaching (6), the sacraments (7–10), the church (11), church discipline (12–13), and the magistracy (14–16). As to our first focus, the article on external/internal preaching was said to take a middle position between the Lutheran emphasis on the external ministry of the word and the sacraments as a "means of grace" and the Anabaptist and Spiritualist view that attributed no salvific signification to these external ministries. Although the article emphasized the external use of the word and the sacraments in the community, it distinctively stressed their ecclesial use as "God's divine grace and operation" for such saving effects as forgiveness of sins.

As to our second focus, the article on the church was preceded by four articles on the sacraments and followed by two articles on church discipline and excommunication. Perhaps reflecting Bucer's then existing position, these articles on the sacraments were clearly conscious of the opposing positions of Luther and Zwingli and also carefully delineated the view of Strasbourg. On the one hand, following the Augustinian notion of "visible signs of invisible grace," the articles called them "visible gospels." On the other hand, they stressed the sacramental character of the signs as a "means of grace." The article on the church was strangely short and did not offer a definition of the church, instead characterizing it with two Bucerian notions, namely, the church as both a eucharistic community and a fraternal association. Accordingly, the church was described as both "a single body and bread in Christ" (*ein leib vnnd brot seind in Christo*) and "brotherly teaching and admonishing" (*brüderlich leren vnnd warren*). From this viewpoint of church as eucharistic and fraternal community of sharing common bread, teaching, and discipline, the following two articles on church discipline were introduced.[21]

As to our third focus, church discipline had been perhaps the most controversial issue in the Strasbourg Reformation of Bucer's times. In the first *Gospel Commentary* (1527), Bucer had already presented his own unique view. On the disciplinary texts (Luke 17:1–4, Matt 18:15–17), he interpreted discipline as fraternal admonition based upon "the love of Christ," asked that "if we cease

21. For the text of the *XVI Articles*, we use the synodical document, *BDS* 5:388–92. For our understanding of the text, the works of Wendel (*L'Église*, 127–61), van't Spijker (*The Ecclesiastical Offices*, 195–213), and G. Hammann (*Entre la secte et la cité: Le projet d'Église du Réformateur Martin Bucer (1491–1551)* [Geneva: Labor et Fides, 1984], 43–59) are mainly consulted. The connection between the Lord's Supper and discipline reflected Bucer's basic church concept. On the one hand, it directly connected the Lord's Supper with discipline in countering the Anabaptist emphasis on the (adult) baptism-discipline connection. On the other hand, by emphasizing communal and fraternal discipline, it tried to erase the magistrates' fear of church discipline as a reintroduction of the "new" papacy.

to admonish one another, what other way is left by which we may demonstrate the love of Christ," and called fraternal discipline "this unique mark of Christianity." On the crucial text of "Tell it to the church" (Matt 18:17), he took "the church" as "a gathering of the faithful" and "the power of the keys" as belonging to that gathering: "therefore, the power of binding and loosening is not to be given, unless in those gathered in Christ's name." As to the practice of such fraternal discipline, especially excommunication, he conceded some difficulties due to the lack of "those who have completely dedicated themselves to Christ" and hoped for the day when such faithful, "together with the magistrate," were raised. In the *XVI Articles*, which reflected the actual situation of Strasbourg, basically the same idea of church discipline was presented, but in a more nuanced manner. As Wendel remarks, two issues behind the disciplinary articles were the legitimacy of the church's own discipline and the question of who was to be primarily responsible for it, the church or the magistrate? Although following the idea of the church's own fraternal "teaching and admonishing" expressed in the preceding article, Article 11 on the church seemed to have avoided referring to the Matthew 18 text. Instead it cited the historical cases of Paul's extraordinary use of apostolic authority (1 Cor 5:1–2) and the apostolic church's practice of removing the derelict from the congregation, connecting these cases to the necessity of "excommunication" in the church. But Articles 12 and 13, both implicitly yet clearly, referred to the binding and loosening "in heaven and on earth" (Matt 18:18) and related the text to the forgiveness of sins in "the church of Christ" (*die kirch Christi*). These two articles clearly claimed the church's own disciplinary process as its exercise of "internal preaching."[22]

As to our last focus, the three articles on the magistrate touched on the second issue mentioned above. Since the previous two articles on church discipline laid claim to the church's own disciplinary process, the question here was the magisterial role in that process and its implication in the community. Without delineating the precise relation between church and state on the matter of church discipline, the three articles positively stressed the magisterial role. For example, Article 14 defined the magistrate as "a minister of God" (*ein dienerin gottes*) in keeping Scripture as God's law and enforcing its teachings. Article 15 described the scope of the magisterial role as covering both "doctrine and practice." Touching on the issue of the magisterial power vis-à-vis that of

22. *BDS* 5:391. Cf. Wendel, *L'Église*, 152–53; *Enarrationum in Evangelion Matthaei, Marci, et Lucae, Libri Duo* (1527, *Bucer Bibliographie*, no. 22), 212v–214v. Quotations in English are, in part, from Burnett, *The Yoke*, 37.

the church, Article 16 considered the magistrate a divinely ordained means for man's salvation. However, an explanatory statement (*Verklärung*) on these three articles, which Bucer and other ministers prepared and presented to the synod (June 1533), spelled a clearer view on the ecclesial-magisterial power issue. While the *Verklärung* on Article 14 attributed "supreme external power" (*die höchsten eusserlichen gewalt*) to the magistrate, on Article 15 it specified that the magisterial power was to be applied only to the "external church" as a mixed body of "true Christians" and those who were not. In the "internal church" of the true Christians, on the other hand, the document affirmed that neither the magistrates nor the church ministers but Christ alone was to rule this church and believers' consciences, and there should be no "mixing" of ecclesiastical and secular powers. This explanation could be interpreted as the appeal of Bucer and other ministers to the magistrates to admit the spiritual and autonomous church of true believers as the manifestation of Christ's kingdom.[23]

(ii) Concerning the *Ecclesiastical Ordinances* (1534) and *Disciplinary Ordinances* (1535), in order to avoid duplicating the issue, the following will not address the complicated history of their formation except for two points. One point concerns the distinctively Reformed character of these *Ordinances*, especially from the Lutheran view of church and state. In the 1533 reform synod, Bucer's view was challenged by a group led by his cominister Antonius Engelbrecht, who was a leader of the "Epicureans," a loosely designated group of intellectual dissidents, in Strasbourg. With the thesis, "the kingdom of Christ stands in heartfelt piety," which partly reflected Luther's view, Engelbrecht criticized Bucer's notion of Christ's kingdom, especially Bucer's defense of the secular power's involvement in spiritual matters as a manifestation of Christ's kingdom.[24] Another point is the contents of the synod's original draft proposal of the *Ecclesiastical Ordinances* that underwent some drastic revisions by the magistracy before the voluminous document of seven chapters was finalized in 1534. Concerning major revisions, for example, as chapter 1 men-

23. *BDS* 5:392. Cf. Hammann, *Entre la secte*, 54–57. For the text of the *Verklärung*, see a portion (*BDS* 5:441–43) of the synodical record on the Engelbrecht case. Wendel (*L'Église*, 169) notes that the *Verklärung* marked a shift from the Zwinglian position and suggests Oecolampadius's influence on Bucer.

24. Cf. Hammann, *Entre la secte*, 320–21; Tuininga, *Calvin's Political Theology*, 57; n. 83 below. For Englebrecht, see Eells, *Martin Bucer*, 157–59. For the "Epicureans," confer M. Lienhard, "Les épicuriens à Strasbourg entre 1530 et 1550 et le problème de l'incroyance au XVIe siècle," and Van den Berg Cornelis, "Anton Engelbrecht: un 'épicurien' strasbourgeois," in *Croyants et sceptiques au XVIe siècle*, pub. M. Lienhard (Strasbourg: Librarie Istra, 1981).

tioned the establishment of the Church Council (*Ersamen Raht*), the highest inquiry commission over matters of the church, the Council's composition became the first point to be revised by the magistrates led by Jacob Strum. The original draft presupposed a church government with the cooperation of its pastors and representatives of the congregation. The draft regarded the "churchwarden" (*Kirchenpfleger*), appointed in 1531 by the city to each parish for overseeing its pastors and parishioners, as a church "elder" following the New Testament examples. Then the draft proposed the Council's composition of eight members (three "churchwardens" as elders, two from the city councils, and three pastors). Rejecting the original draft's idea of the cooperation of pastors and elders, the final document stated the composition of the five-member Church Council (three "churchwardens" and two from the city councils), with only two pastors not as voting members but as advisors to the Council.[25] Another major revision took place in chapter 5, "For the Entire Community," but in reality it dealt with church discipline. Perhaps reflecting Bucer's idea of church discipline, the original draft distinguished matters concerning the external aspect of the faithful (such as observation of Sunday worship, participation in baptism and the Lord's Supper, and moral upkeep) from the internal aspect (such as doctrine, faith, confession of sins, and forgiveness). It combined these two aspects in the concept of church discipline and proposed that the disciplinary process was to be exercised by the parish's pastors and "churchwardens" whose cooperation at the parish level was the basic idea retained in the final document. However, it attributed the right to execute punishment of sins to "the Church Council member" in charge of the parish. Even concerning disciplinary warnings, the original draft's phrase, cooperation of "pastors and churchwardens" was changed to "churchwardens' jurisdiction" and pastors were placed as advisors.[26]

(iii) Many researchers use the publication of the *Strasbourg Ecclesiastical Ordinances* to distinguish the later Bucer from the early Bucer. In his unique book on Bucer's ecclesiology, *Entre la secte et la cité: Le projet d'Église du Réformateur Martin Bucer*, Hammann examines the development of Bucer's church concept in the tense period before and after the *Ecclesiastical Ordinances* (1530–39) and finds there the "double-sided" (*binaire / double face*) concept in both theory and practice. One side is directed to the formation of the "sect" (*secte*), or an ideal congregation of believers patterned after the practices of the New Testament and the ancient church, within the mixed body of the city church. The other side is directed to the reform of the "city church" (*cité*) that

25. *Kirchenordnung*, *BDS* 5:25–26; *Bedacht*, *BDS* 5:402. Cf. Wendel, *L'Église*, 102, 116–17.
26. *BDS* 5:37–38, 415–16. Cf. Burnett, *The Yoke*, 69, 71–72.

is composed of all who have received Christian baptism. Interestingly, Hammann concludes that these two sides are not necessarily always harmonized in Bucer.[27] Following up on Hammann's thesis, this study also finds that in the later Bucer there are two sides that we may call directions of "implicit amplification" and "explicit expansion." The "implicit amplification" is directed to the thorough reform of the Strasbourg Church by means of the practical uses of sermons, the sacraments, and church discipline as the means of grace, and is ultimately directed toward the ideal form of the church that is yet distinctive from the Anabaptists' separatist church. The "explicit expansion" is based upon the reform of the city church, yet it goes beyond it and is directed toward alliance or consensus among the Evangelical churches as well as reunification attempts of the Catholic and Protestant camps. Ultimately, it is directed at the reformation of the Christian world. As Hammann points out Bucer's two-sided and often unharmonious concept of the church, researchers must face this "harmony" issue. After some frustrating and failed attempts to reform the Strasbourg city church, for example, Bucer and his followers were engaged in what was often called the "Christian society" (*christliche Gemeinschafft*) movement (1546–49) to form a sort of "small church" within the framework of the city church. After his exit from the Strasbourg Reformation and taking refuge in England, the aged Bucer wrote a "magnum opus," *Of the Kingdom of Christ* (*De Regno Christi*, 1550), aimed at the realization of Christ's kingdom in England. The question is whether we can view these two examples or the two end points of Bucer's double-sided ecclesiology as integration or simply polarization?[28] As we will examine later, this question remains to be asked in the context of the Bucer-Calvin relationship as well as of the later development of Calvin's ecclesiology after his Strasbourg period.

27. Hammann, *Entre la secte*, 64, 414, 417.

28. Van't Spijker, *The Ecclesiastical Offices*, 306–34, 463–76; M. Greschat, *Martin Bucer: A Reformer and His Time*, trans. S. E. Buckwalter (Louisville and London: Westminster John Knox, 2004), 211–17, 239–44, 265–75; Hammann, *Entre la secte*, 363–86, 414–18; C. Augustijn, "Bucer's Ecclesiology in the Colloquies with the Catholics, 1540–41," in *Martin Bucer: Reforming Church and Community*, ed. D. F. Wright (Cambridge: Cambridge University Press, 1994), 107–21. Concerning the two conflicting aspects seen in Bucer's ecclesiology, on the one hand, van't Spijker regards them understandable from the perspective of Bucer's reconciling stand and Greschat suggests a harmony of the two aspects in the dynamism of Bucer's personality and thought. On the other hand, Hammann considers the "christliche Gemeinschaft" movement a failure and *De Regno Christi* suffering from some ambiguities and antinomies. Augustijn's article on the Catholic-Protestant Colloquies agrees with Hammann's thesis and suggests the existence of "two ecclesiologies" in Bucer. Nevertheless, Augustijn considers Bucer's idea of the reunification of the church in Germany basically sound and even sees in the "christliche Gemeinschaft" movement his "interim ecclesiology."

(2) The Later Bucer: The Reformation of a Local Church

In connection with the theme of "implicit amplification," the later Bucer's ecclesiology shows some important themes, such as his official move from the basic two-marks theory of the church to the three-marks theory, introduction of the Evangelical confirmation, the fourfold ministerial order, presbyterial polity based upon the cooperation of pastors and elders, and the indispensable and autonomous church discipline. For the examination of these themes, we need to consult his major works of this period, especially the third edition of the *Four Gospels Commentary* (*In Sacra Quatuor Evangelia, Enarrationes*, 1536) and *Concerning True Pastoral Care* (*Von der waren Seelsorge*, 1538).

Four Gospels Commentary and Beyond

(i) We will begin by examining the 1536 *Four Gospels Commentary* as a hermeneutical basis for understanding the later Bucer's ecclesiology, primarily focusing on some of its major revisions on the church concept introduced since the 1527 first edition (*Enarrationum in Evangelia Matthaei, Marci, & Lucae*). On the crucial text of Matthew 16, the 1527 edition defined the church as the congregation of believers, interpreted the "rock" (16:16) as the faith of believers and the "keys" symbolizing the power of the church (16:19) as the Holy Spirit sent by Christ to the church, and emphasized the exercise of power to be done by "all those who had received God's Spirit and word." On Matthew 18, the 1527 edition focused on discipline as mutual and brotherly admonitions and corrections. And on the "Tell it to the church" passage (18:17) Bucer admitted the current and impossible stage of practicing any churchly and official discipline due to the recent introduction of Evangelicalism, but encouraged the earnest faithful to exercise mutual fraternal discipline.[29] On the same Matthew 16 text, the 1536 edition shifted the emphasis from the intimate association of the Holy Spirit with believers to that of Christ's kingdom with the church. It interpreted the "rock" as the gospel of Christ and the "keys" as "the duty and power to rule the church of God as Christ's Kingdom according to the word of God."[30] Furthermore, it introduced a distinction between "power"

29. *Enarrationum in Evangelia Matthaei, Marci, & Lucae* (*Bucer Bibliographie*, 22), book 2, 179r–179v, 181r, 182v, 214r–215v. Cf. Burnett, *The Yoke*, 37–38.

30. *In Sacra Quatuor Evangelia, Enarrationes* (*Bucer Bibliographie*, 77), 353: "At regnum caelorum, Ecclesia Christi est: claves igitur estae, id erunt quo Ecclesia Christi aliis clauditur, aliis aperitur, . . . Id autem quid aliud est, quam munus et potestas administrandi Ecclesiam

and "authority" and affirmed that while the power of the keys belonged to the entire congregation, their authority in exercising that power belonged to "presbyters and bishops" according to "the Spirit of Christ and his word."[31] On the Matthew 18 text, moreover, the 1536 edition maintained the earlier edition's emphasis on mutual and brotherly discipline, but added a new sentence to the effect that the disciplinary power of the keys should be exercised according to "the established order and the leaders whom the Holy Spirit sent to the church as pastors and bishops."[32] All these new elements indicated what we may call "church positivism" or emphasizing the significance of the church's ministry of the word, the sacraments, discipline, and ministerial order.

(ii) This new emphasis on the church's ministry was also witnessed in Bucer's shift from the two to three-marks theory of the church. As we have mentioned above, the shift was officially noted in the historical context of the Hessen Reformation (1538) and around this time the new three-marks theory became Bucer's standard position in his major works, such as *Concerning True Pastoral Care* (1538), *Two Writings against Latomus* (1544), and *Of the Kingdom of Christ* (1550). Concerning this shift, there seem to be two convincingly substantiated interpretations: the one sees it as "influence of" or "concession to" the Anabaptists; the other sees it as the end point of Bucer's own ecclesiological development. As to the first interpretation, Burnett's careful examination of Bucer's disciplinary concept indicates that Bucer had developed his concept in the close context of the Anabaptist challenge. Between Bucer and the Anabaptists there were many common concepts as well as phrases concerning discipline, such as "to devote oneself" (*sich ergeben / sich begeben*) to Christ in discipline. That shift could also be explained as the Anabaptist influence on Bucer. As Burnett notices, nonetheless, that the later Bucer's disciplinary concept was a well-integrated and comprehensive plan that included at least four elements; religious education, public confession of faith and oath to the church

Dei, rempublicam Christi, ex verbo Dei." Cf. n. 83 below; van't Spijker, *The Ecclesiastical Offices*, 130–31; Burnett, *The York*, 90–91.

31. *In Sacra Quatuor Evangelia, Enarrationes*, 354: "Haec potestas penes Ecclesiam omnem est, autoritas modo ministeri penes presbyteros et episcopos, ita ut Romae olim potestas populi fuit, autoritas senatus, princeps potestatis huius, ut totius huius reipublicae Christus est, administri eius, qui eam ex spiritu et verbo Christi administrant." Cf. van't Spijker, *The Ecclesiastical Offices*, 132; Burnett, *The Yoke*, 91–92. Concerning the *potestas/autoritas* distinction and the relation between congregation and ministers, Bucer's clearest theoretical formulation can be found in his later work against Latomus, *Scripta Duo adversaria D. Bartholomaei Latomi*, 1544 (*Bucer Bibliographie*, 137), 157, 159.

32. *In Sacra Quatuor Evangelia, Enarrationes*, 386. Cf. van't Spijker, *The Ecclesiastical Offices*, 133–34; Burnett, *The Yoke*, 95–96.

(confirmation), mutual advice and admonition among believers, and public penitence and excommunication in the case of grave sin.[33] For those who take the second interpretation, Bucer's unique and distinguishable elements from the Anabaptists are noticed. For example, the Anabaptists founded church discipline on the baptism of believers and emphasized its significance in their continued observance of the oath they made at baptism, in punishment in the case of the oath broken, and in an excluding device to keep the purity of their congregation. In contrast, Bucer emphasized the aspect of church discipline that concerned the entire life of believers baptized as infants and positively related it to the sacrament of the Lord's Supper.[34] Here, Bucer's unique contribution to introduce Evangelical confirmation to Reformed theology should be noted. As confirmation was made official in the above-mentioned *Hessen Ecclesiastical Ordinances* and was practiced in the Strasbourg Church, his contribution was widely recognized. He stressed its several meanings: as a part of religious education, as an exemplar of the confession of faith in the church, as the ceremonial occasion to express one's loyalty to the church, as an initiation rite to the Lord's Supper that symbolized the communion of believers, as affirmation of obedience to the church's disciplinary process if need arose, and finally, as an effective measure to counter the Anabaptist challenge.[35]

Concerning True Pastoral Care, 1538

The work of Bucer that highlights this theme of the church's ministry is his most well-known publication, *Concerning True Pastoral Care* (*Von der waren Seelsorge*, 1538). It received, on the one hand, such praise as Courvoisier's comment, "the first treatise of pastoral theology in the Reformed Church." On the other hand, a more historically accurate description by Greschat held that, despite being widely acclaimed as a book of the times, it was "deliberately" ignored by the city council and in Strasbourg. It should also be noted here that, despite Bucer's passionate arguments and forcefully presented fresh insights, the work is not always easily understood, especially as to its use of terminology.

33. Burnett, *The Yoke*, 26–86; Burnett, "Church Discipline and Moral Reformation in the Thought of Martin Bucer," *Sixteenth Century Journal* 22 (1991): 440.

34. Cf. van't Spijker, *The Ecclesiastical Offices*, 70–71; Burnett, *The Yoke*, 38.

35. Cf. n. 22 above. Over against the view that attributes the Reformed rite of confirmation to Bucer's contribution, Burnett ("Church Discipline," 440; "Martin Bucer and the Anabaptist Context of Evangelical Confirmation," *Mennonite Quarterly Review* 68 [1994]: 95–122) cautiously places Bucer's theory in the context of his relation with the Anabaptists.

From our ecclesiological focus, however, we will examine it only under the following three points.

(i) The first point concerned its fundamental nature as a "book of criticism." Bucer wrote it at the request of his fellow ministers. It reflected Bucer's critical sentiment toward the city council that had not taken any further steps of reform, especially the implementation of a thorough and effective disciplinary system, since the 1534 *Ecclesiastical Ordinances*. This sentiment was echoed in its title which included the phrase, "from religious split and disintegration, in order to reach the church of good Christian order in a truly unified way."[36] In other words, as a book of the times, it reflected the unreformed reality of the Strasbourg Church, the church's multiconfessional status, and the city's Marsiglian government. Bucer tackled this issue from his unique reformatory concepts of Christ's kingdom or Christ's lordship over the church, pastoral care, and discipline. Since the focal point of Bucer's critical sentiment was on the issue of church discipline, as van't Spijker remarks, Bucer seriously considered the crux of the city's church reform and pastoral care "consisting in the practice of church discipline" and devoted a third of this work "to questions concerning the exercise of discipline." According to Bucer, furthermore, discipline was regarded as "the essence of Christian community" or what was flowing "from the heart of the congregation as *koinonia*." Concerning the actual practice of discipline, as Hammann notes, the work presented it as "a principal constituent of the church" that was regarded as weighty as the ministries of the word and the sacraments. Thus, without making any explicit statement, the work clearly reflected Bucer's three-marks theory. Just as Bucer distinguished five categories of the faithful in the congregation and proposed to apply pastoral care to each category, he also posed three levels of the faithful according to the degree of their Christian commitment and considered discipline to be accordingly applied to each level. The three levels were said to correspond to God's "election" (*electio*), "adoption" (*adoptio*) in Christ, and "sanctification" (*sanctimonia*) of one's life. They roughly corresponded to the three groups of the faithful: those who were baptized members who could hear God's word; those who were practicing a Christian life; and those who showed the fruit of their sanctification. Hammann calls this notion of Bucer "dynamic vision" and clearly sees Bucer's later involvement in the "Christian society" movement as a natural extension of this vision.[37]

36. *Von der waren Seelsorge* (*Bucer Bibliographie*, 81), *BDS* 7:90, 188. Cf. Courvoisier, *La notion*, 115; Greschat, *Martin Bucer*, 150; van't Spijker, *The Ecclesiastical Offices*, 186–87.

37. Cf. van't Spijker, *The Ecclesiastical Offices*, 179–80, 180–86; Gottfried Hammann,

(ii) The second point concerned the basic concept of "pastoral care" (*Seelsorge*) that was closely related to his idea of Christ's kingdom. First, Bucer started his discussions from the "body of Christ" passages in Romans 12, 1 Corinthians 12, and Ephesians 4, defined the "church of Christ" as the "assembly and community" (*versamlung und Gemeinde*) gathered by Christ and through his Spirit and word, and regarded each believer as "servant" (*diener*) to the entire body of Christ. Since each servant was "a member of Christ and instrument of the Holy Spirit," aptitude and ability as well as a position were given to each, and there should be no member who ought not to serve for the salvation of others or to need the help of others for their own salvation. In this respect, for Bucer, "pastoral care" was the concern of the entire body of Christ and not just of a part of the body. Nevertheless, Bucer also understood "pastoral care" in a narrower sense of "church government and polity" (*regiment und policei*). He described those servants who had special ability and were called to the "service for pastoral care and pastor's duty" (*dienst an der seelsorge und dem hirtenampt*) as ministers, and he further comprehensively described their ministry as "teaching and spiritual discipline."[38]

Second, as a complex issue, how did Bucer relate "pastoral care" with the kingdom of Christ? Since he described "Christ's government" (*regiment Christi*) as "maintained and led by himself and his Spirit," he seemed to have assumed Christ's direct rule through his Spirit and word over the church that involved all servants, namely, believers and the ministers of both the church and the magistrates. From this assumption, on the one hand, he denied that any servant could rightly pretend to be "the Lord's deputy" (*herren stathalter*). On the other hand, citing the "without a spot or wrinkle" passages from Ephesians (5:26–27), he assumed that all the servants, especially the ministers of the church and magistrates, were to work toward the manifestation of that reformatory and purifying rule of Christ in the local church. The impression his descriptions gave pointed to the close tie between Christ's kingdom and pastoral care as a manifestation of the kingdom.[39] Here, Bucer introduced an interesting notion concerning the relation of Christ's rule with the ministers. While Bucer designated Christ as the "primary pastor" (*Ertzhirt*), he called both ministers of the church and magistrates the "under-pastors" (*unter-*

"Martin Bucer: Sa vision de l'Église selon le traité 'Von der waren Seelsorge' et les développements de la discipline ecclésiastique à Strasbourg de 1524 à 1549," in *Croyants et sceptiques au XVIe siècle*, pub. Marc Lienhard (Strasbourg: Librairie Istra, 1981), 73–86.

38. *Von der waren Seelosorge*, *BDS* 7:94, 98, 101, 103, 112.

39. *Von der waren Seelsorge*, *BDS* 7:98–107.

hirten). Furthermore, he introduced another distinction between the ministers of the church and those of the magistrates. While he made a clear distinction between "pastoral caretaker" (*Seelsorger*) and "pastor" (*hirt*) and attributed to the minister of the church the comprehensive task of "pastoral caretaker and pastor," he attributed to the magistrate only a task of "pastor," even though he called the magistrate the "highest pastor" (*obristenhirt*).[40] Surprisingly, Bucer chose exactly what distinguished the office of the ministers from that of the magistrates, namely, pastoral care (*seelsorge*), as the title of his book. This subtle distinction perhaps indicated his deep concern that, while the magistrates were inevitably yet indirectly involved in helping the duty of ecclesiastical ministers to be executed properly, they should not be directly involved in the ministers' spiritual duty of the word, the sacraments, and discipline.[41] One can notice here a general parallelism between Bucer's notion of "pastoral care" or "government" under Christ's lordship and Calvin's notion of "church and state" under Christ's kingdom, expressed in chapter 6 of the first *Institutes*.

(iii) The third point concerned the fact that this work so far presented Bucer's most comprehensive concept of ministerial order. Due to some variations in describing ecclesiastical ministers, it is not always easy to correctly understand Bucer's concept, but we will highlight two of its characteristics. The first concerned his general statement: "ministers of the [church] community" whom Christ has given to the church in all ages were "pastors and teachers and servants." Bucer attributed "service of pastoral care" to pastors and teachers and "service of physical needs for the poor" to the servants, identifying them as deacons. Thus, "pastors, teachers, and deacons" were the categories in the church's ordinal ministry. At the same time, to the category of pastor, he added "bishop" (*Bischoff*) whom he called the "highest pastoral caretaker" (*oberen seelsorger*) and "elder" (*Eltist*). On another occasion, furthermore, he considered "elder" to be in the same category as "bishop" or identified "elder" as a generic term for "pastors, bishops, and teachers," and used the term, "pastoral care of elders" (*seelsorge der eltisten*) for pastoral ministry.[42]

The second concerned the difficult issue of whether Bucer included in the category of "elder" the so-called "lay elder" in addition to "pastor, bishop, and teacher." There were several factors that contributed to the difficulty of this

40. *Von der waren Seelsorge*, *BDS* 7:106, 141, 147, 159. Theoretically Bucer's German term, "Seelsorger," can be applied to all believers without distinction. In the limited context of the church's ministry, however, we translate the term as "pastoral caretaker," since the title of the book in English customarily translates "Seelsorge" as "pastoral care."

41. *Von der waren Seelsorge*, *BDS* 7:147, 159. Cf. Hammann, *Entre la secte*, 317.

42. *Von der waren Seelsorge*, *BDS* 7:112, 116, 119–21, 141, 148.

issue. As mentioned above, the original draft of the *Ecclesiastical Ordinances* regarded the "churchwardens" (*kirchenpfleger*), laymen appointed by the city magistracy, as the New Testament office of "elder." In 1534, furthermore, Bucer wrote *Report from Holy Scripture* (*Bericht ausz der heyligen geschrift*) to the Münster Anabaptists in the midst of their revolutionary activities. In this work of his apology and advice, acknowledging the Anabaptist insistence on congregational polity, Bucer referred to the Old Testament case of "elders of the people" (*eltisten des volcks*) along with priest and scribes as well as to the New Testament case of "elders" as representatives of their congregations, and emphasized the comprehensive duty of the elders, including church discipline, oversight of the ministry of the word, and the selection and appointment of pastors. In addition, *Concerning True Pastoral Care* had a few issues itself. For example, curiously, it did not mention "churchwardens" in connection with the office of "elder" at all. Instead, referring to the practice of the New Testament church's election of elders, it affirmed that the elders should be "the most trusted and renowned servants among the faithful and having the true passion to pastor Christ's sheep," a description that might refer to lay elders. This could signal Bucer's rejection of the Zwinglian notion that the New Testament office of elders was abolished when the magistrates became Christians and took their place. As far as the text is concerned, it can be either interpreted that Bucer's "elder" was a generic term for Evangelical pastors, bishops, and teachers, or that Bucer was open to the new idea of lay elders in the Evangelical ministry. However, it seems difficult to assume that Bucer clearly presented the fourfold ministry of pastors, teachers, (lay) elders, and deacons in this work.[43]

The "Christian Society" Movement, 1546–1549

(i) Lastly, we will briefly mention Bucer's controversial involvement in the "Christian Society" or core-church movement, an issue on which the evaluations of researchers have been sharply divided. The movement coincided with Bucer's very last years as a Reformer of Strasbourg and its name was taken from a phrase that often appeared in his writings, "true Christian society" (*ware Christliche Gemeinschafft*). It exerted some visible impact in three of the city's

43. *BDS* 7:122–25. Cf. *Bericht ausz der heyligen geschrift*, 1534 (*Bucer Bibliographie*, 61), *BDS* 5:145–46; Greschat, *Martin Bucer*, 101; Tuininga, *Calvin's Political Theology*, 58, 68. Tuininga remarks on the importance of Bucer's rejection of the Zwinglian notion. Our analysis agrees with his remark: "While Bucer had ambiguously described a fourfold office in the church, Calvin clarified and systematized the concept."

seven parishes, yet as a movement it ended unsuccessfully. In brief, as a result of the Protestant camp's defeat in the Schmalkald War (1546–47), Strasbourg was forced to accept the Augsburg Interim (1548) which included the reintroduction of the Catholic worship (Mass) in the city. The city had also been experiencing an increase of multiconfessional situations, a fresh Anabaptist challenge, and the Lutheran influence. Against this background, Bucer and other church leaders recognized the situation as a crisis for the Reformed character of the Strasbourg church. In their increasing frustration with the city magistracy's indifference to church reform, they took the radical step of becoming involved in the movement. Bellardi's historical study (1934) positively evaluated the movement as the first manifestation of the "small church in the institutional church" (*ecclesiola in ecclesiam*) theme in the Reformed Reformation. He even called it "the second Reformation" and compared it to the rise of Pietism in the Lutheran State Church of the next century, where this theme became prominent. Since then, its evaluation has been the object of many studies.[44]

In 1546, Bucer wrote a critical treatise, *Concerning the Defect and Failure of the Church* (*Von der kirchen mengel vund fähl*), but he could not procure the city's permit for publication, and the text was to remain in manuscript form. In this treatise and others following it, he defended the movement and proposed in concrete terms the way to achieve church reform. Its main theme was the visible manifestation of the "effect" of God's word in the internal life of the church. He listed five fields in which the church's spiritual rule was to see the "effect," namely, gospel proclamation, the administration of the sacraments, confession of sin and forgiveness, excommunication, and ecclesiastical ceremonies. According to him, a Christian society was a small gathering of sincere believers who practiced God's word in these five fields.[45]

(ii) Concerning the evaluation of the "Christian Society," researchers' views have varied widely. On the one hand, there is positive evaluation when seeing the movement as an end point of Bucer's ecclesiological development on the level of the local church. On the other hand, there is negative evaluation when

44. Cf. W. Bellardi, *Die Geschichte der "Christlichen Gemeinschaft" in Strassburg (1546–1550): Der Versuch einer "Zweiten Reformation"* (Leipzig: Heinsius Nachfolger, 1934); van't Spijker, *The Ecclesiastical Offices*, 306–43; Hammann, *Entre la secte*, 363–86; Burnett, *The Yoke*, 180–207.

45. *BDS* 17:163. Cf. "Von der kirchen mengel vund fähl," *BDS* 17:156–95; "Form vff was weiss . . . ," *BDS* 17:245–55; "Kurtzer vnderricht vnd grunde . . . ," *BDS* 17:256–290; "Mehrung götlicher gnaden vnd geists . . . ," *BDS* 17:317–40. Among the above documents of 1546–47, the last treatise was to be later published, without regard to its original context, by a leader of German Pietism of the next century, Jakob Philipp Spener.

seeing the movement as "an abortive effort to institute discipline" or "a contradiction in practice." In other words, it was an ecclesiological bankruptcy for Bucer who had rejected the Anabaptists' separatist challenge and advocated for "a unified civic religion."[46] Even among those who give a positive evaluation, there are various approaches to relate the Christian society or core-church to Bucer's ecclesiology. For example, Wendel relates it with Bucer's claim for the church's autonomy in spiritual matters, especially in discipline. Hammann emphasizes its independent and structural nature as "a small church" in the Strasbourg Church. And Burnett considers it the means or exemplar by which Bucer tried to reform the entire city church of Strasbourg.[47] Exposing the problematic and puzzling aspects of Bucer's ecclesiology, in any case, the Christian Society movement was to disappear from the scene of the Reformation.

(3) The Later Bucer: The Reformation of the European Christian World

One of the above-mentioned designations attributed to Bucer, "the first truly European churchman and theologian," appropriately expresses the second theme of his ecclesiology, that is, "explicit expansion." Among Evangelical Reformers, in fact, there is not even a close match to the scope of his involvement and activity. Examples are numerous: his leadership in the Reformation in southern Germany; his conciliating efforts in the sacramental controversy between the Lutherans and the Zwinglians; his contribution to the Hessen Reformation in which the reversion of the Anabaptists to the state church was achieved; his participation in the Catholic Archbishopric of Cologne; his leadership role in the religious reunification colloquies in Germany; and his bold proposal for the English Reformation to which he poured the passion of his very last years. From these facts, it is natural that the designations of "apostle of church unity" and "ecumenical theologian" are validated. Yet, on the other hand, there was criticism against Bucer as the one who placed diplomacy ahead of his own religious convictions or the so-called horns of a dilemma (*mutatis mutandis*).[48] As to Bucer's bibliographical materials touching on this

46. Among Bucer researchers, Courvoisier, Bellardi, Wendel, Hammann, van't Spijker, and Burnett take the former position, but an example of the latter position is found in James Kittelson's criticism of the positive evaluation ("Martin Bucer and the Ministry of the Church," in *Martin Bucer: Reforming Church and Community*, ed. D. F. Wright [Cambridge: Cambridge University Press, 1994], 83–94).

47. Cf. Wendel, *L'Église*, 168n20; Hammann, *Entre la secte*, 371–79; Burnett, *The Yoke*, 187, 205–6.

48. Cf. M. Greschat, "Bucer, Martin," *OER* 1:223–24; Greschat, *Martin Bucer*, 265–71.

theme, one can count his book advocating for a council between the Catholic and the Protestant camps (*Furbereytung zum Concilio*, 1533), his conciliatory efforts in producing a document of agreement with the Lutherans on the Eucharist, the *Wittenberg Concord* (1536), his major contribution to the *Book of Regensburg* (1541), and his last contribution to the English Reformation, *Of the Kingdom of Christ* (1550). In consideration of the Bucer-Calvin relationship, we will only focus on the *Book of Regensburg* and *Of the Kingdom of Christ* in the following pages.

Book of Regensburg, 1540–1541

The *Book of Regensburg* was occasioned by the deadlock of the unification colloquies of Hagenau and Worms in 1540, both of which had used the Lutheran Augsburg Confession (*Confessio Augustana Variata*) as a basis for discussion. For the next colloquy, scheduled at the Diet of Regensburg in 1541 under imperial auspices, a new basis for discussion was to be secretly prepared. A Catholic Erasmian, Gropper, and Bucer coauthored the document. In April-May 1541, the colloquy quickly agreed on the *Book*'s first four articles (human innocence before the fall, free choice, the cause of sin, and original sin). After the exchange of proposals, the final draft of the fifth article on justification was agreed upon by both sides. The article characteristically avoided the positions of both Luther's justification by faith alone and the Catholic's double justification. Incidentally, Calvin, an official member of the Strasbourg delegation, accepted the article.[49] The *Book*, as the document coauthored by Bucer, revealed interesting insights into his thinking at the unification colloquy. For example, the sixth article, "Marks of the Church," seemed to play an important role as a hinge connecting the first five articles of doctrine with the remaining articles on the three "marks" of God's word (arts. 7–9), the sacraments (arts. 10–17), and bond of love (arts. 18–23). The *Book* did not provide an official definition of the church as such, but Article 6 presented a description of the church that avoided both the Catholic hierarchical concept and Luther's congregation of believers. It did so in this fashion: the church is "the assembly or congregation of people of all places and times, who are called to the unity of the profession

49. Cf. V. Pfnür, "Colloquies," *OER* 1:377–80; Augustijn, "Bucer's Ecclesiology," 107–21; A. N. S. Lane, "Calvin and Article 5 of the Regensburg Colloquy," in *Calvinus Praeceptor Ecclesia*, ed. H. J. Selderhuuis (Geneva: Droz, 2004), 233–63. The five articles are closely examined by Augustijn from the aspect of Bucer's ecclesiology and by Lane from that of Calvin. Lane contends that, since both the papal curia and Luther especially rejected the agreed article 5, the misunderstanding of it as "double justification" was rapidly spread.

of one and the same faith of doctrine and of the sacraments of Christ." In addition, Article 19 defended the God-given character (*de jure divino*) of the historical episcopacy.[50] After having agreed on the first five articles, however, the colloquy stumbled in facing the insurmountable issues of the Eucharist and church authority. As to the *Book*'s evaluation, researchers' views are divided: in the negative it was "ambivalent and ambiguous" and in the positive it was an attempt to tackle the reality of "a church embedded in history."[51]

Of the Kingdom of Christ, 1550

It is not an easy task to analyze *Of the Kingdom of Christ* (*De Regno Christi*, 1550) from an ecclesiological perspective. However, as the ongoing Council of Trent progressed, it is impressive that Bucer's work presented such a wide scope of vision of Christ's kingdom, which reflected his perception of European Christendom as decisively broken into the old and new religions. If we assume the "Christian Society" as a microversion of Christ's kingdom in Strasbourg, certainly the work presents a macroversion of the kingdom's reality in England as well as the end point of his concept of Christ's kingdom.[52] Appointed to the royal professorship of theology in Cambridge, Bucer dedicated the work to King Edward VI, but his clearly claimed intention of making England truly the kingdom of Christ was somewhat of a riddle. It presented neither a theory of the state like *Utopia* (1516), the controversial work of Thomas More, High Chancellor of the previous King Henry VIII, nor political programs to achieve the realization of Christ's kingdom. As Wendel, editor of the work in the *Martini Buceri Opera Omnia*, indicates, it was rather intended to present "a program of reform" that was based upon the concept of Christ's kingdom and was to incorporate various themes both in theology and other fields into a "synthesis."[53]

50. For an analysis of the Regensburg Articles on the church, we have used Calvin's own French translation, *Les actes de la journee imperiale tenue en la cité de Reguespourg 1541* (*BC* 41/1; *CO* 5:509–684). The quotation on the church definition is taken from *CO* 5:527. Also confer Augustijn, "Bucer's Ecclesiology," 111–12, 121.

51. Cf. Hammann, *Entre la secte*, 73–75, 414–15; Augustijn, "Bucer's Ecclesiology," 111, 114–21; V. Ortmann, *Reformation und Einheit der Kirche: Martin Bucers Einigungsbemühungen bei den Religionsgesprächen in Leipzig, Hagenau, Worms und Regensburg 1539–1541* (Mainz: Verlag Philipp von Zabern, 2001), 113–296.

52. A. Gäumann, *Reich Christi und Obrigkeit: Eine Studie zum reformatorischen Denken und Handeln Martin Bucers* (Bern: Peter Lang, 2001), 166.

53. *De Regno Christi*, *BOL* 15, F. Wendel, "Introduction," xxxvi–xl. In the collection of essays *Martin Bucer: Reforming Church and Community* (ed. D. F. Wright [Cambridge:

(i) In the opening chapter, Bucer presented a tentative definition of Christ's kingdom and its goal in the context of England: "the government of people or the nation . . . by those who excel in wisdom and all virtues," and its goal as "toward all virtues, the knowledge of the blessed living, and the formation of wholesome and happy life." From the New Testament passages on the kingdom of God or Christ, he then presented the image of Christ's kingdom as "the Kingdom of the cross" (*regnum crucifixi*), despised and humiliated like Jesus himself in its conflict with the "kingdom of the world" (*regnum mundi*).[54] In reality, however, Bucer presupposed the medieval notion of church and state as "a Christian society" (*societas Christiana*) and assumed princes of the kingdoms of the world to be Christians. Furthermore, Bucer stressed the integration of the two kingdoms, each of which was fulfilling its own duty to the "Christian society,"[55] yet serving commonly.

(ii) Since Bucer often called this "Christian society" the church, the church in a broad sense signified such realities as the city church of Strasbourg and the Church of England. On the other hand, he identified Christ's kingdom with "the administration and procurement of eternal salvation of the elect of God," which was the core of the church in the narrowest sense. The church as Christ's kingdom was understood as an existence related to and contrasted with, yet not completely identified with, the Church of England or the kingdom of the world. As he repeatedly emphasized, this church as a small spiritual gathering was "today" almost lost and forgotten, and its "reality" was uncertain.[56] Furthermore, he considered Christ's kingdom distinguishable by the three marks,

---

Cambridge University Press, 1994]), two contributors present contrasting images of Bucer's *De Regno Christi*. In the context of "Bucer's Influence on Calvin," W. van't Spijker (in *Martin Bucer: Reforming Church and Community*, 42–44) positively notes in this work "the way to a radical Christianization or reformation of the entire people" and that "the deepest motives of his theology and work come to their full development here." He also sees a parallel between Bucer's "wide vision" expressed in this work and Calvin's notion of Europe as a Christian society. In the essay "Martin Bucer in England," B. Hall (in *Martin Bucer: Reforming Church and Community*, 154–58) focuses on the second book of this work, the application of the notion of Christ's kingdom in English society, and concludes that "*De regno Christi* was respected, but its theories and proposals were undermined by English pragmatism." In this limited sense, nevertheless, he acknowledges that the work provided "a fresh and vigorous challenge to the English state on the reform and remodeling of the church, together with a useful account of the principles for the relation of the reformed church with the Christian state."

54. *De Regno Christi*, *BOL* 15:3–6.

55. *De Regno Christi*, *BOL* 15:6–20.

56. *De Regno Christi*, *BOL* 15:20, 40, 54.

God's word, the sacraments, and church discipline. He especially emphasized the third mark that consisted of the education of the children of the faithful, confession of faith, confirmation, and admonition and excommunication as the mark to achieve the "piety and righteousness" of believers as well as that which distinguished Christ's kingdom from the kingdom of the world. In fact, he even claimed that, among the Protestant countries that had escaped Catholic dominion, the restoration of the first two marks had been achieved, but that of the third mark had been insufficient and even faced resistance.[57]

(iii) Book 2 of this work dealt with the English crown's contribution to the realization of Christ's kingdom in its domain, with its responsibility described as being "to restore, establish, and maintain the administration of religion and the entire state according to God's word." In it, Bucer enumerated fourteen regulations that the crown could institute, ranging from religious education, observance of Sunday, religious buildings, ministerial order, and church finance to welfare of the poor, marriage and divorce, agriculture/industry/business, public service, and jurisprudence. His vision was to integrate all of these areas of public life and relate them to the Reformation or the realization of Christ's kingdom in England.[58] In *Of the Kingdom of Christ*, there were many interesting themes and various concourses of the themes, such as the conflicts of Christ's kingdom and the world's kingdom, the narrow and the broad notions of the church, God's election and the public profession of faith, and so forth. These factors often seem to obscure what Bucer precisely intended to communicate in this work. Whether the work as a whole presented a cohesive "integration" of his ideas or not remains a question.

Section 2. Bucer and Calvin

The fact that a second-generation Reformer, Calvin, had spent three years in "Bucer's Strasbourg" and had engaged in various activities both within and outside of the city boundary has been generally understood to be an important formative factor for Calvin's thought and work in the post-Strasbourg period. In particular, among the reformers with whom he had formed close friendships, such as Farel and Viret since his Genevan period, and Capito, Melanchthon, and Bullinger in his Strasbourg period, his relationship with Bucer was exceptional. The "Bucer and Calvin" relationship is an unavoidable

57. *De Regno Christi*, *BOL* 15:40–42.
58. *De Regno Christi*, *BOL* 15:293–94.

issue for understanding Calvin's later theological development, especially his ecclesiology. In the following pages, we will examine this issue under three headings, namely, the so-called "Bucer's influence" theory, Calvin's consistent biblicism and practical activism that we have already partly examined in the previous two chapters, and Calvin's external engagements in France, Geneva, and the Holy Roman Empire during this period.

1. The "Bucer's Influence" Theory

(i) Generally speaking, as Van Oort suggests, any inquiry into "influence" in Renaissance personalities is said to be "an endless and highly speculative matter."[59] Unlike those in the modern period, they considered the works of the past and the contemporary as the common inheritance of their culture, and they used them freely without the feeling of being influenced. Unlike those in the Middle Ages, however, they were independent enough to either accept or reject them in order to establish their own views. For them, the art of such selective enterprises was a mark of their identity as Renaissance personalities. Especially in Calvin's case with Bucer, which does not fit the teacher-disciple patterns of Luther and Melanchthon, Zwingli and Bullinger, and Lefèvre and Farel, the "influence" question becomes complicated. In particular, as we have seen in chapter 1, Calvin was a young humanist lawyer who formed his own theology in a short period of time by privately studying the Bible and church fathers, church history, and contemporary theologians of both camps, including Luther, Zwingli, Melanchthon, and Bucer. In a sense, his most basic theological formation was completed in his first *Institutes*, except for its later amplifications.

In the rise of modern historical research in the early twentieth century, Anrich's Bucer biography noted Bucer's influence on Calvin's teachings on the church and theocracy (Christ's kingdom). Anrich later focused on the connection between Calvin's Strasbourg period and his later ecclesiological development. Doumergue also marked three elements in Calvin's ecclesiological formation, "the influence of Luther and Bucer along with Calvin's own originality." Doumergue especially contrasted Luther's emphasis on the church's objective aspects (such as the word and the sacraments) with Bucer's emphasis on its subjective aspects (such as the church as the number of the elect). In 1933, Courvoisier noticed Bucer's notion of the visible church and

59. J. van Oort, "John Calvin and the Church Fathers," in *The Reception of the Church Fathers in the West: From Carolingians to the Maurists*, ed. I. Backus (Leiden: Brill, 1997), 2:663.

its organization reflected in Calvin's works in this period and especially after 1541. He concluded that "before 1538 he [Calvin] is a Lutheran, after 1541 he is a Bucerian, or better [be called] Reformed." In 1942, Wendel, a Lutheran lawyer and historian specializing in Strasbourg, published a critical study of the Strasbourg Church in its crucial reformatory phase of 1532–35 and concluded that the Strasbourg Reformation was a prototype of the Reformed doctrine and practice. Among areas over which Strasbourg exerted influence, such as Frankfort, Hessen, and Geneva, however, Wendel especially focused on Calvin and his 1541 *Genevan Ecclesiastical Ordinances* as having come under the influence of Bucer and Strasbourg. In a groundbreaking historical study, *Calvin* (1950), he followed up on this thesis and noted the importance of Bucer whom he regarded as "the best negotiator in the service of the new Churches and a first-rate organizer." In particular, he remarked on Bucer's influence, seen in Calvin's emphasis on the church's visible aspects, the concept of church discipline, and the fourfold ministerial order in the second and third editions of the *Institutes*.[60]

Wendel's persuasive theory of Bucer's influence was later shared by Ganoczy, a Catholic theologian who used the same historical methodology in his *Calvin* (1954) and *The Young Calvin* (*Le jeune Calvin*, 1955). In the 1970s, a Bucer scholar, van't Spijker, and in the 1980s, a popular writer on religion and the Reformation, Reardon, and others followed the theory. Reardon even devoted one entire chapter to the formation of Calvin's reformatory thought in the context of Bucer's influence and said that "the close affinity" between Calvin and Bucer "has repeatedly been noted and cannot seriously be disputed."[61]

60. G. Anrich, *Martin Bucer* (Strasbourg: Karl J. Teubner, 1914); G. Anrich, *Strassburg und die Calvinische Kirchenverfassung* (Tübingen: J. C. B. Mohr, 1928); Doumergue, *Jean Calvin*, 5:23–24; Courvoisier, *La notion*, 135–50; Wendel, *Calvin*, 58–59, 113–17, 295–311; Wendel, *L'Église de Strasbourg*, 237–41. Wendel provides a concise description of Calvin's activities in his Strasbourg period in *Calvin*, 58–66.

61. Ganoczy, *Calvin*, 52–53; Ganoczy, *Young Calvin*, 158–68; van't Spijker, *The Ecclesiastical Offices*, 340–41; W. van't Spijker, "Prädestination bei Bucer und Calvin: Ihre gegenseitige Beeinflussung und Abhängigkeit," in *Calvinus Theologus*, ed. W. H. Neuser (Neukirchen: Neukirchner Verlag, 1976), 85–111; B. M. G. Reardon, *Religious Thought in the Reformation*, 2nd ed. (London and New York: Longman, 1995), 136–62; S. Buckwalter, "Possible Influences of Martin Bucer on the *Institutio* of 1539," in *John Calvin: The Strasbourg Years (1538–1541)*, ed. M. Arnold, trans. F. McNab (Eugene, OR: Wipf & Stock, 2016), 90–106; S. M. Manetsch, *Calvin's Company of Pastors: Pastoral Care and the Emerging Reformed Church, 1536–1609* (Oxford and New York: Oxford University Press, 2013), 25. Van't Spijker's original edition (*De ambten bij Martin Bucer* [Kampen: Kok, 1970]) followed Ganoczy's lead on "Bucer's

Beyond the discipline of theology and church history, the theory has also been widely accepted. For example, a work of a historian of political thought, Höpfl's *The Christian Polity of John Calvin* (1982) considers Calvin's Strasbourg period as a time of extensive "reconstruction" in the concept of polity. Although he admits some difficulties in applying the "Bucer's influence" theory in the "reconstruction," Calvin is said to have greatly learned from Bucer's Strasbourg. A historian of the Renaissance, Bouwsma's *John Calvin: A Sixteenth Century Portrait* (1988) sees Bucer as "the paternal authority" for Calvin and notices Bucer's influence on Calvin's biblical exegesis and personal life.[62]

(ii) As the brief survey above indicates, the so-called "Bucer's influence" theory seems to be an established theory today. That influence is said to be widely recognizable in Calvin's theology, and especially in his ecclesiology. As we have said above, our task here is not to examine the evidence of "influence" or affinity per se, but to ascertain historically the exact nature of such "influence" or affinity. For this task we will narrowly focus on Calvin's ecclesiology, on which Bucer's influence has been said to be the strongest. Before commencing our task, however, there are at least two confirmations to be made. One is to acknowledge that both Bucer and Calvin were unique and independent theologians *sui generis* in doctrine and practice. Even though they shared common humanist and Evangelical thrusts, theologically their backgrounds were quite distinct. Bucer, as a professional theologian, came from the Thomistic tradition in Germany, and Calvin was an amateur humanist theologian in the French Reformation. And, as we have briefly sketched Bucer's case in this chapter and rather extensively Calvin's case in the previous two chapters, their ecclesiological formations were historically very different. Our analyses so far indicate a hesitation to make claims about Bucer's overall influence or of Calvin being a Bucerian. Even if we do admit that Calvin learned from Bucer and Strasbourg from 1538 onward, the question "How did he learn?" should be as important as "What did he learn?" For Calvin, Bucer could be a "teacher," a source of different or new ideas for Calvin to take into his own ecclesiology;

---

influence." His later article of 1994 ("Bucer's Influence on Calvin: Church and Community," 32–42) seemed to take a more nuanced view of "Bucer's influence" and noticed the mutual aspects of the influence. Surprisingly, however, van't Spijker neither took Calvin's ecclesiology in the first *Institutes* into serious consideration nor used Bucer's *Theological Advice*, which was already available. Likewise, Buckwalter's more recent article presents a cautious yet selective analysis, indicating Bucer's influence on Calvin's second *Institutes*, especially on the issues of the anti-Anabaptist polemics and the Lord's Supper.

62. Höpfl, *Christian Polity*, 77–90; Bouwsma, *Calvin*, 21–24.

or, Bucer could be a "mirror" in which Calvin could selectively accept or reject ideas and counter them with his own.

(iii) The other confirmation is that "Bucer's influence" should be substantiated in the whole context of Bucer's as well as Calvin's ecclesiology. For those who have contributed to formulate the "influence" theory, firstly, it is possible that some important primary materials were not available for their consideration. Secondly, it is also possible that they have not sufficiently considered some important ecclesiological notions that suggest discord rather than affinity. And, thirdly, some of their evidence of "influence" or affinity might be interpreted otherwise in later historical research.

An example of the first case is Bucer's manuscript document, *Theological Advice* (*Consilium Theologicum*), the existence of which was made known only recently and was not available to the contributors of the "Bucer's influence" theory. As analyzed below, the document indicates Bucer's fundamental ecclesiological perspective of Christianity and the Reformation, which is quite distinct from that of Calvin. As a matter of fact, it includes a refutation of the first epistle of Calvin's *Two Epistles*.

An example of the second case is the notion of the marks of the church. By the time Calvin began his stay in Strasbourg, as we have seen above, Bucer had completed his move from the two-marks theory to the official three-marks theory. In chapter 1, we notice that Calvin's first *Institutes* basically held the two-marks theory, with an ambivalent attitude toward the so-called third mark of church discipline. In his second and third editions of the *Institutes* (1539, 1543) prepared and published in Strasbourg, as we will examine below, he firmly established the two-marks theory upon the distinction of the two marks as relative to the church's "substance/doctrine" or "title," and discipline as relative to its "form." No matter how important or even indispensable church discipline was for the existence of the church, for Calvin, discipline concerned only the matters of the church's "form." If we use the term of his first *Institutes* (ch. 6), it was a matter of "adiaphora," thus implicitly rejecting Bucer's view.[63]

Concerning the third case, we notice a general tendency in recent research on topics such as Calvin's hermeneutics, doctrines, and liturgy to emphasize his unique scholarship, rather than Bucer's "influence" as such. In the com-

63. *CO* 1:543–44. (*Institutio* 4.1.9: *OS* 5:13–14.) Cf. Ganoczy, *Calvin*, 200. Bucer's path to the three-marks theory was already paved in his 1538 work (*Furbereytung zum Concilio* [*Bucer Bibliographie*, 59], 1533: *BDS* 5:306–8). Since this theory was clearly expressed in his *Four Gospel Commentary* (*In Sacra Quatuor Evangelia*, 1536), *Der kürtzer Catechismus* (1537, *BDS* 6/3:189), and the 1538 Hessen disciplinary ordinance (*BDS* 7:261), the process was completed by the time Calvin arrived in Strasbourg in 1538.

parative studies of the Romans commentaries by Calvin and Bucer, for example, researchers have noted the two Reformers sometimes at variance in their teachings on faith, theological anthropology, election, and Christian life. Additionally, the long-held notion that Calvin used the Strasbourg liturgy for his French congregation in Strasbourg, as well as in the Genevan Church after his return in 1541, is being questioned.[64]

(1) Theological Advice

In 1974, the process of revealing the existence of a handwritten document among the materials left in England after Bucer's death, as well as making it available to researchers, began when a well-known scholar of Melanchthon and Johann Eck, Fraenkel, introduced it as "Bucer's Memorandum of 1541" in his "Study-notes." He provided a brief analysis of its content and suggested its significance in connection with the *Book of Regensburg*, but did not explicitly refer to its inclusion of a portion refuting Calvin. When it was officially included in the *Martini Buceri Opera Latina* as *Consilium theologicum privatim conscriptum* in 1988, the editor, Fraenkel, titled its fifth part as "Polemic against Calvin," which was in reality Bucer's refutation of Calvin's first epistle of *Two Epistles*.[65] Of course, as we suggested above, this document was not available to

64. M. de Kroon's 1991 comparative study of Bucer and Calvin in Dutch and its German translation (*Martin Bucer und Johannes Calvin: Reformatorische Perspektiven*; *Einleitung und Texte*, trans. from Dutch by H. Rudolph [Göttingen: Vandenhoeck & Ruprecht, 1991]) examines Bucer's key texts taken from his *Romans Commentary* (1536), *John Commentary* (1527), and other works on political theology. The study also provides some "Reformation perspectives," including the theological perspective of "Bucer and Calvin" (229–36). Against the general tendency of Bucer's "influence," the study portrays each Reformer's unique position in its historical context. In an essay, "Calvin among the Thomists," D. Steinmetz (*Calvin in Context* [New York and Oxford: Oxford University Press, 1995], 141–56) examines Calvin's commentary on Romans 9 in comparison with the interpretations of Thomas Aquinas and Bucer on the same text. He concludes that the thesis (Calvin is the beneficiary of the Thomistic school tradition mediated to him by Martin Bucer) finds no support. J. E. Kok's dissertation ("The Influence of Martin Bucer on John Calvin's Interpretation of Romans: A Comparative Case Study," Duke University, 1993) makes a basic distinction between "Calvin's exegetical detail and doctrinal content" and carefully compares his treatment of the theological loci of Romans with Bucer's. Kok notes "the pattern of continuing differences between Calvin and Bucer" and concludes that, "in Calvin's view, Bucer is exemplary at the exegetical level, but in matters of doctrine, he bends Christian teaching too far in the direction of pagan philosophy." R. Bornert (*La Réforme protestante du culte à Strasbourg au XVI*^e^ *Siècle* [Leiden: Brill, 1981], 199–201) questions Calvin's use of the Strasbourg liturgy.

65. P. Fraenkel, "Bucer's Memorandum of 1541 and a 'Lettera Nicodemitica' of Capito's,"

the contributors of the "Bucer's influence" theory, namely Courvoisier, Wendel, Ganoczy, and van't Spijker. Before we examine *Theological Advice*, however, it seems appropriate to make briefly three preliminary observations.

The first observation concerns the basic nature of *Theological Advice* as a polemical tract that presented a considerably different position from Calvin's on liturgical practice and reform in the Roman Catholic Church. Although the tract contained a section exclusively refuting the main points of Calvin's first epistle, as a whole it intended to present a comprehensive counterproposal vis-à-vis *Two Epistles*. If we point out a basic difference between the two works, while Calvin's work based on two personal letters pointed to the context of Lefèvrianism in the French Reformation, Bucer expanded his polemical scope to the whole of European Christendom. Besides consistently noting Calvin's work, as the editor Fraenkel remarks, Bucer's tract demonstrated his in-depth knowledge of the church fathers, Lombard, Aquinas, Erasmus, and others, and its overall outlook resembled the moderate Catholic position of Beatus Rhenanus, Georg Witzel, and Johannes Gropper. In this respect, the tract revealed another aspect of its basic nature, namely, Bucer's preoccupation with his aspiration for the success of the church unification colloquies. Concerning Bucer's position on liturgical reform in Protestant Evangelicalism, as Tait argues, Bucer took a position between Luther and Zwingli. As to the images of the sacred, such as those in the Roman Catholic Church, Luther considered them neutral in themselves but becoming idolatrous when the faithful trusted in them rather than in Christ. Zwingli regarded any physical representations of the sacred as prohibited by divine law. On the one hand, like Zwingli, Bucer took scriptural authority as law seriously, and from this stance he was able to attack Catholic practices as idolatrous. On the other hand, he had "a subtler argument," the principles of "love of neighbor" and of "the flesh/spirit dichotomy," by which he was able to accommodate himself to the reality of Catholic practices in order to reform them. As a result, in certain circumstances, such as in the context of true faith, the use of images was "free in itself" and admissible, but only in the case of using images as a means for worshipping God did it become idolatrous. On these principles, Bucer attempted the earlier liturgical reforms in the Strasbourg Church, in-

Bibliothèque d'Humanisme et Renaissance 36 (1974): 575–87. Fraenkel revealed that what Carlo Ginzburg regarded as "Capito's Epistle" in his book on Nicodemism (*Il Nicodemismo* [Turin: Guilio Einaudi, 1970]) was indeed a part of Bucer's unpublished manuscripts (*Consilium Theologicum*), and Fraenkel examined the manuscripts' importance in the context of the *Regensburg Book*.

cluding the removal of images. If we take *Theological Advice*, a work of the later Bucer, into our consideration, however, his position was far closer to Luther than Zwingli and was clearly distinct from that of Calvin, who characterized the Roman Catholic religion as "to shape one religion out of Christianity and Judaism and paganism by sewing patches together."[66]

The second observation concerns the relationship between Bucer's addressee who requested his advice and whose identity he kept incognito. While Fraenkel's "Introduction" examines a few possible addressees, such as a secretary of Emperor Charles V, a diplomat of King Francis I, and others, a common denominator of these possible cases is that the addressee was an evangelical Catholic living in a Catholic territory or nation and under pressure to participate in Catholic ceremonies. Since the addressee's condition and the subject of Bucer's advice were similar to those of the first epistle of *Two Epistles*, it can be assumed that Bucer left out the epistle's author and title, as well as Calvin's characteristic expressions and terms, thus making the epistle more like an ordinary treatise.[67]

The third observation concerns the overall subject and goal of *Theological Advice*. The subject was twofold, that is, the origin, history, and current condition of the ceremonies of the Roman Catholic Church, and Bucer's comprehensive proposal to reform them. The goal was to induce an answer to the question: What kind of ceremonies were required for the church to be properly called a Christian church? According to Fraenkel, *Theological Advice* was composed around the time of the *Regensburg Book* (the end of 1540 and beginning of 1541), and Bucer was advising an unidentified person of high position concerning the possibility of avoiding the ultimate schism and advancing church unification.[68] Since he was a leader of the unification colloquies, it is easily assumed that he had already made up his mind on the question of whether the Roman Catholic Church, with its "reformed" ceremonies and even under

66. *Consilium Theologicum*, *BOL* 4, "Introduction," xix; *OS* 1:217. (Battles, trans., *Institution*, 233.) Cf. E. R. Tait, "A Method for the Christian Life: Martin Bucer and the Sermon on the Mount" (PhD diss., Duke University, 2005), 152–212. Tait's careful analysis mainly uses Bucer's earlier works, such as *Das ym selbs niemant* (1523) and *Grund und Ursach* (1525), and the Gospel commentaries. Although the relevant text of *Theological Advice* is available to him, perhaps with reason, he does not use it for his study.

67. Cf. *Consilium Theologicum*, *BOL* 4, "Introduction," xxiv–xxix. For example, Bucer's manuscripts dealing with the first epistle of Calvin's *Two Epistles* did not mention a characteristic term, "Christ-butchers" (*Christi carnifices*), which Calvin applied to the celebrants of the Catholic Mass.

68. Fraenkel, "Bucer's Memorandum," 585–86; *Consilium Theologicum*, *BOL* 4, "Introduction," xix–xxii.

papal rule, could be called a Christian church. Thus, a reason why he included his refutation of Calvin's epistle was that, even though making a distinction between the church catholic and the papal church, the epistle answered the question in the negative. Bucer clearly recognized this as an obstacle to the prospect of reunification.

The edited text of *Theological Advice* was divided into 798 short paragraphs or theses. These divisions were added to the manuscript by a secretary in the early stage of its preservation. The main portions of the text were an introduction (par. 1–84) that began with the document's grand thesis, "Under papal rule the church of Christ exists," and introduced a threefold category of Catholic ceremonies; the main treatise (par. 85–537) that examined the origin, history, significance, and possible reform of ceremonies divided into three categories; the "Polemic against Calvin" (par. 538–769); and a conclusion (par. 770–798). In the following pages, selectively, we will examine only three points: Bucer's definition of the church and a threefold category of the ceremonies, his concept of history and the Mass placed in the third category of the main treatise, and the issue concerning the perspective of the liturgical and church reform in his refutation of Calvin.

(i) In the opening section, which affirmed the churches under papal rule to be Christ's churches, Bucer presented a definition of the church with its conciliatory character:

> Therefore, wherever there are those who truly hold to Christ, and have the communion of the word, the sacraments, and prayer—even if they have them along with observing many other things which they unfortunately agree to be true by faith . . . ,—there the church of Christ as such is recognized. For the church of Christ is none other than the gathering and society of those who truly invoke Christ, and have the communion of the word, the sacraments, and prayer among themselves, no matter how many errors and sins they have committed.

Bucer's expression "gathering and society" was no surprise, and it was reminiscent of Article 6 of the *Regensburg Book*'s "assembly or congregation." Noticeable, however, was his use of "the word, the sacraments, and prayer" as if they were "marks" of the church. The third term, "prayer," was definitely different from his official and ever-stressed mark of church discipline, and it was even different from the *Regensburg Book*'s third mark, "the bond of love." Although it seems difficult to determine why he used "prayer" here, it could be a reference to Luther's *Private Mass and the Consecration of Priests* (1533) in which, as we have mentioned above, Luther listed, besides the preaching of the word and the sacraments, prayer, forgiveness of sins, and ministerial order, and concluded that even under the abominable papal rule, if those marks were present, the "holy church" existed. As far as the church definition was concerned, the overall impression is Bucer's conciliatory posture in the Catholic and Protestant conflict.[69]

In the second section on the "communion" with those churches under papal rule, Bucer added a section dealing with reforming the ceremonies and presented an optimistic vision that was clearly intended to present an alternative to Calvin's pessimistic view expressed in his first epistle. While Calvin titled the epistle negatively as "On Fleeing the Illicit Rites," Bucer counterproposed a positive option for Evangelical believers to remain in the Catholic Church and work together with like-minded Catholics for the reform of the church and its ceremonies. First, Bucer redefined the church with four marks: the word, the sacraments, prayer, and the care of the poor. He both related them "to the manifestation of Christ's kingdom" and regarded them as components of "communion" among the churches. By citing Christ's rebukes against "the Pharisees and the Sadducees," secondly, Bucer pointed out current abominable practices such as the "papal yoke" and appealed to the church to reform them. Notably, he implicitly characterized Calvin's position by the phrase, "rejecting and fleeing from" these papal practices and proposed his own mediating plan. On the one hand, he regarded the "rejecting and fleeing from" them primarily as a magisterial responsibility rather than that of the ministers and the faithful. On the other hand, he emphasized the church's internal duty to reform them on the basis of doctrine and fraternal love.[70]

In the third section, Bucer divided the ceremonies currently practiced "in the Papal church" into three categories. In particular, under the first category, he listed baptism, the Lord's Supper, the (ministerial) order and its related ceremonies, and lastly, church discipline, all ceremonies sanctioned in the Bible and thus having divine right. The second category included ceremonies such

69. *Consilium Theologicum*, *BOL* 4:5: "Proinde, ubicunque tales sunt, qui Christum ita vere tenent, et communionem verbi, sacramentorum, et precum habent—quamquam haec habeant cum observatione multarum rerum, quae cum fide vera male congruent, . . . , ibi tamen ecclesia Christi agnoscenda est. Nam ecclesia Christi aliud nihil est quam collectio et societas eorum, qui Christum vere invocant, et habent verbi, et sacramentorum, ac precum inter se communionem, quantumlibet praeterea errorum et peccatorum illis adhereat." Cf. chapter 2, section 3.2, n. 174 above.

70. *Consilium Theologicum*, *BOL* 4:7–12. Fraenkel's footnote (12n23) indicates Bucer's basic double criterion of "faith and love."

as confirmation, private confession, veneration of saints and relics, and others that could trace their origins to the ancient church and thus could claim their ecclesiastical authority. The third category was headed by what Bucer calls "the abominable Mass" and includes indulgences, celibacy, papal right of granting special forgiveness, and so forth. He considered this category as having no standing in the church and needing reform.[71]

(ii) The second point concerned Bucer's concepts of history and liturgical reform expressed in the threefold division. Although the division of history into biblical times—the ancient church and the medieval church—was just a reflection of the customary humanist concept, what makes his presentation unique was his careful method of analyzing all the Catholic ceremonies, their origins, and significations by dividing them into three categories of biblical authentication, the authorization of the ancient church, and later additions, and then relating them to the notion of reform. His basic assumption was that, though the ceremonies of the first category were directly sanctioned by God's word and those of the second category were authenticated by the church fathers, through history they were corrupted by superstitions and abuse and, therefore, were in need of reform. As to the notion of reform, moreover, he assumed a conciliatory position. Although the ceremonies in the first category were to be maintained pure and authentic, the majority of the second category could be useful in his day by either retaining or restoring them, excluding superstition. Even though they had been extremely corrupted, they could be reformed to be useful.[72]

In spite of his clearly visible Evangelical position, Bucer's optimistic and conciliatory view of reform prevailed throughout the entire text of the tract. As to the first category, for example, he listed baptism and the Eucharist at the beginning as "instituted by the Lord himself" and presented his own Evangelical analyses. Curiously, however, he allocated one of the shortest chapters to the dominical institution of church discipline and only briefly referred to the abuse of Catholic excommunication. As to the second category, likewise, he listed confirmation first and seemed to consider it an important ceremony, suggesting its usefulness in the Evangelical churches. As to the third category, with a clear distinction between the Lord's Supper and the Catholic Mass, he emphasized "the abominable Mass" as a primary and deformed ceremony. Even though he allocated considerable space to cover the Mass, the conclu-

71. *Consilium Theologicum*, *BOL* 4:11–12 (par. 43–48), 4:13–16 (par. 49–77). Cf. Fraenkel, "Bucer's Memorandum," 579–80.

72. *Consilium Theologicum*, *BOL* 4:17 (par. 80–81).

sion that he deduced from the whole discussion was both conciliatory and anti-Calvin. According to him, the Mass retained a glimpse of the Eucharist, and the celebration of the Mass neither destroyed the sacrament's essence nor damaged the church's substance. As to the issue raised by Calvin on the Mass as the "sacrifice" of Christ, Bucer insisted that the sacrificial notion of the Eucharist could be supported by Scripture as well as by the church fathers.[73]

(iii) The third point concerned Bucer's optimistic perspective of church reform in his anti-Calvin polemic. At the beginning of the polemical section, clearly conscious of the title of Calvin's first epistle, "On Fleeing the Illicit Rites," Bucer counterproposed his basic posture on church reform. Citing biblical passages, such as "let each of you lead the life that the Lord has assigned" (1 Cor 7:17) and "to the Jews I became as a Jew" and "to the weak I became weak" (1 Cor 9: 19–22), which was also on the cover page of the document, he urged all those who aspired for the reform of the papal church to remain in that church and to work together with "the saints" in the church "for restoring the kingdom of Christ and glorifying Christ." For Bucer who said in the document's opening that "under Papal rule the church of Christ exists," this was his most optimistic expression on the reform of the papal church.[74]

In order to locate this reasoning of Bucer in its historical context, two documents provided some background information: Bucer's 1536 *Romans Commentary*, to which Calvin's dedicatory epistle to his 1540 *Romans Commentary* gave "praise"; and Calvin's proposed "French Edition of Chrysostom's Homilies" (the project was obviously abandoned by him), of which only its incomplete "Latin Preface" is extant in manuscript. As to the first document, Kok's comparative study of the two Romans commentaries by Bucer and Calvin notes the contrasting images of Paul's apostolic office. While Bucer portrayed Paul as "a teacher who sought every occasion to advance the kingdom of Christ" and who inclusively aimed "all things to all people in order to gain them for Christ," Calvin saw Paul as "a teacher who insisted on the submission to the

73. *Consilium Theologicum*, *BOL* 4:13 (par. 57), 23–26 (par. 90–106), 27–33 (par. 107–50), 65 (par. 302–5); 70–71 (par. 307–11); 22 (par. 86–89), 94–102 (par. 375–417). According to Fraenkel ("Bucer's Memorandum," 583nn38–40) who examined the close relation between the *Regensburg Book* and Bucer's *Consilium Theologicum*, the *Book*'s article 20 deals with the controversial issues of the veneration of saints and the Eucharist as a sacrifice. On the latter issue the *Book* takes the stand that the Eucharist, properly understood and rightly executed, might be called a sacrifice. Bucer's *Consilium Theologicum* (*BOL* 4, ch. 43, "De abominationibus missae," 94–102) basically takes the same position.

74. *Consilium Theologicum*, *BOL* 4:3 (title page citing 1 Cor 3:19–22), 131–32 (par. 538–42, 549).

truth of the gospel" and "right doctrine." As to Calvin's "Latin Preface" to Chrysostom's *Homilies*, Hazlett considers the document originating roughly in Calvin's Strasbourg period and notes "his critique of Chrysostom" as its "most revealing feature." Although Calvin highly praised *Homilies* for its excellence in plainly interpreting God's word and its usefulness for the church and common people, he was critical of Chrysostom's accommodating positions on human free will, the merits of good works, and God's election. In this context, Calvin used two similar references to 1 Corinthians (3:21, 23): "Though everything belongs to us, we however belong to Christ" and "While all things are ours, we belong to the one Christ." Both references were used in such a way that, although all possible interpretations were open to biblical exegetes, they were confined to one standard of Christ and his word. This exclusive position could be interpreted as Calvin's counterargument against Chrysostom's and Bucer's accommodating notion of "all things to all people."[75]

From this basic posture, Bucer's *Theological Advice* refuted Calvin's contention expressed in the first epistle that the Catholic ceremonies represented by the Mass were the idolatrous mixtures of the Christian gospel, Judaism and heathenism and were to be rejected according to the Pauline injunction "flee from the worship of idols" (1 Cor 10:14), and Bucer insisted that participation in the holy ceremonies of the papal church was not idolatry. Citing the apostolic case of Peter restoring himself as an apostle after being rebuked by Paul, Bucer also suggested that the reformers of the papal church should positively use the sacred ceremonies that retained glimpses of the original gospel elements for the reform of that church.[76] As the seemingly most noticeable polemic, furthermore, Bucer properly summarized Calvin's criticism of the Mass in three points: that the significance of Christ's death on the cross

75. Bucer, *Metaphrases et Enarrationes* (*Bucer Bibliographie*, no. 76); Calvin, "Praefatio in Chrysostomi Homilia," *CO* 9:831–38. Cf. J. E. Kok, "The Influence of Martin Bucer on John Calvin's Interpretation of Romans," 43–54; W. I. P. Hazlett, "Calvin's Latin Preface to His Proposed French Edition of Chrysostom's Homilies: Translation and Commentary," in *Humanism and Reform: The Church in Europe, England, and Scotland, 1400–1643*, ed. J. Kirk (Oxford and Cambridge, MA: Blackwell, 1991), 129–50. In particular, Kok (51, notes 86–88) emphasizes that Bucer not only accepts Chrysostom's accommodating position but also defends Chrysostom's notion of the so-called "pious fraud" or "simulation and dissimulation," which is for Calvin a crucial issue of the moderate Catholic reformists. On the other hand, in connection with Calvin's high esteem of Chrysostom as an exegete, Hazlett (146n45) regards the latter as "a representative of the anti-allegorical Antiochene exegetical tradition." The two references to 1 Corinthians in Calvin's "Latin Preface" are found in *CO* 9:832, 836; Hazlett, 141, 146.

76. *Consilium Theologicum*, *BOL* 4:134–36 (par. 552–73; cf. *COR* IV-4:1–18), 137–38 (par. 574–79), esp. n. 4, 139–47 (par. 580–632).

was destroyed, that the promise of the gospel was not given to the faithful, and that the host was raised and adored by the participants. While showing his understanding of the criticism's legitimacy, nevertheless, Bucer defended the Mass as a ceremony retaining the sacrificial elements of the Eucharist. He concluded that the Mass could be regarded as a ceremony instituted by Christ and practiced by the church fathers.[77]

In a final analysis, as the editor Fraenkel indicates, Bucer's apologetic expressed in "Polemic against Calvin" was fully aware of the fact that Calvin's first epistle was addressed not to conservative Catholics but to the moderate Catholic reformists who were interested in the Evangelical Reformation. It dared to challenge Calvin's strict activism that he himself called "our excessive severity," and it offered an alternative for Catholic moderates that we could call a viable defense of Nicodemism. In this connection, it is to be noted that Bucer's defense took the arguments of the moderate reformists into consideration, such as the legitimacy of their participation in ceremonies that they do not regard as evangelical, the distinction between "worship" and "veneration," and the possibility of "truly worshipping Christ" by their participation in these ceremonies.[78] Our concluding impression is that we find here an eloquent apology for the Catholic moderates by Bucer who held a high expectation of the papal church's reform alongside the reunification of the churches, as well as a clear recognition of Calvin's position as an obstacle to the prospect of reunification. Our remaining question is whether the existence of this document was known to Calvin. Since researchers, including Fraenkel, keep silent on this question, we do not have a clear answer. It is possible, however, that the experienced and thoughtful Reformer, Bucer, might have been successful in hiding its existence from Calvin. Above all, the case of *Theological Advice* vividly illustrates an example of the dialectic relationships among Evangelical Reformers in their acceptance, exchange, and rejection of opinions, which cannot be easily characterized as "influencing" or "being influenced" by one another.

(2) Reformation of a Local Church and the Christian World

(i) Despite our problematization of the notion of "influence" in the section above, there is no doubt that the whole outlook of Calvin's ecclesiology finds

77. *Consilium Theologicum*, *BOL* 4:148–51 (par. 633–67). Cf. *COR* IV-4:1–6, 30–38. The section "Le sacrifice de la Messe" (editor's title) shows that Bucer clearly understood the nature of Calvin's attacks against the "Moderators" and his own refutation of Calvin's position in their defense (*BOL* 4:149).

78. *Consilium Theologicum*, *BOL* 4, "Introduction," xx, 147, 161–65 (ch. 68, "Adoratio Christi in sacramento").

its close affinity in no other major Reformer but Bucer. Besides the common Reformed emphases on the concept of the church and its reform, Bucer and Calvin shared similar ideas of Christ's kingdom, the kingdom's relation with the church and state, the importance of the word, the sacraments, and discipline for the church, and their emphasis on practical Christianity. In this context, it bears asking, if Bucer's influence on Calvin is a historically important issue, what are the most pertinent outcomes of this influence? As we have noted above, the period of the later Bucer witnessed a diversion of two distinctive reformatory directions, namely, the theme of "implicit amplification" in the Reformation of a local church and that of "explicit expansion" in the Reformation of the European Christian world. During his three-year stay in Strasbourg, we assume Calvin had inherited these two themes from Bucer. After his return to Geneva, he used them in the Genevan Reformation and, on the basis of the Genevan experience, he applied them to the French Reformation and beyond.[79] In the historical context of this inheritance, we assume that he formulated his Reformed ecclesiology corresponding to the first theme and his Reformation ecclesiology corresponding to the second theme. For example, the former took its clear shape in the third *Institutes* of 1543 and the latter in the extensive reorganization of the previous editions into the final 1559 *Institutes*.

(ii) Before we follow these two themes and ecclesiologies in chapter 4, it seems necessary to mention two preliminary observations in connection with the Bucer-Calvin relationship. As to the first observation, it seems that for his ecclesiological development, Calvin was most interested in the Reformer Bucer of Calvin's Strasbourg period rather than that of Bucer's later years. In other words, Calvin's utmost concern was the Bucer who had been struggling with these two themes both in Strasbourg and beyond its territory during the period of 1538 to 1541, and not the Bucer of the "Christian society" movement and of his last major work, *Of the Kingdom of Christ*. In fact, we are not certain how much Calvin was interested in the "Christian society" movement as the end point of Bucer's first theme. For sure, Calvin had no access to the German materials, including "Concerning the Defect and Failure of the Church." Though *Of the Kingdom of Christ* was presented to the English crown in 1550,

79. Cf. W. van't Spijker, "Bucer's Influence on Calvin: Church and Community," *Martin Bucer: Reforming Church and Community*, ed. D. F. Wright (Cambridge: Cambridge University Press, 1994), 35–44. Basically, taking the "Bucer's influence" theory, especially acknowledging the influence in Calvin's 1539 *Institutes*, van't Spijker sees the influence in two directions, one, corpus Christi: the body of Christ and the other, *Corpus Christianum*: Christian society.

its publication in Latin (as a part of the posthumous *Scripta Anglicana*) was late in 1557.

A crucial question is how Calvin of the Strasbourg period had observed the evolving process of Bucer's two themes and had learned from it. As to the first theme, "the Reformation of a local church," it is said that Bucer had encountered an impasse in Strasbourg. Having considered the settlement of the 1534 *Ecclesiastical Ordinances* insufficient, he kept pressing the magistracy for further actions, as we have seen above. He also wrote the "intentionally ignored" work, *Concerning True Pastoral Care*, implicitly criticizing the city's inaction. And finally, the 1539 church synod's appeal for further reform was ignored by the magistracy. If Greschat calls Bucer "a lonely man" during this process, and Oberman describes it as a cul-de-sac of Strasbourg's City Reformation, it can be assumed that Calvin observed it likewise.[80]

As to the second theme, "the Reformation of the European Christian world," Calvin's evaluation of the religious unification colloquies, in which Bucer took leadership and paved the way for Calvin to participate, can be viewed in both positive and negative perspectives. He viewed the colloquies positively as the last resort in seeking unification in Germany. He expected their positive impact upon the French Reformation on the one hand, yet with cool judgment he was predicting their impasse and failure on the other hand. He participated in the Schmalkald League's Frankfurt assembly in 1539 and two of the religious unification colloquies at Worms and Regensburg in 1540–41. At Worms, he spoke on the issues of justification, the Mass, papal primacy, and others. At Regensburg, though he was an official member of the Strasbourg delegation, his participation was rather limited. In his letters to his friends reporting the progress of the colloquies, however, he often expressed his resentment to the overly reconciliatory attitude on the Evangelical side, especially, of Melanchthon and Bucer.[81] The whole picture of his relationship with Bucer in this period may be seen as a "mirror" or a kind of "reversionary teacher" from whose successes and failures he could learn and use positively for the Genevan Reformation after his return.

(iii) The second observation concerned the existence of noticeable ecclesiological differences between Bucer and Calvin despite the fact that they shared

80. Cf. Greschat, *Martin Bucer*, 127; H. A. Oberman, "*Europa Afflicta*: The Reformation of the Refugees," *Archiv für Reformationsgeschichte* 83 (1992): 177, 182.

81. Confer a well-chronicled article of V. Ortmann, "Calvin and the Religious Colloquia of 1539–1541," in *John Calvin: The Strasbourg Years (1538–1541)*, ed. M. Arnold (Eugene, OR: Wipf & Stock, 2016), 169–82.

many common notions. As to such differences, Bucer's congregational polity, the distinction of "power" and "authority" concerning the power of the keys passages, and others have been noted. Even among the important notions commonly understood as being shared by both, closer scrutiny may reveal some nuanced and significant differences. Such was the case of their notion of Christ's kingdom. In the first edition of his Gospel commentary (*Enarrationum in Evangelia*, 1527), Bucer emphasized the spiritual character of Christ's kingdom as well as its manifestation through the word and the sacraments in the church in history. According to van't Spijker, however, Bucer's exposition on the extensively revised passages on church discipline in the third edition (*In Sacra Quatuor Evangelia, Enarrationes*, 1536) more closely identified Christ's kingdom with a local church properly exercising the power of the keys in discipline.[82] Concerning the direction of church reform, the shift from the basic distinction between Christ's spiritual kingdom and its manifestations in history to a closer identification of both was significant. Interestingly, this shift, which we may call the unitary understanding of Christ's kingdom and the church, took place in the same period in which Bucer was officially moving from the two-marks to the three-marks theory of the church.

An early indication of this shift was Bucer's response to his cominister Anthonius Engelbrecht's challenge in the 1533 synod. Over against Engelbrecht's thesis, "the kingdom of Christ stands in heartfelt piety," which partly reflected Luther's view, Bucer presented his own, "those who believe in Christ are his kingdom" (*die Christo glauben, seind sein reich*). Further, Bucer asked Engelbrecht a question: How was it possible that the magisterial duties, such as the upkeep of "communal good," the believers' "true worship of God," and "the whole scope of human life" could not be involved in Christ's kingdom? His conviction was that both the magistracy and the church could work together as Christ's "organs" to realize his kingdom in the local community. A similar concept of Christ's direct rule over the Christian community was expressed in his *Concerning True Pastoral Care* with a more accented emphasis. As we have seen above, Christ's direct rule was there understood as a realization of "the church . . . without spot or wrinkle" (Eph 5:27), a passage usually viewed as a reference to an eschatological reality, in the local Christian community. In this community, Christ as "the primary pastor" (*Ertzhirt*) used both the church's ministry and the magistracy as "under-pastors" (*unterhirten*) for the

82. *Enarrationum in Evangelia Matthaei, . . .* , 1, 180, 197; *In Sacra Quatuor Evangelia, Enarrationes*, 353 cited in van't Spijker, *The Ecclesiastical Offices*, 131nn88, 89. Cf. Ganoczy, *Young Calvin*, 160.

"pastoral care" of the entire community.[83] In Bucer's last years, the connection of Christ's kingdom and the Christian community was accentuated. His unpublished work "Concerning the Defect and Failure of the Church" defended "Christian society" as a congregation of the elect whose goal was to manifest Christ's kingdom. Furthermore, *Of the Kingdom of Christ* proclaimed to make England the kingdom of Christ.[84]

Over against Bucer's new direction briefly surveyed above, in his Strasbourg period Calvin seemed to have maintained the fundamental distinction of Christ's spiritual kingdom and its manifestation in the Christian community in history, the distinction that we noted in the first *Institutes*, chapter 6. For Calvin, as we mentioned in chapter 1, Christ's kingdom was a notion based upon his Antiochene Christology and was a limiting concept that defined what both church and state ought to be and how they could serve the kingdom. Although it was true that the kingdom could manifest itself in them, each of them as institutions on earth could never be fully identified with the kingdom. By the same token, when either the papal church or the Münster Anabaptists falsely claimed to be Christ's kingdom, Calvin challenged them.[85]

2. *Calvin's Biblicism and Activism*

We have so far surveyed Calvin's basic stand on Reformation and Evangelical theology under the theme of "Catholic ecclesiology" in chapter 1. In chapter 2 we have examined the practice of that ecclesiology in his first Genevan Reformation and have also confirmed his unique biblicism and activism in the Caroli affair and *Two Epistles*. Our question here is whether, through his Strasbourg experiences and communications with Bucer, any substantive alterations could be seen on the essentials of his stance? The question is especially important because in the Strasbourg period Calvin started the process of improving his theological system by publishing the 1539 *Institutes*. He began a series of life-long exegetical works with the *Romans Commentary* as a prototype, deepened his patristic studies, confronted the Anabaptist challenges,

83. "Bucers Wilderlegung des Berichtes von Engelbrecht," *BDS* 5:487–92. Cf. Hammann, *Entre la secte*, 320–21; *BDS* 7:98–107, 147, 159, 317. For Englebrecht, see Eells, *Martin Bucer*, 157–59; Tuininga, *Calvin's Political Theology*, 57. Bucer's identification of "the church" (Eph. 5:26–27), not with the church of the eschatological completion but with the local churches in history, seems bold. For a similar identification in the 1536 *Four Gospels Commentary*, confer n. 30 above.

84. *BDS* 17:156–96.

85. Cf. chapter 1, section 3.2, especially n. 175.

and engaged in the actual building of his own congregation. In particular, the question seems crucial not only for the issue of "Bucer's influence" but also for the formation of Calvin's post-Strasbourg ecclesiologies that we will examine in the next chapter.

(1) Consistent Biblicism

There are not many writings of Calvin's Strasbourg period directly dealing with the issues related to his understanding of the Bible. In the city where the Evangelicalism of Bucer, Luther, and Zwingli, Erasmian humanism, Anabaptism, and Roman Catholicism were intricately coexisting, however, it is unimaginable that Calvin would not have felt an urgent need to firmly establish his own biblicism. While his full-scale engagement in lecturing on the Gospel of John, Romans and other Pauline epistles at the Strasbourg Academy progressed, the theory and practice of Evangelical hermeneutics were his utmost concerns.

To this end, Schreiner notices Calvin's unique contribution in "the exegetical debates about certainty." According to Schreiner, the first-generation Reformers (Luther and Zwingli) and the second-generation Reformer (Calvin) faced the issue of "certitude" of Scripture in the context of both the certitude of the believer's subjective "salvation" and that of objective and exegetical "authority." As to the first issue of "salvation," Reformers such as Luther and Zwingli emphasized the crucial importance of the Holy Spirit illuminating the believer, and their arguments held that "the spiritual man judges all things" (1 Cor 2:15). When Reformers such as Luther and Zwingli faced the second issue of "authority," while their arguments were challenged by the Radical Reformers, using the same principle of the Spirit and the same passages used by the latter to challenge them, or when Luther and Zwingli themselves differed on the interpretation of the Eucharist, and the Catholic apologists, like Eck, challenged them with a choice of "scripture or the Church," their argument for certitude "tended to collapse in upon itself."[86]

While Calvin had inherited Luther's and Zwingli's basic arguments about the certitude of salvation and scriptural authority, Schreiner argues that Calvin freshly reinterpreted his predecessors' arguments. Concerning the subjective certitude of the Spirit, for example, he emphasized "the internal testimony

86. S. E. Schreiner, "'The Spiritual Man Judges All Things': Calvin and the Exegetical Debates about Certainty in the Reformation," in *Biblical Interpretation in the Era of the Reformation*, ed. R. A. Muller and J. L. Thompson (Grand Rapids: Eerdmans, 1996), 189–207.

of the Holy Spirit" who, as the inner teacher, taught the believers and sealed the certainty and confidence in them. He stressed the believers' "union with Christ," by which Christ "outside us" became Christ "inside us." And he insisted that the Spirit could never be separated from but was always anchored in Scripture. Concerning the objective certitude of scriptural authority, in a crucial text on this issue inserted in the 1543 edition of the *Institutes*, he avoided excessive spiritualism and did not even cite the above-mentioned passage ("the spiritual man judges"). As to the interpretation, he laid more emphasis on "the ultimate clarity of Scripture and the persuasive power of good exegesis."[87] Although Schreiner's analysis is not limited to Calvin's Strasbourg period, it provides a good indication of Calvin's search for exegetical certitude. In this respect, the most important text of this period seemed to be an introduction to the exposition of the Apostles' Creed in chapter 4 of the 1539 *Institutes*. We have already mentioned the introduction of the 1536 *Institutes* to the Apostles' Creed (chapter 2) in connection with the Caroli affair. But what was noticeable in the 1539 *Institutes* was the addition of three paragraphs to the introduction, two long and one short. Since the first paragraph dealt with the relation of faith and its certitude, the second with the relation of Scripture and the creed, and the third with the creed's authority in the church, all added paragraphs were related to the certitude issue.[88]

(i) At the beginning of the first added paragraph, Calvin attempted afresh a definition of faith in the context of God's word. He first made clear that his definition of faith made in the first *Institutes*—namely, faith as a "knowledge" (*notitia*), to know God's will that was brought about by "persuasion" (*persuasio*) based upon God's word—could be insufficient when faith encountered doubt and other problems. Then he redefined faith as subjective "cognition" (*cognitio*) in connection with the certitude issue.[89] He presented three theses for assuring its "certitude": faith as the "solid and sure cognition" concerning God's goodwill toward the believer; faith as based upon God's sure promise in

87. Schreiner, "The Spiritual Man," 207–15. Schreiner refers to the final *Institutes* (4.8–9), which is mostly the text added in the 1543 edition. In an examination of Lefèvre's hermeneutics, Oberman (*Forerunners of the Reformation*, 287, especially 295n19) refers to a Lefèvrian overtone in Calvin's teaching of the internal testimony of the Holy Spirit.

88. *CO* 1:455 (#4, De cuius certitudine . . .)–474 (# 35); 477 (# 1)–490 (# 19); 493 (# 23, Esti nomen hypostaseos . . .)–494 (# 24, ll. 1–5). Only the first addition generally survives until the final edition (*Institutio* 3.2.5–6; 3.2.14–40, etc.). Due to the fact that the creedal exposition was abandoned, the second addition only partially survived and the third addition seems to have disappeared.

89. *CO* 1:455. (*Institutio* 3.2.6: *OS* 4:14–15.)

Christ; and faith as shown by the Spirit to the believer's intellect and sealed in one's heart.[90] The three theses of "God's goodwill," "promise in Christ," and "the Spirit," clearly indicated Calvin's determination to base the certitude of faith upon the Trinitarian doctrine. Since the new definition formed the principal portion on faith in the final *Institutes* (*Institutio* 3.2), we will look more closely into these three theses.

The first thesis, the "solid and sure cognition" concerning God's goodwill, was Calvin's fundamental affirmation. Firstly, he affirmed "cognition" as a higher level of knowledge than human "understanding" (*comprehensio/intelligentia*) and corresponding to something more like "acknowledgment" (*agnitio*) in Paul and "wisdom" (*sapientia*) in John. Its "certitude" was to be assured not so much by "rational demonstration" but by "persuasion" based upon God's word as truth.[91] From this affirmation, he proceeded to discuss the problems of doubt, uncertainty, temptation, and the conflict of spirit and flesh that were challenging the certitude of faith. Calvin then introduced an important notion of faith as an "axis/hinge" (*cardo*) connecting what was "outside us" (*extra nos*) and what was "inside us" (*in nobis*). This antithesis had already been used by Luther in his defense of justification by faith against the Catholics and was also used by Calvin in the first *Institutes*. In connection with the second thesis, the "promise in Christ," in particular, Calvin applied this notion to the issue of faith and affirmed that faith was to know this promise "outside us" and not "in us," but by faith it became "in us."[92]

In connection with the third thesis of the Spirit, furthermore, he posed "the internal illumination of the Holy Spirit" as the last resort or absolute necessity to assure the certitude of faith. He acknowledged that human "knowledge" and "intellectual assent" learned from Scripture were subject to depravity and blindness and that "without the Spirit's illumination, the word of God could do nothing." But by "the Spirit's internal illumination," which Calvin called "paradox" or "God's mystery," he affirmed that the certitude that lay "outside us" came to be "inside us," namely, that the "goodwill, promise, and the work" of God, Christ, and the Spirit became what was "inside us," inscribed in our hearts, and assured as solid "cognition." Without doubt, he acknowledged the

90. *CO* 1:456: "si dicamus esse divinae erga nos benevolentiae firmam certamque cognitionem, quae gratuitae in Christo promissionis veritate fundata per spiritum sanctum et revelatur mentibus nostris et cordibus obsignatur." (*Institutio* 3.2.7: *OS* 4:16.)

91. *CO* 1:456–57. (*Institutio* 3.2.14: *OS* 4:24–25.)

92. *CO* 1:458: "Hic praecipuus fidei cardo vertitur, ne quas Dominus offert misericordiae promissiones extra nos tantum veras esse arbitermur, in nobis minime; sed ut potius eas intus complectendo nostras faciamus." (*Institutio* 3.2.16: *OS* 4:26.)

certitude arguments of Luther and Zwingli, such as the Holy Spirit as witness, the solidarity of God's word and the Spirit, and so forth. But he did not consider them final and rather consistently placed the certitude of faith upon the Triune God, what was "outside us," and focused on the internalizing process of the believers' faith becoming their conviction, what was "in us."[93]

(ii) The second added paragraph was inserted just before the core portion of the introduction to Calvin's exposition of the Apostles' Creed. It basically concerned the certitude of Christian doctrine in view of God's word. As we have noted in connection with the Caroli affair, this core portion explained the Trinity (without referring to the Nicene Creed) as "one *ousia*, three *hypostaseis*, that is, one substance, three subsistences in one substance." Concerning "the novelty of word" such as "homoousios," Calvin maintained his position: "would that they had been buried."[94]

In a new addition preceding the core portion, Calvin affirmed that, although its origin was uncertain, the Apostles' Creed was unique in the sense that it did not use any terms unsubstantiated in Scripture. While Luther favored the Creed for the same reason, for Calvin it became the general guideline for all later doctrinal statements of the church and he felt the need to reiterate it here. Then, he added two preliminary remarks concerning the exposition of the Creed.

The first remark concerned the need to interpret the Creed in terms of a perceptive dichotomy of "the visible and the invisible," or "history and the spiritual world." In other words, just like biblical hermeneutics, spiritual and doctrinal teachings were to be deduced from the creedal text's affirmation of Christ's birth, death, resurrection, and ascension.

The second remark concerned the Creed's structure, regarding a distinction between the first three articles (God, Christ, the Holy Spirit) and the fourth article (the church . . . the life everlasting). Calvin called the first three articles a "mystery on which our entire redemption depends" and the fourth article "things in which our salvation is situated." This seemed to indicate his perception of the total structure of theology. In his exposition of the divine "mystery," he stressed the general principle that the "understanding and description" of the mystery should not go beyond "the boundary of God's word."[95] From this principle, the new addition discussed the exegetical problems concerning the first three articles, especially those of Christ's and the Spirit's divinity. As an illustration, for example, Calvin discussed the so-called "eternal generation of

93. *CO* 1:468. (*Institutio* 3.2.33: *OS* 4:44.) Cf. Schreiner, "The Spiritual Man," 207–14.

94. Cf. chapter 2, section 3.1 (Caroli affair), especially n. 144.

95. *CO* 1:479–80; *CO* 1:480.

Christ" theory supported by the church fathers whom he called the "ancient folks" (*veteres*). Without overtly rejecting the theory, he questioned its validity by citing some key biblical testimonies, pointed out subsequent problems that it caused in the church, and expounded on the right relation of God the Father with Christ the Son from Scripture.[96] All in all, he intended to demonstrate his exegetical posture that Christian doctrines should be constructed and interpreted on the basis of and within the boundary of God's word. In this new addition, accordingly, he discussed the issue by consistently citing first Old Testament and then New Testament passages and by referring to neither the Ancient Creeds nor the church fathers.[97]

(iii) The third added short paragraph was inserted just after the core portion, more precisely after Calvin's discussions on terms of the Ancient Creeds not found in Scripture. It mainly concerned his apology about the Caroli affair. From the context of his biblicism, there were two noticeable points. They both affirmed his exegetical posture that the Ancient Creeds and the church fathers should be accepted on the basis of Scripture and its right interpretations. As to the first point, Calvin questioned some Latin fathers who translated the Greek term *hypostasis* as "essence" instead of "person," and who interpreted the "reflection" of God's glory (Heb 1:3) as "essence." Arguing that the essence of God ought to be simple and undivided, he rejected this interpretation as absurd and argued the "reflection" to be referring to the Son's "subsistence" rather than the "essence" of God.[98] As to the second point, he examined the "homoousios" of the Nicene Creed. He argued that the Greek term was effective in refuting the Arian heresy, yet it was usually translated into (the same) "substance," which caused some problems in the West. As an example, he referred to Hilary of Poitiers, an anti-Arian champion, who constantly attributed to each of the Father, the Son, and the Spirit "substance" and even called them "three substances" of the only God. Although he criticized this position in Hilary's earlier work as untenable, he credited Hilary's later work that considered a simpler formula of the faith in the Father, the Son, and the Spirit in the Apostles' Creed better fitting the scriptural testimonies.[99]

96. *CO* 1:482–83. Here Calvin examines several biblical texts (Isa 53:8, Ps 110:23, 1 Cor 10:8, etc.) that some church fathers used for the theory of the Son's eternal generation, but he does not identify the fathers. Since this theory is incorporated in the Nicene-Constantinopolitan Creed, Calvin's challenge seems very bold and can be a reason for his refusal to subscribe to the creed as Caroli requested.

97. *CO* 1:483–89. (*Institutio* 1.13.9–15: *OS* 3:119–29.)

98. *CO* 1:493–94. Cf. *Institutio* 1.13.2: *OS* 3:110.

99. *CO* 1:494. Cf. *Institutio* 1.13.5: *OS* 3:114. Cf. chapter 2, n. 145. It is evident here that

We have examined the three paragraphs and their focus on the certitude issue of faith and doctrine. Although it is not certain whether or not the new paragraphs reflect Calvin's conscious awareness of Bucer's and Capito's biblicism, which is not as strict as his, certainly they show his unique position of "consistent biblicism" and its new emphasis on the certitude issue.

(2) Practical Activism

As far as Calvin's Strasbourg period was concerned, there seemed to be no materials that indicated any change in his position seen in *Two Epistles.* Historically, *Two Epistles* caused sharp reactions both inside and outside of France. In response to this, there were a few noteworthy materials in this period that indicated his efforts to maintain his strict position of practical activism, and to defensively make his apology for what he called "our excessive severity." Focusing on his practical activism, we will briefly survey three points in the following pages.

(i) The first point concerned Calvin's French work, *Small Tract, Showing What the Faithful Living among the Papists Should Do.* The editors of both the *Calvini Opera* and the *Bibliotheca Calviniana* consider the *Small Tract* a free French translation of the first epistle of *Two Epistles* as well as Calvin's first French treatise specifically addressed to his homeland. Although it was published in 1543 in Geneva, he appended an unaddressed letter dated September 12, 1540. From this it could be assumed that Calvin authored the *Small Tract* in Strasbourg, but for some unknown reason postponed its publication, and finally published it after his return to Geneva in the midst of the Nicodemite controversy. Since it carried on the first epistle's basic tone and major points, it could be viewed either as a free "translation" or as a new "adaptation" to a different context with freely edited contents, omitting all references suggesting Duchemin, and adding new apologetic insight. In either case, however, it retained the first epistle's posture of practical activism, and it became the first of Calvin's anti-Nicodemite tracts.[100]

Calvin makes a clear demarcation between the Apostles' Creed and the later Nicene and other creeds.

100. *Petit traicté, monstrant que doit faire un fidele entre les papists*: *CO* 6:537–88. Cf. *CO* 6, "Prolegomena," xxx; *BC* 43/6:133; Droz, *Chemins de l'hérésie*, 42–45; Millet, *Calvin et la dynamique*, 809–20. Droz takes the "adaptation" view and Millet the "translation" view. Even if we accept Calvin's authorship of the tract as the *BC* assumes, the question of when and where he composed it is considered unsettled. Although Millet considers its composition as done after Calvin's return to Geneva in 1541, we assume a possibility of its Strasbourg composition. For our further remarks on the tract, cf. chapter 4, section 1.2.

As to the *Small Tract*'s contents, since it overlaps with the first epistle's contents that we have already examined, we will not repeat them but mention only a few characteristics. Firstly, unlike the first epistle that was addressed to a lay leader (Duchemin) in the church, the *Small Tract* was directed to believers in general, and a noticeable characteristic was that Calvin's discussion was simple, direct, explanatory, and reflected the urgency of the oppressed situation of believers in the church and in society. Secondly, as the *Small Tract*'s apologetic posture shifted from the narrow focus on the moderate evangelical reformists to a general readership, its arguments became more didactic and persuasive. Thirdly, Calvin's two remarks placed at the tract's end were noteworthy. The first concerned a criticism against him, that his advice given outside France was nothing but empty verbiage of a person who had no understanding of those who had been suffering in France. Addressing this, his straightforward advice recognized the possible cases of martyrdom. Yet he added a self-criticism, in a comparison with the lives of these martyrs, "we [the exiled French?] . . . have sufficient information, and by hearing it we are supposed to be on fire, but are colder than ice."[101] In considering the current situation of France as that of "Egypt or Babylon," the second remark asserted that "the premier [choice] will be exiting, if it is possible." As we recall Calvin's final advice in the first epistle suggesting the "fleeing" from the Mass and other Catholic ceremonies, his choice of exile from France reflected a new phase of his activism.[102]

The letter appended to the *Small Tract* revealed Calvin's interesting insight during his Strasbourg period. After having briefly summarized the main contents of the *Small Tract*, he presented a sharper apology for his advice as well as a new way to look at the condition of the church in France. Here, Calvin took up two issues. The one, when a believer was questioning the Mass and other ceremonies, how could he keep "the communion of the church" in which he was baptized? The other, whether the believer in "his private authority" could separate himself from the church? Behind these questions, Calvin suspected criticism that his advice was advocating a schism in the church. Responding to this criticism, he defined "the Catholic church" (*l'Eglise catholique*) as the congregation consisting of God's elect, existing throughout both the Old and

101. *CO* 6:574.

102. *CO* 6:576. The shift from the "fleeing" to the "exile" is emphasized by Millet (*Calvin et la dynamique*, 810) and D. F. Wright ("Why Was Calvin So Severe a Critic of Nicodemism?," in *Calvinus Evangelii Propugnator*, ed. D. F. Wright, A. N. S. Lane, and J. Balserak [Grand Rapids: Calvin Studies Society, 2006], 84–85).

New Testament periods, and united in baptism. He affirmed that the "separation" the Evangelicals were questioning did not concern this "Catholic church" but was limited to "the form of the church" (*forme d'eglise*). He then stressed that the Evangelicals' attack was directed to the papal church as a "form" of the church. Lastly, he mentioned the issue of the Mass (as we have seen in Bucer's *Theological Advice*), writing that "the Mass originated in the Eucharist as the dominical institution." He criticized the papal Mass that profaned and destroyed the Eucharist and turned it into "a pure abomination."[103] Calvin's apology as a whole pointed to the existence of fresh criticisms, partly caused by *Two Epistles*, which he encountered in his Strasbourg period.

(ii) The second point concerned Calvin's actions as the first pastor of the refugee congregation in Strasbourg. In his letters to Farel in March and May 1540, he reported that he had announced to the congregation a week prior to the celebration of the Lord's Supper that those wishing to participate should present themselves to the pastor and that it had so transpired. If we assume that this meeting functioned as the pastoral precommunion examination of the communicants, it would be difficult to determine his intention and its nature and implication. Surprisingly, very little information remained in either the city or church records as Calvin's congregation was still in its formative stage. Unlike the city parishes controlled by the 1534 *Ecclesiastical Ordinances*, the unorganized congregation was seemingly not under the direct control of the magistracy or a churchwarden, and a certain degree of freedom was left to the pastor's discretion. If Calvin considered his action a part of church discipline, it was done on his own authority and discretion as a temporary measure rather than according to the established disciplinary rules and system. Now, when he announced his intended action of pastoral examination, he told the congregation that it was not meant to be a reintroduction of the Catholic sacrament of confession to the priests, but rather for education of the faithful. He said that it was necessary for the coexistence of those in the congregation who understood the proper meaning of the Lord's Supper and those who did not, and that the expectant communicants should follow the action as their exercise of Christian freedom.[104] As far as the interpretations of Calvin's actions are concerned, however, the picture is not unanimous. Due to the paucity of reliable information, many researchers treat it casually. For example, Gordon writes that "now he [Calvin] was also able to implement the church discipline he had proposed in Geneva: in the French Church, admission to communion

103. *CO* 6:582–84.

104. *CO* 11, Ep. 214, 31; Ep. 218, 41. Cf. Herminjard, *Correspondance*, 6:200; 6:224.

was only for those who presented themselves to the ministers for examination." Some researchers, just as we have presented above, go as far as Calvin's letters imply. Others go further and affirm the unique case of Calvin's pastoral examination independent of the Strasbourg system.[105]

(iii) The third point concerned the significance of this pastoral examination for Calvin's practical activism. Theoretically, pastoral examination as a part of church discipline was not strange in light of both Bucer's disciplinary idea partly fulfilled in the 1534 *Ecclesiastical Ordinances* in Strasbourg or Farel's and Calvin's effort to establish discipline in the 1537 *Articles* in Geneva. However, the only unprecedented element was, though as an emergency measure, that he seemed to exercise the examination at his own discretion. Though his sources were silent on this point, we could see a theoretical grounding for this in both Bucer and Calvin. In this period around 1540, as we have noted above, a clear shift was taking place in Bucer's notion of church ministry and discipline. As to the relation of a minister to his congregation, the shift was seen from the early Bucer's emphasis on the Holy Spirit and its collateral emphasis on congregational polity and discipline to the later Bucer's emphasis on the minister to whom Christ entrusted to exercise the power of the keys in preaching, the sacraments, and church discipline.[106] Earlier in the 1527 Gospel commentary on Matthew, he interpreted the church's foundation, "rock" (16:18), as faith of believers, "the power of the keys" (16:9) as the Holy Spirit, and its exercise by "all who hold fast God's Spirit and word." On "tell it to the church" (18:17) in the disciplinary passage, furthermore, he emphasized the mutual discipline of

105. Gordon, *Calvin*, 86; Ganoczy, *Young Calvin*, 127; Parker, *John Calvin*, 68; Wendel, *Calvin*, 60–61; van't Spijker, *The Ecclesiastical Offices*, 341–43. Ganoczy and Parker go as far as Calvin's letters imply, and Ganoczy emphasizes the case's independent nature from the Strasbourg disciplinary system. Both Wendel and van't Spijker see the case in the light of the "Bucer's influence" theory. Wendel considers Calvin's disciplinary action within the context of the 1534 *Strasbourg Ecclesiastical Ordinances* and goes a step further in saying that Calvin implemented Bucer's and Zell's idea in the French congregation. Van't Spijker affirms the case as an example of "mutual influence" between Bucer and Calvin and uses W. Koehler's classical study (*Züricher Ehegericht und Genfer Konsistorium* [Leipzig: Heinsius Nachfolger, 1932/42], 2, 525n100) to the extent that Calvin's case was the exercise of "a church court" composed of Calvin and 12 elders chosen by the congregation. The notion of "a church court" was seemingly not found in Calvin's materials of this period. For the problem of Koeler's use of the Genevan consistorial documents, furthermore, see R. M. Kingdon, "Calvin and the Establishment of Consistory Discipline in Geneva: The Institution and the Men Who Directed It," in *The Reformation: Critical Concepts in Historical Studies*, ed. A. Pettegree (London and New York: Routledge, 2004), 3:67.

106. Wendel, *L'Église*, 192–98; van't Spijker, *The Ecclesiastical Offices*, 127–36.

believers.[107] In the 1536 Gospel commentary, however, he interpreted the same text in the context of the church as the manifestation of Christ's kingdom. Accordingly, the "rock" was interpreted as the Gospel of Christ, and "the power of the keys" as "the ministry and power to govern God's church which is Christ's Kingdom." Making his characteristic distinction between "power" and "authority," furthermore, as to the "power" the whole congregation was to exercise the keys, and as to the "authority" the keys were entrusted to the ministerial order of the "elders and bishops."[108] From this standpoint, Bucer and other church leaders had kept pressing the magistracy for the strict implementation of church discipline. As we have seen above, his *Concerning True Pastoral Care* basically considered discipline either as "pastoral care" or as the joint exercise of the ministers and congregation, independent of magisterial control.[109]

On Calvin's side, the later Bucer's general emphasis on ministerial order could be observed in this period. In connection with the current issue of pastoral examination, however, Calvin's early Genevan catechetical work, the *Instruction* (1537), seemed to provide some background information. As we have noted in chapter 2, his first *Institutes*, written in the context of the Evangelical antithesis to Catholicism, placed the ministerial order in opposition to the Catholic ministerial monopoly and emphasized its ultimate foundation on the power of God's word. Although the *Institutes* affirmed that ministers could exercise the word's power, the authority or dignity given to them was not to "themselves . . . but to the word."[110] Interestingly, the *Instruction* written for the Evangelical church of Geneva contained the section "Of Pastors of the Church and Their Power," and there the indispensability of the work of ministers for the church was stressed. Concerning their ministry in church discipline, for example, it stated "the society of the church, which without a ministry of this sort, can in no way stand." Especially noticeable in connection with the issue of ministerial examination was a description of the pastoral duty "to instruct the people publicly and privately in pure doctrine, to administer the sacraments and to teach them by the best example concerning holiness." In other words, the pastoral ministry was the exercise of the word's power in the comprehensive ecclesial arena of God's word, the sacraments, and disci-

107. *Enarrationum in Evangelia in Matthaei*, . . . , 1, 179r–79v, 214r–15v. Cf. Burnett, *The Yoke*, 37–38.

108. *In Sacra Quatuor Evangelia, Enarrationes*, 353–54. Cf. van't Spijker, *The Ecclesiastical Offices*, 130–32; Burnett, *The Yoke*, 90–92.

109. *BDS* 7:90, 188, 241. Cf. Wendel, *L'Église*, 160–61; van't Spijker, *The Ecclesiastical Offices*, 186–87.

110. *OS* 1:234–35. (Battles, trans., *Institution*, 254.)

pline.[111] Relying on this reasoning, we assume, Calvin on his own authority practiced pastoral examination in the unorganized French congregation as a temporary measure.

3. France, Geneva, and the Holy Roman Empire

In his Strasbourg period, Calvin's official title was Pastor of the French congregation. Several factors had added a new vista to his activities beyond Strasbourg: his church shared the same brand of Evangelicalism with its overlord, the free imperial city-state of Strasbourg; it was located in the outpost city of the Schmalkald League, especially as a strategic point of the League's French strategy; and it was basically a congregation of refugees and exiles from France and its pastor was likewise an exile. In fact, the congregation could be an exemplar of the "foreigner churches" that were increasing in number in Europe and were organized by the refugees and exiles from such countries as France, Italy, and Spain, where anti-Evangelical policies were enforced in the 1540s.[112] In terms of his ecclesiology, his newly acquired vision for Europe inherited "the practice of his Catholic ecclesiology" surveyed in chapter 2 and shared with Bucer the theme of the Reformation's "explicit expansion." From this perspective, we will focus on his activities during this period under three headings: Calvin's role as pastor of the French congregation; letters from and to Du Tillet and Calvin's *Reply to Sadoleto* in the historical context of both the French Reformation and the Genevan Reformation; and his participation in the religious unification colloquies in Germany.

(1) Pastor of the French Congregation

Early in the chapter we described Calvin's personal life in this period as "the most peaceful and satisfactory time in his entire life." Could this description apply to his ministry of the congregation as well as to its members? This period witnessed the rapid increase of executions in France and the arrival of refugees and exiles from France mainly due to the Edict of Fontainebleau (1539) that set a new stage in France's anti-Evangelical policy. The Edict moved heresy

111. *COR* IV-2:103: *OS* 1:413–14. Cf. van't Spijker, *The Ecclesiastical Offices*, 342–43. For English translation, Hesselink's text (*Calvin's First Catechism*, 35–36) is used.

112. A. Duke, "Perspectives on International Calvinism," in *Calvinism in Europe, 1540–1620*, ed. A. Pettegree, A. Duke, and G. Lewis (Cambridge: Cambridge University Press, 1994), 3–6, esp. 5n17.

trials from church courts to the exclusive jurisdiction of the Paris and other provincial Parlements, simplified the juridical process of the trials for swifter judgments, and its Article 8 paved the way for the trials of Evangelicals on charges of treason and staging riots. Accordingly, as the Edict was said to open a new page in the history of the French Reformation, in one estimate, the size of Calvin's congregation in Strasbourg reached four to five hundred.[113]

As the above-mentioned *Small Tract*, probably written in this period, compared the Evangelicals in France with the people of Israel to whom true worship was not permitted during the slavery of Egypt or Babylon, the Strasbourg congregation was seen as the refugee people sojourning in the Sinai. As we have seen, chapter 1 considered Calvin's prefaces to Olivétan's French Bible as his first written confession of faith after his "sudden conversion." In his French preface, he described God as leading the Exodus people to the Promised Land, writing as "he [God] had accompanied them night and day in their flight, just being like a refugee."[114] The triangular relation of refugee God, refugee congregation, and its pastor who was himself an exile had characterized Calvin's ministry in an Exodus congregation. To this congregation he was to proclaim God's word, teach pure doctrines, administer the sacraments, and exercise discipline. In the beginning of this study, we defined him as "a French Reformer." In the Strasbourg congregation he started a life truly fitting to this designation. In the Strasbourg Academy, which was to become the second theological center after Wittenberg, Calvin started to teach the New Testament to those from France and Italy, as well as Germany. One epistolary witness expressed high expectations for Calvin's contributions to the audience's future reformatory work in their homelands.[115] Concerning his French edition (1541) of the 1539 *Institutes*, furthermore, although it was published in Geneva immediately after his return to the city, it was mostly prepared in Strasbourg and was to be the first piece of substantive and Evangelical French theological literature. Besides a French preface translated from the original Latin preface

113. Cf. W. Monter, *Judging the French Reformation: Heresy Trials by Sixteenth-Century Parlements* (Cambridge, MA: Harvard University Press, 1999), 85–87; Ganoczy, *Calvin*, 50–51; Parker, *John Calvin*, 68. Any estimate of the size of the French congregation has to be guesswork. Here we choose Parker's 400–500 over Ganoczy's 1,500.

114. *CO* 9:795. Cf. ch. 1, n. 100. Oberman ("Initia Calvini," 146–47) considers this passage a key to unlocking Calvin's formative period (*initia Calvini*) and interprets it "at the center of the *initia* stands the never forgotten experience of the abyss as the deadly flight *from* God and the growing insight in the lifegiving refuge *with* God." (Italics original.)

115. *CO* 11:106–13, esp. 108. Cf. C. Ocker, "Calvin in Germany," in *Politics and Reformations: Histories and Reformations*, ed. C. Ocker et al. (Leiden: Brill, 2007), 329–30.

of the 1539 *Institutes*, he affixed another short piece, "Outline of Book," in which he expressed his hope of reaping some Evangelical fruit in "our French nation." This first edition of the French *Institutes* contributed to showing a clear unifying direction in the hitherto unorganized French Reformation, to spreading his teachings, and to organizing underground activities, such as Bible studies and evangelical meetings.[116]

(2) The Du Tillet Letter and Reply to Sadoleto

Among many religious issues of the day, a twofold question was most pressing: "Is the Roman Catholic Church, which is in need of reform, a Christian church?" and "Does the Reformation inevitably cause a schism?" Calvin's *Two Epistles* boldly responded to this issue, and as a result, his radicalism was widely known. Surely there were responses both positive and negative, but the negative reactions were perhaps more than what he had expected. As we have seen, Bucer's *Theological Advice* was certainly an example, but prior to that there were two critiques of 1538 and 1539 against Calvin's Evangelicalism and his position on this issue. The first was a French letter addressed to Calvin by Du Tillet. Du Tillet had been with Calvin for three years from their exile in Basel to engagement in Geneva, but had exited from the Genevan reform in August 1537 and returned to France via Bucer's Strasbourg by the end of the year. After Du Tillet's initial letter to Calvin in which he disclosed his defection and resettlement in France, Calvin and Du Tillet exchanged six French letters all written in 1538. To be precise, Du Tillet's initial letter was dated March 10. It was said to have never reached Calvin, who was in transition from his Genevan expulsion to his move to Basel. Unlike letters exchanged afterward between Calvin and Du Tillet, the initial letter most clearly expressed Du Tillet's reasons for his exit as well as his friendly yet severe criticism of Calvin's position on this issue. The second was a famous Latin epistle of Cardinal Jacopo Sadoleto, Bishop of Carpentras. The epistle (Carpentras, April 15, 1539) was addressed to the Evangelical city of Geneva that expelled Farel and Calvin and urged the city to return to the Roman Catholic Church. To this, Calvin responded with his open *Reply to Sadoleto* (Strasbourg, September 1539) and he published it along with Sadoleto's epistle in Strasbourg.[117]

116. *Institution de la Religion Chrestienne*, 1541: BC 41/3, ed. J. Pannier (Paris: Société d'Édition "Les Belles Lettres," 1961), vol. 1, "Argument du livre," 4. Cf. Monter, *Judging the French Reformation*, 112.

117. Cf. G. H. Tavard, "Calvin and the Nicodemites," in *John Calvin and Roman Catholi-*

The Du Tillet Letter and the Sadoleto Epistle

(i) There were a few noticeable similarities between the letter and the epistle. One was the humanist notion of distinguishing the Catholic church from the Roman Catholic Church or, especially in Du Tillet's letter, a Gallican notion of distinguishing the French Church from the Roman Church and the Roman Curia. As to the Du Tillet letter, he was assumed to have returned to the moderate evangelical humanist group represented by Lefèvre and Roussel. His letter was an apology for "the churches" (*les eglises*) in France that Calvin did not consider to be Christian churches. Du Tillet did not attempt to defend the Roman Church. Although the Sadoleto epistle used his official title, "Cardinal of the Holy Roman Church," and referred to the pope as "the Supreme Pontiff" in its beginning, in its main portion he also refrained from defending the Roman Curia. Instead, he used the term the "catholic church" (*catholica ecclesia*, in minuscules), of which Farel and Calvin were said to be destroyers and schismatics and from which the Genevan Church had strayed. In reality, however, it was assumed that the epistle was not a personal letter from the Bishop of Carpentras but was representing a portion of the French Church establishment. By using the term "catholic church" ambiguously, the epistle officially urged the Genevan Church to return to the Roman Catholic Church.[118] Another similarity was that both the letter and the epistle spared no effort to defend the current Catholic ceremonies, especially the Mass, which the Evangelicals had attacked as the object of urgent reform. In the case of the Du Tillet letter, it acknowledged these ceremonies as "abuses, errors, corrup-

---

cism: Critique and Engagement, Then and Now, ed. R. C. Zachman (Grand Rapids: Baker Academic, 2008), 62–69. The *Opera Calvini*, vol. 10, collects 6 letters, and the *COR* VI-1 covers four of them exchanged between Calvin and Du Tillet both using pseudonyms. Tavard, a noted Catholic theologian and the author of *Holy Writ or Holy Church: The Crisis of the Protestant Reformation* (1959), provides a good analysis of the letters exchanged between Du Tillet and Calvin. Focusing on Du Tillet (formerly a canon of Angoulême, a priest of Claix), Tavard examines Du Tillet's return to the Catholic Church and his personal criticism of Calvin's radicalism. Here we examine Du Tillet's first letter (*CO* 10b:163–78: *COR* VI-1:340–59). For Sadoleto's epistle and Calvin's reply, we use the texts of the *Opera Selecta* (*OS* 1:441–56; 457–89).

118. *OS* 1:441. Cf. van't Spijker, *Calvin*, 63; G. Berthoud, *Antoine Marcourt* (Geneva: Droz, 1973), 58n137; R. M. Douglas, "Sadoleto, Jacopo," *OER* 3:467–68. Van't Spijker follows the traditional view that Sadoleto's epistle was written on behalf of the episcopal conference of Lyon. Berthoud considers this view held since Herminjard (*Correspondance*, 5:266) historically untenable, yet he suggests the possibility of the epistle being acknowledged by the prominent leaders of the French Church.

tion, ignorance, and imperfection," but, "nonetheless," it defended the French Church as a true Christian church. In the case of the Sadoleto epistle, it consistently kept the irenic posture of letting the Evangelical criticism on the Mass and other ceremonies slide as being simply an opinion or a judgment on matters of religion and its abuses.[119]

(ii) In a strict sense, the main thrust of the Du Tillet letter was an apology for the moderate humanist evangelicals and their churches, which were attacked by Calvin's *Two Epistles*, and presented an optimistic prospect of the reform efforts of their churches in the French Church. From this limited perspective, it responded to Calvin's accusation of their churches as "being cursed" and at the same time defended Du Tillet's own move to return to their group. Unlike the Sadoleto epistle, it kept a thoroughly evangelical posture and argued that "their churches," though in need of reform because of their abuses and errors, should be regarded as Christian churches since there were many true Christians in them. Thus, the title of the church had not been taken away from them. On the other hand, it argued, they had no choice but to call Calvin "a schismatic" since he encouraged the faithful to "separate" from their churches. Over against Calvin's comparison of "their churches" with the Old Testament people under the corrupted kings Jeroboam and Ahab, furthermore, it appealed to Calvin's own notion of the church's two marks and affirmed that "their churches" had maintained "the true ministry" of God's word and the "effect of baptism." It concluded that "if there has been and now is the true ministry of God in these churches, it follows that they must be true churches of God."[120] Using the biblical notions of the church as "the pillar of the truth" (1 Tim 3:15) and based on "the free grace of God's election," Du Tillet urged Calvin to accept them as the true churches. He himself concluded that he could not judge and reject them "against his own conscience." The letter as a whole was an eloquent apology for moderate evangelicals as well as an optimistic and confident evaluation of their reformatory efforts in the French Church. Its general tone of optimism would resound later in a more elaborate form in Bucer's *Theological Advice*.[121]

119. *COR* VI-1:349–41, 353, 355–56. (*CO* 10b:169–71, 173, 175); *OS* 1:449.

120. *COR* VI-1:346–49, esp. 348 (*CO* 10b:166–68, 171, esp. 168). Although Tavard's article, "Calvin and the Nicodemites" (cf. n. 117 above), weighs Du Tillet's third letter (December 1) that focused on Calvin's lack of episcopal ordination and the crucial importance of the Catholic Church's tradition, we choose his first letter for our examination.

121. *COR* VI-1:350–51, esp. 353 (*CO* 10b:170–71, esp. 173): "De ma part ie ne scaurois ainsi iuger de ces eglises que contre ma conscience." Concerning Bucer's possible advice to Du Tillet, Calvin's letter to Du Tillet (*COR* VI-1:314; *CO* 10b:148) ponders the possibility that

(iii) In clear contrast to the evangelical tone of the Du Tillet letter, the Sadoleto epistle presumptuously demonstrated the Catholic Church's authority to the city and the church of Geneva. It brought Geneva to God's judgment seat and presented it with an either-or choice. It urged the church which had gone astray to return to the bosom of "Mother Church" (*mater ecclesia*). Given this aim, the epistle assumedly used its rhetorical technique to cause a dramatic effect. As far as its apologetic significance was concerned, it represented the same anti-Evangelical posture seen in Budé's *Transition to Christianity*, with fresh additions such as the either-or choice and the dramatic framework. First, the epistle attributed the causes by which Geneva had gone astray to those "advocates of new things," namely, Farel and Calvin. It determined that they sought after "new authority and dignity." And the epistle accused the Evangelicals of attacking "Mother Church" by spreading their own scriptural interpretations, causing controversies, and destroying the Catholic Church's unity and the "consensus and achievement" that had been accepted by all the Catholic churches.[122] After having shown the pathway for Geneva to return to the Catholic Church, it offered three either-or choices: either the Catholic Church that had lasted for 1,500 years, or the church of "cunning fellows" that had only existed in the last 25 years; either the observance of the Catholic Church's constitutions or the agreement with those rebellious and novel men; and finally, the choice before God's judgment seat of either the confession of the penitent who had been nurtured by the Catholic Church, or the confession of the rebellious against the Catholic Church. Concerning the third choice, interestingly, Sadoleto composed examples of the confessions of both the penitent and the rebellious which were long and dramatically contrasted the conservative Catholic and Evangelical positions. Concerning the first choice, he offered a brief definition of the Catholic Church that was characterized by historical catholicity, unity and consensus in Christ, and the presence of the Holy Spirit. And he affirmed that "there should exist no discord" in the Catholic Church. In this definition, which was noticeably like that of Erasmus, there were references neither to the Catholic Church hierarchy nor to the Evangelical marks of God's word and the sacraments.[123]

"certain persons" might have advised him, though unintentionally, to take his stand and action. The editors of both texts (*COR* VI-1:314n14; *CO* 10b:148n7) consider that Calvin had "Bucer and Capito" in mind. On this point, without naming Bucer and Capito, Du Tillet's reply (*COR* VI:347; *CO* 10b:166) acknowledged many points of agreement with them, but denied that their advice was responsible for his actions.

122. *OS* 1:442–44.

123. *OS* 1:450–53. Cf. Ganoczy, *Young Calvin*, 279–82; G. Mannion, "Calvin and the

Calvin's Reply to Sadoleto

This famous open epistle of Calvin has received many positive evaluations, starting with the contemporary and unexpected praise of Luther, continuing to the modern period. Although such evaluations as "a superb apology for Evangelical Christianity," "the best of the rhetorical tradition," and so forth, may have been appropriate, they do not necessarily pinpoint exactly what he had intended. It could be either interpreted widely as an apology for the catholic and nonsectarian character of Evangelicalism, or narrowly as a defense of the Genevan Reformation and his and Farel's involvement in the reform. As to its addressee, Sadoleto, undoubtedly, it was a personal epistle. But can this characterization sufficiently interpret it? What was Calvin's real intention and with whom was he dialoguing? In the following pages, we will analyze Calvin's *Reply* under three headings: its nature and intended addressees; the main theme of the Catholic Church; and another theme, the reform of the French Church.

(i) As we have mentioned Sadoleto in connection with the dedicatory epistle to King Francis I, Calvin had known that Sadoleto's real loyalty was with the Roman Curia. Why then did he praise highly Sadoleto's humanist achievements in the opening of the *Reply*? In its closing words to Sadoleto, why did he mention "you or all the rest" (*tu ac reliqui omnes*), as if he were addressing Sadoleto and his group, and expect that their efforts were for what the Catholic reformists and humanists were most concerned, namely, the unity of the church? Of course, he could assume the capacity in which Sadoleto was acting, as Sadoleto was a high prelate of the Roman Catholic Church who had closely served two popes, was sent to the commission which produced the memorial reformist document, *Consilium de Emendanda Ecclesia* (1537), and was recently promoted to a cardinal. But this was not likely the capacity in which Sadoleto

Church: Trajectories for Ecumenical Engagement Today—Volume Introduction," in *Ecclesiological Investigations, Volume 10: John Calvin's Ecclesiology*, ed. G. Mannion (London and New York: T&T Clark, 2011), 1–12, esp. 2; J. O. Olin, ed., *A Reformation Debate: Sadoleto's Letter to the Genevans and Calvin's Reply* (New York: Harper, 1966), 19–24. Ganoczy's evaluation of the Sadoleto epistle mentions two interesting points: Sadoleto's definition of the "Catholic Church" was substandard even in view of contemporary Catholic theology; on the issue of schism, Sadoleto gravely misjudged Calvin's position. Seeing the Sadoleto-Calvin exchange as "the proto-ecumenical debate," Mannion assumes "the unity of the Christian church" to be the debate's core issue, which both Sadoleto and Calvin accurately understood as such. As the title ("A Reformation Debate") indicates, Olin views the Sadoleto-Calvin debate from the traditional perspective of the two great Reformation issues, the authority of the church or God's word and the doctrine of justification. This study considers the unity of the Catholic Church with its collateral issues of heresy and schism as the debate's cardinal focus.

sent his epistle to Geneva and which Calvin assumed in his reply. Is it possible to assume that he was responding to Sadoleto as representing a certain group or groups in France? One such group could be the bishops conference of Southern France that met in 1538 in Lyon and, with the ousted bishop of Geneva participating, discussed the possibility of restoring Catholicism in Geneva. Another could be a group of prelates in the French Church establishment who were definitely not conservative papists, but reform-minded, humanist-oriented, and perhaps close to the king or Marguerite of Navarre. This group might not be open to the Evangelicalism of Luther or Zwingli, but was interested in humanist reform within the framework of the current church structure in France.[124]

Another possible group could be the one that had been close to both Farel and Calvin and that the Sadoleto epistle personally attacked in connection with the Genevan Reformation. More precisely, this was the moderate reformist group more narrowly associated with the Meaux reform and represented by Lefèvre and Roussel, the group from which both Farel and Calvin extricated themselves and that Calvin's *Two Epistles* called the "mediators." As mentioned above in connection with the Du Tillet letter, this group thought that its members were personally attacked and their church reform totally rejected by Calvin. In addition, there were at least two factors that might suggest the possibility of this group: the one, Calvin's reply contained his apology that clearly recognized the moderate reformists' criticism; the other, very unusually, contained many references to his own person and personal history. For example, at the beginning of the letter he said, "I would not talk freely about myself." But at the end, in response to Sadoleto's dramatic challenge, before God he made one of his most vivid confessions of sin, faith, and conversion, specifically of the conversion from what we have described in chapter 1 as the "moderate evangelical humanist" position to the "radical evangelical humanist" position. If our assumptions above are correct, the *Reply to Sadoleto* was not only an apology for Evangelicalism as the undeniable European force of church reform but also a personal appeal to those who were represented by

124. *OS* 1:457, 489. Olin (*A Reformation Debate*, 12) refers to the possibility of the conference commissioning Sadoleto to write to Geneva. A. Noblesse-Rocher's article, "Jacques Sadolet (1477 to 1547): The Enemy of the Strasbourg Years," in *John Calvin: The Strasbourg Years (1538–1541)*, ed. M. Arnold, 158–68, examines the Sadoleto-Calvin exchange in its historical background of the reform commission of Contarini, which produced *Concilium Emendanda Ecclesia*. It also mentions the Lyon episcopal conference as "the supposed sponsor" of the Sadoleto epistle.

Sadoleto and whom Calvin still expected to be the agents of reform for the Church of France.[125]

The *Reply to Sadoleto* was a comprehensive treatise in which Calvin responded to major reformatory issues of the day as well as particular Genevan issues, both raised by Sadoleto. Since the apologetic stance Calvin exhibited in it was basically the same as in the first *Institutes* and *Two Epistles*, we will neither survey its outline nor analyze his apology against Sadoleto's major arguments. Keeping in mind the above-mentioned real intention of the reply and his intended addressees, whom Sadoleto was representing, we will mainly focus on some new themes in his apologetics. The first will be the general theme of the Catholic church (the main theme of the Sadoleto epistle, as "catholica ecclesia") and its relation with "church reform" and "separation," a theme that can be seen throughout the reply. The second will be a more narrowly conceived theme of the "heresy and schism" issue in the context of the French Reformation, predominantly seen in Calvin's personal response placed at the end of the reply.

(ii) Concerning the first theme of the Catholic church, Calvin's basic apologetic stance contrasted Protestant Evangelicalism, which was the rightful inheritor as well as a legitimate representative of the Catholic church, over against Sadoleto's notion of Evangelicalism as a heretical and schismatic destroyer of the Catholic church. To do so, Calvin presented his basic understanding of the current Christian world scenery:

> We are assailed by two sects, which seem to differ most widely from each other. For what similitude is there in appearance between the Pope and the Anabaptists? And yet, . . . the principle weapon with which they both assail us is the same. For when they boast extravagantly of the Spirit, the tendency certainly is to sink and bury the Word of God, that they may make room for their own falsehoods.

Calvin identified the sects as the pope (or the papal church) and the Anabaptists, and he placed the Catholic church in the middle, including Evangelical Protestantism. From the perspective of his apology, perhaps for the first time, he termed the pope and the papal church as a "sect" vis-à-vis the Catholic church. As we have seen in chapter 1, in the context of the Christ's kingdom theme, the first *Institutes* posed the two extreme positions of the papacy and the Anabaptists: the former was called the pope's kingdom and

125. *OS* 1:460, 480–84.

usurper of Christ's kingdom; the latter was called the pope's "troops in ambush," who stirred controversies in the Evangelical camp and tried to place Christ's kingdom under worldly things. Over against Sadoleto's ambiguous use of the "Catholic church," here tactically he envisioned the Catholic church as being exclusive of the papal church and the Anabaptists and inclusive of Protestant Evangelicalism and the "reformed" French Church.[126]

Secondly, Calvin challenged the shortcomings of Sadoleto's definition of the "Catholic church." We have mentioned his definition above, marked by the church's historical catholicity, its unity and consensus in Christ, and the presence of the Holy Spirit in it, as ambiguous. What Calvin asserted as missing was "the clearest mark of all," the word of God. He further characterized the definition as being in the dangerous position of severing the Spirit from the word and of assuming the church could be led by the Spirit without the word. He concluded with a citation of Ephesians 2:20, which proclaimed that the church was "built upon the foundation of the apostles and prophets." Although he avoided using "the elect" and instead used "the saints" to describe the Catholic church as "a society of all the saints," his main discussions on the church, justification, the sacraments, penance, the intercession of the saints, and purgatory carefully outlined the generally accepted positions of Evangelical Protestantism.[127]

Thirdly, there were a few clear instances in which Calvin responded to the criticism raised against Evangelicalism and further sharpened his defensive position. One such example was his response to Sadoleto's accusation that the new religion had claimed to justify its "secession" from the current "Catholic Church" on the basis of its having restored the teaching and practice of the ancient church. Instead of categorically denying a possibility of "secession," Calvin tactically admitted it "under a much stronger necessity" and described such a necessary situation when "the light of divine truth had been extinguished, the word of God being buried, the virtue of Christ being profoundly forgotten, and pastoral office being turned upside down." Although he cautioned that this necessity was not the case of the "secession" from the Catholic church, apologetically it was a new tactic already suggested by *Two Epistles*.[128]

Lastly, there was a particular reference to the churches under the Bishop of Carpentras, which was puzzling as well as difficult to interpret. Although

126. *OS* 1:465. The block quote is taken from Olin, ed., *A Reformation Debate*, 61. Cf. *OS* 1:233, 250, 259. (Battles, trans., *Institution*, 253, 274, 285.)

127. *OS* 1:464–74.

128. *OS* 1:475.

Calvin did not deny these churches under Sadoleto as "Christ's churches" (*ecclesiae Christi*), Calvin asserted that "the Roman pontiff with his entire herd of pseudo-bishops who have seized pastoral office are ferocious wolves."[129] This reference touched on the entire scheme of Calvin's apology. Could it be interpreted that he distinguished Sadoleto and his group of reform-minded prelates from the pope's "pseudo-bishops" in the same church, for instance, the French Church? Did it indicate his acceptance of the well-known position of Luther, Melanchthon, and Bucer, which acknowledged the Roman Catholic churches with certain evangelical marks to be Christ's churches? Or, was it a tactical expression of his high expectations for the reform of the French Church by means of reform-minded prelates such as Sadoleto and his group? In this case, we assume, he was rhetorically addressing Sadoleto as a reformist, even though he knew that Sadoleto's real identity was not.

(iii) The second theme of the reform of the French Church in connection with the "heresy and schism" issue appeared in the theatrical setting of Calvin's own confession before God's judgment seat. It was his response to Sadoleto's similar setting of a pious Catholic's and a rebellious heretic's confessions, especially of the latter's confession, which admitted that even his rebellion could not overturn the authority of the "Catholic church" but only resulted in guilt over his rebellious schism. Challenging Sadoleto's characterization of the Evangelicals, the jurist Calvin first characterized the above two confessions as simply being Sadoleto's fictitious compositions. Then, in its place, he presented his own nonfictitious and real confession as the "defendant's plea" before God's tribunal, just as he had made the Evangelical cause as the "defendants' plea" before the king's court in the dedicatory epistle to King Francis I in his first *Institutes*. His confession as an apology was composed of two parts: the first was meant to be an apology for the Evangelicals accused of heresy and schism, and the second an apology for the Reformer Calvin. In his confession, it should be noted, he was particularly conscious of the moderate reformist or "mediators" group, and in its second part he mentioned his conversion process, which he later described as "a sudden conversion" in his *Psalms Commentary*.[130] We will only briefly focus on two characteristic features of the confession that indicate his apologetic addressees as the reform-minded prelate group and the moderate reformist group in the French Church.

A characteristic feature appeared in the first part of the confession where Calvin responded to the charge of "heresy and schism." Although he reiter-

129. *OS* 1:476.

130. *OS* 1:480–83, 483–86.

ated his usual defense of orthodoxy against the charge of heresy, as to that of schism, he demonstrated afresh his notion of the church's "unity" as well as that of the "secession" from the church. In the form of a confession to God, for example, he insisted "how I had eagerly pursued unity" and admitted that "the unity of the church should begin with you or end in you." As to his own action of so-called "secession" from the current church, he regarded it not against God's church but against the corrupt leaders of the churches. He referred to the example of the Old Testament prophets who challenged the corrupt priests of their times. His conclusion was that "your prophets were not regarded as schismatics."[131] Moreover, an interesting point appeared at the end of the confession's first part. Obviously in the context of the reform of the French Church, Calvin postulated "two parties" that were eagerly seeking church reform: the one, assumedly the reform-minded prelates and the moderate reformists, and the other, his party of Evangelicals. Instead of fighting each other, he pleaded to God for both parties to work together. The confessional wording was almost a prayer: "all controversies should be decided by your word, that thus 'both parties' might unite with one mind to establish your kingdom; and I declined not to restore peace to the church at the expense of my head."[132]

Another characteristic feature appeared in the confession's second part in which Calvin described his formative process of academic studies, conversion, and Evangelicalism. In this process, he acknowledged that he had been influenced by two groups of teachers that he sharply contrasted. He called the first group "Christian teachers" who had taught God's "mercifulness" but whose teachings on salvation had remained in the Catholic doctrines of work righteousness, satisfaction of sins, and the sacrificial Eucharist. As such, they were unable to offer him a satisfactory resolution. From his descriptions, this group could be that of the evangelical humanists, including Erasmus and Lefèvre. Afterward, he encountered "a totally different form of teaching" and called the teachers who had taught it only anonymously as "they" or "our people." Furthermore, he characterized their teaching as not avoiding the clear confession of Christian faith but rather going back to its original purity, the gospel. Since he highlighted that they rejected the pope who claimed to be "the vicar of Christ, successor of St. Peter, head of the church" as the antichrist, they could be Evangelical teachers such as Luther, Zwingli, and others.[133] Regarding the "secession" or "schism," which was one of the major issues of Calvin's *Reply*

131. *OS* 1:482–83.
132. *OS* 1:483.
133. *OS* 1:484–85.

to Sadoleto, interestingly, he confessed his initial fear that these new teachers lacked respect for the church. However, he soon found his fear groundless for they reminded him "how great the difference is between schism from the church and studying to correct the faults by which the church was contaminated." They showed their respect for the church of Christ and worked for its unity.[134] With this fundamental differentiation between schism and reform, he closed his apology by personally appealing to Sadoleto and his group to understand that "the bond of churchly unity" existed only in Christ who was able to "gather us out of our present dispersion in the fellowship of his body."[135]

In conclusion, the *Reply to Sadoleto* had a double-sided goal: one, an apology for the defense of the Evangelical Reformation against the charge of schism; the other, an apology for the reform of the French Church directed to those whom Calvin had still expected to be the agents of reform, namely, Sadoleto, his group of prelates, and the moderate reformists in France. As our study has focused on the second side, there we notice that Calvin showed a more careful and flexible posture than in the challenging spirit of *Two Epistles* and presented some new responses to the criticism caused by the publication. But his apology as a whole showed no basic change of position. In the historical context of his Strasbourg period, the *Reply to Sadoleto* clearly demonstrated a different apology from the *Theological Advice* that Bucer wrote a year later on the same "church reform and schism" issue.

(3) The Holy Roman Empire

Calvin's Strasbourg period was a "political education" in which he closely observed the conflict of the old and new religions in the Empire, especially the various movements within the Schmalkald League. While the confessional demarcation between Catholic and Protestant territories in Germany under the Habsburg dynasty had been progressing, Strasbourg was not only the "most tolerant" city but also one of the most important communication centers in Northern Europe. Strasbourg was a key city of the Protestant League's anti-Habsburg strategy and an advance post for its policy toward France, Switzerland, the Low Countries, and England. Besides Bucer and Capito, Calvin

134. *OS* 1:185.

135. *OS* 1:489. Cf. D. C. Steinmetz, "Luther and Calvin on Church and Tradition," *Michigan Germanic Studies* 10 (1984): 104. According to Steinmetz's analysis of the *Reply*, Calvin regarded the condition of the Roman Catholic Church at the time of Luther's initial reform as already in a broken state and that the Protestant Reformation had since been restoring the fragmented church to its original state.

benefited greatly from the close friendship of Johann Strum, an expert on the League's French policy, and Melanchthon, an undisputed leader of the Lutheran Reformation.[136] He met Melanchthon for the first time at the League's Frankfurt assembly (1539), which Bucer encouraged him to observe. In that meeting, he discussed the issues of church discipline in the Lutheran churches, the eucharistic dispute between Luther and Zwingli and its aftereffect, and the possibility of the League's intervention for the evangelical cause in France. It is interesting that a young Reformer, whose theological formation owed much to Luther, first raised the issue of church discipline to Melanchthon. This could indicate his preoccupation with the issue as well as his understanding that church discipline was one area in which the Lutheran Reformation had not yet completed its implementation.[137] Above all, unquestionably, he had keenly observed the progress of the religious unification colloquies at Hagenau, Worms, and Regensburg (1540–41). His partial participation in the last colloquy as a member of the Strasbourg delegation must have greatly enhanced his apprehension toward the religious reality of the Empire. In his *Reply to Sadoleto*, he idealistically sketched a road map for church reform, in particular, for the reform of the French Church. By eliminating from consideration the papal party as a "sect," he superposed what he considered the Catholic church over the French Church, appealed to the groups of the reform-minded prelates and the moderate reformists for church reform, and expressed his high expectation for their joining with the Evangelical party to realize the Catholic church in France. However, Germany was nowhere near such a kind of idealism: the Holy Roman Emperor, Charles V, a Catholic, was orchestrating religious unification; both the Catholic and Protestant territories were accomplished facts; and the confessional demarcation was becoming a political as well as religious reality. It is certainly not easy to assess historically how Calvin had observed this reality centered around the religious colloquies. As to his partial participation, especially, two questions need to be answered: What was his motive and expectation for the religious unification colloquies? What was the theological substantiation for his participation?

(i) As to the first question about Calvin's motive and expectation, two problems emerged. A paucity of relevant materials, except his few reports from the colloquy to Farel, Viret, and others, as well as the eventual failure of the last colloquy itself, hinder an easy answer. In addition, there were many

136. Ocker's article ("Calvin in Germany," 313–44) provides a good overall picture of Calvin's activities in Germany.

137. Ocker, "Calvin in Germany," 323; Oberman, *John Calvin*, 25–29.

specific factors that had contributed to the historical context of the progress and collapse of the unification colloquies. For instance, the emperor's leadership was strongly motivated by political necessity for a religiously unified Germany. The colloquies were led by the Catholic reformists, Gropper and Cardinal and papal legate Gasparo Contarini, and Melanchthon and Bucer from the Protestant side, and the doctrinal basis for the first two colloquies' deliberations was the Lutheran *Confession of Augsburg* (*Confessio Augustana variata*). Since the Lutheran confession was formally rejected as a basis for reunification by the Catholic territories by the end of the second colloquy of Worms, under the emperor's directive, Gropper and Bucer secretly prepared the *Book of Regensburg* for the next colloquy. Although the colloquy came to agree on the first five articles, including "justification," the agreement was rejected by Luther and the papal curia via its delegate Eck, and the colloquy failed. Since we assume that Calvin's Strasbourg period was a learning as well as a transitory phase of his formation as a Reformer, his participation in the colloquy and its implication should be interpreted accordingly.[138]

Firstly, it could be viewed from a negative perspective, as exemplified in Wendel's interpretation. Judging mainly from Calvin's epistolary information, he assumes that Calvin first held an optimistic expectation for the colloquies' outcome, but, having seen the colloquies' progress and the excessive compromises made by Bucer and Melanchthon, he reached the conclusion that "division" (schism) between the Catholic and Protestant parties was "unrepairable."[139] Secondly, it could be viewed that Calvin's motive and expectation was not so much in the colloquies' outcome but in their influence upon the French Reformation. This interpretation could be reasonable for the Pastor of Strasbourg's French congregation. There were some indications that Calvin, who was known as the author of the *Reply to Sadoleto*, the 1539 *Institutes*, and the *Romans Commentary*, had actively engaged in his appeal for the French

138. Cf. Lane, "Calvin and Article 5," 233–63. Lane's article on Calvin's participation in the Regensburg Colloquy also provides an excellent historical picture of the Colloquies.

139. Cf. Wendel, *Calvin*, 63–64; Gordon, *Calvin*, 99–102. Wendel's view of Calvin's negative attitude seems to be based upon his analysis of Calvin's two letters (*CO* 11:32–34, 35–37) sent from the colloquy. In the first letter, although Calvin regarded positively the agreement on justification, he considered the colloquy facing "insurmountable obstacles" on the issues of church authority and the Eucharist. In the second letter, Calvin considered the bold compromise put forward by Bucer and Melanchthon being beyond his imagination and unacceptable to his conscience. In the case of Gordon, Calvin's participation in the colloquy itself and his acquaintance with Melanchthon are viewed positively, but his overall assessment of the colloquies is seen negatively as a process of compromise and charade.

Reformation to the League's princes, the Lutheran church leaders and theologians in the colloquies. Despite his expectation, nonetheless, it was also true that there had been no substantive help from the German Protestant side that would influence the future of the French Reformation.[140] Thirdly, one could take Calvin's motive and expectation at face value. According to Ganoczy, for example, Calvin, who had established his Catholic ecclesiology in the first *Institutes* and had been faced with the current most serious issue of schism in Strasbourg, sincerely hoped for the religious unification colloquies. He supported the mediating works of Melanchthon and Bucer as well as Gropper and Contarini, and he considered the intransigence of Eck and the papal curia to be a main reason for the failure of the colloquies.[141]

Although each of the above three interpretations may have its merit, viewed from the context of his *Reply to Sadoleto*, one thing is certain. He did not participate in the colloquies with a disdainful attitude but expected some positive outcome from the colloquies that were to be practically the last interconfessional dialogue before the beginning of the General Council summoned by a pope (1545) and the Schmalkald War (1546–47). It should be noted that immediately after his return to Geneva he published the French version of his report on the Regensburg colloquy in Geneva, and in it he stressed and positively evaluated the Protestant side's efforts for reunification at the colloquy. As Ganoczy suggests, the publication itself indicates Calvin's recognition of schism as the most serious issue facing the French Reformation.[142]

(ii) The second question concerned Calvin's effort to theologically substantiate his participation in the colloquy, especially the existence of any ecclesiological necessity for his participation. The second edition of the *Institutes*, in its new addition to chapter 4 on the exposition of the Apostles' Creed, treated the issue of separation or schism from the church and provided basically the same argument that he later reiterated in the *Reply to Sadoleto*. The argument

140. Wendel, *Calvin*, 63–64; van't Spijker, *Calvin*, 60; Ocker, "Calvin in Germany," 324–25.

141. Ganoczy, *Young Calvin*, 284–85. Unlike Wendel, Ganoczy reads Calvin's first letter (cf. n. 139 above) positively, but curiously does not refer to the second letter in which Calvin criticized the bold compromise presented to the Colloquy by Bucer and Melanchthon on the Eucharist.

142. *Les actes du la journee imperial tenne en la cité de Reguespourg*, 1541: *CO* 5:509–684: *BC* 41/1. Cf. Ganoczy, *Young Calvin*, 285; R. C. Zachman, "The Conciliating Theology of John Calvin: Dialogue among Friends," in *Conciliation and Confession: The Struggle for Unity in the Age of Reform, 1415–1648*, ed. H. R. Louthan and R. C. Zachman (Notre Dame: University of Notre Dame Press, 2004), 89–105.

placed the Catholic church in the middle of the spectrum and considered its two opposite extremes as the "sects" of the papal church and the Anabaptists. In the 1539 *Institutes*, Calvin presented a thesis that there were two methods of Satan against the church's two marks: the one, to take away from the church and destroy the two marks; the other, to despise them and let their believers separate from the church.[143] Without naming the first method, he implied it as that of the papal church, but he identified the second as the sectarianism of the Donatists, Cathari, and Anabaptists. Furthermore, tactically, he treated the second method first and affirmed that, as long as the churches upheld the two marks, they were considered to hold the title of the Catholic church. His apologetic stance against the Anabaptists affirmed that, even though these churches made errors and fell short in the "administration" of the two marks, separation from the churches could not be justified. However, when the Anabaptists considered the two marks insufficient to guarantee the nature of Christ's church and insisted on "perfection" in holiness by means of church discipline, he had to charge them for the error of separatism.[144] In retrospect, this apologetic stance prevented Calvin, in spite of his emphasis on church discipline, to make a move from the two-marks to the three-marks theory.

(iii) Unlike the first case of the Anabaptists, Calvin's apologetic stance against the papal church was more complex. According to him, since papalism had dominated the Catholic church, destroyed the marks, and substituted them with their false teachings and false sacraments, the issues of its "title" and "separation" from it were complicated.[145] He offered a first tentative answer to this issue. In the papal church, the ministry of God's word was substituted by false clerical dominance. The abominable Mass took the place of the Lord's Supper. Its worship was filled with endless superstitions, idolatries, and impious practices. Therefore, "separation" from this papal church should not be regarded as separation from the Catholic church. In comparing the papal church with the corrupted history of God's people under the kings Jeroboam and Ahab, he tackled the issue of the Catholic church's "title." If the papists claimed their churches to hold the "title" and the power of the keys, they could not destroy the word to which the power of the keys was bound. They could not replace the true sacramental "promise" by its substitutes, nor could they persecute and expel true believers from the churches. Then, if the true marks of God's word and the sacraments were not found, their churches lacked the

143. *CO* 1:544. (*Institutio* 4.1.11: *OS* 5:15.)
144. *CO* 1:545–48. (*Institutio* 4.1.12–14: *OS* 5:15–18.)
145. *CO* 1:559–60. (*Institutio* 4.2.10: *OS* 5:40.)

"title" of Christ's church and, accordingly, separation from them should not be considered schismatic.

To this formal conclusion, Calvin added an appendix that perhaps was meant to be his response to the moderate reformists' criticism caused by his *Two Epistles*. If there were "remains" of Christian baptism in these churches, he affirmed that the Catholic church was not completely destroyed. Rather, God had repelled Satan's attacks and kept his own remnants there, and these churches could be regarded as Christ's churches.[146] If we consider the appendix as Calvin's final apologetic stance, it was more flexible and accommodating than *Two Epistles*. In the final analysis, nevertheless, Calvin's stance in the 1539 *Institutes* marked a delicately different approach to the issues from the position that Luther had already taken and that Bucer was soon to take in the *Theological Advice*. To the extent that the marks or their "remains" were being upheld, both Luther and Bucer approved the papal church as Christ's church. By contrast, as far as the church's "title," which was to be strictly judged by the church's two marks, was concerned, Calvin categorically rejected the papal church as Christ's church. Even so, he admitted that, in God's provision, there could be some recognizable "remains" of Christ's church in the papal churches. It can be assumed with this nuanced approach that Calvin had positively participated in the church unification colloquies in Germany and had hoped for the realization of the Catholic church.

Section 3. The Second *Institutes* and the *Romans Commentary*

Unquestionably, the 1539 *Institutes* and the following year's first commentary on Romans were two academic achievements of Calvin's Strasbourg period. They marked the two distinctive starting points of his later theological and exegetical works. Preparations for their publication started in his first Genevan period, progressed side by side in Strasbourg, and were completed by the summer of 1539. As was made clear by the *Institutes*' "Preface to the readers" and the commentary's "Dedicatory epistle to Johann Jacob Grynaeus," the Basel biblical scholar, the two publications were prototypes of two distinctive

146. *CO* 1:559–61. (*Institutio* 4.2.10–12: *OS* 5:41–42.) As we have noted Du Tillet's argument for "the effects of baptism" (cf. n. 120 above), Calvin's reference to baptism, subsequently referred to as "the remaining vestiges" in this portion of his anti-Catholic polemic, may also be intended as an apology against the "Moderators."

yet mutually related academic exercises, working complementarily toward one common goal of Evangelical theology. According to Muller, who has examined this mutual relationship, it is described as "the running exposition of the biblical text in commentary and sermon, coupled with the elicitation of theological *loci* from the text and the gathering of those *loci* together with the important dogmatic *disputationes* of Calvin's time into the form of a basic instruction or *institutio* in theology."[147] From this basic methodological standpoint, as his dedicatory epistle to Grynaeus revealed, he questioned the methodology of both Melanchthon's *Loci Communes* and Bucer's commentaries. Melanchthon emphasized the theological loci drawn from the biblical text at the expense of the text's exegeses, and Bucer compiled the text's translation, paraphrase, and theological loci upon the exegeses. Over against these and other precedents, Calvin was to establish his own two-tier methodology of biblical exegesis and theological instruction. For the development of this methodology, modern researchers have noticed the important influence of Melanchthon's 1535 *Loci communes* and Calvin's own studies on the church fathers, especially on Chrysostom.[148]

1. The Second Institutes

(i) Before we examine Calvin's ecclesiology in the second edition, there are a few preliminary observations that may be helpful. Firstly, the *Institutes* had changed its nature drastically between the first and the second editions. As the "Preface to the readers" revealed, the new edition was meant for "the candidates for sacred theology to study the divine word." That is, the change was from a catechetical instruction to a textbook of theology. The first edition consisted of six chapters divided into "instruction" and "apology" sections, and the second edition was enlarged into seventeen chapters, three times the

147. "Calvinus Lectori," *CO* 1:255–56; "Calvinus Grynaeo," *CO* 10b:402–6. Cf. Muller, *The Unaccommodated*, 27–31, esp. 29; T. F. Torrance, *The Hermeneutics of John Calvin* (Edinburgh: Scottish Academic Press, 1988), 61–71.

148. Cf. Muller, *The Unaccommodated*, 124–30; O. Millet, "Les *Loci communes* de 1535 et l'*Institution de la Religion chrétienne* de 1539–41, ou Calvin en dialogue avec Melanchthon," in *Melanchthon und Europa*, ed. G. Frank and M. Treu (Stuttgart: J. Thorbecke, 2002), 85–96; R. C. Zachman, *John Calvin as Teacher, Pastor, Theologian: The Shape of His Writings and Thought* (Grand Rapids: Baker Academic, 2006), 23–27, 29–53; W. I. P. Hazlett, "Calvin's Latin Preface to His Proposed French Edition of Chrysostom's Homilies: Translation and Commentary," in *Humanism and Reform: The Church in Europe, England and Scotland, 1400–1643*, ed. J. Kirk (Oxford and Cambridge, MA: Blackwell, 1991), 129–50, esp. 135.

volume. Naturally, some previous chapters were turned into multiple chapters, some subsections became chapters, and the division of the "instruction" and "apology" was less noticeable. To be precise, to the previous chapter 1 (Law) the new edition added "The Knowledge of God and That of Man" (chs. 1–2). Chapter 2 (faith) became the separate chapters of faith (exposition of the Apostles' Creed), penance, justification by faith, the Old and New Testaments, and predestination/providence (chs. 4–8). Chapter 3 (prayer) morphed into a new chapter (ch. 9). Chapter 4 (sacraments) turned into three chapters, the sacraments, baptism, and the Lord's Supper (chs. 10–12). The three topics of chapter 6 (Christian freedom, ecclesiastical power, and political administration) became independent chapters (chs. 13–15). Chapter 5 (false sacraments) was moved toward the end (ch. 16), and a new chapter, on the life of the Christian man (ch. 17), was added.

(ii) Secondly, as some researchers have noticed, the second edition reflected Calvin's preoccupations during this period. For example, the above-mentioned Muller's study, which places Calvin's theology in the tradition of late medieval scholasticism, notices the methodological importance of the second edition in the context of this tradition's development into Reformed theology or "the confluence of humanism and scholasticism in the sixteenth century," and considers the second edition the most important in the entire corpus of the *Institutes*.[149] Unlike Muller's focus on theological methodology, some researchers have noticed the substantive importance of the newly added materials. For example, Balke considers the issue of the Radical Reformation headed by the Anabaptists a chief motive for Calvin to revise the *Institutes.* To illustrate this point, he cites Calvin's apology for the Trinity, which was prompted by Servetus's challenge, the analogy of the Old and New Testament partly meant for the defense of infant baptism, and the new materials on predestination and its relation with God's covenant.[150] Another example is provided by Parker, who notes Calvin's intentions in the second edition by citing a phrase in its preface, namely, "embracing a summary of religion in all its parts." According to Parker, in the second edition Calvin enlarged his scope in terms of both *loci communes* drawn from Scripture and the issues of his age. As to the former, it is said that the new edition "is now formally oriented towards the Bible," and as to the latter, that the new edition "belongs to its precise age and speaks to the men of its age."[151]

149. *CO* 1:255–56. Cf. Muller, *The Unaccommodated*, 15, 27–31, 186.
150. Balke, *Calvin and the Anabaptist*, 97–122, esp. 121.
151. Parker, *John Calvin*, 72–74.

(iii) Thirdly, concerning ecclesiology, a few general confirmations are needed. For instance, strictly speaking, it is not the second but the third edition of 1543 that reflected most intensely Calvin's theological thinking and churchly practice of his Strasbourg period. In this sense, as far as his ecclesiology was concerned, the second edition was a transitional work, while the third edition witnessed the most elaborate expansion of his ecclesiology. Although the second edition reflected the first edition, his Genevan period's *Instruction*, the Caroli affair, and *Two Epistles*, it nonetheless showed his keen awareness of the issues and concerns of his Strasbourg period, as well as indicating his ecclesiological move to a new stage that became prominent in his second Genevan period. Since comparison of the second and the third editions will be inevitable in the following analyses, we will cite the first French edition of 1541 that is to be placed between these two Latin editions.[152] Among many ecclesiological issues, we will selectively focus on two issues: his apology for the basic concepts of the church and anti-Anabaptist apologetics that reflected his ecclesiological thinking and concern of this period.

(1) Apology for the Basic Concepts of the Church

Chapter 1 confirmed that Calvin's first *Institutes* presented two basic notions of the church, namely, "the whole number of the elect" as "the holy Catholic church" of the Apostles' Creed and "the congregation of the believers" as the church in history. He presented his Catholic ecclesiology by relating Christologically the former with the latter as its manifestation in history. We have also noticed that Calvin never used the invisible/visible concept of the church and that the relation between the church of the elect and the congregation of the believers was not fully explained there. In the second *Institutes*, however, in order to overcome this shortcoming, he presented a new framework for these basic concepts that will remain until the last *Institutes* of 1559. In the following pages, we will examine the new framework under four points: (1) what we may call "the double concept of the church," which recognizes the church in its two levels of existence; (2) the first level of "the whole number of the elect" and its manifestation in history; (3) "the congregation of believers," which Calvin now calls the "visible" church; and (4) the relation of the church's marks and the issue of schism.

(i) As to the first point, Calvin reconfirmed the two realities of the church presented in the first *Institutes*. He restated them afresh as two interrelated re-

152. Cf. n. 116 above.

alities that could be conceived via two different levels of understanding, that is, "to apprehend the church by faith" and "under our cognition." In the context of the church of the elect, the first expression appeared as "If we wish to enter the kingdom of God, it is necessary for us 'to apprehend the church by faith.'" After a lengthy discussion on the church of the elect, the second expression appeared as "Now we come down to a place where we speak of the visible church which is 'under our cognition' and of which judgment is required."[153] The paired expressions indicated the basic epistemological structure of Calvin's theology that had taken various expressions in his major theological themes. Examples included the (double) knowledge of God (*duplex cognitio Dei*) as God the creator and God the redeemer, the kingdom of Christ and the church, the eucharistic notion of Christ's presence in heaven and in the Lord's Supper.

In this connection, it should be noted that, immediately after the above second expression, the third edition of 1543 made an important insertion, "sacred literatures [Scripture] speak of the church in double fashion." Here too, he did not term the church of the first cognitional level "invisible." He called it instead "before God" (*coram Deo*) and emphasized the process of its manifestation in the historical congregation of believers. As another point of interest, the 1539 edition's "the whole number of the elect," which introduced the church of the first cognitional level, was translated in the 1541 French *Institutes* as "the whole multitude of Christians." Furthermore, it was eliminated in the third Latin edition of 1543. Nonetheless, this double notion of the church, with the predominant emphasis on the visible church in history, was to survive until the final edition of 1559, in which the churches of the two cognitional levels were disproportionally placed in book 4.1.1–3 and the rest of the entire book from 4.1.4 to 4.20.32.[154]

(ii) Concerning the second point, Calvin identified the first cognitional reality of the church as the creedal expression of "the holy, Catholic church." Then, he added two new notions: the first, a traditional Latin distinction of the Apostles' Creed between the "credo in" for confessing the Trinity, and the "credo" for confessing the rest of the Creed, including the church; the second, a notion of the church as "mother." As to the first notion, Calvin explained that the "credo in" indicated the work of the Triune God as the "cause" and the

153. *CO* 1:539: "si in regnum Dei ingressum nobis patefieri volumus, ecclesiam fide apprendere opus est"; 524: "Enimvero de ecclesia visibili, et quae sub cognitionem nostrum cadit, quale iudicium esse debeat, nunc est dicendi locus."

154. The 1543 insertion can be found in *CO* 1:542 (*Institutio* 4.1.7: *OS* 5:12). See also "la multitude des chrestiens" in *Institution* (1541), 2:121.

"credo" as its "effect," and stated that the Triune God's work for our salvation would not be completed "until coming down to the church, the forgiveness of sins, and the life everlasting." This indication could be an early expression of his basic notion by which he later attributed the first three books of the final *Institutes* to the Triune God and book 4 to the church as "the external means" by which God's saving work is applied to us.[155] The second notion of "the church as mother" was inserted immediately after his mentioning the "whole number of the elect," along with the notion that "outside of the unity of the church there is no salvation" (*extra ecclesiae unitatem nullam esse salutem*). These notions and the creedal expression of "the communion of the saints" were all discussed in terms of the first cognitional level of "the holy Catholic church."[156]

(iii) The third point concerned the second cognitional level of the "visible" church. Here the "visible church" was collectively expressed as the "universal church" (*ecclesia universalis*) and its "marks" were discussed. Firstly, Calvin defined the "universal" church as "the collection of multitude of people" dispersed on earth and distinguished by their allegiance to the true doctrine and bond of the Christian religion.[157] Curiously, however, he did not expressly discuss the relationship of the "universal" church with the "Catholic church" but focused strictly on the two marks of the "visible church." In addition, there was an interesting feature in his discussion on the marks. In strictly defining the two-marks theory, he avoided any reference to church discipline as a worthy mark of the church. Although he emphasized the two marks as the basis for the visible church's "unity" and "fellowship," he seemed to exclude church discipline from his discussion on the issue of the church's unity. This point could be due to his regard for the Lutheran *Confession of Augsburg* (art. 7, Latin text), "for the true unity of the church it is enough to agree concerning the teaching of the gospel and the administration of the sacraments," or his apologetic checking of the position of Bucer, who had recently moved from the two-marks to the three-marks theory.[158]

(iv) The fourth point concerned Calvin's discussion, placed at the end of the creedal exposition of the church, on the connection of the power of the keys with the marks of the church. In the context of the unity and schism issue, he

155. *CO* 1:538–39. Cf. *Institutio* 4.1.1: *OS* 5:1.

156. *CO* 1:539–42. As to the two new references to "mother" and "the Church's unity," it can be assumed that Calvin draws the first from Galatians 4:26 ("the other woman corresponds to Jerusalem above; she is free, and she is our mother") and the second from Cyprian's *De catholicae ecclesiae unitate*.

157. *CO* 1:543. Cf. *Institutio* 4.1.9: *OS* 5:13–14.

158. *CO* 1:544. Cf. *Creeds and Confessions*, 2:62.

presented a complex discussion in connection with this double concept of the church. As we have noticed in chapter 1, the first *Institutes* presented a unique twofold division of the biblical texts on the keys: the first texts (Matt 16, John 20) were about the doctrine concerning the fundamentals of Christianity; and the second text (Matt 18) was about the ethical aspects of the believers, or church discipline. However, the second edition kept the discussion on the first texts intact, but revised only that on the second text. The newly added emphasis was that the power of the keys in the second text was strictly limited to the discipline of the "visible church," and that it was to concern only the disciplinary process culminating in possible excommunication. That is, it should not go beyond to "anathema," which concerned the issue of the believer's salvation. In this disciplinary process, furthermore, a disciplined believer was to be regarded as a "brother" in the visible church and a member of the "universal" church.[159]

As we have noted above, Calvin regarded the two marks of the church as the basis of the "visible" unity and communion of the church, and his apology seemed to disregard church discipline as an important concern for the unity and schism issue. In sharp contrast to his treatment of church discipline, he noticeably connected the first keys texts (Matt 16, John 20) with the two marks of the church. By rephrasing the two marks as "the sum of necessary doctrines" and "the use of the sacraments," he emphasized that they were concerns not only for the "Catholic church" but also for the believer's salvation, warning that their destruction was to result in the "ruin of the Catholic church." In the context of this warning, finally, he came to the above-mentioned question of whether "under the papacy" the church of Christ remained, but we will not repeat his negative response here.[160] In retrospect, although the second edition's exposition on the church as a whole marked a new direction in Calvin's apologetics, there were a few unsettled aspects in his discussion, such as the relation of the "Catholic church" with the "universal church" and the direct connection of the two marks with the "Catholic church." For a more cohesive and comprehensive discussion including the double concept of the church, we have to wait for the third edition of 1543.

(2) Anti-Anabaptist Apologetics

As we have seen in chapter 1, Calvin's first *Institutes* placed the church catholic in the middle of the ecclesial spectrum. Since his discussion was concentrated

159. *CO* 1:552–53.
160. *CO* 1:553. Cf. ch. 4, nn. 129 and 130.

on the Roman Catholic Church, his apologetics against the Anabaptists as the Roman Catholic Church's "troops in ambush" was limited. For the preparation of the second edition, this shortcoming was surely an urgent concern. In addition, his pastoral experience with the French refugee congregation, which was said to have had contacts with the Anabaptists, and certainly his close communication with Bucer, who had been known as an expert on the Anabaptist issue, were reflected in the second edition's revisions. According to Balke, almost all of the new additions in the second edition, such as sections dealing with God's word and the Holy Spirit, the relation of the Old and New Testaments, infant baptism, the vows, the Sabbath, universalism, chiliasm, and perfectionism heavily reflected Calvin's concern for the Anabaptists.[161] With this perspective of the anti-Anabaptist apologetics in mind, we will selectively focus on three new sections: the relation of the Old and New Testaments (ch. 7), predestination and providence (ch. 8), and the defense of infant baptism added as an appendix to the general discussion on baptism (ch. 11). Although the second section on predestination and providence is not strictly an anti-Anabaptist topic, it includes a few interesting remarks on the issue.

(i) The first section (ch. 7) was concerned with the Anabaptist notion of Scripture that lay at the foundation of their teachings. Calvin pointed out their disregard of what he considered the first and primary mark of the church, the word of God. Over against the Catholic and the mainstream Protestant view, Anabaptists considered that there were two different covenants or testaments in Scripture and taught the absolute superiority of the New Testament over the Old Testament. Calvin's criticism was focused on what might be termed this "New Testament monism."[162] Before examining the text itself, it should be noted that Calvin's apologetic theme found its parallel expression in his first *Romans Commentary* (chs. 1–8). This was simultaneously prepared with the second *Institutes*, especially on the theme of the relation between the Old and New Testaments. In both publications, he was said to have based his apolo-

161. Balke, *Calvin and the Anabaptist*, 97–122, esp. 97, 121; G. Johnson, "The Development of John Calvin's Doctrine of Infant Baptism in Reaction to the Anabaptists," *Mennonite Quarterly Review* 73 (1999): 803–23. Cf. S. Buckwalter, "Possible Influences of Martin Bucer on the *Institutio* of 1539," in *John Calvin: The Strasbourg Years (1538–1541)*, ed. M. Arnold, 99–101.

162. *CO* 1:802. (*Institutio* 2.10.1: *OS* 3:403.) Cf. G. H. Williams, "The Radical Reformation Revisited," *Union Seminary Review* 34 (1984): 3–5; H. J. Hillerbrand, "Anabaptism and History," *Mennonite Quarterly Review* 45 (1971): 107–22. Questioning the generally accepted view of "restitution" of the New Testament church in Anabaptist scholarship, Hillerbrand finds a key to the Anabaptist notion of history in the "continuity" of "the faithful of all ages."

getics upon Augustine's doctrines of Scripture and grace. In his preparation of the second *Institutes*, he presumably used Zwingli's *Refutation of Anabaptist Tricks* (*In Catabaptistarum Strophas Elencus*, 1527). This Latin work translated the original German text of the *Schleitheim Confession* into Latin and refuted each of its seven "Articles." Interestingly, this work added three appendixes (covenant, election, and the practice of infant baptism in the apostolic church), with the first appendix addressing the theme of the relation between the Old and New Testaments.[163] Furthermore, there was a possibility that Calvin might have also used Bullinger's work *A Brief Exposition on the Unique and Eternal Testament or Covenant of God* (*De Testamento seu Foedere Dei Unico et Aeterno*, 1534). Although some analyses have attempted to prove Calvin's use by parallel evidences, the existence of a basic difference in approaching the issue should also be noted. Bullinger emphasized that God's "unique and eternal testament" took different forms in various periods of scriptural history and that the testament was basically "a bilateral contract," not only binding both the Old Testament people of God and the New Testament church but also binding God himself. In contrast, Calvin followed Augustine's original notion and interpreted the testament as God's sovereign "promise" made to God's people and church.[164]

The starting point of Calvin's anti-Anabaptist apologetics targeted the Anabaptists' insistence that, although the ancient people of Israel received the earthly blessings promised by God, they never received the spiritual blessings of eternal life presented in the New Testament, and therefore basically they shared nothing in common with Christians. Over against this insistence, Calvin affirmed the basic principle: "the covenant made with all the patriarchs is

163. *In Catabaptistarum Strophas Elenchus*: *CR: Zwingli* 6/1:1–196. ("De foedere," 155–72; "De electione," 172–84; "Quod apostoli baptizaverint infantes," 184–94.) Although Zwingli's apology for infant baptism against the Anabaptists is constructed upon the idea of God's election and covenant, in contrast, Calvin does not use the doctrine of election either here in chapter 7 or in his defense of infant baptism.

164. *De Testamento seu Foedere Dei Unico et Aeterno*, 1534. Cf. J. W. Baker, *Heinrich Bullinger and the Covenant: The Other Reformed Tradition* (Athens, OH: Ohio University Press, 1980), "Appendix B: Covenant and Testament in Calvin's Thought," 193–98. A Bullinger scholar, Baker examines Calvin's teaching on covenant expressed in the 1539 edition's chapter 7 and points out that Calvin does not relate covenant directly with his teaching on election. In comparison with Bullinger, while Baker considers Calvin's notion of covenant a traditional Augustinian view that sees the relation of election and covenant as that of God's "primary" and "subsequent" decree, he considers Bullinger's notion, which develops the idea of covenant without referring to God's election at all, a new development in Reformed theology.

so much like ours in substance and reality that the two are actually one and the same. Yet they differ in the mode of dispensation."[165] From this starting point, he advanced three arguments: the people of the Old Testament aspired not for earthly blessings but for the eternal life promised in "[God's] oracles, the law, and the prophets"; the old covenant given to them was not based upon their works but upon God's mercy; and the people were called God's people only in terms of the covenant's mediator, Christ. Throughout his discussion, he emphasized that "the covenant of the law" and "the covenant of the gospel" had one common substance of God's "promise/testament" and one common basis of Christ as the mediator of the covenant.[166] Furthermore, by relating his arguments with the church's two marks, he criticized the Anabaptists for devaluing their importance. For example, he compared the New Testament gospel and the apostles with the "oracles, the law, and the prophets." He also compared the New Testament baptism and the Eucharist with the Old Testament events of the crossing of the Red Sea, "they were baptized in crossing the sea," and of the Passover based upon the New Testament analogy (1 Cor 10: 3–4). His point was that Anabaptists not only devalued the New Testament church's marks but ignored the marks of the Old Testament, and as a result they regarded the people of the Old Testament as having no relevance for the church of the New Testament.[167] For Calvin, the differences in the Old and New Testaments (infancy and maturity, shadow and substance, the covenant of the law and the covenant of the gospel, letter and spirit, and the spirit of slave and the spirit of son) were said to concern only "the mode of dispensation."[168]

(ii) The second section (ch. 8: "Of God's Election and Providence") concerned another fundamental theme of the Augustinian tradition, God's election. Strictly speaking, it was not a polemic against the Anabaptists. As to the theme itself, recognizing that he did not properly treat it in the first *Institutes*, Calvin supplemented one section on it in his *Instruction* (1537), and now he developed it into one chapter in the second *Institutes*. Incidentally, it was one of the main themes of his simultaneously prepared *Romans Commentary*.[169] The theme was also an acute concern among Protestant Evangelicals as to whether it should be regarded as a fundamental doctrine of Evangelicalism. For instance, Calvin had known that Melanchthon and Zwingli had taken

165. *CO* 1:802. (*Institutio* 2.10.2: *OS* 3:404.)
166. *CO* 1:803–4. (*Institutio* 2.10.2–4: *OS* 3:404–6.)
167. *CO* 1:805. (*Institutio* 2.10.5: *OS* 3:406.)
168. *CO* 1:818–30. (*Institutio* 2.11.1–14: *OS* 3:423–36.)
169. The text used here is found in *CO* 1:861–902.

a passive position by considering God's election a mystery, a doctrine to be prudently treated in silence. On the other hand, Oecolampadius and Bucer took it positively as Augustine's main teaching. Against this background, Calvin formulated here what was to be known as a key doctrine of his theology, namely, double predestination, and he distinguished his unique position not only from the positions of Thomas Aquinas, Erasmus, and the Anabaptists but also, to a certain degree, from Melanchthon, Zwingli, and even Bucer.

Calvin began his argument from the experiential fact that the gospel had not been proclaimed always and everywhere, and that, even when proclaimed, a sharp division appeared between those who believed it and those who did not. From this fact, he argued, it was necessary to ascend to God's election in order to determine the cause of salvation initiated by God's grace. Interestingly, he treated first the passive position within Evangelicalism and implicitly criticized Zwingli and Melanchthon: first, Zwingli's notion that human inquiries into God's election could fall into the danger of constricting the divine mystery; and then, Melanchthon's notion that the discussion of election should be altogether buried in order to avoid this danger.[170] We will not follow Calvin's arguments in detail here, but only mention a few points of our own interest. Firstly, Calvin referred to the Anabaptists in the context of their position shared by "the Pelagians, Manichees, Anabaptists, Epicureans." He characterized this position as that which distinguished God's electing "will" from "permission" and thus left room for human meritorious works, which stood over and against Augustine's position that interpreted that "the will of God is the necessity of things." As he combined the Anabaptists with the Pelagians, if he included the semi-Pelagian position of mainstream Catholic theology with the Pelagians, his argument was the same as that of Luther who grouped the Catholics and the Anabaptists by the pivotal connection of work righteousness.[171]

Secondly, Calvin implicitly criticized Melanchthon who, concerning the assurance of salvation, considered the approach based on "faith" better and more certain than that based on divine election, which was uncertain in human understanding. Although he valued this position's legitimate emphasis on faith, he characterized it as "the force of election contingent upon faith in the gospel," calling it "outside the way" (*extra viam*). Furthermore, he considered

170. *CO* 1:861–62, 863. (*Institutio* 3.21.1, 3: *OS* 4:370, 371.)

171. *CO* 1:874. (*Institutio* 3.23.8: *OS* 4:402.) Concerning the Epicureans, Calvin discussed them in the 1550 Latin and French works *De Scandalis* (*BC* 50/9) and *Des scandales* (*BC* 50/12) and used this term to refer to some liberal humanists of his day.

it unable to provide the ultimate certainty of salvation, when faith encountered doubts and was swallowed in "an abyss of sightless darkness."[172]

Thirdly, he implicitly criticized Bucer's position which insisted that, before God's election manifested itself in a believer's calling, the existence of "a seed of election" (*semen electionis*) could be recognized. Earlier he had criticized the Thomistic distinction that good works could not be the cause of "God's election" but could be the cause of the election's result, and he called the distinction "the cunning of Thomas." Questioning Bucer, who was reared in Thomistic theology, Calvin challenged his notion of "a seed of election" as being totally unfounded in scriptural testimonies and Christian experiences.[173]

Among some interesting aspects of Calvin's argument partly mentioned above, from the perspective of ecclesiology, the most unique was his notion of "election in Christ," which he introduced in connection with the assurance of election. As if folding a sheet of paper in half, this notion folded Old Testament history and New Testament history into two halves by the center point of Christ. Furthermore, it applied the same Christocentric scheme to the Old Testament people and the New Testament church. Since God's suprahistorical election manifested in history in the form of a believer's calling, Calvin argued that the believer, who was elected "in Christ" and incorporated into Christ's body, the church, could use Christ as a "mirror" (*speculum*) and, as if ascending salvation history, could meditate on the fountain of "election in Christ" in order to receive the assurance of salvation. By the same token, the believer called into the church, as if descending salvation history, could also secure the future "perseverance" of calling and faith as the goal of "election in Christ."[174] As we have seen above, Calvin, who identified the creedal expression of the holy Catholic church as "the whole number of the elect" in the first *Institutes*, synthesized the twofold notion of "election and salvation history" and "election and the church" into one apology in the second *Institutes*.[175]

(iii) The third section concerned the defense of infant baptism, a topic that Calvin appended to the general discussion of baptism. Since the issue of

172. *CO* 1:879. (*Institutio* 3.24.3–4: *OS* 4:413–14.) According to the editors of the *Opera Selecta*, Calvin's reference here is to Melanchthon's *Loci Communes* (1535).

173. *CO* 1:883–86. (*Institutio* 3.24.10–13: *OS* 4:421–25.) The editors of the *Opera Selecta* consider Calvin's reference here to Bucer's *Enarrationes (perpetuae), in Sacra Quatuor Evangelia* (1530).

174. *CO* 1:880–81. (*Institutio* 3.24.5–6: *OS* 4:415–17.)

175. Cf. D. N. Wiley, "The Church as the Elect in the Theology of Calvin," in *John Calvin and the Church: A Prism of Reform*, ed. T. George (Louisville: Westminster John Knox, 1990), 110–11.

infant baptism was a focal point of the Anabaptist criticism that contended the nonexistence of such practices in the New Testament, for Calvin's consistent biblicism it was a difficult issue to be attended with care. It has been assumed that he used Zwingli's *Refutation of Anabaptist Tricks* and Bucer's *What Is Infant Baptism?* (1533) and that his argument was not completely original.[176] This assumption was affirmed by Calvin's own testimony at the beginning of this section, stating that he was forced to enter the debate for the sake of "the tranquility of the church," because Anabaptist criticism had become a more urgent issue rather than being quieted.[177]

In general, Calvin founded his anti-Anabaptist apologetics strictly on scriptural testimonies without referring either to God's election or to the customs of the ancient church. Its starting point was an affirmation that the issue of infant baptism was nothing but a nonessential matter of baptism's "administration." He justified his point by saying that the essential of baptism or infant baptism was not in its "ceremony" but in its "substance," namely, the "promise" and "spiritual mystery" offered in baptism. Although the works of Zwingli and Bucer mentioned above used the idea of "promise," the combination of promise and mystery seemed to be unique to Calvin.[178] On the "promise," firstly, Calvin defined its substance as the new life and communion with Christ by means of "remission of sins" and "mortification of flesh." He also affirmed that this substance was the same in the Old and New Testaments but took the two different and external forms of circumcision and baptism as different means to assure the same "promise." Citing Christ's blessing of Jewish children as members of the kingdom of heaven and the case of "family baptism" in Acts, he argued that the circumcised children of the old covenant and the baptized infants of the new covenant belonged to the one and same "church."[179] Secondly, he introduced the notion of "spiritual mystery" in connection with the Anabaptist refusal to recognize infant baptism as worthy of the spiritual

176. *In Catabaptistarum Strophas Elenchus*: *CR: Zwingli*, 6/1:29–111; *Quid de Baptismate Infantium*, 1533 (*Bucer Bibliographie*, 60). Cf. Wendel, *Calvin*, 323–29, esp. 323–24; J. W. Riggs, "Emerging Ecclesiology in Calvin's Baptismal Thought, 1536–1543," *Church History* 64 (1995): 29–43, esp. 36–40. Riggs examines Calvin's defense of infant baptism by comparing the 1536 *Institutes* with the second and third editions of 1539 and 1543.

177. *CO* 1:968. (*Institutio* 4.16.1: *OS* 5:304.)

178. *CO* 1:969. (*Institutio* 4.16.2: *OS* 5:305–6.) Cf. *CR: Zwingli*, 6/1:161, 164–65; G. R. Potter, *Zwingli* (Cambridge: Cambridge University Press, 1976), 196. In his appended piece "Concerning Covenant," Zwingli emphasizes the circumcision/baptism and promise connection. For Calvin's use of Bucer's work, see Wendel (*Calvin*, 324–25n87).

179. *CO* 1:969–74. (*Institutio* 4.16.3–10: *OS* 5:306–14.)

blessings accorded to the New Testament baptism. Citing a scriptural reference to baptism as "the circumcision of Christ" (Col 2:11), he affirmed that the spiritual promise God gave to Abraham was commonly shared by the infants both circumcised and baptized. He concluded that, as both circumcision and infant baptism were spiritual, they were "most completely in accord with respect to the inner mystery, the promises, the use, and the efficacy."[180]

In comparison with the argument based upon an analogy of circumcision and baptism, a far more difficult issue for Calvin was the Anabaptist contention concerning the relation of faith and baptism or the infant's ability to understand and believe. Earlier, Balthasar Hubmaier's *On the Christian Baptism of Believers* (1525) argued that Christian baptism should follow the gospel message, repentance, and faith, and that the case of infant baptism could not meet this qualification. While the above-mentioned Latin work of Zwingli refuted Hubmaier with an argument based on God's election and the notion of faith as God's gift, for Calvin, who refrained from directly appealing to election but relied upon scriptural testimonies, the issue was indeed a serious challenge.[181] In fact, Calvin acknowledged the difficulty by granting that infants could neither comprehend the "mystery" symbolized by baptism nor experience the "spiritual renewal." Yet, he put forth an interesting response to this issue. He characterized spiritual renewal as "God's work," which was to go far beyond believers' comprehension, and cited two scriptural references, namely, the case of John the Baptist, who before his birth was "filled with the Holy Spirit" in his mother's womb (Luke 1:15), and the case of Jesus's conception "by the Spirit" (1:35).[182] His argument, emphasizing "God's work" of the Spirit that could bring faith and renewal even to infants, was clearly intended to found his apologetics for infant baptism on the sound basis of the Triune God's work, namely, God's promise, election in Christ, and the work of the Holy Spirit in Scripture. From this assumption, he concluded that the sacrament of circumcision and baptism administered to infants was none other than "the sacrament of repentance and faith."[183]

After having reached this conclusion, Calvin responded to the points raised by the Anabaptists against infant baptism and presented his apologetics based on scriptural testimonies. Concerning the relation of faith with circumcision

180. *CO* 1:974–79, esp. 979. (*Institutio* 4.16.11–16: *OS* 5:314–20.)

181. Cf. *In Catabaptistarum Strophas Elenchus*: *CR: Zwingli*, 6/1:178–79. In opposition to Hubmaier's small work, *Von der christlichen Tauffe der gläubigen* (1525), Zwingli wrote a refutation, *Antwort über Balthasar Hubmaiers Taufbüchlin* (*CR: Zwingli* 4:585–641).

182. *CO* 1:980–81. (*Institutio* 4.16.17–18: *OS* 5:321–22.)

183. *CO* 1:982. (*Institutio* 4.16.20: *OS* 5:324.)

or baptism, he introduced a unique analogy between Abraham and Isaac. Distinguishing the case of Abraham, in whom faith preceded circumcision, and that of Isaac, in whom circumcision preceded faith, Calvin then applied these examples as parallels to the New Testament examples of adult baptism and infant baptism. Another aspect concerned baptized infants who met premature death. Using the notion of God's election, Calvin defended the cases of baptized infants whom God destined to be the elect, with their baptism being the symbol of salvific power through the Holy Spirit. His cautious approach, besides being an argument against Anabaptists, was perhaps meant to provide a contrast with Zwingli's view, which assumed from the notion of God's providence that all the believers' infants who died without having received baptism would be saved. In all, however, Calvin's apologetics seemingly took a unique position that emphasized "God's work" represented by the Holy Spirit and avoided both the Anabaptist overemphasis on faith and the overemphasis on the ceremony of infant baptism as seen among some mainstream Evangelicals.[184]

2. *The* Romans Commentary

The first edition of the *Romans Commentary*, like the second edition of the *Institutes*, inherited Calvin's early exegetical efforts during his first Genevan period. This aspect could be seen in its dedicatory epistle to Basel Reformer Grynaeus, which mentioned their discussion, back in 1535, over the exegetical significance of humanist methodology in interpreting Romans. In Strasbourg, he simultaneously engaged in both the revision of the *Institutes* and the writing of the commentary. He completed the final drafts by the summer of 1539, but the publication of the commentary was delayed until 1540. As we have mentioned earlier, he made a demarcation of two serial works, one for the *Institutes* as a theological textbook and the other as a biblical commentary. Reflecting the more recent interest in Calvin's hermeneutics, the focus of research seems to be the exegetical rather than theological aspect of the 1540 *Romans Commentary*.[185] However, the significance he attributed to the *Romans Com-*

184. Cf. *CO* 1:983–90. (*Institutio* 4.16.21–30, 32: *OS* 5:325–36, 340–41.)

185. Cf. B. Girardin, *Rhétorique et théologique: Calvin, le commentaire de l'Epître aux Romains* (Paris: Beauchesne, 1979); T. H. L. Parker, "Calvin the Exegete: Change and Development," in *Calvinus Ecclesiae Doctor*, ed. W. H. Neuser (Kampen: J. H. Kok, 1978), 33–46; Millet, *Calvin et la dynamique*, 122–51; Gordon, *Calvin*, 103–20; C. Grappe, "Calvin's Commentary on the Epistle to the Romans," in *John Calvin: The Strasbourg Years (1538–1541)*, ed. M. Arnold, 75–95; H. Goudineau, "Luther et Calvin commentateurs de l'Épître aux Romains:

mentary could be seen from the fact that, exceptionally, he revised it rather extensively twice, in 1551 and 1556. Starting with Romans in 1540, he successively published commentaries on the entire corpus of the Pauline epistles, in canonical order, until 1551. More importantly, as Parker remarks concerning the relation of the second *Institutes* and the *Romans Commentary*, almost all of the above-mentioned revisions and additions in the *Institutes* were related to the issues taken in the commentary, and conversely, the issues faced in the commentary were treated extensively in the *Institutes.*[186] Parker's bold conclusion made in the preface to the critical text of the *Renewed Calvini Opera*, that "there is no question of the 1539 *Institutio* consisting only of *loci* culled from Romans," needs to be further examined. Nevertheless, it is important to affirm that the *Romans Commentary*, as well as the second *Institutes*, reflected Calvin's concerns for the vital issues of his Strasbourg period, such as those of the church's unity and schism, biblicism, practical activism, the papal church, and the Anabaptists.[187]

In the dedicatory epistle, among many references used, Calvin listed in particular the three works of Melanchthon, Bullinger, and Bucer on Romans. The list might indicate his consideration of the three works as the exegetical representatives of Protestant Evangelicalism. While he evaluated both their qualities and shortcomings, the list might also suggest his confidence in presenting another better example of his own. In this connection, Gordon's biography of Calvin devotes one entire chapter to the *Romans Commentary* under the heading "'Lucid Brevity' for the Sake of the Church: Romans." It asserts that "Calvin was certain that he could be the voice of the Apostle in his own age" or that "the Paul of the *Romans Commentary* is Calvin himself." It has been well known that, in the preface to his later work on Psalms, Calvin exceptionally mentioned his personal history, and in the commentaries on the text, he implicitly identified King David's struggles with his own as a Reformer. Here in the *Romans Commentary*, likewise, Calvin's apologetic and existential concerns of the Strasbourg period can be discerned.[188] With these preliminary observations, we will proceed to focus on two topics, "salvation history and the church" and "apologetic edge." Because of our focus on Calvin's

---

Une comparison," *Positions luthériennes* 44 (1996): 16–52; A. Demura, "Two Commentaries on the Epistle to the Romans: Calvin and Oecolampadius," in *Calvinus Sincerioris Religionis Vindex*, ed. W. H. Neuser and B. G. Armstrong (Kirksville, MO: Sixteenth Century Journal Publishers, 1997), 165–88.

186. Parker, "Calvin the Exegete," 41–43.

187. T. H. L. Parker and D. C. Parker, *COR* II-13, "Introduction," liv.

188. Gordon, *Calvin*, 110–11.

Strasbourg period, we will primarily examine the 1540 text. As the topics under consideration require, however, we will also refer to the 1551 and 1556 texts.

(1) Salvation History and the Church

In addition to the dedicatory epistle mentioned above, the *Romans Commentary* provided a preface, a brief summary of the contents of Romans, in which Calvin considered the theme of the Pauline epistle's first five chapters as justification by faith, followed by the themes of sanctification (chs. 6–8), the Jewish race (chs. 9–11), and commendations for Christian living (chs. 12–15). Following the epistle's order of chapter and verse, he intended to provide comments in "lucid brevity."[189] First, since the book of Romans was written on the biblical concept of historical narratives, Calvin interpreted the goal of Paul's epistle as "a right and proper use of the sacred histories" to attain "the fruit of sound doctrine," to found faith, and to establish the life of fearing God.[190] If we call "the sacred histories" exhibited in Scripture "salvation history," his notion of history reflected a particular brand of the humanist concept of history in his age. In an examination of Calvin's hermeneutics in his commentaries on the Pauline letters (1540–51), Holder notes "a hermeneutical circle" composed of the three elements of "scripture, history, and the church," and considers them "three intertwining cords" completing the circle. As to the second element of "history," he portrays Calvin neither as an antiquated medieval exegete nor as a historian in the modern sense but rather as "a careful interpreter of human history for theological and ecclesiastical lessons."[191] If Calvin's notion of history reflected the common property of the humanists, however, he considered that Paul's concept of sacred history in Romans did not follow the general pattern of creation, the fall, the chosen people and the law, the gospel, and the end

189. *COR* II-13:7–12; *C. C.*, 8:5–11. For the text in English, we use *Calvin's Commentaries* (vol. 8, *Romans, Thessalonians*), ed. D. W. Torrance and T. F. Torrance, trans. R. Mackenzie (Grand Rapids: Eerdmans, 1960) (hereafter, *C. C.*, 8). For Calvin, "lucid brevity" is an ideal style of commenting on Scripture, which he shared with Grynaeus.

190. *COR* II-13:98 (4:23); *C. C.*, 8:101.

191. R. W. Holder, *John Calvin and the Grounding of Interpretation: Calvin's First Commentaries* (Leiden and Boston: Brill, 2006), 258–71. For the confirmation of his view, Holder cites, among others, S. Schreiner's notion that "for Calvin history represented the realm of salvation" (*The Theater of His Glory: Nature and Natural Order in the Thought of John Calvin* [Durham, NC: Labyrinth Press, 1991], 108) and I. Backus's notion of "the creative role of history" in Calvin as "a decisive factor in the affirmation of confessional identity" (*Historical Method and Confessional Identity in the Era of the Reformation (1378–1615)* [Leiden and Boston: Brill, 2003], 5).

time. Instead, Calvin interpreted its history as a particular pattern of salvation history, namely, the history of justification by faith. From this perspective, according to him, Romans started its arguments from the historical reality of the total corruption of mankind, the human enterprise of self-justification, and the lack of thankfulness toward God's grace. Paul then proceeded to treat Abraham as the beginning of the history of justification by faith, the histories of the law and circumcision, and the completion of that history in Christ's righteousness. From this perspective of Calvin's understanding of Paul's concept of the history of justification by faith, we will focus in the following pages on three points, namely, the relational framework of the history of justification and the church, the salvation of the Jewish race, and the history of justification and the kingdom of Christ.

(i) Concerning the first point of the framework, it is noteworthy that Calvin took the Romans text, "God shows no partiality" (2:11), as the starting point of the relation between justification history and the church. For example, he regarded the possible reason for distinguishing "Jews" (*Judaeos*) and "gentiles" (*Gentium*) solely due to the fact that God chose Jews out of gentiles and that, as far as the two accounts of life brought by justification by faith and death by self-righteousness are concerned, there was no difference between Jews and gentiles.[192] From this starting point, introducing the distinction of justification by faith and justification by works, he divided Jews into two groups: the people of justification by faith or "Abraham and his seed" (4:13) and the people of work righteousness or the people of "the law of works" (3:27). Introducing another framework, furthermore, Calvin considered the Jewish people of justification by faith and the non-Jewish people of justification by faith "all Abraham's seed" (4:16) in Christ, as two parallel developments in salvation history. He concluded that these two peoples constituted the substance of the total church of God. Calvin followed this framework of justification history in his comments on the text.

Firstly, Calvin examined the "privileges" of the Jewish race chosen out of gentiles, interpreting this Jewish privilege as grounded in them being the people of the true worship of God, the law, and circumcision, the people of the covenant God, and "the tribe from which the Redeemer was expected to come."[193] Secondly, he traced the history of this privileged people in their falling into idolatry from the true worship of God, their boasting of having the law but falling into self-righteousness, and their forsaking both the "promise

192. *COR* II-13:44–45 (2:11); *C. C.*, 8:46.
193. *COR* II-13:49 (2:17); *C. C.*, 8:50–51.

and faith" that their circumcision symbolized. As a result, the Jewish race was to be divided into the people of justification by faith and the people of self-righteousness.[194] Thirdly, he illustrated the precise relation of the two peoples via the case of Abraham as an "exemplar." He affirmed that the "principle" of justification by faith shown in Abraham's case was to be commonly applied to both Jews and gentiles (4:1).[195] Introducing a distinction in Abraham's case (4:10) between "before circumcision" and "in (or after) circumcision," he affirmed that Abraham believed God and was made righteous "before circumcision." However, interpreting circumcision as the first step of the righteousness of the law, he held Abraham's way of believing the law, as well as the "promise" that circumcision symbolized, as the way of justification by faith, as sharply distinguished from those who turned their backs to the "promise" and sought self-righteousness by the observance of the law, or the way of justification by works.[196] On the basis of the "promise" (4:13) given to Abraham and his offspring, he commented, not only Jews but also gentiles would be "Abraham and his seed" in Christ. In Calvin's analysis, the Jewish and gentile people of justification by faith was the true reality of the church in salvation history.[197]

(ii) The second point concerned the issue of the salvation of the Jewish race (chs. 9–11), which the apostle Paul introduced in connection with "the calling of gentiles." In his introductory note before commenting on chapter 9, Calvin summarized the criticism of Paul's teachings by his Jewish contemporaries in two points. Over against Paul's assertion that God took the "covenant" away from Jews and gave it to gentiles, Jews accused Paul of the fact that, if his teachings were true, God was not keeping the promise God made with Jews, and they insisted that the Christ whom Paul preached was not the Messiah promised to Jews. In Paul's counterargument against the Jewish criticism, Calvin noted Paul's crucial distinction between two elections of God: the one, the election of Abraham and his descendants, the Jewish race; the other, the election of a remnant among Abraham's descendants. Strictly speaking, only the second election was the object of the history of justification by faith, into which gentiles were later to be called. Following this distinction, Calvin emphasized

194. *COR* II-13:52 (2:25); *C. C.*, 8:54–55.

195. *COR* II-13:79 (4:1); *C. C.*, 8:82–83. Immediately following this text, the 1556 edition adds a section in which Calvin calls Abraham "the example of common rule," his personality "a mirror or exemplar," and his justice by faith the inheritance "belonging commonly to the entire church."

196. *COR* II-13:85 (4:10); *C. C.*, 8:88. Calvin's arguments here parallel his discussions in the 1539 *Institutes* mentioned above (cf. n. 184).

197. *COR* II-13:88–89 (4:13); *C. C.*, 8:91.

that the sovereign God, who separated Jews as the people of his covenant out of gentiles (the first election), could choose the people of justification by faith not only among Jews but also from gentiles (the second election).[198] In order to illustrate this theme, Calvin's comments on the three Pauline passages (9:4; 9:25; 11:26) were particularly noticeable. On the passage in which Paul was proud of the "privileges of Jews," firstly, Calvin's comment stressed that, as Paul confessed later, the privileges were meaningless "without Christ."[199] Secondly, in relation to Hosea's statement that "those who were not my people I will call 'my people'" (Rom 9:26), Calvin's comment rejected Erasmus's interpretation, which applied the oracle only to the election of Israel, as "a little forced" and interpreted it to apply both to Israel and to "the calling of gentiles."[200] Since "the covenant of grace" was to be restored and renewed only in Christ, Calvin's comment was intended to emphasize that, in the New Testament dispensation, Jews lost the status of "God's family" and, like gentiles, were reduced "to a common level" in which they were also required to return to Christ. From the perspective of ecclesiology, it was noticeable that his comment described the returning of both Jews and gentiles to Christ as citizens of the heavenly Jerusalem gathered from all the corners of the world.[201] Thirdly, on Paul's concluding statement concerning the salvation of Jews, "and so all Israel will be saved" (11:26), Calvin claimed to present a "better" interpretation. Acknowledging that many interpreters had taken this Pauline statement exclusively referring to the Jewish race and the eschatological restoration of Israel, Calvin offered another interpretation. Since on the occasion of "the calling of gentiles" the Jews were also to turn to faith in Christ, God has gathered both gentiles and Jews into the new people of justification by faith in Christ and thus "all Israel will be saved."[202]

198. *COR* II-13:10 ("Argumentum"), 186; *C. C.*, 8:190. Cf. Steinmetz, *Calvin*, 150–51.

199. *COR* II-13:189 (9:4); *C. C.*, 8:193–94. Immediately following this sentence, the 1556 edition text is added to emphasize that, despite Israel's disobedience, God kept "the remnant people" and gave to it "the designation of the church."

200. *COR* II-13:208 (9:25); *C. C.*, 8:213. The editor's footnote refers to Erasmus's *Paraphrases* (*Paraphrases in N. Testamentum*, *Opera Omnia*, 7, 809).

201. *COR* II-13:208–9 (9:25); *C. C.*, 8:213–14. At the end of the discussion, the 1556 edition adds a short sentence to highlight that God, in treating the Jews and gentiles on an equal footing, gathered for himself "the church out of the aliens." Here is the interesting notion of "the church of the aliens" (*ecclesia ex alienis*).

202. *COR* II-13:247 (11:26); *C. C.*, 8:155–56. The editor cites Thomas Aquinas, Erasmus, and others among the "majority" interpretations, but does not identify what Calvin calls an "appropriate" interpretation.

(iii) The third point concerned the relation of Christ's kingdom and the church. Modern historical researchers on Calvin's hermeneutics face considerable difficulties in both understanding his concept of Christ's kingdom, which reflects the suprahistorical dimension, and in placing it in his thought as a whole. Although the option to ignore it is open to researchers, some have taken a serious look at this notion. For example, as we have mentioned above, in his view of Calvin's notion of history as an element in his "hermeneutical circle," Holder poses an interesting question. By using the modern concept of the "Historie-Geschichte" distinction, he says that "We have thus far been taking history in its sense of *Historie*, the history of historians. . . . However, it is more fruitful to consider this topic [Calvin's notion of history] under the category of *Geschichte*, which is more broadly the flow of life within history." Although Holder does not refer to Christ's kingdom in connection with Calvin's notion of history, he notes that "Calvin consciously attempted to mediate between the historically-effected nature of the Church as an institution and the unchanging nature of the will of God for the believers."[203] No matter how we picture Calvin's worldview, it is true that he understood Christ's kingdom as both a historical and a suprahistorical and defining concept: Christ's kingdom was to manifest itself in the historical realm of the church and state; and at the same time, it was to define how the church and state in history were to operate. We have noted above Calvin's understanding of Christ's eucharistic "presence" in the Supper based upon the Antiochene approach ("distinction, but not separation") to Christ's resurrected body in heaven and the eucharistic elements in the Supper. Here, we assume, the same Christological teaching was to apply to his understanding of the Christ's kingdom–church relationship.

The concept of Christ's kingdom scarcely appeared in the Pauline text of Romans and only rarely in Calvin's comments. However, his references to this notion revealed a few interesting insights on the topic of "salvation history and the church." In the 1540 text, the term "the Kingdom of Christ or Messiah" was used in his comments on four passages (3:29; 9:25; 11:26; and 15:21; excluding 13:1 in which the term was used in a claim made by the Anabaptists). Calvin's comment connected the questions posed in the first passage—"Is God the God of Jews only? Is he not the God of Gentiles also?"—with the previous passage's notion of a person being "justified by faith." Since Paul applied the principle of justification by faith to both Jews and gentiles, Calvin argued that the Pauline principle was intended to apply "for the Kingdom of Christ through the whole

203. Holder, *John Calvin and the Grounding*, 266–68.

world."[204] As to the second passage that quoted the above-mentioned Hosea, Calvin commented that "where the Kingdom of Christ is raised, there also is lifted up that heavenly Jerusalem." Concerning Hosea's prophecy, Calvin referred to a particular interpretation (perhaps by Erasmus) as being supportable. As the interpretation affirmed a causative relation between God's showing favor first toward Jews, then, upon their failure, toward gentiles, he considered it as too "constricted" and instead offered his own interpretation. He interpreted Hosea's prophecy referring to God's universal favor to both Jews and gentiles, out of which God first chose Abraham among gentiles and showed favor to him and his descendants and, upon the Jewish failure, showed the same favor to gentiles. As a result, Calvin said that the Jewish nation was placed on the same level as gentiles as far as Christ's kingdom was concerned.[205] As to the third and fourth passages, Calvin interpreted them in the context of the historical consummation of Christ's kingdom. On the third passage, also quoted above on "all Israel," Calvin interpreted "all Israel," which was the entire people of justification by faith gathered from both Jews and gentiles, as "the consummation of Christ's Kingdom." As to the fourth passage on the prophecy of Isaiah (52: 15), Calvin interpreted this prophecy as being fulfilled in Paul, the apostle to gentiles, and affirmed that from Paul's time on, the knowledge of "the Messiah's Kingdom" would be spread among gentiles throughout the whole world. The ecclesial reality of Christ's kingdom mentioned in Calvin's comments in the above four passages is no other than what he identifies as the people of justification by faith or "all Israel." If we use his double notion of the church previously mentioned, the people of justification and "all Israel" concern the church of the first level, that is, "the whole number of the elect" and its manifestation in history, "the Catholic church."[206]

(2) Apologetic Edge

In addition to the three commentaries mentioned in the dedicatory epistle, Calvin's *Romans Commentary* was known to have used the commentaries of Luther, Zwingli, Oecolampadius, and others, and was intended to be a work well representing the Evangelical position. In a sense, his intention was recognized by the fact that it was soon listed in the 1543 Index of the Paris Theological Faculty. Unquestionably, it was also intended to meet the high humanist

204. *COR* II-13:77 (3:29); *C. C.*, 8:80.
205. *COR* II-13:208 (9:25); *C. C.*, 8:213–14.
206. *COR* II-13:247 (11:26); *C. C.*, 8:253; *COR* II-13:304 (15:21).

standard of the times in both the hermeneutical and rhetorical sense. In this regard, the editors of the critical text in the *Renewed Calvini Opera* note that Calvin had possibly consulted nearly thirty sixteenth-century works on Romans, in addition to the works of the ancient and medieval periods, and that his comments revealed some discrepancies among his contemporary Evangelical exegetes.[207] As we have earlier noted Gordon's remark that in the *Romans Commentary* Calvin was convinced that he was "a voice of Paul" to his own age, the commentary was at the same time an apology of his own theology. Due to his method of serially separating exegetical works from dogmatic works, the apologetic character was less noticeable in the commentary. Nonetheless, the hermeneutical context seen in his comments was an important key to understanding and evaluating his first biblical commentary. We will call this aspect the "apologetic edge" in his hermeneutics and will examine it in the following two points: the one, his theological apology against the opposing positions of papalism, the Anabaptists, and the moderate Catholic reformists; the other, an apology for his own theological position within Protestant Evangelicalism.

Calvin's Evangelical Apology

(i) Concerning the first point, for Calvin who considered papalism a mixture of Christianity with Judaism and heathenism, the choice of Romans for his first New Testament commentary itself proved his apologetic intention. As Paul's apology against the Judaist Christians crept into the Church of Rome, Calvin juxtaposed the Pauline apology with his own against papalism and its medieval background of Scholasticism. On the passage "if you call yourself a Jew and rely on the law" (2:17), for example, Calvin's comment interpreted Paul's accusation of the Judaists as those who were "abhorring idols yet at the same time robbing temples" (2:22) and were idolaters just like the heathen. In this context, he commented that "so at the present time" superstition instead of God's word, idols instead of God, and pomp and magnificence instead of religion reigned in the papal church.[208] It was true that, as a rule, his comments avoided naming names such as the papists, Anabaptists, and so forth, so they generally left no room for overt criticism of the papal church as such. This tendency remained the same in the commentary's second and third editions (1551, 1556), in which he was conscious of the Catholic counterposition decisively

207. *COR* II-13, "Introduction," lxxv–lxxxi. Cf. Steinmetz, *Calvin*, "Calvin and the Divided Self of Romans 7," 110–21.

208. *COR* II-13:51 (2:22); *C. C.*, 8:53.

taken in the first period of the Council of Trent (1545–47) against Protestant Evangelicalism. One of a few exceptions to this tendency, however, was his comment on Paul's charge in the last chapter of Romans. He interpreted Paul's passage (16:17) as a warning to "all the churches" that "the ministers of Satan [are] constantly watching every opportunity for disturbing the Kingdom of Christ" and commented that the "papists" had no right to quote this passage as a way of describing the Evangelicals as schismatics.[209]

(ii) Although Calvin's direct comments on the Anabaptists were not numerous, a few examples referring to the "spirit of tumult" or the "Anabaptists" could be seen. One such example appeared in his comment on a turnabout of Paul's arguments (7:24–25) from "Wretched man that I am" to "Thanks be to God." Calvin interpreted this turnabout as Paul's "post-conversion" confession of the remnant of original sin within himself and its sharp contrast with salvation in Christ, and then he challenged Anabaptists' perfectionism that interpreted Paul's confession as a "pre-conversion" experience. As we have seen above, in the second *Institutes*, Calvin grouped Anabaptists with the heresies of the Donatists and Cathari. In his comment here he denounced the Anabaptist position as being "the most pernicious dogma of the Purists (*Cathari*)" that "some turbulent spirits are attempting to revive at the present time."[210] Another example appeared in his comment on the divine sanction of magisterial authority (13:1) where he followed his familiar apologetic stand of the first *Institutes* against the *Schleitheim Confession* (art. 6 on sword) and the Anabaptist Münster revolution. His comment described "some restless spirits" and their Anabaptist teachings that Christ's kingdom would not be established unless all earthly powers were abolished and that Christian freedom could not be given unless all human servitudes were taken away.[211] Here, his comment also criticized the Judaist Christians opposed to Paul in the church in Rome as those who, even after Christ's first appearance, were still expecting the earthly reign of another Christ as Messiah. His criticism was obviously directed not only against the Münster revolution, which he regarded as "a Jewish vanity," but also against the papal church, which he considered the usurpation of Christ's kingdom.[212]

(iii) There was practically no evidence of Calvin's overt reference to or critical comment aimed at the moderate evangelical reformists in France with

209. *COR* II-13:68–70 (3:21); *C. C.*, 8:70–73; *COR* II-13:313 (16:17); *C. C.*, 8:124–25.
210. *COR* II-13:151 (7:25); *C. C.*, 8:155.
211. *COR* II-13:271 (13:1); *C. C.*, 8:280.
212. *COR* II-13:271–72 (13:1); *C. C.*, 8:280–81.

whom he had been engaged in dispute since *Two Epistles*. Possible exceptions that might suggest his implicit criticism could be found in his comments on the "confessing" of faith (10:10) and on "seven thousand who have not bowed the knee to Baal" (11:4–5). As to the first passage, he assumed that those who had been saved by confessing faith in Christ were in need of responding to God's work toward the completion of their salvation. Here, he mentioned the case of those with "an imaginary faith," likening them to those who claimed to have a faith like burning fire even though there was evidence of neither flame nor heat there. Furthermore, he denounced them as those who were content with a secret faith in the heart and considered "the confession of mouth" superfluous or unnecessary. This was the theme that he first presented in the first epistle of *Two Epistles*.[213] As to the second passage of "seven thousand" and "a remnant," just like the first epistle, the issue was the physical participation in idolatrous ceremonies. Interestingly, his comment identified "seven thousand" with those "who did not prostitute their body to the worship of idols, even by an outward act of pretense." He further commented that in the days of Elijah, when "the whole [Jewish] people had fallen into idolatry," God kept "a remnant"—the comment clearly reflecting the current condition of France.[214]

Calvin's Hermeneutic Stance

(i) Concerning the second point of Calvin's hermeneutical efforts to establish his own position in the Evangelical circle, Gordon mentions an interesting aspect of the *Romans Commentary* under the theme of "the fellowship of the word." This aspect indicates Calvin's setting of the commentary as a forum of exchange and dialogue with his fellow Evangelical exegetes like Melanchthon, Bullinger, Bucer and others.[215] Besides Erasmus, of whose exegeses Calvin is most conscious, indeed he often refers to Bucer by name, Melanchthon many times although unnamed, but surprisingly Bullinger only in a few instances.[216]

213. *COR* II-13:222 (10:10); *C. C.*, 8:228.

214. *COR* II-13:234 (11:4–5); *C. C.*, 8:241–42.

215. Gordon, *Calvin*, 104–6. Under the heading "The Fellowship of the Word," Gordon considers Melanchthon, Bullinger, and Bucer as the representatives of the Reformation cities of Wittenberg, Zurich, and Strasbourg, and assumes Calvin to be a moderator of various teachings among these cities.

216. Cf. *COR* II-13, "Appendix: Text of Selected References," 319–34. An example of Calvin's comment expressly naming Bucer can be found in his comment on 4:5 (*COR* II-13:82). Since Calvin took some issues with Bullinger on the idea of covenant in the 1539 *Institutes*, the scarcity of reference to Bullinger seems unexpected. Among a few possible references

Concerning the topic of Calvin's "exchange and dialogue" with Melanchthon, Bullinger, and Bucer on Romans, recent researchers have especially focused upon its hermeneutical aspect. Following up on an earlier work by Girardin that examined Calvin's *Romans Commentary* in the tradition of rhetorical exegesis, for example, Grappe's most recent study on this topic focuses on what Girardin called Calvin's search for "Paul's rhetorical gesture" in the Romans text and considers it key to relating Calvin's hermeneutics to those of Melanchthon, Bullinger, and Bucer. In referring to the recent Calvin-Melanchthon and Calvin-Bullinger comparative studies, Grappe points out Calvin's "originality" and concludes that "on this point [Calvin's respect for rhetoric], with Melanchthon, Bullinger, and Bucer, his approach shows an exemplary character."[217]

(ii) As far as the 1540 edition was concerned, Calvin's recognition of Bucer's exegetical contribution, by either referring to him by name or noting his interpretations without naming him, was quite notable. In addition, there seemed to be no comments in which he critically treated Bucer's interpretations or presented alternative interpretations of his own. This tendency could be reflective of his high esteem for Bucer's commentary as expressed in the dedicatory epistle. If we look at the composition of the commentaries as a whole, however, there are some indications of a different approach and emphasis in dealing with the same Pauline text. As to the crucial doctrine of justification by faith in the first five chapters, for example, the editors of the *COR* text say that "while using the same rhetorical terminology as Melanchthon and Bucer, he [Calvin] keeps it to its original place in the law courts." Besides this emphasis on the forensic character of justification, a sharp and consistent distinction between justification and regeneration (sanctification) is another noticeable feature in Calvin's comments. Some researchers find in this distinction an implicit reaction to Bucer's teachings on justification. For example, Grappe points to Bucer's *Romans Commentary* that highlights "the syllogistic development from justification to sanctification" in the Pauline text (1:18–3:31), and De Kroon notes his favorable comment on Cardinal Sadoleto's teaching on justification,

to Bullinger's *Romans Commentary* in the 1540 edition, Calvin's comment on 8:23 (*COR* II-13:171n40) seems to be the only occasion on which he notes Bullinger's interpretation and presents his own alternative one. Gordon (*Calvin*, 105) explains this as "a significant silence" due to the reason that "he avoided direct criticism."

217. C. Grappe, "Calvin's Commentary on the Epistle to the Romans," in *John Calvin: The Strasbourg Years (1538–1541)*, ed. M. Arnold (Eugene, OR: Wipf & Stock, 2016), 75–95. Cf. Girardin, *Rhétorique et théologique*, 168–270, 299. For the Calvin-Melanchthon aspect, see Grappe, 76–79, 89; for the Calvin-Bullinger aspect, see 79–80, 81 (n. 33), 84; for Calvin's "originality," see 83, 90–91, 95.

implying that some of his teachings are the same as those of the Evangelicals.[218] In Calvin's Strasbourg period, his *Reply to Sadoleto* emphasized the doctrine of justification as "the first and keenest subject of controversy between us," and the *Book of Regensburg*, coauthored by Bucer, included a compromising article on justification. With this background, Calvin's 1551 edition added a comment on the crucial text of 1:17 that rejected the view that the text's "righteousness of God" included not only "free remission of sin" (justification by faith) but also "partly the grace of regeneration" (sanctification). The editors of the *COR* edition consider this view shared by Sadoleto and Bucer.[219]

A noticeable exegetical difference of emphasis between Bucer and Calvin appeared on Romans 8:28–30, the text in which Paul dealt with the subject of *ordo salutis*, the gradation of God's election (predestination) and the faithful's calling, justification, and glorification. While Bucer's exegesis treated the subject in general without emphasizing the faithful's afflictions, Calvin focused on and added a fresh emphasis to the issue of their afflictions, especially their bearing the cross, inseparably connected to the *ordo salutis*. Calvin had already expressed this emphasis in the last chapter of his 1539 *Institutes* on the life of the Christian man. The addition of this chapter to the *Institutes* could be, in part, a reflection of his controversy with the moderate French reformists, triggered by the publication of his *Two Epistles*. On the other hand, his commentary on Romans 8:28–29 similarly treated the faithful's afflictions as their following the "image or example" of Christ and their being "the heirs of Christ's Kingdom." On Romans 8:30, in which Paul brought the whole *ordo salutis* into one passage, however, suddenly Calvin started emphasizing the meaning of the cross in conjunction with the entire *ordo salutis*. The cross was said to be ordained for the faithful by God's decree; their bearing the cross was inseparably connected to their calling, justification, and glorification.[220]

218. T. H. L. Parker and D. C. Parker, *COR* II-13, "Introduction," lix; Grappe, "Calvin's Commentary," 80; De Kroon, *Martin Bucer und Johannes Calvin*, 119–24 ("Exkurs: Bucer und Calvin in Auseinandersetzung mit Jacopo Sadoleto"). Cf. Kok, "The Influence of Martin Bucer," 64–67. In chapter 1 (section 3.4.1, n. 206), we have noted Sadoleto's *Romans Commentary* (1535/1536), which appeared just before the publications of Calvin's first *Institutes* and Bucer's *Romans Commentary*, and was recommended for revision by the Paris Theological Faculty for its Pelagian inclination.

219. *COR* II-13:28n52.

220. *CO* 1:1123–52, esp. 1125–43 (*Institutio* 4.6–10: *OS* 4:146–81); *COR* II-13:176 (ll. 33–34, on 8:29), 177 (ll. 31–32, on 8:29), 178 (ll. 1–7, on 8:30). Cf. Kok, "The Influence of Martin Bucer," 133–36; D. S. Sytsma, "The Exegetical Context of Calvin's *Loci* on the Christian Life," *Calvin Theological Journal* 45 (2010): 256–79, esp. 272–74. Using the 1556 edition of Calvin's *Romans Commentary*, Kok remarks on this Bucer-Calvin contrast. Sytsma examines the

As noted above, this was written at the critical time when he was the refugee pastor of the French congregation in Strasbourg, facing across the border the first waves of systematic persecution upon the Evangelicals set in motion by the Edict of Fontainebleau. As we will see in the next chapter, another critical time of his second Genevan reform was the year 1555. In the 1556 edition of the *Romans Commentary*, he drastically revised the entire 8:28–30 section from the emphatic viewpoint of the election-cross connection. On 8:28, for example, he affirmed that, although afflictions could fall upon both the elect and the reprobate, those upon the elect alone were used by God for their salvation; God's decree prescribed afflictions and the cross to them in order for them to conform to Christ. On 8:29, along with God's decree for their calling, justification, and glorification, the cross was said to be ordained "from this other decree." Calvin's final comment (8:30) on the meaning of the faithful's afflictions was none other than their "attaining the celestial glory of the Kingdom" and their "reaching the glorious resurrection of Christ with whom they are now being crucified."[221]

(iii) Although the exegetical details of Calvin's "exchange and dialogue" are not our immediate concern, some of them are noteworthy from the perspective both of his establishing his own position in the Evangelical circle and of his maintaining its hermeneutical solidarity. We examine a few cases below that can be said to be a reflection of his Catholic ecclesiology.

The first case concerned the gift of "prophecy" (12:6), and here, with full recognition of the Evangelical exegetes' interpretations of the passage, Calvin presented his own different view. According to the editors' footnotes in the critical edition, Erasmus, Melanchthon, and Bucer took "prophecy" as the gift of God's oracles or revelatory activities of foretelling limited to the transitional period from the Old to the New Testament dispensation. Calvin preferred the wider connotation of the gift of showing and expounding God's will unlimited to any specific time periods and applicable even to his own "Christian church today" as the office of understanding and explaining the Bible correctly.[222]

Another case of Calvin's "exchange and dialogue" was the passage (1:17) that was a crucial text for Luther, and here Calvin carefully presented his own position. First of all, he considered two verses (1:16–17) as a unit. He intro-

---

correlation between Calvin's dogmatic loci expressed in the newly added chapter on the Christian life in the 1539 *Institutes* and the related exegetical notions in the 1540 *Romans Commentary*, including the references to Romans 8:28–30.

221. *COR* II-13:175 (ll. 27–29, 35), 176 (ll. 26–31, on 8:28), 177 (ll. 21–24, on 8:29), 178 (l. 35)–179 (l. 2, on 8:30).

222. *COR* II-13:261, esp. n. 9 (12:6); *C. C.*, 8:268–69.

duced the notion of the Holy Spirit's internal illumination in connection with the clause "salvation to everyone who has faith" (1:16). Here, he interpreted the Spirit as the "inward teacher" (*Spiritus interior magister*) for believers and placed the clause in the limited framework of the Spirit's internal illumination rather than applying it universally. Although admitting the general principle of the gospel offered indiscriminately to all and of salvation given to all who believed, he nonetheless interpreted the text's "salvation" in the definitive sense of "the eternal life," as he commented that "since then the Gospel delivers from ruin and the curse of endless death, its salvation is eternal life."[223] From this exegetical context he proceeded to verse 17 and presented a rather interesting perspective on the clause, "from faith to faith" (*ex fide in fidem*). While he commented on "from faith" cursorily in the sense of salvation given to believers led by the Spirit, he shifted the weight of his exegesis on "to faith" and emphasized the justified believers' sanctification, which he interpreted as the increase of God's righteousness within the believers through the works of the Spirit.[224] As we have previously noted, in the Strasbourg period, Calvin founded the "assurance of faith" on the works of the Holy Spirit. Here in the *Romans Commentary*, he placed the doctrine of justification by faith in the context of the Spirit's work and presented his own view of emphasizing its connection with the sanctification of believers.

Lastly, there were noticeable cases in which Calvin seemed to have restrained his comments on the passages where the Evangelical exegetes considerably disagreed in treating the contested issues. Such an exemplary case was the main subject of Romans 9, the election of God. As we have noted in the second *Institutes*, he cautiously treated the passive approach of Melanchthon and Zwingli so as to make the doctrine of election a basic teaching of Evangelicalism, although he undoubtedly affirmed the doctrine.[225] While refraining from going into apologetic details, he presented his comments within the limit of the flow of Paul's arguments. His attitude was especially noticeable in his

223. *COR* II-13:26–27 (1:16), esp. 27; *C. C.*, 8:27. Here Calvin is obviously conscious of Luther's position that takes "faith" fundamentally as an act of believing (*fiducia*) and subsequently a "believer" as dialectically defined "simul iustus et peccator." Calvin takes his position that emphasizes "faith" and "justification" as the whole process from the original point of believing the gospel to eternal life.

224. *COR* II-13:28 (1:17); *C. C.*, 8:27–29. The 1556 edition adds a sentence to emphasize "to faith," namely, "[Paul] notes the continuous progress in each believer."

225. Cf. *CO* 1:888. (*Institutio* 3.24.17: *OS* 4:429–30.) The editors of the *Opera Selecta* cite here Melanchthon's *Loci Communes*. Calvin's text itself avoids identifying the reference, but interestingly carries the discussion personally in second person singular.

comments on "I have loved Jacob, but I have hated Esau" (9:13) and on the call of gentiles (9:23–25). This could be understood as his separation of dogmatic and exegetical concerns or simply as his regard for the exegetical difference between Melanchthon and Zwingli.[226]

Concluding Remarks

(1) Calvin's career in Strasbourg, between his expulsion from and then return to Geneva, was a transitional period. It was a preparatory stage for the future "Reformer of Geneva." As a pastor of the French refugee church, he took his first steps toward becoming a "Reformer of France," and in a pivotal city of political and religious communications in Europe, he nurtured his own vision of being a "Reformer of Europe." In other words, he established himself as a unique Reformer. From the perspective of his ecclesiology, this transitional period signified the progress from his basic stratum of "Catholic ecclesiology" to what we will discuss in the next chapter, his "Reformed ecclesiology" and "Reformation ecclesiology."

(2) In view of Calvin's ecclesiological formation, what made his Strasbourg period so meaningful was the close presence of the unique Reformer, Martin Bucer, who took the exiled Calvin in, arranged for him to be called as a pastor of the French congregation, made him a lecturer of the Bible in the Academy, and paved the way for him to meet the Lutheran princes and theologians and even to participate in the religious unification colloquies in Germany. Unlike Luther, from whom the young Calvin had learned the most thorough reading of the German Reformer's writings in Latin, his relationship with Bucer was personal. Since his post-Strasbourg theological formation was said to resemble Bucer's theological outlook, many researchers have associated it with Bucer and developed the "Bucer's influence" theory. Limiting our focus to ecclesiological concerns, we tried to critically reevaluate this theory in the context of such issues as the current Catholic Church under papal rule, the future of the French Reformation, and Calvin's consistent biblicism and practical activism. Especially on the crucial issue of the Roman Catholic Church being the "church of Christ," due partly to having been able to examine Bucer's unpublished manuscript document, *Theological Advice*, which was unavailable

226. Cf. *COR* II-13:197, 203–7 (9:13, 19–23); *C. C.*, 8:208–12. Similarly, the 1539 *Institutes* (*CO* 1:884; *Institutio* 3.24.10: *OS* 4:421) rejects the Scholastic notion of the seed of election that Bucer was said to have held, however, the *Romans Commentary* does not deal with this notion.

to the formulators of the "Bucer's influence" theory, we have noticed a basic difference between Bucer and Calvin.

(3) No matter how we evaluate "Bucer's influence" on Calvin during the Strasbourg period, one clear image of Calvin emerges: that he was his own theologian who had carefully analyzed the reality and shortcomings of urban reformations in Strasbourg, Basel, and Zurich and who had also observed the religious-political scene in Europe and the prospect of religious unification. It is without question that, on the basis of his "Catholic ecclesiology," he started afresh to develop his ecclesiology further in Strasbourg. To acknowledge Bucer's most important contribution to Calvin's ecclesiology, our study indicates two distinctive directions of church reform, namely, the Reformation of the local church and that of the Christian world, especially the latter in the context of the French Reformation. As we will discuss in the next chapter, these two directions were to take the concrete forms of the "Reformed ecclesiology" and "Reformation ecclesiology" in his second Genevan period.

(4) The second *Institutes* and the *Romans Commentary* were two academic achievements of Calvin's Strasbourg period. They marked a beginning of the distinctive two series of dogmatic formulations of theological loci and exegetical expositions of Scripture. The second *Institutes* drastically changed the structure of the first *Institutes* from a combination of the catechetical and apologetic portions into a theological textbook with new supplements, especially those against the Anabaptists. As far as ecclesiology was concerned, the second *Institutes* and its French translation paved the way to the third *Institutes*, which we consider to be the most important *Institutes* of all the editions. The *Romans Commentary* was not just the first commentary to be published, but was meant to be a "prototype" for all the remaining printed works of sermons, lectures, and commentaries on the biblical books. Calvin developed a unique notion of salvation history as the history of justification by faith, as well as the concept of the church based upon this history. In the final analysis, this study will assert that this historical perspective of salvation history provided the framework for both his Reformed and Reformation ecclesiologies.

Chapter Four

Reformed Ecclesiology and Reformation Ecclesiology

This chapter examines Calvin's Reformed ecclesiology and Reformation ecclesiology in sections 2 and 3, respectively. Prior to this examination, in section 1, we will survey his reform activities under the heading of "Reformer of Geneva and Europe" in order to place each ecclesiology in its historical context. The period under consideration is his second Genevan stay (1541–64), and our focus is on tracing some main points in the development of his concept of the church. It is particularly noteworthy that this period is roughly divided into two halves by the year 1555, the pre- and the post-1555 periods. This divide can be seen in that Calvin's main goal for the Genevan Reformation was gradually realized and definitively settled in the first half, while his reform effort for France and Europe, beyond Geneva, was drastically advanced in the second half. As to the publications of his biblical commentaries and lectures, a similar divide can be seen in that the New Testament exegetical works, predominantly on the Pauline epistles, were concentrated in the first half. The Old Testament works of the prophets, including the Psalms, and the Pentateuch, appeared in the second half. Furthermore, what our study calls his "Reformed ecclesiology" took its basic shape in the first half, especially in the third *Institutes* of 1543 and the *First Corinthians Commentary* of 1546. What our study calls his "Reformation ecclesiology" found its clear expression in the commentaries and lectures on the Prophets and especially in the final *Institutes* of 1559, which drastically reorganized and edited the texts of the previous editions.

In section 2, which mainly examines Calvin's concept of the church in his third *Institutes* and his *First Corinthians Commentary*, we will follow up on the theme of "the Reformation of a local church" previously discussed in chapter 3 as his inheritance from the Strasbourg period. The focus of this theme is the actual form, organization, and government of the church in history, that is, Calvin's "Reformed ecclesiology." In section 3, which mainly focuses on his works of the second half of that period, we will focus on his "Reformation ecclesiology," a term that must be more carefully presented. Certainly, his reform activities, which reflected another theme of "the Reformation of the European Christian world," were accentuated in the post-1555 period, and his commentaries and lectures on the Prophets also revealed the same theme. In addition, what is generally called the definitive expression of his ecclesiology in book 4 of the final *Institutes* can be viewed as an integration of his earlier "Catholic" and "Reformed" ecclesiologies. Can we properly call his ecclesiology of the post-1555 period "Reformation ecclesiology" and consider it the final form of his ecclesiology? With this question in mind, we will proceed in section 3 to examine how Calvin viewed the church in his last years and how he had proposed to reform it.

Nearly a quarter-century of Calvin's second Genevan period coincided with the age in which the ideal of one Christian society was broken and the unity of the Christian church was literally torn asunder. This was the age in which Erasmus lamented in the 1530s that "no one will undo this universal tragedy except God." In the 1550s, Calvin diagnosed it as "Europe afflicted." Erasmus feared the coming schism. Calvin acknowledged not only the schism taking place but also the entire religious situation of Europe, in both Catholic and Protestant lands, as being in a state of collapse and a mess.[1] Furthermore, this was the age in which the Roman Catholic Church had officially promulgated the opening of the Council of Trent (1545–63) and had guided it under the spirit of both papalism and Counter-Reformation. In Germany, after the Schmalkald War (1546–47), which marked the failure of the earlier efforts of church unification, the final religious accord was reached in the Peace of Augsburg (1555). While guaranteeing the coexistence of the Catholic and Protestant territories, it also marked the end of the Reformation in Germany. In England, the episcopal settlement of the Church was firmly established with the *Thirty-Nine Articles* (1563). And in the context of the French Reformation, after the clandestine formation of the Reformed Church of France (1559), the Wars of Religion broke out in 1562. In this volatile age in Europe, Calvin had formulated his characteristic concepts of the church, which we call his Reformed and Reformation ecclesiologies, upon the stratum of his earlier Catholic ecclesiology.

1. P. S. Allen, ed., *Opus Epistolarum*, 9, no. 2343, cited in Kelly, *The Beginning*, 6; *Commentarii in Isaiam Prophetam*, *CO* 36:178, 202, cited in H. A. Oberman, "*Europa Afflicta*: The Reformation of the Refugees," *Archiv für Reformationsgeschichte* 83 (1992): 102.

Back in September of 1541, Calvin made a comeback to Geneva with a new vision for reform. From Strasbourg he took a detour to three major Protestant cities in the Swiss Confederation, Basel, Zurich, and Bern. Basel was the only Swiss city that officially accepted the Wittenberg Concord worked out by the Lutherans and the Reformed in Germany and where Oecolampadius had tried to introduce autonomous church discipline ten years before. Zurich and Bern were known for their Zwinglian teachings on the Eucharist and church polity. With these cities the future reformer of Geneva was to endure complicated and arduous relationships.

At this juncture, he had envisioned a new model of the church and state relationship for Geneva. This would be quite different from both the German model of Catholic and Protestant coexistence under the Holy Roman Emperor and the city reformation model of Strasbourg and Zurich, where reform was experiencing an impasse.[2] In fact, the new Genevan ecclesiastical ordinance that Calvin had requested the city to establish was to exert considerable impact upon the future relationship of the Genevan Church and the magistracy. During the course of his second stay in the city, indeed, Geneva was to experience trial and error in its attempts to reach a new model of church-state relationship. In this transformation, which a historian of the Genevan institutions, Kingdon, calls "a revolution," Calvin's concept of reform played a major role and helped to establish a reformation distinct from that in Europe. In fear of Calvin's re-expulsion from Geneva, Strasbourg had initially "loaned" him to Geneva for six months. But his stay lasted longer and he was to end his life in the city as "Reformer of Geneva," "Reformer of France," and "Reformer of Europe."[3]

Section 1. Reformer of Geneva and Europe

It could be seen as absurd to divide Calvin's stormy quarter-century stay in Geneva arbitrarily at the year 1555. However, it should be noted that the year

2. C. Ocker, "Calvin in Germany," in *Politics and Reformations: Histories and Reformations*, ed. Ocker et al. (Leiden and Boston: Brill, 2007), 341. Cf. E. Campi and C. Moser, "'Loved and Feared': Calvin and the Swiss Confederation," in *John Calvin's Impact on Church and Society, 1509–2009*, ed. M. E. Hirzel and M. Sallmann (Grand Rapids: Eerdmans, 2009), 14–34.

3. R. M. Kingdon, "Was the Protestant Reformation a Revolution? The Case of Geneva," in *Church and Society in Reformation Europe*, ed. R. M. Kingdon (London and Freme, Somerset: Variorum Reprints, 1985), 208–15. See also W. G. Naphy's historical reevaluation of Calvin's second Genevan stay, "New Sources and New Ideas on the Life and Career of Calvin, 1541–1557," in *Calvinus Evangelii Propugnator*, ed. D. F. Wright, A. N. S. Lane, and J. Balserak (Grand Rapids: Calvin Studies Society, 2006), 40–53.

was critically important, not only for Calvin's Reformation but also for the city Republic of Geneva and the European theater. On the one hand, the Genevan Reformation, which began with Calvin's recall from Strasbourg in 1541, saw its tentative conclusion with substantive achievements in 1555. Concerning the recall of Calvin, historian Monter's remark that the city leaders did not understand Calvin sufficiently and miscalculated the reform that he was about to introduce is not far off the mark.[4] They were not responsible for their lack of understanding regarding Calvin. He presented his own unique brand of Evangelicalism in his first *Institutes*, defended his stand fiercely during his first stay in the city, maintained his theological position even under the predominant influence of Bucer in Strasbourg, and soon introduced a reform very different from the city reformations that were known to them. In reality, the pre-1555 period was a time of turbulent conflicts, involving various factions of the city, about institutionalizing Calvin's reform concept and applying it to the life of the church and state.

Accordingly, the year 1555 saw the Reformed Church of Geneva firmly established. At the same time, it witnessed a kind of independence from the Zwinglian Bern that had exerted considerable influence over Geneva since the introduction of the reform in 1536. As a matter of fact, the city authority's 1555 verdict against the last opposition group of Ami Perrin and his party, supported by Bern, indicated that the Perrinists plotted "to destroy ecclesiastical discipline and the Reformation."[5] During the post-1555 period, furthermore, Geneva was emerging as an international center of Reformed Christianity. It surpassed Strasbourg, which witnessed the inroad of Lutheranism in the 1550s and even ranked with Bullinger's Zurich. In borrowing sociologist Benedict's expression, during this period Calvin ambitiously expanded his involvement beyond Geneva into the Reformation of Europe with a "refugee's consciousness."[6]

On the other hand, in the same European theater, the year 1555 marked a religious accord in Germany, the Peace of Augsburg, which is generally regarded as the most important achievement in the legal history of early modern Germany. Even legally seen as a tentative measure, the accord was to last for two and a half centuries along with the history of the Holy Roman Empire.

4. E. W. Monter, *Calvin's Geneva* (New York: John Wiley & Sons, 1967), 70. On the Guillermins who took control of the city and moved to recall Calvin, Monter remarks: "But they got a great deal more than they had bargained for. Instead of restoring the church of Farel, they had unintentionally inaugurated the church of Calvin."

5. Monter, *Calvin's Geneva*, 88–89.

6. Cf. P. Benedict, *Christ's Churches Purely Reformed: A Social History of Calvinism* (New Haven and London: Yale University Press, 2002), 109–14.

Although the accord effectively achieved the coexistence of the Lutheran and Catholic territories, according to the faith of their heads of state, it was also a solution that excluded Zwinglianism and Calvinism along with Anabaptism. Besides its positive evaluation as an inevitable compromise, it could be negatively viewed as the institutionalization of "a fiction of one, undivided church."[7] In particular, the German solution could not be an option for Reformed Christianity, which had increasingly hardened its stance against Catholicism. In opposition to both the German solution and the Catholic Council of Trent, internally Reformed Christianity aimed for more thorough church reform, and externally it increased its theological opposition to Lutheranism and its conflicts with Catholicism. Notably, Benedict's book, *Christ's Churches Purely Reformed: A Social History of Calvinism*, also considered 1555 as the dividing year. Benedict regards the years before 1555 as the formative period of the Reformed traditions mainly centered in Zurich and Geneva, and the post-1555 period as the expansion of the Reformed traditions into the European world.[8]

1. The Genevan Reformation

Although the history of the Genevan Reformation in Calvin's time is not a main focus of our study, at least three of its aspects need to be mentioned as crucial to understanding his ecclesiological development in this period. The first is the 1541 *Genevan Ecclesiastical Ordinance* that can be seen as background material for his Reformed ecclesiology. The second focuses on the year 1555 in which the internal conflict over Calvin's ecclesiastical polity was finally settled. And the third is a symbolic year for him, 1559, in which the final *Institutes* was published, the Genevan Academy was established, and the French Reformed Church was organized at the first national synod in Paris.

(1) Genevan Ecclesiastical Ordinance

Beginning with Calvin's request on the day of his arrival in September, through the processes of drafting the original text by a special committee and it being partially corrected by the Small Council, the *Ecclesiastical Ordinance* was finalized on November 20 in the General Assembly of Citizens, the highest

7. Cf. H. Immenkötter, "Augusburg, Peace of," *OER* 1:91–93; H. A. Oberman, "Toward the Recovery of the Historical Calvin: Redrawing the Map of Reformation Europe," in *John Calvin*, ed. Oberman, 75.

8. Cf. Benedict, *Christ's Churches*, 9–120, 121–291.

legislative institution. The title of the final text read, "The Ecclesiastical Ordinances, fundamental to the entire organization and discipline of the Church of Geneva."[9] Swift action on the part of the magistracy suggested that Calvin made the ecclesiastical ordinance a precondition for his return to Geneva. In fact, his farewell to his fellow pastors in 1564 mentioned the city's firm promises of "discipline and catechism" for his return. In addition, it should be noted that the committee's original draft strongly reflected his unique ideas. All six members selected to the committee by the Small Council were Guillermins who had advocated for Calvin's return. Three of them were to be elected in 1542 to the highest executive institution of the four-member Syndic.[10] Since some of the ordinance's expressions were to become points of conflict, however, we will survey its characteristics under the following four points.

(i) The first point concerns the ordinance's nature as a legal document. The ordinance presented important ecclesial notions, without definitions or explanations, as matters of fact in the church. For example, at the beginning of its main text, it affirmed "a fourfold order of offices which the Lord has instituted for the government of the church," listing the offices of pastors, teachers, elders, and deacons. Likewise, their job descriptions covered wide areas of the city's communal life. The duty of pastors concerned the ministry of the word in indoctrinating, admonishing, and exhorting both publicly and privately, the administration of the sacraments, and the exercise of "fraternal corrections" with elders. The office of teachers primarily concerned the teaching of "pure and evangelical doctrine." It also addressed the general education of citizenry for civil and ecclesiastical services and the participation in ecclesiastical discipline as "ministers" along with pastors. The office of elders primarily concerned the care of each of the faithful and the amicable admonitions to those who were in need of it. But, in the case involving discipline, they worked with

9. *Les ordonnances ecclésiastiques, fondement de toute organisation et de la discipline de l'Église de Genève.* The official text is not extant in the Council records of the city archives (*Archives d'État de Genève, Registres du Conseil: AEG, R. C.*). The only existing copy is found at the beginning of *Registres de la Compagnie des Pasteurs de Genève*: *RCP*, vol. 1. We use this text (*RCP*, 1, ed. J. F. Bergier [Geneva: Droz, 1964]) as *Ordonnances ecclésiastiques.* The *Opera Calvini* (*CO* 10a:15–30) cites the Committee's draft text (Projet d'ordonnances ecclésiastiques), which is thought to reflect Calvin's ideas, transcribed from the city archives (*AEG, Pièces historiques*, no. 1384).

10. "Discours d'Adieu aux ministres," *CO* 9:894. Cf. R. M. Kingdon, "Calvin and the Establishment of Consistory Discipline in Geneva: The Institution and the Men Who Directed It," *Nederlands Archief voor Kerkgeschiedenis* 70 (1990): 162; Parker, *John Calvin*, 80–81; W. G. Naphy, *Calvin and the Consolidation of the Genevan Reformation* (Manchester and New York: Manchester University Press, 1994), 84n1.

the "Company of Pastors and Teachers." And the office of deacons was for the double duties of serving the poor and the sick.[11] Since these descriptions were not precisely defined and covered wide aspects of the communal life of the city, the text was easily subjected to criticism.

Another characteristic nature of the document revealed the existence of two distinctive approaches to the ecclesiastical ordinance, one by the committee and the other by the magistracy. In fact, the document seemed to suggest itself as a product of compromise. In the main text prepared by the committee, there was no use of the adjective "spiritual" in describing the "government" or "organization and discipline" of the church. In both the preface and a summary statement at the end of the document, which the city councils added to the committee's text, however, the adjective "spiritual" not only appeared but was emphasized. In the preface, for example, emphasis was laid on the good intention of the magistracy to institute the ecclesiastical ordinance as "the spiritual government." In the summary statement, the magistracy's intention was undisguised: the ministers were in no way to exercise civil jurisdiction but to deal only with "the spiritual sword of the word of God," and the Consistory of ministers and elders should not act like a civil court.[12] In short, the magistracy narrowly conceived of the ecclesiastical ordinance as applying in the spiritual realm centered around the ministry of the word and administration of the sacraments. On the other hand, Calvin's concept of polity reflected in the main text clearly avoided the narrow Zwinglian approach and envisioned the fourfold order of the church's ministry reaching out to the entire community of the city.

A more important characteristic nature of the document was the absence of the terms "discipline" and "excommunication" in the main text. When the text was clearly dealing with matters of discipline, the term "brotherly corrections" was preferred. Referring to the biblical text of Matthew 18:15–17, the text read that "after having admonished three times, it should separate him from the church and it should denounce him to the magistracy." But here the term "excommunicate" was not used. In the drafting stage of the text, perhaps Calvin foresaw the general public's negative reaction to these two terms, which were emphatically used in the 1537 *Ordinance* (*The Articles*) by Farel and Calvin himself, and accordingly he intentionally avoided them.[13]

11. *RCP* 1:1–2, 6–7. Cf. J. E. Olson, "Calvin and Social-Ethical Issues," in *The Cambridge Companion to John Calvin*, ed. D. K. McKim (Cambridge: Cambridge University Press, 2004), 153–72.

12. *RCP* 1:13. To be exact, the main text uses the term "spirituelle" twice (*RCP* 1:7, 9), but not in association with church government.

13. *RCP* 1:12. Cf. *OS* 1:369–70.

(ii) The second point concerned the *Ordinance*'s contents that clearly reflected Calvin's characteristic ideas. For example, the office of pastors and its related topics occupied one third of the entire text. Concerning "the church's government and oversight (police)," moreover, as the text listed two groups of offenses with which the Consistory was to deal, ranging from the major offenses of heresy and schism to the minor offenses of vulgarity and lying, the pastoral office was primarily responsible for evaluating and judging these offenses. Although the Consistory made final evaluations and referred some cases to the magistracy, an emphasis was laid upon the idea of pastoral judgments being based upon and the church being governed by the word of God.[14] In sharp contrast to the emphasis on the pastoral office, another characteristic appeared concerning the role of the congregation in church government, on which the text was almost totally silent. The only reference to the congregational role came in the case of a new ministerial appointment. The candidate, who was selected by the Company of Pastors and Teachers and approved by the magistracy, was to be finally presented to the congregation and appointed "by the common consent of the company of the faithful." By no means was the congregational role presented in a positive and active context. In this connection, it should be noted that the 1537 *Articles*, examined in chapter 2, put forward Farel's idea of congregational polity and even used the phrase "assembly's excommunication." Bucer made a theoretical distinction in church government between ministerial "authority" and congregational "power," and he even advocated for the congregational selection and appointment of ministers in the "Christian Society" movement. Calvin's 1541 *Ordinance* witnessed his unique position within the Reformed Reformation.[15]

(iii) The third point concerned the focal aspect of the *Ordinance*, the practice of church government and discipline by the "Consistory" composed of ministers and elders, and its significance in the history of Reformed Christianity. As we have repeatedly noted before, it has been generally assumed that the 1541 *Ordinance* had achieved a sort of autonomous ecclesiastical discipline that both Oecolampadius and Bucer had attempted earlier, though unsuccessfully. Of course, the Consistory envisioned by Calvin was neither the bishop's court previously extant in Geneva nor the magisterial discipline then practiced in Bern and Zurich. In a letter to Oswald Myconius, successor of Oecolampadius in Basel, sent soon after the *Ordinance*'s enactment, Calvin called it "the elders' court" (*presbyterorum iudicium*), accenting its ecclesial character,

14. *RCP* 1:2–5.
15. *RCP* 1:2.

somewhat independent from the magistracy's direct control of discipline.[16] In particular, the ordinance marked an extraordinary achievement in the legal history of Geneva. For the first time, elders elected from the city councils were officially considered church officers, and, just like ministers of the Company, they were required to take an ecclesiastical oath upon their appointments.[17] Within the historical reality of Geneva, this meant a clear rejection of the Zwinglian position. Although the *Ordinance* reflected Calvin's basic idea of autonomous ecclesiastical discipline, it was far from his ideal. Its significance was to be finally settled, after trial and error, in 1555.

(iv) The fourth point concerned the most problematic aspect implicit in the ordinance, namely, the relation of consistorial discipline and the magistracy. Practically, it concerned the interpretation of two sentences in the main text on the Consistory relating to the biblical reference of Matthew 18. The two sentences in question both assumed the cases in which the consistorial admonitions and warnings had all failed. The first sentence read that "it should forbid him to partake the Lord's Supper, and it should denounce him to the Magistracy." The second sentence was that "it should separate him from the church and it should denounce him to the Magistracy." If we understand the first sentence referring to the debarment of the Lord's Supper and the second sentence to excommunication, the Consistory could exercise its own authority in admonitions and warnings, could determine the cases of

16. *CO* 11:178–79; *COR* II-13:262 on Rom 12:8. Cf. R. M. Kingdon, *Adultery and Divorce in Calvin's Geneva* (Cambridge, MA, and London: Harvard University Press, 1995), 13; Kingdon, "Calvin and Geneva," in *A Companion to the Reformation World*, ed. R. Po-chia Hsia (Oxford: Blackwell, 2004), 109; n. 25 below. Referring to the early exemplary attempt by Basel's Oecolampadius, Calvin described the consistorial discipline codified in the *Genevan Ordinance* as "a sort of the elders' court and form of discipline" that the Council reluctantly accepted but that some members attempted to discredit. Calvin's idea of the consistorial discipline clearly indicated a distinctive perspective from what the Council envisioned. Kingdon, a historian of the Genevan institutions, consistently characterizes the Consistory as "a standing committee" or "a committee of the civil government." His characterization seems to be more applicable to the Council's perspective rather than Calvin's. Already in the first edition of the *Romans Commentary* (1540; *COR* II-13:262 on Rom 12:8) Calvin related the Greek term, "those who preside," to the charge of "governing the church," that is, elders, and implicitly rejected Zwingli's rendering. Following the third edition (1543; *CO* 1:567), the final edition of the *Institutes* (1559; 4.3.8: *OS* 5:50) explicitly rejected Zwingli's rendering of "pious magistrates" and took the rendering of "the elders who were the censors of morals."

17. *RCP* 1:7. Cf. Kingdon, "Calvin and the Establishment," 162–66, esp. 163. The chairperson of the Consistory was an elected elder from the Syndics, assisted by a pastor and an elder. Selection of other elders was done according to the balance of the city Councils and the church parishes.

debarment and excommunication, but was obliged to refer these cases to the magistracy for their final executions.[18] If this was the trend of arguments in the main text, the summary statement inserted at the insistence of the magistracy was intended to counterbalance this trend and to emphasize the magisterial right to oversee church discipline. The summary statement forbade the ministers to exercise civil jurisdiction and made major consistorial decisions such as those mentioned above mandatory, referring them to the [Small] Council. Nevertheless, its ambiguous phrasing seemed to combine the magisterial insistence and the trend of the main text. As Wendel suggests, it resulted in the possibility of two opposite interpretations: Calvin's interpretation of the full consistorial right over discipline and the magistracy's opposite interpretation. Historically speaking, this summary statement could be viewed as the root of all the ensuing conflicts of the next fifteen years.[19]

(2) Settlement of the Conflicts in 1555

The *Genevan Ecclesiastical Ordinance* provided Calvin with the legal status for his reform. Due to the existence of the two claims of the church and the magistracy in it, however, the status was to be finally reconfirmed in 1555 after prolonged conflicts. Concerning researchers' evaluation of the conflicts, there have been many arguments since Wendel, suggesting the crucial importance of the closing summary statement as a focal point of the conflicts. Wendel concluded in 1950 that Calvin's claim of the consistorial right over discipline took "a preponderance over the civil power."[20] As we notice that the period of the conflicts overlapped Calvin's formation of Reformed ecclesiology, instead of surveying the history of the conflicts, we will examine the period's three aspects from this ecclesiological perspective.

18. *RCP* 1:12. Cf. Benedict, *Christ's Churches*, 96. Historically, these sentences provided Calvin and the Consistory's leaders a legal claim for the church's predominant role in discipline.

19. *RCP* 1:13; *CO* 10a:30. Cf. Wendel, *Calvin*, 74; Höpfl, *Christian Polity*, 128, 138; R. M. Kingdon, "La discipline ecclésiastique vue de Zurich et Genève au temps de la Réformation: L'usage de Matthieu 18, 15–17 par les Réformateurs," *Revue de Théologie et de Philosophie* 133 (2001): 343–55; J. W. Baker, "Christian Discipline, Church and State, and Toleration: Bullinger, Calvin, and Basel 1530–1555," in *Reformiertes Erbe: Festschrift für Gottfried W. Locher zu seinem 80. Geburtstag*, ed. H. A. Oberman, Ernst Saxer, A. Schindler, and H. Stuck, Zwingliana 19 (Zurich: Theologischer Verlag, 1993), 2:35–48.

20. Wendel, *Calvin*, 74, 79. Cf. Manetsch's recent work, *Calvin's Company of Pastors*, ch. 7, "The Ministry of Moral Oversight" (182–220), which examines in part Calvin's prolonged conflicts over consistorial discipline.

Achievement of Calvin's Reform Program

(i) Firstly, it has been noted by researchers in history and sociology, such as Kingdon and Benedict, that Calvin's reform during this period had made a considerable impact upon Geneva and had been effective in changing the city's social structure and life. Concerning this Genevan transformation, Kingdon entertains the idea of a social "revolution," and Benedict notes three means effectively used by Calvin's reform, namely, preaching, consistorial discipline, and the municipal laws. He especially emphasizes the far-reaching impact that the Consistory had brought upon the entire city's inhabitants.[21] Especially in the early phase of this period, reform had smoothly advanced under the leadership of the Guillermins, and both the Company of Pastors and Teachers and the Consistory had been filled with Calvin's supporters. As to the increasingly important office of pastors, for example, Calvin was said to have moved those ministers who had remained in the office after his return in 1541 from the city to the rural parishes and had nominated new ministerial appointments, mostly from France, to the Council. According to Manetsch's recent study of Calvin's pastoral ministry, the institution of the Company of Pastors took its shape in the mid-1540s. Swelled with well-educated exiles mostly from France, it "elevated the quality of preaching and brought greater stability to the city's churches." Through the Sunday sermons made obligatory for the faithful to attend and open lectures on the Bible, pastors exerted their influence upon the general public. During the later phase of the period, however, the Company, now filled with French nationals, was to become a point of conflict. In 1542, moreover, *The Form of Ecclesiastical Prayers and Hymns* (*La Forme des Prieres et Chantz ecclesiastiques*) and the French *Catechism* (*Le Catechisme*) were published and a uniformity of worship and children's education was achieved.[22]

21. Cf. Monter, *Calvin's Geneva*, 70–84; Kingdon, "Was the Protestant Reformation a Revolution?," 203–22; Benedict, *Christ's Churches*, 93–109; P. Benedict, "Calvin and the Transformation of Geneva," in *John Calvin's Impact on Church and Society, 1509–2009*, ed. M. E. Hirzel and M. Sullmann (Grand Rapids: Eerdmans, 2009), 5–8; W H. T. Moehn, *"God Calls Us to His Service": The Relation between God and His Audience in Calvin's Sermon on Acts* (Geneva: Droz, 2001).

22. Gordon, *Calvin*, 130–33, 138–40; Manetsch, *Calvin's Company of Pastors*, 40, 44. Cf. R. M. Kingdon, *Geneva and the Coming of the Wars of Religion in France* (Geneva: Droz, 1956), 14–24; Naphy, *Consolidation*, 94–95, 144–66; M. J. Larson's article, "John Calvin and Genevan Presbyterianism," *Westminster Theological Journal* 60 (1998): 43–69, examines Calvin's consistorial polity from the view point of Presbyterianism.

Two recent commendable studies have contributed to the understanding of the process in which Calvin's teachings were translated into the actual reform of Geneva. McKee's study of historical theology of pastoral ministry and worship tries to be "a bridge" between Calvin's theology and practice in this reformatory process. By exhaustive use of Calvin's writings and the city's Consistory and Council records, the study traces the process of the wide range of Calvin's teachings translated through the church's pastoral ministry into the emergence of a worshipping Reformed community. If its own description of the vocation of pastors, "apothecaries of the medicine of life delivering the gospel day in and day out to the whole body and to individuals," reflects Calvin's reformatory vision, this description serves well to illustrate the image of Calvin's aspirational Geneva. On the other hand, however, Spierling's historical study on infant baptism vividly describes the deep tension that existed between Calvin's theological and scriptural incentives and the community's needs. The study takes the issue of infant baptism and documents the complex process of transforming the Genevan sacramental practice from its medieval past to its Reformed present. What it depicts as an emerging practice of infant baptism is definitely distinctive from the Catholic traditions, yet is uniquely complex in both the community's sacramental and civic characteristics.[23]

(ii) In addition to the uniformity of the Evangelical faith, the city was expecting the Company and the Consistory to improve the moral standard of the public that was essential to the maintenance of the city's social life. In this respect, however, there was a tension in both theory and practice concerning the Consistory. The Consistory was presided over by a Syndic, one of the highest executive officers, and it was attended by twelve council members elected each year from two Councils. Since its major cases involving debarment and excommunication were referred to and were decided in the Small Council, the magistracy considered it a part of the civil government. On the other hand, since these council members were regarded as church elders, Calvin and the Company insisted on regarding the Consistory more as an ecclesiastical institution. Thus, it became increasingly difficult to draw a line between these two interpretations.[24] In reality,

23. E. A. McKee, *The Pastoral Ministry and Worship in Calvin's Geneva* (Geneva: Droz, 2016), 13, 29–31, 660; K. E. Spierling, *Infant Baptism in Reformation Geneva: The Shaping of a Community, 1536–1564* (Louisville: Westminster John Knox, 2008), 6, 35, 49–50, 219–27; cf. n. 52 below.

24. Kingdon, *Adultery and Divorce*, 7–30; Gordon, *Calvin*, 134. Kingdon, who considers the Consistory as "a committee of the civil government," offers an excellent overview of its operation. Interestingly, he admits its unique functions, distinctive from the magistracy, as "a hearing court," "a compulsory counselling service," and "an educational institution."

the consistorial deliverances during its early stages, as the record revealed, were largely minor offenses that were mostly met with consistorial admonitions. As the number of people summoned by the Consistory increased significantly and more severe cases involving debarment and excommunication also increased, the problem of these two interpretations had become a tense religious and social issue, as well as a focal point of the conflicts.[25]

(iii) Concerning both Calvin's leadership and consistorial discipline, two points need to be mentioned here. One concerns Calvin's theological stance on ecclesiastical discipline in general, and the other the nature of consistorial deliverances, whether they were equal and impartial disregarding the offenders' social status, whether rich or poor, citizen or noncitizen. As to the first point, it has been assumed that Calvin had inherited the Augustinian view of humanity being in "depravity" and that this theological stance was reflected in his ministry, preaching, and attitude toward discipline. It can be also said that his theological stance became accentuated when his authority as a minister of God's word was challenged. An example can be drawn from his farewell speech to his fellow ministers in 1564. Recalling an episode from 1547 at the Council of Two Hundred when, as the city's chief pastor, he threw himself among the revolting Councilmen and restored order, he nonchalantly commented that "the city is perverse and evil" (*la nation est perverse et meschante*). In his letter of 1547 to Viret, reporting the same incident, he described the Councilmen's rudeness against the minister of the word as "viciousness" in the extreme. Perhaps, he considered disregard and repulsion for the minister as rebellion against the word of God.[26]

Concerning another point of the equality and impartiality of consistorial deliverances, though concerns for favoritism and ministerial advantage were

---

Noticing "a division of authority between the Consistory and the council," Gordon regards the Consistory as "essentially a court in Geneva" and suggests its independent aspect from the magistracy.

25. R. M. Kingdon, "Calvin and Geneva," 109. According to Kingdon, the *Ordinances* originally gave the Consistory the right to scold, but "before long the members of the consistory demanded the right to excommunicate people." This interpretation seems to be consistent with his view of the Consistory as "a committee of the civil government." "Introduction" to the English edition of the original consistorial registers (*Registres du Consistoire de Genève au temps de Calvin*, Vol. 1–, ed. T. A. Lambert et al. [Geneva: Droz, 1996–]), *Registers of the Consistory of Geneva in the Time of Calvin*, Vol. 1, 1542–1544, gen. ed. R. M. Kingdon, ed. T. A. Lambert and I. M. Watt (Grand Rapids: Eerdmans and H. H. Meeter Center for Calvin Studies, 2001), xvii–xviii, mentions an interesting demographic figure: "The Consistory usually summoned from five to seven percent of the adult population each year."

26. *CO* 9:892 (*OS* 2:402); *CO* 12:633 (*Calvinus Vireto*).

raised, researchers of the records generally agree that the principle of equality had been maintained. This was partly due to the Consistory's operational procedure in which an elder responsible for each parish usually brought the cases to the Consistory.[27] Issues arose, however, when the consistorial procedure was applied to the privileged class. These cases were easily tied to public resentment against the Consistory, which was predominantly comprised of pastors and teachers of French origin. In such conflicting cases, Calvin was said to have consistently supported the consistorial decisions on the privileged. His letter of 1546 to Ami Perrin, who had been promoted to Syndic in the previous year, revealed his basic stance on the issue.[28] Although the letter was regarded as an offer of his reconciliation, it was also a letter expressing his determination to repulse the mounting criticism against him and the Consistory, as well as a letter of stern advice, as both a pastor and friend to Perrin, to obey God. Denying any preferential treatment from the Consistory, he warned, "if equality is due in law, how can inequality be tolerated in the church of God."[29]

On the Evaluation of the Conflicts

Recent research on the history of the Genevan Reformation during this period of conflicts has been noteworthy. Among them, there seems to be three interesting studies that are relevant from the perspective of our ecclesiological interest. These are the view of Kingdon, a historian of the institutional history of Geneva; a historical study by Naphy, who tries to rewrite the history of the Genevan Reformation, partly challenging generally accepted views such as Kingdon's; and the unique perspective of theologian and historian Oberman.

27. Cf. Naphy, *Consolidation*, 106–11. Generally speaking, Naphy, who examines the church-city conflict mainly from the city councils' records, takes a critical stance on the documents coming from Calvin and the Consistory. In his comparative examination of both the consistorial and the city's judicial records, however, he recognizes the same tendency in both records and finds no prejudicial tendency unique to the consistorial records.

28. *CO* 12:338–39. Ami Perrin, a Guillermins leader, was an early supporter of Farel and Calvin in the initial phase of the Genevan Reformation. Geneva commissioned him to travel to Strasbourg to recall Calvin in person. In 1546, the head of a prominent Genevan family, François Favre, and his daughter, who was Perrin's wife, were summoned to the Consistory, though in separate cases. Afterward, Perrin gradually became a leader of the anti-Calvinist group.

29. *CO* 12:338. Cf. Naphy, *Consolidation*, 96–98. Calvin's Latin letter is one of a few selective documents that Naphy uses and critically examines from the perspective of the conflict scheme between the native citizens of prominent class versus Calvin, the Company of Pastors, and the Consistory.

(i) Kingdon notices a significant institutional shift taking place in this period, from the pre-1535 Episcopal Monarchy in which the episcopal court and more than one hundred clergymen had maintained the religious and ethical life of the city, to a new system since 1542 in which only nine pastors and the highly controversial institution, the Consistory, had kept fairly efficient control.[30] Calling this shift a "revolution," he concludes that "the ecclesiastical structure" that Calvin envisioned in the 1541 ordinance, especially the consistorial discipline that other city-Reformations had unsuccessfully tried before, "was an outstanding success in consolidating the reformation in Geneva." In echoing Oberman's thesis that "in a very real sense the Calvinist Reformation was a Reformation of refugees," Kingdon acknowledges the support of the new refugee "bourgeois" as "the margin" that made possible the Calvinist victory over the Perrinists in 1555. Nevertheless, he cautions that "the triumph of Calvin's party would not have been possible without substantial native support."[31]

(ii) Naphy's book, *Calvin and the Consolidation of the Genevan Reformation* (1994), is a bold attempt to rewrite the Genevan Reformation mainly using hitherto unused records of the Genevan state archives, especially the Council's records (*Registres du Conseil*) and the Criminal Courts records (*Procès Criminels*), rather than the often-used Consistory records of the archives that Kingdon and others have primarily examined. In this sense, the study focuses on the magisterial perspective on the Reformation. Naphy finds some dominant themes that appear repeatedly in the Council and Criminal Courts records concerning the conflicts. He finds, for example, the sense of resentment on the part of native Genevans and *bourgeois* toward the ministers of French origin and the Consistory's rigid control over religion, "a phobia against foreigners," and their precaution regarding the French immigrants' political influence.[32] The study's basic assumption seems to view the conflicts involving Calvin as basically "political conflicts," and to view Calvin himself as "a major international figure" as well as "an astute politician and propagandist." Methodologically

30. Kingdon, "Was the Protestant Reformation a Revolution?," 207–10, 218.

31. Kingdon, "Was the Protestant Reformation a Revolution?," 219; "Calvin and the Establishment," 163; "Calvin and Geneva," 111–12. According to Kingdon, the three classes of residents in Geneva were: "bourgeois" who owned property and had respectable professions (the native citizens could be elected to the Small Council of 25 and the Syndic); "citizens" (*citoyens*), native Genevans as well as foreigners who earned citizenship (they could be elected to the Council of 60 and that of 200); and other "residents" (*habitants*) who were employees and sojourners (they had no political rights). The problem at issue was the group of foreigners/refugees who could earn citizenship or bourgeois status and exert political influence.

32. Naphy, *Consolidation*, 4–9, esp. 6, 160, 191–97, 230.

speaking, it questions the historical validity of Calvin's own sources (books, sermons, letters, etc.) and even the Consistory records, and accordingly it rarely uses them.[33] As far as the book's contents are concerned, Naphy has surveyed the religio-political history of Geneva starting from the Genevan specialty of "sectarianism," the conflict of the Guillermins and the Berneses, that of the magistracy and the Calvinists, and the assumption of power by the Perrinists and their defeat (1553–55). In particular, he views the defeat of the Perrinists, the last political foe of Calvin, as due to their lack of effective policies and the drastic increase of the political influence of French immigrants. Although he chooses "Calvin and the consolidation" for his title, ironically, in no way does his study seem to present why Calvin's reform was effective in "consolidating" the Genevan Reformation. It also seems to leave an unanswered question, namely, whether or not, as Monter points out, the defeat of the Perrinists was simply due to their being reactionary to Calvinist reform.[34]

(iii) In contrast to the above-mentioned historical studies, Oberman views the conflicts from the historical perspective of theological thought and focuses on some characteristic features of Calvin's reform. In the article "*Europa Afflicta*: The Reformation of the Refugees" (1992), concerning the frame of the conflicts, he notes that, while the opponents of Calvin conceived "peace of the city" as the goal of the reform, Calvin's goal was distinctively different.[35] In place of the traditional city-reformation's goal of "good community," he identified the goal as "salvation of community" or "public salvation." From this perspective, he urged all residents of the city, including its privileged, to live like the refugees.[36] Above all, according to Oberman, Calvin aimed toward the formation of "the core church of the elect" through his sermons and consistorial discipline, and he was well aware that his goal often came into conflict with the ideal of communal unity. Furthermore, Oberman considers Calvin's reformatory stance as seeking "faith" prior to "love," or Luther would say, "faith prior to peace and unity."[37] In short, according to him, Calvin's

33. Cf. Naphy, *Consolidation*, 156–60. Among only a few sermon materials of Calvin cited by Naphy, for example, he examines a series of sermons on Micah (1550) almost exclusively from the viewpoint of native Genevans who considered themselves attacked in them.

34. Cf. Naphy, *Consolidation*, 190–92; Monter, *Calvin's Geneva*, 99–104; P. Benedict, "Calvin and the Transformation of Geneva," in *John Calvin's Impact on Church and Society, 1509–2009*, ed. M. E. Hirzel and M. Sallmann (Grand Rapids: Eerdmans, 2009), 10–12.

35. Oberman, "*Europa Afflicta*," 91–111, esp. 102–4: Oberman, *John Calvin*, 177–94, esp. 187–89.

36. Oberman, "*Europa Afflicta*," 102–3: Oberman, *John Calvin*, 187–88.

37. Oberman, "*Europa Afflicta*," 103–4: Oberman, *John Calvin*, 188–89.

approach to reform, different from that of the traditional city Reformers, was at the root of every conflict.

Ecclesiological Issues

Even though no significant ecclesiological issues were directly raised in the history of the conflicts, there were at least two aspects that had some bearing upon Calvin's concept of the church in this period. The one concerned the fact that Calvin used a contemptuous term, "the Libertines" (*libertins*), for a part of his opposition and described them as the impious, the immoral, and the Devil's agents. The other concerned the fact that Calvin tightened and improved his idea of church discipline.

(i) The first issue is raised by modern Calvin research that questions the historical validity of the term "the Libertines," often used in the historical records of Geneva after 1555 and in the materials related to Calvin. The issue's focal point is the fact that the official use of the term indicated the Libertines as a conspiracy aimed at the destruction of the Reformation, church discipline, and the Genevan Consistory. The issue is further complicated by Calvin's own polemical work, *Against the Fantastic Sect of the Libertines* (1545), in which he described the Libertines as an ideologically defined movement with teachings far more dangerous than the Anabaptists and the Nicodemites. The publication was coupled with another polemical work against the Anabaptists, *Brief Instruction* (1545). Accordingly, Calvin considered these two movements to have a common root, but he uniquely described the Libertines as "those who claim to be spiritual."[38] Concerning the identity of the Libertines, Williams, a Radical Reformation specialist, understands them in connection with radical sects of the Low Countries and France that distinguished themselves by their disinterest in church organizations as well as by their antinomian sentiment. The editor of Calvin's polemical work in the *Renewed Calvini Opera*, Van Veen, considers them the Spiritualist wing of the Radical Reformation and notes their association with Bucer and influence in the French court of Marguerite.[39]

38. *Contre la secte phantastique et furieuse des Libertins. Qui se nomment spirituelz*: *BC* 45/4. For the text, *COR* IV-1:43–171, is used.

39. R. W. Collins, *Calvin and the Libertines of Geneva* (Toronto and Vancouver: Clarke, Irwin & Co., 1968), 153–67; Williams, *The Radical Reformation*, 535–39, 904–12, esp. 909; *COR* IV-1, "Introduction," 10–26. A traditional interpreter, Collins understands "the Libertines" in the narrow context of Genevan reform and identifies them as the city's political and social leaders who felt Calvin's consistorial discipline too constrictive.

Calvin's *Against the Fantastic Sect of the Libertines* took issue with their interpretation of the Bible, which was said to overturn scriptural authority and its main teachings. For example, Calvin charged that their allegorical hermeneutics took the scriptural teachings as if they were fables. In appealing to "the letter kills, but the Spirit gives life" (2 Cor 3:6), they despised the "natural meaning" of the text, and their excessive spiritualizing caused them to appear as if they were seeking "new revelations." Concerning their unorthodox teaching of the Spirit, he accused them of having notions such as "God's word is the spirit" and "Jesus Christ is the spirit."[40] Concerning the practical aspects of their life, he criticized them for taking sin, the devil, and the reality of the world lightly, and for jeopardizing God's law by insisting that their being spiritual and exercising Christian freedom exonerated them from the judgment of the law. They also insisted that their actions should neither be judged by others nor that they should judge the actions of others.[41] The Libertines' perfectionistic notion of the church was the last point of Calvin's criticism. Making reference to "the church without spot or wrinkle" (Eph 5:27) and the nuptial image of Christ and the church, according to him, they claimed to achieve the innocent church just like the original state of Adam and Eve.[42] From this brief survey, it could hardly be mistaken that the Libertines' teaching and practice were extreme opposites of what Calvin had tried to accomplish in Geneva. Strictly speaking, however, none of Calvin's known Genevan opponents, such as the Berneses and the Perrinists, matched the description of the Libertines. Of course, it was possible that Calvin was aware of some Spiritualist influence or teachings of the Libertines among his opponents. Since the Libertines were a well-defined movement, however, it was also possible that he was either warning about their inroads into France, especially among the Evangelicals, or knew of the danger of their radical attack on Calvin's Genevan reform from French soil.

(ii) The second issue concerned the precise theory of the Consistory. An important step was taken in the 1541 *Ecclesiastical Ordinance*: the office of elders was defined as the church's ministry and the elders were, in reality, chosen from the Councilmen and were sent to the Consistory by the magistracy. Beyond this, Calvin did not initially take further steps. Two years later in the third *Institutes*, as the Consistory was gradually recognized as a focal point of the conflicts, Calvin boldly interpreted the disciplinary text of Matthew 18 historically, affirming that "Christ here instituted nothing new but followed the

40. *COR* IV-1:75–76, 79.

41. *COR* IV-1:80, 86–87, 89, 93, 103–4, 119–22.

42. *COR* IV-1:157–59.

custom always observed in the ancient church of his [Jewish] people."[43] In a clear reference to the third and final disciplinary stage of Matthew 18 (17: "Tell it to the church"), furthermore, he affirmed that "Christ commands that he [the person already admonished twice] be called to the tribunal of the church, that is, the assembly of the elders, and there be more gravely admonished as by public authority."[44] It could be easily assumed that the Genevan practice of the Consistory played a part in his interpretation. Since the Consistory's authority and its modus operandi had continuously become a focal issue, when the Perrinists took control of the city in 1553, they even challenged the consistorial right to pronounce debarment of the Lord's Supper. This issue developed into a confrontation between the Small Council and the Company of Pastors and Teachers.[45] In this historical context, Calvin was to finalize his understanding of consistorial discipline. His new interpretation appeared in the *Synoptic Gospels Commentary* (1555). Following up on his position in the third *Institutes*, he commented on "the church" of Matthew 18 and interpreted it as Christ's reference to a council of priests and elders in the Jewish synagogues, the contemporary disciplinary practice in the post–Babylonian captivity period. According to him, this Jewish system exemplified in the Sanhedrin in Jerusalem was later transferred to the newly established Christian church. This was to be his definitive position in the final *Institutes* of 1559.[46] The whole hermeneutical process indicates that Calvin's theory of consistorial discipline had been developed in the context of the Genevan conflicts.

(3) *The Year 1559 in Calvin's Reformation*

The 1555 settlement of the conflicts proceeded to the punishment and eradication of the Perrinist faction from the city. It also indicated the retarding influence of Bern that had been consistently checking the expansion of Calvin's influence and supporting the anti-Calvinist factions, including the Perrinists.[47] At the same time, the city of Geneva had developed into a major international

43. *CO* 1:649. (*Institutio* 4.11.4: *OS* 5:200.)

44. *CO* 1:659. (*Institutio* 4.12.2: *OS* 5:213.)

45. Cf. *RCP* 1:12n1.

46. *Harmonia ex Tribus Evangelistis Composita*: *BC* 55/9, *CO* 45:514: "Scimus, ex quo reversi fuerunt ab exsilio babylonico Iudaei, delecto concilio, quod vocabant Sanhedrin, graece synedrion, mandatam fuisse censuram morum et doctrinae. . . . Quod autem sub lege servatum fuerat, Christus ad nos transmisit, quia nobis communis est ratio cum antiquis patribus." Cf. Maruyama, *The Ecclesiology*, 100–101n108; McKee, *Elders*, 36.

47. Benedict, "Calvin and the Transformation," 10; Gordon, *Calvin*, 209–11.

center with a population of over 20,000 from the modest size of about 10,000 when the reform started in 1535. In post-1555 Calvinist Geneva, especially, the impact of Calvin's reform was widely felt not only in the religious life but also in the sociopolitical life of the city. As mentioned before, internationally, the city equaled Zurich and its influence was recognized as a new force in redrawing the religious map of Europe.[48] Noticeably, the last decade (1555–64) of Calvin's life overlapped the new stage of Genevan history, and the year 1559 marked the apex of his career as a Reformer. In that year, upon the request of the Small Council, he decided to accept the *bourgeois* status, published the definitive *Institutes*, and finally established the Academy of Geneva. While his reputation rose internationally, with its evaluation sharply divided both positively and negatively, the real merit of his reform, theology, and practice were tested during this period. In this context, there also arose many "myths" and "fables" about his person and his reform.

Myth of Geneva

One interesting article, "Le mythe de Genève au temps de Calvin," is authored by a historian of Geneva, Dufour. Although the author considers Calvin's *Reply to Sadoleto* an underlying source of the myth that had made Calvin famous, he finds the real source of the myth in the "sentiment" of the immigrant foreigners in the 1540s, who adored Calvin's "city-church" Geneva. As Dufour relates, for example, a certain historian of French origin called the city "a refuge for the faithful, a shield and fortress against the enemies of truth," and an Italian immigrant acclaimed it "a second Eternal City." Although Calvin severely criticized such "sentiment" and acclaims as fabricating "an idol out of me and a Jerusalem out of Geneva," especially after the Calvinist victory of 1555, the myth continued. Over against the Calvinist myth, the author asserts further, there arose a "counter-myth" by Calvin's opponents, and these two trends exerted certain bearings upon Calvin's theology and reform.[49] In view

48. Cf. Monter, *Calvin's Geneva*, 102–3; Kingdon, "Calvin and Geneva," 114–17; Benedict, *Christ's Churches*, 108–9.

49. A. Dufour, "Le mythe de Genève au temps de Calvin," in *Histoire politique et psychologie historique* (Geneva: Droz, 1966), 72, 84, 90–92, 95. Quotation from Calvin (*CO* 14:363: "faire ung idole de moy, et de Geneve une Ierusalem") is found in his letter to the French congregation in London (September 27, 1552). Interestingly, a recent echo of Dufour's argument may be found in R. A. Muller's "Demoting Calvin: The Issue of Calvin and the Reformed Tradition" (in *John Calvin, Myth and Reality*, ed. A. N. Burnett [Eugene, OR: Cascade Books, 2011], 3–17). For the author "demoting Calvin" means the effort of historical

of the "myth of Geneva," then, how could we assess Calvin's real Geneva and reform historically? To this end, we shall examine the "myth" of Geneva from the following three perspectives.

The first was Calvin's own perspective, expressed in his farewell address to his fellow ministers in 1564. In the address, there were two distinctively opposite propositions. One was his negative affirmation, repeated twice in the same wording, "what all I have done has no value at all," and the other was his positive affirmation, "Concerning my doctrine, I have taught faithfully, . . . and I have done most faithfully not to corrupt even a single passage of Scripture."[50] If the expression, "no value at all" was a reference to his reform as a whole, it simply meant that neither the reform's "completion" nor "termination" were in his perception. Truly the address was not a cohesive document and its contents were far too short and too selective to review his reform as a whole. Nevertheless, it seems to indicate that in his own perspective there was no room for the "myth" of Geneva.

Second, Calvin's reformatory message itself also betrayed the "myth of Geneva." In a study analyzing how Calvin's "message" could have spread so quickly and persuasively into Europe, Oberman notes its three components, namely, the doctrines of total depravity, predestination, and church discipline, which were generally considered to be deterrents to its wide public acceptance. Paradoxically, however, Oberman finds these teachings integrally related to the spread of Calvin's "message." As we have noted, the teaching of total depravity took an opposite position to the humanist ideal of man's integrity as exemplified in the Erasmian reform. The doctrine of predestination caused tension even with Melanchthon's Lutheran and Bullinger's Zwinglian teachings. And the strict observance of church discipline was to cause a break with the traditional city-reformation. In Geneva itself, however, these doctrines, especially discipline, were focal points of the strenuous resistance that Calvin had met. Likewise, another of Oberman's themes, "the Reformation of the refugees," which has been well accepted in recent Calvin research, points to the progressive yet transitory character of Calvin's reform. For example, Kingdon considers Calvin's Geneva as captivated by "the refugee mentality" and becoming a kind of missionary post from which missionaries of the same mentality

contextualization or de-mythologizing to reach the "real" Calvin, distinctive from "ahistorical," "decontextualized, and dogmatized Calvin" as seen among Calvin's contemporaries, in the Reformed tradition, and in current Calvin scholarship.

50. *CO* 9:592–93; *OS* 2:402–3.

had been sent to various parts of Europe as Calvinist agents. Benedict notes the importance of the "refugee mentality" or "exile's fixation" and interprets Calvin's reform as "the sixteenth-century advocate of asylum for persecuted believers" that "secured the transformation of Geneva in his lifetime."[51] These descriptions of Calvin's reform present a quite different image from the "myth" of Geneva.

Third, as recent historical scholarship has noticeably contributed to Calvin research, many studies have "exposed" the real image of Calvin's Geneva as a society in transition from the long history of medieval Catholicism to the nascent Reformed community. As a result, they have effectively challenged the "myth of Geneva" and have rather pictured the unfinished image of Calvin's reform. For example, Kingdon, an expert in Genevan history and archival records (the Councils, the Consistory, and the Company) of Calvin's time, notices a widespread residue of traditional Catholic elements, which he calls "nostalgia for Catholic rituals." Even concerning the crucially important sacramental reform, Spierling's substantive study notices the slow and often painful reform process of the Catholic ritual of infant baptism in the Reformed Geneva. An interesting topic of the study concerns the Catholic practice of baptizing illegitimate children, a practice that was continued after the reform. The study concludes that "this practice was necessary for the stability of both church and city, yet it challenged Calvin's baptismal doctrine." Due to the fact that Geneva neighbored Catholic France and Savoy, furthermore, Maag argues that the city's officially "Reformed" citizenry and immigrants from the Catholic territories were sometimes inconsistent in their practice of the Reformed faith. Their kinship, business network, and travel outside Geneva were factors for their inconsistency and became challenges to Calvin's reform.[52] These studies, though only a few, seem to depict the real image of Calvin's Geneva. They even suggest, instead of the "myth of Geneva," an ensuing theme of Calvin's continuous reform, "semper reformanda," which was often associated with the reform of Calvin's successor, Beza.

51. Cf. Oberman, *John Calvin*, 85; Kingdon, "Calvin and Geneva," 111–17; Benedict, "Calvin and the Transformation," 1, 4.

52. R. M. Kingdon, "Nostalgia for Catholic Rituals in Calvin's Geneva," in *Grenzgänge der Theologie Professor Alexandre Ganoczy zum 75. Geburtstag*, ed. O. Meuffels and J. Bründl (Münster: LIT Verlag, 2004), 209–22; Spierling, *Infant Baptism*, 61–104, 159–92, 225; K. Maag, "Permeable Borders: Cross-Confessional Encounters and Traditions in Reformation Geneva," in *Semper Reformanda: John Calvin, Worship, and Reformed Traditions*, ed. B. Pitkin (Göttingen: Vandenhoeck & Ruprecht, 2018), 15–32.

Genevan Academy

(i) The Genevan Academy followed the educational tradition of biblical humanism in the Strasbourg *Gymnasium* in which Calvin was directly involved during his Strasbourg stay. This tradition was also followed in the cities of Zurich and Basel, with which he was also familiar. In connection with the French Reformation, furthermore, the Academy was to inherit the tradition of theological education and missionary training from the Lausanne Academy. Of course, the Academy was of Calvin's making and was soon to become the academic face of Geneva. It has been said that John Knox, who left the England of Queen Mary and took refuge in Geneva, called the city "a perfect school of Christ." The expression, like Knox's usual hyperbole, might have been quite different from the reality of the city in Calvin's time. Nevertheless, as Gordon notes, the message presented in Calvin's sermons, lectures, and books had been resounding clearly, so powerful and distinctive from what had been recently heard in Europe. Gordon notes that Calvin's "message" transformed the main themes of Erasmus and Luther "into a vision of church life that could be lived in the maelstrom of the early-modern world."[53] It could be said that the accumulation of works over a decade upon this "vision of church life" in sermons, lectures, and catechetical classes of Calvin and other pastors and teachers had finally resulted in the establishment of the Genevan Academy in 1559.

(ii) Besides being Calvin's life-long wish, the Academy's foundation was facilitated by a few unexpected historical events. The one was the sale of Perrinist holdings in the city after their 1555 defeat, of which most of the proceeds were spent for the Academy's new start. The other was an exodus of teachers and students from the Academy of Lausanne under Bernese control to Geneva, occasioned by the dispute over church discipline in 1558. Many of them, sympathizers of Calvin, later joined the new Academy's faculty and student body. One notable teacher was Theodore Beza, who was to become the first rector of the Academy.[54] While the Academy's Latin school for middle education (*schola private*) continued to be open to the Genevan public, its higher institu-

53. Gordon, *Calvin*, 276; C. E. Raynal III, "The Place of the Academy in Calvin's Polity," in *John Calvin and the Church: A Prism of Reform*, ed. T. George (Louisville: Westminster John Knox, 1990), 120–34. Knox's comment "the most perfect school of Christ . . . since the days of the apostles" (John Knox, *Works*, vol. 4, 240) is cited in Benedict's article ("Calvin and the Transformation," 11) referred in n. 34 above. For the Strasbourg *Gymnasium*, see N. S. Amos, "Bucer among the Biblical Humanists: The Context for Practice in the Teaching of Theology in Strasbourg, 1523–1548," *Reformation and Renaissance Review* 62 (2004): 134–54.

54. Cf. Naphy, *Consolidation*, 228; Gordon, *Calvin*, 299.

tion (*schola publica*) was basically for ministerial training open to all qualified auditors, regardless of national origin. As the Rules of the Academy stipulated three professorships in Hebrew, Greek, and classical literature, the "*schola publica*" was to be an international institution for Reformed Christianity and to be widely regarded as a "crown" of Calvin's achievement.

Just as Calvin's lecture on Romans in the first Genevan period resulted in the *Romans Commentary* published in Strasbourg, after his return to Geneva, all his New Testament lectures were to be published as commentaries. In addition, from Isaiah in 1549 to Ezekiel (1–21) in the year of his death, Calvin had lectured on Genesis, Psalms, Hosea, the Minor Prophets, Daniel, Jeremiah and Lamentations.[55] In the cases of his Old Testament lectures, stenographic notes were usually taken from his lectures in Latin, and out of these notes, after Calvin's review, formal lecture notes were prepared. Some lecture notes were polished by Calvin himself and published as commentaries, while others were published as lectures. According to *Bibliotheca Calviniana*, for example, Pentateuch, Genesis, Joshua, Psalms, and Isaiah were published in the form of commentaries, and Jeremiah, Ezekiel, Daniel, the Minor Prophets, and Hosea were in the form of lectures.[56] Noticeably, all these publications in Latin were, as in the case of the Latin Psalms commentary of 1557 and the French Psalms commentary of the next year, translated shortly afterward into French and made available to the readers in Geneva and beyond. In addition, Calvin's Latin lectures themselves were international in nature. According to Wilcox's study on his Old Testament lectures, for example, his Isaiah lecture (1548–50) was attended by three groups of "scholars, ministers, and auditors," and among these "auditors" were many refugees and students from France, Italy, Germany, Hungary, among others. By the more accurate extant record of 1561, among 159 official attendants, three quarters were from France and only three were native Genevans. Forty-three of these French attendants, after completing their studies at the Academy, were sent back to France as Reformed pastors.[57]

(iii) The foundation of the Academy and Calvin's biblical lectures in the post-1555 period are vital factors for understanding the last phase of his ecclesiological development, which our study terms his "Reformation ecclesiology." These factors are especially significant in two respects, both of which are historically related to the background of his Reformation ecclesiology. One

55. Cf. P. Wilcox, "The Lectures of John Calvin and Nature of His Audience, 1555–1564," *Archiv für Reformationsgeschichte* 87 (1996): 138–39; Wendel, *Calvin*, 105.

56. *BC* III, 645–48.

57. Wilcox, "The Lectures," 141–45.

respect was a bold historical step taken by Geneva to openly send pastors/missionaries to France, which appeared in the official city records after 1555 and was carried out not by the magistracy but, with its tacit approval, by the Company of Pastors and Teachers. According to Kingdon's groundbreaking study, the step was systematically executed. Upon receiving requests for pastors from the underground Reformed congregations in France, the Company officially started to supply them in 1557. The numbers commissioned were 11 in 1557, 22 in 1558, 32 in 1559, and the official record between 1560 and 1562 showed 12 in each year. But according to Kingdon, the actual number sent in 1561 was over one hundred. Significantly, almost all of these commissioned pastors were French, had heard Calvin's lectures, and had been trained in the Genevan Academy.[58] The other respect concerned the concentration of Calvin's lectures in this period (ca. 1555–64) on the major prophetic books of the Old Testament, including the Psalms, which he considered a prophetic book. The fact that he was Professor of the Old Testament at the Academy, lecturing on the prophetic books, and was deeply concerned with the prophetic message of Scripture, was to have a considerable impact upon his later understanding of the Christian church in Europe. Along with the theme of the messianic message, his extraordinary self-awareness as its messenger was definitely sharpened in this period. Although this self-awareness appeared in his earlier writings, especially in the preface to *Two Epistles* and throughout the Nicodemite controversy of the 1540s, it was in the last phase of his life that this self-awareness took on exceptional proportions and made his prophetic vision more akin to that of the Old Testament prophets. These aspects will be examined later in connection with his Reformation ecclesiology.[59]

2. *Reformer of France and Europe*

At the beginning of this study, we defined Calvin as "Reformer of France" and assumed that from this perspective he first engaged himself in the Genevan

58. Kingdon, *Geneva and the Coming*, 2, 14–15. Cf. M. Bruening, *Calvinism's First Battleground: Conflict and Reform in the Pays de Vaud, 1528–1559* (Dortrecht: Springer Netherlands Studies, 2005). As Bruening's work substantiates, the earlier training and sending of the French ministers, carried out by the Lausanne Academy with Bernese support, were transferred to Geneva after the establishment of the Academy in 1559.

59. Cf. Oberman, "*Europa Afflicta*," 102: Oberman, *John Calvin*, 187: "Calvin was not a city reformer in any of the usual senses of the term. He regarded himself as a soldier stationed in Geneva, but at the same time as an officer directing a European army"; Balserak, *John Calvin as Sixteenth-Century Prophet*, 88–100.

Reformation and later in the Reformation of Europe. In the case of the French Reformation, however, although he had become the most famous figure in it, he was definitely not the main figure to have led its development. Among recent research in this field, moreover, the French Reformation of Calvin's time is increasingly viewed as "multivocal" and "enigmatic," and the general designation of "Reformed" rather than "Calvinistic" seems to be preferred. In this respect, "the French Reformation and Calvin," is a complex and difficult topic to be tackled.[60] Although it is true that Calvinist Reformation, after Calvin's death, was to be a major form of Protestant Reformation in Europe, any investigation into his relation with the European Reformation as a whole in his lifetime faces great difficulty. Bearing this in mind, and focusing on his ecclesiological development, we will only consider three topics as the background of his Reformed and Reformation ecclesiologies: the French Reformation and Calvin, the organization of the French Reformed Church, and whether he can be considered as Luther's heir.

(1) The French Reformation and Calvin

During his first stay in Geneva, Calvin challenged the early French Reformation by publishing *Two Epistles* in 1537. He was the lone challenger residing in Geneva as a French exile. In his second Genevan period, he became known as both a Reformer of Geveva and a Reformer of France. It is not an easy task, however, to assess how an exiled Reformer of France faced the ongoing reality of the French Reformation and challenged it. With regard to this issue, we will selectively focus on two points: the multivocal character of the French Reformation and the Nicodemite controversy in which he was deeply involved as its main player.

Multivocal Character of the French Reformation

(i) According to the quasi-canonical history of the French Reformed Church, *Histoire ecclésiastique des églises réformées au royaume de France* (1580), the Calvinist Reformed church movement, which distinguished itself as a dominant force of the French Reformation since the mid-sixteenth century, is sharply distinguished from its earlier non-Calvinist movements. This view,

60. Cf. Benedict, *Christ's Churches*, 120; A. Duke, "Perspective on European Calvinism," in *Calvinism in Europe, 1540–1620*, ed. A. Pettegree, A. Duke, and G. Lewis (Cambridge: Cambridge University Press, 1994), 1, 4.

which Reid refers to as "only half the picture," is not an acceptable perspective today.[61] In the early French Reformation, there were some sporadic Evangelical manifestations known as "Lutheranism" as well as the well-known Meaux reform which, after being suppressed in 1525, survived as a movement and even organized the underground church in 1546 on the premise of congregational polity. According to Reid, reform movements led by local priests and monks were recognized in the area surrounding Bourges.[62] Furthermore, as recognized today, there were reform movements that spread from major cities such as Paris and Poitiers, where evangelicals were concentrated and had influence in the courts of Marguerite and her daughter, Jeanne of Navarre.[63] In addition to these reform movements in France, there were church organizations of exiled French centered in Bucer's Strasbourg, of which Calvin was its first pastor, in Farel's Neuchâtel, and in Viret's Lausanne. In Neuchâtel, for instance, sixty French exiles were said to have received ordination between 1530 and 1560. Likewise, before the foundation of the Genevan Academy, many French students had been trained at the Lausanne Academy.[64]

(ii) In the early and formative stage of the French Reformation, properly described as "multivocal," during the period between 1555 and 1560 a significant shift occurred that consolidated the previous reform movements into ecclesial structures. Some researchers describe this shift as a "coagulation" or "metamorphosis," and it remains the most undocumented area in the study of the French Reformation. As an example explaining this shift, Reid notes

61. J. A. Reid, "French Evangelical Networks before 1555: Proto-churches?," in *La réforme en France et en Italie: contacts, comparisons, et contrastes*, ed. P. Benedict, S. Seidel Menchi, and A. Tallon (Rome: École française de Rome, 2007), 106, citing *Histoire ecclésiastique des églises réformées au royaume de France*, I, 97.

62. W. Monter, "France: The Failure of Repression, 1520–1563," in *La réforme en France et en Italie: contacts, comparisons, et contrastes*, ed. P. Benedict, S. Seidel Menchi, and A. Tallon (Rome: École française de Rome, 2007), 472; J. A. Reid, "French Evangelical Networks," in *La réforme en France et en Italie: contacts, comparisons, et contrastes*, ed. P. Benedict, S. Seidel Menchi, and A. Tallon (Rome: École française de Rome, 2007), 108–16, 118.

63. Cf. H. Daussy, "Les élites face à la réforme dans le royaume de France (ca. 1520–ca. 1570)," in *La réforme en France et en Italie: contacts, comparisons, et contrastes*, ed. P. Benedict, S. Seidel Menchi, and A. Tallon (Rome: École française de Rome, 2007), 331–49. Daussy regards the royal lineage from Marguerite (sister of Francis I, Duchess of Alençon, Queen of Navarre) to Jeanne d'Albret (Queen of Navarre), her Calvinist son, Henry (later King Henry IV), and his Huguenot cousin, Henri I of Condé, as forming an important wing of the French Reformation.

64. P. Benedict, "Refugee Churches and Exile Centers in the French Reformation," in *La réforme en France et en Italie: contacts, comparisons, et contrastes*, ed. P. Benedict, S. Seidel Menchi, and A. Tallon (Rome: École française de Rome, 2007), 535–52, esp. 541.

that unorganized circles or congregations of evangelicals rapidly spread in the 1540s. By 1555, they were recognized in more than forty cities and several hundred towns and villages. Between 1555 and 1562, they were organized into more than eight hundred churches. In these organized churches, moreover, regular exercise of Bible studies, the sacraments, and prayers were observed, and some of them were to join in founding the national assembly of the Reformed Church in 1559.[65] Although among these organized churches the direct involvement of Calvin and the Genevan Company was limited, significantly, the increase of unorganized circles or congregations and their "coagulation" into organized churches coincided with the period of Calvin's second Genevan stay. During this period, it is generally assumed that Calvin had exerted considerable influence upon the evangelical movements in France.

(iii) To illustrate this point, we will refer to Calvin's published French works. In the first French *Institutes* (1541) he presented an overview of Evangelical theology. By the *Genevan Ecclesiastical Ordinance* (1541) and *Catechism* (1543) he showed the model of the Evangelical church organization and education. In one of his most famous anti-Catholic polemics on the holy relics, *Advertissement . . . des reliques* (1543), he exposed the reality of the Catholic popular religion. And through a series of his anti-Nicodemite literature (1543–44) he demonstrated the practice of the Evangelical Christian life clearly distinguished from that of the "moderate" reformist groups. It has been assumed that this French literature had been widely spread and read and that it had influenced the direction of the French Reformation in general and the organization of the churches in particular. However, it is not easy to determine the exact occasion on which he shifted his previously reluctant policy to acknowledge the organization of the overtly secessionist churches. His reluctance was mainly due to two concerns: that such an organization of the churches might raise the issue of schism in the French Church and that it might be considered an open act of treason against the King, whose policy was to make Catholicism the state religion. Nonetheless, Salmon notes the importance of the year 1555 in which the last opposing faction in Geneva was defeated. The Company of Pastors and Teachers began to send openly the trained French pastors back to France, and Salmon assumes that "from this point Calvinist churches began

65. Reid, "French Evangelical Networks," 105–8. Cf. Benedict, "Refugee Churches," 545–46. By citing Kingdon (*Geneva and the Coming*, 1–2, 78–80), Reed estimates the total number of ministers sent to France between 1555 to 1562 at 242. By citing Benedict (*Christ's Churches*, 134, 137), he also estimates the total number of churches joined to the Reformed Church by 1570 at 1,240.

to be secretly organized in the main towns."[66] Moreover, as Monter suggests, such historical factors as the collapse of persecution of the Evangelicals by 1550 in France and the increase of exiled French aristocrats and prominent figures in the 1550s in Geneva had contributed to the policy shift.[67]

Nicodemite Controversy

(i) The term "Nicodemite" has been taken from Calvin's last polemical treatise against the moderate reformists in France, *Answer to the Nicodemite Gentlemen* (*Excuse à Messieurs les Nicodemites*, 1544). According to the common understanding of current Calvin researchers, this treatise is the last in a series of Calvin's work. It started with *Two Epistles* (1537) examined in chapter 2, through the French version of its first epistle revised for popular use, the *Small Tract* (1543) mentioned in chapter 3, and concluded with the *Answer to the Nicodemite Gentlemen.* In fact, the *Answer* referred to the other two works by distinguishing *Two Epistles* as a "livre" (book) and the *Small Tract* as a "traicté" (treatise).[68] In the transition from *Two Epistles* to the *Small Tract*, however, Calvin himself changed the nature of the controversy from theological arguments against the Lefèvrian moderate reformists to the general readers who were struggling with their evangelical faith in the French Catholic Church. In this respect, as Monter considers the Nicodemite controversy as the most important aspect of French Protestant history in the 1540s, the controversy was, in a more refined sense, in its later phase. In one sense, Calvin's image of the Nicodemites could be historically applied to a wider European context beyond France, for instance, to "evangelical Roman Catholics" in general. Here we examine it more narrowly against his immediate background of the French Reformation, considering the Nicodemites a reforming force between papalism and Protestant Evangelicalism. As Wright affirms, however, Calvin's stance against Nicodemism was the most severe among all his contemporary Reformers.[69]

66. J. H. M. Salmon, *Society in Crisis: France in the Sixteenth Century* (New York: St. Martin's Press, 1975), 87.

67. Cf. Monter, "France: The Failure of Repression," 473.

68. Cf. *CO* 6:593, 600. We use the text of the *Excuse à Messieurs les Nicodémites* (*BC* 44/9: *CO* 6:589–614). Gordon (*Calvin*, 189) presents an interesting insight on Calvin's attack on the Nicodemites, that it was Calvin's attempt "to wrest control of the evangelical movement in France away from the Navarrists centred around Marguerite."

69. Cf. W. Monter, *Judging the French Reformation: Heresy Trials by Sixteenth-Century*

Two Epistles took issue with the Lefèvrian distinction between "worship/adoration" and "veneration," which was based upon the Catholic dogma of the Second Nicene Council, and urged the moderate reformists to make an either-or choice between papal and Evangelical Christianity. This theoretical distinction, by which the Lefèvrians justified their participation in the Catholic rites of nonevangelical origin, remained the groundwork for later Nicodemism. For example, the *Small Tract* took up the practical issue implicit in Nicodemism to distinguish "the spiritual worship of heart" from the practice of "external adoration." Limiting the arguments exclusively and narrowly to attending the Mass, it questioned the inadvisable practice for evangelical Christians to attend the Mass either in the form of "dissimulation" or that of "simulation." As Calvin said:

> In order to prevent the sophistry of some: we are not on this difficulty, to know if it is wrong to dissimulate: but [it is wrong] to simulate and counterfeit against the truth. Dissimulation amounts to concealing what is in one's heart. Simulation is more, it is to pretend and feign what is not [in one's heart]. In short, just as one would lie by mouth, one simulates fact.

The former position was to hide one's evangelical faith ("what is in one's heart") and to attend the Mass only as an external adoration. Distinct from this feigned idolatry, the latter position gave a false appearance of what one did not believe ("what is not [in one's heart]") by pretending the Mass to be the true worship and a nonissue.[70] Although researchers tend to regard these evangelicals in the 1540s as "atheoretical" and their reform an "amorphous phenomenon" in nature motivated by "fear" of the religious and social pressures, two points should be remembered: Calvin's basic theoretical foundation on this issue was already laid out in *Two Epistles*; his image of the Nicodemites also included the "moderate" Lefèvrian reformists as well as other evangelicals who had been defending their actions with the theoretical arguments.[71]

Parlements (Cambridge, MA: Harvard University Press, 1999), 112: Tavard, "Calvin and the Nicodemites," 72–78; Wright, "Why Was Calvin So Severe," 77–81; ch. 2, n. 188. Tavard takes a wider image of Calvin's Nicodemites as "evangelical Roman Catholics" and considers them forming "a consistent group" within the Roman Catholic Church, including not only French nobles and clerics but also Cardinal Gasparo Contarini, English Cardinal Reginald Pole, etc.

70. Cf. *CO* 6:546; Eire, *War against the Idols*, 256–57; Gordon, *Calvin*, 191.

71. C. M. N. Eire, "Calvin and Nicodemism: A Reappraisal," *Sixteenth-Century Journal* 10 (1979): 45–69; Eire, *War against the Idols*, 251–53; F. M. Higman, "The Question of Nicode-

(ii) The *Answer to the Nicodemite Gentlemen* was the smallest piece among the three mentioned above, but it had the clearest presentation of Calvin's argument. Its noteworthy merit was a clear separation of the known Nicodemites of the 1540s into two groups. One was the group of those who "know their wrongdoing in their hearts and confess it in their mouths and are repentant and continuously asking for God's mercy." This was the group that he tried to console and advise. The other was the group that he variously described as those who "justify themselves with all sorts of subterfuges," "with borrowing the name of Nicodemus," with using him as "a shield," and "hide themselves under the robe of Nicodemus." In short, they were "simulators" against whom Calvin urged to abandon their stances, and asked for their apologies.[72]

Calvin took issue with this second group first and counted four catego-

mism," in *Calvinus Ecclesiae Genevensis Custos*, ed. W. H. Neuser (Frankfurt am Main: Peter Lang, 1984), 168; J. Balserak, "Geneva's Use of Lies, Deceit, and Simulation in Their Efforts to Reform France, 1536–1563," *Harvard Theological Review* 112 (2019): 76–100. Over and against Eire's basic characterization of Nicodemism as "an amorphous phenomenon," "an attitude rather than a movement," "composed of various types of dissemblers," we rather take Higman's view that the Nicodemites had "a defined and coherent theological position" as better fitting to Calvin's own characterization. Balserak, the author of *John Calvin as Sixteenth-Century Prophet* and *Establishing the Remnant Church in France*, is well qualified to write on the two topics of Calvin's Nicodemite controversy and his (and later Beza's) ministry to France. He examines afresh the old integrity issue of Calvin related to these topics. Concerning Calvin's Nicodemite controversy, as one of the article's captions ("Mendacity and Geneva's Judgment of the Nicodemites") indicates, he takes a narrow approach to the controversy and seems to assume its core issue to be the question of morality. For instance, among a few Calvin texts referred to, he cites the *Small Tract*'s definition of dissimulation and simulation (which our main text also cites) and, in his own translation, rather liberally renders its last sentence ("En somme, ce qui seroit mentir de bouche, est simuler de faict") into "and is the moral equivalent of lying." (82) Furthermore, he considers Calvin's "inflexible opposition to lying" (83) as a crux of his anti-Nicodemism. Moral issue was certainly an aspect of the controversy, but we assert that it was not the core issue. Our analyses of *Two Epistles* and the *Small Tract* show that Calvin regarded those who were known later as the Nicodemites as an evangelical reformist force in the French Church, and he challenged them to manifest their evangelical faith by "outward profession" (*professio externa*). His criticism of their "lying" was not primarily directed against their moral integrity but against their "deceiving" their consciences by simulating what they did not believe, in particular by justifying what they simulated to be a truthful fact ("de faict"). For Calvin it was a grave salvific issue of divine worship or idolatry. Although Balserak certainly has a right to historically judge Calvin's integrity and his clandestine ministry to France as deceitful, we wonder, whether his article helps to clarify the issues raised in the already confused field of Nicodemism research or not.

72. *CO* 6:595–96, 608. For a critical English translation of the *Excuse* (*BC* 44/9), see F. Higman, *Three French Treatises* (London: Athlone, 1970), 131–53.

ries of people within it: Catholic priests, court nobles and preachers, literary men including medical doctors, lawyers, and philosophers, and merchants and ordinary faithful. He portrayed the general image of these four categories as having their own subterfuges, such as their duties to minister to the people, social status, freedom of thought, economical stake, and reasoning with which to defend their actions. Another image presented by Calvin was their having a critical attitude toward Calvin and his advice. Concerning the attack and advice that he had made from the safety of Geneva, in particular, they cynically remarked that "since Calvin acts so bravely, why does he not come here to see how it is going?"[73] To these "simulators" who claimed their actions helped to preserve the church, Calvin asked, "Do they consider that God cannot firmly establish his church without the help of their simulation?" To priests who insisted their actions necessary for the church's evangelism, he recommended choosing exile by saying that "the exile of a man sometimes preaches with far greater effect than he can do with his mouth." And to those faithful who could not make such a radical choice, he urged them to "leave everything to the Lord." As we have seen in chapter 2, in *Two Epistles* Calvin seemed to compare himself with the Prophet Ezekiel and sharply attacked the moderate reformists. But his apology against the simulators in the *Answer* was more nuanced and mindful of their conditions and reasonings.[74]

At the end of his advice to the first group, Calvin wrote a fresh apology that examined the notion of the Nicodemites itself and was directed against the second group, especially the simulators' positive use of Nicodemus's case for the justification of their actions. By introducing two images of Nicodemus out of the biblical narratives, namely "imaginary (or false) Nicodemus" and "true Nicodemus," the apology identified the former image with the simulators but clearly distinguished the latter image from the former. In particular, Calvin described the Nicodemus of John's Gospel chapter 3 as an unbeliever who did not know Christ and the Nicodemus of chapter 19 as a confessor of Christ who risked his social status to bury the executed Christ when the disciples were in hiding.[75] Calvin made this distinction a focal point of his apology, and this move could be confirmed in his Latin translations of the *Small Tract* and *Answer* as well as in the *John's Gospel Commentary* (1553). The Latin translations were aimed at introducing the French controversy to German readers for their understanding and were published with Melanchthon's introduction.

73. *CO* 6:597–602, 607. Cf. Gordon, *Calvin*, 181, 192–95.

74. *CO* 6:605–6. Cf. ch. 2, n. 168.

75. *CO* 6:608–9.

For the Latin publication, a part of the title was changed from (*Answer to*) "*the Nicodemite Gentlemen*" to "*the Pseudo-Nicodemites.*"[76]

Among sixteenth-century gospel commentaries, perhaps Calvin's *John's Gospel Commentary* presented the highest evaluation of Nicodemus in chapter 19. In a comment on 19:28, Calvin called Joseph and Nicodemus "disciples of Christ" and described their actions as "that without hesitation they exercised the perpetual fight against their people." In contrast, he called the "false Nicodemites" unworthy of Nicodemus's name, criticizing their actions as exercising superstitions with the simulation of their faith and as unworthy of being Christ's disciples.[77] Although in the original French edition of the *Answer* Calvin did not directly connect the Nicodemites of the first group with this "true Nicodemus," he seemingly advised them from the perspective of the "true Nicodemus." For instance, he encouraged them to have "great courage" [like the true Nicodemus] and "to endeavor to restore the Kingdom of our Lord Jesus and to fight against all the resistance of Satan."[78]

(iii) The middle of the 1540s, in which Calvin's Nicodemite controversy was advancing, was the period when, as Monter demonstrates, official censorship, judicial procedure, an oath of allegiance to Catholicism, and public executions were enforced against the Evangelicals in France. Evangelicalism was in disarray with neither the hope of organizing nor an effective means of survival, except for submitting to persecution or exile. The reason Calvin took on the issue of Nicodemism in this situation was perhaps his recognition that Nicodemism could be a challenging option for the French Reformation as well as a formidable opposition to his Evangelicalism. Here, it should be noted that, besides Calvin's "Reformation of the Refugees," Oberman considers Nicodemism a "courageous alternative to the refugees." For Calvin's prophetic self-awareness, however, this "courageous alternative" was none other than the corrupt religion of the Old Testament people, which the prophets challenged. During the end phase of the Nicodemite controversy, according to Engammare, Calvin recalled the Nicodemites' criticism of his presumptive claim of "making himself a prophet," but he justified his use of prophetic language

76. *De Vitandis Superstitionibus, . . . Eiusdem Excusatio, ad Pseudonicodemos*: *BC* 49/5. Cf. Droz, *Chemins de l'hérésie*, 147; Eire, *War against the Idols*, 246–47. According to the *Bibliotheca Calviniana* (*BC* 45/4, 197), the Latin translation of the *Answer to the Nicodemites* was sent in 1545 to Melanchthon in order to receive his and Luther's endorsement. By Melanchthon's own judgment, however, the translation and Calvin's own letter to Luther were withheld and not sent to Luther. Droz and Eire notice the significance of a change in the title.

77. *In Evangelium secundum Iohannem Commentarius*: *BC* 53/5, *CO* 47:424.

78. *CO* 6:610–14.

by writing that it was God's doctrine that he preached.[79] As chapter 2 above considered the significance of Calvin's *Two Epistles* in the 1530s as his move to prevent the French reform movements from converging with the compromises of the moderate reformists, the same could be said as to the Nicodemite controversy in the 1540s. In fact, an evaluation of Eire, who has examined all of Calvin's publications aimed at this controversy, is worth noticing. He emphasizes that Calvin's motivation was to rescue the reform movements in France from the confusion caused by the compromising simulators, and he concludes that "Calvin's adamant refusal to accept compromise helped establish French Protestantism as a separatist religion, and laid the foundations for a vibrant Huguenot church."[80]

(2) Organization of the French Reformed Church

Eire's evaluation of the Nicodemite controversy poses two derivative issues. One concerns the issue of what Eire calls "necessity of schism." On this premise, any organization of the church other than the Roman Catholic Church is considered schismatic in the mid-sixteenth century. The other concerns the issue of what Eire calls "a prelude to sedition." Since Calvin's uncompromising position in the controversy rejects the Roman Catholic Church as the church of Christ, it could be regarded as an act of resistance to the state that required all its subjects to pledge allegiance to Catholicism.[81] From Eire's point of view, the organization of the French Reformed Church in 1559 was none other than an act of schism and sedition. Calvin had consistently avoided the ideas of "schism" and "sedition" in his concept of the church. However, the organization of a separatist church in France presented him with a fresh theological problem. In the following pages, keeping the issue of "schism" and "sedition" in mind, we will examine two questions: from what point or when did he begin to propose the organizing of the independent churches in France; and what was the nature of his relationship with the organized French Reformed Church in 1559?

79. Monter, *Judging the French Reformation*, 112; H. A. Oberman, "The Nicodemism: Courageous Alternative to the Refugee," in *The Impact of the Reformation* (Grand Rapids: Eerdmans, 1994), 187–200; M. Engammare, "Calvin: A Prophet without Prophecy," in *Calvin Studies IX*, ed. J. H. Leith and R. A. Johnson (Davidson, NC: Davidson College, 1998), 95. The origin of Engammare's reference to "making himself a prophet" in Calvin's sermon on Ezekiel, which Engammare does not identify, may be the preface to *Two Epistles*.

80. Eire, *War against the Idols*, 234–50, esp. 250.

81. Eire, "Prelude to Sedition?," 141–44.

Calvin's Policy Shift and the Organized Church

(i) Concerning the first question, there seems to be no established theory among Calvin researchers on the exact timing of his policy shift on the organized churches. In the 1552 publication of *Four Sermons*, which followed up on the theme of the Nicodemite controversy, Calvin still maintained his hesitant attitude toward the open advocacy of organized churches. He instead encouraged the faithful to avoid idolatrous cults, to endure persecutions, and to pray for the freedom of pure worship. To a cynical remark by a certain French philosopher who claimed that Calvin would not acknowledge anyone as a Christian unless he would take exile in Geneva and listen to Calvin's sermons, Calvin responded: "he would respect a hundred times more" those who, under papal tyranny, studied the Bible at home instead of in church and "strived to live honestly and to serve God than those of us who were enjoying freedom and equality" in exile.[82]

Among some researchers, however, there seems to be a tendency to regard the time around 1555 as when his policy shift on open advocacy occurred. As mentioned above, citing the importance of the Company's decision to openly send pastors back to France in 1555, Salmon holds that "from this point Calvinist churches began to be secretly organized in the main towns."[83] There might also be some historical factors that had contributed to his decision for open advocacy. For example, the Roman Catholic Church in the period of the Council of Trent (1545–63) was increasingly preoccupied with the idea of the Counter-Reformation and closing the door to the reunification of the old and new churches. In addition, the German solution of the Peace of Augsburg (1555) was not considered a viable option for France. Besides these external factors, some internal factors of importance arose in France. Earlier in his career, Calvin sought the French King's favorable view of Protestant Evangelicalism as a viable option. In the time of Calvin after 1541, some high aristocrats and even those of the King's bloodline converted to Evangelicalism. In the 1550s it was said that nearly one third of the minor aristocrats turned to Evangelicalism or exile. Against this background, according to one researcher's assumption, "the massive adhesion of the nobles to the religion of Calvin constituted a decisive trump for the implantation of the Reformed Protestantism in the Kingdom."[84]

82. *Quatre sermons*: *BC* 52/9, *CO* 8:412, cited in Eire, *War against the Idols*, 263.
83. Salmon, *Society in Crisis*, 87.
84. Daussy, "Les élites face a la réforme," 331–39, esp. 338.

Assuming that Calvin became a substantive leader of the reform movements in France after the death of Marguerite, queen of Navarre, in 1549, moreover, Gordon analyzes Calvin's tacit approval of the lifestyle of nobles who had been converted to Calvinism for the sake of France's evangelization, even though their behaviors were not up to his strict standards. As a result of their conversions, in the territories under their rule, Calvinists were protected. This fact had contributed to the phenomenon of the "coagulation" of the mid-1550s.[85] Nevertheless, besides sending pastors from Geneva into France, there was also the issue of the need for elders who were to rule the church with pastors, to constitute a consistory for church discipline, and above all to represent the congregation. Unlike the case of Geneva where elders were chosen from the City Councils, the selection of elders from the congregation posed a serious practical problem. Theoretically, however, as we have seen above, Calvin solved this problem in the third *Institutes* by articulating that both pastors and elders constituted one presbyterial office (*presbyterium*). In the *Synoptic Gospels Commentary* of 1555, furthermore, commenting on the text (Matt 18:17), he interpreted the "church" as a disciplinary institution, a council of priests and elders of the people in the Jewish synagogues. Calvin's decision for open advocacy took into consideration the prospect of having pastors as well as elders from the congregations.[86]

(ii) The second question of Calvin's relationship with the established French Reformed Church remains an area of some unsettled issues. For example, Gordon's Calvin biography places this question in the wider historical context of the French Churches' "great expansion" and the French nobles' contribution to it. Perhaps reflecting the unsettled condition of present scholarship, Gordon treats cursorily the first national synod of the French Reformed Church in Paris and suggests an implicit tension between the synod and Geneva's Calvin.[87] It has been generally assumed that the synod adopted two documents, the *Confession of Faith* and the *Disciplinary Ordinance*. Concerning the *Confession of Faith*, however, the synod actually had examined two confessions: the original confession adopted by the synod and that sent by Calvin, reaching the synod at its last stage.

Though the two confessions could be viewed in the wider sense of Calvin's theology, they differed considerably in their confessional tone and form. The

85. Gordon, *Calvin*, 304–7.

86. Cf. *CO* 1:650; Doumergue, *Jean Calvin*, 5:154. For the *Synoptic Gospels Commentary*, see n. 46 above.

87. Gordon, *Calvin*, 304–12, esp. 305–6.

original confession prepared by the synod took the formal structure of a confession and was expected to be dedicated to the monarch. On the other hand, Calvin's confession bore the tone of the underground and clandestine churches and took an unusual form. Its title began with the words, "The poor faithful who are unjustly slandered and suffered by the Kingdom of France," and opened with an unusual preface in which he defended the Reformed Church of France against the charges of "schism" and "sedition." These two documents represented two distinctive perspectives of the current Reformed churches in France. The *French Confession* was accepted as the official confession by the seventh national synod of La Rochelle in 1571 after going through a process to resolve internal conflicts and assimilating Calvin's confession.[88] Against this historically unsettled background of the early French Reformed Church, especially focusing on Calvin's ecclesiological development, we will examine the following three aspects of this relationship, the first two aspects here and the third aspect under a separate heading. They include the idea of the church in Calvin's preface to his 1559 confession, the articles on the church and the sacraments in the official *French Confession*, and the so-called Morély affair, in which his publication, *Traicté de la discipline et police Chrestienne* (1562), challenged Calvin's ideas of church discipline and polity and caused a protracted controversy in the early history of the French Reformed Church.

(iii) The first aspect concerned an introductory portion of Calvin's confession in the form of a preface, which was in reality a fierce appeal for the reform of the French Church. The preface expressed his understanding of the current situation surrounding the emerging Reformed churches, the significance of founding the French Reformed Church, and an apology dealing with the charges of "schism" and "sedition." Firstly, Calvin analyzed the present churches under persecution as simply following a common "rule" of the entire history of God's church and compared it with the churches of the apostles, who were likewise persecuted, sued in the courts, and called "the useless and mal-

88. Bernard Roussel, "Gallic Confession," *OER* 2:156. Cf. *CO* 9:731–52; *Creeds and Confessions*, 2:372–86. The *Opera Calvini* edition contains Calvin's original "Preface" (731–40) and the early Genevan text of the Confession with 35 Articles (739–52). For our discussion below on church discipline, we use the Niesel edition (*Bekenntnisschriften und Kirchenordnungen der nach Gottes Wort reformierten Kirche* [Zurich: Evangelischer Verlag A. G. Zollikon, 1938]) which, besides "La discipline ecclésiastique" (75–79), has also taken the official Gallican Confession ("Confession de foi des églises de France," 66–75) with forty articles from the so-called official history of the French Reformed Church (*Histoire ecclésiastique des églises réformées au royaume de France*, ed. G. Baum et al. [Paris: Librarie Fischbacher, 1884–89]).

odorous of the world."[89] In spite of the fact that the Reformed churches made their intention of reforming the French Catholic Church known, secondly, he was not ashamed of their being called "foreigners," "outsiders," and "invaders," and urged the critics to read the "confession" as their "apology."[90] Concerning the charges of "schism" and "sedition," thirdly, his apology basically repeated what he had expressed before except adding a fresh affirmation that the Roman Catholic Church, "the synagogue of the Pope" where Christ was repeatedly sacrificed in the Mass, was more heretical and schismatic according to the judgment of the ancient church.[91]

As to the charge of "schism," comparing the current French situation with the time of the Babylonian captivity in which the true worship of God was not officially granted for God's people, he affirmed that God was also currently raising in France "congregations" that were eager to learn from God's word and to propagate the teaching of the salvation of God. In the same manner, as to the charge of "sedition," he affirmed that the founding of the organized church had no intention of changing the "social order" or eradicating existing cathedrals and statues, but only intended the peaceful order of having pastors, praying, and keeping the Evangelical teachings and sacraments. Then, he concluded with the familiar theme, "we are conspiring none to be suspect of sedition," which he expressed in the dedicatory epistle to the French king almost a quarter century previously.[92] One particular argument that he introduced to this end was the legal concept of "peremptory right" (*peremptoire*). This was his apologetic tool to assume that a "plaintiff" who accused the Reformed churches had no right to do so since they as defendants were just exercising God's word and sacraments. This assumption appeared in the context of the charge of "sedition" and was a tacit criticism of the state that made the church of the Babylonian captivity the state religion and thus had no right to persecute the Reformed churches.[93]

In this brief sketch of the newly organized Reformed Church, the most impressive aspect was the way in which Calvin presented the images of the church. The list of images began with the gathering of "the poor faithful" in the title of the confession, went on to a small and scattered congregation, a meeting that worshipped in a "sheep shack," a gathering of those who, just like

89. *CO* 9:731.

90. *CO* 9:733.

91. *CO* 9:734–35.

92. *CO* 9:736: "nous n'attentons rien dont nous puissions estre suspects de sedition." Cf. *OS* 1:35. (Battles, trans., *Institution*, 18.)

93. *CO* 9:736.

Christ's disciples, were hiding in fear and in night, a hidden worship place, and clandestine groups of worshipers hiding in "forests and caves." These unusual images were somehow related in Calvin's mind to the image of the "church of the refugees." As Eire suggests, furthermore, Calvin's understanding of the church expressed in these images was a contributing factor for church reform in other Catholic territories where his message made inroads.[94]

(iv) The second aspect concerned the contents of the official *French Confession* of the Reformed Church (1559/71), especially the articles on the church (25–33) and the sacraments (34–38). On these two topics the confession generally presented notions and expressions characteristic of Calvin's theology. Concerning the topic of the church, without referring to the church's definition and marks, the first article (25) began with "the order of the church" that Christ had established to be "sacred and inviolable" and listed at the head of the "order" the office of pastors for "the ministry and preaching of the word and of sacraments."[95] In the next three articles (26–28), the ministry of pastors was said to maintain "the unity of the church," to teach "the common instruction and yoke of Jesus Christ [discipline]," and to nourish "the true church" and "the company of the faithful." By the exercise of the word of God and the sacraments, in short, the Reformed Church was to be distinguished from "the Papal assemblies."[96] In the following five articles (29–33), the confession recaptured the theme of church government, especially that of ministerial order, and affirmed the order of "pastor, overseers, and deacons" to be primary and indispensable for church government. The word "overseers" (*surveillans*) was obviously used as a descriptive term for "elders" (*anciens*) and the term itself was found in Calvin's confession sent to the first synod.[97]

The articles on the sacraments also generally reflected Calvin's position. This could be illustrated by themes in the articles on the sacraments such as an emphasis of the Holy Spirit's work, the connection of justification and sanctification in the faithful's life, and a definition of the sacraments, especially of baptism, as "a lasting witness that Jesus Christ will always be our justifica-

94. Cf. Eire, *War against the Idols*, 264.

95. *Bekenntnisschriften*, 72; *CO* 9:748 (21); *Creeds and Confessions*, 2:382.

96. *Bekenntnisschriften*, 72–73; *CO* 9:748–49 (22–24). On avoiding any hints of a congregational role, the Confession shared a common stand with the 1541 *Ecclesiastical Ordinance*. According to Roussel ("Gallic Confession," *OER* 2:157), in addition to papalism, the Confession (arts. 25–26) contained the warning against spiritualism and separatism. Translations in English here are our own.

97. *Bekenntnisschriften*, 73; *CO* 9:749–50 (25–26); *Creeds and Confessions*, 2:383–84.

tion and sanctification."[98] As suggested by Roussel, the sacramental articles were said to take into consideration the basic assumptions of the *Consensus Tigurinus* (1549), in which the churches of both Zurich and Geneva came to an agreement on the Lord's Supper. On the crucial article on Christ's presence in the Supper, however, the *French Confession* inserted an important sentence, "by the secret and incomprehensible virtue of the Holy Spirit, he [Christ] nourishes and vivifies us out of the substance of his body and of his blood." Although "the secret and incomprehensible virtue of the Holy Spirit," was Calvin's typical term, the problematic expression, "substance," was the term that the *Consensus Tigurinus* avoided in consideration of Zwingli's eucharistic position. The confessional statement as a whole represented Calvin's own position or reflected the position of the *Wittenberg Concord* (1536) in which Bucer, representing the Evangelical churches in South Germany, initiated the eucharistic agreement with the Lutherans. Incidentally, Calvin in his Strasbourg period personally accepted the concord.[99] Thus, concerning the most controversial issue of Christ's presence in the Supper, the *French Confession* witnessed that the French Reformed Church was a member of the Reformed community, sharing a common understanding with Zwingli and Bucer, and affirmed its catholic communion with the Lutheran Church.

The Morély Affair

(i) The third aspect concerned the Morély affair (1562–72), which became the first internal conflict of the French Reformed Church. As the title of Morély's book (*Traicté de la discipline et police Chrestienne*, 1562) indicated, the focal point of the issue was the Reformed Church's official teachings on church polity, expressed in the *French Confession*, especially in its second part, "Quant a la discipline ecclésiastique." In reality, however, the affair was also a frontal challenge to Calvin's doctrine of church government that he had put forth in his 1543 *Institutes* and finalized in the 1559 *Institutes*. In the same year of its publication,

98. *Bekenntnisschriften*, 74 (35); *CO* 9:751 (31); *Creeds and Confessions*, 2:384.

99. *Bekenntnisschriften*, 74 (36); *CO* 9:751 (32); *Creeds and Confessions*, 2:385. Cf. Roussel, "Gallic Confession," *OER* 2:157. Since the 1543 *Institutes* (*CO* 1:993; *Institutio* 4.17.3: *OS* 5:344), the expression that Christ becomes one "substance" (*substantia*) with believers in the Lord's Supper appeared. According to Roussel, the Zurich representatives at the seventh national synod at La Rochelle (1571) complained about the term "substance" in article 36, but the synod retained it. In the text of the *Wittenberg Concord*, Christ's presence was described: "with the bread and wine the body and blood of Christ are truly and *substantially* present, offered, and received." (*Creeds and Confessions*, 2:799, emphasis added.)

Morély's *Traicté* was hastily judged erroneous by the national synod of Orléans, and in the following year the Genevan Church made a similar judgment against it, holding that it contained fantastic ideas and errors. Nevertheless, the controversy did not die down quickly but was prolonged, after several national and provincial synods, until the national synod of Nîmes in 1572.[100] Since the controversy lasted long after Calvin's death as a serious internal issue, instead of following its historical development, in the following pages we will focus on only two points, Morély's challenge to Calvin's theology at the time of the initial publication of the *Traicté* and the challenge's ecclesiological background.

(ii) The nature of Morély's challenge to Calvin was multifarious. It involved, for example, elements such as Calvin's leadership from Geneva over the French Reformed Church, the native reform movements in France, reactions to the Genevan consistorial discipline, criticism on the still formative stage of the French Confession, including the disciplinary ordinances, debates over the aristocratic and democratic church polity, and hermeneutic problems concerning the biblical teachings on church government and discipline. The most impressive factor in Morély's challenge concerned his understanding of the present state, according to which the theory and practice of the Genevan consistorial discipline were inappropriate for the Christian church and had been thrust upon the nascent Reformed Church in France. His church polity was said to emphasize the church's fundamental nature as a mixture of the monarchic rule of Christ, the aristocratic system of the consistory, and the "republican or democratic" congregation. From this viewpoint, he could have agreed with both the Reformed polity of a consistory chosen by the congregation and the representative system of the provincial and national synods.

However, the problem was the relationship of the democratic congregation and the aristocratic consistory. And here arose Morély's criticism that

100. J. Morély, *Traicté de la discipline et police Chrestienne* (1562). Cf. R. M. Kingdon, *Geneva and Consolidation of the French Protestant Movement, 1564–1572* (Geneva: Droz, 1967), 43–137; Maruyama, "The Morély Affair and Beza," in *The Ecclesiology*, 80–112; P. Denis and J. Rott, *Jean Morély (ca 1524–ca 1594) et l'utopie d'une démocratie dans l'église* (Geneva: Droz, 1993). Kingdon's analysis of the *Traicté* is still useful. He sees the Morély affair in the larger historical context of the Presbyterianism-Congregationalism conflict. Maruyama's analysis examines Morély's work in its immediate background and focuses on the crucial importance of the "Tell it to the church" (Matt 18:17) passage. While Morély takes "the church" as a (Christian) congregation and aligns with the interpretations of Bucer and Viret, Calvin and Beza take it as the disciplinary institution of the synagogues of Jesus's days, a prototype of the later Christian consistory. The most comprehensive study by Denis and Rott attempts a historical reappraisal of Morély and his thought, and includes a chapter (51–72) on the *Traicté* and the Morély affair.

the starting point of Reformed polity, congregational democracy, had been neglected by both the Genevan Church and the French Reformed Church. According to Denis and Rott's critical study on Morély's ecclesiology, his notion of church polity took the basic assumptions of Aristotle's *Politics* and sought after the example of the Athenian democracy.[101] Based upon the Aristotelian distinction between power and authority, just as in the case of Bucer, Morély had attributed the church's "power" to the congregation and its "authority" as derived from the congregational power to the consistory.[102] In addition, his criticism clearly understood that Calvin's interpretation of the disciplinary text (Matt 18:17) underlay the Reformed Church's disciplinary system. As we have noted before, partly reacting to Bucer's interpretation, which sought an extrabiblical hermeneutical key in Aristotle, Calvin sought the root of Christian church discipline in the context of the Old and New Testaments and found it in the disciplinary system of the Jewish synagogue, namely, a council of priests and elders of the people. In strong reaction to this interpretation, Morély insisted that the New Testament texts, including Matthew 18:17, never associated the term "the church" with the council in the Jewish synagogue.[103] On the *French Confession*, furthermore, his criticism was directed to its omission of references to the role of the congregation in church polity and its disregard for congregational power in the election of pastors. He pointed out in concrete terms that the confession (art. 31) referred to the pastoral appointments by "election" but failed to mention its method. The confession's disciplinary ordinances (art. 6) mentioned that the ministers will be elected to the consistory by elders and deacons, and that they will be presented to the "congregation" (*peuple*) for their ordinations. In the case of a conflict between the consistory and the congregation, he further pointed out, the case was to

101. *Traicté*, 183. Cf. Maruyama, *The Ecclesiology*, 99–100; Denis and Rott, *Jean Morély*, 173, 205–6; P. Denis, "Morély, Jean," *OER* 3:91–92. In 1560 Morély criticized the Genevan Consistory and came into conflict with the city authorities, and his critical view on Geneva appeared in the *Traicté* (150–57). In particular, Morély depicted Calvin as "Homeric Jupiter," a divine ruler of the sky, with thunderous lightnings, who threatened the faithful with excommunications, terrified them into submission, and executed a certain one [Servetus?].

102. According to Denis and Rott (*Jean Morély*, 134n17), Morély's unfinished manuscript, "De Ecclesiae Ordine" (II, 3–4), depicted two administrations in the Roman Republic: one superior administration based upon "the universal and supreme power which belonged to the people" and the other "the ordinary administration of power which belonged to the Senate or the magistracy." Morély was said to have applied this distinction to the Reformed polity.

103. *Traicté*, 62. Cf. Maruyama, *The Ecclesiology*, 99n102.

be referred to the provincial synod and decided there.[104] In the brief analysis above, a fundamental difference in church polity between Calvin and Morély could be seen. On the one hand, starting with the notion of Christ's kingdom, the starting point that Morély did not share, Calvin emphasized God's word as the kingdom's power in church polity. Then, he weighed in heavily on the consistory of pastors as the ministers of God's word and elders as the representatives of the congregation. He attributed to the congregation itself a passive role. On the other hand, starting with the principle of congregational power, Morély envisioned a consistory in accordance with it and sought a "utopia of democracy" in the polity of the Reformed Church.[105]

(iii) The French Reformed Church organized at the first national synod manifested its multivocal and fluid nature among the constituent churches. Even though agreeing on the fundamental character of the church, the differences among the churches were accentuated in the practical areas of church government and discipline and eventually became one of the major factors of the prolongation of the Morély affair. According to Denis and Rott, Morély listed the four Reformed ministers from whom he had received instructional influences, namely, Calvin, Bucer, Viret, and Peter Martyr Vermigli. He shared with them, with the exception of Calvin, a common understanding of church government and discipline, especially the notion that the church's basic power resided in the congregation, while its management was entrusted to pastors and elders.[106] In the previous two chapters, we have already mentioned Farel's congregationalist polity inherited from his teacher Lefèvre and the tension existing in Bucer's notions of Christ's kingdom and congregational principle.

However, the case of Viret, whom Morély was said to follow closely, was unique. A native of the French-speaking region of Switzerland, Viret had studied at the Collège de Montaigu at about the same time as Calvin and had come under Lefèvre's influence just as Farel had. As Pastor of the Lausanne Church, he had become a coworker of Farel and Calvin and had contributed to the French Reformation. His congregationalist emphasis in church polity had been well known before and during the Morély affair. And a rumor had surfaced that, in the year before the affair broke out in 1562, Viret's sudden exit from his residence in Geneva to France was occasioned by Morély's previous conflict with the Genevan Company of Pastors and Teachers.[107] In sum, the

104. *Bekenntnisschriften*, 73, 76. Cf. Denis and Rott, *Jean Morély*, 154–55.

105. Cf. Maruyama, *The Ecclesiology*, 82–92; Denis and Rott, *Jean Morély*, 107–203. Denis and Rott use the cited phrase of Morély (*l'utopie d'une démocratie*) in their book's subtitle.

106. Denis and Rott, *Jean Morély*, 109, 148, 206.

107. Denis and Rott, *Jean Morély*, 130. For Viret's disciplinary notion, see Maruyama, *The Ecclesiology*, 97–98. A close correlation between Viret and Morély can be illustrated by the

Morély affair had exposed the multivocal nature of the early French Reformed Church. Even though it ended in the rejection of Morély's particular view, it also proved that in the early Reformed Church, besides Calvin's dominant doctrine of church government (which we will discuss under "the Reformed ecclesiology" in the next section), coexisting trends existed in the ecclesiologies of Lefèvre, Bucer, Farel, and Viret.[108]

(3) Luther's Heir?

In 1546, the death of Luther, who had personified the Protestant Reformation and had exerted his influence at every turn of Reformation history, unquestionably marked the end of an era. Not only the Lutheran Church, but also Reformed Protestantism and the Radical Reformation, all bearing Luther's strong impact, were to step in to the new post-Luther era. As Luther's death coincided with the Council of Trent convoked just the previous year, the consolidation of church traditions based upon confessional distinction became an unavoidable trend in the Protestant camp. In the Lutheran Church, a controversy over the successional right of Luther broke out between the Gnesio-Lutherans and the Philippists. In the Lutheran-Reformed controversy, the issue of the sacraments was rekindled and that of predestination was intensified. Calvin was to be involved in the controversy over both issues. In this new confessional era, the succession of Luther's achievement or tradition was an acute problem in Reformed Protestantism as well. This was felt strongly by Calvin, who was considerably indebted to Luther in his early theological formation. In this new era, he had become an international leader, equal to Melanchthon and Bullinger, who had begun to exert his influence not only in France but also in the Low Countries, England, and elsewhere. Our concern here is to ascertain how a self-taught theologian and a second-generation Reformer, with a background in humanism and jurisprudence, who had never been personally acquainted with Luther the theologian, faced the problem of the Luther-succession issue. Our task is threefold: to ascertain the way by which Calvin understood Luther and his tradition, the substantive contents of Luther's tradition to be succeeded, and whether he was conscious of being "Luther's heir."

(i) Concerning Calvin's conception of Luther and his tradition, mainstream confessional approaches had focused on the contrast between the reception of Luther in Calvin and Calvin's independence from Luther. This question

---

fact that the *Traicté* was published in Lyon, where Viret retired after his sudden exit from Geneva and where both Viret and Morély frequented the palace of the duchess of Navarre.

108. Denis and Rott, *Jean Morély*, 208.

tends to be placed in a strictly historical context by more recent approaches, one of which is the study "John Calvin on Luther" by the prominent Luther scholar Gerrish. Reflecting the confessional studies of the past, Gerrish takes the starting point of the historical perspective that "Calvin was not a Calvinist, but an Evangelical, and what he thought about Luther can only be understood from this viewpoint."[109] He then proceeds to analyze Calvin's viewpoint as both "historical," that is, to see Luther and his Reformation as history and as "objective," that is, to comprehend Luther from what he had written, rather than from a personal relationship. According to him, Calvin had maintained this viewpoint in the fierce eucharistic controversy rekindled in the 1540s between the Lutherans and the Zwinglians.

On the one hand, Calvin requested Melanchthon to restrain the rage of Luther and his friends against the Zwinglians. On the other hand, he reminded Bullinger that Luther was "an illustrious servant of God" who had labored "to destroy the kingdom of the antichrist."[110] Gerrish considers, furthermore, that the core of Calvin's view on Luther was his conviction that Luther was, though being neither "God's oracle" nor "the gospel itself," "a remarkable apostle of Christ," and through his ministry "the purity of the gospel has been restored in our time." Calvin was said to have maintained this core conviction in his eucharistic controversy with the Gnesio-Lutherans after Luther's death, as well as when he successfully concluded the *Consensus Tigurinus*, a basic agreement on the Lord's Supper between Zurich and Geneva.[111] Lastly, Gerrish comes to the difficult problem of the "Luther-succession" in Calvin and proposes two tentative conclusions. One conclusion is that Calvin understood Luther not dogmatically but historically and Luther's Reformation as "a gradual unfolding of the gospel in its various historical relationships." Gerrish insists that Calvin flatly refused to accept Luther's teaching as "dogma," but he acknowledged Luther's achievement as "prophetic" in nature and did not even object to "Luther's being called by the name of Elijah."[112] Another conclusion that Gerrish draws is Calvin's conviction that the whole gospel truth could not be

109. B. A. Gerrish, "John Calvin on Luther," in *Interpreters of Luther*, ed. J. Pelikan (Philadelphia: Fortress Press, 1968), 67–96, esp. 68–69.

110. Gerrish, "John Calvin on Luther," 69–77.

111. Gerrish, "John Calvin on Luther," 77–86, esp. 79. Calvin's phrase, "Christ's apostle," appeared in his refutation of Pighius on the freedom of will (*Defensio Sanae et Orthodoxae*: *BC* 43/3, *CO* 6:250).

112. Gerrish, "John Calvin on Luther," 86–88. Cf. *Ultima Admonitio ad Joachimum Westphalum*: *BC* 57/11, *CO* 9:238: "Atque ut Eliae nomen concedatur Luthero, sacrilegae tamen est temeritatis, asserere ultimum Eliam."

comprehended by one particular Reformer but could be made clearer in dialogue. Gerrish illustrates this point by two examples: the *Consensus Tigurinus*, which was made possible by Calvin's considerable concession to Bullinger in order to avoid discord in the Reformed camp; and his dedicatory epistle to Grynaeus, affixed to the *Romans Commentary*, which expressed this conviction. In Calvin's pluralistic view of the Reformation, therefore, Luther could neither represent the whole Evangelical truth, nor could Calvin "complete" Luther's Reformation.[113]

(ii) The second task concerns the substance of what Calvin had "succeeded" or inherited from Luther's Evangelicalism. It has been widely acknowledged that, in his early theological formation, Calvin had learned from Luther teachings such as Scripture, justification by faith, Christian freedom, and so forth. Instead of individual theological notions, however, our present focus is on the whole outlook of the Protestant Reformation, for which Luther was an initiator and Calvin an inheritor. In this connection, we refer to two articles: "Luther and Calvin on Church and Tradition" by Steinmetz, who is also the author of both *Luther in Context* and *Calvin in Context*; and "*Europa Afflicta*: The Reformation of the Refugees" by Oberman.

The Steinmetz article proposes a thesis that the two 1539 publications *On the Council and the Church* by Luther at the age of fifty-five and *Reply to Sadoleto* by Calvin at the age of thirty shared basically the same concept of the church and its tradition, disregarding their age difference of a quarter-century. Although Calvin could not read Luther's work, which was published earlier but written in German, Luther did read Calvin's Latin work and was favorably impressed by it and, in a letter, even requested Bucer to transmit that impression to Calvin. This was indeed the only epistolary communication, albeit indirect, between the two Reformers. According to Steinmetz, upon reading Calvin's *Reply* Luther recognized that he completely agreed with Calvin and that Calvin could be a spokesperson for the entire Reformation.[114] Proceeding to examine each of the two works, Steinmetz summarizes the thrust of Luther's arguments in three points: that, even in the ancient ecumenical councils, there were many disagreements and contradictions on some doctrines, that these councils could not make new articles of faith unfounded on Scripture, and that the church had no standard other than Scripture for its doctrines. Likewise, Steinmetz lists Calvin's main arguments in his *Reply*: that God commissioned

113. Gerrish, "John Calvin on Luther," 88–91.

114. Davin C. Steinmetz, "Luther and Calvin on Church and Tradition," *Michigan Germanic Studies* 10 (1984): 98–101.

him to the church of Geneva, that church disunity was definitely not due to the inauguration of Evangelical reform because the church before Luther was already in a state of schism, and that the Protestant Reformation was nothing but the restoration of the purer religion of the ancient church.[115]

Steinmetz lists the four main reformatory convictions that were commonly shared by the two works and could represent in what way Calvin "succeeded" from Luther: the church councils and church fathers should occupy subordinate positions to Scripture; the historical concept that the Protestant Reformation caused disruption of the doctrinal unanimity of the past 1,500 years was to be rejected; concerning the teaching office of the church, the Protestant distinction of the office and its bearers as pastors and teachers should be preferred over the Catholic identification of the office bearers (priests) with the office itself; and Christian theology should be founded upon Scripture and not upon philosophy and sophistry.[116]

As Steinmetz's analysis is more or less theological, Oberman tackles the same issue from an interdisciplinary approach to the history of theological thought. Oberman places "Calvin's Reformation of the refugees" in the context of impasses reached by both Luther's Reformation and the city Reformation. On the one hand, Oberman characterizes Luther's Reformation as that "*fides* has priority before *caritas*, the integrity of faith is a higher good than peace and concord." On the other hand, he characterizes the city Reformation of Zurich, Strasbourg, and others as experiencing the impasse caused by the tension between Luther's priority and the city's ideal of civic peace and unity. Although Calvin stood with Luther over Zwingli and the early Bucer on the principle of priority of faith, Oberman concludes, Calvin's Reformation went further than Luther's in applying Luther's principle of priority of faith to "the external practice of charity to be the demarcation line between the true Christians and the hypocrites." Thus, this resulted in directly challenging civic unity as well as in overcoming the impasse reached by the city Reformation.[117] Incidentally, two years later Oberman develops this thesis further in another article, "Via Calvini," in which he mentions the idea of "the incomplete Reformation." This idea concerns Calvin's characteristic teachings on predestination and church discipline. According to Oberman, Calvin understood these teachings as the areas in which both Luther's and Zwingli's reforms made no inroad. In spite of the realization that these teachings could have prevented Calvin's Reformation

115. Steinmetz, "Luther and Calvin," 101–7.

116. Steinmetz, "Luther and Calvin," 107–10.

117. Oberman, "*Europa Afflicta*," 102–7, esp. 104: Oberman, *John Calvin*, 187–91, esp. 189.

from becoming popular, Oberman points to the fact that it had instead become a dynamic reform movement. In connecting this fact with "the Reformation of the refugees," he concludes that Calvin's Reformation envisioned the people of God sojourning in the deserts of the early modern age, led by God's election, practicing discipline, and separated from their homelands as the church of the refugees.[118]

(iii) Our last task concerns the question of Calvin's self-awareness of being "Luther's heir." As far as his extant writings are concerned, there seems to be no evidence of him expressing his being "Luther's heir" either overtly or implicitly. As suggested by Gerrish above, Calvin's historical and objective perception of Luther and his Reformation prevented the "Luther succession" as such. However, it was possible for Calvin to inherit consciously as his own principal notions of Luther's Reformation such as the absolute norm of Scripture, the priority of grace over work, the centricity of Christ in Scripture, and justification by faith. In other words, it could be said that Calvin had found what he needed to succeed in the person of Luther, namely, that Luther had discovered the absolute priority of grace in Augustine against Pelagius and had used the new discovery to break the ecclesiastical fetters of medieval semi-Pelagianism. There is sufficient reason to state that Calvin was Luther's best disciple, as argued by early twentieth-century German church historians Karl Holl and Adolf Harnack.

It is also a fact that Calvin disagreed with Luther on many points of theology. As to the most notable disagreement on Christ's presence in the Lord's Supper, expecting strong reactions from the Lutherans, Calvin dared to agree with the Zwinglians on two crucial issues: that of Christ's bodily presence in heaven, after his resurrection, and that of the noncommunicability of eucharistic grace to the unbelievers. Likewise, he completed the *Consensus Tigurinus* with Bullinger. As we have seen in chapter 1, in light of the ancient church's Christological conflict between the Alexandrian and Antiochene schools, the Luther-Zwingli conflict was unavoidable. Nonetheless, what Calvin, and Bucer before him, had tried to mediate between them was a kind of Chalcedonian solution that did not dissolve the conflict itself but harmonized them in the orthodox periphery of the *Chalcedonian Creed*. In 1539, as Steinmetz affirms, Luther and Calvin shared "the exegetical optimism," a mark of early Protestantism, by which a theology wholly committed to Scripture and excluding all philosophical and speculative arguments, as well as a solution of the

118. Oberman, *John Calvin*, 25, 47.

Luther-Zwingli conflict, were possibilities.[119] Concerning Calvin's "exegetical optimism," Zachman concurs with Steinmetz in his article, "The Conciliating Theology of John Calvin." Focusing on Calvin's notion of teachers who interpreted Scripture and drew "all the essential doctrines of piety" from it, Zachman contends that Calvin regarded the ministry of teachers as the only key, not for total agreement on every biblical teaching, but for the future possibility of doctrinal accord.[120] Furthermore, having this "Luther's heir" issue in mind, one of Oberman's last works, *The Two Reformations*, considers Luther's and Calvin's Reformations as two representative types of the Reformation. Oberman sums up Luther's Reformation in one phrase, the principle of "the triumph of grace," and then characterizes Calvin's Reformation as "the laying bare of the churchly dimension of the triumph of grace."[121] We consider Oberman's insight, that Calvin applied Luther's Reformatory principle to the ecclesiological dimension, as suggestive for our later analysis of Calvin's "Reformation ecclesiology." In a nutshell, Calvin's Reformation was his conscious effort to visibly present the "Luther succession" to the mid-sixteenth-century European world.

Section 2. Reformed Ecclesiology

After the Augsburg Confession of 1530, the Lutheran Church had maintained a basic doctrinal unanimity in spite of a minor confessional revision by Melanchthon (*Confessio Augustana Variata*, 1540). As opposed to this Lutheran tradition in which the dominant theological influence of Luther and Melanchthon's finesse in organizing Luther's thoughts into a theological system played major roles, from the beginning, the tradition generally called "Reformed" had no representative doctrinal expressions. Supposedly, the "Reformed" tradition could claim cohesiveness in pursuing "more thorough reform" than its Lutheran counterpart. Its substantive doctrinal forms were variously represented by the theologies of Zwingli, Bucer, Bullinger, Calvin, and others. Although, among these theologies, there were cohesive emphases in applying doctrine

119. Steinmetz, "Luther and Calvin," 99, 109. Reference to Karl Holl is Steinmetz's.

120. R. C. Zachman, "The Conciliating Theology of John Calvin: Dialogue among Friends," in *Conciliation and Confession: The Struggles for Unity in the Age of Reform, 1415–1648*, ed. H. P. Louthan and R. C. Zachman (Notre Dame: University of Notre Dame Press, 2004), 89–102.

121. H. A. Oberman, *The Two Reformations*, ed. D. Weinstein (New Haven: Yale University Press, 2003), 123.

to practice, the antitransubstantiation stance, and the nuanced distance from the Lutheran position on Christ's presence in the Eucharist, there was no representative Reformed ecclesiology as such. Instead of the more historically accurate expressions of "Reformed" or "Reformed Protestantism," therefore, Zwinglianism, Bucerianism, and Calvinism are often used among researchers. When we use the term, "Reformed ecclesiology," it simply means Calvin's Reformed ecclesiology, which he had formulated in consultation with, as well as in distinction from, other Evangelical Reformers. In the following examination of Calvin's Reformed ecclesiology, we will use two major texts, the third *Institutes* of 1543 and the *First Corinthians Commentary* of 1546. We consider the former to be the most important edition for understanding Calvin's concept of the church's form. The latter, the commentary on the Pauline epistle, which is known for its ecclesial practices, is also important. Our analysis of Calvin's Reformed ecclesiology, based on these two sources, will focus on the church's form and practice.

1. The Third **Institutes***: "The Legitimate Form of the Church"*

Why did Calvin feel the need for and actually publish the third *Institutes* only four years after his major revision in the second edition? What reasons impelled him to start the preparation for a new edition immediately after publishing the second edition in Strasbourg? Although these questions may not bear any meaning for Doumergue, Wendel, and Muller, who do not recognize the third edition's importance, the questions are crucial for our ecclesiological inquiry.[122] To this end, Fraenkel and Zachman call researchers' attention to a significant connection between the religious unification colloquies in Germany (1540–41) and the forthcoming third edition of the *Institutes.* Fraenkel asserts that three chapters newly added to the third edition, namely, religious vows (ch. 4), the creed's article on the church (ch. 8), and human traditions (ch. 13), substantively reflected the three topics of the office of the apostles, that of the bishops, and the papacy, which were hotly debated at the closing period of the Regensburg Colloquy. Zachman contends that Calvin's serious concern at this time was "the continuity of the evangelicals with the older Catholic

122. Cf. Doumergue, *Jean Calvin*, 5:29–37; Wendel, *Calvin*, 83–84; Muller, *The Unaccommodated*, 130–32. Wendel considers the first French edition of 1541 "a masterpiece" but pays little attention to the 1543 *Institutes*. Muller's case is puzzling. Although he notices that newly added "theological locus" to the 1543 *Institutes* is on "Vows" only, the importance of an extensive insertion in the chapter on the church, which we will analyze later, is overlooked.

tradition" and that, due to his dialogues with the Roman Catholics and the influence of Melanchthon and Bucer, Calvin "revised his earlier theological positions." In other words, the new expressions of Calvin's emerging ecclesiology took shape in the period between the religious unification colloquies (1540–41) and the opening of the Council of Trent (1545) and, as suggested by Fraenkel, his emerging ecclesiology was formulated "in the historical process and context" of the Catholic-Protestant dialogues and conflicts.[123]

(1) Ecclesiological Importance of the Third Institutes

As mentioned in chapter 3, the second *Institutes* introduced a few noticeable ideas concerning the basic concept of the church. We highlighted ideas such as the expression "visible church" that appeared for the first time in the *Institutes*, a distinction between the "Catholic" church and the "universal" church, God's work as the "cause" and the church in history as its "effect," and a sincere concern for church unity. In addition, some theological reflections relevant to the concept of the church appeared in the context of Calvin's anti-Anabaptist apologetics, especially in the chapters dealing with the relation of the Old and New Testaments, infant baptism, and the relation between predestination and covenant. Over against the second edition, the third *Institutes* also added several new reflections regarding the creed's fourth article on the church (ch. 8). But the major revision took form at the end of this chapter as an extensive and significant addition. Before examining its major contents, however, it seems useful to make some preliminary remarks about the addition and the sections immediately preceding it under the following three points.

(i) The first point concerns the scale of the addition as well as the framework in which it is made. Noticing the definitive importance of the 1543 *Institutes* for Calvin's ecclesiology, Doumergue asserts: "After 1543 it is finished; 1559 adds nothing." His remark that "a booklet of 1536 written by a young theologian" has evolved into a full work containing "everything useful and necessary to a Reformer of the Genevan Church and of the world" is not an overstatement. In the edition of the *Opera Calvini*, the addition occupies 111

123. P. Fraenkel, "Trois passages de l'*Institution* de 1543 et leurs rapports avec les colloques interconfessionnels de 1540–41," in *Calvinus Ecclesiae Genevensis Custos*, ed. H. Neuser, 149–54; R. C. Zachman, "Revisiting the Reform: What Calvin Learned from Dialogue with the Roman Catholics," in *John Calvin and Roman Catholicism*, ed. R. C. Zachman (Grand Rapids: Baker Academic, 2008), 165–91. Zachman illustrates Calvin's changing position by examining four main topics in the 1543 *Institutes*: baptism, the Lord's Supper, the laying on of hands, and the order of church government.

columns or 171 sections (sec. 34–205). Since it is almost completely carried over into the final edition, in a more easily understood expression, it occupies ten chapters (ch. 3–12), just about one half of book 4 of the 1559 *Institutes*. As to its topical contents, the addition covers the ministerial order, the government in the ancient church and its corruption under the papacy, the papacy and its history, the power to make the articles of faith and its abuse, ecclesiastical councils, the right to make ecclesiastical laws and its abuse (this portion was not from ch. 8 but ch. 13 of the third edition), ecclesiastical jurisdiction, and church discipline. In short, the addition represents what is generally described as church government or polity. In the final *Institutes* it occupies the middle section, sandwiched between the first portion on the basic conception of the church (ch. 1–2) and the last portion on vows, the sacraments, and civil government (ch. 13–20). As to its apologetic nature, the main thrust of all its arguments is the sharp contrast between church government based upon scriptural norm and that of the papal church.[124] This leads to a question about Calvin's intention to make such an extensive revision.

In order to place the extensive addition in its historical context, the key to unlocking the question might be found in the section just preceding the addition where Calvin added a new sentence to the text of the second *Institutes*. Although the second edition, judging from the strict norm of the church's two marks, the word and the sacraments, already denied the "title" of Christ's church to the papal church, it admitted that there remained "some notes of the church" (*aliquot ecclesiae symbola*) or a certain "form" (*forma*). Then, the first French edition of the *Institutes* (1541), based upon the second Latin edition, went a step further and examined the legitimacy of this remaining "form" and concluded that there existed no "legitimate form of the church" (*forme legitime d'Eglise*) under the papacy. Following the lead of the first French edition, then, the third Latin *Institutes* rewrote the text of the second edition, changing "the true form of the church" (*germana ecclesiae forma*) into "the legitimate form of the church" (*legitima ecclesiae forma*), and concluded:

> To sum up, I call them churches to the extent that the Lord wonderfully preserves in them a remnant of his people, however woefully dispersed

124. *CO* 1:561–672. (*Institutio* 4.3.1–4.12.22: *OS* 5:42–237.) Cf. Doumergue, *Jean Calvin*, 5:40; Höpfl, *Christian Polity*, 103–27. Although Höpfl rightly observes the extensive addition on ecclesiology in the 1543 *Institutes* and emphasizes its importance in Calvin's theology by allocating one entire chapter to it, characteristically he notes its "two cognate features" as "aggressive clericalism" and "the centrality of discipline," which we consider his misconstruing of Calvin's addition. For "the centrality of discipline," confer n. 144 below.

> and scattered, and to the extent that some marks of the church remain—especially those marks whose effectiveness neither the devil's wiles nor human depravity can destroy. But on the other hand, because in them those marks have been erased into which (we inquire) in this discourse, (while we search for a church properly ordered,) I say that every one of their congregations and their whole body lack the legitimate form of the church.

Here for the first time, Calvin affirmed that the churches under papal rule were lacking not only the "title" but also the legitimate "form" of Christ's church.[125] The reason for this rewriting, though not easy to ascertain, could be that Calvin emphasized the church's "form" to be lawfully following the norm of Scripture, and that the term "germana" could not properly carry this nuance. From this observation, the framework of the addition was what Calvin considered the church's legitimate form, which he held was lacking in the papal churches but was restored from Scripture in the Evangelical churches. In addition, Calvin's Reformation was most distinctively known by his insistence on the church's "legitimate form," what this study considers the substance of his "Reformed ecclesiology."

(ii) The second point also concerns the sections preceding the addition where the third edition made a few noticeable revisions on the basic concept of the church. There are three general characteristics of those revisions that bear considerable impact upon the arguments of the extensive addition itself. The first characteristic is an emphasis on the "visible church," an aspect of Calvin's ecclesiological orientation that we consider to have shifted in his Strasbourg period. As we will examine later, his "Reformed ecclesiology" is a clear manifestation of this shift.[126] The second characteristic is the appearance of a theoretical demarcation in his apologetics between the discussion leading to the question of truth and falsehood concerning the church that led to the question of the church's form. The former concerns the church's "title" by examining the marks of the word and the sacraments, and the latter concerns the church's "form," whether the form's legitimacy is strictly corresponding to the word and the sacrament.

The third characteristic concerns Calvin's shift in his anti-Catholic and Nicodemite apologetics, especially against the Catholic charge that the Evan-

125. *CO* 1:561; *Institution* (1541) 2:145–46. Cf. *Institutio* 4.2.12: *OS* 5:42. The block quote is based upon the 1543 text. However, we use Battles's translation of the same text in *Institutes*, ed. McNeill (4.2.12), with two exceptions: one, we provide our own translation of the portions in parentheses, which are only found in the 1543 text; the other, we use the term "legitimate" instead of Battles's "lawful" (form of the church).

126. Cf. *CO* 1:542. (*Institutio* 4.1.7: *OS* 5:12.)

gelical churches were both heretical and schismatic. First, Calvin introduced Augustine's distinction between heresy and schism, namely, the former concerning the church's "doctrine" and the latter concerning the "bond" of the believers in the church. Then, he emphasized that the church's unity presupposed doctrinal concord and placed the issue of schism in the context of the prior condition of the church's doctrinal unity. Citing Christ as the church's "head" and "the celestial teacher," he affirmed Christ to be the sole norm for both issues of church unity and schism and concluded that the exit of the Evangelicals from papist churches for the sake of drawing themselves closer to Christ should not be regarded as schismatic.[127]

In a clear recognition of the Nicodemites' challenge, secondly, Calvin posed two questions in the newly added sentences, namely, whether the Evangelicals could participate in "prayers, sacraments, and ceremonies" of papist churches and could respect the "honor, power, and jurisdiction" of papist churches. To these questions, Calvin not only compared papist churches with the Jewish congregations under King Jeroboam but claimed their condition was worse than that of the Jewish congregations. His reason for this accusation was that, while the congregations of Jeroboam's time still upheld circumcision, sacrifices at the temple, and the law of Moses, the tyranny of papist churches in practicing the Mass was "the utmost sacrilege." Furthermore, he defended the Evangelicals by affirming that the "Prophets," who denounced the Jewish congregations that should be God's church, "were strangers to the church of God."[128]

From these affirmations, thirdly, Calvin came to a conclusion on the Catholic charge of schism by partly revising the second edition text. While the second edition denied papist churches as "simply" not being Christ's churches, the third edition made a concluding remark in this fashion: "when we categorically deny to the papists the title of the church, we do not . . . impugn the existence [form] of churches among them." Then, he added a supplementary statement, "Rather, we are only contending about the true and lawful constitution of the church, required in the communion not only of the sacraments but also especially of doctrine."[129] Here Calvin's apologetics supposed the demarcation between, on the one hand, the "title" of Christ's church strictly judged by the existence of the church's marks of doctrine and the sacraments and the "form" or "constitution" of the church that needed to be conformed to these two marks, and the practice of the purer ancient church on the other hand. In

127. *CO* 1:556–57. (*Institutio* 4.2.5–6: *OS* 5:36–37.)
128. *CO* 1:558–59. (*Institutio* 4.2.9: *OS* 5:38–40.)
129. *CO* 1:560. (*Institutio* 4.2.12: *OS* 5:41.)

practical terms, his apologetics to counter the charge of schism had two foci: to establish the form of the church according to the standard of Scripture and the ancient church, and to formulate anew the Evangelical form of the church that could challenge the legitimacy of the Roman Catholic form. The first focus pointed to the direction that Bucer's historical inquiry in *Theological Advice* had already taken. The second focus was the result of Calvin's urgent recognition that the Evangelical church's "form" or "constitution" had not been sufficiently articulated. This was the historical context in which Calvin was urged to revise the second *Institutes*, to formulate the "legitimate form of the church," in order to meet the challenge of Catholicism after the failure of the unification colloquies in 1541 and to counter the increasing challenge of Nicodemism. In a sense, his new apologetics was a "Reformed" response to Bucer's compromising stance, which he had intimately known in Strasbourg and was clandestinely made clear in the *Theological Advice*.[130]

(iii) The third point is the general character of the extensive addition itself. Under the general topic of church government, the addition consists of two parts, the order of ministers and the power of the church, corresponding to book 4 of the final *Institutes*, chapters 3–7 and 8–12.[131] Calvin's comprehension of church government in terms of order and power seemed to indicate a thought pattern that highlighted his training in jurisprudence. As to the first part of the "order," he begins with the biblical order of ministers, then goes on to its abuse in the papal order of ministers. As to the second part of the "power," likewise, he treats first the biblical basis for the church's power in three parts (power to set the articles of faith, to make ecclesiastical laws, and to discipline the faithful) and then goes on to the abuse of each part under the papacy. Throughout the entire argument on church government, the emerging theme is that of the church as Christ's government, the theme that Calvin energetically discussed in the second topic (ecclesiastical power) of chapter 6 of the first *Institutes*. In the extensive addition in the third *Institutes*, however, he pursues the same theme in terms of the church's "legitimate form," which

130. *CO* 1:560. Cf. Zachman, "Revisiting the Reform," 168–91; n. 123 above. Noticing the importance of the 1543 *Institutes* as a "turning point," Zachman focuses on Calvin's appreciation of "the older Catholic tradition" vis-à-vis the Roman Catholic practices of his time.

131. A key to Calvin's classification can be found in the beginning of the discussions on the church's "power" (*CO* 1:628, #137: *Institutio* 4.8.1: *OS* 5:133), which he calls the third "section" (locus). Accordingly, we assume, the first two "sections" (loci) concern "the church's fundamental notions" (the first locus) and "the church's order and government" (the second locus).

is a core of his "Reformed ecclesiology." In order to highlight this aspect, we will selectively focus on two topics only, namely, the order of ministers and the system of church discipline.

(2) Order of Ministers

Calvin presented the order of ministers, especially the ministers of the word, as the first topic of the "legitimate form" of the visible church. As mentioned above, the grounds for this argument was his notion that Christ's governing of the church, the manifestation of his kingdom, was indirect and through his word: "because he [Christ] does not dwell among us in visible presence, . . . he uses the ministry of men to declare openly his will to us by mouth, as a sort of delegated work."[132] Furthermore, he asserted that between the ministers of the word and the faithful there should be "the strongest means of keeping unity" and cited one of his key passages for the ministerial order, Ephesians 4 (11–16).[133] The whole discussion led by this small section was almost entirely carried into the final *Institutes* and was to be known as his distinctive notion of church ministry. Topics such as the fourfold order of ministers, the extraordinary and ordinary ministers, the analogy between the apostles and pastors, the office of elders, that of deacons, the ministerial elections and ordinations, and so forth, were treated here. Instead of surveying each topic, we will selectively focus on three points that are thought to be characteristics of his "Reformed ecclesiology."

(i) The first point concerned the basic nature of Christ's governing of the church that Calvin characterized as "logocracy," the rule of God's word through "delegated work" of the ministers. As we examined in chapter 1, this notion was further amplified here and was highlighted by his two-marks theory and pneumatology. Since his first *Institutes* adopted the Augustinian notion of the sacraments as "the visible word" of God, as to the two-marks theory, the third *Institutes* and later editions increasingly identified the two marks simply as "the word" or "doctrine."[134] As to the relation of Christ's logocratic rule over the church with the work of the Holy Spirit, it was well known that Calvin defined the Holy Spirit as Christ's Spirit and elsewhere emphasized the Spirit's work whenever Christ's word was preached and heard. In the section on ministerial order in the third *Institutes*, however, the ministry of the Spirit was

132. *CO* 1:561. (*Institutio* 4.3.1: *OS* 5:42–43.)
133. *CO* 1:561–62. (*Institutio* 4.3.1: *OS* 5:43–44.)
134. *OS* 1:119. Cf. *Institutio* 4.14.6: *OS* 5:263.

less emphasized than that of the word, perhaps due to the section's focus on the "form" of the church.[135]

(ii) The second point concerned the fourfold order of pastors, teachers, elders, and deacons, the order that Calvin considered as founded by Christ for the New Testament church. These four offices represented the permanent and ordinary ministries, in distinction from the temporal and extraordinary ministries of the apostles, the prophets, and the evangelists. Interpreting two series of the texts—Ephesians (4:11) and Romans (12:7–8), and 1 Corinthians (12:28)—Calvin drew the offices of pastors and elders from the first and those of elders and deacons from the second series.[136] It has been assumed that Calvin inherited the notion of the fourfold order from Bucer. In Bucer's *Concerning True Pastoral Care*, however, the ministerial offices were not delineated as clearly and often with variant terms. In addition, despite his elaborate arguments on the fourfold ministry, Bucer's founding of the four offices on Scripture was not as clear as Calvin's later reduction of them from the two series of biblical texts. It could be said that, in line with Bucer's notion of the ministerial order, Calvin had developed his own notion with precision.[137] In this connection, he interpreted "those who lead" (*gubernatores*, 1 Cor 12:28) as "elders chosen from the people." This notion of so-called "lay elders," which he claimed to be his own interpretation, has been noted by researchers as his distinctive view. This notion could also be understood from what he had practiced in his French congregation in Strasbourg, or from what he had presented in the 1541 *Genevan Ecclesiastical Ordinance*, according to which the consistorial members chosen from the city councils were assumed to be the lay elders of the church.[138]

135. Cf. Wendel, *Calvin*, 302; W. Niesel, *The Theology of Calvin*, trans. H. Knight (Philadelphia: Westminster, 1956), 200.

136. *CO* 1:563–64, 567. (*Institutio* 4.3.4; 4.3.8: *OS* 5:45, 50.)

137. Cf. chapter 3, section 1.2 above, esp. nn. 42, 43. For Bucer's notion of the ministerial order in the *Concerning True Pastoral Care*, see W. van't Spijker (*The Ecclesiastical Offices*, 171–76). It is a knotty issue to compare the notion of ministerial order in Bucer's work and Calvin's 1543 *Institutes*. If we assume that both share the notion of the fourfold office of the ministers, Bucer seems to reduce it from the perspective of the "joint pastorate of the ministers and congregation," and Calvin places it in the context of the church's "order and government."

138. *CO* 1:567. (*Institutio* 4.3.8: *OS* 1:50.) Battles (*Institutes* 4.3.8, ed. McNeill) translates "*gubernatores*" as "governors" instead of "leaders." Cf. McKee, *Elders*, 25–39; E. A. McKee, "Exegesis, Theology, and Development in Calvin's *Institutio*: A Methodological Suggestion," in *Probing the Reformed Tradition*, ed. E. A. McKee and B. G. Armstrong (Louisville: Westminster John Knox, 1989), 160–61. McKee examines Calvin's notion of eldership from the

(iii) The third point concerned the issue of the presbyterial office or order (*presbyterium*), which combined ordained ministers of the word and elders elected from the people into one order for the joint governance of the church. This issue was partly caused by Calvin's insistence that the New Testament terms of "pastors," "bishops," and "elders/presbyters" designated one and the same office and that another term, "leaders/governors," designated another office of the lay elders. It was also caused by the need to provide the theoretical foundation for the consistorial system instituted in the 1541 *Genevan Ecclesiastical Ordinance*. As to its background, Bucer's original draft proposal of Strasbourg's 1534 ecclesiastical ordinances considered the city's "churchwardens" as the church's "elders." His *Concerning True Pastoral Care* held the ministry of pastors, bishops, and teachers as one office of the "pastoral care of the elders."[139] In this historical background, the extensive addition in the third *Institutes* presented the principle of joint church government and discipline by the ministers of the word and the representatives of the people. It illustrated the principle by referencing the ancient church's practice, namely, that "from the order of presbyters (*ordo presbyterorum*) part were chosen pastors and teachers, the remaining part were charged with censure and correction of morals."[140] A later discussion on the church's jurisdictional power also described this principle by which the elders in charge of discipline "were joined with the pastors in the spiritual rule of the church" or, in citing the "double honor" text of First Timothy (5:17), "those who labor in the word and those who do not carry on the preaching of the word yet rule well."[141] In the section on church discipline, furthermore, the twofold presbyterial order of those who were "ordained to teach" and "to be censors of morals" was described as "the assembly of the elders" and "the senate of the presbyters."[142] From the above, as observed by Doumergue, Calvin had completed his notion of the twofold presbyterial order in the third *Institutes* and elaborated it further in his *First Corinthians Commentary* (12:28, 1546) and *First Timothy Commentary* (5:17, 1548).[143]

---

history of his biblical hermeneutics. Concerning the origin of the so-called "lay elder," in addition to the *Ecclesiastical Ordinance* of 1541, McKee notices the importance of the 1540 *Romans Commentary*, in which Calvin is said to have explored the possible interpretation of lay elders due to the absence of Christian magistrates in the Pauline churches.

139. Cf. *Von der waren Seelsorge*, *BDS* 7:116, 119–21, 141, 188; chapter 3, section 1.2.

140. *CO* 1:572. (*Institutio* 4.4.1: *OS* 5:58.)

141. *CO* 1:648. (*Institutio* 4.11.1: *OS* 5:195.)

142. *CO* 1:650. (*Institutio* 4.11.6: *OS* 5:201–2.)

143. Cf. *CO* 49:507; *CO* 52:315; Doumergue, *Jean Calvin*, 5:154.

(3) The System of Church Discipline

The new addition in chapter 8 of the third *Institutes* treated church discipline as the third and last topic of the church's jurisdictional power. The treatment of jurisdiction was divided into two parts, its theory (sections 169–83; roughly corresponding to *Institutio* 4.11) and practice (sections 184–205; *Institutio* 4.12). Since the main theme of the entire addition was the church's "legitimate form," our question is how Calvin comprehended the legitimacy of church discipline.

(i) The first aspect of this question concerned the way in which Calvin conceived the relation between his two-marks theory and church discipline. As noted above, his apologetic demarcation between the church's "title" and "form" implied the distinction of the church's two marks, the word and the sacraments, as the matters concerning the "title" and discipline as the matters concerning only the "form." As a result, their relation needed to be theoretically delineated. The second *Institutes* defined the "visible church" strictly by the two-marks theory and described church discipline as just the "fruit" of the two marks. Perhaps, this unique view was Calvin's reaction to and checking of Bucer's three-marks theory in which church discipline had been considered a constitutional element of the church. Following this line of thought, the third *Institutes* introduced a new argument that appeared in connection with the ministerial order. In addition to the ministry of the word and the sacraments, pastors had the duty of personal chastisement and correction in which they were to work together with lay elders according to the "order of presbyters." In this way, Calvin distinguished the pastors' primary ministry of the word and the sacraments and the secondary ministry of discipline. As far as the arrangement of topics in the extensive addition was concerned, the ministry of pastors and teachers that appeared at the beginning of the discussion was theoretically separated from the topic of discipline that appeared at the very end of the addition. This development implied that his understanding of the relation between the two marks and discipline had evolved from the first Genevan reform, which made church discipline a primary focus of the reform in the *Articles*, to the present position in the third *Institutes*. It could also imply a shift in his apologetic stance due not only to the Anabaptists, who made discipline an essential mark of the church, but also to Bucer's three-marks theory.[144]

144. *CO* 1:565, 566–67, 572, 648. (*Institutio* 4.3.6; 4.3.8; 4.4.1; 4.11.2: *OS* 5:48, 50, 58, 198.) As noted in n. 124 above, Höpfl (*Christian Polity*, 103–27) considers "the centrality of discipline"

Concerning Calvin's understanding of the relation between the two marks and discipline, the views of researchers have varied widely. For example, Wendel understands the relation as the issue of the church's definition and its organization and notes Calvin's equal emphasis on the two marks and discipline. With a different emphasis, Milner defined discipline simply as "an appendage of doctrine" and makes light of the significance of discipline in Calvin's ecclesiology.[145] Following the example of the 1541 *Genevan Ecclesiastical Ordinance*, which presented Calvin's reform as characteristically disciplinary, however, it should be emphasized that his understanding of this relation was basically dialectical. The two marks and discipline were to be clearly distinguished but never separated; rather they were to be integrated in order to make the church the living body of Christ or its "legitimate form." Only in this dialectical relation could his remark in the third *Institutes* be understood: "as the saving doctrine of Christ is the soul (*anima*) of the church, so does discipline serve as its sinews (*nervi*) through which the members of the body hold together, each in its own place."[146] In the same manner, his *Synoptic Gospels Commentary* (Matt 18:18) regarded discipline as "an appendage of doctrine," and his *First Corinthians*

as one of the two "cognate features" in the extensive addition of the 1543 *Institutes*. In the section "the visible church," he is puzzled by the fact that Calvin, who learned about the visible church from Strasbourg's Bucer, did not make church discipline the third mark of the church as Bucer did. Under another section, "the purposes of the discipline" (115–27), Höpfl extensively covers various points made in Calvin's discussion. Despite this extensive coverage, however, he does not seem to provide any clue as to why and how Calvin made discipline central in his entire church polity as Höpfl claims. We consider that Calvin tried to show "the legitimate form" of the practice of discipline that was warranted by scriptural testimonies. We also see no attempt by Höpfl to examine Calvin's hermeneutic context. Instead of "centrality," we rather assume that Calvin tried to "marginalize" discipline in church polity. By distinguishing the church's "title" and "form," (thus, categorically separating the church's two marks of the word and the sacraments from discipline as a matter of its "form"), and by placing discipline at the very end of his discussion, we assume that Calvin was reacting to Bucer's three-marks theory and its implications and was allocating discipline a proper place in what we consider his "Reformed ecclesiology."

145. Cf. Wendel, *Calvin*, 298–300, esp, 299; Milner, *Calvin's Doctrine*, 175–79, esp. 175. Wendel, who takes the "Bucer's influence" theory, places Calvin's notion of church discipline in "a continuation of the ways opened up by Oecolampadius and Bucer, but nowhere does he mention that Bucer in his later years officially took discipline as the third mark of the church. Despite his emphasis on Calvin's "two marks" (99–133), Milner's treatment on discipline is rather cursory. His quotation (*appendix doctrinae*) is taken from Calvin's *Synoptic Gospels Commentary* (*CO* 45:515 on Matt 18:18).

146. *CO* 1:658. (*Institutio* 4.12.1: *OS* 5:212.)

Commentary, which considered the ministry of the word as "the mysteries of God," even called the sacraments "appendages" of these mysteries.[147]

(ii) The second aspect of the question regarding the legitimacy of church discipline concerned Calvin's apologetic stance on Zwingli's view. In the third *Institutes*, at the beginning of the treatment on the church's jurisdictional power, he distinguished the two "power of the keys" passages of Matthew 16 and 18 and then, attributing the former to the ministry of the word and the latter to the ministry of censure and discipline, he treated Zwingli's view as one of the issues within the Reformed camp.[148] Basically he joined the criticism of Oecolampadius and Bucer on Zwingli's view that attributed a major role in church discipline to the magistracy. A focus of their criticism was a hermeneutical question regarding Matthew 18:17. They held that Zwingli's view might infer "tell it to the magistracy" rather than "tell it to the church." The first point of Calvin's criticism was directed at Zwingli's notion that the "power of the keys" in Matthew 18 gave power to the church when there were no Christian magistrates extant and, in the Christian era, this "power" properly belonged to the Christian magistrates. Distinguishing the magisterial power from the church's jurisdiction, which exercised no force in coercion but aimed for spiritual correction, Calvin interpreted the Matthew 18 text as "a set and permanent order of the church (instituted by Christ), not a temporary one." Then he affirmed that this order was "the ancient custom always observed in the ancient [Old Testament] church of his people."

In this context, particularly noticeable was Calvin's seeming awareness of Zwingli's successor, Bullinger's historical analysis of the Old and New Testaments from the concept of God's "covenant," in which the historical distinctiveness rather than the integrity of the two covenants was stressed. Calvin boldly asserted that in the Matthew text "Christ here instituted nothing new but followed the custom always observed in the ancient church of his people" and that Christ's intention was for the use of the people of the new covenant.[149] Here, he identified Christ's institution with "the senate of presbyters" and "the assembly of elders" of the ancient church. Furthermore, he characterized this disciplinary power as being "only by the word of the Lord" and requiring no physical force but being "content with the power of God's word." In this intermural challenge, his search for legitimate discipline was clearly presented.[150]

147. *CO* 49:362. Cf. *CO* 45:515.
148. *CO* 1:648–51. (*Institutio* 4.11.3–6: *OS* 5:199–201.)
149. *CO* 1:649. (*Institutio* 4.11.4: *OS* 5:199–200.)
150. *CO* 1:649–51. (*Institutio* 4.11.4–6: *OS* 5:199–202.)

2. *The* First Corinthians Commentary: *The Practice of Reformed Ecclesiology*

First Corinthians was the text that Calvin chose for his lectures in the Strasbourg Academy. As a sequence of his first and renowned commentary on Romans, the publication of the *First Corinthians Commentary* was considerably delayed. While Farel urged its quick appearance, Calvin excused its delay due to his active involvement in the Genevan reform. According to Parker, Calvin completed the writing in November 1545 and published it at the beginning of the next year in Strasbourg.[151] From this brief history, it could be said that the commentary held his Strasbourg lectures as its basic stratum, and, consequently, urgent issues at that time such as church unification, schism, the Eucharist, and church discipline in the Protestant Reformation were reflected in the commentary. Since 1 Corinthians was the most practically oriented text of the Pauline epistles, the commentary's direct background was none other than Calvin's second Genevan reform in which he inaugurated an ambitious yet practical plan of reform by means of the 1541 *Ecclesiastical Ordinance*.

Chapter 3 has noted Calvin's methodological demarcation of two serial works, the *Institutes* as theological text book and commentaries as the practical implications of the biblical texts, and illustrated this claim using the second *Institutes* and the *Romans Commentary*. The third *Institutes* and the *First Corinthians Commentary* followed this methodological pattern. As to the notion of the church, for example, the former presented an overview of the church's "legitimate form" and the latter focused on the practical applications of the "legitimate form" in the church.[152] As the apostle contextualized Christ's gospel in the first-century city of Corinth, in a sense Calvin contextualized "the legitimate form of the church" in the Reformation age of the sixteenth century. As the third *Institutes* placed "the legitimate form" in clear opposition to papal church structure and presented his own understanding of it as distinctive from the forms of Luther, Zwingli, and even Bucer, so the *First Corinthians Commentary* presented its practical applications with his own distinctive emphases. An example to illustrate this point could be found in his comments on

151. *Commentarii in priorem epistolam Pauli ad Corinthios*: *BC* 46/2. Cf. Parker, *John Calvin*, 106; T. H. L. Parker, *Calvin's New Testament Commentaries* (Louisville: Westminster John Knox, 1993), 19. For the Latin text, we use the *Opera Calvini* (*CO* 49:293–574) and for the text in English, we use *Calvin's [New Testament] Commentaries*, vol. 9, trans. J. W. Fraser (Grand Rapids: Eerdmans, 1960), cited as *C. C. 1 Corinthians*.

152. Cf. R. W. Holder, "Calvin as Commentator on the Pauline Epistles," in *Calvin and the Bible*, ed. D. K. McKim (Cambridge: Cambridge University Press, 2006), 232–37.

the Eucharist text (11:23–26). As expected, they focused on the crucial issue of the age, Christ's presence in the Lord's Supper, and typologically presented the Roman Catholic, Lutheran, and Reformed views on it. Interestingly, however, Calvin represented the Reformed view as his own without any thoughtful consideration of the Zwinglian emphases.[153] In short, it could be said that Calvin had completed his Reformed ecclesiology in the period between his third *Institutes* and *First Corinthians Commentary*.[154]

The *First Corinthians Commentary* took issue with the Anabaptists (15:18), the spiritualistic "Libertines" (15:1), and the Nicodemites (8:13), but its apologetic aim was decisively directed toward the doctrines, liturgies, and customs of the papal church. In his criticism of the Catholic Mass, for example, Calvin delivered his verdict on the current abuses in the Catholic Church in this fashion: "the only remedy for removing and correcting corruptions is to get back to the unadulterated institution of God." In calling this "unadulterated institution" "an inviolable law" and identifying it with the Lord's Supper, he asserted that the prospect of reform for both the Catholic and Protestant sides lay in the restoration of the Lord's Supper as "the common standard."[155] The dominical institution of the Supper was an exceptionally clear case, and his appeal for restoring the "legitimate form" was easily understood. In general, however, it could be noted that his overall apologetic thrust can be seen clearly in the parallelism between his understanding of the church of Corinth in the midst of religious syncretism of the first century and that of Catholicism, which he once described as "to shape one religion out of Christianity, Judaism, and paganism." As the apostle Paul had shown the "legitimate form" of the Christian church to the Corinthian church, which was suffering from internal problems of immorality, heresy, and schism, Calvin challenged Christian Europe to restore the same "legitimate form" as "the common norm." With this perspective in mind, in the following pages, we will focus on three themes in the commentary, namely, "the legitimate form of the church," the church's internal characteristics, and the church in history.

(1) "The Legitimate Form of the Church"

In order to assess Calvin's ecclesiological perspective in the commentary, it is essential to know his understanding of the Corinthian church's general con-

153. Cf. *CO* 49:483–91 (11:23–26).
154. McKee, "Exegesis, Theology, and Development," 162.
155. *CO* 49:484 (11:23); *C. C. 1 Corinthians*, 242.

dition. This can be illustrated from his comments on Paul's two testimonies, regarding "the church of God that is in Corinth" (1:2) and Paul's commendation of the church (11:2). As to the first testimony, Calvin asked a rhetorical question: how could the apostle call the Corinthian church "the church of God," when it was rumored that Satan, rather than God, ruled it and there were "various corruptions both of teaching and manners?" His concluding remark was that the apostle's reasoning acknowledged the existence of "the doctrine of the gospel, baptism, and the Lord's Supper" or "the fundamental teaching" in the Corinthian church. In other words, according to the apologetic stance of the third *Institutes*, Calvin understood that the Corinthian church retained the "title" of Christ's church. In this connection, it should be noted that he rejected "a dangerous temptation to think that there is no church where perfect purity is lacking."[156] As to the second testimony, even though perplexed by the apostle's praise of the Corinthian church, Calvin made a concluding remark that "as far as the public form of the church is concerned, the institutions of Christ and the apostles are kept in being."[157]

From the comments above, it could be said that, acknowledging the "title" to the Corinthian church, Calvin understood the apostle's focus to be on the "maintained" form of the church. Here, his comment on the text, "if anyone builds on the foundation [Christ] with gold, silver, precious stones, wood, hay, straw" (3:12), was illuminating. In the context of the "title" and "form" distinction, he said that "by gold, then silver and precious stones," Paul meant "teaching that is not only in keeping with Christ, but is also a *superstructure* in harmony with such a *foundation*."[158] Furthermore, his comments affirmed that, in the history of the Western Church, Cyprian, Ambrose, and Augustine had built the structure upon the foundation of the "pure word of God," and that the medieval churchmen, Gregory the First and Bernard of Clairvaux, had tried the same but oftentimes deviated "from the right building method."[159]

156. *CO* 49:307 (1:2); *C. C. 1 Corinthians*, 17–18. Cf. Eva-Maria Faber, "Mutual Connectedness as a Gift and a Task: On John Calvin's Understanding of the Church," in *John Calvin's Impact on Church and Society, 1509–2009*, ed. M. E. Hirzel and M. Sallmann (Grand Rapids: Eerdmans, 2009), 130–31. According to Faber, Calvin's *First Corinthians Commentary* indicates his rejection of "the search for the perfect church." We interpret the text, however, as indicating Calvin's fundamental apologetic posture against both the Roman Catholics and the Anabaptists. Against the former, he took issue with the church's "title" based upon the church's two marks, and against the latter, the issue of the church's perfect purity.

157. *CO* 49:473 (11:2); *C. C. 1 Corinthians*, 228.

158. *CO* 49:355 (3:12); *C. C. 1 Corinthians*, 75. (Italics added.)

159. *CO* 49:357 (3:15); *C. C. 1 Corinthians*, 77–78.

In short, an overall focus of the commentary was on what the third *Institutes* termed "the legitimate form" of the church. In the following pages, we note three aspects of this overall focus.

(i) The first aspect concerned the starting point of Calvin's focus on the "legitimate form," in which "only Christ ought to rule in the church."[160] On the passage that exposed the schismatic activities in the Corinthian church, "I belong to Paul, Apollos, Cephas, and Christ" (1:12), for example, Calvin commented that "the unity of the church rests mainly on this one thing: that we depend on Christ alone, and that men therefore take, and remain in, lesser place."[161] On the passage, "the kingdom of God depends not on talk, but on power" (4:20), he assumed that Christ's rule over the church through his gospel was often called the kingdom of God. Then he interpreted the "power" in the text as the church's "soul" or "majesty" of preaching the gospel and "talk" as human wisdom or eloquence. Without this "majesty," he concluded, "preaching is dead, and has no force at all."[162]

(ii) The second aspect concerned Calvin's insistence on "the legitimate form" being worthy of the two marks by which the church was to be recognized as Christ's church. Concerning this correlation, generally speaking, the commentary followed what the third *Institutes* had theoretically already covered, yet it provided some interesting practical applications. As to the two marks, for instance, there was a noticeable logocratic tendency to comprehend the two marks as "the word of God" or "doctrine." As noted above, "the doctrine of the gospel, baptism, and the Lord's Supper" was rephrased as "the fundamental teaching."[163] On the text (4:1) where ministers like Paul were regarded as "stewards of God's mysteries," Calvin interpreted "mysteries" as the gospel and ministers as its stewards. Interestingly he commented that "the sacraments

160. *CO* 49:316 (1:13); *C. C. 1 Corinthians*, 28.

161. *CO* 49:316 (1:12); *C. C. 1 Corinthians*, 28.

162. *CO* 49:375 (4:20); 49:376 (4:20); *C. C. 1 Corinthians*, 107. Tuininga's *Calvin's Political Theology* (see chapter 1, nn. 169, 174) appropriately cites Calvin's comment on 1 Cor 4:20 (184n10) in discussing "Christ's spiritual government." The citation is one of a few texts that Tuininga uses for describing Calvin's notion of Christ's kingdom and in which the word of God or Christ's gospel is emphatically identified with the power of Christ's kingdom. In view of Tuininga's fair use of the Calvin texts, we wonder why his basic understanding of Calvin's notion of Christ's kingdom emphasizes only one side of it, such as its immanent and eschatological nature, at the expense of its other and primary side. When he says that "the power of the kingdom is that of the Holy Spirit" and "the kingdom completes creation's eschatological purpose" (119–20), we wonder why the kingdom's power of the word and its prophetic character are not sufficiently emphasized.

163. *CO* 49:307 (1:2); *C. C. 1 Corinthians*, 18.

are connected with these mysteries as appendages."[164] He also commented on the text where the sacraments of both the Old and New Testaments were compared (10:1–6) in the same manner as in the third *Institutes*. He interpreted the "crossing" of the Red Sea and the "cloud" protecting the people in Sinai as prefiguring baptism and the "manna" as prefiguring the Lord's Supper.[165] However, the practical applications of his eucharistic theory predominated in the commentary, especially in his anti-Catholic apologetics. On the unique eucharistic text (11:23–26), for example, Calvin's comments refuted the Catholic claim of the dominical institution of the Mass. Interestingly, the typological presentation of Catholic, Lutheran, and Reformed views on Christ's presence in the Supper appeared in this section. Here, he represented the Reformed view by his own interpretation of Christ's presence as "metonymy." Just as John's Gospel (1:32) told of the Spirit appearing in the form of a dove, Christ used metonymy in "a sacramental way of speaking, when the Lord applied to the sign [bread] the name of the reality signified [his body]."[166] Another interesting comment appeared on the crucial text of "This is my body" (11:24). At the beginning of the comment, he lamented that the meaning of these words had caused "the unhappy battles which have been disturbing the church in our time," but he said not to recount them. Then he expressed his undisguised wish to God that "I only wish it were possible to bury all remembrance of them [battles] in everlasting oblivion." This expression reminds us of another expression of his in the first *Institutes*, which we have noted in connection with the Caroli affair in chapter 2. Over the unbiblical terms of "one *ousia*, three *hypostaseis*" on the Trinity and of "*homoousios*" on Christology used in the Nicene orthodoxy, he expressed his feeling, "Would that they had been buried."[167] Concerning the doctrine and practice of the Lord's Supper that the apostle presented to the Corinthian church in the first century, Calvin could not believe that Evangelical Christianity, which was supposed to have restored the "legitimate form of the church," could have "conflicts" over the form of Christ's presence in the Supper.

(iii) The third aspect concerned the topic of the ministerial offices and duties, which corresponded to the topic of the order of ministers in the third *Institutes*. As noted above, the *Institutes* generally shared with the *First Corinthi-*

164. *CO* 49:362 (4:1); *C. C. 1 Corinthians*, 85.

165. *CO* 49:451–56 (10:1–4); *C. C. 1 Corinthians*, 200–205. Cf. *CO* 1:804–6. (*Institutio* 2.10.5–6: *OS* 3:406–8.)

166. *CO* 49:486 (11:23); *C. C. 1 Corinthians*, 245.

167. *CO* 49:486 (11:24); C. C. *1 Corinthians*, 244. Cf. *OS* 1:75. (Battles, trans., *Institution*, 65.)

ans Commentary the notion of the "logocracy" in the church and, in particular, used the 1 Corinthians passage (11:28) for its fourfold order of ministers. In a comparison to the third *Institutes*, however, the Corinthians commentary seemed to underscore a new emphasis, the correlation of the Holy Spirit and the ministerial offices. On the text (3:5–7) in which Paul referred to the ministers' works for the building up of the Corinthian church, for example, Calvin called the gospel of Christ the "instrument of the Holy Spirit" and Christ's ministers the dispensers of this instrument. Concerning the triad relation of Christ, the Holy Spirit, and a minister, in one sense, a minister as "the minister of the Spirit" could work "for the regeneration of souls, thereafter for feeding them into eternal life, for remitting sins, for renewing of the mind of men, for setting the Kingdom of Christ, and destruction of Satan's." On the other hand, the work of a minister as Christ's "servant" was dead and powerless "unless the Lord gives effective power to it by his Spirit."[168] Furthermore, Calvin connected Paul's notion of the ministry with another text (9:1), in which the apostle claimed the Corinthian church as his "work." He commented that "God is the efficient cause, while man, with his preaching, is an instrument, which is futile by itself."[169] On the theme of the "legitimate form of the church," while he emphasized the notion of the rule of Christ's word, logocracy, in the topic on ministerial order of the third *Institutes*, his *Corinthians Commentary* focused on the operation of the Spirit, making the ministers "Spirit's instruments," and their works only efficacious by Christ's power and through the Spirit's operation. From his notion of the mutually supplemental relation between the *Institutes* and the commentaries, what we consider his "Reformed ecclesiology" could be surveyed under the two themes of "the rule of Christ's word" and "the operation of his Spirit."

(2) Internal Characteristics of the Church

Paul's first letter to the Corinthians is known for its theme of the church as "Christ's body," an organism with Christ as its head and the believers as its members. The letter provides a richer imagery of the organism (12:12–26) than the similar one in his letter to the Romans and, in particular, connects the organism with the ministerial offices (12:27–31). Our task here is not to survey Calvin's comments on chapter 12 but to focus on some characteristic remarks that appeared in its introductory portion and concerned the church's "legitimate form." Citing the ancient example of using the term "body" for a political

168. *CO* 49:349 (3:5); 49:350 (3:7); *C. C. 1 Corinthians*, 68–70.
169. *CO* 49:438 (9:1); *C. C. 1 Corinthians*, 183.

institution, Calvin remarked that Paul's use of the term was quite different from the ancient use. He specifically indicated the group of believers as "the spiritual and mystical body of Christ." When Calvin's first *Institutes* used a similar term, "the mystical body of Christ," for the "holy Catholic church" in the Apostles' Creed, the reference was to "the whole number of the elect." However, the reference here was to the actual and visible congregation of believers. Here he also emphasized comprehending "the body of Christ" from the "connectedness (*coniunctio*) in Christ," namely, all the believers with various gifts merging into one body in Christ.[170] If the third *Institutes* focused on the "legitimate form" in its full scope, the *First Corinthians Commentary* identified the "legitimate form" as the living and visible organism of the body of Christ.

(i) The first characteristic notion concerned the internal and unifying nature of the Spirit's operation. On the text concerning Christ's connectedness with believers (1:5–6), Calvin commented that "the gifts of the Spirit are bestowed for the upbuilding of all, . . . as gifts common to the whole church." On the text of "spiritual gifts" (12:1–11), furthermore, his comment described "the function of the Holy Spirit to send out the power of God, and keep it at work, by bestowing these gifts on men, and distributing them among them."[171]

(ii) The second notion concerned the cooperation and unity in the church worked out by the ministers and congregation together. This notion could be illustrated by Calvin's comments on chapter 5, the text which included difficult passages such as those that called the church to hand a member "over to Satan." Calvin understood the presbyterial system of government in this text. On the passage (5:4) where the congregational assembly in Corinth and Paul's "presence in spirit" were to make the final judgment of "handing over," Calvin commented that the judgment was made according to Paul's "consulting with the church" and was based upon "common authority." Since Paul had prejudged the case (5:3) before consulting the Corinthian congregation, Calvin interpreted this type of church government as the precedent to the ancient church's "institution of presbytery" that had the power of prejudging the case and bringing it to the congregation for consultation. Moreover, he considered this system an effective countermeasure against the spiritual tyranny of Rome.[172] On Paul's expression, "handing over to Satan" (5:5), he took issue with Chrysostom's interpretation of it as the infliction of a severe punishment

170. *CO* 49:501 (12:12); *C. C. 1 Corinthians*, 264. Cf. Faber, "Mutual Connectedness," 222–44; chapter 1, n. 148.

171. *CO* 49:310–11 (1:5–6); *C. C. 1 Corinthians*, 20–21; 496–500 (12:1–11), esp. 498 (12:4); *C. C. 1 Corinthians*, 258–63, esp. 260.

172. *CO* 49:379–80 (5:4); *C. C. 1 Corinthians*, 107–8.

upon the body, as well as this interpretation's adoption by the Roman Catholic Church. Instead, he interpreted the Pauline expression as excommunication and cited Augustine's saying that "while Christ reigns within, so Satan reigns outside, the church."[173] Furthermore, he accused the Roman Catholic Church of expanding the text's meaning beyond severe physical punishment into the system of "Interdiction," which he termed as "not strictness of discipline, but arbitrary and savage cruelty."[174]

(iii) The third notion concerned Calvin's fresh interpretation of the most illustrious chapter of the epistle, the chapter on love (*caritas*; 13:1–13), which was said to symbolize the internal unity of the church. His interpretation was prima facie traditional, but it was in reality a fairly radical redefining of "love" from the two principles of faith and the ministry of the word. It also indicated that his search for the "legitimate form" went beyond the church's external system into internal religiosity. Above all, he was keenly aware of the fact that this chapter occupied a crucially important place in Catholic apologetics against Protestantism. This could be illustrated by his comment that, if the Protestants claimed "justification by faith," the Catholics boasted "that, if faith justifies, therefore love, which is described as greater, does it much more" and attacked Protestantism as an inferior religion.[175] Or he might have been aware of the early Luther's struggle in his *Psalms Lectures* (1513–15) to found the faith-based ecclesiology over against the Catholic ecclesiology that treasured the caritas passages in chapter 13. In the case of Luther, the believer was formed "in the Spirit and by faith" and lived in the church "in the Spirit and by faith." According to Hendrix, as noted before, Luther's "faith-ecclesiology" was set against the Catholic "love-ecclesiology."[176]

With this background in mind, we will briefly examine Calvin's bold reevaluation of this chapter. Calvin interpreted the passage "if I have all faith, so as to remove mountains" (13:2) as a reference to a "special kind" of faith, or the "faith of Judas," which was without the Spirit's sanctification and sharply distinguished it from faith that had comprehended Christ fully, was formed in justification, and was to result in sanctification.[177] On another passage, "in a mirror, dimly" (13:12), his interpretation was conscious of the Catholic theory

173. *CO* 49:380–81 (5:5); *C. C. 1 Corinthians*, 108.

174. *CO* 49:386 (5:11); *C. C. 1 Corinthians*, 115.

175. *CO* 49:516 (13:13); *C. C. 1 Corinthians*, 283.

176. *WA* 4:450; *WA* 3:150. Cf. S. H. Hendrix, *Ecclesia in Via: Ecclesiological Developments in the Medieval Psalms Exegesis and the Dictata super Psalterium (1513–1515) of Martin Luther* (Leiden: Brill, 1974), 161–62, 179–215.

177. *CO* 49:509 (13:2); *C. C. 1 Corinthians*, 275.

of the knowledge of God and particularly noted the Vulgate's term, "in obscurity" (*in enigmate*). In response, he cast the "obscurity" as a contrast between the knowledge of God through Scripture and the face-to-face knowledge promised to be given in the last day. Citing another Corinthian passage, "for we walk by faith, not by sight" (2 Cor 5:7), he identified the former knowledge through Scripture as gospel knowledge through faith, which was given in the word, the sacraments, and the church's ministry.[178] On the crucial passage, "the greatest of these is love" (1 Cor 13:13), furthermore, his reevaluation presented two arguments, the first of which examined the relationship among "faith, hope, and love" from the perspective of "faith." He interpreted "hope" as nothing but "perseverance of faith" and "love" as the "effect of faith," thus establishing the superiority of "faith." The second argument noted a significant commendation that Scripture gave to "faith" but not to "love," namely, "the victory that conquers the world" (1 John 5:4). He then concluded that "faith" was to hold "a primary role in keeping the church in being."[179] A glimpse of Calvin's bold reevaluation of the chapter from the principle of faith showed the religiosity of the Evangelical churches, which was an integral part of his Reformed ecclesiology.

(3) The Church in History

Holder, who has examined Calvin's hermeneutics in his commentaries on the Pauline epistles, notes Calvin's "hermeneutical circle, made up of the three elements of scripture, history, and the church." Calvin was said to have interpreted Scripture not from the church's tradition but from history (God's providence, the history of salvation and of the church), and then to have applied the truth revealed in that history to the church of his day.[180] From Calvin's *First Corinthians Commentary*, in particular, Holder cites his comment (3:15) mentioned above that Cyprian, Ambrose, and Augustine had attempted to build up the

178. *CO* 49:514 (13:12); *C. C. 1 Corinthians*, 290.

179. *CO* 49:515–16 (13:13); *C. C. 1 Corinthians*, 283.

180. R. W. Holder, *John Calvin and the Grounding of Interpretation: Calvin's First Commentaries* (Leiden and Boston: Brill, 2006), 11, 258–71. Holder uses such recent authors on Calvin's view on salvation history as S. E. Schreiner (*The Theater of His Glory: Nature and the Natural Order in the Thought of John Calvin* [Durham, NC: Duke University Press, 1991]) and I. Backus (*Historical Method and Confessional Identity in the Era of the Reformation (1378–1615)* [Leiden: Brill, 2003]), and others. We may add another work of R. C. Zachman (*Image and Word in the Theology of John Calvin* [Notre Dame: University of Notre Dame Press, 2007], 73–104) published after Holder's work.

church upon the foundation of gold, namely, the word of God. Furthermore, Holder considers that Calvin signified "the church" in his hermeneutical circle as "the present culmination of the stream of history," a contextual attempt to apply scriptural and historical truth in the church.[181] Although his *Corinthians Commentary* was not as interested in history as his *Romans Commentary*, which presented "the history of justification," in the following pages we will present some examples of his historical contextualization.

In 1 Corinthians 4:15, Paul claimed that while there were "ten thousand tutors in Christ," his role was as "father through the gospel" in building up the Corinthian church. Commenting on this passage, Calvin asserted that, "today, indeed, the condition of the universal church is like the Corinthian Church then." Thus, his general hermeneutical guideline to compare the universal church of his day to the Corinthian church was set. Clearly referring to the Evangelical "tutors" and not to the Roman Catholic "tutors," he commented that many among the Evangelical "guardians" were too busily occupied with their own causes rather than those of Christ.[182] On other passages (7:12–16), in which Paul dealt with a married couple with one unbelieving spouse and concluded the marriage was holy, Calvin's comment recognized the existence of those who, in the Reformation era, considered the marriage as unholy and regarded the couple as guilty of fornication. Calvin criticized them and urged them to distinguish always between "the nature of a thing and its abuse."[183] Furthermore, concerning Paul's saying that "if food is a cause of their falling, I will never eat meat" (8:13), Calvin took issue with the current Nicodemites who had used this passage for the defense of their actions. He acknowledged that the abstinence from food in Paul's day involved far less peril than the current abstinence from participating in the Catholic Mass. He criticized the Nicodemites' use of Paul's example of regarding weaker brothers as justification for their participation in the Mass simply as "simulation."[184] On the issue of celibacy in chapter 7, furthermore, Calvin considered the idealizing of celibacy "a superstition" that Satan had brought in the earliest stage of the church, as seen in the Corinthian church. His comments criticized the Catholic teaching of ministerial celibacy as a system that had closed the door for many able believers to become ministers of the gospel.[185] In general, his comments aimed

181. Holder, *John Calvin and the Grounding*, 267–71.

182. *CO* 49:373 (4:15); *C. C. 1 Corinthians*, 98.

183. *CO* 49:411–12 (7:14); *C. C. 1 Corinthians*, 148–49. Here, Calvin's criticism is aimed at the Anabaptists.

184. *CO* 49:436 (8:13); *C. C. 1 Corinthians*, 180–81.

185. *CO* 49:400 (7:1), 406–7 (7:9); *C. C. 1 Corinthians*, 135–36.

at rejecting the wrong, rectifying the impure, and supplementing the lacking, in short, at searching the practical and "legitimate form of the church." It could be said that the spirit of Calvin's *First Corinthians Commentary* as a practical example of his Reformed ecclesiology could be summed up in the reformatory phrase, "it therefore stands in need of correction."[186]

Section 3. Reformation Ecclesiology

"Reformation ecclesiology" is not a theological but a historical concept. As we have noted that Calvin's *Romans Commentary* saw the biblical scheme of history as the history of justification, his Reformation ecclesiology, in concrete terms, was an attempt to conceive of the same salvation history in the church of the Reformation era. Yet Calvin conceived of it within a prophetic perspective that had been especially accented in his writings of the period from 1555 to 1564. As we will see in our examination of the Psalms commentary and Daniel lectures, this perspective became a distinctive characteristic of his Reformation ecclesiology. In a sense, it is true that the theological framework of the so-called "Calvin's ecclesiology" in book 4 of the 1559 *Institutes* defined his Reformation ecclesiology. Yet, Reformation ecclesiology as a historical concept indicates his understanding of the entire church and its reform from Luther's time to his own. In this historical concept, he took into consideration the realities of the Roman Catholic Church, the Nicodemites, the Anabaptists, and others, as well as the English Reformation and the Evangelical Reformations of Luther, Zwingli, Bucer, and his own. The aim of his Reformation ecclesiology was to conceive of the entire Evangelical church of his age as the "Reformation church" from a prophetic perspective, as well as in the framework of God's salvation history, and to place his own idea of the Evangelical church and its reform in that frame. The presentation of his own ideas was not meant to be a completion of other Reformations but to supplement and integrate them into a representative image of the entire Evangelical Reformation.

(i) From the viewpoint of the history of doctrine, Calvin's Reformation ecclesiology was but the last phase of his developing ecclesiology. It was the culmination of his "Catholic ecclesiology," which we consider the founding stratum of his ecclesiology, and "Reformed ecclesiology," which mainly focused on the church's "legitimate form." How can we, then, define Reformation ecclesiology historically? As we have seen in the previous three chapters of our

186. *CO* 49:484 (11:23): "correctione igitur, opus est"; *C. C. 1 Corinthians*, 242.

study, his "Catholic ecclesiology" excluded the papal church and the Anabaptists as two extremes and placed Protestant Evangelicalism in the center as a manifestation of the Catholic church. His Nicodemite controversy rejected the Nicodemite position as a viable part of Evangelicalism. Moreover, his "Reformed ecclesiology" presented his unique understanding of the church's form as quite distinctive from the forms presented in the Reformations of Luther, Zwingli, and even Bucer. As we have noted, his ecclesiology manifested many facets that were complex and often seemingly contradictory. Can we assume that the facets that were seen in his apology of the high estimate of the church's catholicity in his *Reply to Sadoleto*, his participation in the church unification colloquies in Germany, his signing of both the *Wittenberg Concord* and *Consensus Tigurinus*, and his controversy with the Lutherans over the Lord's Supper were to be harmonized in his Reformation ecclesiology? In the inquiry "Toward the recovery of the historical Calvin," Oberman postulates Luther's and Calvin's Reformations as two distinctive Reformations, yet he affirms each Reformation as commonly and deeply rooted in the historical Luther and Calvin. On the one hand, he remarks that Luther's "catholic" conviction allocated the common "birthright" in the body of the church to both "reformed" Lutheranism and "unreformed" Roman Catholicism. On the other hand, he remarks that, although Calvinism established a separate church at the exclusion of the Catholic and Nicodemite elements, along with the Roman Catholic Church, Calvinism was "vying for the same birthright."[187] Thus, the question is whether Calvin could, with the recognition of the difference between Luther's Reformation and his own, assume one "Reformation church" as such.

(ii) In the dedicatory epistle to Grynaeus affixed to his *Romans Commentary*, Calvin delineated his basic mode of scriptural interpretation in accordance with the hermeneutical tradition from the ancient church to his contemporaries, Melanchthon, Bullinger, Bucer, and others. He affirmed that God never favored "his servants" (interpreters) in providing them "with a full and perfect knowledge in everything" and that God's purpose for this was to "keep them humble" and "render them disposed to cultivate brotherly exchange" with other interpreters.[188] In his 1550 work, *Concerning Scandals*, Calvin acknowledged the existence of major disagreements over the Lord's Supper within the Evangelical side. Referring to the Marburg Colloquy (1529) in which the German reformers (Luther, Melanchthon, etc.) and the Swiss reformers (Zwingli,

187. H. A. Oberman, *The Two Reformations*, ed. D. Weinstein (New Haven: Yale University Press, 2003), 102.

188. *COR* II-13:5.

Oecolampadius, etc.) tried to reach an Evangelical consensus, he depicted the current Evangelical position as a whole as being united in "the principal sum of Christian doctrine" yet only having some disagreements on the Lord's Supper. Even concerning the disagreements, he avoided emphasizing the issue as a "stumbling block" to Evangelical unity and optimistically presented the possibility of reaching an accord through earnest efforts.[189] These two affirmations on scriptural interpretation and theological consensus illustrated Calvin's vision of the Evangelical Christianity of his day as a sort of single entity.

(iii) There is yet another dimension that we will call the prophetic perspective in Calvin's Reformation ecclesiology. During the period of 1555 to 1564, his ecclesiological vista became increasingly focused on the perspective of prophetic vision and his own prophetic self-awareness. In a sense, this perspective was nothing new and its manifestations could be traced back to the 1536 *Institutes*, the 1537 *Two Epistles* and its "Preface to the readers," and the anti-Nicodemite tracts of the 1540s, as well as to his naming Luther as a prophet. Ganoczy summarizes Calvin's earlier position on this issue: "the reformer continues to maintain the analogy between the pioneers of the reform [such as Luther] and the prophets of the Old and New Testaments, but at the same time he wishes to avoid the idea that one can take an analogy for a pure and simple identification." As far as Calvin's theory of New Testament ministry was concerned, since the 1543 *Institutes* his position had been clear: the offices of apostles, prophets, and evangelists were "extraordinary" in the sense that they were limited to the initial founding of the New Testament church; those of pastors and teachers were "ordinary" offices in the church. As to the particular office of prophets, he narrowly associated it with God's "revelation." Interestingly, however, he made his interpretation rather flexible: as God "now and again revives them [apostles, prophets, and evangelists] as the need of the times demands," the office of prophets "either does not exist today or is less commonly seen." In recent Calvin scholarship, we have seen considerable interest in Calvin's commentaries, sermons on the Old Testament prophetic books, and the particular issue of his own prophetic self-awareness. As seen in the case of Balserak's study, which defines Calvin as a "sixteenth-century prophet," there is even a tendency to stretch the issue of prophetic self-awareness to that of self-identity. No matter how we interpret this complex issue, it remains an important element for interpreting his Reformation ecclesiology.[190]

189. *De Scandalis*, *OS* 2:215. Cf. *Jean Calvin: Des scandales*, ed. O. Fatio (Geneva: Droz, 1984), 171–72.

190. *CO* 1:563–64 (*Institutio* 4.3.4: *OS* 5:45–46); Ganoczy, *Young Calvin*, 298; J. Balserak,

With this background in mind, in the following pages, we will examine his Reformation ecclesiology in the two major publications of this period, the *Psalms Commentary* (1557) and the final *Institutes* (1559). In the former, we will focus on the prophetic images of the church in salvation history and, in the latter, on the vision of the Reformation church, of which we will also use in part his *Lectures on Daniel* (1561).

1. *The* Psalms Commentary: *The Prophetic Image of the Church in Salvation History*

The *Psalms Commentary* was a unique work even among Calvin's commentaries and published lectures on Scripture of this period. It was based upon his Psalms lectures (1552–56) and its draft was prepared by at least three auditors who transcribed his extemporaneous lectures in Latin. However, its final draft was completely written by himself through what he described as "a

John Calvin as Sixteenth-Century Prophet, 66–101, esp. 88–100; ch. 2, n. 168. Balserak's study is commendable in the sense that it successfully places the issues of Calvin's prophetic self-awareness in the historical context. Especially, its treatment of the issue in Calvin's background (ch. 2) and in the context of his reformatory works in the French Reformation (chs. 4–5) is persuasive. As to the crux of the study, Calvin's prophetic self-identification as an Old Testament prophet, however, its argument is not so convincing. For example, its first proof taken from Calvin's dedicatory epistle to the French king is questionable. Although its text cites a passage from Isaiah along with four New Testament passages, the text shows no indication of Calvin's prophetic self-awareness as such. The author's reduction from the text, Calvin "does believe himself to be one who has been invested with [prophetic] authority," seems to be overstated. The second proof consists of a cluster of Calvin's references to the OT prophets' messages in his anti-Nicodemite tracts of the 1540s. Although we admit a close relationship between Calvin's message taken from the OT prophetic books and his prophetic self-awareness, the author's conclusion, "Calvin, it may be asserted, self-identifies with the old covenant messengers," seems an overreach. Knowing Ganoczy's balanced concluding remark which our text cites, we also question the author's footnote reference to Ganoczy (*Young Calvin*, 287–97, a section that deals with "Calvin's consciousness of a divine call") for his conclusion. As the third proof, the author states that "Calvin addresses the question [of self-identification] specifically in material produced in the last decade of his life." Although this could be the author's strongest proof, however, he seems to provide no proof texts in which Calvin clearly "identifies" himself as the Old Testament prophet. The fourth proof is taken from Calvin's preface to the Psalms commentary where he makes an analogy of the life and work of David and himself. From this the author makes a case of "Calvin's sense of prophetic calling." There should be no question that the preface witnesses a strong case of Calvin's prophetic self-awareness. At the same time, however, it should be noted that the preface also states a clear distinction between David as "king and prophet" and himself as "a preacher and minister of the gospel." (For this, confer n. 192 below.)

long and extremely difficult labor." Although three commentaries on Isaiah (1551), Genesis (1554), and Psalms (1557) were placed in the background of the final *Institutes*, the *Psalms Commentary* was by far the work on which he exerted himself most and that was the most important to our interest in his ecclesiology.[191] Focusing on his concept of the church in the commentary, in the following pages, we examine its three characteristic aspects, namely, the *Psalms Commentary* and salvation history, the relation between Christ's kingdom and the church, and the images of the Reformation church as the "orchestra" and "under the cross."

(1) The Psalms Commentary *and Salvation History*

(i) One of the unusual features of the commentary was that, as noted in chapter 1, Calvin recollected his life in its preface. The recollection, which included the expression "a sudden conversion" compared the life and work of David, the main author of the Psalms, and his own life and work. Making a comparison between "that most illustrious king and prophet" and "the honorable office of a preacher and minister of the gospel," which undoubtedly reflected his acute prophetic self-awareness, Calvin began the recollection of his own life with the open acknowledgment that "if I have any things in common with him [David], I have no hesitation in comparing myself with him." Since his comments on Psalm 18 described David's life at length, the recollection in the preface served as Calvin's intended parallelism.[192] As he used this parallelism throughout his comments on the Psalms, he aimed to show that David and he were from different ages but shared the same faith in God, salvation, church, and struggle as believers. In fact, some of his comments not only expressed

191. *In librum Psalmorum commentarius*, 1557: *BC* 57/4, 629–32. Cf. Parker, *John Calvin*, 130; P. Wilcox, "Calvin as Commentator on the Prophets," in *Calvin and the Bible*, ed. D. K. McKim (Cambridge: Cambridge University Press, 2006), 107. For the text, we use the *Opera Calvini* (*CO* 31:13–842; 32:1–442). For the text in English, we use *Calvin's Commentaries* (the Calvin Translation Society edition) (Grand Rapids: Eerdmans, 1989), vols. 4–6, cited as CTS, *Psalms*. According to the historical notes of the *Bibliotheca Calviniana*, among three transcribers of Calvin's original lectures were Jean Budé, a son of the famous French Humanist, Guillaume Budé, and Nicolas Des Gallar, later a Calvin biographer. However, Calvin's own "Preface" (*CO* 31:13, 15) reveals a rather unusual origin of the commentary, suggesting the possibility that he used his own fresh writings independent of the transcribed lecture notes in some cases. Despite Wilcox's contention that Calvin did not write down this commentary, we take Parker's assessment that Calvin consistently wrote it down and that the case of the *Psalms Commentary* was exceptional among his exegetical works of the Old Testament.

192. *CO* 31:21; CTS, *Psalms*, 4:xl. Cf. *CO* 31:169–70 (18:1); CTS, *Psalms*, 4:256–57.

that both of them shared belief in the Triune God and salvation in Christ but also consistently used the same term, the church (*ecclesia*), for God's people in David's time and the church in the sixteenth century, without distinguishing the difference of ages and conditions. If we consider this view of history to be that of salvation history, it can be said that Calvin applied the same method of interpreting Romans as "the history of justification" to the Psalms so as to reach a hermeneutic principle of "Christ and his church" in the Psalms text. Since Psalms is an Old Testament book, this principle was to ground the whole scope of God's promise made to Abraham and the people of his descendants, the promised fulfillment in Christ and his church, and its continuing fulfillment in the sixteenth century church. In this respect, among the many Psalms commentaries that Calvin used, he might have consulted Lefèvre's biblical work on the Psalms (*Quincuplex Psalterium*, 1509) and Luther's first Lectures on the Psalms (*Dictata super Psalterium*, 1513–15). Both of them used salvation history as a hermeneutical prop and interpreted the text Christologically, with the congregation of believers being the church of the Old and New Testaments. For Calvin's basic understanding of Psalms as a prophetic book and David as a prophet, however, Lefèvre's preface to the 1509 Psalms commentary might have been his inspiration. It is certainly possible to characterize Calvin's Psalms commentary as a work focusing on the faithful believers in history and on their sufferings and consolations. However, we consider its main theme as something beyond individual histories, namely, the relation of Christ and the church in salvation history.[193]

(ii) In the *Psalms Commentary*, Calvin approached the beginning of "the history of the church" not as starting in the Garden of Eden, but, rather, as in his *Romans Commentary*, as being founded in the history of Abraham. In other words, the church's beginning was in God's election as seen when "God adopted Abraham freely" or "God adopted for himself a church from

193. Cf. W. de Greef, "Calvin as Commentator on the Psalms," in *Calvin and the Bible*, ed. D. K. McKim, 101; Gordon, *Calvin*, 285–88; D. C. Steinmetz, "Calvin as an Interpreter of Genesis," *Calvinus Sincerioris Religionis Vindex*, ed. W. H. Neuser and B. G. Armstrong (Kirksville: Sixteenth Century Journal Publisher, 1997), 53–66. Greef notes "David/Christ/the church" as the commentary's chief motif and places it in the tradition of Augustine's Psalms commentary. Using the Genesis text of the divine-human encounter (32:24–32), Steinmetz examines a similar Jacob/Christ/the church theme. Gordon characterizes Calvin's commentary as a book of consolation by a quotation from Calvin, "a far-fetched consolation." For Lefèvre's "Preface" and his remark concerning David as a prophet, see its Latin text in *The Prefatory Epistles*, ed. Rice, 192–97, esp. 194 and its English translation in Oberman, *Forerunners of the Reformation*, 297–301, esp. 298. For Luther, confer Hendrix, *Ecclesia in Via*, 5–8.

the posterity of Abraham." God made the "covenant" with the church on the premise of the church remaining in "pure and holy obedience" to him. In this respect, he understood salvation history as the history of the church. In the center of this history, he placed Christ's advent, emphasizing that "Christ beautified the church by his advent." Calvin illustrated this central period of Christ's advent as when the God of Scripture began to be worshipped in the different languages of all nations, believers were gathered "in the holy unity of faith," kings of nations came to obey under Christ's yoke, and the gifts of the Spirit were poured upon the faithful. With this idealized image of the apostolic age, Calvin concluded that "the body of the church was also gathered together out of different countries and was increased and preserved in a wonderful manner." In addition, he distinguished two periods of the preadvent and post-advent and called them "puberty" and "adulthood."[194] Even though the two periods formed a continuum in the history of the church, he distinguished the former as the period for "expecting" the advent and the latter as the period for "restoring" the glorious stage of the advent. In this prophetic scheme of salvation history, he justified the coupling of the church of the David-Solomon period and that of his own time, as well as of David and himself personally.

(2) Christ's Kingdom and the Church

For our understanding of the relation between Christ's kingdom and the church in Calvin's *Psalms Commentary*, two pieces of research on Calvin's hermeneutics on the Prophets, which have examined this relation, are useful. One is Muller's article, "Hermeneutic of Promise and Fulfillment in Calvin's Exegesis of the Old Testament Prophecies of the Kingdom," and the other is Wilcox's article, "Calvin as Commentator on the Prophets."

Having surveyed modern research on Calvin's exegetical principle, Muller selects the theme, "the Old Testament prophecies of the kingdom," as a test case for establishing Calvin's exegetical principle, namely, "the hermeneutic of promise and fulfillment." According to him, Calvin interpreted prophetic texts to show "the relation of the text, historically interpreted, to the New Testament fulfillment of Old Testament prophecy and, with fulfillment as logical pivot, to the present day life of the church." Referring to Calvin's phrase, "the whole course of the kingdom of Christ," furthermore, Muller calls this principle "a

194. *CO* 31:143 (15:1); CTS, *Psalms*, 4:203–4. Cf. *CO* 31:720 (78: argumentum); CTS, *Psalms*, 5-b:225; *CO* 31:723 (78:5); CTS, *Psalms*, 5-b:230–31; *CO* 31:799 (87: argumentum); CTS, *Psalms*, 5-b:395. *CO* 32:331 (129:1); CTS, *Psalms*, 6-b:122–23.

hermeneutic of multiple fulfillment." In this promise/fulfillment scheme, some promises in the prophetic texts were fulfilled in the Old Testament times, and other promises in "the coming of Christ and the new age inaugurated by him and, by extension, to the life of the present-day church."[195]

Similarly, yet in a more general and schematic approach, Wilcox examines Calvin's hermeneutics on the Prophets and notes the "two hermeneutic emphases" of "the progress of Christ's Kingdom and salvation history" and "the restoration of the church." Concerning the first emphasis, he writes that Calvin identified the beginnings of Christ's kingdom in the period between the Babylonian captivity and the return from it and the actual consummation of the kingdom in Christ's advent and the apostolic age. Yet Calvin understood the kingdom to be completed in the last day, and he saw the period between the first advent and the last day as the time for the kingdom's "progress." Wilcox concludes that for Calvin "the progress of Christ's kingdom is manifest in the events of the mid-sixteenth century." As to the second emphasis, he argues that Calvin used the terms "restoration" and "reformation" synonymously and interpreted this progress as restoring the original integrity of the church.[196] In particular, Muller's notion of multiple fulfillment and Wilcox's "two hermeneutic emphases" are helpful for our understanding of the *Psalms Commentary*. With this background in mind, in the following pages, we will examine three points concerning the relation between Christ's kingdom and his church. How did Calvin distinguish them, how did he relate them to one another, and how did he relate them to his "Reformation ecclesiology"?

(i) The first point concerned Calvin's basic stance that the "spiritual" kingdom of Christ should be distinguished from the "visible" church in history. Although the visible church could be a manifestation of the kingdom, as we have noted in the first *Institutes*, his apologetic stance rejected the *a posteriori* identification of the visible church with the kingdom as "an error" in the case of the papal church and "a Jewish folly" in that of the Münster Anabaptists. We assume that this distinction was a reflection of his Christological understanding, namely, the Antiochene position of Christ's two natures to be "distinguished, but not separated," and that he carefully maintained this distinction in his *Psalms Commentary*. Although we take this clear distinction of Christ's kingdom and the church in history as Calvin's basic hermeneutic stance, due

195. R. A. Muller, "The Hermeneutic of Promise and Fulfillment in Calvin's Exegesis of the Old Testament Prophecies of the Kingdom," in *The Bible in the Sixteenth Century*, ed. D. C. Steinmetz (Durham and London: Duke University Press, 1990), 68–82, 214–21.

196. P. Wilcox, "Calvin as Commentator on the Prophets," 120–30.

to the nature of the text on which he was commenting, he came exceptionally close to identification rather than distinction. This was the case of his comment on Psalm 87, in which, as mentioned above, he idealized the period of Christ's advent and the apostolic age, "which may be called the golden age," and then said that the church "was truly the heavenly Kingdom of God."[197]

As we have seen, his commentary on 1 Corinthians, the most ecclesial text among the Pauline epistles, did not have much to say on the church's relationship with Christ's kingdom. What, then, was the reason that, almost ten years later in his *Psalms Commentary*, the close relationship of Christ's kingdom and the church had become such a prominent theme? Of course, the difference of the biblical texts could be one explanation. Another reason could be that the period of Calvin's lectures on the Psalms and the publication (1552–57) coincided with some of the crucial stages of his life, such as the critical phase of the Genevan Reformation, the volatile situation of the French Reformation, and the Council of Trent and Catholic counterreform movement, surveyed in section 1 above. In the previous chapter, furthermore, we noted two ecclesiological themes, "implicit amplification" (the Reformation of a local church) and "explicit expansion" (the Reformation of the European Christian world), which Calvin had inherited from Bucer. As this post-1555 period witnessed his deep concern for the latter theme, "the Reformation of the European Christian world," the church's eschatological dimension, especially its relation with Christ's kingdom, had become a prominent theme. In this respect, he had now expanded his ecclesiological vista beyond his "Catholic" and "Reformed" ecclesiologies in his studies of the Old Testament texts, especially the prophetic books including the Psalms. As suggested by Muller and Wilcox, Calvin's understanding of the current Reformation history had unquestionably acquired an extra emphasis on the prophetic and eschatological dimensions of Christ's

197. *CO* 31:800 (87: argumentum); CTS, *Psalms*, 5-b:395. Cf. chapter 1, n. 175. P. Wilcox's other article ("The Progress of the Kingdom of Christ in Calvin's Exposition of the Prophets," in *Calvinus Sincerioris Religionis Vindex*, ed. W. H. Neuser and B. G. Armstrong [Kirksville: Sixteenth Century Journal Publishers, 1997], 315–22, esp. 320) makes a similar affirmation. Referring to Calvin's *Lectures on Amos* (9:13, *CO* 43:172) and others, he insists that Calvin can assert without qualification that "the Church is Christ's Kingdom." In the Amos text, Calvin compared the happy and blessed conditions of the kingdom of Christ in his advent with the church and said "which means the same thing" (*quod idem valet*). Wilcox might interpret "idem" as a categorical identification of Christ's kingdom and the church. We feel this interpretation is not as certain. We consider, however, his further affirmation that "this identification is of the Kingdom of Christ not with 'the elect' (the invisible Church), but with the institutional (or visible) church" is simply an overstatement without sound textual support.

kingdom. In an article, "The 'Extra' Dimension in the Theology of Calvin," Oberman focuses on Calvin's Old Testament commentaries and lectures and finds there the theme of Christ's kingdom, a vision of the Reformation going far beyond the boundaries of cities and nations, and what he calls "a political eschatology." On the relation of Christ's kingdom and the church, Oberman concludes that "the rule of Christ obtains *etiam extra ecclesiam*." Likewise, Engammare's analysis of Calvin's prophetic self-awareness highlights the aspect of a prophet as "admonisher of the government" or "advisor" to kings and princes. He illustrates Calvin's self-awareness by drawing attention to "Calvin's first printed text as a Protestant," his Latin preface to Olivetan's French Bible, which begins with "to all emperors, kings, princes, and gentlemen who are under Christ's sovereign power, greetings."[198] The above analyses suggest a prophetic aspect of what we call Calvin's Reformation ecclesiology.

(ii) The second point concerned the way in which Calvin related the spiritual kingdom of Christ with the church in history, especially its reflection of the motif of his Antiochene Christology, "being distinguished, but not being separated." In his comment on Psalm 85:10–13 praising God's "love, faithfulness, righteousness, and peace," Calvin interpreted these as the four attributes ("mercy, truth, peace, and righteousness") of Christ's spiritual kingdom. He related these four virtues to the church, saying that the church's wellbeing was "comprehended in these gifts."[199] Regarding his comment on the "fruit" that land was to yield (85:12), he rebuffed an objection that "the spiritual Kingdom of Christ and the fruit of the land" for the sustenance of humans should not be improperly mixed. For him both the church's "virtues" as "gifts" from Christ and earthly blessings were to be properly distinguished and then related to Christ's spiritual kingdom.[200] Another example could be taken from his comment on "the psalm of David" (110), which Jewish commentators usually interpreted as a reference to the prosperity of the Davidic kingdom. Calvin, however, took this as a Messianic psalm referring to the eternal and universal rule of the coming Christ. At the beginning of his comment (110:1–2), he defined the Davidic kingdom and the current church, to which he believed David was a member, as indicators of the coming kingdom of Christ. On the text of the king's "youth" (or "seed"; 110:3), Calvin commented that "under his [Christ's] reign the church is promised to enjoy an immeasurable pros-

198. Oberman, *The Dawn*, 235–39; Engammare, "Calvin: A Prophet without Prophecy," 100–103; cf. chapter 1, n. 89.

199. *CO* 31:790 (85:11); 31, 790 (85:13); CTS, *Psalms*, 5-b:377.

200. *CO* 31:790 (85:13); CTS, *Psalms*, 5-b:378.

perity."[201] As indicated by the above two examples, Christ's spiritual kingdom and the church identified as the kingdom's "gifts" or "seed" on earth were not only to be distinguished but also to be intimately associated.

(iii) The third point concerned the nature of this intimate association between Christ's spiritual kingdom and the church. From the first to the third *Institutes*, we have noted that Christ's kingdom was a "mirror" in which the church in history could see its image, as well as a "defining concept" by which the church could know whether it was manifesting the kingdom or failing to do so. In his comment on the Psalm 21, for example, Calvin made an analogy between the Davidic kingdom and Christ's kingdom, and affirmed that the Davidic kingdom and the people of Judah as the church were an "image" for Christ's kingdom. In this analogy, he affirmed that "the kingdom of Christ . . . is never without enemies in this world." Attacks on the Davidic kingdom were considered attacks against Christ's kingdom, because Christ was the head of that church.[202] In this analogy, the church was to be an "image" of Christ's kingdom.[203] On Psalm 20, which he defined as "a prayer of the church on behalf of the king," Calvin commented that "since Christ our King, being an everlasting priest, never ceases to make intercession with God, the whole body of the church should unite in prayer with him."[204] In spite of the close association, however, the modus vivendi of the church was by nature different from that of Christ's kingdom. The church could face fall and extinction and, therefore, be desperately in need of Christ, who was "sent by his Father for the redemption of the church."[205] Throughout the commentary, Calvin described the church with terms such as "external," "human," and "temporal" and Christ's kingdom with "spiritual" and "celestial." As to the church's existence in history, he emphasized its solid and indispensable foundation on God's word and its need to be restored to its original "form."

(3) The Images of the Reformation Church: The "Orchestra" and "under the Cross"

The images of the church that Calvin's *Psalms Commentary* drew on were historically the images of God's people in the Psalms from the times of Da-

201. *CO* 32:159–63, esp. 163 (110:3); CTS, *Psalms*, 6:303.
202. *CO* 31:216 (21:9); CTS, *Psalms*, 4:350.
203. Cf. *CO* 31:169 (18: argumentum); CTS, *Psalms*, 4:256.
204. *CO* 31:208 (20:2); CTS, *Psalms*, 4:335.
205. *CO* 32:210 (118:25); CTS, *Psalms*, 6:392.

vid and Solomon to the Babylonian captivity and the postexilic period. Since Calvin considered the Psalms a prophetic book and its main author, David, a prophet, the images were coupled with those of Christ's advent and the period of his apostles, which the text's messianic messages projected. By way of application, the commentary reflected the images of the church in Calvin's own time, especially of Evangelical people and churches in France. In his comment on Psalm 44, which described the massacre of the Jewish people in connection with their captivity, Calvin recollected the history of Jewish sufferings from the time of David to Christ's advent. Concerning the scriptural teaching on those sufferings, he pointed to the need "to apply this doctrine to our circumstance" and then affirmed the sufferings to be "the perpetual destiny of the church."[206] In the following pages, we will follow some characteristic images of the church as the Reformation church in Calvin's commentary.

(i) The first characteristic images were a pair of two distinctively opposite images appearing in the commentary. One appeared in Calvin's comment on Psalm 135, in which he compared the whole world to a theater where God's justice, wisdom, and power were in full play and where "the church is a more illustrious part, just like the orchestra." The other appeared in his comment on Psalm 129, in which he recommended that the faithful learn from the Old Testament church that the church had "always toiled under the cross."[207] As Calvin said that "the whole world" was the theater of God's providence, the church as the "orchestra" was a more specific reality than the universal church or Christendom in Europe. It was the reality of Christ's kingdom or of "the holy Catholic church" of the Apostles' Creed, and it was the image that appeared in Calvin's comment on the psalm (22:31) where the church's perpetuity was defined as the "fruit" of "the incorruptible seed" of God's word.[208] On the other hand, the church "under the cross" was the image most often recognized in the commentary. For example, Calvin's comment that defined the "sufferings" as "the perpetual destiny of the church" was followed by another comment (44:23), whereby being "under the cross" was more positively described as "a state of continual warfare in bearing the cross is enjoined upon us by divine appointment."[209]

206. *CO* 31:447 (44:23); CTS, *Psalms*, 5:170.

207. *CO* 32:361 (135:13): "Et certe sicuti totus mundus theatrum est divinae bonitatis, sapientiae, iustitiae, virtutis: pars tamen illustrior, instar orchestrae, est ecclesia"; 32, 330 (129:1): "si oculos referant ad vetusta ecclesiae certamina, agnoscant semper laborasse sub cruce"; CTS, *Psalms*, 6-b:178, 120.

208. *CO* 31:236 (22:31); CTS, *Psalms*, 4:388. Cf. Zachman, *Image and Word*, 87–92. According to Zachman, Calvin identifies the church with "both the orchestra in the theater and the theater itself."

209. *CO* 31:447 (44:23); CTS, *Psalms*, 5:170.

What made it noteworthy was that these two images, orchestra and cross, were not presented as two separate realities but as two sides of the same reality. They could be the same church seen "in the sight of God" (*coram Deo*) and "in the eyes of the world" (*coram mundo*). An illustration for this point was found in Calvin's comment quoted above in which he idealized the period of Christ's advent and the apostles in saying that "Christ beautified the church by his advent." "At the time when (the church) flourished most," Calvin commented, "not purple, gold, and precious stones . . . but [it was] the blood of martyrs which shined." Then, he continued by saying that the church being spiritually blessed was materially poor and, being holy in the face of God, was despised and surrounded by enemies in the world.[210] In short, for Calvin, the two opposite images of the church were understood as the Reformation church of his day.

(ii) Secondly, the images of the church in Calvin's *Psalms Commentary* were in sharp contrast to those in the third *Institutes*, which focused on the legitimate "form" of the church. The new images depicted the church as a living, dynamic, and historical organism that was active in the theater of God's providence, playing the role of the design or manifestation of Christ's kingdom, and bearing both Christ's glory and cross. Researcher Selderhuis draws these images together succinctly in his article title "Church on Stage: Calvin's Dynamic Ecclesiology."[211] However, what was most prevalent in the commentary was the theme of eschatological vision, that God had led his church in each epoch of salvation history through Christ and his Spirit and had upheld it toward its consummation. This theme could be recognized in a comment (90:16) in which he asserted that God's providence was working "internally" in the church and "externally" in the world. In another comment (125:1), God as the shepherd of the church spoke to "the whole people" as well as "to individual members" according to circumstances.[212] Concerning the theme of God's providential care over the church, Calvin consistently interpreted the church of the New Testament in terms of that of the Old Testament. On the Psalm 22, for example, Calvin commented that Christ's advent not only opened the door to the salvation of gentiles but also provided the way for God "to graft

210. *CO* 31:800 (87: argumentum); CTS, *Psalms*, 5-b:325. Cf. n. 200 above. Cf. H. Selderhuis, "Calvin's Theology of the Psalms," in *Calvin Studies IX*, ed. J. H. Leith and R. A. Johnson (Davidson, NC: Davidson College, 1998), 10. In examining the theme of God's hiddenness in Calvin's Psalms commentary, Selderhuis notices the importance of the "coram Deo / coram mundo" contrast.

211. Cf. H. J. Selderhuis, "Church on Stage: Calvin's Dynamic Ecclesiology," in *Calvin and the Church*, ed. D. Foxgrover (Grand Rapids: Calvin Studies Society, 2002), 46–64.

212. *CO* 31:842 (90:16); 32:313 (125:1); CTS, *Psalms*, 5-b:476; 6-b:90.

them [gentiles] onto the body of the [Jewish] church." On Psalm 47, furthermore, he commented on the inheritance of God's covenant by the gentiles and interpreted it not as removing Jews from the covenant but rather as "joining us to them [Jews]."[213] In the same manner, Calvin interpreted the New Testament church as the church where the wall separating Jews and gentiles was removed with the church's perpetual nature based upon the reality that "Christ must be viewed as living in his members to the end of the world."[214]

(iii) The third characteristic set of images came from Calvin's own understanding of the church in the Psalms as the Reformation church itself. In general, by reading the *Psalms Commentary* we have the impression that Calvin did not attribute a special significance to the Reformation era but considered it simply as an epoch in God's salvation history. Certainly, he had no intention of equating the Reformation era with salvation history's opening period of Abraham, its apex of Christ's advent and his apostles, and its end period of the church's consummation. However, he did signify that the Reformation era had an important parallel relation with the David-Solomon era of the church's history. He also understood that the churches of these two eras shared similar experiences: they had faced the issue of church corruption, encountered its internal problems, and endeavored to restore its original form.

Calvin's *Psalms Commentary* presented his own images of the church peculiar to the Reformation era. For example, he depicted the church of his day as being attacked by its "internal" as well as "external" enemies. As to enemies, he cited most frequently "the Papacy," "the papists," "the Nicodemites," and "the Libertines." In his critical comment on the papal church in the Psalm 122, for example, he raised the issue of the church's "title," which was for him the most fundamental element of the church's identity or true religion. "How foolish are the papists," he criticized, "who have overthrown the doctrine of the gospel, yet mightily boast of the church's name [title]."[215] Although he never mentioned the country by name, the most unique image of the church appeared in the historical context of France, where Evangelicalism was severely suppressed and persecuted under the papal church establishment. While he pictured the Evangelical churches as hindered from hearing the true word of God,

213. *CO* 31:234 (22:28); 31:471 (47:10); CTS, *Psalms*, 4:384; 5:214. Cf. D. L. Puckett, *John Calvin's Exegesis of the Old Testament* (Louisville: Westminster John Knox, 1995), 12–18. From what he calls "the Jewish/Christian polarity in Calvin's exegesis," Puckett examines the implication of Jewish and Christian exegetical traditions, which Calvin had learned, in his sixteenth-century religious world.

214. *CO* 31:583 (61:7); CTS, *Psalms*, 5:415.

215. *CO* 32:307 (122:9); CTS, *Psalms*, 6-b:79.

from participating in the sacraments, and from being expelled from the papal church, in his comment on David's psalm ("Hear my cry, O God: listen to my prayer," 61:1), he recommended to Evangelicals who were in similar situations to follow the example of David in prayer. In his comment on Psalm 63, which depicted David's flight and hiding from King Saul, he made a veiled reference to France and the French monarch, that "tyrannical power" forcefully robbed the Lord's Supper and other reinforcements of our warfare.[216] Concerning the theme of the church "under the cross," his comments emphasized that "we may with greater alacrity glory in bearing the cross with Christ." Under this theme, Calvin taught that the church's sufferings, such as persecution, danger of apostasy, death, ridicule, and the slaughterhouse, signified not only "severity of the cross" and "weariness or dread of the cross" but also the "glory" of the cross.[217] This theme also reflected his prophetic view of history and was certainly a vital element of his "Reformation ecclesiology."

2. *The Final* Institutes*: Vision of the Reformation Church*

In spite of the illness and overwork of his last years, Calvin had attempted to make a comprehensive survey of his theology by rearranging and reediting the materials in the previous editions of the *Institutes*. According to Beza's *Life of Calvin*, while in the poorest of health Calvin had completed both the definitive and final Latin edition, *Institutio Christianae religionis* (1559), and its final French edition, *Institution de la religion Chrestienne* (1560).[218] It is generally recognized that the final *Institutes* is his chief work among the entire corpus of his literary accomplishments and that it is not only one of the representative works of Reformed theology but also one of the most distinguished books of the Protestant Reformation. Since he did not offer any explanation worthy of the name for the composition of the entire *Institutes* and book 4 as the final expression of his ecclesiology, the question of the reasons for rearranging previous materials into the final form has been a point of controversy among researchers.

From our ecclesiological perspective, there seem to be two main concerns: one is the formal composition of the four books of the *Institutes* and its relation to book 4; the other is the internal structure of book 4 and its governing

216. *CO* 31:581 (61:1); 31:594–95 (63:3); CTS, *Psalms*, 5:411, 435.

217. *CO* 31:447 (44:23); CTS, *Psalms*, 5:170.

218. *Institutio Christianae religionis*: *BC* 59/4. Cf. *CO* 21:33 cited in Wendel, *Calvin*, 118. For the final Latin edition, we use the *Opera Selecta* text and its English translation by Battles in *Institutes*, ed. McNeill.

principle. Since the second concern will be discussed later, in this introductory section, we will briefly cover the first concern with reference to some representative interpretations. First of all, the traditional interpretation has followed the scheme of the Apostles' Creed, which Calvin's first *Institutes* used, that of the four articles of God, Christ, the Holy Spirit, the church, and so on. Accordingly, this interpretation uses the four articles for the four books of the final *Institutes* and attributes a rather independent position to book 4. Over against this interpretation, Wendel considers the relation with the Creed to remain rather "external and formal" in the *Institutes.* As to the theological contents of the *Institutes*, instead, he divides it into two main parts: book 1, "doctrine of God"; and books 2–4, "the historic revelation and the plan of salvation." Accordingly, Calvin's ecclesiology in book 4 is to be understood in its close relation with book 2, the doctrine of Christ, and book 3, that of the Holy Spirit.[219]

Taking the two-part theory in a similar way to Wendel, but focusing on the new materials added in the last edition, Dowey proposes that Calvin abandoned the Apostles' Creed as the structural guide for the *Institutes* and, instead, employed the scheme of the "double knowledge of God" (*duplex cognitio domini*) or of the two kinds of revelation, namely, "the revelation of God as Creator, and as Redeemer." According to Dowey, book 4 is to be understood in the context of "the knowledge of God the Redeemer" (books 2–4) and, especially, of the immediately preceding book 3, on the Holy Spirit.[220] On the other hand, unlike Wendel and Dowey, Parker finds the coexistence of two schemes, literary and theological, in the final *Institutes.* As to its literary scheme, the *Institutes* used the creed's four articles for the four books on God the Father, Christ, the Holy Spirit, and the church. As to its theological scheme, however, Parker analyzes the two parts of the *Institutes*, book 1 and books 2–4, corresponding to the division of "knowledge of God" and "knowledge of man," the division that Calvin first used in the opening of the first *Institutes.*[221]

Although there are other interpretations, the above representative interpretations seemingly suggest at least two issues: the question of whether Calvin abandoned the creedal scheme remains unsolved; book 4 is to be placed in the context of Christology (book 2) and pneumatology (book 3). In the following pages, we will survey what we consider the final expression of Calvin's ecclesiology, Reformation ecclesiology, under three points. The first point concerns the unique title of book 4, the second point analyzes its internal structure

219. Wendel, *Calvin*, 120–21.

220. E. A. Dowey Jr., *The Knowledge of God in Calvin's Theology* (New York and London: Columbia University Press, 1965), 41–49.

221. Parker, *John Calvin*, 130–31.

as well as Calvin's intention in arranging the final form, and the third point focuses on the images of the church in the Reformation era or what we may call his vision of the Reformation church. Since the *Institutes* did not freely describe the church's images as in the *Psalms Commentary*, as to the third point, we use his *Lectures on Daniel* as a supplement.

(1) The Title of Book 4: "The Society of Christ" and "the External Means or Aids"

Generally known as Calvin's ecclesiology, book 4, "The External Means or Aids by Which God Invites Us into the Society of Christ and Holds Us Therein," noticeably did not contain the word "church." This alone made the title unusual, but the two expressions, "the society of Christ" (*Christi societas*) and "the external means or aids" (*externa media vel adminicula*), were also peculiar. What was his intention behind these terms?

(i) Calvin's choice of the first term, "the society of Christ," suggested something new in his intention. He used neither "the whole number of the elect" nor "the spiritual kingdom of Christ." In the first *Institutes*, he used two basic concepts of the church, "the whole number of the elect," which he identified with "the holy Catholic church" of the Apostles' Creed, and "the congregation of believers." Furthermore, he effectively related these two concepts to "the kingdom of Christ" as a reality, simultaneously superhistorical yet manifested in history. He called "the whole number of the elect" "one church and society and one people," and he also called "the congregation of believers" "the common society of Christianity." As far as the first *Institutes* was concerned, he could relate "society" with either "the whole number of the elect" or "the congregation of believers."

(ii) The fact that Calvin used two new terms, "the society of Christ" and "the external means or aids," in the title of the final *Institutes*, book 4 suggested his fresh ecclesiological perspective. In a preamble to book 4 (4.1.1–3), he made his intention clear. First of all, recapitulating the gist of books 2 and 3 in the sentence, "it is by faith in the gospel that Christ becomes ours and we are made partakers of the salvation and eternal blessedness brought by him," Calvin affirmed that "in our ignorance and sloth we need outward helps to beget and increase faith within us, and advance it to its goal." In this connection, he presented a list of his discussions in this fashion: "our plan of instruction now requires us to discuss the church and its government, order and power; then the sacraments; and lastly the civil order."[222] If the list's three divisions

222. *Institutio* 4.1.1: *OS* 5:1. Cf. n. 131 above. As to the first division of the list, we consider the church's "government" (polity) subdivided into the "order" of ministry and "power." In

indicated the entire scope of his ecclesiology and if he summarized the spectrum of three divisions in the humble phrase "external means or aids," then what was the reality of "the society of Christ" envisioned by Calvin? How was this reality related to his image of the creed's "holy Catholic church" or that of the "orchestra" of the European theater and "the spiritual glory of Christ's Kingdom" in his *Psalms Commentary*?[223]

(iii) In the preamble, Calvin worked over the texts of the 1539 and the 1543 *Institutes* and reduced their rather extensive arguments on the creed's two terms, "the holy Catholic church" and "the communion of saints," into two concise sections (4.1.2–3). Over against the previous texts that basically treated the creedal terms from the perspective of God's election with a resulting emphasis on the church's invisibility, he treated them more cautiously and introduced a nuanced distinction between them.

As to "the holy Catholic church," Calvin closely related the church's catholicity and unity to two notions of God's election and the elect's union with Christ in history. On the identity of "the multitude of the elect," for example, he concluded that "we must leave to God alone the knowledge of the church, whose foundation is his secret election." At the same time, he affirmed that "all the elect are so united in Christ that, as they are dependent on one Head, they also grow together into one body."[224] Along with the balance of these two notions, it should be noted that Calvin dropped two assertions prominently held in the previous texts. One concerned the causal relationship between the creed's first three articles (*credo in*) and the fourth article (*credo*), or between the Triune God's work as the "cause" and the church and so forth as its "effect." In the previous editions, he stated that the Triune God's work for our salvation would not be completed "until coming down to the church, the forgiveness of sins, and the life everlasting." The other assertion concerned Calvin's high view of the Catholic church's unity, which he had expressed in a fashion similar to a famous Cyprianic formula: "scripture pronounces that without the unity of the church there is no salvation."[225] These two omissions were coordinated with Calvin's intent in the title and were indications of allowing no foundation

the main text, we see the church's "power" further subdivided into the power to formulate articles of faith, to make laws, and to exercise jurisdiction, including discipline.

223. *CO* 32:361 (135:13); 31:805 (87:7).

224. *Institutio* 4.1.2: *OS* 5:2–4. Cf. chapter 1, n. 136. The precise expression since the 1536 *Institutes*, "the whole number of the elect" (*universus electorum numerus*) is replaced by a more nuanced expression, "the multitude of the elect" (*electorum turba*).

225. *CO* 1:538–39: "nisi ad ecclesiam, peccatorum remissionem, et vitam aeternam, descendat"; "quando extra ecclesiae unitatem nullam esse salute scriptura pronunciat."

of the church's existence other than the Triune God. They also witnessed his strong conviction that the church, even the creed's "holy Catholic church," was but one of the "external means or aids."

As to "the communion of saints," in the last section of the preamble (4.1.3), Calvin made his intention clearer by freshly introducing two points of emphasis. The first point appeared in his discussion on the creed's fourth article. Since the article's "holy Catholic church," he said, "also applies to some extent to the outward church, . . . 'the communion of saints' is added." In this context he used the term "the society of Christ" for the first time in the main text: "the saints are gathered into the society of Christ on the principle that whatever benefits God confers upon them, they should in turn share with one another." The second point appeared in Calvin's discussion on the certainty of "the communion of saints." Since this communion "stands in God's election," he affirmed, "we are not bidden to distinguish between reprobate and elect—that is for God alone, not for us, to do." In order to make this certainty established in our hearts, he emphasized our necessary recognition of the Triune God's operation and concluded that the communion of saints consists of "all those who by the kindness of God the Father through the working of the Holy Spirit, have entered into fellowship with Christ."[226] These two points of emphasis were coordinated with Calvin's intent in the title and were indications of allowing no foundation other than the Triune God for the church's reason for being as "the society of Christ."

(2) Internal Structure and Intention of Rearrangements

To analyze the internal structure of book 4 theologically is not an easy task and it is not our design to do so here. To help our understanding, however, a casual and descriptive survey of its contents can be presented in five sections: (a) an introductory section dealing with the fundamental issues of the church concept (chs. 1–2); (b) the section corresponding to the extensive addition of the third *Institutes*, what we have called the "form" of church government (chs. 3–12); (c) a single chapter on vows (ch. 13); (d) a section dealing with the issues of the sacraments including the Evangelical sacraments, the Catholic

226. *Institutio* 4.1.3: *OS* 5:4–7. Cf. *CO* 1:541–42. Cf. M. C. Sanchez, *Calvin and the Resignification of the World: Creation, Incarnation, and the Problem of Political Theology in the 1559 Institutes* (Cambridge: Cambridge University Press, 2019), 43–82. Under the general theme of Calvin's "resignification of the world," Sanchez defines the 1559 *Institutes* as Calvin's "writing reform" and says that it is meant to be "a gift for the benefit of 'God's Church.' In some important way, this text is for community's formation and its use" (49).

Mass, and so-called "five false sacraments" (chs. 14–19); (e) the last section on civil government (ch. 20). A prima facie survey of book 4 gives us an impression that its freshly added materials are surprisingly not as extensive as the new additions made in both the second and third *Institutes*. Of course, there are some exceptions: the opening portion of chapter 1 (4.1.1–6) that we will discuss later, Calvin's refutation of Servetus's view on infant baptism (4.16.31), a discussion on Christ's corporeal presence in the Lord's Supper (4.17.30–34), and a small yet important addition in the last chapter concerning the resistance to civil power (4.20.32). Since, besides the rearrangement of the old materials, there are numerous revisions that he has made in both strengthening and supplementing the arguments of the previous editions, book 4 is a fresh work worthy of the last expression of his ecclesiology. In the following pages, we will selectively examine some of the newly added materials and extensive rearrangements of old materials in order to assess Calvin's intention for book 4.

Fundamental Notions of the Church in Chapters 1–2

(i) As noted above, Calvin considered the first three opening sections (preamble: 4.1.1–3) an independent introduction to the entire book 4. His intention was to show a framework of his ecclesiology by briefly describing the church's reason for being, the contents of book 4, and two ecclesiological themes of God's secret election and the Triune God's operation, drawn from the fourth article of the Apostles' Creed.

In the first section (4.1.1), following the logical flow of book 2 (salvation achieved in Christ) and book 3 (salvation brought to the faithful through the work of the Holy Spirit), Calvin opened book 4 with an affirmation of the church's reason for being, that God would use the church as the "external means and aids" in order to accomplish salvation in the faithful. Then, he briefly described the contents of book 4, what he called "plan of instruction" (*docendi ratio*). His description could be summarized as the fundamental notions of the church (chs. 1–2), and its government, namely, the ministerial "order" (chs. 3–7) and "power" (chs. 8–13), "the sacraments" (chs. 14–19), and "the civil order/administration" (ch. 20).[227] Here, he called for the reader's attention to "those corruptions by which Satan, in the papacy, has polluted everything God had appointed for our salvation." Interestingly, he reaffirmed his old conviction, expressed in the first *Institutes*, of the conflict between Christ's kingdom and the kingdom of Satan and popes, thus placing the entire book 4

227. *Institutio* 4.1.1: *OS* 5:1.

in the context of this historical conflict. He introduced here the notion of the church as "mother of the faithful" (*mater ecclesia*). His closing sentence (4.1.1), "for those whom he [God] is Father the church may also be Mother," moreover, was not a reference to Cyprian, as every reader would have expected, but only to Paul's testimony of the heavenly Jerusalem as "our mother" (Gal 4:26). This was an indication of Calvin's consistent biblicism that was to govern the entire scope of his discussions on the church of the Reformation era.[228]

In the following two sections of the preamble (4.1.2–3), Calvin referred to two phrases, "the holy Catholic church" and "communion of the saints" of the Apostles' Creed. Strictly speaking, however, there he neither explained the creedal expressions nor made an invisible or visible distinction, but considered the two sections a kind of device to introduce a certain conclusion. In section 2, he argued that the foundation of either the creed's "holy Catholic church" or "the universal church" in history was only in God and concluded that "we must leave to God alone the knowledge of his church, whose foundation is his secret election."[229] In section 3, likewise, he discussed the "communion of the saints" that was generally understood as an entity visibly identifiable. Thus, on the one hand, God alone was entitled to discern the elect, and we were not bidden to do so; on the other hand, we were bidden "to establish with certainty in our hearts that all those who by the kindness of God the Father, through the working of the Holy Spirit have entered into fellowship with Christ are set apart as God's property and personal possession." As noted above in connection with the title, this conclusion balanced his two ecclesiological themes of God's secret election and the Triune God's operation.[230]

228. *Instituto* 4.1.1: *OS* 5:1–2. According to Oort (J. van Oort, "John Calvin and the Church Fathers," in *The Reception of the Church Fathers in the West: From the Carolingians to the Maurists*, ed. I. Backus [Leiden: Brill, 1997], 2:684, 687), the final *Institutes* witnesses the predominant citations of Augustine. After Augustine, Gregory the Great, Chrysostom, and Cyprian are among the most frequently cited Fathers. Oort also notes that Cyprian is "particularly quoted in the ecclesiastical sections" of the *Institutes*. As far as the basic notion of the church in book 4 is concerned, however, a remark of I. Backus (*Historical Method and Confessional Identity in the Era of the Reformation (1378–1615)* [Leiden and Boston: Brill, 2003], 52–54) is noteworthy: "One striking feature of both these theologians' [Calvin's and Beza's] concept of the Church is that Augustine is hardly mentioned at all." On Calvin's reference to "mother," here, the editors of the *Opera Selecta* and *Institutes*, ed. McNeill, refer to Cyprian's *De Catholicae Ecclesiae Unitate* (251). Unlike the traditional Catholic use of the notion "mater ecclesia" as the indispensable, salvific institution, however, Calvin radically reinterprets it in the context of the church's "education" rather than of "salvation" and as "an external" rather than "indispensable" aid.

229. *Institutio* 4.1.2: *OS* 5:2–3.

230. *Institutio* 4.1.3: *OS* 5:5–7.

Since Calvin made the bold statement "it is now our intention to discuss the visible church" at the very beginning of the section (4.1.4) immediately following the preamble, this conclusion was significant for the formative history of the *Institutes* as well as for his own ecclesiology. While he excluded the topic of "the whole number of the elect" or "multitude of the elect" from the scope of his ecclesiology in the final *Institutes*, he allocated the entire twenty chapters of book 4, starting from chapter 1, section 4, to the loci of the church in history. To be precise, this was the church where the Triune God would be active in forming the faithful as members of "the society of Christ." What was Calvin's motive behind this ecclesiological shift? It could be said that he was reinforcing his apologetic stance of "the legitimate form of the church" that was presented first in the third *Institutes* and was positioned over and against the Catholic ecclesial hierarchy. It could also be said that his apologetics for the Evangelical churches would focus not on the identity of the true church of the elect but instead on presenting them as one historical entity, which we may call "the Reformation church."

(ii) The first topic on the visible church was a very unique portion of three sections (4.1.4–6) that defined the church's mission as "education" through God's word and the ministers of the church. Although "education" was the common theme, each section characteristically described it from a unique angle. For instance, section 4 recaptured the "mater ecclesia" notion of section 1 and called the church that mother's "school" and the faithful its "pupils." It affirmed that "away from her bosom one cannot hope for any forgiveness of sins or any salvation, as Isaiah and Joel testify." This section was Calvin's rewriting of the text of the 1539 *Institutes*, and the last sentence quoted above was his replacement of Cyprian's famous saying (*extra ecclesiae unitatem nullam esse salutem*). In replacing Cyprian's "outside the church's unity" by "away from her [mother's] bosom" and in quoting all scriptural supports exclusively from the prophetic books including the Psalms, Calvin sharpened both his apologetic edge against Catholic ecclesiasticism and its effective appeal to Cyprian's authority. By so doing he reinforced his consistent biblicist stance.[231]

Section 5 was the longest of the three and contained the expression "the education of the church" as well as a paraphrase of the Ephesian text (4: 10–13),

231. *Institutio* 4.1.4: *OS* 5:7. Cf. n. 228 above; *CO* 1:539. For the whole history of Calvin's "reception" of the Cyprian text, confer A. Zillenbiller, *Die Einheit der Katholischen Kirche: Calvins Cyprianrezeption in seinen Ekklesiologischen Schriften* (Mains: Verlag Philipp von Zabern, 1993).

which we have previously considered as a concise expression of his ecclesiological vision. The paraphrase affirmed that Christ had appointed the apostles, prophets, evangelists, pastors, and teachers to the church "for equipment of the saints, for the work of the ministry, for the building up of the body of Christ, until we all reach the unity of the faith and of the knowledge of the Son of God, to perfect manhood, to the measure of the fully mature age of Christ."[232] Then, Calvin added a lengthy discussion on the notion of God's "accommodation" and its relation to the church's "education." He defined "accommodation" as God's way of accommodating his power to the conditions of the church and believers so as to achieve the intended goal. Such statements as "God, who could in a moment perfect his own, nevertheless desires them to grow up into manhood solely under the education of the church" and "although God's power is not bound to outward means, he has nonetheless bound us to this ordinary manner of teaching" only indicated Calvin's vision of the Evangelical churches as humble and as "external means."[233]

The last section concerned the Evangelical camp's internal conflict concerning a key element of the church's "education": the preaching of God's word. Researchers and the editors of the text have identified what Calvin called the "great controversy" as the conflicting views between Luther and Zwingli. Following his usual manner of not naming controverters, he summarized their conflicting views on the preaching ministry in this fashion: "Some exaggerate its dignity beyond measure. Others contend that what belongs to the Holy Spirit is wrongly transferred to mortal men—if we suppose that ministers and teachers penetrate into minds and hearts and so correct both blindness of mind and hardness of heart." Instead of refuting them, he followed his own approach proposed in his dedicatory epistle to Grynaeus in the *Romans Commentary*, namely, to search for a better and more correct interpretation in order to resolve the conflict. Indeed, he took a middle ground and tried to reach an acceptable understanding of the preaching ministry in Evangelical Christianity.[234] It could be assumed that behind this controversy he saw the danger of two opposite and extreme positions—Catholic clericalism and the

232. *Institutio* 4.1.5: *OS* 5:7–8.

233. *Institutio* 4.1.5: *OS* 5:8–9; M. de Kroon, *The Honour of God and Human Salvation*, trans. J. Vriend and L. D. Bierma (Edinburgh and New York: T&T Clark, 2001), 147–70. In the chapter titled "God's Honour and the External Means of Salvation," Kroon presents a good analysis of Calvin's notion of "external means" mainly taken from book 4 of the final *Institutes*.

234. *Institutio* 4.1.6: *OS* 5:11–12.

Anabaptist submission of preaching under the congregational power—and he presented the unified Evangelical position, including the conflicting views of Luther and Zwingli.

(iii) What was Calvin's intention when he placed chapter 2, "A Comparison of the False and the True Church," in this introductory portion of book 4? The title expressed nothing new, but what was new consisted mainly of two aspects: he identified "the false church" exclusively with the Roman Catholic Church and even omitted references to the Anabaptists, which he had occasionally mentioned in various editions of the *Institutes*; by adding a new caption to the chapter and placing it here, he declared that the entire scope of his ecclesiology was squarely set against the Roman Catholic Church. As far as its ecclesiological analysis was concerned, we will not repeat here what we have discussed with regard to the third *Institutes*, but will instead focus on two concluding remarks that Calvin made in the last section (4.2.12) of the chapter. The first was the above-mentioned notion that "we categorically deny to the papists the title of the church." This judgment was based upon the church's two marks of God's word and the sacraments, in this regard, the term "title" represented the church's essential identity as Christ's church.[235] Having denied the "title" to their church, he acknowledged that in "form" there remained a church which they claimed to be Christ's Catholic church. Then he introduced the second conclusion that "we are only contending about the true and lawful constitution of the church, required in communion not only of the sacraments but also especially of doctrine." In other words, he was presenting newly defined apologetics that critically compared the "form" of the Roman Catholic Church and the "legitimate form" of the Evangelical churches.[236] In addition, under the "legitimate form," his new apologetic stance encompassed the rest of the entire book 4 including the ecclesiological loci of the sacraments (4.14–19) and political administration (4.20), which the third *Institutes* did not include under the scope of the "legitimate form." His presentation here was the "legitimate form" of the Evangelical churches over against what he considered the "false form" of the papal church, which the Council of Trent (1545–63) was currently reconfirming in full force. This was a definite reason for his rearrangement of book 4 and, we assume, it reflected the vision of his "Reformation church."

235. *Institutio* 4.2.12: *OS* 5:41. Cf. *CO* 1:560, n. 129 above.
236. *Institutio* 4.2.12: *OS* 5:42.

New Additions and Rearrangements in the Rest of Book 4

There are a few noteworthy new additions and rearrangements in the main body of book 4. However, we will examine only two loci, church jurisdiction (discipline) and the Lord's Supper, as representative cases.

(i) As to the first case, our study has traced Calvin's notion of church discipline from his first *Institutes* onward and has focused on the development of his interpretation of the "church" in Matthew 18:17. His final and refined expression appeared in the beginning of his discussions on ecclesiastical jurisdiction (4.11.1). On the power of the keys passage in Matthew 18, he affirmed that this "passage does not deal with the general doctrinal authority, as do Matt. 16:19 and John 20:23, but that the jurisdiction of the Sanhedrin is for the future transferred to Christ's flock." In essence, this statement was recapitulating what he affirmed in his third *Institutes*, that Christ's reference was to the disciplinary custom of the Jewish synagogues, namely, a council of priest and elders from the people. It was also recapitulating what he stated in his *Synoptic Gospels Commentary* of 1555 that, after the return from Babylonian captivity, this custom of the "elected council" of elders was called the "Sanhedrin" and that, by referring to the "church" in "Tell it to the church" (Matt 18:17), Christ intended that same order under the Law was to be kept in his church of the new covenant. This presbyterial system of discipline was formally presented as an integral part of the church's "legitimate form" in the final *Institutes*.[237]

(ii) As to the second case of the Lord's Supper, Calvin polished his twofold apologetic stance of his anti-Catholic polemic and his irenic approach to mediate the Protestant discord, the stance he had maintained since his first *Institutes*. On the one hand, he highlighted the meaning of the Supper as "a spiritual banquet," "the life-giving bread, upon which our souls feed unto true and blessed immortality," and a "high mystery." By contrast, he accused the papists of preventing the faithful from partaking of this spiritual blessing and for causing the controversies over the Supper. Further, he boldly attributed the real cause of the controversies, involving the Catholic errors and obstructions as well as even the Protestant discord, to "Satan," who not only had deprived the church, and especially "simple folk," of the true Supper but also had "tried the same trick in our own day." On the other hand, he characterized his "irenic approach" as such: "after summarizing the matter in a way intelligible to the unlearned, I shall resolve those difficulties with which Satan has tried to

237. *Institutio* 4.11.1: *OS* 5:342. Cf. *CO* 1:649; *CO* 45:514–15; Maruyama, *The Ecclesiology*, 100–101; McKee, *Elders*, 34–37.

ensnare the world."[238] If by "the unlearned" he had in mind "the simple folk" within both the Catholic and the Protestant folds, and by resolving "those difficulties" he intended to include both his anti-Catholic polemics and his mediating effort to solve the Protestant discord, this might indicate his new apologetic vista that was reflecting his vision of the Reformation church.

What was Calvin's new apologetic vista? As we have seen in the first *Institutes*, Calvin started his doctrine of the Lord's Supper from the notion of the God-given "promise," and mediated the conflict between Luther and Zwingli from a "framework," which was a kind of Chalcedonian orthodox solution to harmonize the conflicting schools of Alexandria and Antioch. In this respect, book 4, chapter 17 on the Supper presented his own view, which was also his mediating effort to solve the discord. The same spirit prevailed in a newly added portion (4.17.30–34) that served as his response to an unfortunate controversy with Westphal, the Lutheran apologist. Starting from his own Antiochene Christological stand of "distinction, but not separation," he presented his case, which was to refute two crucial points of the Lutheran emphasis, the "ubiquity" of Christ's resurrected body and the reception by the unbelievers of its grace in partaking of the communion. But his presentation had to do more with persuasion than refutation. In concluding this portion, furthermore, he appealed to the authority of Augustine, whom he considered close to the Chalcedonian orthodox solution.[239]

(3) Vision of the Reformation Church

Our study has finally come to the last question. What was the reality of the church Calvin envisioned in his last years, especially in his doctrinal summa, the 1559 *Institutes*, supplemented by the lectures on the prophetic books of Daniel, Jeremiah, and Ezekiel? As we have already examined, he had established both the "Catholic" and the "Reformed" ecclesiologies, affirmed the universal, Evangelical church to the exclusion of papalism and Anabaptism as two extremes, and refined the church's Catholic principles as well as its "legitimate form" as the Reformed polity. Upon these ecclesiologies, we assume, he had drawn up a vision of what we may call "the Reformation church" in his last *Institutes* and published lectures on Daniel (1561), Jeremiah (1563), and Ezekiel (1565). In the following pages, we shall selectively examine three themes that we assume to be his fresh reflections on the Reformation church:

238. *Institutio* 4.17.1: *OS* 5:342.
239. *Institutio* 4.17.30–37: *OS* 5:387–98.

the Reformation church's internal unity, symbolized even in the most controversial doctrine of the Lord's Supper; its external harmony and tension existing in the church-state relationship; and its prophetic dimension expressed in the relationship between the extrahistorical kingdom of Christ and the church in history. The first two themes are drawn from book 4 of the final *Institutes* and the last from the lectures on Daniel, which coincided with the final stage of the editing and publishing of the 1559 *Institutes* and revealed his prophetic self-awareness as well as his most illuminating picture of the kingdom-church relationship.[240]

The Reformation Church's Internal Unity in the Lord's Supper

Since we have already mentioned Calvin's doctrine of the Lord's Supper expressed in book 4, chapter 17 in connection with the "legitimate form" of the Evangelical churches, here we focus on it as a symbol of the church's internal unity. In the first *Institutes*, Calvin tried to harmonize variant eucharistic teachings within the Evangelical churches into the Catholic tradition of the ancient church. Over the two decades since then, he had engaged in dialogues with Melanchthon, Bucer, Bullinger and others, and in controversies with the Catholic apologists as well as the Lutheran theologians, notably Westphal and Hesshus. In addition, he personally signed an important Lutheran-Reformed agreement, the *Wittenberg Concord*, and he negotiated with Bullinger an intramural Reformed agreement, the *Consensus Tigurinus*. Against this background, he made some substantial revisions and refined his final position. As the result of the revisions, we assume, he tried to portray the vivid and mysterious character of the Reformation church as one eucharistic community.

(i) At the opening of chapter 17, Calvin revised the previous texts and presented a threefold aim, namely, to orient the Lord's Supper in the Trinitarian framework, to highlight God's household character of the church as the eucharistic community, and to emphasize the reality of the Supper as "high mystery" as well as the importance of its proper teaching in the church. In keeping the

240. *Praelectiones in Librum Prophetiarum Danielis*; *BC* 61/20, 1561. Cf. T. H. L. Parker, *Calvin's Old Testament Commentaries* (Edinburgh: T&T Clark, 1986), 219; P. Wilcox, "The Lectures of John Calvin," *Archiv für Reformationsgeschichte* 87 (1996): 140. Disregarding the canonical order, Calvin lectured on the book of Daniel ahead of Jeremiah (1560), Lamentations (1560–62), and twenty-one chapters of Ezekiel (1563–64). As the editors of the *Bibliotheca Calviniana* indicate (*BC* 59/4, 709), Calvin finalized the last *Institutes* in the winter of 1558–59, and its preface was dated August 1, 1559. Calvin's Daniel lectures began in June 1559 and continued to April 1560.

Christological framework of prior editions intact, firstly, the newly revised text affirmed God as the initiator of the Supper, then Christ as God's viceroy present at the Supper, and further the Holy Spirit that by "the secret power" made it effective to the faithful.[241] Secondly, the goal of the Supper was clearly defined as God's forming of "the household of the Father" (*patrisfamilia*), "the society of his Church" through Christ the Son. An overwhelming emphasis was laid here on the oneness and unity of God's household through God's goodness and Christ's intermediary works.[242] As to the Supper's mystical character, thirdly, Calvin combined the emphasis of the previous editions, "the mystery of Christ's secret union with the devout," which was by nature "incomprehensible," with the new edition's emphasis on Christ's presence and "the secret power of the Holy Spirit" in the Supper. Then he emphasized the importance of the right understanding of the Supper not only by the learned but also by the unlearned "simple folk."[243] His intention behind the threefold aim in the revision seemed to reflect his vision of the Reformation church as one eucharistic community.

(ii) Although Calvin's presentation in this chapter was genuinely his own, it should be noted that he carefully avoided making it overly polemical, but instead orchestrated his discussions into what he believed to be the common ground for the entire Evangelical camp. To illustrate this point, for example, twice in the 1559 text (17.1, 9) he referred to the current discord and confusion over the Lord's Supper as Satan's work and urged more serious and careful efforts to resolve difficulties, as if he were presenting his own as an example. With regard to the Lutheran emphases on the real presence and real eating of Christ's body in the Supper, he seemed to go as far as the *Wittenberg Concord* could affirm. By calling some Lutheran theologians "good masters" and "good zealots" (17.23, 24), however, he carefully yet firmly delineated his position over the points of difference (17.16–31). With regard to the Zwinglian position, he affirmed the core points of the *Consensus Tigurinus*, but seemingly subdued the differences between the Zwinglian and his own position. In 17.6 he even said that "I now pass over those who would have the Supper only a mark of outward profession." In this regard, one section (17.32) was particularly unique. He used the texts of all five major editions of the *Institutes* and weaved them to express his own conviction on the real presence of Christ's body in the Supper, not just an alternative to the Lutheran ubiquity, but as a highly mystical yet comprehensive opinion of the real presence. The section began with the 1543

241. *Institutio* 4.17.1, 10: *OS* 5:342–43, 351. Cf. *CO* 1:991–92.

242. *Institutio* 4.17.1: *OS* 5:342.

243. *Institutio* 4.17.1–10: *OS* 5:343–54.

text, which sounded as if it were his personal confession: "that it [the real presence] is a secret too lofty for either my mind to comprehend or my words to declare, . . . I rather experience than understand it." More notably, however, he connected the analogy of Christ's spiritual kingdom and the church in history with the question of the real presence: "For as Christ's whole Kingdom is spiritual, whatever he does with his church must not be subjected to the reason of this world . . . such is the presence of the body."[244] As we have examined before, Calvin's scope of the kingdom-church relation was universal or, at least, pan-European. Thus, we might assume from this analogy that he envisioned the visible reality of the European Evangelical churches as a whole in celebrating this life-giving mystery of Christ's real presence in the Supper. We might properly call this reality Calvin's vision of the Reformation church.

External Harmony and Tension in the Church-State Relation

As we have noted in chapter 1, historians of political thought usually view Calvin's contribution to it rather minimally, if not negatively. Reflecting this trend, Oakley acknowledges the importance of the mainstream Reformers' reinterpretations of the medieval *Corpus Christianum*. But he summarizes Calvin's position in two points, namely, "a clear note of reserve about the role of the temporal authority in matters religious" and "the independence and superiority of the clerical authority."[245] However, our examination of the 1536 *Institutes* has found the young humanist's interpretation to be not a defense of the medieval status quo but a fresh interpretation of the church-state relation from the notions of Christ's kingdom and Christian freedom. It reflected his conviction of the "inviolable order" set in Scripture, in God's theocratic rule of the Old Testament, as well as the Christ's kingdom–church scheme of the New Testament.

(i) The fact that Calvin had kept the topic of "political administration" basically intact throughout the various editions, ending in the final edition's book

244. *Institutio* 4.17.32: *OS* 5:390–91. Cf. *OS* 1:143. (Battles, trans., *Institution*, 146.) For Calvin's relationship with the Swiss Reformed churches, see B. Gordon's article "Calvin and the Swiss Reformed Churches," in *Calvinism in Europe, 1540–1620*, ed. A. Pettegree, A. Duke, and G. Lewis (Cambridge: Cambridge University Press, 1994), 64–81. Gordon highlights Calvin's "accommodating" stance and his interest in achieving a closer tie between the Swiss alliance and his French interests.

245. F. Oakley, "Christian Obedience and Authority, 1520–1550," in *The Cambridge History of Political Thought, 1450–1700*, ed. J. H. Burn (Cambridge: Cambridge University Press, 1991), 185. Cf. chapter 1, n. 182.

4, chapter 20, was somewhat curious, since during this period he had observed the unsettling situations in the Evangelical camp. In the Lutheran lands, Luther's initial theological insight of the two kingdoms theory had been largely compromised. On the Reformed side, he himself had witnessed the failing of Bucer's reform efforts in Strasbourg, the Zwinglian formula under the leadership of Bullinger, which had never been a satisfactory model for him, and his own efforts in Geneva having taken more than a decade to achieve a workable solution. Above all, he had been facing the rapidly changing and critical situations in his homeland, France. Nonetheless, he did make some revisions in the final edition which, though by no means major, seemingly reflected his deep concern for what he considered "inviolable order" being challenged and somewhat broken. If this assumption was correct, it was reflected in two focal points of the revisions. One appeared in the opening section (20.1) on the general scheme of a twofold government of the spiritual and the temporal, and the other was in the closing sections (20.30–32) on the particular issue of obedience and resistance to political authority.[246]

(ii) In the opening section, by saying "necessity compels me," Calvin acknowledged an urgent need to counter two opponents. He inserted in the original 1536 text the following sentence: "from one side, insane and barbarous men furiously strive to overturn this divinely established order; while, on the other side, the flatterers of princes, immoderately praising their power, do not hesitate to set them against the rule of God himself." Both the *Opera selecta* and McNeill's edition of the *Institutes* note the first adversary to be the Anabaptists and the second Machiavelli's *The Prince*.[247] As far as the 1559 revisions are concerned, this inserted sentence has considerable bearing, since

246. Although Oakley ("Christian Obedience," 186) considers these revisions "a few ambivalent sentences" and Höpfl (*Christian Polity*, 147) offers a negative summary ("Calvin had nothing new to teach, and he was certainly quite unwilling to learn"), our study finds in the revisions Calvin's genuine sense of the crisis that the entire Evangelical camp was facing in Europe.

247. *Institutio* 4.20.1: *OS* 5:471–72nn9–10; *Institutes*, ed. McNeill, 1548n4. Höpfl (*Christian Polity*, 149n81) challenges the *Opera Selecta* editors' judgment on the reference to Machiavelli and, without offering an alternative reference, concludes that "Calvin himself nowhere deigned to notice that work [*The Prince*] or to formulate a reply to it; it is not apparent that he had ever heard of it." Since Calvin's short second sentence does not use any phrase from *The Prince*, Höpfl may have a basis for the challenge. However, R. Bireley (*The Counter Reformation Prince: Anti-Machiavellianism or Catholic Statecraft in Early Modern Europe* [Chapel Hill: University of North Carolina Press, 1990], 14) indicates the increasing influence of Machiavelli's book, especially in France, the availability of its French translation besides many Italian editions and a Latin translation, and the fact that it was placed on the

he followed up the first adversary in a completely fresh section (20.5) and the second in at least two revised sections (20.8–9). If the second reference was indeed to Machiavelli's work, the combination of the Anabaptists and Machiavelli seemed rather strange. As we have examined the 1536 *Institutes*, Calvin regarded Christian society as an ellipse with two foci of church and state, and above it he placed Christ's spiritual kingdom. For him, God's "inviolable order" meant the harmonious balance in the triangular relationship of Christ's kingdom–church, Christ's kingdom–state, and church-state. As to the first relation of Christ's kingdom–church, he considered papalism, by its claim of spiritual dominion, guilty of usurpation of Christ's kingdom. As to the second relation of Christ's kingdom–state, he blamed the Münster Anabaptism's claim of Christ's Messianic rule on earth as "Jewish folly." From this background, we assume, what Calvin faced in the 1559 revisions was the issue of the third relation, church-state. As a matter of fact, immediately after the fresh insertion quoted above, he resumed the 1536 paragraph in which appeared a definitive sentence, "Christ's spiritual Kingdom and the civil jurisdiction are things completely distinct."[248]

Calvin's apologetics against the Anabaptists showed nothing new in substance. However, his placing the Anabaptists exclusively in the perspective of the church-state relation was something new. He accused the Anabaptists of "anarchy," which would be brought about through their argument that there is a "servile kind of government totally incompatible today with the perfection which Christ brought with his gospel." Perhaps his allusion was to the *Schleitheim Confession* (art. 4), where "sword" (magisterial power) was said to be "an ordering of God outside the perfection of Christ." Further, he interpreted this as a rejection of the magistracy as the protector of Christianity and accordingly accused the Anabaptists of "anarchy."[249] Against the second adversary, Machiavelli, however, his defense (20.8–9) seemed more complex. Already in an earlier section (20.2) of the 1536 text on the "appointed end" of civil government, he added a fresh qualifying sentence, "to cherish and protect the outward worship of God, to defend sound doctrine of piety and the position of the church." If he also had in mind here Machiavelli's teachings that claimed

Index of Pope Paul IV in 1559. We assume it extremely hard to theorize that Calvin did not or failed to recognize the adverse effects of Machiavelli's work, especially in France.

248. *Institutio* 4.20.1: *OS* 5:427. Cf. chapter 1, section 3.3 above.

249. *Institutio* 4.20.5: *OS* 5:475. Cf. *Creeds and Confessions*, 2:699. Both the *Opera Selecta* and *Institutes*, ed. McNeill (1490n16) consider Calvin's remark on Christian perfection a reference to Zwingli's work of 1525, *De Vera et Falsa Religione Commentarius* (*CR: Zwingli* 3:875), the work that Calvin had already used for the 1536 *Institutes*.

all religions to be man-made, with Christianity as an inferior religion due to its end to serve the state, Calvin's defense affirmed civil government to be the defender of the church's worship and moral teachings.[250]

In section 8, where the classical discourses on the ideal forms of democracy, aristocracy, and monarchy were treated, his preference of "aristocracy or a system compounded of aristocracy and democracy" was well known. Immediately after this, however, he added the 1559 qualifying text "because it is very rare for kings so to control themselves" and defended his preference as "safer and more bearable" than monarchy.[251] In section 9, the 1559 text dealt with the same challenge to the traditional notion of the magistracy as the defender of Christianity, but Calvin defended it with a twist. He expressed his concerns in rhetorical form: "if Scripture did not teach that it [the office of the magistrates] extends to both Tables of the law," and he suggested to learn from the "secular writers" and "philosophers" of the classics, who taught religion as their primary concern. Then, he added an exclamatory sentence: "let Christian princes and magistrates be ashamed of their negligence." If this sounded unusual, more striking was a concluding remark: "this proves the folly of those who would neglect the concern for God and would give attention only to rendering justice among men."[252] To sum up, these fresh revisions in the opening sections revealed Calvin's urgent concerns for the divine order being challenged especially from political quarters, including the possible challenges of Machiavelli.

(iii) Another concentration of noticeable revisions appeared at the chapter's end (20.30–32), where Christian obedience to political authority, with questions of its limit or the possibility of resistance, was the focal point. As many researchers have agreed, this is expressed in the first *Institutes*, in which Calvin penned an apologetic note, "we, from whom not one seditious word was ever heard," in its dedicatory epistle to the King, and retained it up to the last *Institutes*. He had steadily maintained the guideline of obedience, not because of political expediency but due to the demand of the divine order. As far as private persons were concerned, he did not change his strict teaching against political resistance, even in the late 1550s when his followers in the French

250. *Institutio* 4.20.2: *OS* 5:473. The sentence can be meant to be against the Anabaptists as well.

251. *Institutio* 4.20.8: *OS* 5:478. This section may reflect both Calvin's resentment against Machiavelli's preference of political realism over any ideal political forms and his shared conviction with the humanists who generally viewed Machiavelli negatively.

252. *Institutio* 4.20.9: *OS* 5:479–80.

Reformed circle, under the duress of persecutions, began to waver and move beyond that teaching.[253]

This was the background against which Calvin made the final adjustments to his position. The revision in section 30 occurred in the 1539 text that described God's dealings with the ancient kingdoms surrounding the Old Testament people of God, Judah, and Israel. The focus of this section was God's deliverance of his people by using two methods for the punishment of oppressors. One method was using his own "servants," such as Moses against Pharaoh (Exod 3:7–10) and Judge Othniel against the Syrian King (Judg 3:9), and the other, the dynasty changes of non-Jewish nations such as the Egyptians, the Assyrians, the Medes and the Persians. Calvin did not follow up on the second method, but on the first he made a small yet important revision. In describing the acts of such avengers as Moses and Othniel, he revised the previous text of "in rebelling against kings" (*in Reges incurrendo*) with "in taking up arms against kings" (*in Reges arma sumendo*), and he inserted the clause "armed from heaven" (*a caelo armati*) before the sentence "they subdued the lesser power [kings] with the greater [God]."[254] Could this revision suggest an adjustment, if not a change, in his teaching? Could this also suggest a move, for example in the French context, toward possible armed resistance to the king by such Huguenot princes of the Reformed movement as Gaspard de Coligny, Louis de Condé, and others? Incidentally, a related question appeared in the final French translation (1560) of the 1559 *Institutes*, which was generally regarded as Calvin's own work but did not follow the Latin text of the above revisions and instead used the previous text. If this was Calvin's doing and not a translator's unintentional omission of the revisions, and since the final stage of publishing the French edition coincided with the period immediately after the conspiracy of Amboise in March 1560, this might reflect his hesitation over

253. *OS* 1:35. (Battles, trans., *Institution*, 18.) Cf. Doumergue, *Jean Calvin*, 5:486–90; Oakley, "Christian Obedience," 187; R. M. Kingdon, "Calvinism and Resistance Theory, 1550–1580," in *The Cambridge History of Political Thought, 1450–1700*, ed. J. H. Burns (Cambridge: Cambridge University Press, 1991), 193–218.

254. *Institutio* 4.20.30: *OS* 5:500–501. Cf. *CO* 1:1122. Cf. W. R. Stevenson Jr., "Calvin and Political Issues," in *The Cambridge Companion to John Calvin*, ed. D. K. McKim (Cambridge: Cambridge University Press, 2004), 185–86. Both the *Opera Selecta* and *Institutes*, ed. McNeill, do not record this 1559 revision in their textual footnotes. Doumergue (*Jean Calvin*, 5:499) calls this revision "double correction" and its implication as Calvin's "manifestation" of the armed resistance. Referring to Calvin's notion of "open avengers," Stevenson considers it as Calvin's "warning to tyrants" and especially relates it to Calvin's French interests expressed in his lectures on Daniel.

the revisions' possible adverse effects in France.[255] In short, the whole matter of the revisions of the last Latin and French editions seemed to illustrate the precarious nature of the balance that he proposed over and against the rapidly changing and challenging French scene.

In section 31, Calvin retained the exact original 1536 text in which, although a private person's case was categorically denied, the constitutional right of magistrates and institutions to check and resist the tyranny of kings was affirmed. For nearly a quarter century since the first edition appeared, the fact that Calvin had maintained his high hope for the role of the French Three Estates for the remedies of the current religious and political situations was in itself noteworthy.[256] In the very last section of the entire *Institutes* (20.32), however, he inserted an extensive addition to the 1536 text and expanded the discussions onto a new level of what we might call a "prophetic dimension." The revision began with a response to the dictum of the 1536 text, "if they [kings] demand anything against, let it go unesteemed." He affirmed that "on this consideration, Daniel denies that he has committed any offense against the king when he has not obeyed his impious edict." "Conversely" the revision dealt with the case of "a false modesty," in which the people of God, forsaking his command, followed the king's edict and received Hosea's prophetic condemnation. Finally, the revision closed with these climactic statements: "As if God had made over his right to mortal men, giving them the rule over mankind! Or as if earthly power were diminished when it is subjected to its Author, in whose presence even the heavenly powers tremble as suppliants!"[257] In this way, the entire *Institutes* came to a close in the prophetic air of God's majestic presence, and this image witnessed Calvin's acute prophetic self-awareness, and was also a part of his vision of the Reformation church.

(4) The Daniel Lectures: Prophetic Dimension of the Reformation Church

As we have seen, in the last three sections of the 1559 *Institutes*, Calvin had focused on the cases of religious leaders such as Moses and Judge Othniel,

255. Cf. Doumergue, *Jean Calvin*, 5:499; M. Yardeni, "French Calvinist Political Thought, 1534–1715," in *International Calvinism, 1541–1715*, ed. M. Prestwich (Oxford: Oxford University Press, 1985), 315–37. *BC* 60/8 (759, 762) states that the request for publication was made in May 1560 to the Genevan authorities and Calvin's "Advice to the readers" was dated August 1. Benoît, ed., *Institution* (Book 4, 535n3) leaves this question open as either a translator's mistake or Calvin' s hesitation. We consider the latter case more likely.

256. *Institutio* 4.20.31: *OS* 5:501. Cf. chapter 1, n. 200.

257. *Institutio*, 4.20.32: *OS* 5:502. Biblical references are Dan 6:22–23 and Hos 5:13.

the constitutional magistrates, and the prophetic figures of Daniel and Hosea over the question of obedience to the tyrannical kings. This study's last section explores his image of the mid-sixteenth-century church and its surrounding world. To facilitate the question, we choose his *Lectures on Daniel* (1561) because of a few of its unique features, its French context in particular. In addition to the coincidence of the period of the lectures (June 1559 to April 1560) and the completing and publication phases of the last *Institutes*, he disregarded the canonical order and lectured on Daniel ahead of Jeremiah and Ezekiel. As Parker notes, he gave his first lecture immediately after the first national synod of the French Reformed Church (May 1559). Above all, the "Greetings" of the published lectures dated August 1561 was titled "To all God's faithful servants who long for Christ's kingdom to be well ordered in France."[258] The lectures revealed the aged Reformer Calvin's understanding of Christ's kingdom, history, and the church, especially the church in France.

In the opening "Greetings," Calvin summarized Daniel's prophesies that explicitly referred to the Babylonian and Persian (Chaldean) Empires, and he implicitly referred to the Greek (Macedonian) and Roman Empires prior to the advent of Christ. Then he underlined both the prophesies themselves and the usefulness of studying them for the contemporary church as follows: "For what was foretold of the fluctuating and ephemeral splendor of the monarchies and of the perpetual state of Christ's kingdom is no less profitable to know nowadays than of old."[259] From this, we assume, Calvin's orienting theme expounded in the lectures was on the triad of Christ's perpetual kingdom, the earthly kingdoms, and the people of God, the church. Furthermore, the lectures revealed yet another feature that was of his utmost concern, namely, the French context. His choice of the book of Daniel, the nature of his expositions of the texts, and their applications to the current historical contexts all

258. *CO* 18:614; *C. C. Daniel I*, 1. Cf. *B.C.* 61/20, 843; Parker, *Calvin's Old Testament Commentaries*, 219; Muller, "The Hermeneutic of Promise and Fulfillment," 71; Balserak, *John Calvin as Sixteenth-Century Prophet*, 102–26; P. Wilcox, "The 'Restoration of the Church' in Calvin's 'Commentaries in Isaiah the Prophet,'" *Archiv für Reformationsgeschichite* 85 (1994): 68–96. By using Calvin's commentary on Isaiah and not focusing on the concept of Christ's kingdom, Wilcox focuses on Calvin's vision of the church's "restoration, restitution, and reformation," the vison that is close to what this study calls the "prophetic dimension of the Reformation church." For the English translation of Daniel 1–6, we use the Rutherford House translation: *Calvin's Old Testament Commentaries*, vol. 20, *Daniel I (chs. 1–6)*, trans. T. H. L. Parker (Grand Rapids: Eerdmans, 1993), cited as *C. C. Daniel I*. For that of Daniel 7–12, we use the Calvin Translation Society edition, *Calvin's Commentaries*, vol. 13 (Grand Rapids: Baker, 1993), cited as CTS, *Daniel II*.

259. *CO* 18:617; *C. C. Daniel I*, 4.

seemed to reflect the volatile conditions of his homeland, where the Reformed Evangelicals, who were beginning to be called Huguenots, found themselves in anxious suspension with no clear direction of their future.[260] In the lectures, however, the French Reformer's eyes seemed to transcend the historical realities and to focus steadily on Christ's spiritual kingdom vis-à-vis the earthly kingdoms and the church in history. Yet, instead of staying speculatively in the transcendental sphere, he descended to the historical arena, especially to the church as "the visible image of Christ's Kingdom," an expression that may come close to what we may call "the Reformation church."[261] In the following pages, as our last inquiry into Calvin's ecclesiology, we will focus on two main points of the above-mentioned triad relationship. The first is the focus on Christ's kingdom, especially in its relation with the earthly kingdoms. The second is that of the church as "the living image of Christ's Kingdom," especially in its relation with the secular powers.

Christ's Kingdom and the Secular Kingdoms

(i) For Calvin, the first point of Christ's kingdom was a spiritual yet historical concept. In the Daniel lecture (7:14), he commented that, under the providential rule of God the Father, Christ the Son was commissioned to reign over his kingdom (Matt 28:18) in order "to subdue all powers to himself . . . , to restrain the devil, and by God's help to protect and preserve the church as well as all the elect of God the Father."[262] In this quotation, the triad of Christ's kingdom, what he called "the earthly monarchies" (alternatively, "empires/kingdoms"), and the church conceptually distinguished from the elect, were presented. As to Christ's kingdom itself, firstly, Calvin considered its fundamental nature to be "perpetual," while that of the earthly kingdoms to be temporal or perishable. On the prophecy and Daniel's interpretations of "a great statue" in chapter 2, for example, Calvin interpreted the four successive monarchies of Babylon,

260. Cf. n. 240 above. Parker (*Calvin's Old Testament Commentaries*, 219–21) provides a sketch of the political scene in France as the background to Calvin's lectures. The period of the lectures coincided with the last phase of Henry II's repressive policy and was not yet to see the more irenic policy pursued by Catherine de Médicis, the Queen mother of Francis II. Two major achievements of Catherine's religious policy were the Colloquy of Poissy (September 1561), in which a royal audience was granted for the first time to the Huguenot delegation headed by Theodore Beza and the Edict of Saint-Germain (January 1562), which granted to the Huguenots freedom of worship with some limitations.

261. *CO* 41:82 (7:27); CTS, *Daniel II*, 73.

262. *CO* 41:62–63 (7:14), esp. 62; CTS, *Daniel II*, 44.

Persia, Macedonia, and Rome together as that which "under a single image is depicted the condition of the whole earth." On the prophecy that a God-appointed kingdom "shall crush all these kingdoms and bring them to an end, and it shall stand forever" (2:44), furthermore, Calvin's discussions brought forth the conclusion, "whatever was against the only-begotten Son of God must of necessity vanish and perish miserably."[263]

(ii) For Calvin, secondly, Christ's kingdom was neither visible nor visibly identifiable and was also beyond the perception of human eyes and intellect. He rejected the Jewish interpretations of the prophecy in chapter 2 as the visible and earthly Messianic kingdom, just as he had rejected the Münster Anabaptists' claim for their realization of Christ's kingdom.[264] Nevertheless, thirdly, the manifestation of Christ's kingdom in history, just as its commencement and completion, was real and was to be really experienced. With regard to the prophecy (2:33–35) of the statue's "feet partly of iron and partly of clay" and "a stone" that struck the feet and broke the upper statue of gold, silver, and bronze in pieces, Calvin interpreted the feet as the Roman Empire and the stone as the historical manifestation of Christ's kingdom in the Advent. He identified the kingdom's commencement in history roughly with the Advent, the gospel proclamation, and especially Christ's ascension after the resurrection. Although before the commencement, the person of Christ, the Son of God, as well as his kingdom was active, the commencement marked the preeminent manifestations of Christ's rule through the gospel, especially in subduing the earthly kingdoms and protecting the church until its completion at his second Advent.[265]

(iii) As to Calvin's understanding of Christ's kingdom, we assume that he had never changed his basic assumption expressed in the 1536 *Institutes*, "Christ's spiritual Kingdom and the civil jurisdiction are things completely distinct," as well as his criticism of the Münster Anabaptists for their mixing of the two.[266] Due to the subjects of the Daniel prophecies, however, Calvin's lectures did not focus on the Anabaptists but on the political usurpation of Christ's kingdom by the temporal powers themselves. A quarter century after penning his first theological work, he was facing the issue of temporal powers, which he now considered to be as great a threat to the church as the spiritual threat of papalism.

263. *CO* 40:589–92 (2:31–35), esp. 592; 40:609 (2:44); *C. C. Daniel I*, 88, 106.

264. *CO* 40:605 (2:44–45); *C. C. Daniel I*, 102. *CO* 41:82 (7:27); CTS, *Daniel II*, 73. Cf. *OS* 1:258–59. (Battles, trans., *Institution*, 285); chapter 1, n. 185.

265. *CO* 40:589–90 (2:31–35); 40:607–8 (2:44); *C. C. Daniel I*, 84–91, 100–101. *CO* 41:60 (7:13); 41:81 (7:27); CTS, *Daniel II*, 41, 75.

266. Cf. *OS* 1:258 (Battles, trans., *Instruction*, 285); chapter 1, n. 185.

As a basic premise, Calvin maintained the vertical relation between Christ's kingdom and the earthly kingdoms of the entire world, in which God had entrusted to political governments as "God's ministers" or "ministers of God's justice." However, what he saw as a critical issue was this very premise being challenged. On the prophecy of "a great statue" (2:31–35) against which "a stone" [Christ] was to strike, Calvin stated two propositions: "For if kings perform their office well, it is certain that Christ's kingdom is not against their rule"; but the fact that Christ struck them did prove that they were against his kingdom "because their pride is untamable and they lift up their heads above the heavens and would like, if they could, to drag God down off his throne."[267] In particular, since he interpreted the four monarchies of the statue representing all earthly powers regardless of their times and places, the second proposition was in the forefront in the lectures. By calling national pride "a disease" hard to be cured, for instance, he depicted the present-day monarchs as usurpers of God's honor by forgetting their human status, by boasting of "God's blessing" without acknowledging their rule as simply his "gift to them."[268] As a counterbalance to the second proposition, Calvin made the statement that whatever stood against Christ was necessarily to vanish and perish, even though Christ's kingdom was by nature "contemptible and mean in the eyes of the world." From this notion of Christ's kingdom, in the "Greetings," Calvin advanced the sternest denunciations against the French monarchs, who had been traditionally claiming to be "the best defenders of the Catholic faith," for their contempt. As Calvin saw it, when the gospel promulgation caused commotion among the people, the magistrates rejected it for the sake of public safety and, by seeing their refusal to submit to the yoke of Christ, even the people joined them to reject the gospel.[269] In this historical context, he made a personal apology for the French Reformed movement, contending that he was not responsible for the current unrest because of his utmost efforts to avoid the turmoil and his careful warnings against any private persons transgressing for resistance. However, he described the current condition of the Reformed movement in France as "the restoration of his [God's] church further than I have dared to hope."[270]

267. *CO* 40:592 (2:31–35); *C. C. Daniel I*, 88. Cf. *OS* 1:261 (Battles, trans., *Institution*, 288), chapter 1, section 3.3.

268. *CO* 40:670 (4:25).

269. *CO* 40:602 (2:40–43); *C. C. Daniel I*, 99. *CO* 18:617–18 (Greetings); *C. C. Daniel I*, 4.

270. *CO* 18:619–20 (Greetings); *C. C. Daniel I*, 6–7.

The Reformation Church as the Living Image of Christ's Kingdom

The second main point concerning the church as "the living image of Christ's Kingdom" or prophetic image of the Reformation church was by far the most interesting theme in the Daniel lectures. Since, as Calvin said, "Christ has inaugurated his Kingdom by the gospel promulgation," the kingdom-church relationship had defined the innermost nature of the church in history.[271] In his lectures, he seemed to have pictured three distinctive images of the church. The first was the church as "the living image of Christ's Kingdom" and the second was "the church in resistance" to the temporal powers. By combining these two images, the third was the sixteenth-century reality of the prophetic church, the Reformation church.

(i) Immediately after affirming the impossible perception of Christ's kingdom through human eye or intellect, Calvin's concept of the church as "the living image of Christ's Kingdom" appeared in the lecture on 7:27 ("the kingship and dominion . . . shall be given to the people of the holy ones of the Most High"). Using "an analogy between the things earthly and visible and the things spiritual and most blessed," he interpreted "the visible image" as being that "God began to give the Kingdom to the elect people, wherever, by the power of the Holy Spirit, the teaching of the holy gospel was received in the world."[272] He then explained the kingdom-church relationship in terms of the New Testament image of the church as the body of Christ. He said the kingdom to be perpetual both "in the whole body of believers" and "in each believer." Furthermore, he related "the visible image" with both God's "elect people" and "the remnant."[273] In short, the Daniel lectures seemed to indicate Calvin's twofold conception of "the visible image," one image rooted in the primary cause of God's election, and the other in the secondary cause of the believer's incorporation into the body of Christ by faith. On the one hand, due to the close analogy of Christ's kingdom and its image, the church in history, he used two conceptually distinguishable notions interchangeably, the elect people and believers in history. Thus, the church as the kingdom's image was viewed as a universal reality, transcending historical, confessional, and national boundaries.[274] On the other hand, as far as the individual believer was concerned, he urged the believer to be content with being "inserted into

271. *CO* 41:84 (7:27); CTS, *Daniel II*, 75.
272. *CO* 41:82–83 (7:27); CTS, *Daniel II*, 73.
273. *CO* 40:608 (2:44–45).
274. *CO* 41:62 (7:14); 41:83 (7:27). Cf. nn. 264, 272 above.

the body of Christ" and to exercise "the outward testimony of the conduct." Although God's secret election was the superior cause for salvation, what he urged upon the believer most was the historical importance and certainty of the believer's union with Christ by faith in the gospel, even as the secondary cause in itself.[275]

(ii) The second image of "the church in resistance" represented Calvin's most militant image of the church so far. On the prophecy of 11:33–34, where "the wise" of God's people "shall fall by sword and flame, and suffer captivity and plunder," "shall receive a little help," and "many shall join them insincerely," Calvin's comments depicted the church facing extreme trials as well as that of "active resistance." He interpreted "the wise" as "the elect" or "the teachers and rulers of the church," illustrated "a little help" by the Maccabees' armed revolt, and identified "many" with those who joined the wise "in flatteries." More interestingly, he pictured this whole process of resistance as God's act of "purging his church" and juxtaposed the ancient example to the present condition of the church, especially in France. Here, the idea of resistance might well point in the direction of the political armed resistance that we have examined in relation to the final revision of the 1559 *Institutes*. Throughout the lectures, Calvin threatened God's judgment upon tyrants, without naming the French. As to the faithful's armed resistance against them, however, he carefully restrained himself from inciting rebellion. Instead, the focal point of resistance in the lectures was directed toward the religious context.[276] He questioned, for example, "the whole Papacy is called the church of God, we are few in number: what a mixture exists even among us?"[277] He said, "but in that small number who have withdrawn themselves from the papal idolatries," "the greater part is full of unfaithfulness and deceit." "So if God quickly tests his church," he went on, "as he attempted some years ago in Germany, and as he may attempt shortly even to us," the Evangelical churches, especially in France, could hardly stand at ease.[278] For him, God's purging or testing the church meant the coming of

275. *CO* 18:623 (Greetings); *C. C. Daniel I*, 10. *CO* 41:289 (12:1); CTS, *Daniel II*, 372.

276. *CO* 41:258–60 (11:33); CTS, *Daniel II*, 326–31. Calvin's sixty-first lecture on this text was likely delivered around the beginning of 1560, just before the conspiracy of Amboise, and possibly reflected the French Reformed Church's critical condition, in which the issue of armed resistance was one of the most urgent concerns.

277. *CO* 41:261 (11:33); CTS, *Daniel II*, 331.

278. *CO* 41:262 (11:34); CTS, *Daniel II*, 334. Calvin's reference to the experience of the Evangelicals in Germany appeared in the context of his somber view of the condition of the current Evangelical churches. The reference can be either to the Augsburg Interim (1548), which partially enforced the Catholic practices of the church and sacraments, or to the Peace

the most oppressive time in which under Christ's kingdom "God would treat his church far more strictly than before, and submit it to far more excruciating trials."[279] Yet he affirmed that the church in resistance was called to the pursuit of pure worship and piety and was forced to be "a remnant" or "a small company" of the elect people even in the Evangelical churches. Accordingly, this was a new direction in which he took a step further than those he had taken in *Two Epistles* and the Nicodemite controversy. This was also a direction into the prophetic dimensions of the church. In this context, he called Daniel and his companions "the choicest flower of the elect people."[280]

(iii) Lastly, we assume that "the visible image of Christ's Kingdom" and "the church in resistance" comprised Calvin's final vision of sixteenth-century Evangelical Christianity as a prophetic and eschatological reality. Assuredly, he did not, and perhaps would not, write a book like Bucer's *Of the Kingdom of Christ*, by which the author intended to make England a kingdom of Christ. Nor did he ever try Bucer's Strasbourg experiment of "the Christian societies" either in the Genevan Church or in the French Reformed Church. Both Reformers in their last years had faced the same reality of the church and shared similar ideas of God's election, Christ's kingdom, and the manifestations of the kingdom in the church in history. Bucer, however, "the first truly European churchman and theologian" of Strasbourg was optimistic and irenic. Calvin, on the other hand, the French Reformer of Geneva, was pessimistic and militant in his vision. Moreover, what made Calvin's vision so unique was its thoroughly prophetic and eschatological features inspired by those prophetic books. In the dedicatory epistle to the faithful in France, referring to the Maccabee's revolt, for example, he remarked that "the enemy was far superior in men and munitions and there was nothing left for all who had taken arms in defense of the Church than to hide in the dens of wild beasts."[281] Adding the testimonies of Isaiah and a psalmist, then, he remarked further that "the prophet did not encourage us to hope and patience simply by examples from those days. He added exhortation, dictated by the Spirit, which extends to the entire kingdom of Christ and belongs to us."[282] This was his prophetic and

of Augsburg (1555), which was perpetuating the Catholic-Lutheran confessional division, yet excluding the Reformed faith. His other reference, "to us," must be the French case, but the exact condition that he was expecting to see is not clear.

279. *CO* 41:288 (12:1); CTS, *Daniel II*, 370.

280. *CO* 18:615 (Greetings); *CO* 40:608 (2:44); *CO* 41:262 (11:34).

281. *CO* 18:621 (Greetings); *C. C. Daniel I*, 8. Cf. Martin Greschat, "Bucer, Martin," *OER* 1:223.

282. *CO* 18:622 (Greetings); *C. C. Daniel I*, 8–9.

eschatological vision of the Evangelical churches in France expressed just a year prior to the coming Wars of Religion, as well as that of the Reformation church in the entire European theater. Calvin had lived in and experienced the violent age of transition from the medieval to early modern periods, and had keenly anticipated the forthcoming changes surrounding the church. His final concept of the Reformation church, however, manifested that the French Reformer in his entire career had maintained the same prophetic and eschatological vision of the church, suffering afflictions yet hoping for its final survival under the kingdom of Christ who had been and was the head and defender of the church.[283]

Concluding Remarks

(1) Our study in the history of doctrine has come to the last chapter. Chapter 1 examined Calvin's first *Institutes* and found his "Catholic ecclesiology" as foundational stratum. Chapter 2 traced the practice of "Catholic ecclesiology" both in the early Genevan Reformation and in his apologetics in the Caroli affair and *Two Epistles*. And chapter 3 analyzed his Strasbourg period as a transitional stage for his new ecclesiological development. In a sense, all three previous chapters serve as background material for the last chapter on Calvin's Reformed ecclesiology and Reformation ecclesiology. To illustrate this point, for example, we assumed in chapter 3 that he had inherited from Bucer two themes concerning the direction of church reform, namely, implicit amplification (the Reformation of a local church) and explicit expansion (the Reformation of the European Christian world), and developed them into his own "Reformed ecclesiology" and "Reformation ecclesiology" during his second Genevan Reformation.

(2) Although Calvin's new Reformed ecclesiology and Reformation ecclesiology were integral parts of the ecclesiological development examined in the previous chapters, they were formulated over nearly a quarter century (1541–64) in the historical context of his second Genevan Reformation. During this period, as section 1 of this chapter assumes, he had literally become a Reformer of Geneva, France, and Europe. It also assumes that this period can be divided into two halves, roughly centering in the year 1555 corresponding

283. See Calvin's lecture on 12:1 (*CO* 41:286; CTS, *Daniel II*, 370). He interprets the biblical text's "Michael" as either "a prince of God's people" or "an Archangel," and considers him to be "the guardian of the church" under the rule of Christ, the head of the church.

to the development of each of the two ecclesiologies. This division, though it may sound artificial, is based upon our analyses of European history, the history of the Genevan Reformation, and the history of his exegetical works, concentrating in the first half on the New Testament books and in the second half on the Old Testament, especially on the prophetic books.

(3) Although the focus of section 2, Reformed ecclesiology, is undoubtedly an ecclesiology in the Reformed theology, it does not simply mean a locus of the Reformed theology. Having experienced the Strasbourg period and participated in the church unification colloquies, Calvin had now come to realize an urgent need for formulating the external "form" of the Evangelical churches that would be able to counter the Roman Catholic hierarchy. His realization was partly based upon the conviction that the first-generation Reformers, successful in formulating the basic scriptural teachings on the church's nature and identity, had not sufficiently presented such a "form." As a second-generation Reformer, Calvin presents his "Reformed ecclesiology" in the 1543 *Institutes*, which we consider the most important edition as to his ecclesiological development, and the *First Corinthians Commentary* as a test case for the practice of Reformed ecclesiology. It was his new attempt to formulate "the legitimate form of the church" based upon Scripture and the ancient church tradition, and it was intended to be acceptable to the Evangelical churches of the Reformation era.

(4) The subject of section 3, Reformation ecclesiology, is at the culmination of his ecclesiological development, yet its legitimation is more difficult than the cases of his "Catholic ecclesiology" and "Reformed ecclesiology." Since it predominantly appears in the latter part of his second Genevan Reformation, its historical context can be placed in the steady achievements of the Genevan Reformation under his leadership, in his emergence as a leading Reformer in post-Luther Europe, and in his significant imprint on the French Reformation as exemplified by the founding of the Reformed Church in France. As to its substance, however, our study has focused on his exegetical works on the prophetic books, especially the Psalms, and the substantive revisions in the form of rearranging the previous materials and supplementing with new materials, which take place in book 4 of the final *Institutes*.

As a result, our study assumes that Calvin had reached a comprehensive picture of Christianity in Europe, in which the emergence of the Evangelical churches and the prospect of reforming the Roman Catholic Church were in foresight, as well as the vision of the Reformation church as a part of European Christianity. First of all, his vision of the Reformation church was based upon his prophetic self-awareness which, like the Old Testament prophets, addressed prophetic messages to his contemporary Christian world. His vision then presupposed God's salvation history unfolding in the historical process, assumed the Reformation church a unified reality despite some discords such as over the Lord's Supper in the Evangelical churches, and defined the church in history strictly under the leadership of the Triune God, with subservience to the gospel of Christ as "the external means or aids" for the salvation of the faithful. Above all, his vision placed the reality of "church and state" under the spiritual kingdom of Christ, and, accordingly, the triangular relationship (Christ's kingdom–church, Christ's kingdom–state, and the church-state) assumed prophetic and eschatological features. On the one hand, the Reformation church was viewed as "the orchestra" in the European theater and "the living/visible image of Christ's Kingdom." On the other hand, it was viewed as "a remnant" or the church "under the cross" and "in resistance." Thus, his prophetic and eschatological vision of the Reformation church surmised his "Reformation ecclesiology."

Selected Bibliography

For primary sources concerning the Reformers, including Calvin, see "Abbreviations" at the head of this book.

Arnold, Matthieu, ed. *John Calvin: The Strasbourg Years (1538–1541)*. Translated by Felicity McNab. Eugene, OR: Wipf & Stock, 2016.

Augustijn, Cornelis. "Bucer's Ecclesiology in the Colloquies with the Catholics, 1540–41." In *Martin Bucer: Reforming Church and Community*, edited by D. F. Wright, 102–21. Cambridge: Cambridge University Press, 1994.

———. "Calvin in Strasbourg." In *Calvinus Sacrae Scripturae Professor: Calvin as Confessor of Holy Scripture*, edited by Wilhelm H. Neuser, 166–77. Grand Rapids: Eerdmans, 1994.

Augustijn, Cornelis, Christoph Burger, and Frans P. van Stam. "Calvin in the Light of the Early Letters." In *Calvinus Praeceptor Ecclesia*, edited by Herman J. Selderhuis, 139–57. Geneva: Droz, 2004.

Backus, Irena, ed. *The Reception of the Church Fathers in the West: From the Carolingians to the Maurists*. 2 vols. Leiden: Brill, 1997.

———. *Historical Method and Confessional Identity in the Era of the Reformation (1378–1615)*. Leiden and Boston: Brill, 2003.

Backus, Irena, and Claire Chimelli, eds. *La vraie piété: Divers traités de Jean Calvin et Confession de foi de Guillaume Farel*. Geneva: Labor et Fides, 1986.

Baker, J. Wayne. "Christian Discipline and the Early Reformed Tradition: Bullinger and Calvin." In *Calviniana: Ideas and Influence of Jean Calvin*, edited by Robert V. Schnacker, 107–19. Kirksville: Sixteenth Century Journal Publishers, 1988.

———. "Christian Discipline, Church and State, and Toleration: Bullinger, Calvin, and Basel, 1530–1555." In *Reformiertes Erbe: Festschrift für Gottfried W. Locher zu seinem 80. Geburtstag*, edited by Heiko A. Oberman, Ernst Saxer, Alfred Schindler, and Heinzpeter Stucki, 2:35–48. Zwingliana 19. Zurich: Theologischer Verlag, 1993.

———. *Heinrich Bullinger and the Covenant: The Other Reformed Tradition*. Athens, OH: Ohio University Press, 1980.

Balke, Willem. *Calvin and the Anabaptist Radicals*. Translated by William J. Heynen. Grand Rapids: Eerdmans, 1981.

Balserak, Jon. "Geneva's Use of Lies, Deceits, and Simulation in Their Efforts to Reform France, 1536–1563." *Harvard Theological Review* 112 (2019): 76–100.

———. *John Calvin as Sixteenth-Century Prophet*. Oxford: Oxford University Press, 2014.

Barth, Karl. *The Theology of John Calvin*. Translated by Geoffrey W. Bromiley, Grand Rapids: Eerdmans, 1995.

Battles, Ford L. *Interpreting John Calvin*. Edited by Robert Benedetto. Grand Rapids: Baker Books, 1996.

Bedouelle, Guy. "Jacques Lefèvre d'Etaples (c. 1460–1536)." In *The Reformation Theologians: An Introduction to Theology in the Early Modern Period*, edited by Carter Lindberg, 19–33. Oxford: Blackwell, 2002.

Benedict, Philip. "Calvin and the Transformation of Geneva." In *John Calvin's Impact on Church and Society, 1509–2009*, edited by Martin E. Hirzel and Martin Sallmann, 1–13. Grand Rapids: Eerdmans, 2009.

———. "Refugee Churches and Exile Centers in the French Reformation." In *La Réforme en France et en Italie: contacts, comparisons, et contrastes*, edited by Philip Benedict, Silvana Seidel Menchi, and Alain Tallon, 535–52. Rome: École française de Rome, 2007.

———. *Christ's Churches Purely Reformed: A Social History of Calvinism*. New Haven and London: Yale University Press, 2002.

Benoît, Jean-Daniel. "Calvin à Strasbourg." In *Calvin à Strasbourg, 1538–1541*, Commission synodale de l'Église réformée d'Alsace et de Lorraine, 11–36. Geneva: Éditions Labor, 1938.

Berthoud, Gabrielle. *Antoine Marcourt: Réformateur et Pamphlétaire du "Livre des Marchans" aux Placards de 1534*. Geneva: Droz, 1973.

Bohatec, Josef. *Budé und Calvin: Studien zur Gedankenwelt des französischen Frühhumanismus*. Graz: Verlag Hermann Böhlaus, 1950.

Bornert, René. *La Réforme Protestante du culte a Strasbourg au XVIe siècle (1523–1598): Approche sociologique et interpretation théologique*. Leiden: Brill, 1981.

Bouwsma, William J. *John Calvin: A Sixteenth Century Portrait*. New York and Oxford: Oxford University Press, 1988.

Boyle, Marjorie O. *Erasmus on Language and Method in Theology*. Toronto and Buffalo: University of Toronto Press, 1977.

Brady, Thomas A., Jr. *Protestant Politics: Jacob Strum (1489–1553) and the German Reformation*. Atlantic Highland, NJ: Humanities Press International, 1995.

Breen, Quirinus. *John Calvin: A Study in French Humanism*. 2nd ed. Hamden, CT: Archon Books, 1968.

Bruening, Michael W. "Pierre Viret and Geneva." *Archiv für Reformationsgeschichte* 99 (2008): 175–97.

Bruening, Michael. *Calvinism's First Battleground: Conflict and Reform in the Pays de Vaud, 1528–1559*. Dortrecht: Springer Netherlands Studies, 2005.

Buckwalter, Stephen. "Possible Influences of Martin Bucer on the *Institutes* of 1539." In *John Calvin: The Strasbourg Years (1538–1541)*, edited by Matthieu Arnold, 96–106. Eugene, OR: Wipf & Stock, 2016.

Budé, Guillaume. *De Transitu Hellenismi ad Christianismum, Libri Tres*. First published 1535. Reprinted in *Opera omnia Guileilmei Budaei*, 4 vols., 1557. Reprint, Farnborough: Gregg Publishing, 1966.

———. *De Transitu Hellenismi ad Christianismum*. Translated by Maurice Lebel. Sherbrooke: Éditions Paulines, 1973.

Burnett, Amy N. *The Yoke of Christ: Martin Bucer and Christian Discipline*. Kirksville, MO: Northern Missouri State University Press, 1994.

Campi, Emidio, and Christian Moser. "'Loved and Feared': Calvin and the Swiss Confederation." In *John Calvin's Impact on Church and Society, 1509–2009*, edited by Martin E. Hirzel and Martin Sallmann, 14–34. Grand Rapids: Eerdmans, 2009.

Church, William F. *Constitutional Thought in Sixteenth-Century France: A Study in the Evolution of Ideas*. Cambridge, MA, and London: Harvard University Press, 1941.

Collins, Ross W. *Calvin and the Libertines of Geneva*. Toronto and Vancouver: Clarke, Irwin & Co., 1968.

Courvoisier, Jaques. "Bucer et Calvin." In *Calvin à Strasbourg, 1538–1541*, Commission synodale de l'Église réformée d'Alsace et de Lorraine, 3–66. Geneva: Éditions Labor, 1938.

———. *La notion d'église chez Bucer dans son développement historique*. Paris: F. Alcan, 1933.

Daussy, Hugues. "Les élites face à la Réforme dans le Royaume de France (ca. 1520–ca. 1570)." In *La Réforme en France et en Italie*, edited by Philip Benedict, Alain Tallon, and Silvana Seidel Menchi, 331–49. Rome: École française de Rome, 2007.

Demura, Akira. "Calvin's and Oecolampadius' Concept of Church Discipline." In

Calvinus Ecclesiae Genevensis Custos, edited by Wilhelm H. Neuser, 187–89. Frankfurt am Main: Peter Lang, 1984.

———. "Church Discipline according to Johannes Oecolampadius in the Setting of His Life and Thought." ThD diss., Princeton Theological Seminary, 1964.

———. "Two Commentaries on the Epistle to the Romans: Calvin and Oecolampadius." In *Calvinus Sincerioris Religionis Vindex: Calvin as Protector of the Purer Religion*, edited by Wilhelm H. Neuser and Brian G. Armstrong, 165–88. Kirksville: Sixteenth Century Journal Publishers, 1997.

Denis, Philippe, and Jean Rott. *Jean Morély (ca 1524–ca 1594) et l'utopie d'une démocratie dans l'Église*. Geneva: Droz, 1993.

Doumergue, É. *Jean Calvin: Les hommes et les choses de son temps*. 7 vols. Lausanne, 1899–1917; Neuilly: G. Bridel, 1926–27.

Dowey, Edward A., Jr. *The Knowledge of God in Calvin's Theology*. New York and London: Columbia University Press, 1965.

Droz, Eugenie. *Chemins de l'hérésie: Textes et documents*. Vol. 1. Geneva: Slatkine Reprints, 1970.

Dufour, Alain. *Histoire politique et psychologie historique*. Geneva: Droz, 1966.

Duke, Alastair. "Perspective on European Calvinism." In *Calvinism in Europe, 1540–1620*, edited by Andrew Pettegree, Alastair Duke, and Gillian Lewis. Cambridge: Cambridge University Press, 1994.

Eells, Hastings. *Martin Bucer*. New Haven: Yale University Press, 1931.

Eire, Carlos M. N. "Antisacerdotalism and the Young Calvin." In *Anticlericalism in Late Medieval and Early Modern Europe*, edited by Peter A. Dykema and Heiko A. Oberman, 583–603. Leiden: Brill, 1993.

———. "Calvin and Nicodemism: A Reappraisal." *Sixteenth Century Journal* 10 (1979): 45–69.

———. "Prelude to Sedition? Calvin's Attack on Nicodemism and Religious Compromise." *Archiv für Reformationsgeschichte* 76 (1985): 120–45.

———. *War against the Idols: The Reformation of Worship from Erasmus to Calvin*. Cambridge: Cambridge University Press, 1986.

Elwood, Christopher. *The Body Broken: Calvinist Doctrine of the Eucharist and the Symbolization of Power in Sixteenth-Century France*. New York and Oxford: Oxford University Press, 1999.

Engammare, Max. "Calvin: A Prophet without a Prophecy." In *Calvin Studies IX* (Paper Presented at the Ninth Colloquium on Calvin Studies, 1998), edited by John H. Leith and Robert A. Johnson, 88–107. Davidson, NC: Davidson College, n.d.

Faber, Eva-Maria. "Mutual Connectedness as a Gift and a Task: On John Calvin's Understanding of the Church." In *John Calvin's Impact on Church and So-*

ciety, 1509–2009, edited by Martin E. Hirzel and Martin Sallmann, 122–44. Grand Rapids: Eerdmans, 2009.

Farel, Guillaume. *Du vray usage de la croix de Iesus-Christ*. Geneva: Jules-Guillaume Fick, 1865.

———. *Le Sommaire de Guillaume Farel*. 1534. Edited by J.-G. Baum. Reprint, Geneva: Jules-Guillaume Fick, 1867.

Farge, James K. *Biographical Register of Paris Doctors of Theology, 1500–1536*. Toronto: Pontifical Institute of Mediaeval Studies, 1980.

———. *Orthodoxy and Reform in Early Reformation France: The Faculty of Theology of Paris, 1500–1543*. Leiden: Brill, 1985.

Fraenkel, Peter. *Testimonia Patrum: The Function of the Patristic Argument in the Theology of Philip Melanchthon*. Geneva: Droz, 1961.

Fraenkel, Pierre. "Bucer's Memorandum of 1541 and a 'Lettera Nicodemitica' of Capito's." *Bibliothèque d'Humanisme et Renaissance* 36 (1974): 575–87.

———. "Quelques observations sur le 'Tu es Petrus' chez Calvin, au Colloque de Worms en 1540 et dans l'*Institution* de 1543." *Bibliothèque d'Humanisme et Renaissance* 27 (1965): 607–28.

Fudge, Thomas A. "Icarus of Basel? Oecolampadius and the Early Swiss Reformation." *Journal of Religious History* 21 (1997): 268–85.

Fulop, Timothy E. "The Third Mark of the Church? Church Discipline in the Reformed and Anabaptist Reformations." *Journal of Religious History* 19 (1995): 26–42.

Ganoczy, Alexandre. *Calvin: théologien de l'église et du ministère*. Paris: Éditions du Cerf, 1964.

———. *The Young Calvin*. Translated by David Foxgrover and Wade Provo. Edinburgh: T&T Clark, 1987.

Gäumann, Andreas. *Reich Christi und Obrigkeit: Eine Studie zum reformatorischen Denken und Handeln Martin Bucers*. Bern: Peter Lang, 2001.

Gerrish, B. A. "John Calvin on Luther." In *Interpreters of Luther*, edited by Jaroslav Pelikan, 67–96. Philadelphia: Fortress Press, 1968.

Girardin, Benoît. *Rhétoique et théologique: Calvin, le commentaire de l'Épitre aux Romains*. Paris: Beauchesne, 1979.

Gordon, Bruce. "Calvin and the Swiss Reformed Churches." In *Calvinism in Europe, 1540–1620*, edited by Andrew Pettegree, Alastair Duke, and Gillion Lewis, 64–81. Cambridge: Cambridge University Press, 1994.

———. *Calvin*. New Haven and London: Yale University Press, 2009.

———. *The Swiss Reformation*. Manchester and New York: Manchester University Press, 2002.

Grappe, Christian. "Calvin's Commentary on the Epistle to the Romans." In *John*

Calvin: The Strasbourg Years (1538–1541), edited by Matthieu Arnold, 75–95. Eugene, OR: Wipf & Stock, 2016.

Greef, Wurfert de. "Calvin as Commentator on the Psalms." In *Calvin and the Bible*, edited by Donald K. McKim, 85–106. Cambridge: Cambridge University Press, 2006.

Greschat, Martin. *Martin Bucer: A Reformer and His Time*. Translated by Stephen E. Buckwalter. Louisville and London: Westminster John Knox, 2004.

Hammann, Gottfried. *Entre la secte et la cité: Le projet d'Église du Réformateur Martin Bucer (1491–1551)*. Geneva: Labor et Fides, 1984.

Hazlett, W. Ian P. "Calvin's Latin Preface to His Proposed French Edition of Chrysostom's Homilies: Translation and Commentary." In *Humanism and Reform: The Church in Europe, England, and Scotland, 1400–1643*, edited by James Kirk, 129–54. Oxford and Cambridge, MA: Blackwell, 1991.

Hendrix, Scott H. *Ecclesia in Via: Ecclesiological Developments in the Medieval Psalms Exegesis and the Dictata super Psalterium (1513–1515) of Martin Luther*. Leiden: Brill, 1974.

Herminjard, A. L. *Correspondance de réformateurs dans les pays de langue française*. 7 vols. Geneva and Paris: H. Georg, 1866–86.

Hesselink, I. John. *Calvin's Concept of the Law*. Allison Park, PA: Pickwick Publications, 1992.

———. *Calvin's First Catechism: A Commentary*. Louisville: Westminster John Knox, 1997.

Heyer, Henri. *Guillaume Farel: Essai sur le développement de ses idées théologiques*. Geneva: Ramboz et Schucherdt, 1872.

Higman, F. M. "The Question of Nicodemism." In *Calvinus Ecclesiae Genevensis Custos*, edited by Wilhelm H. Neuser, 165–70. Frankfurt am Main: Peter Lang, 1984.

Higman, Francis M. *The Style of John Calvin in His French Polemical Treatises*. Oxford: Oxford University Press, 1967.

Higman, Francis. "Bucer et les Nicodemites." In *Martin Bucer and Sixteenth Century Europe*, edited by Christian Krieger and Marc Lienhard, 645–58. Leiden: Brill, 1993.

———. *Lire et découvrir: La circulation des idées au temps de la Réforme*. Geneva: Droz, 1998.

———. "New Forms of Religious Engagement circa 1540." In *Charting Change in France around 1540*, edited by Marian Rothstein, 119–40. Selinsgrove: Susquehanna University Press, 2006.

———, ed. *Three French Treatises*. London: Athlone, 1970.

Hillerbrand, Hans J. "Anabaptism and History." *Mennonite Quarterly Review* 45 (1971): 107–22.

Holder, R. Ward. "Calvin as Commentator on the Pauline Epistles." In *Calvin and the Bible*, edited by Donald K. McKim, 224–55. Cambridge: Cambridge University Press, 2006.

———. *John Calvin and the Grounding of Interpretation: Calvin's First Commentaries*. Leiden: Brill, 2006.

Höpfl, Harro. *The Christian Polity of John Calvin*. Cambridge: Cambridge University Press, 1982.

Hughes, Philip E. *Lefèvre: Pioneer of Ecclesiastical Renewal in France*. Grand Rapids: Eerdmans, 1984.

Johnson, Galen. "The Development of John Calvin's Doctrine of Infant Baptism in Reaction to the Anabaptists." *Mennonite Quarterly Review* 73 (1999): 803–23.

Kelley, Donald R. *The Beginning of Ideology: Consciousness and Society in the French Reformation*. Cambridge: Cambridge University Press, 1981.

Kingdon, Robert M. *Adultery and Divorce in Calvin's Geneva*. Cambridge, MA: Harvard University Press, 1995.

———. "Calvin and Church Discipline." In *John Calvin Rediscovered: The Impact of His Social and Economic Thought*, edited by Edward Dommen and James D. Bratt, 25–31. Louisville and London: Westminster John Knox, 2007.

———. "Calvin and Discipline among French and Italians." In *La réforme en France et en Italie*, edited by Philip Benedict, Alain Tallon, and Silvana Seidel Menchi, 553–62. Rome: École française de Rome, 2007.

———. "Calvin and Geneva." In *A Companion to the Reformation World*, edited by R. Po-chia Hsia, 105–17. Oxford: Blackwell, 2004.

———. "Calvin and the Establishment of Consistory Discipline in Geneva: The Institution and the Men Who Directed It." *Dutch Review of Church History* 70 (1990): 158–72.

———. "Calvinism and Resistance Theory, 1550–1580." In *The Cambridge History of Political Thought, 1450–1700*, edited by J. H. Burns, 193–218. Cambridge: Cambridge University Press, 1991.

———. *Church and Society in Reformation Europe*. London and Freme, Somerset: Variorum Reprints, 1985.

———. "La discipline ecclésiastique vue de Zurich et Genève au temps de la Réformation: L'usage de Matthieu 18, 15–17 par les Réformateurs." *Revue de Théologie et de Philosophie* 133 (2001): 343–55.

———. *Geneva and the Coming of the Wars of Religion in France, 1555–1563*. Geneva: Droz, 1956.

———. "A New View of Calvin in the Light of the Registers of the Genevan Consistory." In *Calvinus Sincerioris Religionis Vindex: Calvin as Protector of the Purer Religion*, edited by Wilhelm H. Neuser and Brian G. Armstrong, 21–33. Kirksville: Sixteenth Century Journal Publishers, 1997.

———. "Nostalgia for Catholic Rituals in Calvin's Geneva." In *Grenzgänge der Theologie Professor Alexandre Ganoczy zum 75. Geburtstag*, edited by Hans O. Meuffels and Jürgen Bründl, 209–22. Münster: LIT Verlag, 2004.

———, ed. *Registers of the Consistory of Geneva in the Time of Calvin*. Vol. 1, *1542–1544*, edited by Thomas A. Lambert and Isabella M. Watt. Translated by M. Wallace McDonald. Grand Rapids: Eerdmans and the H. H. Meeter Center, 2001.

———. "Was the Protestant Reformation a Revolution? The Case of Geneva." In *Church and Society in Reformation Europe*, edited by Robert M. Kingdon, 203–22. London and Freme, Somerset: Variorum Reprints, 1985.

Kok, Joel E. "The Influence of Martin Bucer on John Calvin's Interpretation of Romans: A Comparative Case Study." PhD diss., Duke University, Durham, NC, 1993.

Kroon, Marijn de. *The Honour of God and Human Salvation: A Contribution to an Understanding of Calvin's Theology according to His Institutes*. Translated by John Vriend and Lyle D. Bierma. Edinburgh and New York: T&T Clark, 2001.

———. *Martin Bucer und Johannes Calvin: Reformatorische Perspektiven; Einleitung und Texte*. Translated by Hartmut Rudolph. Göttingen: Vandenhoeck & Ruprecht, 1991.

Kuhr, Olaf. "Calvin and Basel: The Significance of Oecolampadius and the Basel Discipline Ordinance for the Institution of Ecclesiastical Discipline in Geneva." *Scottish Bulletin of Evangelical Theology* 16 (1998): 19–33.

Lane, Anthony N. S. "Calvin and Article 5 of the Regensburg Colloquy." In *Calvinus Praeceptor Ecclesia*, edited by Herman J. Selderhuis, 233–63. Geneva: Droz, 2004.

———. *John Calvin: Student of the Church Fathers*. Edinburgh: T&T Clark, 1999.

Lang, August. *Der Evangelienkommentar Martin Butzers und die Grundzüge seiner Theologie*. Leipzig: Dieterich'sche Verlagsbuchhandlung, 1900.

Larson, Mark J. "John Calvin and Genevan Presbyterianism." *Westminster Theological Journal* 60 (1998): 43–69.

Lefèvre d'Étaples, Jacques. *Épistres & Évangiles pour les cinquante & deux semaines de l'an*. Facsimile of the first edition of Simon du Bois. Edited by M. A. Screech. Geneva: Droz, 1964.

———. *Jacques Lefèvre d'Étaples and the Three Maries Debates*. Edited and translated by Sheila M. Porrer. Geneva: Droz, 2009.

———. *Quincuplex Psalterium*. Facsimile of the 1513 edition. Geneva: Droz, 1979.

———. *S. Pauli Epistolae XIV ex Vulgata, adiecta intelligentia ex graeco, cum commentariis*. Facsimile of the 1512 edition. Stuttgart: Frommann-Holzboog, 1978.

Lefèvre d'Étaples, Jacques, et ses disciples. *Epistres et Evangiles pour les cinquante et deux dimenches de l'an*. The edition of Pierre de Vingle, edited by Guy Bedouelle and France Giacone. Leiden: Brill, 1976.

Lewis, Gillian. "The Geneva Academy." In *Calvinism in Europe, 1540–1620*, edited by Andrew Pettegree, Alastair Duke, and Gillian Lewis, 35–63. Cambridge: Cambridge University Press, 1994.

Lienhard, Marc. "Strasbourg in Calvin's Time." In *John Calvin: The Strasbourg Years (1538–1541)*, edited by Matthieu Arnold, 1–22. Eugene, OR: Wipf & Stock, 2016.

Littell, Franklin H. "What Calvin Learned at Strassburg." In *The Heritage of John Calvin*, edited by John H. Bratt, 74–86. Grand Rapids: Eerdmans, 1973.

Locher, Gottfried W. *Zwingli's Thought: New Perspectives*. Leiden: Brill, 1981.

Maag, Karin. "Permeable Borders: Cross-Confessional Encounters and Traditions in Reformation Geneva." In *Semper Reformanda: John Calvin, Worship, and Reformed Traditions*, edited by Barbara Pitkin, 15–32. Göttingen: Vandenhoeck & Ruprecht, 2018.

Manetsch, Scott M. *Calvin's Company of Pastors: Pastoral Care and the Emerging Reformed Church, 1536–1609*. Oxford and New York: Oxford University Press, 2013.

Mann, Margaret. *Érasme et les débuts de la réforme Française (1517–1536)*. Paris: H. Champion, 1934.

Maruyama, Tadataka. *The Ecclesiology of Theodore Beza*. Geneva: Droz, 1978.

McGrath, Alister E. "John Calvin and Late Mediaeval Thought: A Study in Late Mediaeval Influences upon Calvin's Theological Development." *Archiv für Reformationsgeschichte* 77 (1986): 58–78.

———. *A Life of John Calvin*. Oxford: Blackwell, 1990.

McKee, Elsie A. *Elders and the Plural Ministry: The Role of Exegetical History in Illuminating John Calvin's Theology*. Geneva: Droz, 1988.

———. "Exegesis, Theology, and Development in Calvin's *Institutio*: A Methodological Suggestion." In *Probing the Reformed Tradition*, edited by Elsie A. McKee and Brian G. Armstrong, 154–72. Louisville: Westminster John Knox, 1989.

———. *The Pastoral Ministry and Worship in Calvin's Geneva*. Geneva: Droz, 2016.

McNeil, David O. *Guillaume Budé and Humanism in the Reign of Francis I*. Geneva: Droz, 1975.

Millet, Olivier. *Calvin et la dynamique de la parole: Étude de rhétorique réformée*. Paris: Classiques Garnier, 2019.

Milner, Benjamin C. *Calvin's Doctrine of the Church*. Leiden: Brill, 1970.

Monter, E. William. *Calvin's Geneva*. New York: John Wiley & Sons, 1967.

Monter, William. "France: The Failure of Repression, 1520–1563." In *La Réforme en France et en Italie*, edited by Philip Benedict, Silvana Seidel Menchi, and Alain Tallon, 465–79. Rome: École française de Rome, 2007.

———. *Judging the French Reformation: Heresy Trials by Sixteenth-Century Parlements*. Cambridge, MA, and London: Harvard University Press, 1999.

Muller, Richard A. "Demoting Calvin: The Issue of Calvin and the Reformed Tradition." In *John Calvin, Myth and Reality: Images and Impact of Geneva's Reformer*, edited by Amy N. Burnett, 1–17. Eugene, OR: Cascade Books, 2011.

———. "The Hermeneutic of Promise and Fulfillment in Calvin's Exegesis of the Old Testament Prophecies of the Kingdom." In *The Bible in the Sixteenth Century*, edited by David C. Steinmetz, 67–82. Durham, NC: Duke University Press, 1990.

———. *The Unaccommodated Calvin: Studies in the Foundation of a Theological Tradition*. New York and Oxford: Oxford University Press, 2000.

Mullett, Michael A. *John Calvin*. London and New York: Routledge, 2016.

Naef, Henri. *L'ère de la triple combourgeoisie, l'épée ducale et l'épée de Farel*. Vol. 2 of *Les origines de la réforme a Genève*. Geneva: Droz, 1968.

Naphy, William G. *Calvin and the Consolidation of the Genevan Reformation*. Manchester and New York: Manchester University Press, 1994.

———. "New Sources and New Ideas on the Life and Career of Calvin, 1541–1557." In *Calvinus Evangelii Propugnator*, edited by David F. Wright, Anthony N. S. Lane, and Jon Balserak, 40–53. Grand Rapids: Calvin Studies Society, 2006.

Niesel, Wilhelm, ed. *Bekenntnisschriften und Kirchenordnungen der nach Gottes Wort reformierten Kirche*. Zurich: Evangelischer Verlag, 1938.

———. *The Theology of Calvin*. Translated by Harold Knight. Philadelphia: Westminster, 1956.

Nijenhuis, W. *Ecclesia Reformata: Studies on the Reformation*. Leiden: Brill, 1972.

Oakley, Francis. "Christian Obedience and Authority, 1520–1550." In *The Cambridge History of Political Thought, 1450–1700*, edited by J. H. Burns, 159–92. Cambridge: Cambridge University Press, 1991.

Oberman, Heiko A. "Calvin and Farel: The Dynamics of Legitimation in Early Calvinism." *Journal of Early Modern History* 2 (1998): 32–60.

———. *The Dawn of the Reformation: Essays in Late Medieval and Early Reformation Thought*. Edinburgh: T&T Clark, 1992.

———. "*Europa Afflicta*: The Reformation of the Refugees." *Archiv für Reformationsgeschichte* 83 (1992): 91–111.

———. *Forerunners of the Reformation: The Shape of Late Medieval Thought*. New York: Holt, Rinehart & Winston, 1966.

———. *The Impact of the Reformation*. Grand Rapids: Eerdmans, 1994.

———. "Initia Calvini: The Matrix of Calvin's Reformation." *Mededelingen van de Afdeling Letterkunde* 54 (1991): 109–47.

———. *John Calvin and the Reformation of the Refugees*. Geneva: Droz, 2009.

———. *Masters of the Reformation: The Emergence of a New Intellectual Climate in Europe*. Translated by Dennis Martin. Cambridge: Cambridge University Press, 1981.

———. *The Two Reformations*. Edited by Donald Weinstein. New Haven: Yale University Press, 2003.

Ocker, Christopher. "Calvin in Germany." In *Politics and Reformations: Histories and Reformations*, edited by Christopher Ocker, Michael Printy, Peter Starenko, and Peter Wallace, 313–44. Leiden and Boston: Brill, 2007.

Olin, John C., ed. *A Reformation Debate: Sadoleto's Letter to the Genevans and Calvin's Reply*. New York: Harper & Row, 1966.

Olson, Jeannine E. "Calvin and Social-Ethical Issues." In *The Cambridge Companion to John Calvin*, edited by Donald K. McKim, 153–72. Cambridge: Cambridge University Press, 2004.

Oort, Johannes van. "John Calvin and the Church Fathers." In *The Reception of the Church Fathers in the West: From the Carolingians to the Maurists*, edited by Irena Backus, 2:661–700. Leiden: Brill, 1997.

Opitz, Peter. "Calvin in the Context of the Swiss Reformation: Detecting the Trace." In *Calvinus Pastor Ecclesiae*, edited by H. J. Selderhuis and Arnold Hijgen, 13–28. Göttingen: Vandenhoeck & Ruprecht, 2010.

Ortmann, Vokmar. "Calvin and the Religious Colloquia of 1539–1541." In *John Calvin: The Strasbourg Years (1538–1541)*, edited by Matthieu Arnold, 169–82. Eugene, OR: Wipf & Stock, 2016.

Oyer, John S. "Bucer and the Anabaptists." In *Martin Bucer and Sixteenth Century Europe*, edited by Christian Krieger and Marc Lienhard, 603–13. Leiden: Brill, 1993.

Pabel, Hilmar M. *Erasmus' Vision of the Church*. Kirksville: Sixteenth Century Journal Publishers, 1995.

Parker, T. H. L. *Calvin's New Testament Commentaries*. Louisville: Westminster John Knox, 1993.

———. *Calvin's Old Testament Commentaries*. Edinburgh: T&T Clark, 1986.

———. *Calvin's Preaching*. Edinburgh: T&T Clark, 1992.

———. "Calvin the Exegete: Change and Development." In *Calvinus Ecclesiae Doctor*, edited by Wilhelm H. Neuser, 33–46. Kampen: J. H. Kok, 1978.

Parker, Thomas H. L. *John Calvin: A Biography*. Philadelphia: Westminster, 1975.

Parsons, Jotham. *The Church in the Republic: Gallicanism and Political Ideology in Renaissance France*. Washington, DC: Catholic University of America Press, 2004.

Partee, Charles. *Calvin and Classical Philosophy*. Louisville: Westminster John Knox, 2005.

Payton, James R., Jr. "Calvin and the Legitimation of Icons: His Treatment of the Seventh Ecumenical Council." *Archiv für Reformationsgeschichte* 84 (1993): 221–41.

Pelikan, Jaroslav. *The Christian Tradition: A History of the Development of Doctrine*. 5 vols. Chicago and London: University of Chicago Press, 1971–89.

Piaget, Arthur, ed. *Les actes de la Dispute de Lausanne 1536, publiés intégralement d'après le manuscript de Berne*. Neuchatel: Secrétariat de Université, 1928.

Pils, Holger, Stephan Ruderer, and Petra Schaffrodt, eds. *Martin Bucer (1491–1551) Bibliographie*. Gütersloh: Gütersloher Verlag, 2005.

Potter, G. R. *Zwingli*. Cambridge: Cambridge University Press, 1976.

Poythress, Diane. *Reformer of Basel: The Life, Thought, and Influence of Johannes Oecolampadius*. Grand Rapids: Reformation Heritage Books, 2011.

Puckett, David L. *John Calvin's Exegesis of the Old Testament*. Louisville: Westminster John Knox, 1995.

Reid, Jonathan A. "French Evangelical Networks before 1555: Proto-Churches?" In *La Réforme en France et en Italie*, edited by Philip Benedict, Silvana Seidel Menchi, and Alain Tallon, 105–24. Rome: École française de Rome, 2007.

Renaudet, Augustin. *Humanisme et Renaissance: Dante, Pétrarque, Standonck, Érasme, Lefèvre d'Étaples, Marguerite de Navarre, Rabelais, Guichardin, Giordano Bruno*. Geneva: Droz, 1958.

Reuter, Karl. *Das Grundverständnis der Theologie Calvins: Unter Einbeziehung ihrer geschichtlichen Abhängigkeiten*. Neukirchen: Neukirchner Verlag, 1963.

Rice, Eugene F., Jr., ed. *The Prefatory Epistles of Jacques Lefèvre d'Etaples and Related Texts*. New York and London: Columbia University Press, 1972.

Riggs, John W. "Emerging Ecclesiology in Calvin's Baptismal Thought, 1536–1543." *Church History* 64 (1995): 29–43.

Rothstein, Marian. Introduction to *Charting Change in France around 1540*. Selinsgrove: Susquehanna University Press, 2006, 9–36.

Salmon, J. H. M. *Society in Crisis: France in the Sixteenth Century*. New York: St. Martin's Press, 1975.

Sanchez, Michelle C. *Calvin and the Resignification of the World: Creation, Incarnation, and the Problem of Political Theology in the 1559* Institutes. Cambridge: Cambridge University Press, 2019.

Schreiner, Susan E. "'The Spiritual Man Judges All Things': Calvin and the Exegetical Debates about Certainty in the Reformation." In *Biblical Interpretation in the Era of the Reformation*, edited by Richard A. Muller and John L. Thompson, 189–215. Grand Rapids: Eerdmans, 1996.

———. *The Theater of His Glory: Nature and the Natural Order in the Thought of John Calvin*. Durham, NC: Duke University Press, 1991.

Selderhuis, Herman J. "Calvin's Theology of the Psalms." In *Calvin Studies IX*, edited by John H. Leith and Robert A. Johnson, 1–15. Davidson, NC: Davidson College, n.d.

———. "Church on Stage: Calvin's Dynamic Ecclesiology." In *Calvin and the Church*, edited by David Foxgrover, 46–64. Grand Rapids: Calvin Studies Society, 2002.

Spierling, Karen E. *Infant Baptism in Reformation Geneva: The Shaping of a Community, 1536–1564*. Louisville, KY: Westminster John Knox, 2008.

Spijker, Willem van't. "Bucer's Influence on Calvin: Church and Community." In *Martin Bucer: Reforming Church and Community*, edited by David F. Wright, 32–44. Cambridge: Cambridge University Press, 1994.

———. *Calvin: A Brief Guide to His Life and Thought*. Translated by Lyle D. Bierma. Louisville: Westminster John Knox, 2009.

———. *The Ecclesiastical Offices in the Thought of Martin Bucer*. Translated by John Briend and Lyle D. Bierma. Leiden: Brill, 1996.

———. "Prädestination bei Bucer und Calvin: Ihre gegenseitige Beeinflussung und Abhängigkeit." In *Calvinus Theologus*, edited by Wilhelm H. Neuser, 85–111. Neukirchen: Neukirchner Verlag, 1976.

Staehelin, Ernst. *Das theologische Lebenswerk Johannes Oekolampads*. Leipzig: M. Heinsius Nachfolger, 1939.

Stam, Frans P. van. "Die Genfer Artikel vom Januar 1537: aus Calvins oder Farels Feder?" *Zwingliana* 27 (2000): 87–101.

———. "Farel und Calvins Ausweisung aus Genf am 23. April 1538." *Zeitschrift für Kirchengeschichte* 110 (1999): 209–28.

———. "The Group of Meaux as First Target of Farel and Calvin's Anti-Nicodemism." *Bibliothèque d'Humanisme et Renaissance* 68 (2006): 253–75.

Steinmetz, David C. *Calvin in Context*. New York and Oxford: Oxford University Press, 1995.

———. "Luther and Calvin on Church and Tradition." *Michigan Germanic Studies* 10 (1984): 98–111.

Stevenson, William R., Jr. "Calvin and Political Issues." In *The Cambridge Companion to John Calvin*, edited by Donald K. McKim, 173–87. Cambridge: Cambridge University Press, 2004.

Sytsma, David S. "The Exegetical Context of Calvin's *Loci* on the Christian Life." *Calvin Theological Journal* 45 (2010): 256–79.

Tait, Edwin R. "A Method for the Christian Life: Martin Bucer and the Sermon on the Mount." PhD diss., Duke University, Durham, NC, 2005.

Tavard, George H. "Calvin and the Nicodemites." In *John Calvin and Roman Catholicism: Critique and Engagement, Then and Now*, edited by Randall C. Zachman, 59–78. Grand Rapids: Baker Academic, 2008.

———. *Holy Writ or Holy Church: The Crisis of the Protestant Reformation*. New York: Harper, 1959.

Torrance, Thomas F. *The Hermeneutics of John Calvin*. Edinburgh: Scottish Academic Press, 1988.

Tuininga, Matthew J. *Calvin's Political Theology and the Public Engagement of the Church: Christ's Two Kingdoms*. Cambridge: Cambridge University Press, 2017.

VanDrunen, David. *Natural Law and the Two Kingdoms: A Study in the Development of Reformed Social Thought*. Grand Rapids: Eerdmans, 2010.

Wallace, Ronald S. *Calvin, Geneva and the Reformation: A Study of Calvin as Social Reformer, Churchman, Pastor and Theologian*. Edinburgh: Scottish Academic Press, 1988.

Wendel, François. *Calvin: The Origins and Development of His Religious Thought*. Translated by Philip Mairet. New York and Evanston: Harper & Row, 1963.

———. *L'Église de Strasbourg, sa constitution et son organisation 1532–1535*. Paris: Presses universitaires de France, 1942.

White, Robert. "An Early Doctrinal Handbook: Farel's *Summaire et briefve declaration*." *Westminster Theological Journal* 69 (2007): 21–38.

———. "Oil and Vinegar: Calvin on Church Discipline." *Scottish Journal of Theology* 38 (1985): 25–40.

Wilcox, Peter. "Calvin as Commentator on the Prophets." In *Calvin and the Bible*, edited by Donald K. McKim, 107–30. Cambridge: Cambridge University Press, 2006.

———. "The Lectures of John Calvin and the Nature of His Audience, 1555–1564." *Archiv für Reformationsgeschichte* 87 (1996): 136–48.

———. "'The Progress of the Kingdom of Christ' in Calvin's Exposition of the Prophets." In *Calvinus Sincerioris Religionis Vindex: Calvin as Protector of the Purer Religion*, edited by Wilhelm H. Neuser and Brian G. Armstrong, 315–22. Kirksville: Sixteenth Century Journal Publishers, 1997.

———. "'The Restoration of the Church' in Calvin's 'Commentaries in Isaiah the prophet.'" *Archiv für Reformationsgeschichte* 85 (1994): 68–96.

Wiley, David N. "The Church as the Elect in the Theology of Calvin." In *John Calvin and the Church: A Prism of Reform*, edited by Timothy George, 96–117. Louisville: Sixteenth Century Journal Publishers, 1990.

Williams, George H. *The Radical Reformation*. 3rd ed. Kirksville, MO: Truman State University Press, 2000.

Willis, E. David. *Calvin's Catholic Christology: The Function of the So-Called Extra Calvinisticum in Calvin's Theology*. Leiden: Brill, 1966.

Wright, D. F., trans. and ed. *Common Places of Martin Bucer*. Appleford, Abingdon: Courtenay Press, 1972.

———, ed. *Martin Bucer: Reforming Church and Community*. Cambridge: Cambridge University Press, 1994.

Wright, David. "Why Was Calvin So Severe a Critic of Nicodemism?" In *Calvinus Evangelii Propuganator*, edited by David F. Wright, Anthony N. S. Lane, and Jon Balserak, 66–90. Grand Rapids: Calvin Studies Society, 2006.

Yardeni, Myriam. "French Calvinist Political Thought, 1534–1715." In *International Calvinism, 1541–1715*, edited by Menna Prestwich, 315–37. Oxford: Oxford University Press, 1985.

Zachman, Randall C. "The Conciliating Theology of John Calvin: Dialogue among Friends." In *Conciliation and Confession: The Struggle for Unity in the Age of Reform, 1415–1648*, edited by Howard P. Louthan and Randall C. Zachman, 89–105. Notre Dame: University of Notre Dame Press, 2004.

———. *Image and Word in the Theology of John Calvin*. Notre Dame: University of Notre Dame Press, 2007.

———. *John Calvin as Teacher, Pastor, and Theologian: The Shape of His Writings and Thought*. Grand Rapids: Baker Academic, 2006.

———. "Revisiting the Reform: What Calvin Learned from Dialogue with the Roman Catholics." In *John Calvin and Roman Catholicism: Critique and Engagement, Then and Now*, edited by Randall C. Zachman, 165–91. Grand Rapids: Baker Academic, 2008.

Zillenbiller, Anette. *Die Einheit der Katholischen Kirche: Calvins Cyprianrezeption in seinen Ekklesiologischen Schriften*. Mainz: Verlag Philipp von Zabern, 1993.

Zuidema, Jason, and TheodoreVan Raalte. *Early French Reform: The Theology and Spirituality of Guillaume Farel*. Farnham, Surrey: Ashgate, 2011.

Index of Authors

Index of Subjects

Index of Scripture